Who Are We Now?

Blaise Agüera y Arcas

Who Are We Now?

Hat & Beard Editions
Los Angeles

Contents

Preface

→ Cover of Campbell and Sharp, *Dick and Jane: Fun with Our Family*, 1962.

This is a book about human identity: the frontline in today's culture wars. The book's backbone consists of a set of surveys I conducted between 2016 and 2022, asking tens of thousands of anonymous respondents all over the United States simple but at times intimate questions about their identity and behavior, and especially about gender and sexuality. The surveys open a window into people's lives a bit like the one opened in the middle of the 20th century by sex researcher Alfred Kinsey and his collaborators. Their wonky, questionnaire-based reports scandalized postwar America. Though methodologically flawed, the Kinsey reports correctly concluded that, to use today's language, people were a lot queerer than had been assumed, and less easily categorized. Cracks were showing in the façade of the white, middle class, heterosexual "normalcy" on display in popular media— Dick and Jane in the 1950s, the Flintstones and the Jetsons in the 1960s, the Brady Bunch in the 1970s.

By the 2020s, it has become clear not only that the cracks have widened, but that the whole edifice was an artifact of its historical era, long gone. We're living in a different world now, and probably, under the social surface, we always were. Sex and gender are complicated. Suppressing their complexity with received moral wisdom about what is and isn't "natural" has become increasingly untenable. Young and urban people, especially, aren't buying it.

But what motivated *me* to conduct these surveys? My own gender, sexuality, and family life are unremarkable, even by last century's standards. Neither am I a sexologist, sociologist, or anthropologist. I work on artificial intelligence at a big tech company, which on the face of it seems unrelated. Digging a bit deeper, though, the rapid advance of AI has forced my colleagues and I to think hard about humanity. How do we envision our future? Who *are* "we," anyway? Does *we* include collective identity groups as well as individuals? Nonhuman animals and plants? Governments and corporations? Will it soon include robots?

Such questions are far from academic. Regarding the last, for instance: computers have become enmeshed in our personal lives, moving in just a few years from being office furniture to living in our

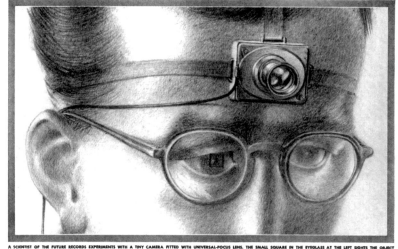

A SCIENTIST OF THE FUTURE RECORDS EXPERIMENTS WITH A TINY CAMERA FITTED WITH UNIVERSAL-FOCUS LENS. THE SMALL SQUARE IN THE EYEGLASS AT THE LEFT SIGHTS THE OBJECT

AS WE MAY THINK

A TOP U. S. SCIENTIST FORESEES A POSSIBLE FUTURE WORLD IN WHICH MAN-MADE MACHINES WILL START TO THINK

purses and pockets, mediating our most intimate relationships. The intersection of AI and privacy, one of my team's main areas of research, has thus become an urgent concern. Beyond that, computers are starting to look less like tools than like extensions of our bodies and minds, always on and always connected, as if telepathically. Online, our presentation can become increasingly decoupled from our physical selves. Neural nets are now able to model human language and interact with us on our own terms, which will soon lead to all sorts of novel human-AI relationships. What kind of strange hybrid world will our kids grow up in?

It's telling that "the future" and "our children" seem like phrases joined at the hip. Their association, suffused with nurturing, protective values, has sometimes been called *reproductive futurism*.[1] It's hard to argue against being "pro child," especially if the alternative sounds selfish, uncaring, or short-sighted. Children are sweet, and we hold them in a state of grace, because they either haven't had the chance yet to make truly bad choices, or they aren't old enough to take full responsibility for them.[2] For obvious evolutionary reasons, many of us are powerfully compelled to nurture and protect them, especially when we believe they're "ours"—which might mean nationally or tribally, and can of course include adoption, but most often means genetically. In this sense, reproductive futurism is bound up in heterosexuality, in having and raising kids who will propagate our genes—and in the old days, the more the better.

1 Edelman, *No Future: Queer Theory and the Death Drive*, 3, 2004.

2 Legally, this is the very definition of childhood.

Increasingly, though, it's becoming clear that for civilization on our planet to survive, we need *fewer* kids, not more. This isn't about curtailing our future, but about embracing it. Civilization comprises far more than the sum of its human reproductive lineages; it's about our relationships with one another, the knowledge and cultures we've built up over thousands of years, our institutions, our cities and our countryside, our sciences and technologies, our languages and our art.

This implies a shift from reproductive futurism to something more like ecological and civilizational futurism. The shift implies that gender and sexuality have a different role to play now, with biological reproduction no longer center stage—which is precisely what we see happening. Is that a coincidence? Queer and trans identities are rapidly on the rise. Nontraditional relationships of all kinds are becoming far more common too, and many of them aren't focused on making babies. Even for young people who are heterosexual and fairly traditional, the likelihood of marrying and having kids is in sharp decline worldwide, especially in cities and in the more economically developed countries.[3]

3 Kulu, "Why Do Fertility Levels Vary Between Urban and Rural Areas?," 2013; Ortiz-Ospina and Roser, "Marriages and Divorces," 2020; Roser, "Fertility Rate," 2014.

Not everyone is happy with these changes. One of the more traditionally minded survey respondents wrote, "all these homos will burn in hell. What would happen to a animal species that went gay, I'll tell you, they would all go extinct... bunch of dipshits."[4] Birth control and access to abortion have of course played a much larger role in the shift than "going gay," so unsurprisingly, these practices, too, have become flashpoints in the culture wars. Meanwhile, despite (or perhaps, partly, because of) ubiquitous connectivity, loneliness and isolation have become endemic, both in small towns with dwindling populations and in increasingly anonymous big cities. Sexuality itself, both partnered and solo, seems to be in decline.[5] Is this the way we're meant to live?

4 A 33-year-old man from Kalamazoo, Michigan. When quoting survey respondents, I'll usually do so verbatim, neither correcting spelling and grammar nor adding the obnoxious "[sic]" disclaimer.

At their core, the culture wars are about who we are now, how we define what's "natural" and whether that's actually desirable, and to what extent we can redefine ourselves over time without becoming something entirely *unnatural*, alien... *other*. Since everyone alive today would likely seem thoroughly alien to a paleolithic human, perhaps our cultural divide is about differences in people's maximum comfortable rates of change.

5 Herbenick et al., "Changes in Penile-Vaginal Intercourse Frequency and Sexual Repertoire from 2009 to 2018: Findings from the National Survey of Sexual Health and Behavior," 2022.

Consider, for example, how the struggle to define and delimit humanity in some elusive "natural" state animates a long-simmering debate about the Olympics. Such high-stakes physical competitions are fraught with contradiction, in that they harness human ingenuity and our capacity for self-modification to select for and continually expand the limits of what bodies can do. Somewhat arbitrarily, caffeine and high altitude training are allowed, but blood doping[6] and steroids aren't.

6 Meaning: taking drugs or getting transfusions to increase an athlete's red blood cell count.

7 Intersexuality is a complex topic, discussed in Chapters 11–13 of this book. Women with certain intersex variations have elevated androgens, which are strongly correlated with elite athletic performance; see Bermon et al., "Serum Androgen Levels Are Positively Correlated with Athletic Performance and Competition Results in Elite Female Athletes," 2018 and Bermon and Garnier's "Serum Androgen Levels and Their Relation to Performance in Track and Field: Mass Spectrometry Results from 2127 Observations in Male and Female Elite Athletes," 2017.

8 Jensen, Schorer, and Faber, "How Is the Topic of Intersex Athletes in Elite Sports Positioned in Academic Literature Between January 2000 and July 2022? A Systematic Review," 2022.

Meanwhile, the Paralympic games, originally a gesture toward greater human inclusivity, have turned the tables. Paralympians with prosthetics are now beating Olympians at running, and as technology improves, they'll doubtless do so in other events too. Where do we draw the line? Decisions to allow or prohibit specific technologies will come to look increasingly absurd—as will decisions to allow or prohibit people, or to classify them "fairly."

For instance, in order to allow women to compete meaningfully as runners, their events have been segregated from men's since the early 20th century; yet doing so made it likely that people with intersex characteristics would rise to the top of certain women's events.[7] Over the years, committees were then put in place to attempt to rigorously define and enforce sex boundaries—a practice, this book will argue, that is not only humiliating for athletes, but downright impossible.[8] Similar controversies have broken out on a much more local scale over trans kids competing in gendered school sports programs.

Zdeněk Koubek (born Zdena "Zdeňka" Koubková) set world records in running events, winning two medals at the 1934 Women's World Games and several national titles in 100–800m running, long jump, and high jump. In 1936, he underwent gender reassignment surgery and retired from athletics.

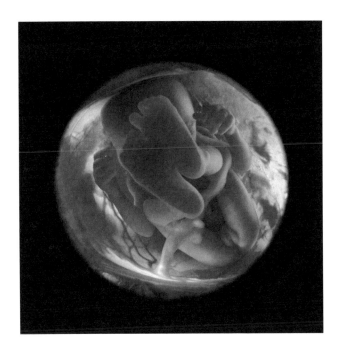

Swedish photographer Lennart Nilsson's groundbreaking photograph of a fetus in its amniotic sac, featured in *Life* magazine, April 30, 1965.

At some point, we'll need to admit to the futility of trying to police categories like women versus men, or natural versus augmented. We're *all* augmented in so many ways—physically, intellectually, and societally.

I hope that we can think and act soon on a planetary scale, because the great challenges we now face are all planetary in scale too—and largely of our own making: climate collapse, pollution, pandemics, loss of habitable land, surging inequality, desperate mass migrations. We live in the Anthropocene, a geological era defined by human activity.

We've gotten into this pickle thanks to the advanced technologies civilization has developed over thousands of years, enabling us to explode in numbers, burn fuels, and consume resources far in excess of what can be sustained. It's not just human bodies that are burning and consuming too much, but cows, factories, jet engines, and crops—a multispecies, cyborg lichen whose reach has, for the moment, exceeded its grasp. Major changes will be needed—and they are possible, with ideas and partial solutions already glimmering here and there. Our challenge is that while our technologies may be products of our collective imagination, our actions, our will, and the ways we identify are still not collective enough.

Introduction
Anonymous Identity

Bild Lilli, a German
fashion doll in pro-
duction from 1955 to
1964, when Mattel
acquired the rights
and relaunched her
as "Barbie."

Ours is a world in vertigo. [...] We are all alienated – but have we ever been otherwise? It is through, and not despite, our alienated condition that we can free ourselves [...] nothing is so sacred that it cannot be reengineered and transformed so as to widen our aperture of freedom, extending to gender and the human. To say that nothing is sacred, that nothing is transcendent or protected from the will to know, to tinker and to hack, is to say that nothing is supernatural.
Laboria Cuboniks, *Xenofeminist Manifesto*, 2018

You will find your answers in the secrets of strangers.
Frank Warren, creator of *Postsecret*, 2004

An anonymous caller's voice played over the laptop's speakers. "Hi, Dan. This is a 26-year-old bisexual man in New York, and I have a somewhat strange question. Watching the HBO show *Westworld*, I've been thinking… if there were hyper-advanced sex robots and you were to have sex with one, would that be cheating? I mean, isn't it just like a really fancy sex toy? Or is there some other component, like, if you had an emotional connection that means something else. I don't know. What do you think?"

The recording clicked off. Dan Savage, looking both mischievous and a bit world-weary, waited a beat, then leaned into his microphone and spoke. "Joining me in our studio today to help tackle this very important question about robots, *Westworld*, and AI is Blaise Agüera y Arcas, who is the head of Google's machine intelligence effort here in Seattle."

Cutting politely through my equivocations, Dan took this one into his more capable hands—"It's cheating if your partner thinks it's cheating, period, the end"—then shifted the conversation into territory I'm slightly more qualified to have opinions on: the state of machine learning today, the way we project personhood onto inanimate things, and what the Turing test might look like—in bed. Bad puns about uncanny valleys were made.

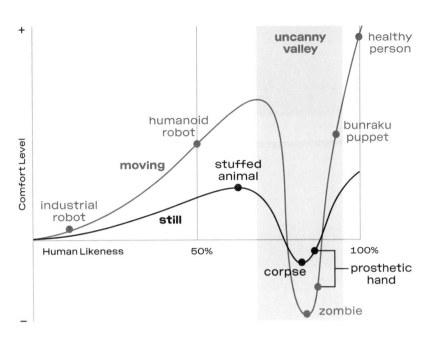

The uncanny valley.

(In case you're not familiar with it: the Turing test, which will come up again in Chapter 14, was a thought experiment proposed by computing pioneer Alan Turing in 1950. He pointed out that, since we have no objective way of determining when a machine goes from being an "it" to a "who," we may as well simply ask it to convince us that it can stand in for a human in an online chat. As for the "uncanny valley," the phrase was invented by Japanese robotics professor Masahiro Mori in 1970 to refer to that in-between situation in which something humanoid is *just* realistic enough to be creepy—without being realistic enough to be convincing. The characters in the 2004 animated movie *The Polar Express* are an oft-cited example.)

As I gamely struggled to answer Dan's rapid-fire followup questions ("Do you guys talk about how everyone's going to be fucking what you're working on?"), I remember hoping I wouldn't get in too much trouble with my employer when this episode of the Savage Lovecast aired.[1] Sometime after we'd wandered off into the thickets of whether consciousness is an illusion, and when people with *Avatar* kinks would get their very own giant blue sexbots, Nancy Hartunian, the Lovecast's long-suffering producer, rolled her eyes and signaled for us to wrap it up.

The recording stopped, but conversation continued. The ethical conundrum of how advanced a sex toy needs to be before we start having to ask for its consent was a welcome distraction, but I didn't really have robots, sexy or otherwise, on my mind that day. I was thinking about people. How were they voting? It was Election Day: Tuesday, November 8th, 2016. It was hard to think of anything else.

[1] The segment aired a few weeks later, on Episode #526 of the Lovecast.

Voters wait in line to cast their ballots on Election Day, November 8, 2016, in Alexandria, Virginia.

Dan, normally a worrywart, was uncharacteristically confident that Hillary had it in the bag. So was everyone else in Seattle, a famously/notoriously progressive little blue dot near the upper left corner of the US map. Despite an unspoken agreement not to jinx it, the mood was expectant, even festive. Parties were being planned for the evening, including one at my place. Champagne was chilling in the fridge. Nancy and her family would be dropping by.

I was less certain. I'd been checking Nate Silver's FiveThirty-Eight polling website obsessively, and while it, too, favored Hillary, her lead was far from decisive. Everyone seemed to be ignoring the margin of error... and it was substantial.

Although not on the same scale as all of those big national polls, my own data had me wondering, too. As a side project, I'd been running surveys using Amazon's Mechanical Turk platform, which lets you code up questionnaires and crowdsource responses from people all over the country. Having learned about Mechanical Turk as a frequently used tool for generating AI training data, I wanted to use it to satisfy my curiosity instead. At first, my questions were straightforward. They ran along the lines of: Who will you vote for? What issues do you care about? What do you believe? Who are you?

I didn't want to be exploitative, so I was paying my respondents decently—and this was turning into an expensive hobby. Still, it was cheap and easy compared to the phone banking or field operation needed to run such a survey a few years ago. Now it could all be done from a laptop, and with a turnaround time of mere hours. I felt like I was learning a lot about my fellow human beings. Every insight suggested more questions I wanted to ask, hence a new survey, more graphs, more analysis. It was addictive.

As soon as I'd begun these experiments, in the summer of 2016, it had become clear that the way people would vote had less to do with policy positions than with identity; "Who are you?" turned out to be the key. It was about "us" versus "them." Granted, it's no news that tribalism is a part of human nature, but it seemed like an especially powerful driver during this election cycle. Much of Donald Trump's brand was based on the idea of building a wall to protect "us" from "them," and it had become increasingly clear that "they" included not only undocumented border crossers, but minorities of all kinds within the United States. "They" included immigrants, people of color, LGBTQ+ people, academics, people who aren't Christian. At times, women seemed to be included too, and anybody with a disability, and everybody living in the city.[2] Of course the resulting "majority" then turns out to be a minority—but one that held the reins of economic and political power last century, during the half-real, half-mythical era people had in mind when they chanted "Make America Great Again!"

In response to the free text question I had begun adding to my surveys ("Is there anything you'd like to add?"), I had seen comments like:

I believe that as a society we have moved in a positive direction regarding inclusion in recent years and this will only benefit everyone in the long run.[3]

On the other hand, I had also seen:

I am an Anglo Saxon European American male. The most hated discriminated group in America. I am looking forward to the civil war. Oh, and not the Anglo Saxon side which conspired with these Jews to rip Americans off. I am from the side that didn't get paid.[4]

Beyond the numbers, responses like these were going through my head as I confessed to a skeptical Dan and Nancy in the podcast studio that I thought Trump might win. We'd been debating whether we'd need to empathize with machines in the future, but in the meantime we humans weren't even managing to acknowledge each other.

The *Stranger*, Seattle's alt-weekly newspaper, has been home to Dan's sex advice column, Savage Love, since its first issue in 1991. Nancy

2 Bellafante, "Why the Big City President Made Cities the Enemy," 2020.

3 A 28-year-old from Burnsville, Minnesota.

4 A 55-year-old from Raleigh, North Carolina.

Seattle's alt-weekly newspaper, the *Stranger*, February 2017.

had cajoled him into podcasting when that medium was still new, in 2006. The *Stranger*'s smart, cheeky, lefty, and often smutty sensibility feels much like the voice of the city itself; it's much like the voice of many US cities. In places like Seattle, sentiments like those of my Anglo Saxon European American respondent could seem distant and irrelevant. But my statistics told me that he was far from alone.

The empty and barricaded Seattle Police Department headquarters at the heart of the Capitol Hill Autonomous Zone (CHAZ), June 14, 2020.

I was thinking about him as I unlocked my bike in front of the *Stranger*'s offices, on a street that would briefly become, four years later, part of the Capitol Hill Autonomous Zone. The call for civil war was still in my head when, a few hours later, my family and friends huddled around the kitchen table, listening soberly to the returns coming in from one swing state after another, our drinks untouched.

"Who are these people?," someone asked quietly.

This question presupposes something profound about what it means to be human—something far deeper and more enduring than election cycles, political parties, nationalities, religions, or robot kink communities.

It's a remarkable intellectual achievement to be able to respond to questions about who you *are*. To understand why, consider first the language needed to make such questions precise. "Did you vote for Jill Stein?" and "Do you use the men's bathroom?" are straightforward enough, but what about "Do you identify as liberal?" or "Are you bisexual?" The last two questions are about identity, not about behavior. To understand why the difference matters, let's imagine what life was like for our pre-human ancestors, and what it's *still* like for our non-human cousins.

If you were, for instance, a chimpanzee, you would be able to communicate, and even, to a degree, use language. However, questions about identity likely wouldn't make any sense to you, because as a chimp you'd lack the ability to "identify" in any collective way—what I'll call having an "anonymous identity."

You wouldn't lack an *individual* identity, or meaningful relationships with others. I'm pretty sure you would feel like a *person*, and would understand that other people have their own experiences, just as you do. It's hard to imagine otherwise, after spending some time watching old documentary footage of the groundbreaking primatologist Jane Goodall interacting with the chimps in Tanzania's Gombe National Park. As a chimp, you'd have a rich inner life, experiencing much the same range of emotions humans do. You'd love, quarrel, scheme, form alliances, and problem solve. When Frans de Waal, another prominent primatologist, wrote the bestselling *Chimpanzee Politics* in 1982,[5] the shenanigans described were so instantly familiar to US Speaker of the House Newt Gingrich that he put it on a recommended reading list for his colleagues in Congress.[6]

5   De Waal, *Chimpanzee Politics: Power and Sex Among Apes*, 1982.

6   De Waal, *Different: Gender Through the Eyes of a Primatologist*, 82, 2022.

Jane Goodall and a fellow primate in Tanzania's Gombe National Park.

Not that any of these behaviors are unique to higher primates. If you have a cat, dog, or parrot at home, you probably feel that much of this holds for your nonhuman friend too. We're animals ourselves, and in almost every respect we're much like the other big-brained creatures we share our planet with.

Koko gives the "to listen" sign, telling (then graduate student) Francine Patterson she wants to use the phone.

However, two important characteristics make humans unusual. One is complex language, and the other, which is closely related, is our ability to identify collectively to form large "anonymous societies."[7]

We all know what language is, though it's not accurate to claim that complex forms of communication are *uniquely* human. There are unanswered questions about advanced communication among whales and dolphins, for example; chimps and gorillas can be taught elements of sign language; and prairie dogs, amazingly, can warn each other about the color and shape of an invader.[8] Parrots can even learn our spoken languages, albeit not with adult human proficiency. Researchers and animals who have established true symbolic interspecies communication—like Koko the gorilla with Francine Patterson, or Alex the parrot with Irene Pepperberg[9]—should convince us that humans don't hold a copyright on speech.

However, these rare connections also highlight a gulf in depth and degree. Humans have a talent for language that's probably unparalleled on Earth, and has been key to developing the cooperative strategies, technologies, and cultures that, over the course of many generations, have turned us from a niche species into a world-shaping force.

Symbols are at the heart of language. These are abstractions that "digitize" the analog world around us, turning a welter of continuous

Alex the parrot counts red and blue objects at the behest of Dr. Irene Pepperberg.

perceptual impressions into discrete entities with names: fruit, tree, rock, chimp. Recognizing individual people and assigning them names—like "Alex" or "Irene"—is an especially important case. We have every reason to believe that many animals with big brains have individual recognition, and some can even use names. (In 1983, for example, Koko the gorilla asked for a cat for Christmas, and was eventually allowed to choose a kitten from an abandoned litter. She named him "All Ball," and loved him.) In a primate troop, everyone recognizes everyone else individually. However, there's no evidence that nonhuman primates have anonymous societies, the way humans do.

Koko, known for her fondness of cats, adopted two kittens on her 44th birthday— Ms. Gray (pictured) and Ms. Black.

In an anonymous society, people aren't (or aren't only) identified by their individual names, but by symbolic markers of group identity, such as race, nationality, tribe, class, sexuality, profession, membership in a club or guild, political party, and so on. I call these associations "anonymous identities"—a seemingly paradoxical phrase, but an apt one, since when we say that a person "identifies" as, for example, "a Christian Gen Xer," they have both identified themselves *and* remained anonymous.

Curiously, we find anonymous societies mostly in animals with tiny brains, like ants and bees. In the distant past, these insects roamed individually or in small groups, but eventually, many different lineages independently evolved the same highly beneficial trait: collective identity. Ants, for instance, can live in a colony with a large number of individuals, cooperating closely within the colony—while being at war with ants in *other* colonies. They distinguish "us" from "them" using pheromones. There's really no other way to do it, since their numbers are so large (and their brains are so small) that it would be impossible to distinguish "us" from "them" using individual recognition. So instead, they use the chemical equivalent of team jerseys.

In this important respect, humans are more like social insects than like other primates. Psychologist Jonathan Haidt had a similar idea in mind when he called us "90 percent chimp and 10 percent bee." A chimp colony could never grow to the size of an ant colony or beehive—let alone a human city—because chimps rely on individual recognition.

Relationships based on individual recognition can still result in something like in- and out-groups. When Jane Goodall and her colleagues observed a troop of chimpanzees they referred to as the "Kasakela community" undergo a violent splintering into

7 Moffett, *The Human Swarm: How Our Societies Arise, Thrive, and Fall*, 2019.

8 Dennis, Shuster, and Slobodchikoff, "Dialects in the Alarm Calls of Black-Tailed Prairie Dogs (*Cynomys ludovicianus*): A Case of Cultural Diffusion?," 2020.

9 Patterson, "The Gestures of a Gorilla: Language Acquisition in Another Pongid," 1978; Pepperberg, *The Alex Studies: Cognitive and Communicative Abilities of Grey Parrots*, 2002.

A column of *Eciton* army ants on the march.

two communities, afterward referred to as the "Kasakela" and the "Kahama," they may have been mistakenly projecting a human idea onto a non-human situation. Consider Frans de Waal's description of this "Gombe Chimpanzee War," written 30 years later:

> [C]himpanzees [that] had played and groomed together, reconciled after squabbles, shared meat, and lived in harmony [...] began to fight nonetheless. Shocked researchers watched as former friends now drank each other's blood [...] us-versus-them among chimpanzees is a socially constructed distinction in which even well-known individuals can become enemies if they happen to hang out with the wrong crowd or live in the wrong area. In humans, ethnic groups that used to get along reasonably well may all of a sudden turn against each other, as the Hutus and Tutsis did in Rwanda and the Serbs, Croats, and Muslims in Bosnia. What kind of mental switch is flipped that changes people's attitudes? And what kind of switch turns chimpanzee group mates into each other's deadliest foes? I suspect the switches operate similarly in humans and apes [...].[10]

10 De Waal, *Our Inner Ape: A Leading Primatologist Explains Why We Are Who We Are*, 142, 2005.

De Waal has written a number of books about how the behavior of other primates offers profound insight into human behavior, but here, he may be making an unwarranted leap. Chimps aren't friendly to other chimps by default. They distrust strangers, but may over time develop a bond, or at least a relationship with established parameters (with one dominant over the other, for example). These dynamics, together with the bonds that arise from mating and child-rearing, naturally lead to evolving clusters of individuals that are comfortable—or comfortable enough—being near each other. Scientists who study animal behavior use the term "fission-fusion societies" to characterize the result. The clusters are more or less stable, but can change either over the course of a day (for example, as foraging parties go out in the morning but reconvene at night) or over longer periods of time (as when a few individuals decide to strike out on their own, or, with careful deference, join an existing group).

A human observer might identify a cluster of chimps who get along as a community, and give it a name. However, from the inside, there's no evidence that collective identity exists; no community name, tribal flag, or team jersey. Upon re-analyzing Jane Goodall's field notes, social scientist Joseph Feldblum noted that the split seemed to have been precipitated by the death in 1970 of a single senior male, Leakey, who "seems to have been a bridge between the northern and southern chimps."[11] What looks from the outside like one community

11 Barras, "Only Known Chimp War Reveals How Societies Splinter," 2014.

Lantern slide of Woureddy, native of Bruny Island, Tasmania. The 4,000 or so Tasmanians are thought to have been isolated from the Australian mainland for about 10,000 years.

12 Diamond, *Guns, Germs, and Steel*, 312–13, 2005.

splintering into two factions might feel, from the inside, like a web of relationships that has frayed, in which friendships don't have enough force to overcome enmities, and in which individuals who no longer hang out together become estranged over time. We might still say that troops or colonies "exist" as a phenomenon we can observe, in the same way that clouds or patches of clover exist, but they may not correspond to a concept in the minds of the chimps themselves.

As far as we know, chimps don't explicitly identify with communities. Nor do any other primates, aside from us. Hence, events like the Gombe Chimpanzee War can only occur locally, on a scale of dozens of individuals, unlike the "mental switch" that flipped between the Tutsis and the Hutus, or between the Serbs, Croats, and Muslims, both of which led to genocide.

One could argue that community is just as fundamental to humanity as language. This isn't just for the reasons everyone talks about—because we need friendship, love, and emotional support; chimps need and have those relationships too. It's because, as the last section of this book will explore, the development of culture and technology requires the concentrated interaction of many people. Language is *how* those interactions take place; community is *with whom*.

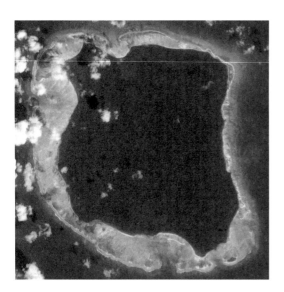

Community size matters. Throughout our history, wherever the number and density of interacting humans is very low, we not only find that technologies and cultures develop more slowly, but that they can regress. The isolated Tasmanian people, for example, forgot over the generations how to fish and make many of the tools their ancestors on the Australian mainland used.[12] By the 19th century, the Andamanese, inhabitants of an island archipelago in the Indian Ocean, had forgotten how to make fire. As far as we understand, they continually tended lit embers in hollowed-out trees, and would need to rely on "harvesting" wildfire from a

Glassblowing in a Dutch lightbulb factory, 1936.

13 Goodheart, "The Last Island of the Savages," 17, 2000; Man, "On the Aboriginal Inhabitants of the Andaman Islands. (Part II.)," 150, 1883.

14 Moffett, "Human Identity and the Evolution of Societies," 39–40, 2013.

← North Sentinel Island, the most isolated of the Andaman Islands, with (per the 2018 Indian census) an estimated 39 inhabitants.

lightning strike if those embers were to go out.[13] They didn't end up in this situation because they're any less intelligent than anyone else. It happened because knowledge, like those glowing embers, must be nurtured and passed down from generation to generation. With too few people, the risk of loss with every generation comes down to a roll of the dice.

It follows that the answer to the question "how many humans does it take to screw in a lightbulb" is probably a few million, given the complexities of mastering electricity and industrial manufacturing. Yet we can't achieve the critical mass needed for evolving this kind of advanced technology without anonymous societies to allow for large, stable communities.

When we consider that no vertebrate on Earth other than us has societies larger than 200 individuals or so,[14] we should wonder whether our individual intelligence is really humanity's special sauce. To an alien visiting the Earth 100,000 years ago, small bands of human hunter-gatherer-scavengers might not have stood out relative to the planet's other large-ish fauna.

On the other hand, we're animals that talk. While nobody knows for sure how anonymous human societies first arose, my guess is that they've been with us for a very long time—specifically, since language *itself* arose. If there ever was a Tower of Babel time in which we all spoke the same language (unlikely), it wouldn't have taken long for this one language to splinter into many. Over generations, language evolution produces linguistically differentiated populations in much the way genetic evolution produces new species. Language, culture, and group identity would have co-evolved and reinforced

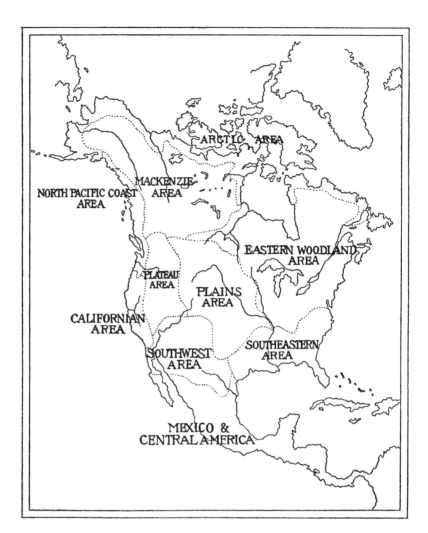

Map of "culture-areas" in North America by Clark Wissler, who theorized that cultural diffusion explained these vast regions over which closely related artifacts can be found, 1913.

There's evidence of this same process in some other animals too, e.g. in resident orca populations, per Filatova et al., "Call Diversity in the North Pacific Killer Whale Populations: Implications for Dialect Evolution and Population History," 2012. These researchers found that language among killer whales evolves slowly, is transmitted from one generation to the next, and can split into mutually incomprehensible dialects; also, bigger populations seem to support more complex languages.

one other, creating rifts in the process. Everyone would have become aware of an "us" (people who speak the same language) and a "them" (people who don't).**15**

The latter would often have been further divided into those speaking different recognizable but incomprehensible foreign languages. Hence, the names of many of today's most popular languages are also the names of the people who first spoke them: French, Vietnamese, English, and so on. That these terms also correspond to the names of countries defined by clearly delineated polygons on the world map is a more recent development.

Native North American tribes offer a catalog of evidence about how such names generally work. For instance, Kwakwaka'wakw (the tribe commonly known today as Kwakiutl), means "speakers of our language"; "Cherokee" or "Tsalagi" derives from a Muskogee word for "speakers of another language."

16 Wissler, "The Culture-Area Concept in Social Anthropology," 1927. Per Graeber and Wengrow: "At first, the most prominent exponent of the culture area approach was Franz Boas. [...] Boas's student and successor at the [American Museum of Natural History], Clark Wissler, tried to systematize his ideas by dividing the Americas as a whole, from Newfoundland to Tierra del Fuego, into fifteen different regional systems, each with its own characteristic customs, aesthetic styles, ways of obtaining and preparing food, and forms of social organization. [...] Boas was a staunch anti-racist. As a German Jew, he was particularly troubled by the way the American obsession with race and eugenics was being taken up in his own mother country. When Wissler began to embrace certain eugenicist ideas, the pair had a bitter falling-out. But the original impetus for the culture area concept was precisely to find a way of talking about human history which avoided ranking populations into higher or lower on any grounds [...]." *The Dawn of Everything*, 171–72, 2021.

17 There have been large-scale societies that didn't rely heavily on farming, but spent part of the year roaming over a large area, only convening seasonally to create "temporary cities," as described by Lowie, "Some Aspects of Political Organization Among the American Aborigines," 1948. Obviously, this way of life requires a shared anonymous identity as well.

The word for "person" or "people" in a tribe's language has itself often turned into the name of the people who speak that language. For instance, Dena'ina, Dene, Dine'e, Gwich'in, Innu, Inuit, Iyiniwok, Lenape, L'nu'k, Maklak, Mamaceqtaw, Ndee, Numakiki, Numinu, Nuutsiu, Olekwo'l, and Tsitsistas are all tribes whose names simply mean "people" or "the people." So, ironically, the one word that ought to encompass everyone—"people"—spoken in many languages immediately implies many distinct tribes. Moreover, it suggests the ultimate "othering": that foreigners *aren't even* people.

Unlike species membership, though, belonging to one language group does not preclude membership in another. Multilingualism means that certain people, in any era, belong to multiple linguistic groups, literally able to "code switch" between accents, dialects, or languages. During the long stretches of prehistory when people spent their lives roaming over vast distances, this undoubtedly eased cooperation, trade, and knowledge exchange, and may have been key to allowing practices and technologies to diffuse over "culture areas" spanning whole continents.[16]

Over the last 10,000 or so years, though, certain populations became increasingly dependent on farming and the year-round settled lifestyle that implied. Such conditions would have caused anonymous identities to further crystallize. Regardless of ideas about property and ownership (it was often collective), individuals would have begun to think of themselves as tied to permanent dwellings, and to the surrounding cultivated land. Hence place names became common symbolic markers of anonymous societies.

Farming could support larger concentrations of people in one place—more than could have known each other personally. A shared anonymous identity would have been at least as important a "technology" as farming itself to allow for the cohesion of large communities with common norms, customs, and laws.[17] Settled societies also gave rise to increasingly fine-grained division of labor, which would have produced yet more anonymous identities—of the kind eventually institutionalized into so-called "voluntary associations" like guilds, councils, and clubs. Finally, farming would have allowed (or required) big extended families to grow in place over many generations without the continual fission and fusion that characterizes a more mobile lifestyle. This is presumably how clans arose.

Today, compound names often comprise an "individual symbol" (first or given name) and a "team symbol" (family, clan, or surname) based on one of the above properties: place (as in Jack London), profession (as in Anita Baker), and ancestor (as in Sinéad O'Connor). Notice that anonymous identities almost from the start would have been multiple: an individual would have identified in all of these overlapping ways at once. An ancestral O'Connor might not only have been a member of the O'Connor clan, but also a blacksmith, and a resident of Dublin.

Anonymous identities often don't emerge as an organic, bottom-up social phenomenon, though. Rather, they tend to be imposed from above, as detailed by political scientist and anthropologist James C. Scott. In his 1998 book *Seeing Like a State*, Scott describes the social machinery required by any government to perform its usual functions: taxation, military conscription, representation (maybe), and prevention of rebellion (as needed). To exert power over its people, the state must first render those people "legible," meaning that they must be identified, counted, classified, and quantified. The state will want to know where you live; this is why, once sedentary farming has made statehood possible, and an aspiring state has marked out its borders, life within those borders becomes increasingly difficult for wanderers, nomads, travelers, gypsies, and the houseless—anyone whose coordinates (not to mention allegiances, property rights, and obligations) can't be pinned down.[18]

Even more fundamentally, in a large organization or modern state, your *name* must be standardized. This is no small feat, given that in many traditional societies, names are far from stable:

> [...] [I]t is not uncommon for individuals to have different names during different stages of life (infancy, childhood, adulthood) and in some cases after death; added to these are names used for joking, rituals, and mourning and names used for interactions with same-sex friends or with in-laws. Each name is specific to a certain phase of life, social setting, or interlocutor.[19]

Hence, legal names and permanent surnames (in patriarchal societies, typically patronymic) have often been government-imposed—whether during the Qin dynasty in China, the European Middle Ages, or more recently, the Philippines under Spanish rule.[20] Paradoxically, it's precisely a state or other large organization's ability to individually identify inhumanly large numbers of people that allows it to issue passports, driver's licences, ID badges, uniforms, and membership cards vouchsafing anonymous identities for citizens, employees, or club members. In other words, it's only by becoming individually legible to the state that we can become anonymous to each other.

Insect colonies offer a striking parallel. Calling the large reproductive female at the heart of a colony its "queen" is a misnomer, as she doesn't rule, but she does, like a state, play a key role in defining colony membership through anonymous identity. Ants have "smells" that, as with human anonymous identity, derive in part from a place (a common

18 Nowadays, digital credentials, and especially a mobile phone number, are increasingly supplanting a home address as an enduring coordinate system for uniquely identifying people. While this enables new forms of digitally mediated nomadism (see Marquardt, *The New Nomads*, 2021), it also gives the state unprecedented new powers to contact, track, and surveil "digital nomads."

19 Scott, *Seeing Like a State*, 64, 1998.

20 In the Philippines, the colonial government imposed surnames *en masse*, with entire towns sometimes assigned last names starting with the same letter, and whole regions of the map laid out alphabetically as if the land itself were an enormous collage made out of cut-up pages from a telephone book.

21 In a telling exception, a 2005 paper found that ant queens can individually recognize other queens, which may be beneficial in maintaining dominance hierarchies among the queens. Some larger-brained social insects, such as paper wasps, have also been shown to be capable of individual recognition. See D'Ettorre and Heinze, "Individual Recognition in Ant Queens," 2005; Sheehan and Tibbetts, "Specialized Face Learning Is Associated with Individual Recognition in Paper Wasps," 2011.

environment and diet), from their version of a profession, or "caste" (worker vs. drone, for instance), and from a genetic line (chemical markers inherited from common ancestry). In this sense, while chimps have only first names, ants have only last names, something like "London-Baker-O'Connor."[21]

As Jonathan Haidt's "chimp plus bee" formula implies, modern humans combine both kinds of identity; and unlike ants or bees, we have repurposable mental machinery—language—allowing us to coin new symbols and form new identity groups at will. Hence for us, identities don't develop at the leisurely pace of biological evolution, but at the increasingly breakneck speed of cultural evolution. Today, every new social media hashtag offers a potential identity marker.

The onslaught of new and overlapping identities can be exhausting. You might be fantasizing about how life would be without identity politics, but insular, "first name only" societies are far from peaceable paradises. Inequality and oppression still exist in the context of individual relationships—just as for our chimpanzee cousins. Squabbles can turn violent, murder can be commonplace, escaping an abusive situation can be near-impossible, and bonds of friendship or kinship with wronged parties can lead to cycles of revenge and feuding. Life is precarious, whether you're a bullied underdog or a paranoid "alpha," on top for now but always looking over your shoulder.

In anonymous societies, broader social cohesion, shared norms, division of labor, and sheer scale (which allows for more consistent resource sharing, diversification, greater mobility, and risk pooling) can give us significantly more individual security. Laws, customs, rights, and social safety nets can let us live together without having to rely on continual one-on-one negotiation, patronage, and goodwill—or under the constant threat of random violence. On the whole, this seems like progress.

However, such progress comes at a price, as we've seen. With its greater social control over a population that has been pinned in place, the state can be benevolent or tyrannical—and is typically both at once; an individual's experience will depend on their position and caste or class within the society. A monopoly on violence allows powerful states to oppress their own people in ways that would be inconceivable to our mobile hunter-gatherer ancestors, who could always pull up stakes and move somewhere else if things got ugly. Moreover, even if life in a big city feels safer than worrying about being picked off by an enemy raiding party, it can come at a cost of personal freedom, disconnection and alienation.

Describing a termite colony, the late English scientist James Lovelock noted,

22 Lovelock, *Novacene*, 50, 2019.

23 Many ethnographic accounts support this view; for instance, American linguist Daniel Everett wrote of the Pirahã hunter-gatherers in the Amazon, "The Pirahãs show no evidence of depression, chronic fatigue, extreme anxiety, panic attacks, or other psychological ailments common in many industrialized societies. But this psychological well-being is not due, as some might think, to a lack of pressure [...]. [T]hey do have life-threatening physical ailments [and] love lives [... and] they need to provide food every day for their families. They have high infant mortality. [...] They live with threats of violence from outsiders who frequently invade their land. [... But] I have never heard a Pirahã say that he or she is worried. In fact, so far as I can tell, the Pirahãs have no word for worry in their language. One group of visitors [...], psychologists from [MIT's] Brain and Cognitive Science Department, commented that the Pirahãs appeared to be the happiest people they had ever seen." Everett, *Don't Sleep, There Are Snakes: Life and Language in the Amazonian Jungle*, 278, 2008.

The individual worker who once lived freely on the plains now spends a lifetime gathering mud, mixing it with shit and sticking the smelly bundle into gaps in the walls of the nest or anywhere their in-built programme instructs. Is something akin to this egalitarian paradise a model of future urban life? Passing a contemporary office tower, it is hard to ignore the termite analogy—in glass boxes everybody is doing exactly the same thing, not mixing shit but staring at computer screens.[22]

Perhaps, then, it's unsurprising that depression seems to be increasingly common in modern, affluent, anonymous societies.[23]

Worse, the moment there's an anonymous collective identity, there's also an "us," or in-group, and a "them," or out-group,[24] on a scale that dwarfs individual friendship or enmity.[25] Super-colonies of Argentine ants might seem peaceful and cooperative, until we find the places where one super-colony borders another; there, the carnage is brutal, an invisible boundary shifting in a slow tug-of-war over the bodies of the dead.

It recalls the trenches of World War I. Individual German and English people in that war had no quarrel with each other, as the famous Christmas truce of 1914 vividly demonstrated. For a short time, soldiers on opposing sides of the Western Front put down their arms, played football, and sang carols together; but their national identities soon prevailed, turning every Hans or Gunter back into the anonymous "Jerry," every William or Robert back into the anonymous "Tommy." Dehumanized once more, neither individual empathy nor the shared norms of an anonymous in-group inhibited the ongoing violence.

Artist's impression of the Christmas truce of 1914 in the *Illustrated London News*, 1915.

Anonymous identity matters: in 1943, this ID card allowed American sculptor Ruth Asawa to leave the Rohwer Relocation Center, where she was held along with eight thousand Japanese Americans—among the ~122,000 "Persons of Japanese Ancestry" who were detained by the US War Relocation Authority and resettled into concentration camps between 1942–1946.

24 Haldane, "Population Genetics," 1955; Smith, "Group Selection and Kin Selection," 1964; Hamilton, "The Genetical Evolution of Social Behaviour. II," 1964; de Waal, *The Bonobo and the Atheist: In Search of Humanism Among the Primates*, 2014.

25 Consistent with this, strong evidence exists of a dramatic overall decline in violence throughout human history, as measured in violent deaths per capita; however, given exploding population numbers and the mechanization of warfare, the absolute numbers of people killed since 1900 dwarf those of historical conflicts. Further, five of the top ten most deadly mass killings in human history have taken place after 1900, in terms of death *rate* per capita per unit time: World War II (number one), World War I (number three), the Russian Civil War (number eight), the Rwandan genocide (number seven), and Chinese famines associated with Mao's Great Leap Forward (number ten). Sapolsky, *Behave: The Biology of Humans at Our Best and Worst*, 619, 2017.

Can there ever be an "us" *without* a "them"? Our future may depend on the answer to this question.

Today, one of the most important functions of language is forming communities—negotiating their boundaries, naming them, identifying with them. Those overlapping communities are the social laboratories where culture, specialized knowledge, and technology develop. Certain communities may have widely agreed-on prerequisites for membership, some of which are hard to change, such as skin color or sex characteristics. Some, like language, accent, skills, clothes, and hairstyles, can be acquired to one degree or another, though it may be costly. Yet other communities may be quite abstract. When membership in a community relies on a document for proof, like a passport or a union card, it has clearly become so unmoored from an individual body that it has entered a realm of pure ideas.

Chimps, then, wouldn't be able to answer questions on a survey about identity, because even though they can acquire enough symbolic language to understand "first names," they don't live in anonymous societies, hence they lack anonymous identity. Their natural mistrust of strangers isn't softened by the idea that the stranger, because of some kind of team marker, is "one of us"; on the other hand, neither are they *especially* prejudiced against a stranger who is "one of them."

That's why, despite the popularity of *Chimpanzee Politics* in Washington, neither the "build a wall" campaign nor the characterization of an opposing group as a "basket of deplorables" (to use the tribal language in play in the 2016 election) would work on real chimps. Unlike ants or people, it would be hard to convince chimps to go to a rally or march in the street, let alone die for a country, political party, or cause—because that would require *identifying* with a country, political party, or cause.

There's a difference in *purpose* between a population that has anonymous societies and one that doesn't. It's an oversimplification to claim that everything we do is driven by *any* single purpose, but let's suppose, as Darwin did, that an organism "succeeds" insofar as it manages to reproduce. For a chimp, success means raising baby chimps. For ants, success means reproduction of the whole colony, which is not the same—it's entirely compatible, for example, with sacrificing many individuals in war.

Social gathering of six bonobos at the San Diego Zoo.

A colony can be thought of as a single body rather than a collection of individuals. We wouldn't say that a large person is "more successful" than a smaller person, just because a larger body is made up of more cells. Nor do we mourn the death and sloughing-off of our skin cells, or worry about the short lifespans of our white blood cells (those only last a couple of weeks). Since ants within the same colony are genetically very similar (or even clones!)[26] and their brains aren't wired for individual relationships with other ants, the analogy between ants and cells in a body is quite close. Arguably, the colony *is* the organism.

So where does all this leave humanity? I would argue that we're in the midst of a great transition. "Humanity 1.0" was more

[26] Fournier and Aron, "Evolution: No-Male's Land for an Amazonian Ant," 2009.

[27] Firestone, *The Dialectic of Sex: The Case for Feminist Revolution*, 2, 1970.

chimp-like, while "Humanity 2.0" is increasingly ant-like—though we remain a mixture of the two. Can we really still think of ourselves as "90% chimp," though? Success for us used to mean biological reproduction. Now, it's shifting toward cultural reproduction.

We can easily see this transition playing out in front of our eyes, once we know where to look: trends in the birth, death, and reproduction of our bodies; and trends in the birth, death, and reproduction of our identities. This is why, in my own research, I eventually began to ask questions about gender and sexuality, which lie right at the crossroads between reproduction and identity.

The chapters that follow tell a story about human identity and how it's evolving, based on six years of surveys answered by tens of thousands of people in the US. It's a story I've pieced together by combining data analysis, my bread and butter as a researcher, with study and consultation from experts in fields where I have no formal training—including ethnography, sociology, psychology, anthropology, demography, gender studies, and medicine. I've also learned directly from thousands of pages of candid comments from a wide range of survey respondents. The picture that emerges by bringing all of these elements together has surprised me at every turn, and feels important to share.

Feminist writer and activist Shulamith Firestone (1945–2012).

A few disclaimers are in order, though. To focus so much of this book on gender and sexuality may puzzle some readers, given the many other identities fraught with marginalization and systemic bias—especially, in the American setting, race. While I'll touch on race in the context of urbanization, I'll do so only tangentially. I focus on gender because it's so tightly bound to the fundamentals of biology and reproduction. As the controversial feminist writer Shulamith Firestone put it in her 1970 book *The Dialectic of Sex*,

The division yin and yang pervades all culture, history, economics, nature itself; modern Western versions of sex discrimination are only the most recent layer. [...] [F]eminists have to question, not just all of Western culture, but the organization of culture itself, and further, even the very organization of nature.[27]

28 Lewis, "Shulamith Firestone Wanted to Abolish Nature—We Should, Too," 2021.

Modern readers of Firestone have noted her obliviousness to the racist dimensions of the culture she critiques—yet remains embedded within.[28] I'll elaborate on some of these dimensions in Chapter 4, and take a step back from "Western" ideas about sex, gender, and the family to consider a wider historical context.

Nonetheless, Firestone's central insight is worth taking seriously. Beyond biology's "yin and yang," modern societies have accumulated a great tangle of gender, sexual, and relationship models, power structures, taboos, preferences, kinks, and orientations. Yet these cultural structures are built on a foundation tracing all the way back to the evolution of sex itself by single-celled lifeforms that pre-date even the distinctions between animals, plants, and fungi.

In this sense, the biological reproduction-focused "Humanity 1.0" is not only far older than the US, but far older than humanity itself. Our ongoing transition to "Humanity 2.0," the reproduction of identities, may be a shift as profound as the emergence of multicellular organisms 600 million years ago, in which language serves as the new DNA.

You may be wondering how it's possible to draw broad conclusions about humanity based on a sample of respondents from just one country. In general, that should arouse skepticism, and yes, these conclusions should be regarded as tentative.

29 The historical materials, too, focus on the United States and Western Europe, both because of my own limitations as a researcher and to offer timely context for the survey data.

My focus on the United States emerged as a result of two constraints: practical limitations in my surveying methods, and the way cultural barriers complicate apples-to-apples comparisons between countries. While many of the trends we can see in the US data are being felt elsewhere too, asking the right questions to get at those underlying patterns would require nuanced local knowledge.[29] The US is itself far from culturally uniform, and as you'll see, plenty of evidence indicates that even here, we don't entirely agree on what even the most basic words mean.

Still, as a large country with disproportionate influence around the world, whose language is spoken by the largest number of people on Earth, and whose technical infrastructure allows for this kind of surveying, the US is a reasonable place to begin. As we start to make out the deeper patterns in the US data, it'll also become clear that many of these are functions of demography, urbanization, technology, and new media—trends that are increasingly global, not local. Where applicable, I'll supplant survey data with publicly available international and historical data to support the broader conclusions.

Although neither I nor anyone else can claim to have a "view from nowhere," I'm writing in a spirit of open-ended inquiry.

The research that went into this book has been, for me, an extended and at times thrilling process of discovery. I would like to take you on a guided tour of the insights, as I experienced them. This means doing more than just offering up unattributed conclusions or factoids to bolster an argument; the idea is to show, not tell.

That's why this book has so many graphs, rather than just citing a percentage here and there. Graphs are harder to fudge than out-of-context "lonely numbers," to use public health expert Hans Rosling's term:

> **It is instinctive to look at a lonely number and misjudge its importance. [...] Never, ever leave a number all by itself. Never believe that one number on its own can be meaningful. If you are offered one number, always ask for at least one more. Something to compare it with.[30]**

30 Rosling et al., *Factfulness*, 128–30, 2018.

Amen! A graph can tell a nuanced story, show margins of uncertainty, and even reveal how the same raw information could be used (or misused) in the service of different agendas. By showing my work, I hope to convince you of some findings that, frankly, I wouldn't have found believable had *I* not seen the data myself.

In approaching the evidence both openly and critically, you will become a data scientist too. This will let us explore questions about causality, sources of error, and different possible explanations for what we see. It feels more honest—and it's more interesting—to delve into ambiguities when we find them, rather than sweeping them under the rug to make the narrative tidier. Reality is often surprising, but seldom simple.

If you're more of a stories person than a numbers person, I hope you, too, will find much to enjoy here. There'll be no equations (except in the *Appendix for Data Nerds*), and everything will be explained in plain English. Also, in the "show, don't just tell" spirit, the book is full of quotes and accounts directly from respondents, domain specialists, and historical sources. No citation or quotation should be mistaken for endorsement. Sometimes, what the supposed "experts" have had to say over the years needs to be seen to be believed.

However, open-mindedness is important too. We're living in a time of such rapid and uneven changes in norms that it's easy to become disconnected from those not in our geographic, generational, and cultural cohort. We can feel disoriented when confronting the views and lived experiences of people outside our bubbles, especially when these seem outlandish but are (or were) mainstream within their own communities. Yet this exposure feels crucial, both to understand the bigger picture, and to counteract the forces pulling us apart today.

Many of us are finding ourselves bewildered, unable to understand large segments of our society. Most of us do not understand, either, how alien the recent past was. This is an opportunity to listen, learn, and place our own views in context.

Who Are We Now? comes in three parts, mirroring my own journey through this territory and working like the stages of a rocket. Fueled by data and stories, each of them will lift us into a higher orbit; then detach, allowing us to take a breath, reorient ourselves; then fire up a new stage and venture farther out.

The first stage, Chapters 1–3, is like a booster rocket to get us off the ground: _Handedness._ The majority status of right-handedness is built into our biology. Across many cultures, it has almost universally resulted in a right-handed in-group and left-handed out-group, with real social consequences. This often unnoticed human trait may seem inconsequential—but it isn't. If you're left-handed, you're probably nodding knowingly as you read. If you're right-handed, you're probably puzzled. That's partly the point.

Beyond raising our consciousness, handedness offers us a practice run for a second rocket stage: _Sex and gender,_ covered in Chapters 4–15. This is the heart of the book, treating the aspects of identity that many people consider the most private, and that are in dramatic transition, particularly for young city dwellers. This stage brings us from the familiar territory of (apparent) sexual and gender-conforming majorities to a population overview that reveals a more unfamiliar reality. It's as if we'd begun at ground level on Main Street, USA, but the houses and storefronts were revealed to be a Potemkin village from above: many people's private lives and selves are not as they present them publicly.

For our final stage, _Humanity,_ we'll be in a position to study ourselves literally from outer space. Chapters 16–21 zoom out to consider the forces that attract people to each other, not just individually but collectively, and how the action of those forces over time has resulted in profound changes to our planet that can easily be seen from orbit—especially on Earth's night side, our cities glowing in the dark like skeins of fairy lights. Accelerating urbanization in the past couple of centuries has generated unprecedented cultural innovation and has been fundamental to the creation of the new identities explored in earlier chapters. Urbanization is also polarizing us culturally and politically in dangerous new ways. The book concludes with some guesses about (and hopes for) a broader, more inclusive future, predicated on a broader, more inclusive human identity.

Southern Scandinavia lit up at night, as seen from the International Space Station; the Aurora Borealis is visible.

In the quiet moments after each of these rocket stages has finished its burn and fallen away, I hope you'll experience something like what I felt at certain points throughout the project. The feeling is like the so-called "overview effect" astronauts have described when they look back at Earth from outer space and confront the reality that we're all living on a tiny, fragile ball hanging in the void. As the anonymous, collective voice of Wikipedia puts it:

> **From space, national boundaries vanish, the conflicts that divide people become less important, and the need to create a planetary society with the united will to protect this "pale blue dot" becomes both obvious and imperative.[31]**

31 Wikipedia, "Overview effect," 2020.

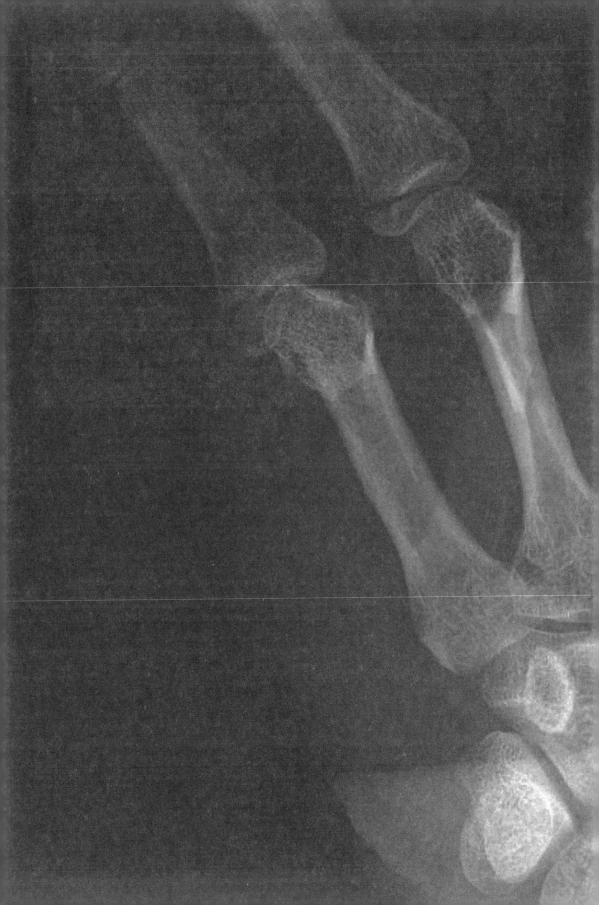

Part I

Handed-ness

Survey Handedness

These are the questions I asked participants taking the handedness survey. They're in random order, as they would have been for a respondent.

Are you living in your own place?

Was your father left-handed?

Do you live with depression?

Do you identify as Filipino / Filipina?

Are you ambidextrous?

Do you have cerebral palsy?

Do you live with an anxiety disorder?

Is your right hand bigger than your left?

Do you identify as Latino / Latina
    or Hispanic American?

Was your father right-handed?

When you use a computer mouse or trackpad,
    do you tend to use your right hand?

Do you identify as male?

Do you work in the arts?

Are you making enough money?

Do you identify as Native American?

When you type, do you usually
    use the right shift key?

Do you identify as White / European American?

Do you live with bipolar disorder?

When you clasp your hands, is your right
    thumb on top?

When you cross your arms, is your left fore-
    arm on top?

Are you alcoholic?

When you wink, does your left eye close?

When you clasp your hands,
    is your left thumb on top?

Were you born in May or June?

Do you identify as Black / African American?

Do you identify as Native Hawaiian or Other
    Pacific Islander?

Were you born in January or February?

Are you left-handed?

Did you have trouble with handwriting as a
    child?

Do you work in tech?

Do you play a musical instrument?

Do you have a left hand?

Is your left hand bigger than your right?

When you cross your arms,
    is your right forearm on top?

Are you right-handed?

Was your mother born in the US?

Do you identify as South Asian / Indian American?

Do you normally hold scissors in your right hand?

Do you identify as female?

Were you born in July or August?

Were you born in September or October?

Do you identify as Asian American?

Can you write equally well with
    your left and right hands?

Do you normally hold scissors in your left hand?

Were you born in the US?

Are you looking for a job?

Were you born before 1983?

Was your mother left-handed?

Are you a strong verbal communicator?

Do you live with schizophrenia?

When you type, do you usually
    use the left shift key?

Is English your first language?

Were you made to change your
    dominant hand as a child?

Do you write with your left hand?

Are you currently employed?

Are you on the autism spectrum?

When you use a computer mouse or trackpad,
    do you tend to use your left hand?

Do you write with your right hand?

Are you good at drawing?

Were you born in March or April?

Was your father born in the US?

When you wink, does your right eye close?

Were you born outside the US?

Were you born in November or December?

Do you have a right hand?

Have you ever had a bone fracture?

Was your mother right-handed?

Do you have a heart disease?

Do you live with Parkinson's disease?

1 Whom to believe?

While language and anonymous societies give humans our superpowers, they can also limit our thinking. Those limitations can be hard to see, because social discourse—"the conversation," as many people have taken to calling it—defines many of the building blocks of thought itself.

First, by identifying with abstract, discrete symbols like "Palestinian" or "Israeli," "straight" or "gay," we can impose arbitrary thresholds on properties that usually come in many shades of in-between. We may struggle to notice when people don't fall neatly into categories. The result can be uncomfortable for those in the ambiguous middle. When a continuous human landscape coalesces into opposing camps—tribalism—the consequences can be severe, even deadly, especially when those camps are unequal in size or privilege.

When I started to think about how to run online surveys about identity in 2016, I puzzled over the technical problem of how to map both the human landscape and the tribal encampments on it. Ultimately the surveys would have to rely on language to ask questions and get answers. It seemed a bit like trying to lift yourself up by your own bootstraps. Language is all about categories. How could I explore the continuum underneath language *using* language? Would I need to ask respondents to use sliders or knobs?

I tried to simplify. First, I decided to go in the opposite direction, and stick to plain, yes/no questions. Second, I hit on the idea of trying out my method by exploring handedness before tackling anything trickier. Both of these decisions need some explaining.

Why handedness? I knew that I wanted to figure out how to ask and reason about identity categories like gender and sexuality, which involve majorities and minorities, blur the lines between the biological and the cultural, and involve both visible signs and behaviors. But gender and sexuality are complicated and politically fraught. Debates rage today about the definitions of words and identities in these domains, the harms that language can or can't cause, who has the right to use words that may offend, and even about grammar (capitalization of races, the singular "they"). Before wading into such landmine-strewn territory, I needed what physicists call a "toy problem" with lower stakes.

Handedness seemed like the perfect solution. Something in human neurophysiology makes a majority of us right-handed, but some of us are left-handed. Handedness strongly influences everyday behavior, such as which hand you write with, and how you hold tools.

It's a trait, but it's also an identity—something people say that they "are." With a survey on handedness, I could begin to explore how identity works in a simplified setting—one that seemed less likely to land me in hot water during the learning process. There's no talk radio about deporting left-handed people, no grave offense taken for guessing someone's handedness incorrectly, no epic debate over terminology, no moral panic about whether left-handed couples should be allowed to reproduce—or adopt, lest their left-handedness rub off on an innocent child.

I sensed, on running the first handedness surveys, that the experiment had pretty much worked as planned. There was no blowback. Dozens of respondents wrote some variation on "I liked this survey, thanks!"[1] Some were also bemused. "What are you testing for? I'm curious!"[2]

1 A man from Charlotte, North Carolina.

2 A woman from Odessa, Florida.

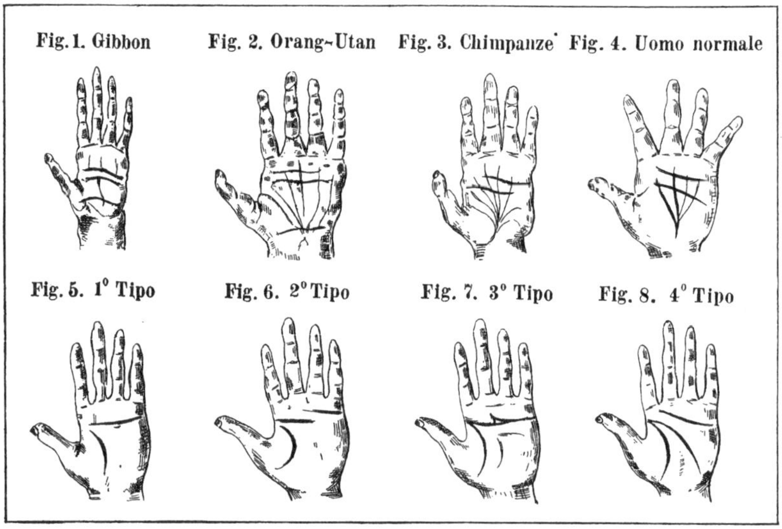

Fig. 1. Gibbon   Fig. 2. Orang-Utan   Fig. 3. Chimpanzè   Fig. 4. Uomo normale

Fig. 5. 1° Tipo   Fig. 6. 2° Tipo   Fig. 7. 3° Tipo   Fig. 8. 4° Tipo

Supposed abnormalities in the palms of criminals compared with the palms of "less evolved" nonhuman apes, from Lombroso, *L'Uomo Delinquente*, 1897.

Partly, what made the survey fun and quick to take was the other simplification—its format. It consisted almost entirely of short yes/no questions, with no assumptions made and no definitions given. Finding out people's handedness and which hand they write with required asking not one or two, but *four* yes/no questions:

Are you left-handed?
Are you right-handed?
Do you write with your left hand?
Do you write with your right hand?[3]

3 In practice, these would turn up in random order.

4 This respondent was, in fact, a non-binary 23-year-old from Chicago.

At first glance, this simpleminded approach might seem like a head-scratcher if the goal is to get at nuance. As one respondent put it, "A very binary test for nonbinary concepts."[4] Answering seemingly unnecessary questions could be annoying for some people, too—in the words of a man from Morrison, Illinois, "This could really be condensed into a short set of multiple choice questions." Yes, and no.

Normally, all four yes/no questions would be presumed to follow from a single, two-choice question: "Are you (a) left-handed, or (b) right-handed?" This would give us a single "bit" of information for every person. ("Bit" is short for "binary digit," meaning a zero or a one, or equivalently an (a) or (b).) Since each yes/no question also gives us a single bit of information, using the "yes/no method" with the four questions above produces *four* bits per respondent instead of one, which works out to 16 different possibilities ($2 \times 2 \times 2 \times 2$) instead of just two. The man from Morrison might argue that all of these extra possibilities are redundant, because if someone answers "yes" to being left-handed, they will also answer "no" to being right-handed, "yes" to writing with their left hand, and "no" to writing with their right hand. Isn't that what being left-handed *means*?

In real life, we make assumptions like these all the time. They are, however, just that—assumptions. Put another way, they're testable hypotheses.

To test them, we just have to ask thousands of people the same four questions. Then, we can see how well our assumptions match the data. Here's the breakdown of answers to the first two questions ($2 \times 2 = 4$ possibilities), from a total of 5,590 respondents:

	Not left-handed	Left-handed
Not right-handed	1.14%	11.93%
Right-handed	85.89%	1.04%

Unsurprisingly, a large majority of people—about 86%—answer "yes" to right-handed, and "no" to left-handed. A minority, just under 12%, answer "yes" to left-handed, and "no" to right-handed. This accounts for about 97.8% of the population, which tells us that the assumption that a person is either left- or right-handed, but not both or neither, is generally correct. However, it doesn't cover everyone. About 1 in 46 people answer either "yes" to both or "no" to both.

Michelangelo's David rendered with dithering, allowing shades of gray to be approximated using only black and white pixels.

These people belong to an "excluded middle." By answering as they have, they've opted out of our usual multiple-choice, either/or assumption about left- and right-handedness. One in 46 isn't such a small number, either. If the sample is representative of the US, this works out to about 7.2 million people. That's more than the combined population of LA and Chicago.

That we can see this excluded middle in the response statistics shows us that yes/no questions are not as binary as they seem. Or rather, each individual question *is* binary, and forces each respondent to "round up or down" with every answer. However, looking at the aggregated answers of multiple yes/no questions over many subjects reveals the excluded middle in the *pattern* of yeses and nos.

This is analogous to the old printing and graphics technique known as "halftoning" or "dithering," which allows a black and white printer or display to render images in shades of gray—even if each pixel can only be black or white. I'll explain shortly how one can produce a "halftoned" portrait of some nuanced human characteristic using only the unpromising ingredients of binary (and redundant-seeming) yes/no questions.

But first, you may be wondering: what if these 1 in 46 people are *wrong*—misguided, delusional about their handedness, or just sloppy at answering the questions? The last, at a minimum, is definitely a fair concern. I automatically paid all who completed the survey, even if they clicked at random, because I didn't want to get into a petty dispute with a Mechanical Turk worker over a dollar and change. I figured that I was paying for their time, and hoping that by paying fairly they'd reciprocate by answering carefully and honestly.

As a social experiment, this was interesting in its own right. The results were, on the whole, affirming. The great majority of respondents took obvious care with their work—pride, even—clarifying any apparent contradictions in their answers using the free response section, or sometimes even by sending me explanations by email. As you've seen, they didn't hesitate to let me know if they felt I might have overlooked something in the survey design (this feedback was often valuable), or when they worried they might have taken the same survey twice (this happened when I revised my methods and ran an updated version).[5] In an era that sometimes seems

5 After some initial experimentation to get survey designs right, I used a Mechanical Turk feature called "qualifications" to make sure that nobody could take a survey twice (unless they went to the trouble of creating a fake second account, which is against the site's policies).

characterized by abusive behavior online, it was reassuring to see that decency, reciprocity, and a work ethic seemed the norm.

A cynic might argue that this is a function of the power dynamic between Amazon and its gig workers on Mechanical Turk—that they're kept on a short leash, subject to a harsh reputation economy. I'm not a romantic about either people or corporations, but I think this view does both a disservice. Reputation probably does matter, online just as in real life, and the anonymity of burner accounts almost certainly does undermine social accountability on the internet, but my experiences with Mechanical Turk have left me with the impression that most people, regardless of their identities or beliefs, are wired for decent social behavior by default.

Nonetheless, I did set some "traps" in the surveys, to filter out respondents who weren't answering carefully. More details, along with a careful look at the demographics of Mechanical Turk workers, are in the *Appendix for data nerds*. As will soon become clear, there's good reason to believe that for the 90% or so of survey respondents who made it through the filter, the excluded middle is unlikely to be the result of random clicking. Most of them meant to answer as they did.

So what does it mean to be neither exclusively left-handed nor exclusively right-handed? As noted earlier, when their answers aren't self-evident, people often elaborate on them in the free response field at the end of the survey. I left the wording of this final question deliberately vague, along the lines of "Is there anything else you'd like to add?," to encourage elaboration. Its open-endedness helps make up for the rigidity of the yes/no questions. The tradeoff is that while those yes/no questions are perfect for statistical analysis, free text isn't so quantifiable. Stories do give us insight, though, like this one, from a 62-year-old woman living in a small town in rural Washington:

> **Due to an industrial accident ten years ago, I lost half of my right hand, so [some] of these questions were hard to answer because I've had to "adapt" by learning how to use my left hand for things like writing, etc. I wouldn't necessarily call myself [ambidextrous], though, because if that hadn't happened, I would still be strictly right-handed.**

6 Ziegler-Graham et al., "Estimating the Prevalence of Limb Loss in the United States: 2005 to 2050," 2008.

7 A 36-year-old man from Henderson, Kentucky.

Injuries leading to outcomes like these aren't as uncommon as one might think. A recent paper in a medical journal estimated that "One in 190 Americans is currently living with the loss of a limb."[6] Many respondents described other, more commonplace injuries affecting handedness: "I badly burnt my left hand as a kid and was forced to [learn] to write with my right hand"[7]; "When I was young I was

8 A 35-year-old man from Springville, Utah.

9 A 67-year-old woman from Kearney, Nebraska.

10 A 34-year-old woman from Bellevue, Nebraska.

becoming ambidextrous, but due to an injury my right hand became dominant"**8**; "I was forced to switch when I got [juvenile rheumatoid] arthritis at 13"**9**; or simply "I can write reasonably well with my right hand because I broke my left wrist for a while."**10**

Although some hand or arm problems are chronic or congenital, most injuries are acute, meaning that they happen at a particular moment, and may affect life from then onward. This makes it interesting to look beyond overall percentages, and start to break down people's responses by age.

1.0 **Handedness** % by age

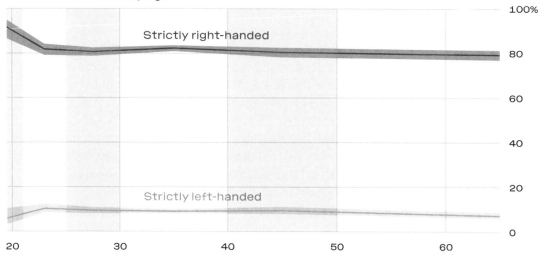

11 These bins or intervals are "half-open" and would be written in mathematical set notation as [18,21), [21,25) and so on, meaning that someone aged exactly 21 would fall in the [21,25) bin, not the [18,21) bin. Questions about birth month ("Were you born in January or February?"), together with age in years, allow the ages of respondents to be calculated to within two months. Bin sizes are chosen to ensure that each bin contains enough samples for the error bar to be reasonably small, while still capturing significant changes by age, as described in the Appendix.

I'll be using age breakdowns a lot, so some explanation is in order. These graphs are generated by dividing responses into age brackets or "bins," which are shown in alternating shades. Here, the bins are ages 18–21, 21–25, 25–30, 30–40, 40–50, and 50–80.**11** For each labeled series, straight solid lines connect values from the center of one bin to the next, showing how these quantities vary with age (hence the left edge of the graph is at the midpoint of the first bin, 19.5, and the right edge is at the midpoint of the last, 65). The "Strictly left-handed" line shows the percentage of people who both answered "yes" to "Are you left-handed?" and "no" to "Are you right-handed?"; the "Strictly right-handed" line is the converse. Putting multiple quantities on the same graph this way can help us see patterns in the combined data.

If you look closely, you'll spot shaded regions just around the lines. When you zoom out to look at majorities like right-handedness, they look small, but when you zoom in to look at minorities like left-handedness, they look much bigger. These shaded regions are important. They're what data scientists call "error bars." They represent the 90% confidence interval, meaning that if one assumes every bin contains a random sample from a much larger candidate population, then 90% of such random draws of the same size would produce an estimated percentage within the shaded range.[12]

12 I've chosen a generous 90% confidence interval rather than the more common 68% confidence interval (one "standard deviation") both in order to emphasize uncertainty where it exists and, where the regions are tight, to make clear how many of the effects I'll describe are so large that they're highly unlikely to be statistical artifacts.

Nobody can say for certain that the *real* percentage of the candidate population falls within this (or any) range, because it's only possible to sample a tiny fraction of, say, all of the 18- to 21-year-olds in the United States, and it's impossible to guarantee that any given sample isn't biased—though I have taken pains to make *my* sample as unbiased as possible, using "stratified sampling" methods as described in the *Appendix for data nerds*. Still, the error bars are useful in showing how seriously to take the estimate. When they're tight around the solid lines, as they are here, it means those numbers are pretty reliable, statistically speaking.

So what *are* the patterns in the data? There's more going on than tables of numbers like the one earlier in this chapter can reveal. For one, a large proportion of the youngest adults, probably over 90%, characterize themselves as strictly right-handed, while only a small proportion (a bit over 5%) say they're strictly left-handed. However, this rapidly shifts to only about 80% strictly right-handed by the mid-20s, and from there, the number of strictly left- or right-handed people declines subtly but steadily with age.

Big meta-analyses of the scientific literature suggest that about 10% of people are left-handed on average, and that left-handedness is about 23% more common in men (so, about 9% of women and 11% of men).[13] It's been theorized that left-handedness is due to some

13 Papadatou-Pastou et al., "Sex Differences in Left-Handedness: A Meta-Analysis of 144 Studies," 2008.

1.1 **Strict left-handedness in women and men** % by age

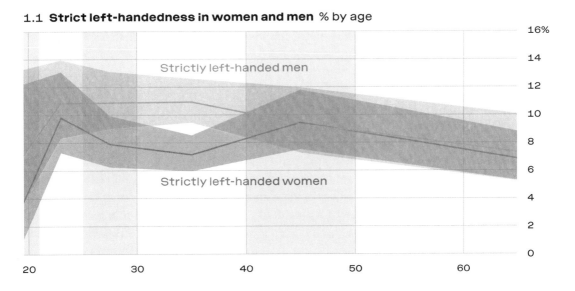

inherent sex-linked difference in brain development. There may be such a factor, but zooming in on the strictly left-handed curve and breaking it down by sex reveals something interesting.

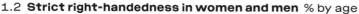

1.2 **Strict right-handedness in women and men** % by age

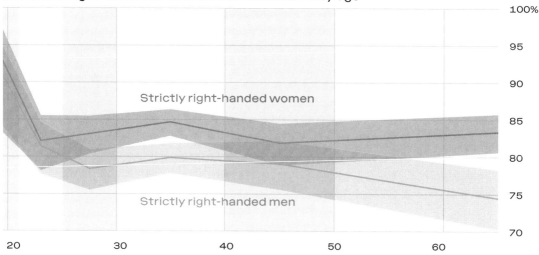

Strictly right-handed women

Strictly right-handed men

On the whole, the survey data are consistent with big studies in the research literature—showing 9.6% of women are strictly left-handed, and 11.7% of men.[14] However, that difference may only be significant before middle age; by 45, men and women seem pretty much alike, with both below 10% and falling. What's going on here?

Looking more closely at strict *right*-handedness broken down by sex adds some further color.

Now, it's *young* men and women who are all but indistinguishable; but as they age, fewer and fewer men report being strictly right-handed. By age 65, only about 75% are, as compared to about 83% of women. Those 90% confidence intervals show us that this effect is probably quite significant.

It has been well-established that, on average, men are more accident prone than women. They use (and misuse) more power tools, fall off more roofs, lose more limbs, and are even (somewhat bafflingly) struck by lightning more often![15] Perhaps they lack the good sense to stay indoors during a thunderstorm. As a cohort, *young* men are—it will surprise nobody to learn—especially unwise in their life choices, likely due to a complex stew of biological, cultural, and behavioral factors.

Regardless of initial handedness, with every passing year, men have on average a greater likelihood of needing to *change* their handedness due to injury. Even if women and men started off with equal (and very low) probabilities of left-handedness at birth, this would result not only in an excess of left-handed men by age 18 due to disproportionate

14 Later I'll delve into the non-binariness of sex and gender. For purposes of the analysis here, "women" is a shorthand for those who answer "yes" to "Do you identify as female?" and "no" to "Do you identify as male?," and vice versa for "men." There are a number of other possible definitions based on the survey questions, but none of them materially affect these results.

15 Jensenius, "A Detailed Analysis of Lightning Deaths in the United States from 2006 Through 2019," 2020; Sorenson, "Gender Disparities in Injury Mortality: Consistent, Persistent, and Larger than You'd Think," 2011.

childhood injuries, but also would result in more sharply declining numbers of both strictly left- *and* strictly right-handed men over time—especially since injury of the dominant hand is more common, as it's in harm's way more often. And this is exactly what the graphs show.

The evidence mounts further on considering the excluded middle. With declines in both strict left- and strict right-handedness, it follows that an increasing number of people are answering the handedness questions ambiguously. This is true; that curve is similar to the rate at which people answer "yes" to "Are you ambidextrous?," and consists largely of the same population (though "ambidextrous" seems to be a somewhat stronger statement, as it's used a tad less often, at every age).

1.3 Ambidexterity % by age

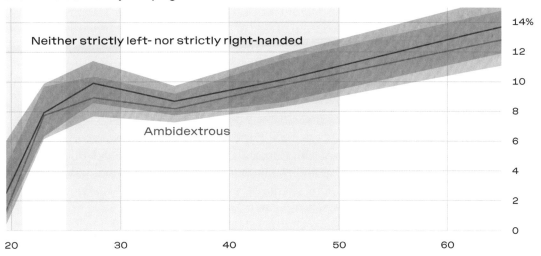

When people say they're ambidextrous, they often include an account of injury, as in "I have severe deficiencies with my right arm I've had 9 surgeries so I became ambidextrous"[16] or "ambidextrous in some things due to having a severely broken right hand wrist, in a cast/pins for 6 months"[17]. So, injuries likely account for the increasing numbers with age.

None of this means that there's no innate biological component to handedness. There is evidence for at least *some* heritability of handedness (based on studies of twins), and there may well be inherently sex-linked differences too.[18] Eventually, our understanding of neuroscience and genetics might pinpoint a sex-linked developmental mechanism. However, given the variations by age and sex in the survey data, the burden of proof would be on medical researchers to demonstrate such an effect—and show that differences in overall

16 A woman from Elkton, Maryland.

17 A woman from Kansas City, Kansas.

18 Porac, *Laterality: Exploring the Enigma of Left-Handedness*, 2016.

handedness averages between the sexes can't be accounted for simply by different rates of injury over time. This is a good illustration of the old saying "correlation is not causation."

And so, we've arrived at this book's first run-in with medical authority. It won't be the last.

We have much to thank physicians for. Many of us would die young were it not for everyday miracles like antibiotics, perinatal care, insulin, even modern dentistry. (In the last chapters of this book, I'll return to the key role these innovations have played in the larger human story.)

However, as with any in-group, the medical community has its preconceptions, biases, and blind spots. Medical history is rife with long-held assumptions that turned out to be wrong, and with at least the usual share of expert overconfidence in those assumptions. We often entrust doctors with our bodies and our lives. Maybe that's why we invest them with a kind of intellectual and even moral authority that we don't tend to extend to other researchers or knowledge specialists.

I reflexively reached for that authority when, in wondering what ambidexterity "really means," I consulted medical sources—many people would do the same to resolve a dinner table dispute as to the "official" definition. So many people claiming to be ambidextrous puzzled me; I had assumed it was less common. Indeed, according to much of the medical literature, ambidexterity or mixed-handedness is a fairly rare condition "afflicting" about 1% of infants and "associated with atypical cerebral laterality" resulting in "a greater likelihood of having language, scholastic, and mental health problems" later in life.[19]

Older research ascribes similar woes to the left-handed. As an influential 1977 paper on measuring handedness by psychologists Curtis Hardyck (of UC Berkeley) and Lewis Petrinovich (of UC Riverside) put it,

> **Reaction to the problems of explanation posed by the left-handed has followed two courses. Perhaps the most common approach has been to assume that left-handedness is a signal that something is wrong—that the left-handed represent an aberrancy or abnormality and can thus be excluded from consideration in theories of normal cerebral functioning. Certainly the search for deficit associated with left-handedness has been both extensive and unceasing. [...] A second approach has been to disregard the left-handed [...].[20]**

Despite a lack of evidence that left-handed people have "something wrong," this attitude filters into people's lives in a variety of ways.

[19] Rodriguez et al., "Mixed-Handedness Is Linked to Mental Health Problems in Children and Adolescents," 2010.

[20] Hardyck and Petrinovich, "Left-Handedness," 1977.

For instance, a 24-year-old survey respondent from Wewahitchka, Florida wrote, "I was left-handed at birth but the doctor encouraged my parents to train me right-handed due to me being on the spectrum, the doctor said I would have enough problems without adding left-handedness to them." Speaking from the majority's point of view, a 42-year-old from East China, Michigan wrote, "I seem to be right-handed dominant. I think I have less emotional problems than left-handed people."

I included questions on the survey about depression, bipolar disorder, alcoholism, and a number of other conditions that have been at one time or another associated with left-handedness. The results are underwhelming, with the exception of cerebral palsy—one case where a link with left-handedness has long been well established.[21] Left-handed people are also slightly overrepresented among the bipolar population, though the effect is modest.

On the whole, though, the survey doesn't support the idea that either left-handedness or ambidexterity are "aberrant or abnormal" traits. Ambidexterity in childhood may indeed be rare, perhaps as low as 1% or even less, based on the youngest respondents (unfortunately I couldn't survey people under 18). But as we've seen, by middle age it also rises, and to well above 10%—even more common than strict left-handedness. That's a pretty big excluded middle. The survey data are also inconsistent with the idea that ambidexterity is a rare medical condition you're either born with or not. By middle age, at least ten times more people say they're ambidextrous than were born that way. So whom should we believe, the doctors or the survey respondents?

21 Only 14 people surveyed have cerebral palsy, but 4 of those are left-handed, which at about 29% is much higher than the expected rate of left-handedness. This is consistent with the medical literature.

2 The excluded middle

Left-handed and right-handed side-bent scissors.

Does the idea of an "official definition" of ambidexterity even make sense? Official, says who? Ambidexterity isn't a mathematical concept; it doesn't refer to something that has an objective meaning independent of our language and culture.

In fact, the term "ambidextrous" is used in various communities—not just medicine, but also sports and music, for example—and in each it means something a bit different, sometimes rare, sometimes commonplace. If we think that one of these communities holds a copyright on what ambidexterity means, then we'd be creating a hierarchy of authority to police the term. If we went with the medically sanctioned "1%" definition, then we'd be claiming that 90% of those who say they're ambidextrous are just confused—not a case I'd be keen to make. Instead, I'll focus on being *descriptive*, not *prescriptive*—a stance I'll try to maintain throughout the book.

I'm aware that this argument skirts difficult territory. We're living through a period of "alternative facts," conspiracy theories, and the devaluation of science by large segments of the population. I stand firmly with science—paying close attention to data when exploring fuzzy, socially defined concepts, rather than relying on orthodoxy or arguments from authority.

It has long been known that handedness is such a fuzzy concept. Noticing the wide range of left-handedness estimates at the time, Hardyck and Petrinovich wrote that handedness "is most appropriately regarded as a continuum"—what we might today call a "spectrum." In the survey data, there aren't any continuous measures, like grip strength or hand size, but quite a few yes/no questions about handedness allow one to render a continuous "halftone" picture of it:

Do you have a right hand?

Do you have a left hand?

Is your right hand bigger than your left?

Is your left hand bigger than your right?

Do you write with your right hand?

Do you write with your left hand?

Can you write equally well with your left and right hands?

When you use a computer mouse or trackpad,
do you tend to use your right hand?

When you use a computer mouse or trackpad,
do you tend to use your left hand?

When you cross your arms, is your right forearm on top?

When you cross your arms, is your left forearm on top?

When you clasp your hands, is your right thumb on top?

When you clasp your hands, is your left thumb on top?

When you wink, does your right eye close?

When you wink, does your left eye close?

When you type, do you usually use the right shift key?

When you type, do you usually use the left shift key?

Do you normally hold scissors in your right hand?

Do you normally hold scissors in your left hand?

Was your mother right-handed?

Was your mother left-handed?

Was your father right-handed?

Was your father left-handed?

Did you have trouble with handwriting as a child?

Were you made to change your dominant hand as a child?

Do you work in tech?

Do you work in the arts?

Are you a strong verbal communicator?

Do you play a musical instrument?

Are you good at drawing?

1 Sometimes the supposed "aberrancy" of left-handedness is given a romantic gloss, associating it not only with mental imbalance but also with artistic talent or creative eccentricity. Ellen Forney writes movingly about the "mad artist" trope in her graphic memoir, *Marbles: Mania, Depression, Michelangelo, and Me: A Graphic Memoir*, 2012.

All of these are potential "handedness correlates." Some of the questions seem like they should correlate strongly—such as whether you write with your left hand—while others are speculative and based on possibly bogus theories—such as whether you're good at drawing or play an instrument.[1] Is it *really* true that artists tend to be left-handed? Let's find out!

Imagine making a composite left-handedness "score" for a given respondent by counting the "yes" answers that seem to support left-handedness ("Is your left hand bigger than your right?," "Do you write with your left hand?," and so on). Perhaps this score could be improved by subtracting the number of "yes" answers that argue *against* left-handedness ("Is your right hand bigger than your left?," "Do you write with your right hand?"). Each question, then, would contribute a +1 or –1 to an overall left-handedness score. Let's call the +1 or –1 number for each question its "weight" for calculating that score.

This procedure might give a reasonable first approximation of a "left-handedness spectrum," but it has some obvious drawbacks. Some questions, like "Do you work in tech?," *might* be correlated with handedness, but it would be dangerous to assume so. It might be safest simply not to count them after all; put differently, maybe their real weight should be zero.

Then, too, it seems obvious that certain questions, like "Do you write with your left hand?," ought to count for a lot more than "Was your mother left-handed?" So, ideally, questions should have a *range* of different weights, not just the +1, 0, and –1 weights of the simpler "bookkeeping" approach. But now we're in trouble. How can one guess what those weights should be?

Luckily, no guessing is required. Instead, canny data scientists can use a mathematical technique called "optimal linear estimation," which allows the weights to be calculated directly from the data. It requires a cheat sheet, which in this case, the survey itself supplies: weights combine with the answers to questions like "Do you write with your left hand?" and "Was your mother left-handed?" to predict the answers to handedness questions. An "optimal" set of weights for right-handedness aims to produce a positive score for everyone who answered "yes" to "Are you right-handed?," and a negative score for everyone who answered "no." The optimal weights for left-handedness, conversely, aim to produce a positive score for everyone who answered "yes" to "Are you left-handed?," and a negative score for everyone who answered "no."

Branches of applied math are dedicated to solving "optimization problems" like these. A fancier version, "nonlinear optimization," is the foundation of most modern AI, so very much part of my day job. Linear optimization is more straightforward, though. My laptop spit out optimal weights in about a millisecond, sorted from most positive (shown here as the longest bar extending to the right) to most negative (the longest bar extending to the left).[2] Unsurprisingly—though it did not have to work out this way—the strict right-handedness and strict left-handedness weights are nearly perfect mirror images of each other.

There are no big surprises in the weights themselves either. The hand you write with, and the hand you hold scissors with, make the strongest contributions to predicting strict left-handedness, both positive ("Do you write with your left hand?") *and* negative ("Do you write

2 Numerical weights aren't shown, because the scale is arbitrary; doubling all of the weights, for example, wouldn't change the prediction. What matters here is the overall pattern: whether a question is positively or negatively correlated, and how important it is relative to the others.

3 Nobody knows exactly why this is so, but it's consistent with the literature. Herron and James, *Neuropsychology of Left-Handedness*, 171, 1980.

2.0 **Predictors of strict left-handedness** Questions sorted by weight, from most positive to most negative

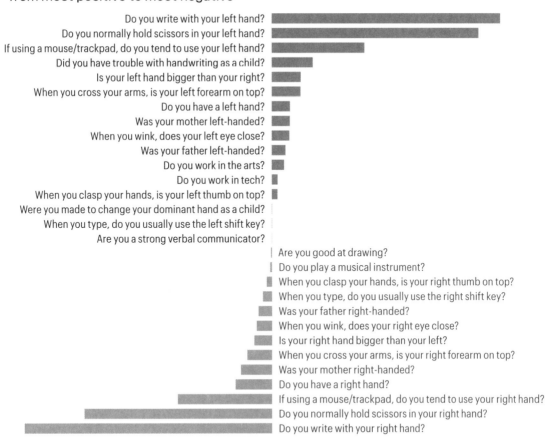

Do you write with your left hand?
Do you normally hold scissors in your left hand?
If using a mouse/trackpad, do you tend to use your left hand?
Did you have trouble with handwriting as a child?
Is your left hand bigger than your right?
When you cross your arms, is your left forearm on top?
Do you have a left hand?
Was your mother left-handed?
When you wink, does your left eye close?
Was your father left-handed?
Do you work in the arts?
Do you work in tech?
When you clasp your hands, is your left thumb on top?
Were you made to change your dominant hand as a child?
When you type, do you usually use the left shift key?
Are you a strong verbal communicator?

Are you good at drawing?
Do you play a musical instrument?
When you clasp your hands, is your right thumb on top?
When you type, do you usually use the right shift key?
Was your father right-handed?
When you wink, does your right eye close?
Is your right hand bigger than your left?
When you cross your arms, is your right forearm on top?
Was your mother right-handed?
Do you have a right hand?
If using a mouse/trackpad, do you tend to use your right hand?
Do you normally hold scissors in your right hand?
Do you write with your right hand?

4 Once again, the numerical values on the *x* axis don't matter here; they're just a function of the arbitrary way the weights are scaled. If the weights were all doubled, for example, then the overall score would also be doubled, but the predictions would be the same; only the proportions matter. The error bars in this histogram are calculated by rerunning the whole procedure many times with random subsets of respondents "held out," giving an estimate of how reliable the calculation is, or more precisely, how much variability is due to the limited size of the sample.

with your right hand?"). The opposite holds for strict right-handedness. Parental influence is a factor too, though it's much weaker, with mom's handedness playing a stronger role than dad's.[3] Questions about drawing, music, working in tech, and being a strong verbal communicator are so close to zero as to be uninformative—those theories indeed look bogus.

With this ability to calculate a strict left-handedness score, a nuanced, "halftoned" rendition of strict left-handedness emerges, as promised. In practice, this looks like a histogram of left-handedness scores, with error bars as usual. For each bin, it shows, in different colors, the percentage of respondents who report being strictly left-handed, strictly right-handed, or whose responses are ambiguous (meaning that they answered "yes" to both, or "no" to both).[4] Since there are no other possibilities, those three percentages add up to 100%.

The predictor isn't perfect (nothing ever is), but it does pretty well! When the score is low (here, below about 0.5), the likelihood that the respondent self-identified as strictly left-handed is virtually zero.

2.1 Likelihood of being left-, right-, or ambiguous-handed as a function of strict left-handedness score % by score

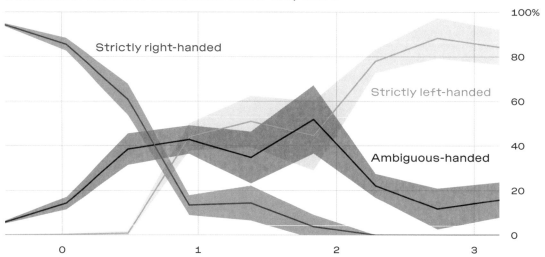

When the score is high (here, above about 2.2), the likelihood that the respondent self-identified as strictly *right*-handed is virtually zero, and they're about 85% likely to have identified as strictly left-handed.

For a data nerd like me, there's something reassuring about visualizations like these. Yes, language is fuzzy, almost everything is a "spectrum," and "reality," whatever that means, is hard to pin down. However, the data reveal a strong underlying degree of agreement about what people *mean* when they talk about their own handedness. Put another way: handedness is real.

I'd argue that it's just as real as height or grip strength, but, as with any continuous landscape we reduce to named categories—say, "short" or "tall," "strong" or "weak"—there's some individual "measurement error." More significantly, people's personal thresholds vary. Just as there's no objective definition of "tall," there's no objective place to put the threshold distinguishing left- from right-handedness.

Interestingly, even when the left-handedness predictor is maxed out, about 15% of respondents still give ambiguous handedness answers. They're not in the majority, but are they "wrong"? In cases like these, the variety of answers isn't a human imperfection, but an essential feature of the way language is used to mark out and constantly renegotiate the way we all think about things. Without that give and take, language couldn't evolve. There will be many more examples of this effect in the second and third parts of the book.

To accommodate the flexibility of language, I avoided putting definitions into the survey questionnaires, though that did frustrate some people—especially when, in later surveys, I used words like "intersex" and "non-monogamous," which not everybody knows.

A 64-year-old woman from Houston, Texas let me have a (virtual) earful about it. "How come you did not include definitions for all these weird words? I spent a lot of time just looking up definitions. Are you just too hip to let us little people know WTF you are talking about?"

Dear Madam: if you're reading, I apologize. I didn't define the words because part of the point of the survey was to find out what they actually mean to people! This is true even for seemingly boring terms like "left-handed" and "ambidextrous." If I had tried to define them, I'd have needed to pick a definition, and then it would likely have shifted the ground of many comments toward debates about these definitions (sometimes this happened anyway), and in the yes/no section, I'd have ended up with some unknown number of "well, technically..." answers at odds with what people would have selected otherwise. In short, I didn't want my finger on the scale.

Now let's return to the "ambiguously handed" curve. Remember that the weights behind calculating this strict left-handedness score are based only on predicting the responses of people who were *unambiguously* left-handed. So, when people whose responses were ambiguous actually *do* fall in the blurry region between the strictly right-handed and strictly left-handed groups, this offers powerful evidence that those respondents aren't making mistakes or clicking at random—they really are an excluded middle. For most of those respondents, identifying as ambiguously handed goes along with ambiguous answers to a series of other handedness questions relating to bodies, histories, and behaviors.

The same technique produces optimal question weights for strict *right*-handedness. The results are similar, though in mirror image. A high score correlates strongly with right-handedness and makes the probability of strict left-handedness zero, while a low score correlates strongly with left-handedness, and makes the probability of strict right-handedness zero. One subtle but significant difference, though, is that there's a lower likelihood of an ambiguous response when the right-handedness score is high, for reasons that will soon become clear.

There's something much less intuitive about the optimal predictor of *ambiguous*-handedness (again, this is a "yes" to both, or a "no" to both handedness questions).

Predicting ambiguity doesn't work quite as well as the left-handed or right-handed predictions, which perhaps isn't news—since in handedness as in anything else, there are few ways to be *unambiguous*, but many ways to be *ambiguous*. More surprisingly, scoring high on the "ambiguity scale" not only rules out strict right-handedness, but also does a better job of predicting strict *left*-handedness

2.2 Likelihood of being right-, left-, or ambiguous-handed as a function of strict right-handedness score % by score

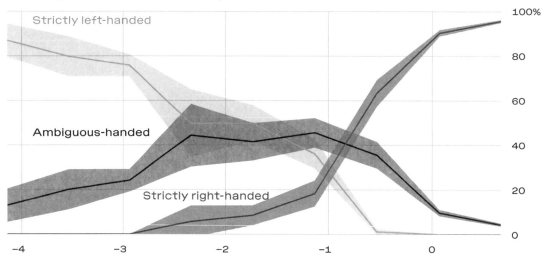

2.3 Likelihood of being ambiguous-, right-, or left-handed as a function of ambiguous-handedness score % by score

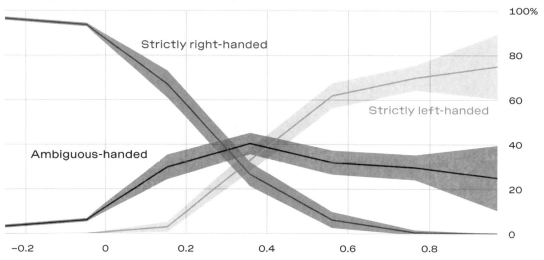

than of predicting ambiguity! This is a weird result. It tells us that if we start with "average" answers to every question and begin to slowly modify them to increase the ambiguity score, we'll *also* be increasing the left-handedness score. If we keep going, we can overshoot, and end up in more *strictly left-handed* than ambiguous territory.

So in this sense, it's more accurate to call handedness ambiguity "a little bit left-handed" than "a little bit right-handed," since right-handedness *is* the average; it's the default, and variations are defined relative to it. This isn't just a mathematical subtlety, but a basic consequence of majority and minority—a recurring theme throughout this book.

The question weights for ambiguous-handedness are broadly similar to those for strict left-handedness—with one important exception: "Were you made to change your dominant hand as a child?" got virtually zero weight for predicting strict left-handedness, but it's the second most positive predictor of ambiguous-handedness, just behind "Do you write with your left hand?"

2.4 Predictors of ambiguous-handedness Questions sorted by weight, from most positive to most negative

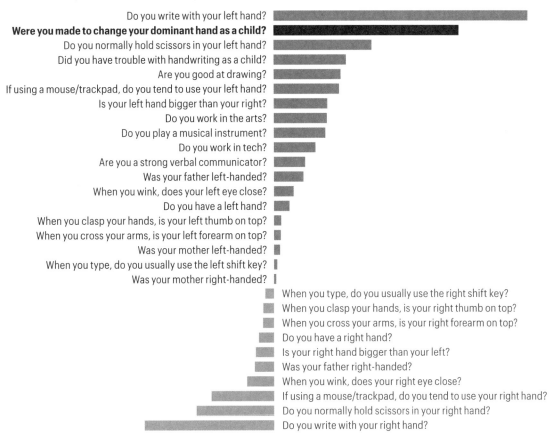

An implication is that many of the ambiguous respondents were left-handed to one degree or another in childhood, but were made to switch their dominant hand. For completeness: "Were you made to change your dominant hand as a child?" has a strong *negative* weight for the strict right-handedness predictor. So, strongly right-handed children are made to change their dominant hand much less often—because it's already the "right" one!

The difference becomes obvious by separately graphing the proportion of strictly right-handed people who were made to switch and the *non* strictly right-handed people who were made to switch.

2.5 **Handedness in people forced to switch** % by age

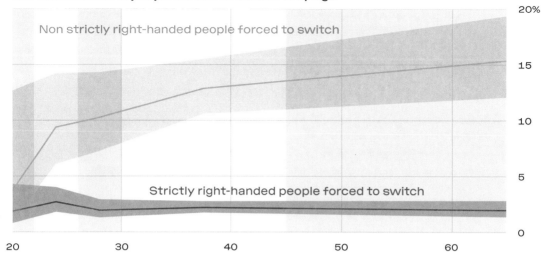

Non strictly right-handed people forced to switch

Strictly right-handed people forced to switch

20%

15

10

5

0

20   30   40   50   60

The full effect is probably even larger than the plot shows, since many people's handedness scores fall somewhere in the middle, even if they identify as strictly right-handed on the survey. After all, if you have some flexibility with regard to handedness as a child, you may as well go with the right-handed majority, and reap the social benefits.[5]

In fact, depending on where, when, and how you grew up, you may be *compelled* to switch, whether by parents, siblings, teachers, nuns, or other authority figures. As a 27-year-old from Phoenix, Arizona put it, "ambidextrous as a child and pushed to choose right-handedness." Or, in the words of a 54-year-old from Southwith, Massachusetts,

> **My sister took the pencil out of my left hand, put it in my right hand, and said 'You're a (family name). We write with our right hands.' I was in first or second grade. I used my right hand from there on.**

It's likely that many people who were similarly pushed to choose right-handedness didn't notice it as kids or don't remember it as adults; they just adapted. Latent signs of left-handedness may remain in these cases, whether the respondent is conscious of them or not.

People seem to remember the pressure to conform when there's embarrassment or trauma involved, though, or when adaptation is especially hard. Those who answered "yes" to "Were you made to change your dominant hand as a child?" often had stories to tell:

6 A 58-year-old woman from Palmyra, New York.

> **Early school teachers often taped one hand to my waist to force me to always use the other. It was strange and [embarrassing] to be selected for this punishment.[6]**

Classroom at the Old Sun Indian Residential School, Blackfoot Reserve in Gleichen, Alberta, Canada, 1945. Conditions were especially harsh at these religious boarding schools in the US and Canada, set up to forcibly "civilize" Native American or First Nations children.

It's tempting to think of such negative experiences as stories from less enlightened times, long ago. That had certainly been *my* assumption. A 32-year-old from Long Beach, California wrote, for instance,

> **I believe [my mom] *did* have to change, cause people were crazy back then, so I couldn't really answer yes or no to her handedness either way, so I just said no to both.**

A 67-year-old from McKinney, Texas speaks for that previous generation:

> **I was naturally left-handed, but in 1950 you couldn't get scissors, etc. for left-handed people, so my mother forced me into using my right hand. I still do many things left-handed [...] So I would, to some extent, call myself ambidextrous.**

There's a likely age trend in the "forced to switch" question for non-strictly right-handed people, suggesting a generational shift underway. The large error bars suggest taking this with a grain of salt, though; the population graphed is a minority of a minority, so the counts are low. Still, very few of the youngest strictly left-handed adult respondents reported having been made to switch—under 5% between ages 18 and 22—while the number rises past 10% by age 26, and 15% by middle age. If there were enough data in the sample to add an additional age bin, the "forced to switch" percentage among older people might be even higher.

The data suggest that there's a change afoot in how we treat left-handed children, but also that the practice of forced switching is far from ancient history. Speaking for many, a 26-year-old man from Shelburn, Indiana wrote, "I was beat by nuns as a child to change what hand I wrote with" (yes, nuns do figure in a surprising number of these accounts). A 30-year-old woman from Sterrett, Alabama expressed her surprise that this was even a thing:

> I can't believe the situation where I was made to change hands as a child was a question on here! I figured I was the only one in the world that my biological father spanked me when I picked things up with my left hand and until I used my right hand to pick it up with. Is there other people like me out there? I'm not alone on that?

As the numbers show, she is very much not alone.

Although I'm not suggesting any equivalence, it's hard not to notice a parallel with the stories of people who have been subjected to "conversion therapy," the pseudoscientific practice of trying to change someone's sexual orientation through social pressure, psychology, or spiritual indoctrination. There, too, of course, the conversion attempt is always from the ("queer") minority to the ("straight") majority.

We have no good evidence that conversion therapy actually works. Many of the leaders and proponents of conversion programs over the years eventually admit that they themselves are still gay, and end up apologizing for putting so many other people through those programs. John Paulk, for example, wrote in the *Advocate* in 2013,

> For the better part of ten years, I was an advocate and spokesman for what's known as the 'ex-gay movement,' where we declared that sexual orientation could be changed through a close-knit relationship with God, intensive therapy and strong determination. At the time, I truly believed that it would happen. And while many things in my life did change as a Christian, my sexual orientation did not. [...] Today, I do not consider myself 'ex-gay,' and I no longer support or promote the movement. Please allow me to be clear: I do not believe that reparative therapy changes sexual orientation; in fact, it does great harm to many people.[7]

7 Brydum, "John Paulk Formally Renounces, Apologizes for Harmful 'Ex-Gay' Movement," 2013.

8 Other prominent ex-ex gay figures include Günter Baum, Michael Bussee and Gary Cooper, Ben Gresham, Noe Gutierrez, John Smid, Peterson Toscano, Anthony Venn-Brown, McKrae Game, and David Matheson.

Paulk is just one among at least a dozen prominent "ex-ex-gay" former leaders of such organizations.[8] Clearly the question of how malleable sexual orientation may be is both ideologically charged and can have major real-life implications. I'll revisit this topic (as well as the deep history of conversion therapy) in later chapters.

For now, let's consider the lower-stakes question of whether trying to change the handedness of children "works." Adaptation *does*

In the belief that the left hand was the devil's hand, nuns sometimes punished left-handed children at residential schools by tying one or both wrists, dangerously constricting blood-flow and causing the hands to turn purple.

seem possible for some people, especially if they're in the middle of the spectrum, as with a 66-year-old in Lakeland, Florida who wrote, "I did use both as a child, but nuns in Catholic Kindergarten changed that. Glad they did actually."

However there are also many responses like the one below, from a 31-year-old in Dumont, New Jersey, suggesting that "handedness conversion therapy" on a left-handed kid often doesn't produce a happily right-handed adult:

Just wanted to say thank you. So many people don't realize that when we were forced to change our hands at a young age ("This is a right-handed world") it forever tainted handwriting/drawing ability.

From the survey data alone, it's impossible to guess how many people could have been left-handed tradespeople or visual artists, but never developed their gifts because they were forced to use their right hands. Clearly, harm has been done.

It's reassuring to see that forced handedness switching is less common in the United States nowadays, though sobering that the change is so recent. Questions about the "natural" range and balance of handedness over a human lifetime may only be answerable in another generation, by which time we'll perhaps have seen a whole cohort grow up without the pressure to switch. Or else, it could be that trying to find this "natural state of things" is a fool's errand, because we're such an inherently social species. Pressures to conform are ever-present, as are shifts in language and behavioral norms.

Stenciled hands at the Cueva de las Manos ("Cave of the Hands") in Argentina, created in waves between 7,300 BCE and 700 CE. Left hands predominate, indicating a right-handed majority in pre-Columbian South America (as people will generally use their dominant hand to hold the painting tool, here probably a bone spray pipe).

3

Stigma and inferiority

Handedness seems pretty inconsequential compared to gender and sexuality, race, class, and myriad other anonymous identities with real stakes. Nobody cares if you're left-handed—that had been my assumption, and that's why I thought handedness would be a good toy problem.

Then again, I'm right-handed. Many other right-handed people taking the survey either minimized handedness, or in some cases, even failed to notice the *existence* of the left-handed. A 27-year-old man from Miami, Florida, for example, wrote only, "I am exclusively right-handed and so is everyone else I know." Given the statistics (about one in ten men are strictly *left*-handed at his age), this is hard to believe. In another typically blithe comment, a 58-year-old from Fort Lauderdale wrote, "Being right-hand dominant I often try to chuck a Frisbee with my left hand to improve skill. [...] Otherwise, I never think about 'handedness'. Good luck with your research!"

The left-handed are acutely aware of the asymmetry here: "It is more difficult than right-handed people realize to be a left-handed person."[1] At a purely practical level, many awkward scenarios were described concerning scissors, can openers, pots and measuring cups, desks, light switches, and, most of all, our writing system. It *is* a right-handed world, so we talk about "left-handed scissors" but not "right-handed scissors": the majoritarian default again. For parents, educators, and numerous nuns, an understanding that "the left-handed curse is real"[2] has motivated efforts to push left-handed children toward right-handedness.

Accommodating the left-handed properly is possible, but it takes thoughtfulness and resources. As a 34-year-old from Marietta, Georgia put it,

> **I was ambidextrous as a child and was forced to learn to write with only my right hand. My writing was so sloppy that I had to take a special class. Eventually they gave up and put a computer in the classroom just for me, which was expensive and a big deal in the 80's!**

1 A 41-year-old from Carlinville, Illinois.

2 A 35-year-old from Terre Haute, Indiana.

This example illustrates how the "enlightened" treatment of left-handed kids was as much about evolving technology as about changing attitudes. The two go together. Technologies, even simple kinds like scissors and can openers, are a kind of prosthetic, and it takes either sophisticated design or large consumer markets (or both) to make these prosthetics work well for everybody. Until recently, most societies have followed something like the "80–20 rule," the truism that often you can get a "good enough" solution to work 80% of the time (or for 80% of the population) with 20% of the effort it would take to solve the full problem.

In fact, 80–20 is often too optimistic, because there are so many combinations of minority and majority, and intersections of minorities have a fractal quality. How do we design a can opener that remains useful for a strictly left-handed person with low grip strength due to arthritis *and* severe cerebral palsy? Designers do sometimes think about such problems nowadays, but there are still too many "corner cases," as they're often called, to think through, to test, or to be compatible with making a profit. Regulation can help, but it, too, relies on something like a "marketplace" of advocacy for specific needs. It seems unlikely that the project of universal inclusion will ever be complete. But we can chip away at it.

In 1656, English Quaker James Naylor was publicly tortured and branded on the forehead with a "B" for blasphemer.

IAMES NAYLOR

Of all the Sects that Night, and Errors own
And with false Lights possesse the world, ther's none
More strongly blind, or who more madly place
The light of Nature for the light of Grace.
708

The practical aspects of majoritarian "privilege" and minoritarian "curse" are far from the whole story, though. Beyond how you write or throw a Frisbee, handedness is an identity, which brings with it all of the social machinery of tribalism, in-groups, and out-groups. "Proud to be right-handed," wrote a 36-year-old from Monmouth Junction, New Jersey. Or, "LEFTIES RULE," according to a defiant 28-year-old from Hebron, Indiana.

However when a visible majority exists, and the world is set up to favor that majority, these "tribes" are unevenly matched. Social stigma inevitably ensues: per Wikipedia,[3] "the disapproval of, or discrimination against, a person based on perceivable social characteristics that serve to distinguish them from other members of a society."

3 Wikipedia, "Social stigma," 2020.

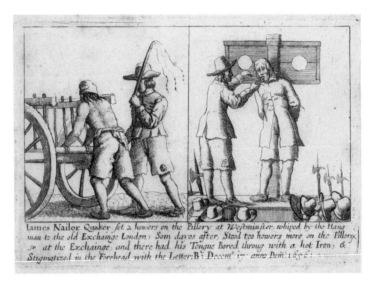

"Iames Nailor Quaker set 2 howers on the Pillory at Westminster, whiped by the Hang man to the old Exchainge London, Som dayes after, Stood too howers more on the Pillory at the Exchainge, and there had his Tongue Bored throug with a hot Iron, & Stigmatized in the Forehead with the Letter: B: Decem: 17 anno Dom:1656:"

Iames Nailor Quaker, set 2 howers on the Pillory at Westminster, whiped by the Hang man to the old Exchainge London; Som dayes after, Stood too howers more on the Pillory in at the Exchainge, and there had his Tongue Bored throug with a hot Iron, & Stigmatized in the Forehead with the Letter:B; Decem: 17 anno Dein:1656:

When I set out to explore handedness, I didn't fully appreciate the way stigma follows inexorably from the social logic of majority and minority. Respondents' comments were eye opening. They included many variations on "As a child I was told that doing things with my left had was bad,"[4] as well as tropes familiar from other contexts, like "I don't really believe in handedness"[5] and even "some of my best friends are left-handed."[6] I didn't know whether to laugh or wince at this last one. Was it meant ironically? An emoji might have helped, if so!

The Greek word "stigma," dating back at least to the 6th century BCE, originally referred to the branding, tattooing, or cutting of symbols into the skins of slaves or criminals, to make it impossible for them to move through society without advertising their low status. Similar practices were documented in the colonial slave trade, two thousand years later. As Imogen Tyler writes in her 2020 book *Stigma: The Machinery of Inequality*,

> **Penal tattooing involved the inscription of words, symbols, and sometimes full sentences into the skin. These tattoos 'usually consisted of the name of a crime' inked into the face. Records of common stigmas include 'Thief' or 'Stop me, I'm a runaway', tattooed on the forehead. If you survived the torture of being tattooed (without antiseptic) you would never be free of the stigma, the 'disgrace, humiliation and exclusion' remaining 'indelibly written on one's face for all to see.'[7]**

Hence these marks were never just about subordination or ownership, as in cattle branding (though the parallel with the treatment of livestock has always been clear, and highlights both the

4 A 28-year-old from Evansville, Indiana.

5 A 34-year-old from Orange, California.

6 A 38-year-old from Lanham, Maryland.

7 Tyler, *Stigma: The Machinery of Inequality*, 35, 2020.

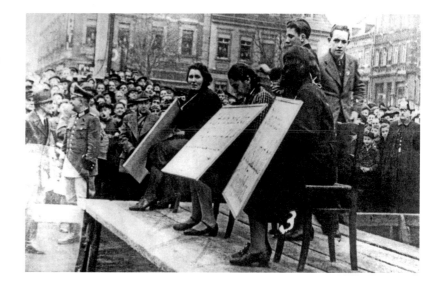

dehumanization of the act and the stark power inequality behind it). The tattoos were also ways of literally writing shame into the skin. They indelibly marked someone as blemished, morally polluted, and lesser than, in a way that would forever change the way that person was seen—both by others and, worse still, by themselves. It was why, during the Kristallnacht pogrom of November 1938, Jewish women in Linz, Austria were made to exhibit themselves in public with cardboard signs reading "I have been excluded from the national community [*Volksgemeinschaft*]."[8] It was why Jews were forced to wear yellow star of David badges in public, and were eventually tattooed on the arm with coded numbers in concentration camps.

8 Gruner, "The Forgotten Mass Destruction of Jewish Homes During 'Kristallnacht,'" 2019.

    In the past century, our understanding of stigma has broadened. While the word was originally associated with tattooing or otherwise permanently marking the skin, this practice is more the exception than the rule. Such a marking was "needed" by the ancient Greeks, because their slaves (and criminals) could be ethnically Greek too, making their subordinate status otherwise impossible to spot.

    Similarly, despite Nazi pseudoscience and propaganda cartoons suggesting that Jewish faces were distinctive or even monstrous, it was often impossible to tell Jews and Christians apart based on bodies, clothes, languages, or behaviors. Plenty of "Aryans" had big noses, and plenty of Jews had blond hair. The same held for gay people, Gypsies, and other populations Nazi Germany sought to isolate and eliminate, despite these populations often not being well defined. These examples reveal how tattooing, branding, and other kinds of permanent physical marking are simply ancient technologies that an in-group may press into service to reinforce social categories, especially when the signs of belonging or exclusion are not otherwise obvious.

In 1844, Captain Jonathan Walker's right hand was branded with "SS" for "Slave Stealer" by a US Marshal for attempting to help seven runaway slaves.

Today, stigma is no longer a sign *per se*, but the meaning behind it. That meaning—"your kind are inferior"—has attached to a wide range of out-groups throughout history, whether of race, caste, sexuality, culture, class, or much else—including, yes, handedness.

An 1845 daguerreotype (hence, in mirror image) of Walker's branded palm.

For evidence of the handedness stigma, one need only look to language itself— the words we use to identify the majority and the minority. Though they've lost their power, these words are like the eroded features of a dormant volcano. They hint at a violent past during which the stigma of handedness was more active than it is today.

Consider: the word "left" derives from the Anglo-Saxon word for "weak," *lyft*, while *riht* meant "good, proper, fitting, straight." "Right" of course still means something proper or correct, both in English and in many other languages. Remarkably, a similar pattern holds in languages unrelated to English: the Chinese word for right, 右 (yòu), also means "respect," "esteem," or "value,"[9] while the word for left, 左 (zuǒ), means "queer," "unorthodox," "wrong," "devious," "dishonest," or historically, simply "inferior position."[10]

Dexter, the Latin for right, connotes skill and adroitness, as per the English word "dextrous." In fact "ambidextrous," skilled with both hands, literally means "having two right hands"! Compare this with

9 Wiktionary, "右," 2020.

10 Wiktionary, "左," 2021.

sayings like having "two left feet," which means being clumsy. The same expression works in a number of other languages too, as in the French *deux pieds gauches*. For that matter, *gauche* itself means not only "left" but also "awkward or lacking in social graces." The Latin for left is *sinistram*, from which we derive "sinister."[11]

In boxing, a right-handed fighter is referred to as "orthodox," which comes from Greek *orthos*, meaning "straight" or "right," and *doxa*, "opinion." The modern Spanish word for left, *izquierda*, comes from the Basque *ezkerretara*, whose original meaning is probably "clumsy or crooked hand."[12] In a number of different cultures, the right hand is traditionally used to eat, while the left hand is used for... the opposite. Hence expressions like the British and Australian "cack-handed," which can mean either clumsy or—of course—left-handed.

This litany is far from exhaustive, but you get the idea.

It may be surprising, today, to notice the overwhelming linguistic evidence of implicit bias against the left-handed. In many historical sources, wherever handedness comes up, the bias is more explicit. The Old Testament, for example, refers hundreds of times to right and left hands, and where these are distinguished, the right hand represents honor and strength, the left sin and wickedness. Per Ecclesiastes, "A wise man's heart is at his right hand; but a fool's heart at his left."[13] God's right hand is often described as powerful and "full of righteousness"; "The right hand of the Lord is exalted: the right hand of the Lord doeth valiantly".[14]

11 In researching the literature on handedness, I ran across papers with titles like "The Sinistral Child," which just refers to left-handed children but sounds more like the title of a horror movie.

12 Anders, "Etimología de Izquierda."

13 Eccles. 10:2 (King James Version).

14 Pss. 48:10, 118:16 (KJV).

A sixth century mosaic of the Last Judgment in the Basilica of Sant'Apollinare Nuovo, Ravenna, Italy. Notice how right hands are shown, while left hands are concealed.

The New Testament is perhaps even starker, per the Gospel of Matthew:

And before him shall be gathered all nations: and he shall separate them one from another, as a shepherd divideth his sheep from the goats:
And he shall set the sheep on his right hand, but the goats on the left.
Then shall the King say unto them on his right hand, Come, ye blessed of my Father, inherit the Kingdom [...].[15]

15 Matt. 25:32–34 (KJV).

16 In real life goats are of course perfectly lovely.

17 Per the introduction by Mary Gibson and Nicole Hahn Rafter of their 2006 translation of Lombroso's *Criminal Man*.

In the Christian tradition, sheep have always been considered saintly, to the point that Jesus himself is referred to as *Agnus Dei*, the Lamb of God. Naturally, the "goats" exiting to stage left represent the damned.[16]

But this is ancient history, long predating the Enlightenment, the Scientific Revolution, the Industrial Revolution, and modernity as we know it. How did we get from Iron Age prejudices to institutionalized medical ideas that still held sway within living memory about the left-handed being "aberrant or abnormal"—hence to widespread attempts by 20th century parents, nuns, and school teachers to save the at-risk youth with "handedness conversion therapy"?

Cesare Lombroso.

Cesare Lombroso (1835–1909), physician, anthropologist, criminologist, and arguably the most famous Italian thinker of his era,[17] played a significant role in this turn—as well as in this book's larger story of human identity and the "othering" that so often accompanies attempts to distinguish "us" from "them." Lombroso's starting point was medical. He sought to bring new rigor to the quantitative study of the human body, both in its healthy or "normal" state and in its "aberrations"—an admirable goal, though a difficult one in an era with few lab tests and little idea of what caused most illness.

Victorian doctors may not have been able to quantify what went on inside the body, but they could at least inspect our outsides. Physical measurements, distances and angles, weights and volumes could be tabulated. Surely such variables correlated with health in some manner? Where previous generations of doctors had relied

A couple viewing the head of Lombroso preserved in a jar of formalin at an exhibition in Bologna, 1978.

on lore and intuition, the "modern" doctor now could analyze statistics, and start treating medicine as a science. That was the theory, anyway.

Lombroso worked in prisons and asylums, which prompted him to concentrate on mental disorders, and hence to focus especially on the measurement of the head and facial features. Intuitively, we note that animals with bigger heads relative to their bodies seem to be among the more intelligent; also, certain congenital problems like microcephaly (in which the brain and the head are underdeveloped) usually result in intellectual disability. The head houses the brain, after all. Might the signs of other cognitive impairments—or even gifts, signs of genius—also be detectable through careful physical measurement of the head? What about a predisposition to criminal behavior?

The "logic" proved irresistible. Lombroso came to champion physiognomy, the pseudoscientific belief (to be explored further in

LARGE AND SMALL INTELLECTS.

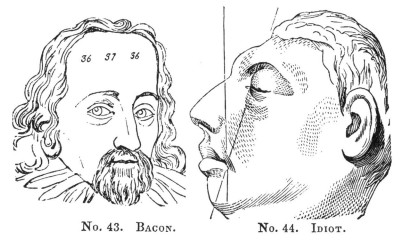

"[C]ontrast the massive foreheads of all giant-minded men—Bacons, Franklins, Miltons, etc., with idiotic heads." From Fowler and Fowler, *The Illustrated Self-Instructor in Phrenology and Physiology*, 1853.

No. 43. Bacon.   No. 44. Idiot.

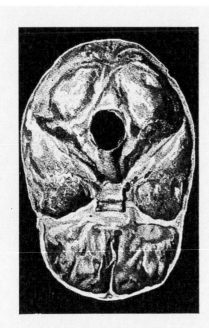

Fossette Occipital

Occipital fossa from
*Criminal Man, According
to the Classification
of Cesare Lombroso,
Briefly Summarised
by His Daughter Gina
Lombroso Ferrero*, 1911.

Chapter 14) that people's physical features reveal their essential nature—and their value to society.

I know, I'm making this chain of reasoning sound a bit far fetched. Perhaps it's best to let Lombroso tell the story in his own words. Luckily, we have a colorful first person account, written shortly before he died, in a 1911 book published by his daughter Gina introducing "scientific criminology" to an eager American audience:

[I]nspiration came to me when [...] I applied to the clinical examination of cases of mental alienation the study of the skull, with measurements and weights, by means of the esthesiometer and craniometer. [...] I, therefore, began to study criminals in the Italian prisons, and, amongst others, I made the acquaintance of the famous brigand Vilella.[18] This man possessed such extraordinary agility, that he had been known to scale steep mountain heights bearing a sheep on his shoulders. His cynical effrontery was such that he openly boasted of his crimes. On his death one cold grey November morning, I was deputed to make the *post-mortem*, and on laying open the skull I found on the occipital part, exactly on the spot where a spine is found in the normal skull, a distinct depression which I named *median occipital fossa*, because of its situation precisely in the middle of the occiput as in inferior animals, especially rodents. This depression, as in the case of animals, was correlated with the hypertrophy of the *vermis*, known in birds as the middle cerebellum.

This was not merely an idea, but a revelation. At the sight of that skull, I seemed to see all of a sudden, lighted up as a vast plain under a flaming sky, the problem of the nature of the criminal—an atavistic being who reproduces in his person the ferocious instincts of primitive humanity and the inferior animals. Thus were explained anatomically the enormous jaws, high cheek-bones, prominent superciliary arches, solitary lines in the palms, extreme size of the orbits, handle-shaped or sessile ears found in criminals, savages, and apes, insensibility to pain, extremely acute

18 Gina Lombroso referred to Vilella, rather hyperbolically, as "an Italian Jack the Ripper, who by atrocious crimes had spread terror in the Province of Lombardy." As far as we know, he was in fact a laborer from Calabria who had been imprisoned for the theft of two kid goats and five ricotta cheeses. See Assandri, "Il Cranio Del 'Brigante' Villella Può Restare Al Museo Lombroso," 2017.

19 Gina and Cesare Lombroso, *Criminal Man*, xii–xv, 1911.

sight, tattooing, excessive idleness, love of orgies, and the irresistible craving for evil for its own sake, the desire not only to extinguish life in the victim, but to mutilate the corpse, tear its flesh, and drink its blood.[19]

It's hard not to connect this account, with its preternaturally lithe monster scaling steep mountainsides, post-mortem dissections, flaming epiphanies, and anthropophagous horrors, with the Gothic vibe of Mary Shelley's *Frankenstein* (1818). The enduring popularity of Lombroso's works and those of his followers must have owed something to Romanticism's lurid flair.

At any rate, Vilella's remains supplied Lombroso with "evidence" confirming his belief that *brigantes* (brigands) were primitive or "degenerate" types, prone to crime. Hence criminality, Lombroso maintained, is inherited, and carries with it inherited physical characteristics that instruments like calipers and craniographs can measure. Incidentally, this belief conveniently justified his assumption that southern Italians (like the Calabrian Vilella) were racially inferior to northern Italians (like himself).

20 Lombroso, *L'uomo delinquente*, 1876.

21 Darwin, *The Descent of Man, and Selection in Relation to Sex*, 1871.

22 His reticence to point out this obvious conclusion had been borne of anxiety over a religious backlash, which did occur and is still ongoing.

While physiognomy was already an ancient tradition in 1876, when Lombroso first published his ideas in *The Criminal Man*,[20] he gave it new life by attaching it to the most groundbreaking scientific discovery of the age: Charles Darwin's theory of evolution. *The Criminal Man* followed on the heels of *The Descent of Man*[21] (1871), wherein Darwin belatedly acknowledged that evolutionary theory, which he had introduced more than a decade earlier in *On The Origin of Species* (1859), applied to people too:

> **[M]an bears in his bodily structure clear traces of his descent from some lower form.[22]**

With these words, Darwin didn't just affirm human evolution; he articulated a grand unifying idea of *progress*, of life marching ever onward and upward—with humanity representing nature's most recent (hence most transcendent) crown jewel.

A century later, in 1973, Darwin's idea inspired mathematician and polymath Jacob Bronowski's BBC series about the history of everything, cleverly entitled *The Ascent of Man*. For Darwin and Bronowski both, this ascent had intellectual, artistic, and moral dimensions, blurring the distinction between biological evolution and cultural history. Darwin was, unfortunately for his posterity, explicit in drawing these connections. He went on to write:

> [N]or is the difference slight in moral disposition between a barbarian, such as the man described by the old navigator Byron, who dashed his child on the rocks for dropping a basket of sea-urchins, and a Howard or Clarkson; and in intellect, between a savage who does not use any abstract terms, and a Newton or Shakspeare. Differences of this kind between the highest men of the highest races and the lowest savages, are connected by the finest gradations.[23]

23 While Bronowski was less explicitly racist, his perspectives on vanished civilizations are similarly animated by the sense of progress from a state of savagery and primitivism toward a European Enlightenment featuring debates between bewigged intellectuals Newton and Leibniz over a Bach soundtrack. Despite the grandeur of Machu Picchu, for instance, Bronowski's disdain for the Inca is evident as he castigates them for being so backward that they hadn't even conceived of the stone arch.

Left to right: Darwin's tubercle, from Darwin, *Descent of Man*, 1871; Darwin's tubercle on a crab-eating macaque.; Illustration of a "Criminal's Ear" from Gina Lombroso, *Criminal Man*, 1911.

As with Lombroso's racism, this is another illustration of homophily, the pervasive cognitive bias whereby we tend to associate with and favor people similar to ourselves. Darwin's apex of humanity was thus peopled by the physicist Isaac Newton, the playwright William Shakespeare, the abolitionist Thomas Clarkson, and the philanthropist John Howard. All were English, Christian, white, male, and from the educated classes—that is, much like Darwin himself!

Still, Darwin's views were in step with those of his peers, and in some ways more liberal; hence his staunch opposition to slavery, evident even here in his inclusion of Clarkson among the great and the good. On the other hand, *The Descent of Man* lent scientific authority to the idea of a racial hierarchy differentiating humans who are "more human" (more evolved, physically, intellectually and behaviorally) and "less human" (less evolved, physically closer to the other great apes, less intelligent, and less "civilized").

Thus inspired, it wasn't such a big step for Lombroso to venture beyond "scientific" racism, and seek out those "clear traces of [man's] descent from some lower form" specifically in the bodies of the people deemed "lowest" within his own society—beginning with convicts and the mentally ill. For instance: Darwin had pointed out the presence

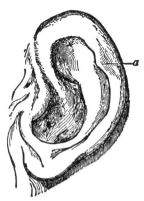

Fig. 2. Human Ear, modeled and drawn by Mr. Woolner.

a. The projecting point.

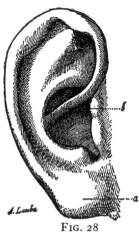

FIG. 28
Criminal's Ear

24 More modern anthropometric research tells us that about 18% of the Spanish adult population, 40% of adults in India, and 58% of Swedish school children exhibit this feature. Rubio, Galera, and Alonso, "Anthropological Study of Ear Tubercles in a Spanish Sample," 2015; Singh and Purkait, "Observations of External Ear—an Indian Study," 2009; Hildén, "Studien über Das Vorkommen Der Darwinschen Ohrspitze in Der Bevölkerung Finnlands," 1929.

25 Gina Lombroso, *Criminal Man*, 14–15, 1911.

in some people of a "peculiarity in the external ear," a "little blunt point, projecting from the inwardly folded margin, or helix" which he believed to be the "vestiges of the tips of formerly erect and pointed ears" found in monkeys. Building on this rather flimsy observation,[24] Lombroso claimed that

> **Twenty-eight per cent. of criminals have handle-shaped ears standing out from the face as in the chimpanzee: in other cases they are placed at different levels. Frequently too, we find misshapen, flattened ears, devoid of helix, tragus, and anti-tragus, and with a protuberance on the upper part of the posterior margin (Darwin's tubercle), a relic of the pointed ear characteristic of apes.[25]**

The next time you look in the mirror, you may want to check whether your ears, too, feature this apish protuberance!

As you might have guessed by now, Lombroso deemed left-handedness a marker of "degeneracy" too:

(Figura 1.)

(Fig. 2.)

Ladro milanese, condannato 13 volte.

> **Compared to normal individuals, criminals show an almost twofold prevalence of left-handedness; in this they resemble children, primitives, and idiots, who are commonly ambidextrous [...]. Everyone agrees that left-handedness is a result of the prevalence of the brain's right hemisphere over the left, as opposed to the normal prevalence of left over right,**

26 The observation that the right brain is "wired" mainly to the left side of the body, and the left brain to the right, is correct.

which results in right-handedness.[26] While the honest person thinks with the left brain, the criminal thinks with the right [...]. When people shy away from the left-handed person and refer to him as "sinister," they simply confirm Italian folk wisdom about left-handed people. Lengthy research will be needed to confirm the popular belief, prevalent especially in Emilia and Lombardy, that swindlers tend to be left-handed. But my own findings provide preliminary proof that left-handedness is more prevalent among swindlers (33 percent) than among other types of criminals.[27]

27 Lombroso, Criminal Man, 211, 2006.

Needless to say, none of this "preliminary proof," which was based on a very small number of samples and hopelessly biased, stood up to later scrutiny. Nonetheless, the stigma, mired as it was in age-old folk wisdom, stuck—especially once it acquired a scientific veneer.

Given the association of right-handedness with the "normal" dominance of the "good" left brain, and left-handedness with "pathological" dominance of the "bad" right brain, many 19th century thinkers began to similarly associate every other property or character trait that had "good/strong" and "bad/weak" polarities with lateralization, including sex and gender. According to the American phrenologist Orson Squire Fowler (1809–1887), for instance, "seeds from the right testicle [impregnate] only an egg from the right ovary, which produces only boys, while girls are created by the left."[28]

28 Shafer, Man and Woman; Or, Creative Science and Sexual Philosophy, 1882. How Fowler arrived at his many weird conclusions is anyone's guess; they were easily disproved by noticing that people with a single testicle or ovary were perfectly capable of having children of any sex.

Inevitably, this resulted in sexual orientation also becoming associated with handedness, since here, too, there was a "right" majority and a "wrong" minority. Hence the Australian vernacular for left-handed likely dating to the 1930s, "mollydooker," from slang for effeminate ("molly") and fist ("dook" or "duke," as in "put up your dukes"), or, in US English, the use of the sports term "switch hitter" (meaning an ambidextrous baseball batter) for bisexuality. Austrian physician and psychologist Wilhelm Stekel, one of Sigmund Freud's earliest and most distinguished followers, wrote in *The Language of Dreams* (1911),

29 Die sprache des traumes, 466, 1911, quoted in Freud, "The Interpretation of Dreams," 374, 1938.

The right-hand path always signifies the way to righteousness, the left-hand path the path to crime. Thus the left may signify homosexuality, incest, and perversion, while the right signifies marriage [...].[29]

Freud's closest friend for a time, the physician Wilhelm Fliess (1858–1928), took this belief a step further, writing in *The Course of Life* (1906),

The emphasis on the two halves of the body always changes, so that effeminate men and masculine women are wholly or partially left-handed; and vice versa, left-handed men are invariably more effeminate and left-handed women are more masculine than those who are right-handed.[30]

Both Stekel and Fliess, like many other 19th and 20th century thinkers, regarded homosexuality along with any tendency to flout the (highly rigid) gender norms of their day as "perversions" and "aberrations" expressing traits of the "wrong gender." They also associated these traits with criminality, as will be discussed further in Part II.

Sigmund Freud (1856–1939) and Wilhelm Fliess (1858–1928).

30 Fliess, *Der Ablauf des Lebens: Grundlegung zur exakten Biologie*, 1906. Translation mine.

31 Fausto-Sterling, *Myths of Gender*, 67, 2008.

Sloppy thinking about handedness and its relationship to gender and sexuality continued throughout the 20th century, and persists even in the 21st, as discussed in detail by Anne Fausto-Sterling in her 2008 book *Myths of Gender*. Prominent brain lateralization researcher Jerre Levy (1938–), for instance, popularized the notion of the left hemisphere as specializing in "linear reasoning," while the right hemisphere is more "holistic," adding that since speech in women is less lateralized than in men (there is some evidence for this), women's brains must function less efficiently—a claim for which there is no evidence. As Fausto-Sterling points out, Levy's (unsubstantiated) theory "actually holds that left-handed men resemble women in this regard."[31]

Let's look at real data before wrapping up handedness and moving on to more delicate topics. Since some genetic evidence links handedness with sex (albeit, per Chapter 1, there are confounding factors given the greater propensity of men to injure themselves), it's reasonable to wonder about the validity of the supposed connection between handedness and sexual orientation.

If so, the effect is weak, as evidenced by comparing the numbers of strictly left- and right-handed women and men who are strictly same-sex attracted. (This framing avoids the complications that come from relying on self-identification, e.g. as lesbian or gay, since as later chapters will show, the definitions of those terms vary over time and with age.) Strict same-sex attraction is defined here as either sexual or

3.0 **Handedness in women who are strictly same-sex attracted** % by age

3.0 **Handedness in women who are strictly same-sex attracted** % by age

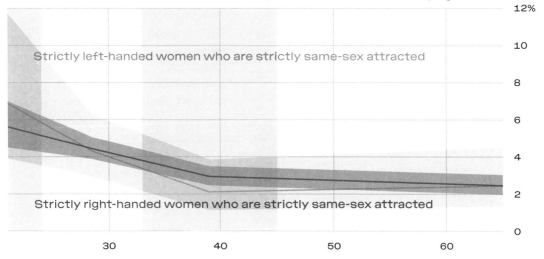

Strictly left-handed women who are strictly same-sex attracted

Strictly right-handed women who are strictly same-sex attracted

3.1 **Handedness in men who are strictly same-sex attracted** % by age

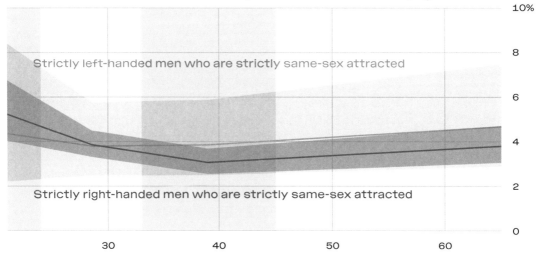

Strictly left-handed men who are strictly same-sex attracted

Strictly right-handed men who are strictly same-sex attracted

32 Once again, this somewhat awkward framing (as opposed, for example, to "trans man" or "trans woman") avoids to the degree possible the confounding effects of the shifting definition of identities like "trans" across ages and between populations, a topic explored in Chapter 13.

romantic attraction to the same sex, and no attraction of either kind to the opposite sex; it's only graphed for people who answer "yes" to exactly one of "Are you a man?" or "Are you a woman?"

Notice that the left-handed and right-handed curves fall within each other's error bars across all ages, showing no significant difference in the rate of strictly same-sex attraction by handedness. Nor is there any statistically significant association between handedness and identifying as a man in adulthood if assigned female at birth, or as a woman, if assigned male at birth[32] (though for the latter group especially, for reasons discussed in Chapters 12 and 13, the numbers are small; since these graphs involve minorities of minorities of subsets of the population, the error bars are large).

3.2 Handedness in men who were assigned female at birth % by age

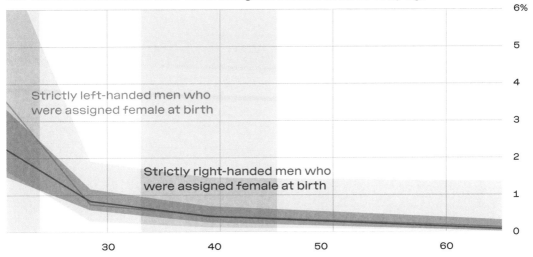

3.3 Handedness in women who were assigned male at birth % by age

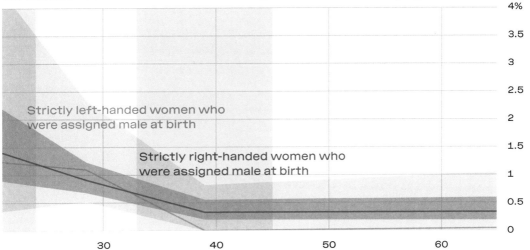

In a recurring pattern, that influential 19th and 20th century thinkers lacked the thousands of datapoints required to test their hypotheses didn't prevent them from making some highly confident claims. With modern surveying and data analysis techniques, it's now possible to check whether any of those claims hold water. Often, they don't.

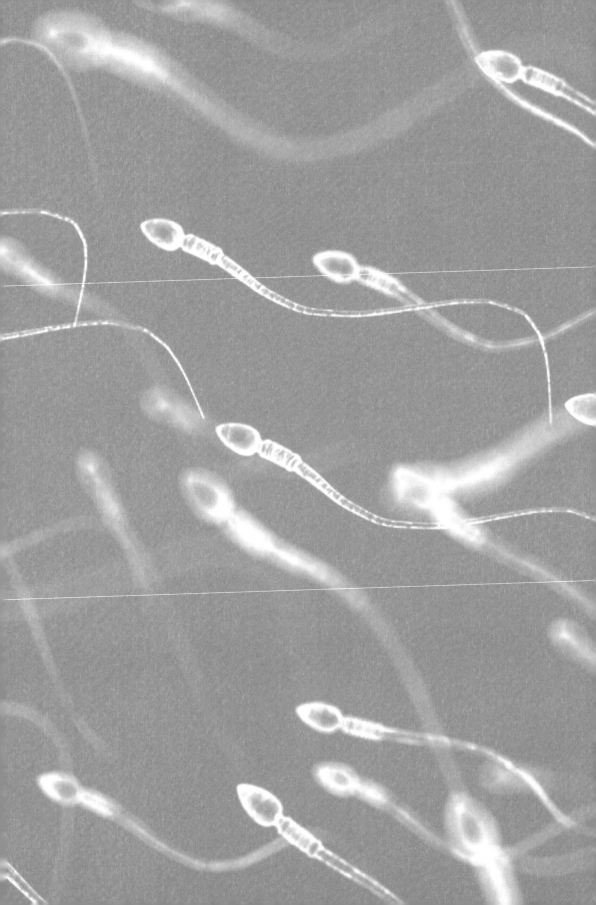

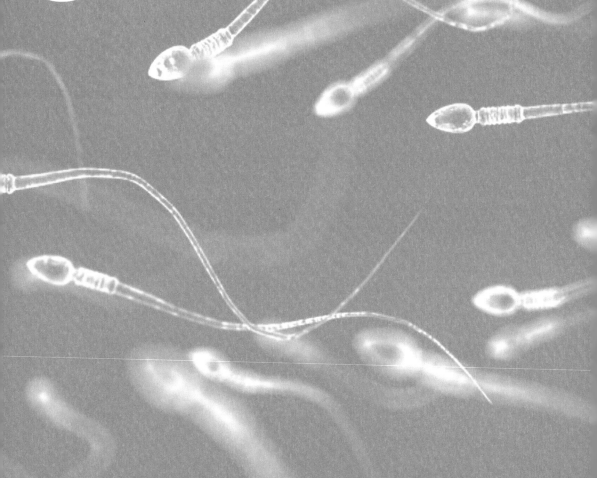

Part II
Sex and gender

Survey **Sex and Gender**

These are the questions I asked participants taking the sex and gender
survey. They're in random order, as they
would have been for a respondent.

Were you born in September or October?

Do you have short hair?

Do you menstruate?

Do you wear colorful clothes?

On paper, do people assume from your
name that you are female?

Are you romantically attracted to men?

Are you demiromantic?

Do either of your parents identify
as homosexual, gay, or lesbian?

Are you intersex?

Do you identify as South Asian/
Indian American?

Do you identify as agender?

Do you live in the countryside?

Do you ever wear a bra?

Have you ever been pregnant?

Do you shave your legs?

Are you Buddhist?

Were you born outside the US?

Do you ever wear ties?

Do you live in the city?

Do you wear dresses/skirts?

Do you identify as gender fluid?

Were you born in March or April?

Were you born in November or December?

Do you identify as Native Hawaiian or
Other Pacific Islander?

Do you identify as Native American?

Were you born before 1983?

Do you identify as Black/
African American?

Are you non-monogamous?

Is the right pronoun for you "they"?

Do you have an ear piercing?

Are you atheist or agnostic?

Do you play shooter video games?

Are you homosexual, gay, or lesbian?

Do you work in tech?

Do you ever wear high heels?

Are you demisexual?

Do you identify as trans?

Are you Christian?

Do you wear pants?

Do you identify as White/
  European American?

Do you live in an urban environment?

Is the right pronoun for you "he"?

Do you have a beard or mustache?

Do you shave your face?

Do you have a penis?

Were you born in May or June?

Do you identify as Latino/
  Latina or Hispanic American?

Do you have long hair?

Do you identify as Filipino/Filipina?

Are you pansexual?

Is the right pronoun for you something
  other than he/she/they?

Do you identify as Asian American?

Are you sexually attracted to women?

Were you assigned male at birth?

Do either of your parents identify as
  heterosexual or straight?

Are you monogamous?

Are you married?

Were you born in the US?

Do you identify as non-binary?

Do you identify as queer?

Are you aromantic?

Do you ever wear boxer shorts?

Do you use the men's bathroom?

Are you bisexual?

Are you Muslim?

Have you had breast reduction surgery?

Do you use the women's bathroom?

Do you ever wear panties?

Were you born in July or August?

Do you identify as female?

Do you ever use colored lipstick?

Do you get pedicures?

Are you asexual?

Were you assigned female at birth?

Have you ever lactated (produced milk)?

Are you right-handed?

Do you get manicures?

Are you romantically attracted to women?

Are you Catholic?

On paper, do people assume from
  your name that you are male?

Are you polyamorous?

Are you left-handed?

Do you have a vagina?

Do you use public urinals?

Is the right pronoun for you "she"?

Do you wax?

Are you heterosexual or straight?

Are you Jewish?

Do you shave your armpits?

Do you identify as male?

Are you Hindu?

Do you ever use makeup?

Have you ever menstruated?

Have you had breast augmentation surgery?

Do you live in the suburbs?

Do you have long nails?

Are you sexually attracted to men?

Do you identify as gender queer?

Do you ever wear stockings?

Were you born in January or February?

4 Family models

Haber, *The Walt Disney Story of Our Friend the Atom*, 1956.

In particle physics, the so-called "Standard Model" is a flawed yet widely accepted picture of how the universe works—the rules and formulas governing elementary particles like electrons and quarks, the forces holding together atoms and molecules, the theoretical basis of electricity and magnetism. It's been in development since the Atomic Age in the mid-20th century, continually tweaked and refined but never upended, and it accounts so precisely for so much of what we can observe in the lab that alternative theories are often regarded as exotic, even fringe. For now, it has no serious competitors.

Still, we know that it really can't be complete or even correct, because it has no way of accounting for the big picture: the force of gravity that tells us which way is up, the mysterious dark matter that holds together galaxies, the accelerating expansion of the universe. It's a convenient fiction.

When it comes to sex, relationships, and reproduction, something like a Standard Model also exists, and it, too, found a name in the Atomic Age: the Nuclear Family. This supposedly elementary social building block consists of one man and one woman in a sexually and romantically exclusive relationship, typically having children together and raising them in a house until they're ready to move out and eventually settle down with spouses of their own to repeat the cycle.

In a Nuclear Family, the man has a paid job and brings in money, while the woman runs the household.[1] People (men especially) are defined by specialized work and valued for their individual achievements. Ownership of assets is individual or "joint" (meaning belonging to the couple), and one of life's main goals is to amass as much wealth as possible. People are free to dispose of their assets more or less as they wish, with their legal children inheriting any remaining loot when both parents die.

[1] The "man alone is the breadwinner" aspect is the most dated, but disparities in income continue to cast a long shadow, as we will see.

Hanna-Barbera, *The Flintstones*, 1960–66.

→ Hanna-Barbera, *The Jetsons*, 1962–63.

Sexual or romantic liaisons outside the exclusive pair bond are *verboten*. When pursued furtively, they're a source of both guilt and, if exposed, shame. Any children known to have been born of such an unsanctioned liaison face inheritance challenges and lifelong stigma as "illegitimate" or, to use an older and even uglier term, "bastards."

These rules and norms doubtless all sound familiar. Many of us were brought up to think of them as not just familiar, but universal. Whether ironic or not, the endless reruns of Hanna-Barbera cartoons I remember watching—*The Flintstones, The Jetsons*—embraced the premise that from the Stone Age to the Space Age, however much the technological trappings may evolve, the Nuclear Family has always been and will always be the fundamental unit of human sociality.

Hanna-Barbera cartoons were hardly an isolated case. The edifice of mainstream 20th century media, from Norman Rockwell paintings to *Leave it to Beaver* sitcoms, all agreed. More broadly, much of Western society was built on the presumption of this kind of domesticity: laws, institutions, customs, entertainment, housing, transportation, jobs, infrastructure, and even—as with handedness—the very language we think with.

Nuclear Families may not be a law of physics, but neither did they come out of nowhere. To understand their underlying logic, we can ask: Why and when did they arise? And what's really at stake when we start questioning them?

Norman Rockwell (1894–1978), *Freedom From Want*, 1943.

In his 1837 book *The Philosophy of Marriage*, the physician Michael Ryan summarized the widely held view—especially then, and still today—that the monogamous pair bond underlies not only our entire political economy, but the reproductive future of humanity. There are some obvious wrinkles: the monogamous pair bond is far from universal today, it's not the historical norm, and it's "unnatural," insofar as it doesn't come easily to many, requiring constant legal, social, and moral enforcement.

I'll quote from Ryan at length, in the spirit of showing rather than telling:

> **POLYGAMY, or Polygyny, is sanctioned by laws of eastern nations [...]. Although polygamy is interdicted by our laws, it does not exist the less in the hearts of most men who profess to be monogamous, but who are no less polygamous**

by their actions. [...] St. Augustin, Grotius, and other moralists, admit this truth, but declare it would be contrary to morals, the interests of society, and the increase of population. Nevertheless, polygamy, or concubinage, is common among the higher classes in all civilised countries. [...] [The] promiscuity of the sexes would be justifiable according to many writers (Pliny, Diodorus, Siculus, &c.), and [...] there are some few eastern countries in which a community of women was, and even now is tolerated. [...] It is easy to adduce many valid reasons to prove that this community of women, and promiscuous intercourse of the sexes, can never be tolerated in any enlightened country. It must be obvious to the commonest understanding, that without marriage, neither paternity, nor family, nor patrimonial possession, nor division of landed property, nor legitimacy could be accurately determined; and thence it would follow that all would belong to all, every one would be benefitted in common, no one would exert himself for all his race, and the result would be a state of barbarism as in savage nations, and all the laws of society would be overturned.

You read that right: monogamy must be enforced so that capitalism and patriarchy can be preserved! What might an alternative look like? Ryan continues:

This perfect community of women and property, if it could take place, could only exist among people living as savages, and among a very small number on a vast territory. Suppose the community of women was established, what man would willingly allow an infant to be affiliated to him, of which he had any right to doubt that he was the father? The woman would violate the sacred duty of nursing her own infant only, and in a few centuries the human race could not be preserved; there would also be incessant desertions of infants, and a great increase of infanticides, crimes unfortunately too common; even under existing laws, but which would be innumerable in proportion as the people and their morals became more corrupted, and where no asylums would exist for the fruits of universal debauchery. Every fine feeling of paternal and natural love would be destroyed; all cares and protection of children would be at an end, and the mortality would become so great as in a few ages to exterminate the human race.[2]

2 Ryan, *The Philosophy of Marriage*, 91–93, 1837.

Whew, that's a lot to unpack!

For starters, Ryan's curious phrase "community of women" read differently in 1837 than it does today. He didn't mean a sisterhood or community *among* women, but that they'd be communally *owned*—meaning the communal property of men, who are clearly the intended readers here. Ryan would have considered it nonsensical to talk about a "community of men"! So, he can imagine non-monogamy—it looks a lot like communism—but if anything, it's even more patriarchal than the monogamous alternative, in which a woman "belongs" to *one* man, rather than to *all* men. A grim picture.

Despite Ryan's chauvinism and catastrophizing, there are elements of truth here. Among documented societies, sanctioned polygyny (sexual relationships between one man and multiple women) is a good deal more common than sanctioned polyandry (sexual relationships between one woman and multiple men),[3] and polygynous societies do tend to be highly patriarchal.[4] Also, as we'll see, a relationship between communism and non-monogamy *does* exist, both in traditional societies and among the freethinking sexual pioneers advocating "free love" who had begun to spring up in Ryan's day—much to his dismay.

3   Starkweather and Hames, "A Survey of Non-Classical Polyandry," 2012.

4   White and Burton, "Causes of Polygyny: Ecology, Economy, Kinship, and Warfare," 1988; McDermott and Cowden, "Polygyny and Violence Against Women," 2015.

5   McCammon, Arch, and Bergner, "Early US Feminists and the Married Women's Property Acts," 2014; Chused, "Married Women's Property Law: 1800–1850," 1982.

This passage also reminds us that the 20th century Standard Model had already departed in significant ways from its 19th century precursor (itself a recent invention), mainly due to the slow but steady progress of the women's rights movement. It wasn't until the 1848 Married Woman's Property Act, passed in New York and used as a model in other states, that a married woman could enter into contracts, collect rent, receive inheritances, or enter into lawsuits on her own.[5] Such basic obstacles to independence survived far into the 20th century; until 1974, many American banks required married women's husbands to cosign any credit application, and in Ireland, women only won the right to own their own homes in 1976. Legally and financially, a married woman in the 19th century really *was* her husband's property.

An 1854 critique of marriage by Thomas Low Nichols (1815–1901) and Mary Sargeant Gove Nichols (1810–1884), just the kind of free love activists Ryan was railing against, described the state of marriage in the starkest possible terms:

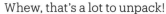

Mary Gove Nichols (1810–1884), American writer, women's rights activist, hydrotherapist, and vegetarian.

In the early ages slave and wife were convertible terms. The slave became the wife of her master, the wife no less became

his slave. In both cases they were sometimes purchased, sometimes taken captives in war; sometimes they were presents, given as the hostages of peace and friendship. [...] The great wrong of slavery consists in the power which it gives to one human being over another. A husband has almost precisely the same power over the wife that the master has over the slave.[6]

6   Nichols and Nichols, *Marriage: Its History, Character, and Results*, 91–92, 1854.

A century later, this comparison would have been less appropriate; Mary Nichols might have kept her original name, Mary Neal, and she would have been able to vote, sign contracts, and own her own assets, whether married or not. Then again, she was white, educated, and lived in New England. Gender inequalities like those of the 19th century US, and worse, still hold in many parts of the world. In 2017, the International Labour Organization first classified forced marriage as slavery, estimating that nearly 22 million women are thus enslaved.[7] In every country, women's equality remains very much an incomplete project.

7   International Labour Organization, Walk Free, and International Organization for Migration, "Global Estimates of Modern Slavery: Forced Labour and Forced Marriage," 2022.

In traditional American marriages with one wage-earner, that earner is still more likely to be the husband than the wife, though the balance has started to shift.[8] Even when a woman works a paying job, her wage is likely to be significantly lower than a man's. Numbers from the Bureau of Labor Statistics tell the story.[9]

Here the dots are raw data from the Bureau, and the lines are smoothed versions to make trends easier to see amid the random year-to-year fluctuations.

8   Pew, "The Rise in Dual Income Households," 2015.

9   U.S. Bureau of Labor Statistics, "Highlights of Women's Earnings in 2020," 2022.

4.0 Women's income as a fraction of men's income % by year

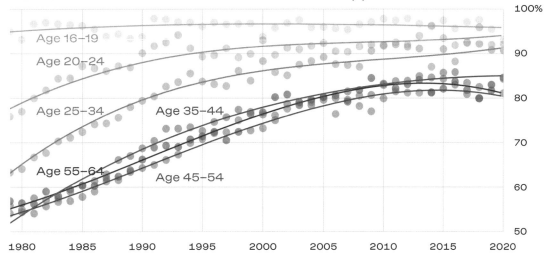

On average, women of all ages, from 1979 until 2020 (the year these data were released), earn at most 95% or so of what men earn. Despite gradual improvement over those 38 years, the gap has stubbornly refused to close. To many, like Cris, a woman in her forties from Tennessee, this isn't news:

> **I was born on a day that was a huge step forward for womans rights, while my full name indicates female, i have never went by it, nor was I raised with my parents calling me by it. They done this so it would be easier on me in life for the job market.**

Women of high school age have been consistently earning about 95% of men's income for decades, while older women have been catching up to, but never exceeding, that plateau. In dollar terms, incomes are much lower at younger ages, so even those modest gaps for 16- to 24-year-olds can make the difference between being able to scrape by on their own and not. Among older people making more money, the differences become far greater, both in dollars *and* in percentages. If you were a 50-year-old woman earning an average wage in 1979, that amounted to less than 55% of what the average 50-year-old man earned. By 2020 the figure had risen to about 80%—an improvement, but still not great.

Now, consider this difference in terms of accumulated savings, with compound interest, over a lifetime; you'll start to appreciate why women have so much less wealth at retirement than men, and fall below the poverty line at far higher rates.[10]

10 Inequality.org, "Gender Economic Inequality."

Such considerations would have strongly incented a young Wilma to marry Fred Flintstone, even if she worked full-time and wasn't all that into him. Of course people can remain in less-than-happy marriages for many reasons. Money and motherhood tend to curtail women's choices disproportionately, though. When Wilma's baby came along, the case for keeping her Nuclear Family together might strengthen, given the primary role mothers play in providing for their children. Was Fred shouty and unhelpful—abusive, even? Did he spend his weekends reclining on the La-Z-Boy watching football? Did he get caught messing around with Betty next door? In a patriarchal world, there are still hard economic realities. Alimony notwithstanding,[11] many unhappy wives have stayed married for the kids' sake, or because there was simply no viable alternative.

11 In 2001, only 52% of divorced mothers in the United States received their full child support payments. For women who had children out of wedlock, the figure was about 32%. These data are per Dominus, "The Fathers' Crusade," 2005.

12 Hrdy, *Mothers and Others: The Evolutionary Origins of Mutual Understanding*, 2009.

Despite these powerful social forces, the Standard Model for US families has never been as universal as it was made out to be on TV— with working moms, grandparents, and other relatives living under

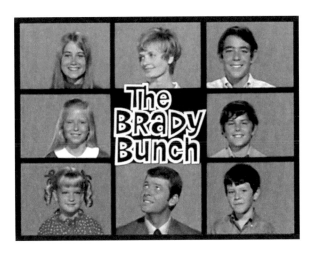

From the title sequence of *The Brady Bunch*, season 2, 1970.

P.L. Travers's vision of the ideal alloparental help: fictional nanny Mary Poppins, played by Julie Andrews in Disney's 1964 musical, *Mary Poppins*.

the same roof, communal arrangements, children moving back in after college or never moving out in the first place, divorce and blended families, adoption and surrogacy all commonplace. For that matter, it's hard to ignore the whiteness, suburban-ness, and middle-classness of this supposed standard. In the Antebellum South, the "standard" certainly didn't apply to the enslaved population; nor have Black, Native, and immigrant communities of later generations necessarily fit the mold.

The mismatch with reality goes beyond minority and immigrant populations in the United States today. Confronted with a wealth of historical evidence from still-extant traditional societies, researchers working at the intersections of evolutionary biology, psychology, economics, and anthropology have finally begun to realize how peculiar the Nuclear Family really is.

Traditional societies, which is to say, nearly *all* societies until recently, tend to be built instead around clan structures, with high rates of cousin marriage continually reinforcing extended kinship networks. The old-fashioned phrase "kith and kin" is sometimes used, emphasizing that these networks include both genetic relatives, or kin, and so-called "fictive kin," or "kith." (If you had "uncles" or "aunties" as a kid who were in fact not related by blood or marriage, these were kith.) Such social networks are at once stable and fluid, meaning that dense interconnectedness maintains a sense of belonging and community stability even as people occasionally join or wander off to seek their fortune elsewhere.

How does family life work in such a setting? Anthropologist and primatologist Sarah Blaffer Hrdy has convincingly argued that much of what makes humans special (and unique among the great apes) is made possible by alloparenting—our habit of caring for each others' young—and in particular cooperative breeding, in which the babysitters aren't themselves mothers; they may be young or post-menopausal females, or males.[12] Our survival likely depended on alloparenting for hundreds of thousands of years, since in a traditional society, it's extremely difficult for a mother alone to procure the thirteen million calories needed to raise a child to

Emperor Tamarin babies ride piggyback on their father or older brother, Schönbrunn Zoo, Vienna, 2021.

maturity. It helps to have dads, grandmas, and friendly neighbors bearing snacks.

And not just snacks. Humans are born helplessly inept. Unlike other animals with more complete (though also more limited) instinctual behavioral repertoires, we must learn a great deal from others to become self-sufficient. This requires an investment in time and mentorship from multiple adults, older siblings, cousins, and so on. Raising children truly does take, if not a village, at least a committed social network of helpers.

Poster created in response to the controversial 1834 New Poor Law, depicting forced labor and corporal punishment.

Hrdy also points out a related, darker finding: "Along with humans, marmosets and tamarins are virtually the only primates where mothers have been observed to deliberately harm their own babies or leave newborns to die."[13] As it turns out, these species also stand out as the most cooperative breeders among our primate cousins. The mothers tend to commit infanticide when they know they won't have the community support they need to raise their offspring successfully.

Consider the high rate of infanticide and baby abandonment that so horrified Michael Ryan (the pearl-clutching author of *The Philosophy of Marriage*) in this light. The 18th and 19th centuries saw a dramatic rise in these practices throughout Western Europe.[14] The rise coincided with the start of a great migration of people away from a more traditional life in the countryside and into cities, far from kith and kin. Those cities, in turn, did not yet provide anything like the state assistance, food banks, social services, daycare centers, kindergartens, and so on that might have taken up the alloparental slack for the displaced poor.

The English Poor Laws were important steps toward organized state assistance, but gave rise to Victorian-era workhouses designed to be punitive, with revolting food, forced family separation, and other disincentives making life in such an institution a last resort. Since poor working people were already immiserated, ensuring that the workhouse remained strictly worse often meant truly grim conditions.

Ryan likely had it backwards, then, when he claimed that free love communes would result in wholesale infanticide. It was the rapidly industrializing, capitalist, and Nuclear Family-oriented London of his day that did so.

Engraving of London's infamous Seven Dials slum by Gustave Doré in *London: A Pilgrimage*, 1872.

In traditional "kith and kin" societies, where extended relationship networks are paramount, individualism plays a more modest role than in modern urban life. Work tends to be less specialized. As we've seen, child rearing is a collective effort. Housing and property ownership (when they exist) are often collective too, and are usually controlled by men—patriarchy being perhaps the one Flintstones-Jetsons motif that *does* have a long history.

Such patterns persist even in the lives of white city-dwelling Westerners today, and are especially evident in the (underrepresented) accounts of the contemporary poor and working class. For instance, English activist and author D. Hunter writes in his 2018 autobiography, *Chav Solidarity*,

As a seven year old I was shown how to be a lookout during a robbery, and not long after, my cousins taught me how to steal a car. All of the rewards for this were collectivised [...]. One of my uncles was fiercely respected for the amount of money he brought into our family, but he lived in a one bedroom flat which was furnished with a mattress, a TV and nothing else. I only have a thin recollection of the flat but I'm not convinced it had a bathroom. This was acknowledged, but never challenged, it was raised by others as an example

13 Hrdy, 99.

14 Fuchs and McBride-Schreiner, "Foundlings and Abandoned Children," 2014.

of how we all should be. [...] The money went to uncles and aunts with children instead, so that those kids wouldn't go short. [...] My grandfather took whatever he wanted from the collective pot, and I'm sure he would say, that as the responsibility for everyone else was with him, it was only right. [...] If one of my cousins was given something, they would share it without a second thought. Nothing was saved for later; nothing was personal property.[15]

15 Hunter, *Chav Solidarity*, 2018.

When a dominant society enforces norms and creates institutions at odds with the traditional cultures of families like Hunter's, those families tend to be marginalized. Often, they live in undocumented ways and outside the law, rendering the underlying structures that have organized their lives for countless generations invisible to outsiders. They might get by mainly with cash, in a black- or gray-market economy. Many of the resources cities offer their middle classes become harder for such communities to tap into, locking them into cycles of intergenerational poverty. Schools, governments, banks, potential employers, and social services demanding that forms be filled out (parent or guardian, permanent address, occupation, income, etc.) require semi-fictional responses.

Similarly, while legal marriages do exist, the many and varied intimate relationships and sexual encounters Hunter recounts often don't occur within them, or within any of the parameters considered

↓ Fela Kuti and his wives.

→ The five Pandava brothers with their common consort, Draupadi, by the Ravi Varma Press, ca. 1910.

socially or even legally acceptable today. They certainly don't follow the monogamous Nuclear Family model.

Non-monogamous sexual relationships (meaning, anything outside a sexually exclusive long-term pair bond) are also the norm in traditional societies, whether settled, nomadic, or somewhere in between. The specifics vary widely, but tend to be more fluid and less patriarchal among hunter-gatherers or other societies with temporary (often seasonal) settlements.

Nomadic or seasonally settled societies are also less dependent on property ownership. In such settings, polyandry may be a good idea: a mother's vagueness about the paternity of her children won't cost them an inheritance, but might offer a fine strategy for expanding the network of alloparents (including potential fathers and *their* kin— a bonanza of indulgent aunties, uncles, and grandparents).**16**

16 Ryan and Jethá, *Sex at Dawn: The Prehistoric Origins of Modern Sexuality*, 2010.

Persian emperor Naser al-Din Shah Qajar with some of his 84 wives, from a collection of 19th century photographs at the Golestan Palace in Tehran, Iran.

In traditional agricultural societies, though, land and livestock tend to be owned by men. Fixed settlements of varying grandeur can be built on that land, and the labor needed to farm it can itself become a commodity. Then, patriarchy tends to predominate. Number of wives, as much as access to land, livestock, and labor, signifies a man's social rank, and since assets pass from fathers to sons, paternity is all-important. Given roughly equal numbers of women and men, many women end up sharing a high-status male partner, while large numbers of lower-status men remain single. Some version of this more patriarchal traditional model still holds in many places today.

So where did Nuclear Families come from? Joseph Henrich, chair of the Department of Human Evolutionary Biology at Harvard, argues

17 Henrich, Heine, and Norenzayan, "The Weirdest People in the World?," 2010.

18 The Old Testament is full of patriarchs and kings with multiple wives, including Esau, Abraham, Jacob, Elkanah, David, and Solomon. Exodus 21:10 advises that if a man takes another wife, then of the first one, "her food, her raiment, and her duty of marriage, shall he not diminish"; Deuteronomy 21:15–17 clarifies the rules of inheritance for sons in polygynous marriages.

that they're a defining feature of what he memorably calls WEIRD societies: Western, Educated, Industrialized, Rich, and Democratic.[17]

Monogamy and the suppression of cousin marriage, both key to establishing the Nuclear Family model, were Christian religious policies, advanced with varying success throughout Europe in the Middle Ages as natural laws and expressions of God's will (despite numerous Biblical counterexamples[18]). These policies had profound economic and political consequences. As a somewhat cynical 26-year-old survey respondent put it,

> **I do not believe in monogamy or marriage. I believe they are created by those in power (government and religion) to keep people under control. The government needs couples to buy homes, create children and keep the economy humming. And religion uses marriage and monogamy for power, control and access to money.**

4.1 Legality of polygamy by country

- Legal
- Customary
- Legal for Muslims

While there's a whiff of conspiracy theory about the way this is put, it's... not wrong. (Though of course non-monogamous arrangements have their own politics, and their own ways of perpetuating power.)

Beyond offering avenues for social control by the church or the state, though, WEIRD societies foster social stability in other ways. Several lines of evidence suggest that large numbers of unpartnered males with little to lose drive higher rates of violence and instability in traditional societies, which might be one reason that enforced monogamy created a competitive advantage for the WEIRD.

A Christian belief in the universality of God's strictures may have kept most Westerners from realizing how unusual their Nuclear Family model was, even when, as with the Flintstones and Jetsons, Christianity wasn't overt. Or maybe it was hard to notice how atypical this model was simply because the worldwide influence of WEIRDness has grown so pervasive over the past several centuries.

Scientific research, technology, political power, and wealth are all overwhelmingly WEIRD-dominated today.[19] WEIRD media, social norms, and psychology have also infused many other societies globally, both through imposition from outside (which we might call cultural hegemony), and through voluntary copying, appropriation, or local adaptation, as humans have always done. These phenomena have all created feedback loops, perpetuating and reinforcing each other. Still, it's important to remember that WEIRD people remain a minority, and represent a small fraction of humanity historically.

The real Flintstones, then, were decidedly not WEIRD; Paleolithic people's daily lives wouldn't have made for family-friendly TV in 1960s America. But what about the Jetsons?

Let's assume a non-dystopian scenario in which future generations are at a minimum educated, industrialized, and rich ("EIR"). Even so, far from being a universal norm, the Nuclear Family may turn out to be a short-lived historical footnote, a transitional step between a "kith and kin" past and an emerging model whose outlines we can just start to make out.

What are those outlines? That's one of the central questions Part II of this book will attempt to answer. Chapter 5 focuses on emerging patterns in romantic and sexual exclusivity—in a way, the least radical of the changes we'll explore, since this exclusivity has always been preached more than practiced. In Chapters 6 and 7, we'll take a closer look at the decline of heteronormativity, the force that binds Nuclear Families together, and in Chapters 8 and 9, we'll delve into the implications for (and about) women's sexuality. Finally, in Chapters 10 to 15, we'll see how biology and culture are interacting to redefine sex and gender.

Today, many people aren't romantically or sexually exclusive; aren't having children, or are approaching parenthood in different ways; aren't heterosexual; aren't as reliant on property ownership;

19 China is now poised to surpass the West in a number of ways, and lacks the "D" as well as the "W," though significantly, during its "modernization" in the 20th century, it systematically adopted a number of WEIRD social norms and concepts, as did many other countries.

and aren't living in either multigenerational or nuclear households. Even conservative columnist David Brooks knows something is up; his 2020 think piece in the *Atlantic*, "The Nuclear Family Was a Mistake," points out that it has been "crumbling in slow motion for decades."[20] Feminist writer Sophie Lewis goes further in a 2022 book, spicily entitled *Abolish the Family*.[21] To her, as journalist Marie Solis writes, the call for abolition means "caring for each other not in discrete private units (also known as nuclear households), but rather within larger systems of care that can provide us with the love and support we can't always get from blood relations [...]."[22]

Increasing numbers of people are also questioning, tweaking, or entirely discarding the gender binary that has underpinned both the Nuclear Family and earlier, more traditional social structures. Gender Abolition, too, is an old social movement now gaining mainstream traction.

Though historical context can help us find antecedents to, and make sense of, these trends, they're far from a return to a preindustrial past. They represent something new.

20 Brooks, "The Nuclear Family Was a Mistake," 2020.

21 Lewis, *Abolish the Family: A Manifesto for Care and Liberation*, 2022.

22 Solis, "We Can't Have a Feminist Future Without Abolishing the Family," 2020.

A cylindrical space colony designed to support a population of over a million, as envisioned in the 1970s by Princeton physicist Gerard O'Neill.

But *how* new? Seen from a certain perspective, changes to family, sex, and gender can have radical, even posthuman overtones. Science fiction writers like Octavia Butler, Pat Cadigan, Justina Robson, Annalee Newitz, and Kim Stanley Robinson have imagined futures in which gender is just one of many fluidly alterable bioengineered variables for our descendants... who may also range from three to ten feet tall, splice in the DNA of other species, merge with robots, and adapt themselves to live anywhere from the dark side of Mercury to the moons of Saturn.[23] Human lifetimes may become unconstrained by any inbuilt biological clock; babies may become rare, and may be grown in artificial wombs.

23 Robinson, *2312*, 2012.

Even these versions of posthumanity are conservative compared to "uploading," in which we all scan our brains and become virtual beings, unmoored from bodies or the constraints of the physical world. What could human or personal identity even *mean* in a universe like that?

Imagining such futures can induce a kind of vertigo, even horror. Then again, *our* lives would be equally alien to our recent ancestors. It helps to remember that we humans are a uniquely culturally constituted species. So much about our lives and bodies is already a product of our cumulative culture and technology—from our lack of fur (due to the invention of clothes) to our short gut (due to cooking with fire) to our ability to drink milk in adulthood (still a work in progress, or if we all end up vegan, an evolutionary spur).[24]

24 Pagel and Bodmer, "The Evolution of Human Hairlessness: Cultural Adaptations and the Ectoparasite Hypothesis," 2004; Wrangham, "Control of Fire in the Paleolithic: Evaluating the Cooking Hypothesis," 2017; Leonardi et al., "The Evolution of Lactase Persistence in Europe. A Synthesis of Archaeological and Genetic Evidence," 2012.

In this sense, we're already highly engineered, and we have ourselves been the unwitting engineers. Profound culturally induced changes in gender and sexuality may, then, just be the next steps on a long road we began walking millions of years ago when we tamed fire, our brains began growing rapidly, and cultural development began to snowball over generations, radically reshaping not only our bodies but Earth itself.

Interlude

Planetary consciousness

Donna Haraway,
from *Donna Haraway:
Story Telling for
Earthly Survival*, 2016.

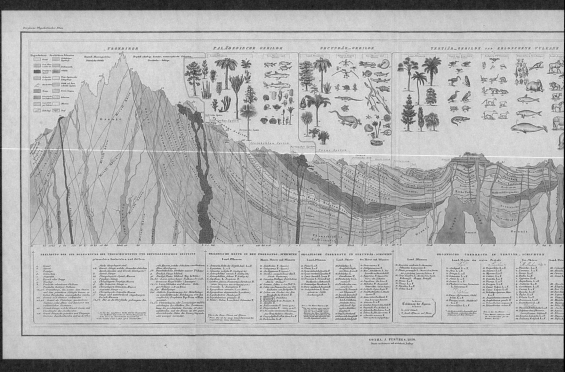

For billions of years, life has written itself into the very structure of our planet, making any sharp distinction between biology and geology murky at best. As the often brilliant, often cryptic cyberfeminist scholar Donna Haraway put it in 1995,

> [...] the whole earth [is] a dynamic, self-regulating, homeostatic system; the earth, with all its interwoven layers and articulated parts, from the planet's pulsating skin through its fulminating gaseous envelopes, [is] itself alive.[1]

1   Haraway, "Cyborgs and Symbionts: Living Together in the New World Order," xiii, 1995.

In the Western scientific tradition, geologist and naturalist Alexander von Humboldt (1769–1859) became an early advocate of this holistic view. It led him to sound alarms about ecological destruction and human-induced climate change as early as 1800.

Humboldt's observations, based on phenomena like the desiccation of the landscape following clearcutting in Venezuela's Aragua Valley, were at once obvious and visionary. He was rowing against both prevailing scientific currents and millennia of religious dogma. Scientific progress had lately been advancing rapidly through controlled experiments, analysis, and classification, all of which worked by isolating and simplifying phenomena, studying them in the lab rather than observing them in context as parts of larger systems. Biblical doctrine, too, discouraged whole-system thinking, instead

Humboldt, *Diagram of a Cross-Section of the Earth's Crust*, 1841.

Humboldt, *Selbstportrait in Paris*, 1814.

Illustration of the
Great Chain of
Being by Diego
Valadés, *Rhetorica
Christiana*, 1579.

2   Lovejoy, *The Great
Chain of Being: A Study of the
History of an Idea*, 1964.

insisting on the static hierarchy of a Great Chain of Being that began
with God above, then descended through the ranks of angels, people,
animals, plants, and minerals.[2]

According to *Genesis*, the Earth was only a few thousand years
old (though contrary evidence was mounting), and God had separately created everything on it to serve a specific end: *Man*. Man was
both distinct from Nature and rightly held dominion over her. The
lower orders served the higher—like a military chain of command, or
a corporate org chart. Hierarchies are certainly easier to reason
about than the realities of mutually interdependent networks with
no center, top, or bottom.

The traditional genders here—humanity (or "Man") as male, Nature as female—aren't accidental. In 1603, laying the foundations for the coming knowledge revolution, Francis Bacon had entwined religious and scientific doctrines in a Latin essay whose title can be translated as *The Masculine Birth of Time, Or the Great Instauration of the Dominion of Man over the Universe.* Writing from the vantage of a future scientist with godlike power exhorting his young apprentice, Bacon thundered,

3 Bacon, *Temporis Partus Masculus*, 1603; translation in Anthony Wilden, 1972; see also Farrington, 1951.

> **I am come in very truth leading Nature to you, with all her children, to bind her to your service and to make her your slave [...]; so may I succeed in my only earthly wish, namely to stretch the deplorably narrow limits of man's dominion over the universe to their promised bounds [...].**[3]

This chilling passage frames science and technology as the rape of a femininized, subordinate Nature by Man, righteous in his lust for knowledge and power. Much is implied: that science and technology, as active arts, are the enterprises of men, not women; that Nature and the feminine are passive resources for male usufruct; that Man's manifest destiny won't be fulfilled until he has dominated literallyeverything in the observable universe.

Lord Bacon,
Newfoundland
stamp, 1910.

Bernini, *The Rape of Proserpina*, Galleria Borghese, Rome, 1621–22.

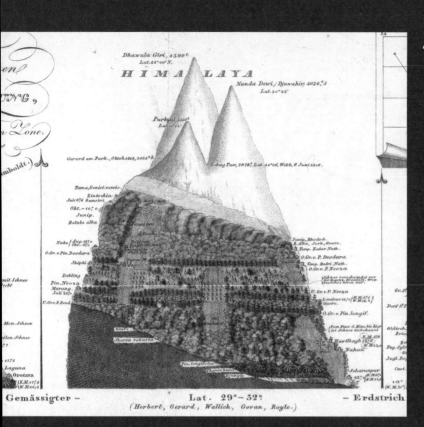

Himalaya section of
"Umrisse des Pflanzen-
geographie" (Outlines of
Botanical Geography)
from Berghaus, *Physikal-
ischer Atlas*, 1851.

Although the posthumously published *Masculine Birth
of Time* is among the more obscure writings in Bacon's storied
career, it's also a rare moment of candor, an unobstructed
glimpse of the black hole whose gravitational well we're still
struggling to escape: patriarchy.

"Man dominating Nature" is not the only way to do science.
Humboldt—obsessively measuring temperature and barometric
pressure on every shore and mountain slope, talking to indigenous
farmers, gathering samples and drawing connections—perceived
the entanglement of living systems, the way nature resists simplification; how we must dance with it, not plunder it.

He came to understand the suicidal consequences of ecological colonialism and unfettered resource extraction through lengthy
travel in the New World, far from home. It's unlikely that he would
have developed these insights had he stayed in Germany, among
the long-cultivated fields of Saxony or in the coffeehouses of Jena.
Understanding required distance and perspective—and time.

Many years later, astronaut William Anders also attained such
a planetary perspective. On Christmas Eve of 1968, in orbit around

Michael Maier, Emblema II: "Nutrix ejus terra est" (The Earth is His Nurturer) in *Atalanta Fugiens*, 1617.

Earthrise, taken by Apollo 8 astronaut Bill Anders on December 24, 1968.

the moon, he exclaimed, "Oh my God! Look at that picture over there! There's the Earth coming up. Wow, that's pretty." The photo he took with his boxy modified Hasselblad, now known as *Earthrise*, galvanized the environmental movement. As the world shrank, Humboldt's vision had become more accessible.

Dawning popular awareness of the finite nature of our world, its fragility, and the interconnectedness of all its systems inspired researchers James Lovelock and Lynn Margulis to develop the Gaia Hypothesis, first articulated by Lovelock in a famous 1972 paper, *Gaia as Seen Through the Atmosphere*:

> **[T]he sum total of species is more than just a catalogue, "The Biosphere," and like other associations in biology is an entity with properties greater than the simple sum of its parts. Such a large creature, even if hypothetical, with the powerful capacity to homeostat [regulate] the planetary environment needs a name; I am indebted to Mr. William Golding for suggesting the use of the Greek personification of mother Earth, "Gaia."[4]**

4 Lovelock, "Gaia as Seen Through the Atmosphere," 1972.

Oberon Zell, *The Millennial Gaia*, 1997.

Though initially Lovelock made his case hesitantly, couching it in qualifiers like "hypothetical," his was a stronger statement than Humboldt's. Beyond pointing out interrelations between lifeforms and the mutual shaping of biology, atmosphere, and geology, he was proposing that we view Earth as a single great organism, that we call her *Gaia*, and that we consider ourselves part of that organism.

Margulis, whose groundbreaking findings as a cellular biologist established symbiosis (or mutual interdependence) as fundamental to all life on Earth, was nonetheless deeply skeptical of the name Lovelock had chosen:

5 Margulis, "Gaia Is a Tough Bitch," 140, 1995.

The Church of All Worlds," *Green Egg*, Vol. 1, No. 1, 1968.

> The Gaia hypothesis is a biological idea, but it's not human-centered. Those who want Gaia to be an Earth goddess for a cuddly, furry human environment find no solace in it. [...] Gaia is a tough bitch—a system that has worked for over three billion years without people. This planet's surface and its atmosphere and environment will continue to evolve long after people and prejudice are gone.[5]

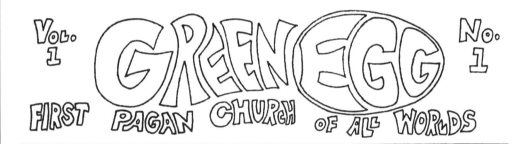

The Church of All Worlds is what is called a modern "Pagan" religion. By this is meant that it is basically a life-affirming religion without supernatural elememts, such as the Dionysians, the Epicurians, the Stoics, the Druids, the Transcendentalists and the Existentialists. The Church regards metaphysical questions as irrelevant, and leaves them up to the individual to ask as well as to answer. The theological position of the Church of All Worlds takes the step beyond Humanism (which states that God is Mankind) by affirming that man <u>individually</u> is God — but only to himself, as every other individual is also.

We teach that man is himself ultimately free, ultimately responsible — for his life, his actions, and his salvation (which is defined however he wishes). We reject utterly the concept of original sin and inherent human evil. The three basic commandments of the Church of All Worlds are: Know yourself; Believe in yourself; Be true to yourself. These are set forth as a guide towards becoming more fully human and self-actualizing, which is regarded as necessary before one can hope to function fully with his brothers. In this context, it is accepted that hypocrisy is the only sin, and that the Golden Rule is the basic ethical imperative. Again, the metaphysical questions, such as that of life after death, the purpose of the universe, and the possibility of a guiding intelligence behind natural phenomena, are not regarded as relevent to the Church of the human community, and the individual, if he so chooses, may treat them howsoever he wishes. Consequently, on those issues, Pagans have a large variety of opinions which are still, however, accepted as <u>only</u> opinions.

Pagans believe that each individual must work out his or her own faith by which to live. Consequently, we are a "free" church with no creeds. The priest or speaker is granted complete freedom of the lecturn, and this freedon also extends to the listeners. The only guides for Pagans in their faith are reason, conscience and experience. We congregate for stimulation, friendship, service and self-expression.

Welcome to the First Pagan Church of All Worlds! Our meetings are currently being held on Thursday nights at our Agora lounge above The Exit, at the

It turned out that Gaia had already been given an incongruously cuddly name the year before—*Terrabia*—by Timothy Zell, founder and Primate of the Neopagan Church of All Worlds. Though Lovelock and Margulis were almost certainly unaware of it, they had been scooped by Zell's 1971 article, *TheaGenesis: The Birth of the Goddess*, in the Church's (decidedly non-peer-reviewed) journal *Green Egg*. Influenced by science, but also borrowing liberally from Eastern and indigenous belief systems where planetary-scale animism goes back thousands of years, Zell had written:

> We now know that our planet, Mother Earth, is inhabited not by myriad separate and distinct organisms, each going its own way independent of all the others, but rather that the aggregate total of all the [living] beings of Earth comprises the vast body of a single organism—the planetary Biosphere itself. Literally, we are all One. Further, we now realize that the being we have intuitively referred to as Mother Earth, The Goddess, Mother Nature, The Lady, is not merely a mythical projection of our own limited visions, but an actual living entity, Terrabia, the very biosphere of Earth, in whose body we are mere cells. Forced by this discovery to re-examine our religious language and conceptualizations, we have arrived at the following definition of Divinity (which, incidentally, includes within it the essential nature of the Divine as expressed by all other religions): "Divinity is the highest level of aware consciousness accessible to each living being, manifesting itself in the self-actualization of that being." Thus the living Biosphere is Goddess in Her evolving self-actualization. As in the corporate body of the great planetary organism we are all One, so are we all God! (More correctly, we are all Goddess, since Mother Earth is of feminine gender.) This concept has been recognized, though not heretofore fully understood, in the basic aphorism of Neo-Pagan religion; the phrase "Thou art God."[6]

So, the hippies beat the scientists to the punch—at least, in the modern West.[7]

The hippies and scientists *both* committed a seemingly obvious category error, though, by persisting in thinking of the Earth as female. After all, sexual differentiation is just a reproductive trick particular to certain branches of Earth-life—including *Homo sapiens*, most other animals, and many plants, but these account for just a fraction of Earth's biomass.

6 Zell, "TheaGenesis: The Birth of the Goddess," 1970.

7 Contested wizardly spelling alert. In November 2022, Zell wrote (personal communication): "[I]n all my own references (except the statue, for marketing reasons) I [use] the traditional and universal (prior to Lovelock) Latin spelling of 'Gaea' (Greek Gē)—from which we derive all our Earth-terms (geography, geology, geometry, geocentric, geode, etc.). The 'Gaia' spelling with an 'i' was a misunderstanding on Lovelock's part of the word he heard from his friend William Golding, and he just spelled it phonetically, having, as he himself said, 'no Classics.' Indeed, he first thought Golding had said 'gyre.' But the diphthong 'ae' can be pronounced either 'eh' or 'eye' (I have all this in Lovelock's own words, quoted in my recent book: *GaeaGenesis: Conception and Birth of the Living Earth*—which should be listed in the bibliography of this book)." With thanks, it has been duly listed. However, Lovelock's misspelling has stuck, and is now more common by far, so in keeping with this book's theme of embracing cultural evolution, I, too, have stuck with "Gaia."

The split gill fungus *Schizophyllum commune.*

Our planet also hosts vast numbers of cells and larger constituent organisms that are unsexed, hermaphroditic, or based on reproductive schemes so profoundly queer (in multiple senses of the word) that our provincial notions of sex and gender are upended.[8] According to biologist Merlin Sheldrake,[9] the split gill fungus, *Schizophyllum commune*, "has more than twenty-three thousand mating types, each of which is sexually compatible with nearly every one of the others"! Even among our closer animal relatives, surprises abound. Some fish, for instance, change sex as they age, and the white-throated sparrow appears to have four sexes with distinct genotypes and mating behaviors.[10]

So, it makes little sense to talk about Earth as a whole in gendered (not to mention binary) terms. Perhaps we can call it progress, though, for a syncretic Neopagan mythology about an all-encompassing Earth-mother to supplant an Iron Age mythology starring a domineering and vindictive patriarch-God.

Gaia isn't an easy concept. For one thing, it's squicky to think about lifeforms living *inside* other lifeforms. The chest-bursting xenomorph of the *Alien* movie franchise may come to mind, and the real-world endoparasitic horrors that inspired it—tiny wasps laying their eggs inside the bodies of bigger wasp species, or *Cordyceps* fungi controlling the minds of ants. Ugh, boundaries!

In reality, though, life is never isolated from other life; living worlds within worlds nest like *matryoshka* dolls. It has become a trope to point out that you have ten times as many bacteria living in your gut as you have cells of "your own" in your entire body.

8   Kaishian and Djoulakian, "The Science Underground: Mycology as a Queer Discipline," 2020.

9   Sheldrake, *Entangled Life*, 2020. See also Kothe, "Tetrapolar Fungal Mating Types: Sexes by the Thousands," 1996.

10   Tuttle et al., "Divergence and Functional Degradation of a Sex Chromosome-like Supergene," 2016.

Lynn Margulis
(1938–2011).

The rabbit hole goes far deeper. *Within* every one of your 30–40 trillion cells, there are anywhere from dozens to hundreds of thousands of tiny sausage-ish mitochondria, which may dynamically split, fuse, and form intricate layered structures.[11]

Mitochondria in turn contain the folded-up membranes or *cristae* whose electric charge, maintained by trans-membrane ion pumps, powers all animal life. Unfolded, the *cristae* in your body would cover five football fields, and store the power of a lightning bolt.[12] As yet, human-engineered power generation and battery technologies can't even approach this biological marvel.

Lynn Margulis was the first to realize that mitochondria (as well as chloroplasts, their photosynthetic counterparts in plant cells) were once free-swimming bacteria. In fact they're *still* bacteria, with their own DNA and their own reproductive cycle, albeit by now mutually dependent on their host cells—much the way we both depend on and have reshaped our host planet.

Margulis's epiphany was mind-blowing—maybe *too* mind-blowing. In response to one grant application, a reviewer wrote, "Your research is crap. Don't ever bother to apply again."[13] Her now-classic 1967 paper, *On the Origin of Mitosing Cells*, was rejected by fifteen journals before finally being accepted, maybe on a slow day, by *The Journal of Theoretical Biology*.[14]

In a 1991 book, *Two Plus Two Equals One: Individuals Emerge from Bacterial Communities*, Margulis and a coauthor wrote a sentence that sums up much of *this* book:

Identity is not an object; it is a process with addresses for all the different directions and dimensions in which it moves, and so it cannot so easily be fixed with a single number.[15]

In 1999, toward the end of her stormy career, she was finally awarded the National Medal of Science. She died in 2011, aged 73.

While revising this chapter in the summer of 2022, I learned that her old collaborator, James Lovelock, had also died, at 103 years of age. He wrote his last book, *Novacene*, at 100. Though the Gaia hypothesis was also long mired in controversy, the scientific establishment was quicker to recognize Lovelock's contributions than those of Margulis. Lovelock was made a Fellow of the Royal Society in 1974, and later, a Companion of Honor and a member of

11 Cole, "The Evolution of Per-Cell Organelle Number," 2016.

12 Lane, *Transformer*, 68, 2022. In fact Lane's figure is "four football pitches," which translates into about five American football fields.

13 "Obituary: Lynn Margulis," 2011.

14 Sagan, *Lynn Margulis: The Life and Legacy of a Scientific Rebel*, 2012.

15 Margulis and Guerrero, "Two Plus Two Equals One: Individuals Emerge from Bacterial Communities," 50, 1991.

the Most Excellent Order of the British Empire: thus, a knight.

Not to be outdone, the man once known as Timothy Zell, now 80 years old and styling himself Oberon Zell-Ravenheart, is no mere honorific knight, but "a true Wizard in the traditional sense," according to his website.[16] He's also the Headmaster of the Grey School of Wizardry, open to "all seekers, young and old," and offering "more than 500 classes in 16 Departments," from "Alchemy, Healing, and Divination to Ceremonial Magick and Defense against the Dark Arts."[17]

Let's rewind.

Throughout the '70s, Zell continued to write and speak in public about his TheaGenesis epiphany. With a nod to Lovelock and Margulis, he had replaced

Oberon Zell, Co-Founder, Primate, Council of Elders, High Priest, President, ERA, H.O.M.E., and Nemeton.

Terrabia with *Gaia* by the time he delivered the keynote address at the 1973 Gnosticon Aquarian festival. Pagans, witches, druids, shamans, astrologers, and seekers of every other stripe had converged on the unlikely city of St. Paul, Minnesota for this happening.

Morning Glory, a young witch in the audience, was smitten. Although already in an open marriage, she immediately resolved

→ Oberon and Morning Glory, 1974.

to leave her husband and join her life to the charismatic Zell's. They were married the following year in a handfasting ceremony at the Spring Witchmeet, presided over by High Priestess Carolyn Clark and the Archdruid Isaac Bonewits, the latter a skinny Pagan activist who had recently graduated from UC Berkeley with a degree in Magic (sadly, the last they would ever grant).

16 Zell, "Oberon Zell – Master Wizard," 2018, https://oberonzell.com/.

17 "The Grey School of Wizardry," https://www.greyschool.net/.

Green Egg collating party, 1974.

Soon afterward, Morning Glory became the Assistant Editor of *Green Egg*, hosting collating parties in St. Louis at which an often naked crew of volunteers met to staple together and mail out the quarterly journal. Following a period of study lasting the customary year and a day, Morning Glory was ordained High Priestess of the Church of All Worlds. Their Midwestern idyll proved fleeting, though; the Zells felt the call of the West.

In 1975, they outfitted a schoolbus, christened the Scarlet Succubus, for a one-way road trip to California. They eventually settled on a ranch in Mendocino County, opening a magic shop in a nearby town and developing a technique for creating "unicorns" by performing horn surgery on baby goats. These were kept as pets, exhibited at Renaissance Faires, and licensed for a time to the Ringling Brothers and Barnum & Bailey Circus.

Surprise: the Zell-Ravenhearts were never a conventional Nuclear Family. They lived communally with a slowly evolving cast of additional partners and occasional children, all of whom were involved in the commune's upkeep and collective enterprises.

This mingling of communal, religious, sexual, reproductive, and commercial concerns in an intentional lifestyle has a rich, if fringe, history in the United States.[18] The term "free love," for instance, was coined by John Humphrey Noyes, founder of the Oneida Perfectionist community in upstate New York in 1848.[19] The Perfectionists practiced group marriage and rigorous birth control, lived in the collectively owned Mansion House, and earned income from a variety of cottage industries, including Oneida silverware, which is still in production today.

The Nicholses, whom we have already encountered, also advocated free love, in addition to universal suffrage, opposition to capital punishment, full access to education for women, vegetarianism, and many other then-radical ideas. In a lightly fictionalized autobiography written in 1855, Mary Gove Nichols railed against the strictures of her day:

> I must move among all men as sepultured alive, because a man *owned* me by law. [...] [T]he fact that we received a gentleman as a boarder in our family was an evidence of evil in me,

18 In their 2021 book *The Dawn of Everything*, David Graeber and David Wengrow make the case that the American continent was a laboratory for social experimentation long before European colonists arrived, and indeed, that this tradition informed the United States's founding Enlightenment ideals.

19 Wayland-Smith, *Oneida: From Free Love Utopia to the Well-Set Table*, 2016.

to ultra-moralists, that was irrefragable. I could conform to no such code of morals. [...] I had always been a lover, but [...] I had thought that all love was sinful that was not according to law, that had not the stamp of property, the "ear-mark" of ownership upon it. If a man were pleasant to me, it had been a reason for shunning him. If the touch of his hand or the sound of his voice sent a thrill through [my] heart, it was a sufficient reason why I should not touch the one nor listen to the other. I lived for a long time under a solemn vow to allow no pleasant friend of the opposite sex to hold my hand. And in this horrible asceticism, this suffocation of my life's life, I had lived, [...] and had thrown all my energies into efforts for the good of others.. [20]

20 Nichols, *Mary Lyndon, Or, Revelations of a Life: An Autobiography*, 210–11, 1855.

As well as being an unusually reliable source of information in print about birth control, Thomas Low Nichols's 1853 book *Esoteric Anthropology* also found much to critique in the patriarchal and monogamous norms of the time—though, as with many utopian thinkers, his idealism tended to deny inconvenient social and psychological realities. In describing sexual jealousy, he wrote:

I believe it to be a morbid, mean, bad feeling, caused by poverty, lack of self-esteem, distrust, suspicion, and a

Young women and men born during the Oneida Community's eugenics program, 1887.

The children's hour" at the Oneida Community from Ellis, *Free Love and Its Votaries*, 1870.

craving for more than we fear we have an honest right to. It is a feeling every one is ashamed of and disclaims, which is proof enough of its badness. It is everywhere a subject of ridicule, because men are conscious that it is a shabby feeling. It grows, in most cases, out of the idea of property in each other. As long as a man thinks he owns a woman, he will guard her like any other piece of property, and consider any intercourse with her a trespass, only so far as he permits: and the same of women. [...]

I have seen women who assured me that they had no power to love but one man at a time, though capable of a succession of amours. Others believe that one love is enough for a lifetime. There are others who seem to love two, three,

Rowan and Gray, The world-map of patriarchy," 1987.

—System of Patriarchy

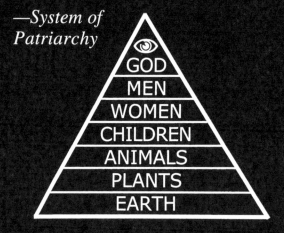

or even more, with various degrees of passion, but all amatively. I knew one woman who slept with two men on alternate nights, and she declared that she loved them both, and could not endure the thought of parting with either. They were two respectable business men in New York, satisfied with her, and not jealous of each other. She had a child, and each believed it his, and loved it accordingly. But, then, a man generally loves the child of a woman he loves, whether he believes it his or not. I think men are, at least, equal to women in this respect. [...] I believe liberty to be the truest bond, and best security for love.[21]

21 Nichols, *Esoteric Anthropology*, 207–10, 1853.

These were remarkably modern ideas, of which the Zell-Ravenhearts would doubtless have approved.

Reunion of the original members of the Church of All Worlds at the Heartland Pagan Festival, Kansas, 1990.

Green Egg underwent a long hiatus after the move to California. Eventually, aided by the newfangled personal computer and desktop publishing software, it was revived under the editorship of Diane Darling, a member of the Ravenheart commune from 1984 to 1994. The topics covered ranged from the cosmic to the personal, as described by Darling in a retrospective anthology:

Why did we [publish *Green Egg*]? What were we thinking? I thought we were saving the world by reviving human consciousness of the sacred living Earth and of our true ancestral roots. [...] By displaying and discussing our own,

22 Zell-Ravenheart, *Green Egg Omelette: An Anthology of Art and Articles from the Legendary Pagan Journal*, 2008.

23 Henrich, Heine, and Norenzayan, "The Weirdest People in the World?," 2010; Henrich, Heine, and Norenzayan, "Most People Are Not WEIRD," 2010; Henrich, Heine, and Norenzayan, "Beyond WEIRD: Towards a Broad-Based Behavioral Science," 2010; Apicella, Norenzayan, and Henrich, "Beyond WEIRD: A Review of the Last Decade and a Look Ahead to the Global Laboratory of the Future," 2020.

24 A phrase trademarked by TED Conferences, LLC, in 2015.

25 Zell-Ravenheart, "A Bouquet of Lovers: Strategies for Responsible Open Relationships," 1990.

26 While Morning Glory was probably unaware of it, these Greek and Latin roots had been fancifully combined in print a few times before, though never in a way that stuck. For instance, on page 283 of Italian Futurist Tommaso Marinetti's 1921 book *L'alcòva d'acciaio: Romanzo vissuto*, "*Sono io che ti bevo e mangio tutta di baci minutissimi rapidissimi, Italia mia, donna-terra saporita, madre-amante, sorella-figlia, maestra d'ogni progresso e perfezione, poliamorosa – incestuosa, santa – infernale – divina!*" Translation: "I am the one who drinks and eats you all with very small, very quick kisses, my Italy, delicious woman-land, mother-lover, sister-daughter, mistress of all progress and perfection, polyamorous – incestuous, holy – infernal – divine!"

then-radical lifestyle experiments, we hoped to turn the wheel of social evolution for the benefit of our Mother. [...] We were surfing the bleeding edge of cultural shift [...].[22]

This conflation of cosmology with lifestyle is characteristic of many intentional communities. It can whiff of grandiosity, doubtless contributing to the marginalization of such movements… even if, at the core, their practices and beliefs are no stranger than anyone else's.

Intentional communities have arisen in every era, but their numbers seem to have exploded in recent Western history. Perhaps this owes to WEIRD propensities for individualism, disregard for the authority of elders, and a taste for "rational" behavior, meaning a through-line whereby external actions are anchored by internally consistent beliefs about the way the world works, as opposed to received wisdom.[23]

Thus, in questioning and reimagining the principles that govern the universe, intentional communities also reimagine the social norms governing daily life—and vice versa. To the WEIRD way of thinking, the cosmic *is* personal. And, perhaps especially to the American way of thinking, good ideas are "ideas worth spreading."[24] The United States has always leaned evangelical—whether the ideas are temperance or free love, spiritualism or the gospel of prosperity, Mormonism or TED talks.

At Diane's suggestion, Morning Glory contributed an article to *Green Egg* in 1990 about the norms underpinning her commune's lifestyle, and lessons learned. As she put it,

> **Having been involved all my adult life in one or the other Open Marriages (the current Primary being 16 years long), I have seen a lot of ideas come and go and experimented with plans and rules to make these relationships work for everyone involved. [...] [T]here are some sure-fire elements that must be present for the system to function at all and there are other elements that are strongly recommended on the basis that they have a very good track record.**[25]

This essay, *A Bouquet of Lovers*, became an instant (albeit cult) classic. In it, Morning Glory coined an odd, half-Greek, half-Latin word to describe consensual non-monogamous relationships: *polyamorous*.[26]

She prophesied thusly:

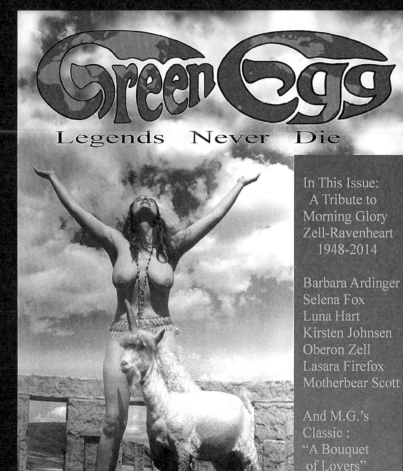

Cover of *Green Egg*, No. 163, June 2014.

I feel that this whole polyamorous lifestyle is the avant garde of the 21st Century. Expanded families will become a pattern with wider acceptance as the monogamous nuclear family system breaks apart [...]. In many ways, polyamorous extended relationships mimic the old multigenerational families before the Industrial Revolution, but they are better because the ties are voluntary and are, by necessity, rooted in honesty, fairness, friendship and mutual interests. Eros is, after all, the primary force that binds the universe together; so we must be creative in the ways we use that force to evolve new and appropriate ways to solve our problems and to make each other and ourselves happy.

5 Nuclear meltdown

5.0.0 Number of children claimed by all respondents
Average (and median) by age

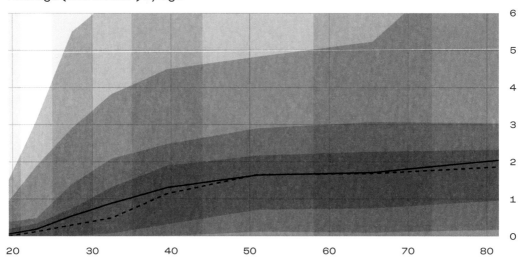

How many of us are committed to the traditional Nuclear Family today, and how is this changing? A first clue can be gleaned from the family's most traditional "output": the number of children we're having.[1]

When graphed as a function of age, number of children gradually rises, as one would expect, from near zero as a young adult to a plateau around menopause, at age 45 or so. The solid line is the average, the dashed line is the median, and the four concentric shaded regions, from narrowest to widest, enclose 38.3%, 68.2%, 95.4%, and 99.7% of the answers at every age (the 99.7% range goes off the chart, and is noisy, but plateaus somewhere between 8 and 12 children).[2] Zooming in on the inner 38.3% shaded region makes the graph easier to read. It's also helpful to break the data down by the respondent's sex assigned at birth, since the people actually *giving birth* to those children must have uteruses.[3]

Notice how women report having significantly more children than men, at *all* ages. On the face of it, this seems impossible, since every child must have a biological mother and father... right?

1 Some of these data are from a parallel population survey I ran in 2020 asking 12,000 respondents, among other questions, how many children and siblings they had.

2 If you're a data nerd, you may recognize these numbers as a half, one, two, and three standard deviations or "sigmas." I make no assumption here, though, that the data are "normally distributed" or follow a bell curve (in fact they can't, since it's not possible to have fewer than zero children).

5.0.1 Number of children born to those assigned female at birth and claimed by those assigned male at birth Average (and median) by age

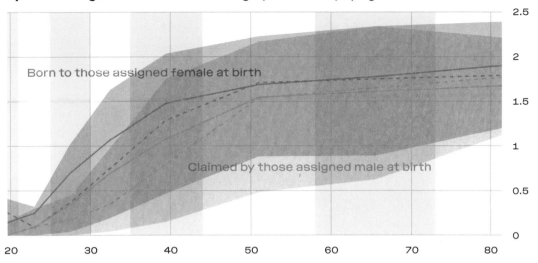

Born to those assigned female at birth

Claimed by those assigned male at birth

3 I was careful to frame the questions being graphed here as precisely as possible. As we'll explore in Chapter 11, being assigned female at birth isn't a guarantee of having a uterus, let alone of being fertile, but for these purposes it's a reasonable proxy. The "Born to those assigned female at birth" curve plots responses to "How many children have you personally given birth to?" for those unambiguously assigned female at birth. "Claimed by those assigned male at birth" plots responses to "How many children do you have?" for those unambiguously assigned male at birth. Using only "How many children do you have?" for both sexes, and relying on "Are you female?" and "Are you male?" produces very similar curves, though.

4 Surrogate pregnancies are such an exception; however, they account for significantly fewer than one in 1,000 births today.

5 Osterman et al., "Births: Final Data for 2020," 2022.

Our lived reality is a little different. When a mother gives birth, she *knows* she's had a child, and with rare exceptions, she can be certain that the baby is hers.[4] That's never been true of men. If anything, their answers to the question graphed—"How many children do you have?"—will *overestimate* the number they believe to be their biological children, while the question for potential mothers—"How many children have you personally given birth to?"—leaves no room for ambiguity with respect to children by marriage or adoption. Men may have one-night stands with unexpected consequences, or split up with their partners soon after conception, or commit rape without using a condom. Or they may donate anonymously to a sperm bank, allowing a single mother somewhere to conceive.

Centers for Disease Control (CDC) data[5] show that about 40% of births in the US happen outside marriage, but this persistent gap reveals something more interesting: that a significant number of births don't involve the biological father at all. So, many men have children they don't know about! This might come as a surprise, but there's no reason to believe it's a new phenomenon. Nor is the finding specific to any one demographic (I checked).

Setting aside men's undercounting of their offspring, 1.7 or so children per woman, today's plateau at menopause, still implies a rapidly shrinking population. With a moment's thought, you can see how, assuming equal numbers of females and males (and zero childhood deaths), women would need to have two children on average for the next generation to be of the same size.

5.1.0 **Married women and men** % by age

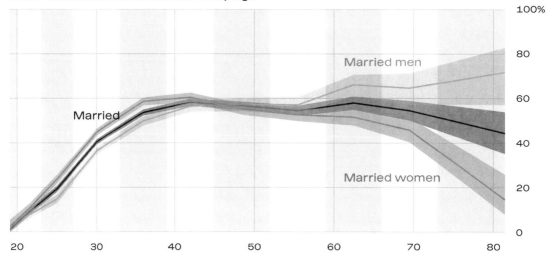

An average lower than two leads to an exponential decline in population over time, a phenomenon we'll explore in more detail in Part III. So children are in decline. What about marriage?

While it remains a mainstream institution, the historical notion[6] that marriage is "normal," and that unmarried middle-aged adults are unusual, is negated by the data. "Peak marriage" for women—which is around age 42—is still just 60% or so. It only crosses 50% to become a majority in the mid-30s.

Evidently, young men tend to marry a few years later than young women, reflecting the traditional small age gap between an older husband and younger wife (about 2.2 years on average, in the US).[7] This age gap becomes larger for people marrying later in life, though, consistent with the folk adage that "a wife should be half the age of her husband with seven years added"[8]—likely part of a larger patriarchal pattern.

Combined with women's longer life expectancy, the age gap results in a dramatic divergence in marriage among the older population. Only about 20% of 80-year-old women are married; and by their mid-'80s, nearly half are widows. While older surviving men are scarcer (hence the larger error bars), a steadily increasing proportion are married, perhaps precisely because being married increases their odds of survival to an advanced age! Older men aren't always so great at taking care of themselves.[9]

Why do women live longer than men? This still isn't perfectly understood, but researchers have some theories. Unlike the Y chromosome, which we can live without, the X chromosome carries critical

6 Schweizer, Valerie, "Marriage: More than a Century of Change, 1900–2018," 2020; Allred, "Marriage: More than a Century of Change, 1900–2016," 2018.

7 Ausubel, "Globally, Women Are Younger than Their Male Partners, More Likely to Age Alone," 2020.

8 There are many other 19th and 20th century formulations, but this one is from Locker-Lampson, *Patchwork*, 1879.

9 Manzoli et al., "Marital Status and Mortality in the Elderly: A Systematic Review and Meta-Analysis," 2007; Jia and Lubetkin, "Life Expectancy and Active Life Expectancy by Marital Status Among Older U.S. Adults: Results from the U.S. Medicare Health Outcome Survey (HOS)," 2020.

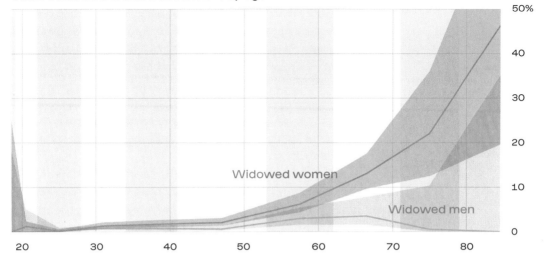

50%

40

30

20

10

0

Widowed women

Widowed men

20   30   40   50   60   70   80

10 Klein and Flanagan, "Sex Differences in Immune Responses," 2016; Oertelt-Prigione, "The Influence of Sex and Gender on the Immune Response," 2012; Caruso et al., "Sex, Gender and Immunosenescence: A Key to Understand the Different Lifespan Between Men and Women?," 2013.

genes. Men generally have only one copy, while women generally have two; this redundancy may confer health benefits. Men's and women's immune systems differ too, which could play a role.**10** You might also remember, from way back in Chapter 1, that men are more accident prone than women—maybe at least partly due to testosterone-linked risk-taking behavior.

However, the best explanation may not be mechanistic, but evolutionary: grandmothers are more useful than grandfathers, as far as Darwinian selection is concerned. This may seem counterintuitive, given that women stop being fertile in middle age, while men can continue to have offspring until late in life (though their fertility does decline). However, as discussed in Chapter 4, humans alloparent;

A grandma and her grandchild, Besaran Village, Kurdistan, Iran, 2017.

it takes a village to raise a baby. In most traditional societies, grand-mothers, far more than grandfathers, play a key role in raising their grandchildren—so much so that, in traditional societies, the presence of a grandmother raises a child's odds of survival substantially.[11]

11 Hrdy, *Mothers and Others: The Evolutionary Origins of Mutual Understanding*, chap. 3, 2009.

Menopause may even be an evolutionary "innovation" to avoid resource competition between the offspring of successive generations: once she's done having her own babies, grandma can dedicate her undivided effort to the grandkids. So, since grandchildren also carry grandma's genes, evolutionary selection will keep pressure on genes that bestow long life on women.

Because older men are less helpful in raising grandchildren, they don't benefit from the same degree of evolutionary selection pres-sure; therefore, over many generations, mutations leading to earlier death specifically in men will pile up unchecked.[12] The proximal cause may be anything—heart failure, stroke, cancer, poor judgment, even suicide. The *underlying* cause is nature's relative indifference to men's lifespan beyond their most reproductive years. In fact, it's conceivable that the same evolutionary force that has prolonged women's lifespans has actively worked to shorten men's—since grandma will have more time to devote to the grandkids if she doesn't have to take care of frail old grandpa too.

12 Hamilton, "The Moulding of Senescence by Natural Selection," 1966.

But let's return to marriage.

5.2 **Rate of marriage among respondents overall and with minority identities** % by age

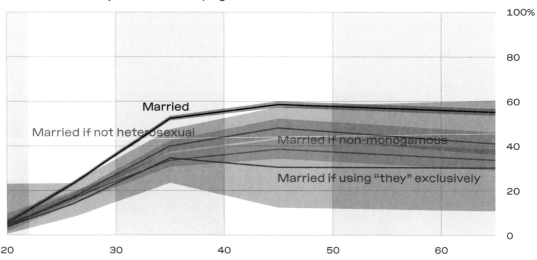

Breaking down the marriage data based on responses to other survey questions shows that many minority identities and behav-iors—such as not being heterosexual, being non-monogamous, or using "they" pronouns—are associated with significantly lower odds of marriage, across all ages. Marriage, in other words, is a traditional practice, and often goes along with being traditional in other ways. As traditions are upended, fewer people are getting married.

So was Morning Glory right about the looming breakdown of the Nuclear Family, and the rise of polyamory? Three questions on the survey bear on this directly: "Are you monogamous?" "Are you non-monogamous?" and "Are you polyamorous?" These terms weren't familiar to every respondent, especially "polyamorous," which should be unsurprising, since it was so recently coined by a Neopagan witch to describe a practice that was (at least in 1990) far outside the mainstream.

5.3 **Polyamorous, non-monogamous, and "not monogamous"** % by age

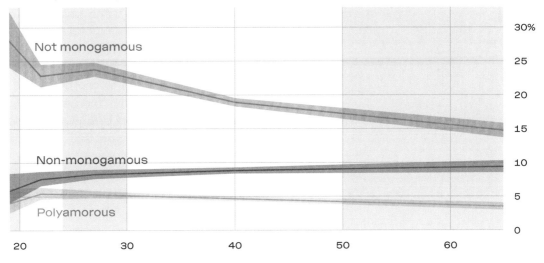

13 This figure is fairly consistent with other studies. Haupert et al., "Prevalence of Experiences With Consensual Nonmonogamous Relationships: Findings From Two National Samples of Single Americans," 2017; Rubin et al., "On the Margins: Considering Diversity Among Consensually Non-Monogamous Relationships," 2014; Conley, Moors, and Matsick, "The Fewer the Merrier?: Assessing Stigma Surrounding Consensually Non-Monogamous Romantic Relationships," 2013.

Remarkably, three decades later, around 5% of American respondents, or 1 in 20, self-identify as polyamorous, across a wide range of ages.[13] That's about as common as naturally blond hair! It's also notable that so many more people answer "no" to "Are you monogamous?" than answer "yes" to "Are you non-monogamous?"— a thread we'll pick up shortly. But first, polyamory.

The need for a term to acknowledge loving and honest sexual relationships among more than two people clearly predated 1990; Thomas and Mary Nichols were writing about such relationships in 1854, and they in turn could point to far older precedents. On the other hand, having newly minted language for the idea clearly has aided its recent rise in popularity—which has in turn triggered some of the same kind of conservative backlash that has accompanied rising acceptance of other sexual minorities. A frustrated 32-year-old man from Boise, Idaho, wrote, "If i went with the gays and polynomous and the non-monagoumas, and homosexual route, I'd might be more accepted into society."

The association between non-monogamy and homosexuality is not entirely off-base, as a number of relationship models and practices that are now becoming increasingly mainstream were either pioneered by or accepted earlier in gay communities. A 25-year-old from Elizabeth, Colorado, wrote about this aspect of gay culture:

I think a lot of times sexual behavior depends in part on the "culture" of the group of individuals that you fit into, if that makes sense. For example, I find it extremely common among heterosexual individuals [to] just end up having monogamous relationships with the expectation to be together for the rest of their lives (it may be that they both feel that way, or just one feels that way and the other ends up either accepting it and living monogamously or if not then engaging in sexual activities with others without their "partner's" knowledge). I have found that, at least in the gay male culture, it is much, much more common for individuals to have non-monogamous relationship[s] and to speak freely about all of those relationships with all their partners.

Three World War I soldiers.

14 Ortiz-Ospina and Roser, "Marriages and Divorces," 2020.

15 Perel, *Mating in Captivity: Sex, Lies and Domestic Bliss*, 2007; Barker, *Rewriting the Rules: An Integrative Guide to Love, Sex and Relationships*, 2012; Savage, *American Savage: Insights, Slights, and Fights on Faith, Sex, Love, and Politics*, 2013; Fern, *Polysecure: Attachment, Trauma and Consensual Nonmonogamy*, 2020.

16 Quoted at greater length in Chapter 4: Ryan, *The Philosophy of Marriage*, 91, 1837.

Large age differences, kink, friends with benefits, sex parties, roleplay, safewords, pride parades, and many other practices were also once strongly associated with gay culture, but have now become less so. As these practices have diffused throughout society, though, they haven't entirely shed the connection with their origins. A sense that gay people were the original cool kids (even if they're still, in some settings, stigmatized) may help explain the recent strain of self-pitying straight resentment, the sense of being left behind—or of digging in heels and refusing to budge.

Quite a few more people answer "yes" to "non-monogamous" than to "polyamorous," which makes sense, since non-monogamy is generally understood to be a broader category than polyamory—including, for instance, simultaneous but compartmentalized relationships, swinging, cheating, and "don't ask, don't tell" arrangements. In this vein, a cheerful 38-year-old woman from Wisconsin wrote, "I live in a rural area, I am not polyamorous but my husband and I have threesomes together with other women because I enjoy women as well sexually. It is a perk for both of us!"

Postcard, ca. 1910.

The age patterns are revealing here. At age 18, non-monogamy begins just above polyamory, at around 6%, but rises steadily with age to nearly 10%, more than double the rate of polyamory, which declines slightly to just below 4%. One likely contribution: a fair number of initially monogamous people become non-monogamous over time, as it becomes clear to them that their needs or wants can't be met by a single partner. Somewhere between a third and a half of marriages in the US end in divorce,[14] and marriages often represent the more committed end of monogamy, suggesting that a great many people realize at some point that their needs can't be met by their *current* partner.

Esther Perel, Dan Savage, and a number of other relationship experts whose work has brought them into contact with struggling couples have pointed out the obvious but often unacknowledged conflict between societal expectations of monogamy (accompanying the stigma of non-monogamy) and the lived realities of many people's needs and desires.[15] As Michael Ryan pointed out in 1837, "polygamy is interdicted by our laws, [but] it does not exist the less in the hearts of most men who profess to be monogamous, but who are no less polygamous by their actions."[16] Contrary to Ryan's belief, this is just as true of women. Speaking for many, a 27-year-old from Canoga Park, California, put it succinctly: "Hard to remain monogamous."

Belgian psychotherapist and author Esther Perel.

→ American sex advice columnist, author, podcaster, and activist Dan Savage.

Although non-monogamy is somewhat less common among the young, a far greater proportion of those who *are* non-monogamous appear to identify with the honest, consensual, and emotionally committed polyamorous approach espoused by Morning Glory. As a 26-year-old woman from New Orleans, Louisiana put it, "I considered 'non-monogamous' and 'polyamorous' to be so close they were interchangeable so I gave the same answer." (In her case, that answer was "yes.")

This becomes less true of older people, though. Hence, while 70–80% of polyamorous people of all ages report being non-monogamous, the fraction of non-monogamous people who are polyamorous declines from around 50% among young people to under 30% among 65-year-olds.

5.4 Overlap of non-monogamy and polyamory % by age

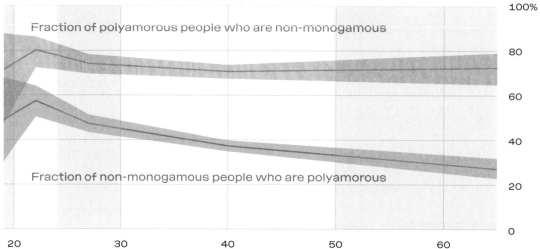

Given that the stigma associated with non-monogamy appears to be higher among older people, one likely factor is the unwillingness or inability of many older couples to be transparent with each other about their needs. Of course satisfying those needs can lead to non-consensual non-monogamy (read: affairs), but *not* satisfying them may imply a potential or desire on the part of one partner that the other will never know, as for the 31-year-old woman from Jacksonville, North Carolina, who wrote, "While I am married, and we are monogamous, I am open to being in a triad, but only with another man. I wouldn't admit this to my husband though." Obviously such an admission can be frightening, and can have very real negative consequences. On the other hand, it's hard not to wonder how many couples could be having a better time ("It is a perk for both of us!") if they overcame their reticence to communicate. Such openness would be easier, too, if the risks and social stigma associated with sex outside marriage were lower, especially for women.[17]

17 Conley, Ziegler, and Moors, "Backlash From the Bedroom: Stigma Mediates Gender Differences in Acceptance of Casual Sex Offers," 2013.

5.5.0 **Polyamorous men and women** % by age

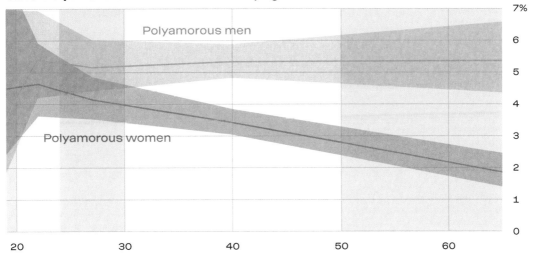

5.5.1 **Non-monogamous men and women** % by age

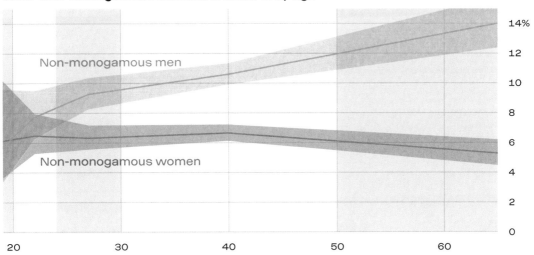

Breaking down polyamory and non-monogamy by gender reveals an obvious asymmetry, becoming increasingly pronounced as respondents get older. At age 19, polyamory and non-monogamy are about 4% and 6% respectively, with no difference by gender, but by age 65, both curves show men answering "yes" nearly three times as often as women. For polyamory, the gap grows because the number of men saying "yes" remains constant, while the number of women saying "yes" declines steadily. For non-monogamy, the gap grows because the number of women saying "yes" remains constant(ish), while the number of men climbs all the way up to 14%. What to make of this?

Part of the story might be an old, patriarchal pattern. Recall from Chapter 4 how many traditional agricultural societies practiced

18 The term was coined by researchers who claimed to have found evidence of Genghis Khan's Y chromosome, though this is contested. See Wei et al., "Whole-Sequence Analysis Indicates That the Y Chromosome C2*-Star Cluster Traces Back to Ordinary Mongols, Rather Than Genghis Khan," 2018.

19 Pollet et al., "The Golden Years: Men from the Forbes 400 Have Much Younger Wives When Remarrying than the General US Population," 2013.

polygyny; in such societies, a man's social status correlates with his number of wives. Historical records offer some extreme examples, like Ismail al Sharif, a Sultan of Morocco from 1672 to 1727, whose harem numbered over 500 women, and Aztec ruler Montezuma II, who reportedly kept four thousand concubines. In the sixth century, King Tamba of Banaras (more commonly known today as Varanasi, in northern India) is believed to have presided over a harem of sixteen thousand women. The very large number of descendants fathered by such men can leave genetic traces on whole populations, especially in the Y chromosome, which passes from father to son. Such traces are known in the literature as "Star Clusters."[18] In all of these cases, as the man acquires wealth and power—and ages—he also "acquires" consorts, who are typically younger... and younger. (Though it should be noted that in many traditional societies, polygyny involves higher-status men not so much maintaining harems as providing alimony to a succession of ex-partners.) Among very wealthy American men today, a similar pattern still seems to hold: the wives of men on the Forbes 400 list are younger than average, and when they remarry, their new wives are *far* younger than average. There's no equivalent pattern for Forbes 400 women.[19]

If this is also true (to a more modest degree) among more ordinary people, we'd expect the result to look as it does—a gendered "non-monogamy gap" that increases with age—especially since men die younger than women do. It's possible that such patriarchal patterns are in decline among young people. It's also possible that men are simply more willing to acknowledge their non-monogamy because in a patriarchal setting it may confer higher status ("conquests"), while for many women, having multiple partners remains a source of shame.[20]

Regardless of gender, older non-monogamous people may also be less eager to *identify* as polyamorous. That is, it's likely that a greater number of older people whose approach to non-monogamy is *de facto* polyamorous just don't relate to what they may, with some historical justification, consider trendy or New-Agey jargon. No matter how they go about it, it's certainly the case that older people tend to be more closeted about their non-monogamy, making it a hidden (thus underestimated) minority. Their non-monogamous behavior

The Bloomsbury Group and their purported relationships.

20 In a number of studies, men have reported having about twice as many opposite-sex sexual partners as women on average, which on its face seems inconsistent. There are a number of likely causes, including social stigma, but also other factors—such as missing or underreported data from sex workers, most of whom are women catering to men. Mitchell et al., "Why Do Men Report More Opposite-Sex Sexual Partners Than Women? Analysis of the Gender Discrepancy in a British National Probability Survey," 2019.

21 Also known as: cheating.

may be opaque not only to colleagues and friends, but even to their own partners.[21]

Polyamory, on the other hand, is for many not just a practice, but a community, a language, and a culture openly acknowledging and supporting the practice. Hence the 20–30% or so of people of all ages who report being polyamorous but *not* non-monogamous often appear to be identifying with the community or movement, even if that's not reflected in their current behavior. As a 31-year-old from Woburn, Massachusetts, put it,

> **My partner and I are both exploring the idea of polyamory but have been thus far monogamous in our relationship. I Identify as poly in that I do not experience jealousy and am interested in having multiple romantic and sexual partners, but have not yet had a "polyamorous relationship."**

This can all be quite confusing. Naïvely following the logic of double negatives, the finding that about 6% of young people are *non*-monogamous would lead one to conclude that 94% are *monogamous*... but that would be wrong. Only about 70% of 19-year-olds report being monogamous. This number rises above 85% by age 65.

18–20 years old	No to monogamous	Yes to monogamous
No to non-monogamous	23.13%	71.04%
Yes to non-monogamous	5.03%	0.79%

50+ years old	No to monogamous	Yes to monogamous
No to non-monogamous	7.83%	82.72%
Yes to non-monogamous	6.94%	2.51%

Let's explore the counterintuitive difference between "being non-monogamous" and "not being monogamous." Consider all four possibilities: (A) those who answer "no" to both "monogamous" and "non-monogamous," (B) those who answer "yes" to "monogamous" but "no" to "non-monogamous," (C) those who answer "no" to "monogamous" but "yes" to "non-monogamous," and (D) those who answer "yes" to both.

The majority at all ages, despite the moral panic of a certain frustrated "monagoumas" respondent from Boise, is still the conventional (B) "yes" to "monogamous" and "no" to "non-monogamous"; for the most part, these are people in monogamous, pair-bonded relationships.

Since these are the only four possible responses to two yes/no questions—hence options (A), (B), (C), and (D) add up to 100%—the whole picture can be gleaned from the three minority combinations,

5.6 **Responses to "monogamous" and "non-monogamous"** % by age

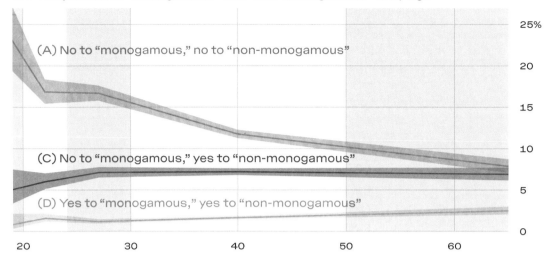

(A), (C), and (D). The second most frequent response is (A), "no" to "monogamous" and "no" to "non-monogamous," as typified by a 41-year-old respondent from Elk Grove Village, Illinois: "I'm faithful to who I'm with at the time, but I'm not with anyone now. So I answered no to both." As one might expect, this number declines with age, from near 25% at 19 to only about 7% by age 65, as more people end up partnered over time.

Over the same period, the number of (C) "not monogamous" *and* "non-monogamous" people rises from 5% to 7%, in keeping with what we've already seen. Notice that the largely unpartnered group (A) and the multiply partnered group (C) end up tied by age 65, despite (A) being five times likelier at age 19.

The lowest likelihood combination—(D) "yes" to both questions—is the most counterintuitive. It can arise from varying interpretations of the two terms, as in the case of a 26-year-old woman from Ormond Beach, Florida: "I am currently monogamous, but there have been times I have been with women that my husband is aware of. If it were to present itself, I would be sexual with another woman and or have a love triangle poly relationship." In other words, this is a situation in which one of the terms—"monogamous"—is interpreted as a behavior that applies in the moment, while "non-monogamous" is interpreted as an identity or orientation, which may not be reflected in one's current behavior.

There's a parallel here with a finding we'll soon explore at more length: many (especially younger) bisexual people do not stop identifying as bisexual even if they're in an exclusive long-term relationship with a man or woman. Here and elsewhere, identity is more typically associated with a minority behavior than with the majority—which makes sense, since the majority, being a default, doesn't need any separate community, language, or culture. As we'll explore in the following chapters, personal identity has become increasingly *distinct from* behavior, especially in urban settings. Uncoupling identity from behavior opens the door to many combinations of responses that can appear contradictory by a more literal, purely behavioral standard.

Why do minority labels, cultures, and identities exist, if they aren't reflected in people's behaviors? Put another way, why would anyone feel the need to signal that they are a card-carrying member of a club they may never intend to set foot in?

Some critics find such signaling performative and annoying. The harshest critique tends to come from people *within* those communities, who may feel that "non-practicing members" are posers, talking the talk but not walking the walk—and, perhaps, not paying the price of admission. Such "gatekeeping" can feel painful, as for this 31-year-old from Woodridge, New York: "Because I'm in a heterosexual marriage people assume that my queerness is not real or genuine and this makes me feel invalid and lost in the queer community. Almost erased."

As a consequence—beyond individual feelings of erasure by the excluded or dilution by "practicing members"—invisibility can make the prevalence of an identity trait hard to guess. How many queer or bisexual people are there, really?

The answer will vary dramatically depending on whether we count only those who are "practicing" or include everyone who identifies as such. Hence our choice of questions to ask, and the way we interpret responses, can change our perspective on a phenomenon dramatically. It can even make the difference between a minority and a majority.

A "Bidentification Card" distributed by the US based Bisexual Resource Center.

BIDENTIFICATION CARD

This card certifies the bearer as an official, card-carrying bisexual and confers upon the bearer all the rights and privileges of bisexuality. The bearer may display the bi colors, wear bi-positive adornments, and may contemplate and/or engage in sexual activity with persons of all genders.

Authorized Signature   Member Since

No expiration date ~ No renewal required

6

The true mission of sex

Elizabeth Blackwell.

Priests, moralizers, politicians, lawyers, and policemen have been branding non-heterosexual orientation and behavior as pathological for thousands of years—but nobody out-pathologizes doctors. A number of strong opinions by MDs in this vein have already come up; in order of appearance so far: Cesare Lombroso, Wilhelm Stekel, Sigmund Freud, Wilhelm Fliess, Michael Ryan, Thomas Nichols—a frock-coated and bewhiskered panel of learned men. It's easy to understand why doctors have assumed this role. They traditionally consider the body in terms of organs and systems with well-defined functions, and it's their job to diagnose and, when possible, address *dys*functions.

Elizabeth Blackwell (1821–1910), the first woman to receive a medical degree in the United States, offered a humbler take on our understanding of function in the human body in her 1894 book *The Human Element in Sex*:

The Christian physiologist [...], knowing that there is a wise and beneficent purpose in the human structure, seeks to find out the laws and methods of action by means of which human function may accomplish its highest use. This task can only be carried out gradually. Ultimate function is not revealed by structure, nor ultimate use by function. [...] Ignorance of facts, preconceived notions, or fanciful theories as to "vital spirits," "cold and hot humours," &c., long delayed the attainment of correct knowledge of physiological facts. Neither does physical knowledge of individual function reveal the developed use of which it is capable. [...] Function and use are only proved by observation, reflection, and rational

1 Blackwell, *The Human Element in Sex: Being a Medical Inquiry into the Relation of Sexual Physiology to Christian Morality*, 1–2, 1894.

experiment patiently carried on age after age, with generalisation based upon accurate and accumulated facts.[1]

Where Blackwell's Christianity led her to advocate caution in presuming to understand the ultimate functions of human bodies, most of her (male) contemporaries drew the opposite conclusion—also on religious grounds. For them, the detailed workings of, say, the uterus might remain mysterious, but its *purpose* is spelled out clearly enough

2 Gen. 1:28 (KJV).

in the Bible: to "be fruitful, and multiply."[2] Unfortunately, Blackwell's views were—and remain—in the medical minority.

Philosophers refer to the idea that everything is *for* something as *teleology*. Why should a doctor not apply this idea to sex? It's a seemingly powerful yet circular argument: if a body part cannot fulfill its natural function, then you have a physical disorder. If it *can* do so but you are not using it to fulfill its natural function, then you're *mentally* disordered, committing a crime against nature. You're doing it wrong. And there will be consequences, since our health as individuals and as a species depends on these natural functions. As the phrenologist Samuel Roberts Wells (1820–1875) put it when dispensing "scientific" marriage advice,

[W]hen art and nature are thrown into positions of antagonism, as they often are under the present order of things, deterioration and decadence are the results. Man has dominion over nature. The unphysiological habits and

3 Wells, *Wedlock; Or, the Right Relations of the Sexes: Disclosing the Laws of Conjugal Selection, and Showing Who May, and Who May Not Marry*, 22, 1884.

pernicious systems of education so prevalent at the present day, especially in cities, tend to produce precocity and a depreciation of vital stamina. The natural order of development is often subverted [...].[3]

So, it falls to medical professionals to tell us what is natural and what is pathological or "unphysiological." By drawing this distinction, they tell us both who we *are* and who we are *not*—that is, who falls outside the boundaries of the acceptable.

While medicine is an ancient field with roots in traditional practices dating back to Ice Ages, we should keep in mind that beyond herb-lore, lancing boils, and the like, it's only over the last two centuries that surgery and "physic" have merged into an organized profession endowed with the skill and knowledge to reliably

4 Schneider, *The Invention of Surgery*, 2021.

cure disease,[4] rather than philosophizing and conducting magic rituals, whether shamanic (like dancing) or pseudo-scientific (like bloodletting).

As medicine has become more effective, physicians have gained moral authority, arguably surpassing that of the church,

Lavinia Dock.

especially when we consider how universally their judgment is trusted, and how consequential that judgment can be. Doctors wield scalpels, administer treatments, and prescribe drugs, both with and without patients' consent—for consent is not the norm when those patients are minors, or when they're deemed incompetent.[5] Doctors can also determine people's legal status as competent or incompetent, normal or deranged, safe to be in public or condemned to an institution... where their consent also ceases to matter. With or without ill intent, this power has often been abused. The next several chapters will feature some vivid examples, continuing up to the present day.

Lavinia Dock (1858–1956), a feminist pioneer in nursing education, characterized this frequent overreach in her notes on a 1902 conference in Brussels on the regulation of prostitution. Like Blackwell, Dock critiqued a patriarchal medical establishment that was not only ignorant outside a narrow purview, but blind to its own ignorance:

This [...] conference [was] very remarkable not only for the facts brought out, but also as showing, along with the rapidly advancing tendency of the best medical thought to think in unison with social moralists [...] two things especially: one, the immense handicap of involuntary, unconscious sex dominance and egotism to men discussing these problems: the other, the conspicuous ignorance of many great medical specialists in matters of sociology. It is a mistake to suppose that an eminent authority in one line will be equally eminent as an authority in another. As a matter of fact, the general esteem and confidence proffered to the medical profession by the public has sometimes encouraged its members to believe that their pronouncements on social conditions are as final as their definitions of medical knowledge.[6]

To see the trick in action—medical knowledge morphing into teleology, and then into moral judgment, and then into social prescription—consider Henry Stanton's 1922 book *Sex: Avoided Subjects Discussed in Plain English*,[7] a typical and popular pamphlet of its era designed to help parents instruct their children in the "facts of life":

5 Or, worse, undesirable, like the Jewish women in Linz in 1938, wearing placards in the public square announcing that they had been "excluded from the national community" (see Chapter 3). In the United States, such "undesirability" has motivated forced sterilization campaigns for Black, Native, and Latin American men and women.

6 Dock, *Hygiene and Morality: A Manual for Nurses and Others, Giving an Outline of the Medical, Social, and Legal Aspects of the Venereal Diseases*, 84–85, 1910.

7 Stanton, *Sex: Avoided Subjects Discussed in Plain English*, 1922. Many, many other 19th and 20th century books could illustrate the point equally well.

As we mount the ascending ladder of plant and animal life the unit-cell of the lower organisms is replaced by a great number of individual cells, which have grown together to form a completed whole. [...] Philosophically it may be said that [the egg and sperm] cells directly continue the life of the parents, so that death in reality only destroys a part of the individual. Every individual lives again in his offspring.[8]

8   Stanton, 8–9.

Queen Victoria and the members of the royal family, 1877.

So far, so good. There *is* something beautiful and true in this grand picture, a hint of the way our individual bodies aren't so individual, but are connected through the generations, as with a spacetime spiderweb, by the tiny strands of our germline. A chicken is just an egg's way of making another egg, as the old saying goes.

But, like any description, this isn't a view from nowhere. It again evokes the Great Chain of Being familiar to the theologians and natural philosophers of previous centuries, in which complex multicellular animals like us are at the top of the hierarchy of living things on Earth. It also prescribes the role, or natural function, of egg and sperm cells.

Now comes the rub. For them to fulfill this natural function, the organism as a whole has to do *its* bit. So, Stanton gets down to business:

THE TRUE MISSION OF SEX
This rebirth of the individual in his descendants represents the true mission of sex where the human being is concerned. And reproduction, the perpetuation of the species, underlies all rightful and normal sex functions and activities.[9]

9   Stanton, 9.

Victorian children at Crumpsall Workhouse, Manchester, England, ca. 1895–97.

Syrian immigrant children, ca. 1910–15.

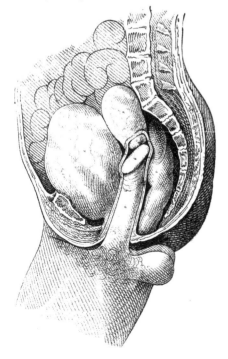

Plate 22 from *Kalogy-nomia*, T. Bell, 1821.

This short passage, neatly harmonizing religious, scientific, and medical doctrines, encapsulates historical attitudes to lesbian, gay, and trans people: they're unnatural and disordered because their sex lives aren't furthering the reproductive mission.

Nationalism, racism, and classism play a part here too. Sexual reproduction, says Stanton, "underlies the vigor and racial power of every nation."[10] Hence shirking one's reproductive duty has overtones not only of self indulgence, but of betraying race and country. At the time, anxieties were running high about the sexually restrained bourgeoisie being out-reproduced by foreigners and poor people—and indeed, the correlation between poverty and high birth rate is real, as Part III of this book will explore. Conversely, the trend toward sharply lower birth rates described in the previous chapter holds not only in the US, but in all economically developed countries. This correlation was already apparent to scholars by the end of the 18th century, and had become something of a demographic panic by the early 20th.

→ Richard von Krafft-Ebing (1840–1902).

10 Stanton, 50.

11 Quotes are from Krafft-Ebing, *Psychopathia Sexualis with Especial Reference to Contrary Sexual Instinct: A Medico-Legal Study; Authorized Translation of the Seventh Enlarged and Revised German Edition*, 1893.

12 *Psychopathia sexualis* cites Lombroso's work 25 times.

13 Krafft-Ebing, *Psychopathia Sexualis*, 225, 1893.

Sándor Vay (1859–1918).

Stanton's widely held perspective carries many other implications, too. For one, the enjoyment of sex should be secondary to thinking of it as a duty. Thus, birth control (at least, by the wealthy) is monstrous, as is, obviously, any kind of sex that can't result in conception, such as oral or anal sex, or even masturbation (hence the old time euphemism for it, "self abuse"). Thus the original meaning of sexual "deviancy" or "perversion": any activity that perverts or deviates from the "naturally" reproductive function of sex.

The most widely read work on "sexual deviancy" of its generation was pioneering sexologist Richard von Krafft-Ebing's 1886 book *Psychopathia sexualis*.[11] Profoundly influenced by Lombroso,[12] it's full of lurid "medico-legal" case studies, peppered with Latin to project a scholarly veneer (and maybe to keep its titillations out of reach of women, children, and the vulgar masses). Krafft-Ebing introduced English readers to many new terms, including "heterosexuality," "homosexuality," "bisexuality," "sadism," and "masochism."

Like Lombroso, he considered homosexuality, in particular, "a functional sign of degeneration, and [...] a partial manifestation of a neuropsychopathic state, in most cases hereditary."[13] In other words, just as "criminality" was deemed evidence of being degenerate or primitive, so was being lesbian, gay, trans, or anything else Krafft-Ebing regarded as "deviant"; all were steps down the Chain of Being, and into the non-reproductive gutters of society.

The consequences were severe. Given the draconian sodomy laws in force at the time, LGBT people *were* legally criminals—a textbook instance of circular reasoning.

Many case studies in *Psychopathia sexualis* vividly illustrate these points. They also make for

14 See also Mak, "Sandor/Sarolta Vay: From Passing Woman to Sexual Invert," 2004.

heartbreaking reading today. Case 131, for example, is the story of "Count Sandor V," who was arrested in 1889,[14] and discovered to be "no man at all, but a woman in male attire":

> **Among many foolish things that her father encouraged in her was the fact that he brought her up as a boy, called her Sandor, allowed her to ride, drive, and hunt, admiring her muscular energy. [...] At thirteen she had a love-relation with an English girl, to whom she represented herself as a boy, and ran away with her. [...] She recognized the abnormality of her sexual inclinations, but had no desire to have them changed, since in this perverse feeling she felt both well and happy.[15]**

15 Krafft-Ebing, *Psychopathia Sexualis*, 311, 1893.

After a youth in which Count S. "became independent, and visited cafés, even those of doubtful character," "was a very skillful fencer," "carried on literary work, and was a valued collaborator on two noted journals," she found:

> **A new love [...] Marie, and her love was returned. Her mother and cousin tried in vain to break up this affair. [...] In April, 1888, Count S. paid her a visit, and in May, 1889, attained her wish; in that Marie—who, in the meantime, had given up a position as teacher—became her bride in the presence of a friend of her lover, the ceremony being performed in an arbor, by a false priest, in Hungary. S., with her friend, forged the marriage-certificate. The pair lived happily, and, without the interference of the step-father, this false marriage, probably, would have lasted much longer.[16]**

16 Krafft-Ebing, 312.

If only this passage had ended with the sentence "The pair lived happily ever after," we'd have a sweet, gender-expansive love story; then again, if the couple had remained undiscovered (as must have happened in some cases) we also wouldn't have a medico-legal record.

We don't know what became of Marie, but we do know that upon being outed, Count S. fell victim to the legal, psychiatric, and medical institutions of the day, and was imprisoned.

> **The first meeting which the experts had with S. was, in a measure, a time of embarrassment to both sides; for them, because perhaps S.'s somewhat dazzling and forced masculine carriage impressed them; for her, because she thought she was to be marked with the stigma of moral insanity.**

Professor Robert Burger-Villingen, a "race scientist," measuring heads at Humboldt University, Berlin, 1930.

The ordeal must have been both terrifying and humiliating. A lengthy, chillingly invasive examination ensues, much abbreviated here:

> She is 153 centimetres tall, of delicate skeleton, thin, but remarkably muscular on the breast and thighs. Her gait in female attire is awkward. Her movements are powerful, not unpleasing, though they are somewhat masculine, and lacking in grace. [...] Feet and hands remarkably small, having remained in an infantile stage of development. [...] The skull is slightly oxycephalic, and in all its measurements falls below the average of the female skull by at least one centimetre. [...] The circumference of the head is 52 centimetres; the occipital half-circumference, 24 centimetres; the line from ear to ear, over the vertex, 23 centimetres; the anterior half-circumference, 28.5 centimetres; the line from glabella to occiput, 30 centimetres; the ear-chin line, 26.5 centimetres; long diameter, 17 centimetres; greatest lateral diameter, 13 centimetres; diameter at auditory meati, 12 centimetres; zygomatic diameter, 11.2 centimetres. [...] Genitals completely feminine, without trace of hermaphroditic appearance, but at the stage of development of those of a ten-year-old girl. [...] The pelvis appears generally narrowed (dwarf-pelvis), and of decidedly masculine type. [...] On account of narrowness of the pelvis, the direction of the thighs is not convergent, as in a woman, but straight.
>
> The opinion given showed that in S. there was a congenitally abnormal inversion of the sexual instinct, which,

Sarah Bernhardt plays Hamlet, London, 1899.

indeed, expressed itself, anthropologically, in anomalies of development of the body, depending upon great hereditary taint; further, that the criminal acts of S. had their foundation in her abnormal and irresistible sexuality.[17]

Count S. was lucky—and doubtless benefited from high socioeconomic class, a university education, literary talent, and eloquence:

"Gentlemen, you learned in the law, psychologists and pathologists, do me justice! Love led me to take the step I took; all my deeds were conditioned by it. God put it in my heart.
"If He created me so, and not otherwise, am I then guilty; or is it the eternal, incomprehensible way of fate? I relied on God, that one day my emancipation would come; for my thought was only love itself, which is the foundation, the guiding principle, of His teaching and His kingdom."
[...] The court granted pardon. The "countess in male attire," as she was called in the newspapers, returned to her home, and again gave herself out as Count Sandor. Her only distress is her lost happiness with her beloved Marie.

Carousing, love affairs, duels, and financial troubles aside, Sándor Vay went on to become a prolific and successful writer, ultimately collecting 400 stories and publishing them in 15 volumes. In 1908, two years before his death, a street in his native town of Gyón was named Count Sándor Vay in his honor.

Many of the subjects of Krafft-Ebing's case studies weren't so fortunate; their stories often ended in suicide or internment in an asylum for life.

Remarkably little seemed to have changed by the time the American Psychiatric Association published the first edition of the Diagnostic and Statistical Manual of Mental Disorders (DSM) in 1952. It, too, defined "sexual deviation" as a form of criminal pathological behavior—not drawing distinctions based on harm or violation of consent, but on violation of social norms:

The term includes most of the cases formerly classed as "psychopathic personality with pathologic sexuality." The diagnosis will specify the type of the pathologic

17 Krafft-Ebing, 316–17.

18 American Psychiatric Association, *Diagnostic and Statistical Manual: Mental Disorders (DSM-I)*, 39, 1952.

behavior, such as homosexuality, transvestism, pedophilia, fetishism and sexual sadism (including rape, sexual assault, mutilation).[18]

The DSM's characterization of homosexuality as a mental illness reflected the views of the foremost psychoanalytic theorist of homosexuality in the 1940s and '50s, Dr. Edmund Bergler. He coined the term "writer's block" in 1947, and wrote books on gambling, self-harm, midlife crises, and (albeit rather humorlessly) the basis of humor. He was also a strong proponent of conversion therapy—and for a psychiatrist to offer such a service, there needed to be a diagnosis. The DSM delivered exactly that.

Bergler's popular 1956 paperback, *Homosexuality: Disease or way of life?* answers the titular question right on the cover, with an inset reading, "A world-famous psychoanalyst's inquiry into the causes of homosexuality and the possibilities for its cure." In the opening chapter, *What is a homosexual?*, he writes,

March for equal rights, Philadelphia, July 4, 1967.

> **For nearly thirty years now I have been treating homosexuals, spending many hours with them in the course of their analyses. I can say with some justification that I have no bias against homosexuals; for me they are sick people**

requiring medical help. […] Still, though I have no bias, if I were asked what kind of person the homosexual is, I would say: "**Homosexuals are essentially disagreeable people, regardless of their pleasant or unpleasant outward manner. True, they are not responsible for their unconscious conflicts. However, these conflicts sap so much of their inner energy that the shell is a mixture of superciliousness, fake aggression, and whimpering. Like all psychic masochists, they are subservient when confronted with a stronger person, merciless when in power, unscrupulous about trampling on a weaker person […] you seldom find an intact ego (what is popularly called 'a correct person') among them.**"[19]

19 Bergler, *Homosexuality: Disease or Way of Life?*, 26, 1956.

This passage reveals the way moral judgment can be inflicted while gaslighting: Bergler is "unbiased," because he's writing dispassionately and authoritatively, as a celebrated doctor and researcher. Any critical response to his judgment, in particular *from* a gay person, would doubtless be interpreted as evidence of just the kind of "denial," "aggression," and "neurosis" that he claims characterize gayness.

Perhaps most gallingly, Bergler's brisk business in conversion therapy (by 1959 he claimed to have "treated" over a thousand gay patients[20]) both preyed on and amplified his victims' internalized homophobia:

20 Bergler, *One Thousand Homosexuals: Conspiracy of Silence, or Curing and Deglamorizing Homosexuals?*, 1959.

Newer psychiatric experiences and studies have proved conclusively that the allegedly unchangeable destiny of homosexuals (sometimes even ascribed to nonexistent biological and hormonal conditions) is in fact a *therapeutically changeable subdivision of neurosis* […] today, psychiatric-psychoanalytic treatment can cure homosexuality.

The homosexual of either sex believes that his only trouble stems from the "unreasonable attitude" of the environment. If he were left to his own devices, he claims, and no longer needed to fear the law or to dread social ostracism, extortion, exposure (all leading to constant secrecy and concealment), he could be just as "happy" as his opposite number, the heterosexual. This, of course, is a self-consoling illusion. Homosexuality is not the "way of life" these sick people gratuitously assume it to be, but a neurotic distortion of the total personality […] *there are no healthy homosexuals.*[21]

21 Bergler, *Homosexuality: Disease or Way of Life?*, 9, 1956. Emphasis is in the original; Bergler was fond of italics.

From a 21st century perspective, the cartoonish awfulness of these passages might tempt one to believe that Bergler's views were unusually bigoted; however, this isn't the case. While nascent gay rights publications critiqued the book, it was squarely within the medical, psychiatric, and popular mainstream of the 1950s. *Time* magazine, for instance, reviewed his work positively on its publication in 1956 and again in 1959, concluding,

> **Dr. Bergler holds that every homosexual can be cured in about eight months of psychiatric treatment. All he needs is the will to change, and the willingness to accept that what he really seeks is not synthetic sex but self-punishment. But if he wants to persist in self-punishment, homosexuality is certainly the most efficient means to that unhappy end.[22]**

22 "Medicine: The Strange World," 1959.

The DSM-II, published in 1968, made no significant change, but amid mounting pressure from gay rights groups to de-pathologize homosexuality, the APA issued a rather tortured revision memo in 1973. The memo tried to split the difference, keeping "Sexual orientation *disturbance* (Homosexuality)" (emphasis mine) listed as a disorder:

> **This category is for individuals whose sexual interests are directed primarily toward people of the same sex and who are either disturbed by, in conflict with, or wish to change their sexual orientation. This diagnostic category is distinguished from homosexuality, which by itself does not constitute a psychiatric disorder.[23]**

23 American Psychiatric Association, "Homosexuality and Sexual Orientation Disturbance: Proposed Change in DSM-II, 6th Printing, Page 44, Position Statement (retired)," 1973.

The absurdity soon devolved into ridiculousness and internal contradiction. In justifying the change, the memo acknowledged that not *all* gay people think of themselves as mentally ill, and allowed that this *might* be true, though in the process it still managed to condemn

Gay rights activists Barbara Gittings, Frank Kameny, and Dr. H. Anonymous (Dr. John Fryer, member of the American Psychiatric Association) at an APA panel, "Psychiatry: Friend or Foe to Homosexuals?", Dallas, 1972.

THE CHICAGO GAY CRUSADER

♀ ♂

25¢

JANUARY, 1974   THE TOTAL COMMUNITY NEWSPAPER ®   **NUMBER NINE**

20,000,000 GAY PEOPLE CURED!

Ann slanders less?

Advice columnist Ann Landers may be slowly changing her opinion that gay is sick, though she has not explicitly said so.

On Jan. 8 she devoted an entire column to a letter asking her whether she is "big enough to reverse yourself and give the gay population a clean bill of health" in light of the American Psychiatric Association's vote on homosexuality.

She answered: "I have said homosexuals are sick, in the sense [of] a dysfunction, a form of aberrant behavior. My opinion has not changed. When the APA says homosexuality is 'not normal' they are saying, in a different way, what I have been saying all along. But labels can be dangerously misleading, and here-in lies part of the problem."

After equating her position with that of the APA (which in fact said gays are not necessarily sick, despite Landers' earlier claim that they are), she went on at length to say that she "had something to do" with Illinois' 1961 sodomy law repeal and that she is "fighting to protect homosexuals from job dismissal or demotion." She concluded: "In my opinion, the heterosexual who is at war with himself, abuses others, engages in orgies, excessive drinking or drug abuse is sicker [sic] than the homosexual who is at peace with himself and is a productive member of society."

The next day, she printed another letter from a gay who disagreed with her on some points but praised her for providing a forum for varying views on homosexuality. In her reply, she again noted that for 18 years she had preached that homosexuals should not be "harassed or ridiculed or discriminated against."

As evidenced by a December letter, however, she feels that demonstrations like the Gay Pride parades are bizarre and a discredit to gay people. She did not explain how she thought that gay rights issues would have achieved their present public attention without demonstrations or Gay Liberation activities.

Ann Landers has long praised psychiatry. A psychiatrist might suspect from her recent breastbeating and slippery terminology that she sees a past error but can't face up to it openly. --W.B.K.

PSYCHIATRISTS DROP 'SICK' LABEL

In what may be the biggest gay news event of 1973, the American Psychiatric Association's Board of Trustees voted Dec. 15 without dissent to remove homosexuality from its list of mental disorders.

The trustees also voted to urge the repeal of laws against homosexual behavior and the passage of new laws to ban discrimination against gay people.

And in Chicago, syndicated *Sun-Times* advice columnist Ann Landers has begun to retreat from her own position that gays are "sick."

But, in a last-ditch move, some APA diehards are trying to reverse the trustees' action.

* * * * * *

New Category Created

To replace homosexuality as a disorder, the APA defined a new illness--"sexual orientation disturbance"--for gays who "are either disturbed by, in conflict with, or wish to change their sexual orientation." The definition went on to say that homosexuality "by itself does not necessarily constitute a psychiatric disorder [but] is one form of sexual behavior and, like other forms... which are not by themselves psychiatric disorders, is not listed in this nomenclature of mental disorders."

However, no similar catch-all category exists for heterosexuals troubled by their sexual orientation.

Result of Gay Pressure

The reversal of position by the APA caps a long drive by gay activists for abandonment of its official view that being gay is sick. The drive got under way in earnest when San Francisco gay activists disrupted an APA convention in 1970, and succeeding years saw panel discussions, exhibits, and lectures on the correct psychiatric stand toward homosexuality.

In 1972 a committee was established to study dropping homosexuality from the APA sickness list, and a member of the committee, Dr. Robert L. Spitzer, eventually drafted the two resolutions which passed Dec. 15.

Spitzer said that homosexuality does not fit the two criteria for defining a psychiatric disorder--that it either "regularly cause emotional distress or regularly be associated with generalized impairment of social functioning"--and was therefore dropped from the diagnostic manual.

Opponents Ask Referendum

But a group of psychiatrists long known for their view that gays are sick has launched a campaign to conduct a poll of the APA's entire membership on reversal of the trustees' stand.

The group includes Drs. Irving Bieber and Charles Socarides, who made a special trip to Washington to plead with the trustees not to adopt the resolutions. After the vote, the group filed a petition in early January requiring the referendum question to be included in a February issue of *Psychiatric News* for all APA members to vote on.

Wide News Coverage

Members of the National Gay Task Force had received advance indication of the APA vote and were on hand for a news conference afterward at Washington APA headquarters. The psychiatrists' action received nationwide news coverage, though some of it was inaccurate.

An unusually accurate and comprehensive story was filed to the *Chicago Sun-Times* by its Washington correspondent William Hines, in which he quoted long-time gay activist Franklin E. Kameny as challenging the newspaper's Ann Landers to reassess her attitude toward homosexuality in light of the APA action. Kameny's comments were also mentioned by the *Sun-Times'* Irv Kupcinet in his daily column.

But the *New York Times* (America's "newspaper of record") and United Press International carried garbled accounts of the action, in which they stated that it involved reclassification of homosexuality (per se) as a "sexual orientation disturbance." The *Times* corrected itself in subsequent editions but repeated the error the following Sunday in its review of the week's news.

The UPI reportedly issued a clarification after being contacted by Kameny in Washington and the Chicago Gay Alliance's president William B. Kelley, but no clarification appeared in the *Chicago Tribune* (which had printed the misleading UPI dispatch) even though the *Tribune* was also advised of the error.

Significance of Decision

In an accompanying position paper, Spitzer pointed out: "In the past, homosexuals have been denied civil rights in many areas of life on the ground that because they suffer from a 'mental illness,' the burden of proof is on them to

(Continued on page 4)

---

142   II   Sex and Gender

homosexuality as a "failure to function optimally"—for good measure, throwing celibacy, revolutionary behavior, male chauvinism, and vegetarianism under the same bus.[24]

24 Of course, like any organization with more than a handful of people, the APA had many members who were themselves gay; they were almost without exception deeply closeted at the time. A 1998 article in the *New York Times*, for instance, details the coming-out of a prominent psychoanalyst, Dr. Ralph Roughton, former director of the Emory University Psychoanalytic Institute. It was not until 1996 that "he looked around at his profession and recognized that the need for secrecy, for pretending to be someone that he was not, was no longer so urgent." Goode, "On Gay Issue, Psychoanalysis Treats Itself," 1998.

25 None of the six officers of the APA were women, but perhaps Henriette R. Klein contributed this item, as the only woman among the 14 trustees and 17 ex-officio non-voting members of the board?

26 American Psychiatric Association, "Homosexuality and Sexual Orientation Disturbance: Proposed Change in DSM-II, 6th Printing, Page 44, Position Statement (retired)," 1973.

The *Chicago Gay Crusader*, January, 1974.

> **Clearly homosexuality, per se, does not meet the requirements for a psychiatric disorder since [...] many homosexuals are quite satisfied with their sexual orientation and demonstrate no generalized impairment in social effectiveness or functioning. The only way that homosexuality could therefore be considered a psychiatric disorder would be the criteria of failure to function heterosexually, which is considered optimal in our society and by many members of our profession. However, if failure to function optimally in some important area of life as judged by either society or the profession is sufficient to indicate the presence of a psychiatric disorder, then we will have to add to our nomenclature the following conditions: celibacy (failure to function optimally sexually), revolutionary behavior (irrational defiance of social norms), religious fanaticism (dogmatic and rigid adherence to religious doctrine), racism (irrational hatred of certain groups), vegetarianism (unnatural avoidance of carnivorous behavior), and male chauvinism (irrational belief in the inferiority of women).[25] [...]**
>
> **[By] no longer listing [homosexuality] as a psychiatric disorder we are not saying that it is "normal" or as valuable as heterosexuality. [...]**
>
> **What will be the effect of carrying out such a proposal? No doubt, homosexual activist groups will claim that psychiatry has at last recognized that homosexuality is as "normal" as heterosexuality. They will be wrong.[26]**

The 1973 DSM revision is celebrated to this day as an important milestone in gay rights, when millions of Americans were suddenly "cured," per a snarky headline in the *Chicago Gay Crusader*. By maintaining that homosexuality was abnormal and less "valuable" than heterosexuality, though—and by keeping a diagnosis on the books for gay people who were dissatisfied with their "failure to function optimally"—the Dr. Berglers of the world got to keep plying their trade.

The idea that homosexuality or bisexuality were disorders at all was finally dropped with the publication of the DSM-III-R in 1987. So, when I was being taught sex ed at school in a suburb of Baltimore in 1986, "sexual orientation disturbance (homosexuality)" was still "officially" a mental disorder in the US. It's unsurprising, then, that a 35-year-old man from Nashville, Tennessee, would write in the survey, unprompted, "tranny and gay are forms of mental illness most likely stemming from childhood abuse (possibly sexual)." Mainstream psychiatrists within living memory had no compunctions about expressing similar views.

Some key aspects of our sexual identity and orientation (including how flexible these are) seem to be wired into our developing brains even before we're born, as the next several chapters will show—though the underlying mechanisms are still poorly understood.[27] That's probably why "gay conversion" has so consistently failed, despite decades of attempts.

The "Bergonic chair," a World War I era device "for giving general electric treatment for psychological effect, in psycho-neurotic cases."

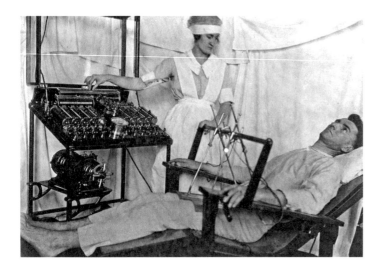

Conversion attempts haven't been limited to talk therapy. They have included hypnosis and aversion therapy—exposure to physical discomfort, pain, or traumatic stimuli. Of course if the intervention is blunt and drastic enough, sexuality, and other aspects of the self, can be damaged or broken. Castration[28] and so-called "chemical castration" have been used. Lobotomy was used frequently, as were electroshock treatments; a 1935 presentation to the APA noted that converting homosexuals required electroshock intensities "considerably higher than those usually employed on human subjects."[29]

In a particularly bizarre 1972 experiment by Robert Heath, the founder of Tulane University's Department of Psychiatry and Neurology, a gay 24-year-old who had been institutionalized for suicidal depression had electrodes implanted deep into his brain. These were stimulated, first prior to masturbating to heterosexual porn, then just before being coaxed into having sex with a female sex worker whom Heath had hired for the purpose and brought into the lab. According to one of the papers in which Heath published this "research" (amidst impressive but incomprehensible graphs of recorded brain activity before, during, and after orgasm), "the patient began active participation and achieved successful penetration, which culminated in a highly satisfactory orgasmic response, despite the milieu and the encumbrances of the lead wires to the electrodes."[30] Yikes!

27 Mbūgua, "Reasons to Suggest That the Endocrine Research on Sexual Preference Is a Degenerating Research Program," 2006.

28 Guy T. Olmstead underwent voluntary castration in 1894 to "overcome" his homosexuality, per Katz, *Gay American History: Lesbians and Gay Men in the U.S.A.; A Documentary*, 1976.

29 Katz, 252.

30 Heath, "Pleasure and Brain Activity in Man: Deep and Surface Electroencephalograms During Orgasm," 1972.

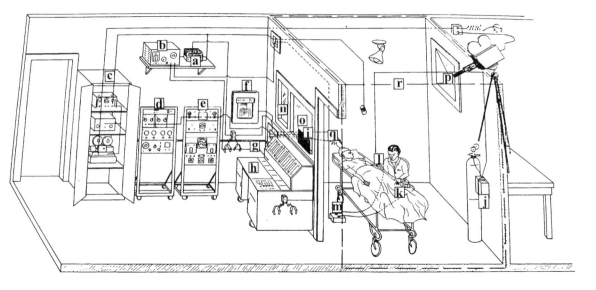

Diagram of Dr. Robert Galbraith Heath's lab at Tulane University showing the patient and instrument room, ca. 1954.

Importantly, Robert Heath, like Edmund Bergler, was not a fringe figure, nor was this, at the time, generally regarded as fringe science. Heath wrote 420 articles and 3 books, collaborated extensively, and chaired his department until his retirement in 1980, concluding a long research career. In 1985 Tulane awarded him an honorary doctorate and created an endowed lectureship and professorship in his honor.

As of this writing, the rather dusty website of The Robert Heath Society, the alumni association of the Tulane University School of Medicine Department of Psychiatry and Neurology, is still online.[31] In the Society's Spring 2005 newsletter, a "Historical Perspective" is offered under the heading "Robert G. Heath: 'A Perfect Gentleman.'" It begins, "Confucius said that the three virtues of a 'perfect gentleman' were wisdom, courage, and benevolence," and goes on to make the case for these qualities. His colleagues, it seems, remember him fondly.

31 "Robert Heath Society," 2013, http://www.heathsociety.org/.

Photographs of a patient who underwent Heath's Deep Brain Stimulation therapy for schizophrenia, showing the plastic headpiece with an electrode connector exposed (left) and with dressing (right), ca. 1954.

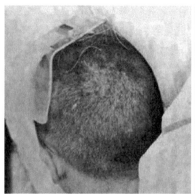
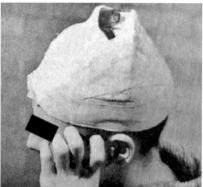

Modern human subject research protocols forbid such gruesome experiments, and as described in Chapter 2, the most prominent contemporary gay conversion programs have all imploded. However, we are still arguing about what is "natural" and what is not.

It's tempting to dismiss the entire teleological premise by affirming our humanism, our agency to do with our bodies anything we want, and "nature" be damned. We're not just animals! Our internal organs might perform their monotonous yet essential life-support functions, whether we will them to or not, but when it comes to behaviors we can consciously control, freedom and the human spirit prevail. In this view, our sex organs are "for" procreative sex no more or less than our hands are "for" picking fruit, squishing lice, or whatever else our ancestors did with them millions of years ago. Not everything has to have a "for" anymore. Evolution may have given us our bodies, but we're human precisely because we can do with them as we please. We get to choose our own lifestyle.

In its pure form, this argument isn't much more defensible than Stanton's moralizing, though. For one, the idea that we humans are so different from the rest of nature is dubious. If we have agency, so too, surely, do our close cousins the bonobos (or "pygmy chimpanzees," as they were once called), and they have lots of non-procreative sex, as well as engaging in frequent play and other humanlike activities. Homosexual behavior, too, is commonplace in other species.[32] Yet when we see nonhuman animals participating in such activities, we're unsatisfied with the individualistic justifications we reserve for ourselves—choice and pleasure—instead reaching for collective, functional explanations such as "troop bonding and cohesion," presuming that these are instinctive behaviors that must serve some larger evolutionary purpose. Indeed, when we look closely enough, we can often find one.

So do we choose how to behave, or is it chosen for us by our essential nature? Seemingly, we want to have it both ways. Modern liberal values are predicated on safeguarding our freedom to choose how to live. On the other hand, the lesbian, gay, and trans rights movements have at times been at pains to point out how *little* choice we have in our gender or sexual orientation—hence the failures of conversion therapy. How much sexual choice and freedom we each really have is a profound question with real-life implications. The survey data can offer some insight here.

[32] Bagemihl, *Biological Exuberance: Animal Homosexuality and Natural Diversity*, 2000.

7 Naturecultures of attraction

Natureculture: **a playful hybrid word,** coined by Donna Haraway, meaning "a synthesis of nature and culture that recognizes their inseparability in ecological relationships that are both biophysically and socially formed."[1] Just as urgently as we need to understand the inseparability of humanity from the rest of nature, we also need to understand that *human* nature and culture are inextricable.

1 Malone and Ovenden, "Natureculture," 2016.

What do the data have to say about the natureculture of sexual attraction? Let's begin with the basics. In 2015, the US Census estimated that only 3.8% of the population are LGBT, but for a variety of reasons—likely including concerns about anonymity—this number falls well short of reality. A 2017 Gallup poll found that 4.5% of adults in the US identify as LGBT—5.1% of women, and 3.9% of men.

7.0 **Heterosexuality and heteronormative attraction** % by age

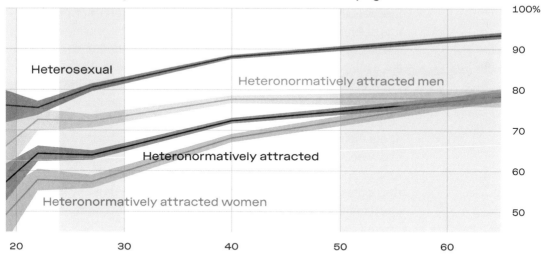

This "1 in 20" number has been widely cited, and is roughly comparable with the way older adults responded in the survey. However, looking across ages, a sharp decline in traditional heterosexuality is evident among the young. While nearly 95% of 65-year-olds report being heterosexual, only 76% of 19-year-olds do. This is an enormous change, and alarming to some: from 19 out of 20 at the older end to only 3 out of 4 young people!

This graph and others like it illustrate why it's so important to break such statistics down by age, and where possible, to use smaller age bins at the younger end of the scale, where the changes are often most rapid. Especially in highly developed countries like the US, the population is heavily skewed toward older people. Averages will thus be dominated by those older people and won't reveal how different the numbers are among the young. Yet arguably, the statistics of the young may tell us more about the shape of the future.

For younger women, it's not even clear that sexual and romantic attraction exclusively to men (which I'll abbreviate to "heteronormative attraction") is a majority at all. The data show heteronormative attraction among women falling all the way to 50%, with the error bars suggesting that the real number might be even lower. As a 29-year-old woman from Alpharetta, Georgia, wryly put it, "Nowadays, being heterosexual is in the minority. Just an observation." Although the numbers for men aren't quite so dramatic, a 58-year-old bemoaned that he was "VERY unusual. I am a male that was born a male and is heterosexual. You never [hear] of people like that anymore. No really."

You may find these numbers hard to believe, especially if you're over 40. For two obvious reasons, our intuitions can lead us astray. First, we tend to associate with people in our own age cohort. Second, unlike hair length or height, we can't generally tell someone's sexual orientation at a glance. Talking about it outside a close friendship can be socially taboo, and, as with handedness (but more so), a minority status generally carries stigma. These observations apply especially among older people, amounting to a recipe for rendering the minority invisible, much as for non-monogamy.

Still, in recent years, we've seen high-profile public debates about topics such as the legalization of same-sex marriage, the status of gay people in the military, and trans rights. It's easy, then, to see how someone in an older or more conservative cohort might harbor the impression that a lot of fuss is being kicked up by a tiny but vocal minority. Within such a cohort, even a person *belonging* to a minority might dramatically underestimate its prevalence, since they're likelier to be closeted and not know—or not *know* that they know—anyone else like them. This puts in context occasional comments like the following, from a 58-year-old in North Carolina:

Yes, I am normal. I just wanted to mention this to the researchers as this represents 97% of the general population. I think the Trans/gender fluid people blew their

wad and lost because of after 20 years of being beat over the head by the homosexual agenda, people are sick of the brain washing. I want the researchers to know just how normal [people] feel about this gender foolishness. These people are mentally retarded and they need to shut up and get out of everyone's face with their personal problems. People just want them to shut up and get out of the way. Enough of them and their idiocy. They are mentally ill people who need to be slapped back into their proper place of being and that is not catering to their stupidity and allowing these fools to set public policy. We don't care what they want. They should be institutionalized.

This jeremiad against the "homosexual agenda" ends with a cheery "Great survey.//Thanks." Hateful responses are less common, though, than bemusement or plain bewilderment, like that of a 63-year-old straight man from Pulaski, New York, attracted exclusively to women, who wrote, "I don't know exactly what many of these terms mean. I am a definite no on those. [N]othing that needed extra explaining thanks."

Despite overwhelming heterosexual majorities among older people, the "heteronormatively attracted" curve never goes above 80% at any age—that is, significant numbers of people, at all ages, identify as heterosexual but don't report being exclusively sexually and romantically attracted to the opposite sex.

7.1 **Not sexually attracted to anyone** % by age

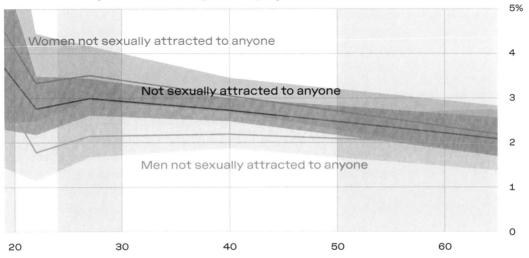

Some of them are not sexually attracted to either men or women. Though these numbers are comparatively small, they aren't negligible, amounting to about 3.5% among the young and gradually dropping to about 2% by age sixty.

While both the overall percentage and the difference between men and women shrink with age, notably more women than men report a lack of sexual attraction to anyone. A similar pattern holds for asexuality, meaning a low or absent sex drive.

7.2 **Asexuality** % by age

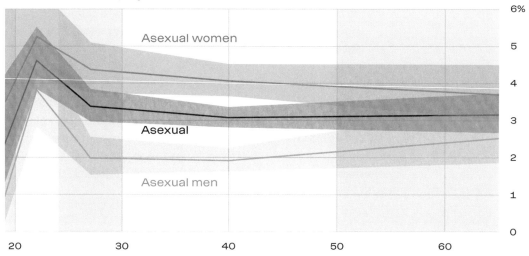

In this area as in some others, asexual respondents often express different views about whether they see their minority status as a medical abnormality, an identity, or somewhere in between. A 22-year-old woman from Illinois wrote of her asexuality, "I'm tired of people saying I'll grow out of it or thinking there's something wrong with me." Contrast her response with the way an asexual 27-year-old from Florida characterizes *her* asexuality as a dysfunction: "I have hormone issues and thus greatly reduced sex drive."

Of course it could be said that all of us have sexual urges influenced by our hormone levels, and our hormone levels can be welcome or prove inconvenient in any number of ways. We can believe our hormonal settings are normal or abnormal, wish they were different or embrace them, think of them as a malady or as part of our identity. There is no objectively right answer.

Evidently asexuality is less common—or, judging by the previous graph, less acknowledged—for the youngest cohort, even among those who don't find themselves attracted to anyone. Identifying the *absence* of something can be tricky for a young person, in that it's hard to distinguish not having the psychological or hormonal "circuitry" for strong sexual attraction from simply not having experienced it yet: "I think I'm asexual, but I don't even know."[2] Or, in the words of a 23-year-old woman from Michigan,

2 A 27-year-old woman.

> **I've identified myself as aromantic/asexual on this survey because I have never been attracted to anyone in my life. However, I am constantly questioning this and am unsure if this is influenced by my lifestyle/health issues, and if this will change in the future.**

For a 24-year-old from New York, this is precisely what happened:

> **If it's worth anything, I've mistaken myself for asexual. Turns out I'm just a late bloomer and I hate it. I mean, it feels good, but it's so much easier not having sex on my radar much at all.**

Asexuality peaks in the early twenties at about 4% of men and nearly 5% of women, then settles down to about 3% by age thirty. The gap between women and men is large between ages thirty and forty, though, when twice as many women report being asexual.

Multiple factors are in play here. Some older people lose interest in sex or romance, despite still thinking of themselves as heterosexual; their identity hasn't changed, but their drives have. As a woman from Oregon explained,

> **The older I get (67) I seem to feel less and less emphasis on how I look and more emphasis on how comfortable I am as in comfortable clothes, less fuss about how I look. Of course ones libido takes a hit after menopause, but for me that is not a great loss as my husband has lost his too due to illnesses and medications. One finds in old age that sexual orientation and its importance gives way to what matters in your life more such as love for life in general and those around you.**

A 70-year-old woman from East Hartford, Connecticut, put it more succinctly: "no longer interested in men or anyone in that way." On the other hand, younger people may identify as asexual despite having *some* sexual or romantic feelings, or engaging in sex:

3 A 23-year-old woman from Michigan.

> **I am asexual but have sexual relations with who I love/am in a relationship with. I do not have sexual urges though.[3]**

Like any other identity, asexuality is defined socially, based on the labels and norms of a peer group. These expectations change with age, and for a 23-year-old woman today, lacking sexual urges is notable, while for a 70-year-old, it may not be.

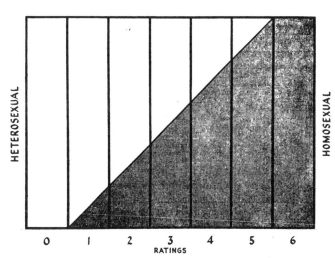

Figure 161. Heterosexual-homosexual rating scale

Based on both psychologic reactions and overt experience, individuals rate as follows:

0. Exclusively heterosexual with no homosexual
1. Predominantly heterosexual, only incidentally homosexual
2. Predominantly heterosexual, but more than incidentally homosexual
3. Equally heterosexual and homosexual
4. Predominantly homosexual, but more than incidentally heterosexual
5. Predominantly homosexual, but incidentally heterosexual
6. Exclusively homosexual

The Kinsey Scale, as first published in Kinsey et al., *Sexual Behavior in the Human Male*, 1948.

Interestingly, some young respondents identify as both asexual *and* as bi- or pan-sexual.[4] This can be confusing to those of us who think of sexuality in terms of a simple dial, with "gay" at one end, "straight" at the other end, and "bi or pan" somewhere in the middle. In the 1940s, pioneering sexologist Alfred Kinsey and his collaborators came up with just such a model, which came to be known as the Kinsey Scale. Even today, it's often invoked as a counterargument to the idea of attraction being binary, either strictly homosexual or heterosexual ("I'm around kinsey 4 lol," wrote a 20-year-old from Poquoson, Virginia). The Kinsey Scale may be the archetypal "spectrum."

Although more nuanced than a simple dichotomy, the model falls short in many ways. Even when gathering their data, Kinsey and collaborators found that they had to define a special off-scale category that they called "X"—which today we'd associate with asexuality. The need for the "X" category illustrates a problem with thinking about orientation one-dimensionally: being less attracted to the same sex does not automatically make you more attracted to the opposite sex, or vice versa. A two-dimensional sexual attraction scale, considering same-sex and opposite-sex attraction as independent variables, accounts for asexuality more naturally, and doesn't presume a zero-sum tradeoff between heterosexuality and homosexuality.[5]

Models are always simplifications, and they always smuggle in assumptions. Hence the two-dimensional picture, like any model, still remains incomplete (for instance, it presumes that same and opposite sexes can be clearly defined, which as I'll explore further in Chapter 11, isn't always the case), but at least it allows an asexual "X" to be placed on the map—somewhere near the lower left—rather than awkwardly

4   Pansexuality is a more recent term for attraction to all people regardless of gender.

5   Something close to this idea was also proposed by Anne Hale, Lindsay B. Miller, and Jason Weaver in their paper "The Dual Scales of Sexual Orientation," 2019.

Sketch of a 2D sexual attraction scale, showing how asexuality and bisexuality can be modeled as a continuum.

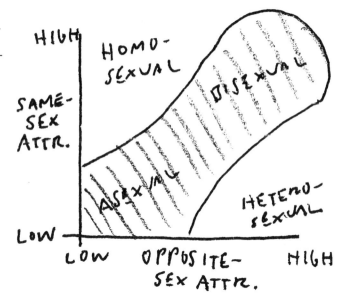

off it. The model also reveals the way asexuality and bisexuality can be regarded as a continuum, ranging from the lower left to the upper right. Describing his position near the asexual end of this continuum, a 39-year-old from Moorhead, Minnesota, wrote,

> **I could very easily see myself as registering as either asexual—which is a thing, or possibly pan. It's not quite as clear cut as all that. I don't really have a preference, except that I'd rather avoid sex altogether.**

Both the Kinsey Scale and its more nuanced two-dimensional cousin fall short in assuming a person can be pinned down to a fixed point on the map. Even setting aside daily ups and downs, life is long, and for most people, sexual attraction waxes and eventually wanes; a life is better described as a trajectory than as a fixed point.

How we identify tends to remain more stable than our actual feelings or behaviors, though. There's social value in maintaining (and presenting) a consistent self-concept, independent of time, place or context—especially in WEIRD societies—even if that self-concept is at odds with facts on the ground.[6] Given the stigma of asexuality as a minority identity, it's unsurprising, then, that many older people with little or no libido don't identify as asexual, or, indeed, as anything other than "normal"—so, usually, heterosexual.

Presumed heterosexuality by default also holds for many older women despite non-heteronormative impulses or inner lives, even if unrealized or long-buried. A 67-year-old woman from Mohawk, New York, reminisced,

6   By contrast, many non-WEIRD societies put greater emphasis on social adaptability, as they value relationships above individuals. Henrich, Heine, and Norenzayan, "The Weirdest People in the World?," 2010.

I have had sexual relationships with women three times when I was in college, but I don't know if that qualifies me as bisexual or not? It hasn't happened since.

In another characteristic comment, a 41-year-old woman from Salt Lake City wrote,

I am married and only recently realized an attraction to women, also. Wonder if religion of my upbringing held that part of me back and so I never really experimented.

A couple on a porch in Germantown, New York, 1977.

The frequency with which women, especially, express these feelings when asked anonymously is a topic I'll return to in the next chapter.

In addition to sexual attraction, the survey also asks questions about romantic attraction. Although they're often in alignment, sexual and romantic attraction work differently for some people. The breakdown of romantic attraction by age and gender certainly looks very different from sexual attraction.

As with lack of sexual attraction, the numbers converge to roughly 2% for older respondents, but at younger ages a lack of romantic interest is far more prevalent among men—rising above 12% for

7.3 **Not romantically attracted to anyone** % by age

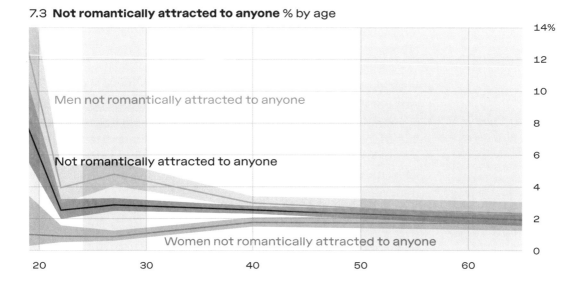

the youngest men. Men appear to become more interested in romance as they get older, while women become less so.

Differences like these between younger and older people can be explained in two very different ways: as an effect of the respondent's age at the time of the survey—let's call this the "age hypothesis"—or as an effect of their generation—the "era hypothesis." According to the age hypothesis, any variations are a function purely of the respondent's age, so if the survey were run again in 20 years, the resulting graph would look exactly the same. As a 57-year-old from Cold Brook, New York, put it,

We were once the younger generation and some of us were wild and crazy but not all. In so many ways the different generations are more alike than people want to believe.

Lovers, date unknown.

The age hypothesis can be thought of as the "nature" end of natureculture. It's hard to imagine it doesn't apply at least to some degree, and for some variables. For instance, declines in sex drive over time must be at least partly due to the biology of aging, and intuitively, it seems likely that young men have always been more interested in sex than in romance.[7]

The era hypothesis, on the other hand, would hold that each individual's response to a survey question will remain constant as they age—in which case, if someone were to rerun the same survey with respondents drawn from the same population in 2040, the whole graph would shift to the right by 20 years, alongside a new cohort of younger respondents on the left with potentially different answers (and a vanishing cohort on the right who are no longer among the living). The era hypothesis is also the expected behavior for variables one might assume correspond to some essential, changeless property of an individual's body, identity, or personality, such as race, gender, or sexual orientation.

It's impossible to disentangle age and era effects by looking only at the kinds of graphs shown so far. Making that distinction requires measuring responses over time as well as across ages.

Unfortunately, I don't have 20-year-old survey data— I was barely out of college 20 years ago, and my research interests were very different back then. However, I've been working on this project long enough to have been able to run the gender and sexuality survey four times at yearly intervals, in December 2018, December 2019, December 2020, and December 2021.

7 The age hypothesis *doesn't* imply that individuals of a given age are all the same; they vary, and for an individual, often there will be strong correlations over time. For instance, someone who is tall for their age at 18 will probably still be tall for their age at 80; height is nonetheless a variable that follows the age hypothesis perfectly in the survey data.

The research still covers a relatively short period, and can only provide a local, noisy window on long-term trends. We may also be in a period of unusually rapid historical change. Nonetheless, the results are interesting. For variables like height and weight, the data precisely follow the age hypothesis, with the 2018, 2019, 2020, and 2021 curves plotting these variables as a function of age lying right on top of each other (see the Appendix for examples).

I should note here that Mechanical Turk allows the experimenter to create and assign "qualifications" to workers, as well as offering an option to specify qualification requirements for performing a task. By assigning a qualification to everyone who took the survey in a given year, I was able to screen out those respondents in subsequent years; that is, Mechanical Turk did not offer them the survey if they'd already taken it in a previous year. Hence the 2018, 2019, 2020, and 2021 cohorts don't overlap.[8] Nonetheless, I was able to verify that, even if the *individual* respondents each year were all different, the basic demographics of the population they were drawn from remained the same. Put another way, demographic variables behaved according to the age hypothesis.[9]

So, upon comparing heteronormative attraction over these four years, do responses look like (a) a pure function of age, or (b) a pure function of historical era? Or, perhaps, (c) a mixture of the two? For many variables, including heteronormative attraction, the answer turns out to be a surprise: (d), none of the above.

To simplify comparison, I've combined the 2018 and 2019 data into one pool, and the 2020 and 2021 data into another, as well as using coarser age bins. This way, the graphs allow comparisons between two curves with smaller error bars, rather than four curves with larger ones.

8 "Cheating" is possible. Workers are anonymous and can make up multiple identities, using them to bypass this mechanism. I didn't find evidence of this occurring any statistically significant number of times, though. Workers on Mechanical Turk generally unlock tasks by acquiring qualifications, reaching milestones, and earning good reputations, which tends to disincent switching identities.

9 As shown in the Appendix, age *itself* also follows the age hypothesis, meaning that the age distribution of Mechanical Turk workers is stable from one year to the next.

7.4 Heteronormative attraction in 2018–19 and 2020–21 % by age

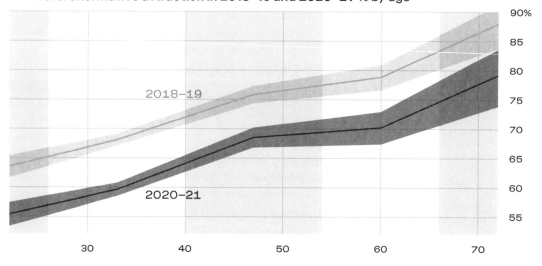

Evidently, heteronormativity across age ranges is significantly lower in 2020–21 than it was in the previous two years, 2018–19. Incidentally, this suggests another reason the literature tends to overestimate heteronormativity in the US. Since survey data are always historical, their numbers—along with our perceptions—lag reality on the ground. The question is, how fast is that reality changing? The answer: *very* fast.

Keep in mind that *any* change over time is incompatible with the age hypothesis, which would hold that lower heteronormativity among the young is just about *being* young (i.e., perhaps experimenting or questioning more, before "figuring it out"). However, the data are *also* incompatible with the era hypothesis, which would predict that the 2020–21 curve ought to look like the 2018–19 curve shifted rightward by two years.

So, it's not (a) or (b). What about (c)? That can't be the case either, because if the data merely showed a mixture of age and era effects, one would expect to see a rightward shift over this period somewhere between the zero years predicted by the age hypothesis and the two years predicted by the era hypothesis. Instead, the 2018–19 curve would need to shift to the right by *almost two decades* to lie on top of the 2020–21 curve. The curves look consistent with a version of the era hypothesis in which time itself is fast-forwarding by nearly 10x! Seen another way, it looks more like the 2020–21 curve is a downward-shifted version of the 2018–19 curve, rather than a rightward-shifted one. What could this mean?

For one, it means that any preconceptions one might have about the essential or unchanging nature of people's responses to questions like these—about same- and opposite-sex attraction—are wrong. In fact, it's very difficult to find *any* questions relating to identity or behavior where the slow rightward shift predicted by the era hypothesis actually holds. Yes, the youngest people are different from year to year, but older people are changing their answers over time too, presumably in response to a changing social environment. Natureculture, indeed.

The data offer strong evidence of an effect sometimes referred to in the social sciences as "social contagion," although the term of art is unfortunate. I prefer "social transmission," since "contagion" connotes disease, whereas our human ability to learn from and be influenced by others throughout life is hardly pathological. Beyond its obvious negative connotations, "contagion" as a metaphor revives the old trope of "sexual deviance" and provides cover for new incarnations of "conversion therapy." As legal scholar Kenji Yoshino has written in a widely cited *Yale Law Journal* article,

Even as the concept of homosexuality as a literal disease (i.e., a mental disorder) waned, a concept of homosexuality as a figurative disease (i.e., a disfavored social condition that was contagious) remained. [...] The metaphorical contagion model captures a fundamental fear about homosexuality [...]. Whether framed as contagion, as recruitment, as seduction, or as role-modeling, the fundamental fear about homosexuality is the apocalyptic "fear of a queer planet," the fear that homosexuality can spread without being spread thin.

Because it so closely tracks popular fears, the contagion model has proved an extremely effective anti-gay rhetorical device. The utility of this conception of homosexuality is that it figures homosexuals as themselves engaging in a kind of conversion therapy, converting wavering individuals into gays.[10]

10 Yoshino, "Covering," 2002.

Even as we reject the metaphors of "disease" and "contagion," however, we should acknowledge that human beings do continually influence each other's beliefs, behaviors, and identities through their social networks. That's how culture works; it is, in the words of Joseph Henrich, "the secret of our success" as a species.[11] While the effect is often strongest among the young, perhaps because their uncertainty, plasticity, or susceptibility to changing social inputs is highest, social transmission is evident at all ages. We influence each other all the time, even when it comes to traits most people consider "essential."

To return briefly to the previous chapter's topic, a similar pattern is evident in the shift away from monogamy between 2018–19

11 Which isn't to say that culturally transmitted ideas are always good ones; this book documents many ideas strongly held by experts over the past two centuries that most of us would abhor today.

7.5 **Monogamy in 2018–19 and 2020–21** % by age

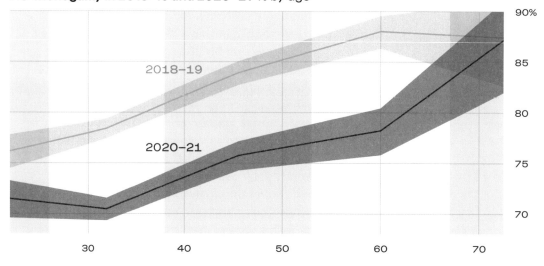

and 2020–21 (though here, younger people may be reaching a lower plateau at about 70%; given the error bars, more years of observation will be needed).

The shift across this two year gap would correspond to even more than two decades of change under the era hypothesis. Much like the decline in heteronormativity, the decline in monogamy (one might call it "Morning Glory's Prophecy") can be attributed to rises in a number of alternative models and behaviors, all of which chip away at the historical norm.

Such rapid change highlights the power of modern human sociality as a kind of accelerated evolutionary engine. Consider: the era hypothesis can be understood as an upper limit on the speed of *genetic* evolution, since once we're born, we're stuck with the genes we have.[12] Generational turnover is also a limit on the speed of most learning in traditional societies, which typically involves younger people learning from their elders during a period of apprenticeship. While this allows humans to evolve skills and accumulate knowledge far in excess of our genetic inheritance, it does not allow us to break the generational speed limit.

When we become lifelong learners, though, and especially when older people can learn new tricks from the young, generational turnover no longer constrains the rate of cultural evolution. Urbanization, cafes, journals and newspapers, TV, the web, social media, and many other features of modern life seem almost tailor-made to boost cultural evolution both within and across age cohorts.

12 In reality evolution is much slower, since factors like mutation rate limit how much a generation can differ genetically from the previous one.

13 The dynamics of human population growth and decline will be explored in much more detail in Part III.

14 There are still hungry people in the world. However, as the statistics in Chapter 18 will show, the number of people for whom caloric shortfalls limit survival has been falling steeply for many decades, and now represents a relatively small minority. In many places, though—including "food deserts" in otherwise developed countries, like the US—the most readily available calories come from fast food or junk food. Starvation is rare, but diabetes is prevalent.

A comment on evolution is in order here. Remember the survey respondent I quoted at the beginning of this book, both bigoted and perhaps honestly alarmed by this same trend, writing, "What would happen to a animal species that went gay, I'll tell you, they would all go extinct." While my own feeling is that unbounded exponential population growth[13] is a greater threat to human survival—hence, if many of us did indeed "go gay" (or at least stop reproducing) now, we'd be *improving* our collective odds—there's a valid observation lurking under the surface here.

Prodigious social transmission, together with intense competition between societies at every scale for thousands of years, has certainly boosted human fitness in the Darwinian sense; so much so that we've now achieved something like escape velocity from Planet Darwin. With plummeting mortality among the young and calories cheaply available, individual survival no longer depends so much on individual Darwinian fitness.[14]

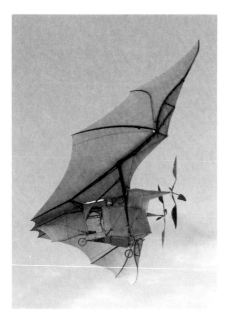

Ader Avion III, an experimental steam-powered monoplane designed and built by Clément Ader between 1892 and 1897, France.

→ The Concorde's maiden flight, Fairford, Gloucestershire, England, April 10, 1969.

15 Blackmore, *The Meme Machine*, 2000.

16 Blackmore's use of the word "meme" long predates internet memes, though they, too, undergo something like an evolutionary process, complete with Margulis-style symbiosis as images are colonized and repurposed by words, or vice versa.

Nonetheless, the mechanisms of accelerated cultural evolution are still busily at work, tinkering with our sexuality along with our politics, our languages, our diet, our technologies, and everything else. Susan Blackmore, in her book *The Meme Machine*,**15** has referred to ideas that propagate as "memes," by analogy with genes, hence to this process as "memetic evolution."**16** It operates much faster than genetic evolution, and has a far larger palette of tools to work with: consider how long it took genetic evolution to develop flight, compared with how long it took us to invent airplanes, then evolve them into a Cambrian explosion of flying machines of all sizes and shapes.

This brings us in a full circle back to the question posed by the previous chapter: how "rational" are genetic and cultural evolution, really? We've already seen the dangers of teleology, which can cut both ways here.

Conservative people often argue that evolution, i.e. "nature," is inherently rational because only the fit survive, while cultural evolution, unfettered by the survival imperative, is prone to all sorts of irrational excesses. Those making this argument tend to be reacting to a cultural development they disapprove of, whether recreational drugs, gay nightclubs, women's colleges, or selfie sticks—in general, urban-first trends. Recall the phrenologist S.R. Wells from Chapter 6, for example, who railed against the "unphysiological habits and pernicious systems of education so prevalent at the present day, especially in cities," subverting the "natural order of development."

From the progressive or techno-optimistic perspective, the emphasis is instead on how humanity can now engineer rationally, correcting the arbitrariness (and, often, cruelty) of nature. Hence such wonders as: Braille, surgery to correct cleft palates, antibiotics, transfusions, birth control, and perhaps eventually, full editorial control over our own genome. It would be nice to edit out Huntington's disease, sickle cell anemia, and other obviously undesirable legacies. Maybe that will mark the start of a takeover of genetic evolution *by* cultural evolution!

Looking dispassionately at these mirror-image arguments, it becomes clear that they both cherry-pick "rational" and "irrational" examples based on appeals to personal taste or values. Further, "rationality" isn't particularly objective, no matter which way you slice natureculture.

Arguing that cultural evolution is always "rational" neglects the overwhelming number of cultural developments that really don't serve some grand purpose. (If you insist on defending the utility of the selfie stick, try doing the same for the Tide pod challenge.[17])

But the same is true of genes; consider the beautiful but absurd peacock's tail, or the fact that vertebrate retinas are inexplicably wired back-to-front, requiring that our visual systems Photoshop out the big blind spots and nests of blood vessels we're peering through.[18] In short, though genetic evolution is slow, the idea that it works "rationally" seems dubious. If it were, much of the strangeness, beauty, and impracticality of nature—its orchids, sea dragons, and peacock tails—would be far more utilitarian. And that would make the world a drab place.

17 To readers of the future who may be (blessedly) ignorant of this ephemeral craze: in 2017, US Poison Control Centers fielded over ten thousand calls about children chomping on concentrated dishwasher detergent pods, due in part to social media "challenges" encouraging the gullible to eat them. Chokshi, "Yes, People Really Are Eating Tide Pods. No, It's Not Safe," 2018.

18 Octopus eyes evolved independently, and they got it right, with the photoreceptors in front and the rest of the machinery behind. Serb and Eernisse, "Charting Evolution's Trajectory: Using Molluscan Eye Diversity to Understand Parallel and Convergent Evolution," 2008.

An adult male mandarin duck.

Female flexibility

Over the past fifty years, there's been an explosion of gender and sexual minorities—lesbian, gay, bi, trans, queer, questioning, asexual, aromantic, and many more.

The LGBTQ+ rainbow is, unsurprisingly, most embraced by the young, more than a quarter of whom claim at least one of those letters. Even among older respondents, though, the survey suggests that significantly more people identify with a sexual minority than commonly cited statistics suggest.[1] The changes are especially dramatic among women. In this chapter, I'll explore why that might be.

Before proceeding, though, a word about methodology and the slipperiness of definitions. As in the handedness analysis in Part I, "women" and "female" are used here as shorthand for those who answer "yes" to "Do you identify as female?" and "no" to "Do you identify as male?"; vice versa for "men." This is not intended to suggest logical equivalence. We can be sure that, had the survey additionally asked "Are you a woman?," a "yes" would usually—but not always—have been answered the same way as "Are you female?"

1   The National Bureau of Economic Research has concluded that the non-heterosexual population has been significantly underestimated in surveys using traditional questioning methods, even if anonymous. Coffman, Coffman, and Ericson, "The Size of the LGBT Population and the Magnitude of Antigay Sentiment Are Substantially Underestimated," 2017.

8.0 LGBTQ identification, broken down by some of its subpopulations % by age

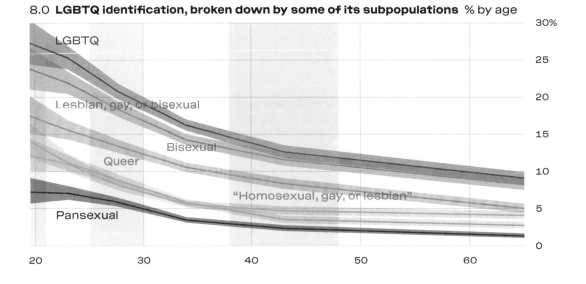

Due to that "not always," we can't make assumptions about individuals without running roughshod over an excluded middle.

However, it's still possible to meaningfully analyze differences between *populations*. The statistical findings distinguishing "men" from "women" in this book aren't sensitive to the choice of criterion, because the excluded middle between these two populations remains a minority, as Chapter 14 will show. Graphs based on pronoun use, for example, look much the same. With appropriate care, inferences about populations can be made reliably, even if they're based on approximate or noisy working definitions.

This statistical approach remains robust even when language and categories are a great deal blurrier. Much of Part III will be about population-level differences between people living in cities and in rural areas; with so many Americans living in the suburbs and so little standardization in terminology, this classification is hardly precise or binary. (Is Parker, Pennsylvania, population 695 according to the 2020 Census, really, per its official designation, a "city"?) Yet those differences can still be quantified and studied by focusing on changes as a function of a correlated variable—such as population density based on ZIP code, or self-reported answers to questions like "Do you live in the city?" Moreover, exploring these effects doesn't require any commitment to rigid definitions of words like "city" or "rural."

Now, let's dive in.

Bisexuality, despite its frequent invisibility, accounts for well over half of the rainbow, over all ages. Women, in turn, make up the majority of the bisexual population, especially among the young.

Graphing female and male bisexuality separately reveals a striking difference. Roughly 5% of men are bisexual, with only modest variation by age. Among women, though, the variability is extraordinary. Nearly 34% of 19-year-old women are bi (about 1 in 3), but by age 66 it's only about 2.15% (1 in 46). There are, in other words, about 15 times more 19-year-old bisexual women than 66-year-old bisexual women. Further, 4 out of 5 bisexual 19-year-olds are women, while only 1 in 3 bisexual 66-year-olds are.

What to make of this? Thinking in terms of the Kinsey Scale, one might imagine that women are on average closer to the middle than men, that is, "more bisexual"; but this wouldn't explain why there's such an impressive *change* in women's bisexuality as a function of age. In theory, this change could be age-related; perhaps something about women's physiology, more so than men's, changes as they age?

Remember, this "age hypothesis" is testable simply by comparing the 2018–19 data with the 2020–21 data. Although the error bars are large, the percentages appear to be in flux, which isn't consistent with the age hypothesis.

8.1 **Bisexuality accounts for over half of the LGBTQ population** % by age

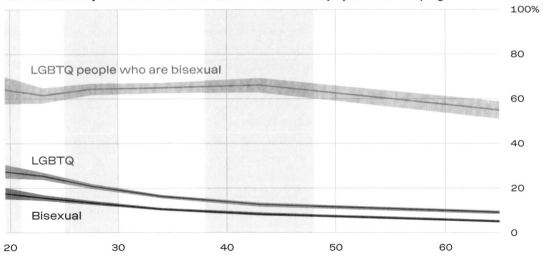

8.2 **Bisexuality in women and men** % by age

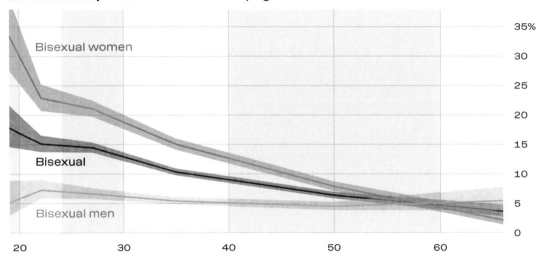

Among women across a wide range of ages, bisexuality has risen by somewhere between 1% and 4%—probably a significant change, but not dramatic. A rise in bisexuality is also evident among men across all ages. Although the absolute increase is only a bit larger, it's *much* larger in relative terms, since fewer men are bisexual to begin with; around age 45, a 5% change has amounted to a *doubling* in the number of bisexual men.

Here are four potential factors explaining the discrepancy between bisexuality in women and in men:

1   Maybe women are more flexible in their sexual attraction than men, resulting in a far greater proportion of younger women identifying as bisexual.

8.3.0 **Bisexuality in 2018–19 and 2020–21** % by age

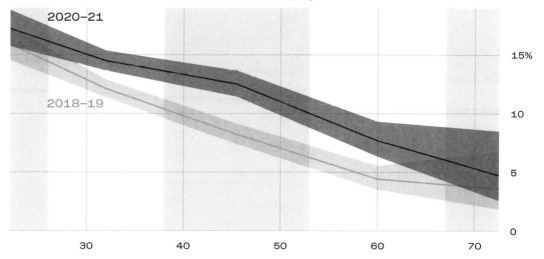

8.3.1 **Bisexuality among women in 2018–19 and 2020–21** % by age

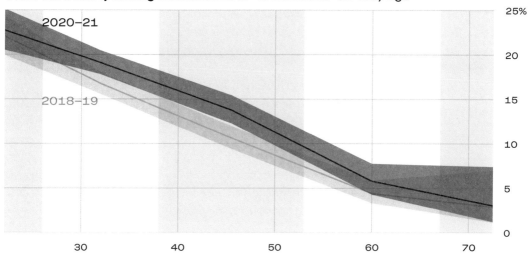

8.3.2 **Bisexuality among men in 2018–19 and 2020–21** % by age

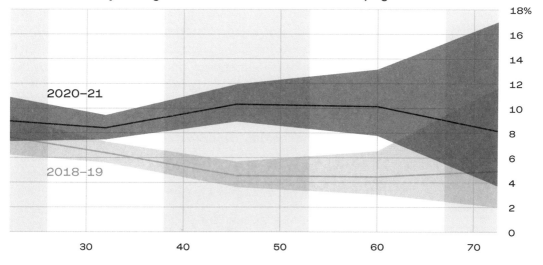

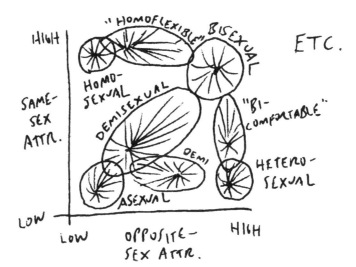

Sketch of a 2D sexual attraction scale, where a person's "default position" is a point, and the region around the point illustrates their "flexibility."

2   Maybe male bisexuality carries a greater stigma than female bisexuality at *all* ages, resulting in only a fraction of potentially bisexual men acknowledging their bisexuality—though over time, the stigma for men is decreasing. Absent uneven stigma, the curves for women and for men might look more alike.

3   Maybe, even if women aren't inherently more flexible than men, they have been forced to compromise more—that is, exercise whatever flexibility they have—especially in the past, due to social and economic disadvantage.

4   Maybe female sexuality as a whole has been systematically devalued, especially in the past, resulting in lower expectations of sexual attraction and pleasure.

2 This isn't an exhaustive list of potential factors, just the ones for which I have evidence based on the survey data. For example, it's also conceivable that sexual attraction varies more as a function of age in women than in men for physiological reasons (to be clear: no evidence I'm aware of supports this idea).

Evidence supports all four factors.**2** This chapter focuses on sexual flexibility and stigma—numbers one and two above—since the techniques I've introduced offer several ways to see these effects, and the implications are both interesting and wide-ranging. In particular, sexual flexibility bears on the question of essential nature versus "lifestyle choice"—that is, free will—broached in the previous chapter. The next chapter will delve into the third and fourth factors, exploring gender asymmetries in the role of economics and in societal expectations about sexual fulfillment.

Flexibility cannot be fully described using a single point on the one-dimensional Kinsey Sscale, or even the two-dimensional "Kinsey diagram"—yet another limitation of those models. The 2D model can be extended, though, to imagine a person as being tethered to a "home position" on the diagram by a spring, which might be tight or loose, or perhaps even loose in one direction (say, attraction to the same sex) but tight along another (say, attraction to the opposite sex). A highly flexible person may live in an entire fuzzy region of the Kinsey diagram.

Most people seem to have *some* flexibility in their sexual "wiring," allowing them to adapt to varying environments. Studies have documented this kind of flexibility, for example, among otherwise heterosexual men in prisons, on naval ships, and under other prolonged single-sex living conditions.[3] It's also common for gay and lesbian people to have a history of early opposite-sex relationships before coming out, and while those early relationships may not have been entirely satisfying, they imply some flexibility too.

The survey comments include many accounts of sexual flexibility, but, as the numbers also show, they're a lot more frequent among women, regardless of whether they identify as straight, lesbian, bi or pan, or otherwise:

> **There were a couple questions that may seem contradictory, to clarify: I am both hetero and bi, a little bit… Meaning I'm not like fully bisexual because it's only a physical attraction towards women sometimes. I would consider myself more "bi-comfortable" than bisexual, if that makes sense.[4]**

> **I have had homosexual and bisexual experiences and attractions to women in the past. I consider myself heterosexual, but could change my mind if the right woman came along.[5]**

> **I am mostly lesbian, but once in a blue moon I am attracted to a man. It doesn't happen often enough for me to consider myself bisexual, but it happens.[6]**

One implication is that many women with male partners (including ones who think of themselves as straight) easily could have been bisexual or pansexual, or even lesbian, had they grown up without the pressure to conform to heteronormative expectations—reminiscent of the way many people whose behaviors suggest they're ambiguously handed seem to have taken the path of least resistance to become right-handed. Comments from 20- to 40-year-old women offer many examples:

> **I am a slightly closeted bisexual woman who is happily married to a man.[7]**

> **I consider myself bisexual because I am attracted to both men and women, but I've only ever dated men.[8]**

3 Hensley and Tewksbury, "Inmate-to-Inmate Prison Sexuality: A Review of Empirical Studies," 2002.

4 A 29-year-old woman from Bargersville, Indiana.

5 A 40-year-old woman from Dallas, Texas.

6 A 37-year-old woman from Austin, Texas.

7 A 26-year-old woman from Eureka Springs, Arkansas.

8 A 39-year-old woman from Pittsburgh, Pennsylvania.

9 A 34-year-old woman from Thomson, Georgia.

10 A 29-year-old woman from Huntersville, North Carolina.

11 A 21-year-old woman from Rensselaer, New York.

12 A 34-year-old woman from Winnetka, California.

13 A 35-year-old woman.

14 A 36-year-old woman from Westland, Michigan.

I'm bisexual, married to a man, living a hetero-normative life.[9]

Bisexual but in a heterosexual partnership.[10]

Bisexual, don't show it much.[11]

Closeted bisexual.[12]

I guess I could be classified as bisexual because I am physically attracted to women. But have never acted on it and doubt I ever will.[13]

I don't identify as bisexual, but find myself attracted to women.[14]

These sentiments are so common, it can almost make one wonder whether *truly* exclusively opposite-sex attracted women might be a rarity, as one less flexible 33-year-old from Kennesaw, Georgia, wryly points out:

> **It seems like everyone is so touchy [nowadays] about their sexuality, and it [seems] like women are supposed to be attracted to other women. but I'm not, [it's] almost confusing.**

This comment implicitly observes that, as with other sexual minorities, same-sex attraction and bisexuality are much less stigmatized now than they used to be—especially for women, among young people, and (as Part III will show) in cities. A 38-year-old woman in San Francisco, a city famous for its progressive attitude to sex, celebrated this in her response, writing,

> **I was born female and have always identified as a heterosexual woman. But I am very blessed to live in a city/community that is the most diverse, open, and beautiful in this world and I feel so very lucky to live [in] a place where everyone is allowed to be who they truly are in every sense.**

It's still worth remembering that this isn't always the felt reality, though. A fellow resident demurred,

> **I consider myself heterosexual because I don't want to deal with being gay or bisexual in our current society, but every once in a while I'll be attracted to another woman. I suppose that could make me bisexual then, but I don't really consider myself that.**

Given these are the sentiments of a 32-year-old woman who also lives in San Francisco, it's easy to imagine that for an older man in a more conservative rural ZIP code, the closet is still the norm.

The recent and contentious idea of "demisexuality" can be understood as another manifestation of sexual flexibility. Per Wikipedia,

Painting for *Cosmo*, 1971, by Frank McCarthy.

> The term 'demisexual' comes from the concept being described as being "halfway between" sexual and asexual. [...] A demisexual person does not experience sexual attraction until they have formed a strong emotional connection with a prospective partner. The definition of "emotional bond" varies from person to person. Demisexuals can have any romantic orientation. People in the asexual spectrum communities often switch labels throughout their lives, and fluidity in orientation and identity is a common attitude.[15]

The apparent vagueness of demisexuality as a phenomenon or identity has attracted a certain amount of ridicule in some quarters, especially considering the ever-lengthening "alphabet soup" of finely parsed LGBTQ+ identities. Is a lack of lust for anyone you haven't bonded with emotionally really a sexual minority deserving of a letter, like being lesbian or gay—or is it just, to use a contentious word, "normal"? On the other side of the coin, some feminist critics argue that demisexuality whiffs of a patriarchal fantasy: a woman being reluctantly wooed by a man, awakening sexually to her suitor only once she has been "made" to fall in love. Whichever way one feels about such stories, it's undeniable that they sell—and men aren't the main audience.

More to the point, though, claiming that there's no such thing as demisexuality is a stretch when so many people *say* that they're demisexual: between 2% and 5% of men, and between 5% and 10% of women. To assert that one "doesn't believe in" demisexuality is like saying one "doesn't believe in" ambidexterity, whether because vanishingly few people are "truly" ambidextrous or because nearly all of us are, a little bit. Here, as elsewhere, we should listen to what people are telling us about themselves, and follow the data where it leads.

Recall that asexuality is more common among women than men. I've also hypothesized that women tend to be, on average, more flexible in their sexuality than men. So, it's unsurprising to find that

15 Wikipedia, "Gray asexuality," 2021.

8.4 **Demisexuality in women and men** % by age

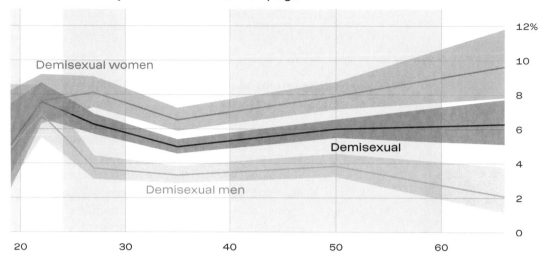

demisexuality is more common among women too, since demisexuality can be thought of as an asexual anchor point along with a high degree of flexibility. This is consistent with the usual self-description of people who identify as demisexual: asexual by default, but able to become *more* sexual under the "right" circumstances, and with the "right" partner.

The way asexuality and bisexuality are neighbors on the 2D Kinsey diagram might also shed light on why demisexual people are often fluid in their orientation. For example, a 27-year-old woman from Batavia, New York, wrote, "I identify as demisexual and have only had relationships with men, but that doesn't mean I'd be opposed to a relationship with a woman."

In comparing the percentage of women who are lesbian with the percentage of men who are gay, more evidence emerges of greater sexual flexibility among women and also, perhaps, of greater stigma among same-sex attracted men.

Notice that the percentage of men who are gay at different ages only varies by a bit over a factor of two, from a high of 10% around age 22 to a low of 4–5% among the youngest and the oldest adults in the sample. It's reasonable to suppose that about 5% of men are so unambiguously gay that they identify that way regardless of which generation they belong to, which is to say, despite the inexperience of younger men, and the greater stigma experienced by older men. It seems that an additional 5% or so of young men who don't identify as gay at age 19 decide that they are by their early twenties, which suggests a greater degree of flexibility among this group; in earlier generations, when the stigma was stronger, many of them likely would never have identified as gay.

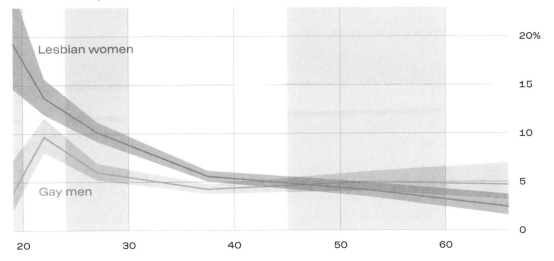

8.5 **Percentages of women who are lesbian and of men who are gay** % by age

Lesbian women

Gay men

20%

15

10

5

0

20   30   40   50   60

By contrast, lesbians only comprise about 2.5% of 66-year-old women (1 in 40). Yet among young women, lesbian identification rises to 20% (1 in 5), a factor of *eight* higher! The curious result is that older lesbians are half as common as older gay men, while 19-year-old lesbians are four times *more* common than 19-year-old gay men.

Comparing the proportion of gay men who are exclusively same-sex attracted[16] with the proportion of lesbian women who are exclusively same-sex attracted reveals further evidence supporting the case for women being more flexible.

16 These calculations are based on both sexual and romantic attraction. Exclusive same-sex attraction here means "yes" to both sexual and romantic attraction to the same sex, and "no" to the opposite sex. As in other plots where numbers are broken down by binary gender, people whose gender identification is ambiguous are left out of the analysis.

Only 25% or so of young lesbians are *exclusively* same-sex attracted, implying some combination of sexual flexibility and a broader umbrella for lesbian identity, as one would expect given lower stigma nowadays. Among the (much smaller) population of 66-year-old lesbians, though, nearly 90% are exclusively same-sex attracted; most of them presumably felt no ambiguity or flexibility, and would have had the greatest trouble conforming to heterosexual expectations in a repressive environment. (Many, in fact, grew up in just such an environment.) On the other hand, a majority of gay men of all ages, roughly 60–80%, are exclusively same-sex attracted, with the lowest proportion around age 22, coinciding with the peak in gay male identification.

Recall, from the graphs at the end of Part I of this book, that percentages of women and men who are exclusively same-sex attracted show far less variability, both by age and by gender, than the percentages identifying as lesbian and gay. Even in the same-sex attraction graphs, though, there's some evidence of greater female flexibility; the range for exclusive same-sex attraction among women varies from a low of about 2.5% above age 50 up to nearly 6% at age

8.6.0 Lesbian and gay people who are exclusively same-sex attracted % by age

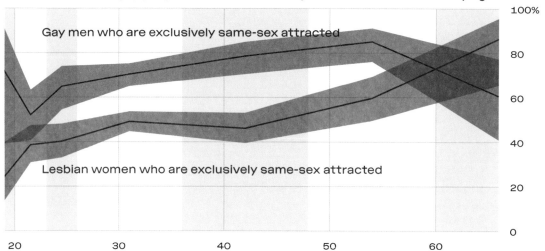

Gay men who are exclusively same-sex attracted

Lesbian women who are exclusively same-sex attracted

8.6.1 Lesbian and exclusively same-sex attracted women % by age

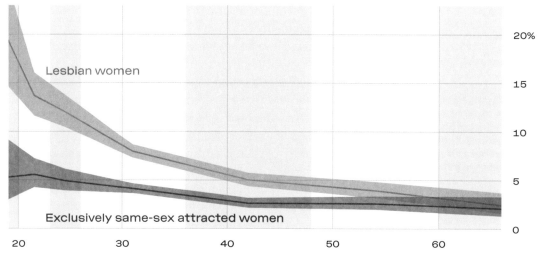

Lesbian women

Exclusively same-sex attracted women

8.6.2 Gay and exclusively same-sex attracted men % by age

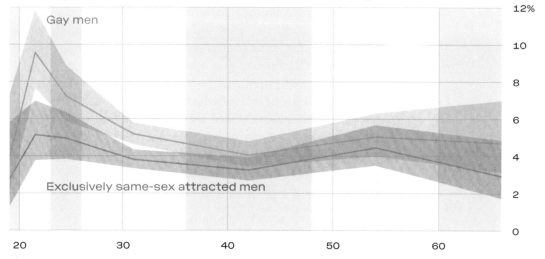

Gay men

Exclusively same-sex attracted men

8.7 **Exclusively same-sex attracted men and women** % by age

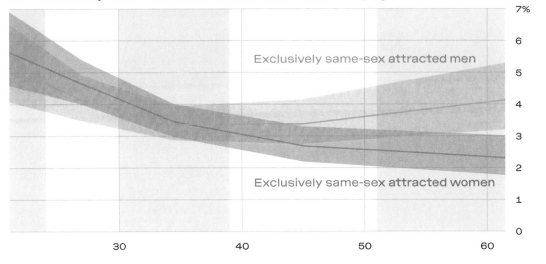

Exclusively same-sex attracted men

Exclusively same-sex attracted women

21 (a 2.4x difference), whereas among men it doesn't vary as much by age, ranging from about 3.5% to about 5% (a 1.4x difference).

Under the age of 40, the percentages of exclusively same-sex attracted women and men look very similar. This is interesting in that it suggests far less of a difference between male and female same-sex attraction once we look beyond the evolving meanings (and differing stigmas) of terms like "lesbian" and "gay." While you've hopefully been convinced by now that it's unwise to speculate on what humanity in "a state of nature" might look like (remember natureculture: the inseparability of nature and culture), the numbers among the young are probably less distorted by historical stigma or economic privilege.

Whew, that's a lot of graphs.

To sum up the picture so far: with less social stigma, more men might be gay or "heteroflexible," or put another way, women's apparently greater flexibility is at least partly a function of the lower stigma surrounding female same-sex attraction.

Italia und Germania
by Johann Friedrich
Overbeck, 1828

9

Pressure to conform

Oscar Wilde and
Lord Alfred Douglas,
May 1893.

1   A 23-year-old woman
from Galena, Ohio.

2   Robb, *Strangers: Homosexual Love in the Nineteenth
Century*, 2004.

3   In case you're dying to
know whom Alfred had *his* love
affair with: it was renowned
Irish poet and playwright
Oscar Wilde. The ensuing campaign of harassment and legal
attacks instigated by Queensbury ultimately led to Wilde's
sentence—two years of im-
prisonment with hard labor—
followed by self-exile and an
untimely death in France.

The reclamation of the umbrella term "queer"
in recent years is partly a response to the ever-
thickening LGBTQ+ alphabet soup—an effort to
create more solidarity across that archipelago
of minority identities. This reclamation coincides
with a sharp rise in queer identification among
the young, plainly visible even between 2018–19
and 2020–21.

Queer generally means "not on the mainland."
It says, "I don't conform." But it's also an acknowledgment that sexual flexibility and other kinds of
fluidity can render some of those fine alphabetic
distinctions tenuous, at least as a stable basis for
identity: "I'm queer and categories don't fit and sometimes answers sound conflicting when they aren't."[1]

Queerness has become disproportionately
common among younger women—under the age
of 30, about two thirds of queer people are women,
about a quarter are men, and about 10% identify
as both or neither, whereas above middle age roughly equal numbers
of queer people are women and men, with a negligible number of people (queer or not) identifying as both or neither.

Where did the term come from? In its older sense, it meant unnatural or off-kilter, and usually not in a good way. By the end of
the 19th century, "queer" had also become a slur referring specifically
to gay and lesbian people. This usage is often traced to John Sholto
Douglas, the 9th Marquess of Queensbury (1844–1900), a boxing
enthusiast and inveterate bully whose sons had love affairs with other
men, much to Queensbury's disgust.[2] The eldest son, Francis, was
engaged as a private secretary (with... benefits) to Archibald Primrose,
the 5th Earl of Rosebery, who briefly served as the Prime Minister of
the UK in 1894–95. When Francis died under suspicious circumstances
at a shooting party, Queensbury sent an enraged letter to his younger
son, Alfred, blaming the death on "Snob Queers like Rosebery."[3]

9.0 Queerness in 2018–19 and 2020–21 % by age

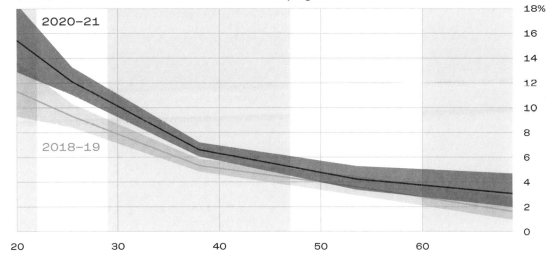

9.1 Gender identification of queer people % by age

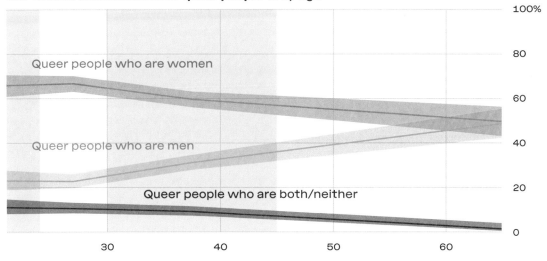

4 Shifting usage and attitudes in the US have been influential globally, though it would be wrong to assume that the term has precisely equivalent meanings in other countries.

5 A somewhat antique-sounding phrase today, which I cribbed from the US Census to allow for apples-to-apples statistical comparison.

The survey shows how the meaning of "queer" in the US has continued to shift in more recent history.**4** While three quarters of queer people over the age of 50 identify as "homosexual, gay or lesbian,"**5** this figure drops to around half among younger people. At the same time, older lesbians and gay people are somewhat *less* likely to identify as queer—not so much because they don't believe the word was intended to apply to them, but because many still find it offensive, hence reject the usage. As a 59-year-old man from Jacksonville, Florida, put it, "I identify as homosexual or gay, but not queer."

Studying the same pattern with respect to bisexuality offers further evidence of the way "queer" has become more inclusive and less offensive over time. Among the young, nearly 60% of queer

9.2 **Identifying as queer and "homosexual, gay, or lesbian"** % by age

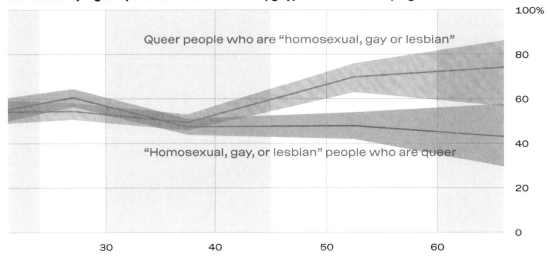

people are bisexual, while less than 30% of queer people older than 55 are bi. Conversely, while 40% of the 21-year-old bisexual population consider themselves queer, fewer than 15% of bisexuals over the age of 50 do.

There's more going on here than a mere shift in language. Most older lesbian, gay, and bisexual people seem to have less *use* for the flexibility implied by the term "queer," because while fewer

9.3 **Identifying as queer and bisexual** % by age

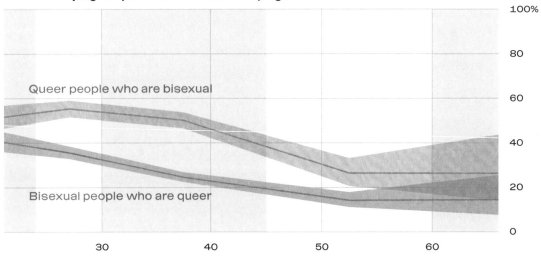

in number, a greater proportion are (and, typically, always were) among the least flexible: unwilling or unable to conform to heterosexual expectations even at a time when the social pressure to do so was far more intense than it is for young people today.

Cover of a 1960 pulp novel, *Warped Desire*.

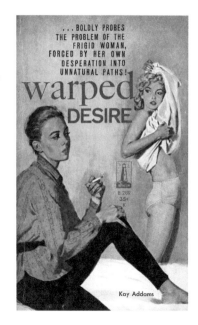

The previous chapter made the case that women tend to be more sexually flexible, or adaptable, than men, and that the stigma associated with same-sex attraction seems to be easing. Before accepting this as a sufficient explanation for the upward trends in same-sex attraction among women, though, it's important to take stock of the economic picture. After all, stigma isn't the only mechanism by which social pressure can force "who we are" to conform to a societal norm. Lack of resources can constrain us just as powerfully.

Recall the income data from Chapter 4, showing how much less money women used to make than men (an earnings gap that still hasn't closed). Their lower expected earnings strongly incent women to marry men, and stay married to them, especially if they're committed to the costly project of raising children. Many women might make this choice even if they're far from heterosexual—and perhaps even if they're not particularly flexible. These economic considerations didn't escape the notice of Edmund Bergler, who set aside a chapter on lesbianism in his 1956 book, writing:

The ratio of visible to camouflaged Lesbians is probably one to one hundred, and most of the camouflaged Lesbians are married. [...] Male homosexuals habitually overplay, female homosexuals habitually underplay the perversion. [...] [F]emale homosexuals of the majority group (those who have married for social or economic reasons) [...] tend to "prove" that the whole thing is child's play, for aren't they married? [...] In observing and studying women patients for nearly thirty years, I have always been amazed at the frequency with which one finds protracted or sporadic, transitory Lesbian episodes in the histories of frigid women.[6]

Bergler's glancing reference to the likely "economic reasons" for this asymmetry hardly does justice to the profound difference in means between men and women historically, and why this might have mattered. Lesbians were never well represented in the trendy gay neighborhoods of San Francisco, New York, or Seattle;[7] when I once asked

6 Bergler, *Homosexuality: Disease or Way of Life?*, 261–62, 1956.

7 This is part of the reason that in 2021, there were only 21 remaining lesbian bars in the United States, out of roughly 1,000 bars catering to gay men and LGBTQ+ people more generally. During the general downturn of the COVID pandemic, lesbian and Black-owned gay bars were hit hardest, due to the greater economic precarity of both their owners and their patrons. See "The 21 Bars —The Lesbian Bar Project"; Compton, "A Year into Pandemic, America's Remaining Lesbian Bars Are Barely Hanging On," 2021.

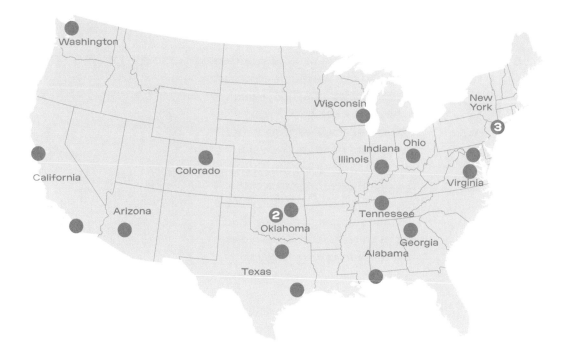

The 21 remaining lesbian bars in the US in 2021.

a lesbian friend why that was, she replied acidly, "Do you think we could afford the rent?"**8**

In the survey, a 91-year-old woman from Seffner, Florida, wrote, "I am attracted to other women, but do not act on it." This is likely true for the majority of lesbian or bisexual women of her generation, and earlier. Especially for women far from the heterosexual end of the scale, like this 49-year-old from Johnson City, Tennessee, repression can manifest as a lack of interest in sex:

Comedian Lea DeLaria and Cubby Hole owner Lisa Menichino in the 2021 documentary *The Lesbian Bar Project*.

8 Nowadays it's a common refrain that gay neighborhoods "aren't what they once were." Partly, as the stigma of being LGBTQ+ decreases (and more social life moves online), there's less pressure on sexual minorities to move to such enclaves. Relatedly, it has become hard to counteract the dilution caused by an onslaught of straight people attracted to the vibrant nightlife in these neighborhoods.

9 A 67-year-old woman from Mishawaka, Indiana.

10 Stekel, *Frigidity in Woman: In Relation to Her Love Life*, 1926.

> **I consider myself asexual at this point in my life. All my life I have been attracted to males and females. Mostly females. As a female I conformed to my family and societal norms and no one has ever known I have been attracted to females. I believe years of marriage to a male has a great deal to do with why I now feel nearly completely asexual.**

Such survey responses are common. Some, like the above, are clear-sighted, while others are profoundly confused: "Female looking, now asexual, maybe my whole life but pretending?"[9]

Beyond issues of economic privilege, expectations have also shifted over time regarding female sexual pleasure. The fact that leading 20th century psychiatrists like Sigmund Freud, Wilhelm Stekel, and Edmund Bergler considered "frigidity" in women a problem (Stekel wrote a two-volume monograph on the subject[10]) represented progress of a sort, as a pervasive belief in the 19th century had been that women didn't, or shouldn't, actually enjoy sex.

British medical doctor and author William Acton (1813–1875) was a towering figure during this earlier period. His book *The Functions and Disorders of the Reproductive Organs in Childhood, Youth, Adult Age, and Advanced Life, Considered in Their Physiological, Social, and Moral Relations* was an international bestseller, going through dozens of editions and reprintings in London and Philadelphia from 1857 until 1903, more than a quarter century after his death. *The Lancet* and other prominent medical journals of the day were effusive in their praise. The following is from the third edition, printed in London in 1867:

11 Acton, *The Functions and Disorders of the Reproductive Organs*, 144, 1867.

> **[The] majority of women (happily for them) are not very much troubled with sexual feeling of any kind. What men are habitually, women are only exceptionally. It is too true, I admit, as the divorce courts show, that there are some few women who have sexual desires so strong that they surpass those of men, and shock public feeling by their exhibition. I admit, of course, the existence of sexual excitement terminating in nymphomania,* a form of insanity that those accustomed to visit lunatic asylums must be fully conversant with; but, with these sad exceptions, there can be no doubt that sexual feeling in the female is in abeyance, and that it requires positive and considerable excitement to be roused at all; and even if roused (which in many instances it never can be) is very moderate compared with that of the male.[11]**

The footnote on "nymphomania" is perhaps even more remarkable, in that it spells out the potential consequences for a woman who admits to too much sexual pleasure:

> *I shall probably have no other opportunity of noticing that, as excision of the clitoris has been recommended for the cure of this complaint, Kobelt thinks that it would not be necessary to remove the whole of the clitoris in nymphomania, the same results (that is destruction of veneral desire) would follow if the glans clitoridis had been alone removed, as it is now considered that it is in the glans alone in which the sensitive nerves expand. This view I do not agree with [...].

12 The full extent of the clitoris wasn't well understood in the 19th century, but we can assume that Acton's "excision of [...] the whole" implied more extensive mutilation than removal of the glans.

13 Kellogg, *Plain Facts for Old and Young*, 1881; Graham, *A Lecture to Young Men on Chastity: Intended Also for the Serious Consideration of Parents and Guardians*, 1838; Kimmel, *The History of Men: Essays on the History of American and British Masculinities*, 50, 2005.

One of Victorian London's secret brothels, from *The Swell's Night Guide Through the Metropolis*, 1841.

Acton, in other words, wasn't content to cut off the exposed tip of the clitoris to "treat" cases of excessive female pleasure, but felt it necessary to excise "the whole" organ[12] in order to extinguish sexual pleasure—the same reason female genital mutilation is still practiced in some places today. On the other side of the pond, America's most famous doctor, the KFC-looking John Harvey Kellogg (of breakfast cereal fame), recommended the same procedure for the "treatment" of masturbation in girls. In his doomed quest to eradicate lustful urges and "self abuse" by means of wholesome grains, cereals, and genital mutilation, Kellogg was inspired by temperance preacher Sylvester Graham (of Graham cracker fame) and in turn inspired Charles William Post (of competing breakfast cereal fame). To my knowledge, no other country's contributions to the culinary arts were so deliberately designed to suck the joy out of life.[13]

Returning to economics, what Acton had to say about the role of social class in female sexual desire is noteworthy too:

[Y]oung men [...] form their ideas of women's feelings from what they notice early in life among loose or, at least, low and vulgar women. There is always a certain number of females who, though not ostensibly in the rank of prostitutes, make a kind of trade of a pretty face. [...] Any susceptible boy is easily led to believe [...] that she, and therefore all women, must have at least as strong passions as himself. Such women, however, will give a very false idea of the condition of female sexual feeling in general.

Association with the loose women of London streets, in casinos, and other immoral haunts (who, if they have not sexual feeling, counterfeit it so well that the novice does not suspect but that it is genuine), all seem to corroborate an early impression such as this, and [...] it is from these erroneous notions that so many young men think that the marital duties they will have to undertake are beyond their exhausted strength, and from this reason dread and avoid marriage.

Married men—medical men—or married women themselves, would tell a very different tale, and vindicate female nature from the vile aspersions cast on it by the abandoned conduct and ungoverned lusts of a few of its worst examples. [...] The best mothers, wives, and managers of households, know little or nothing of sexual indulgences. Love of home, children, and domestic duties, are the only passions they feel.*

As a general rule, a modest woman [...] submits to her husband, but only to please him; and, but for the desire of maternity, would far rather be relieved from his attentions.[14]

14 Acton, *The Functions and Disorders of the Reproductive Organs*, 144 45, 1867.

15 Acton, *Prostitution, Considered in Its Moral, Social, and Sanitary Aspects, in London and Other Large Cities: With Proposals for the Mitigation and Prevention of Its Attendant Evils*, 1857. These extremely high figures have been questioned by modern scholars, per Flanders, "80,000 Prostitutes? The Myth of Victorian London's Love Affair with Vice." Much of the debate turns on the precise definition of "prostitution," which may have encompassed many sexual relationships out of wedlock— relationships that might not be recognized as sex work today, but that were similarly stigmatized at the time.

Portrait of a sex worker, Storyville, New Orleans, by E.J. Bellocq, ca. 1912.

The association of lust with poverty hints none too subtly that Acton imagined the Great Chain of Being to be reflected in the social order, with the upper classes more angelic in their pursuits, while the "low and vulgar" rutted like animals. There's something self-fulfilling in this grim picture. It's undoubtedly true that some lower-class women feigned or exaggerated sexual interest in order to secure support from wealthier men. Given the marginal economic prospects for a single working-class urban woman in the 19th century, this would have offered a route, albeit a precarious one, to better prospects—and it must have made the line between professional sex work and mere "survival while female" somewhat blurry, as it often has been under patriarchy.

The sex trade did in fact flourish in this age of extreme repression, rapid urbanization, and rising economic inequality. According to an 1857 article in *The Lancet*, there were 80,000 sex workers and 5,000 brothels in London ("one house in sixty"),[15] generating a torrent of lurid reportage and hand-wringing

Illustration of severe syphilitic lesions by Christopher D'Alton, 1862.

16 As sociology lecturer Phil Burton-Cartledge put it, "Zombies as a horror staple are the result of some unfathomable biological or supernatural crisis that cannot be reversed. They are mindless. They are faceless. They are ugly. And they want to invade your home and feast on your flesh. If this does not work as an allegory for bourgeois attitudes to and fears of the working class, I don't know what does." Burton-Cartledge, "Zombies and Ideology," 2010.

17 As has often been remarked, pre-Victorian attitudes toward sex in "Merry Old England" (and elsewhere in the West) were far less repressive.

policy debates among clergy, politicians, doctors, lawyers, reformers, and moralizers—many of whom, being older, male, and moneyed, were undoubtedly also regular clients.

With no antibiotics and scant use of condoms (for these were still primitive and costly), epidemic waves of syphilis and other "social diseases" swept through the cities, disfiguring, sterilizing, and sometimes killing poor and rich alike. Artwork of this period often reprised, in a sexier key, the *danse macabre* (or dance of death) themes popularized in earlier centuries during outbreaks of the Black Death. The body horror in such imagery, reminiscent of something from a zombie movie, is hard to imagine today, especially in the developed world. To those who believed lust was a sin, the "pox" must have seemed like divine punishment, a foretaste of the tortures of the damned in a Hieronymus Bosch painting.

Like zombie horror today, a powerful undertone of class anxiety also played a role.**16** The association of frank sexuality with poverty, disease, and rotting flesh amplified Victorian sexual shame, turning pleasure into pathology. Perhaps, indeed, the sharp rise in horrific sexually transmitted infections associated with urbanization was the real driver of the sex-negativity that characterized the era's pearl-clutching "purity literature."**17**

At any rate, female desire, whether feigned or real, was associated with the lower classes and their moral depravity, with animalistic "ungoverned lusts." Bourgeois and upper-class women would ostensibly be far removed from all that, and if they weren't, they would likely claim to be, the better to avoid social stigma, institutionalization, and perhaps even mutilation. Once again, Acton adds an eye-opening footnote to the passage quoted earlier, expanding on the correspondence of women's sexuality with that of beasts:

> ***The physiologist will not be surprised that the human female should in these respects differ but little from the female among animals. We well know it, as a fact, that the dog or horse is not allowed approach to the female except at particular seasons. In the human female, indeed, I believe, it is rather from the wish of pleasing or gratifying the husband than from any strong sexual feeling, that cohabitation is habitually allowed. Certainly, it is so during the months of gestation. I have known instances where the female has during gestation**

evinced positive loathing for any marital familiarity whatever. In some of these instances, indeed, feeling has been sacrificed to duty, and the wife has endured, with all the self-martyrdom of womanhood, what was almost worse than death.

If respectable women can't admit to sexual pleasure, greater female sexual flexibility is hard to distinguish from the expected—and required—"self-martyrdom of womanhood." That would make it hard to tell the difference, from the outside, between a straight woman avoiding any great show of desire in her marriage for propriety's sake, an asexual woman, and a woman who, whether straight or not, simply isn't with a sexually compatible partner, and is thus "not very much troubled with sexual feeling of any kind."[18]

As one of the few female doctors seeing patients in the 19th century, Elizabeth Blackwell offered a different perspective:

> **The affectionate husbands of refined women often remark that their wives do not regard the [...] sexual act with the same intoxicating physical enjoyment that they themselves feel, and they draw the conclusion that the wife possesses no sexual passion. A delicate wife will often confide to her medical adviser [...] that [...] when her husband's welcome kisses and caresses seem to bring them into profound union, comes an act which mentally separates them, and which may be either indifferent or repugnant to her. But [...] [it] is well known that terror or pain in either sex will temporarily destroy**

18 Of course, if you suspected your husband might be visiting sex workers, your desire for intimacy might also be tempered by fear of contracting the pox.

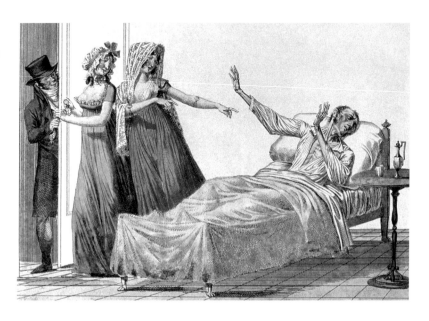

French caricature of a syphilitic man on his deathbed lamenting the cause of his illness, ca. 1800–1810.

all physical pleasure. In married life, injury from childbirth, or brutal or awkward conjugal approaches, may cause unavoidable shrinking from sexual congress, often wrongly attributed to absence of sexual passion. [...] It [...] is also a well-established fact that in healthy loving women, uninjured by the too frequent lesions which result from childbirth, increasing physical satisfaction attaches to the ultimate physical expression of love. [...] The prevalent fallacy that sexual passion is the almost exclusive attribute of men, and attached exclusively to the act of coition—a fallacy which exercises so disastrous an effect upon our social arrangements, arises from ignorance [...]. A tortured girl, done to death by brutal soldiers, may possess a stronger power of human sexual passion than her destroyers.[19]

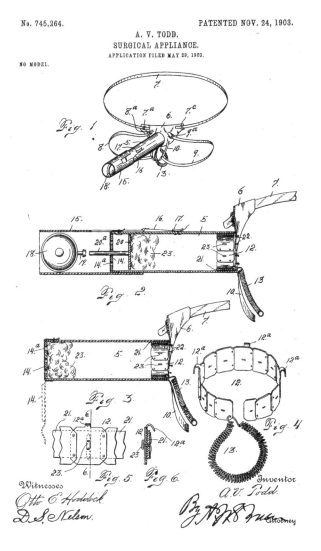

No. 745,264.

A. V. TODD.
SURGICAL APPLIANCE.
APPLICATION FILED MAY 29, 1903.

NO MODEL.

PATENTED NOV. 24, 1903.

As Blackwell hints when she writes of "*increasing* [...] satisfaction," figuring out what's pleasurable, what works and what doesn't, is an active process of exploration, learning, and even of self-creation—what Dan Savage has referred to as carving neural pathways.[20] In an environment where that kind of learning is discouraged, one's own sexuality may remain undeveloped; sexual orientation itself may remain uncertain or undefined. This may account for a good deal of the asexuality reported by older women today.

To be fair, Victorian society also regarded "excessive" *male* sexuality as a problem. However, judgments in that quarter were more lenient,[21] and "treatments" were generally less grisly, though they did sometimes involve dubious tinctures, running current through electrodes inserted into the urethra, administering cold enemas, blistering the penis with harsh chemicals, and other activities not to everyone's taste.[22]

In curbing excess male sexuality, the main goal was to avoid overtaxation, leading to (the theory went) a premature decline in virility, which would in turn

19 Blackwell, *Essays in Medical Sociology*, 52–54, 1902.

20 Savage, "Savage Love: Fresh Starts," 2018.

21 For example, while US Surgeon General William Hammond wrote in *Sexual Impotence in the Male*, "That the civilized man is in general excessive in the matter of sexual intercourse admits of no question," he then hedges vaguely: "The question then arises, what is excess? There are men who think it entirely within bounds to have sexual intercourse once every twenty-four hours; others, again, indulge regularly twice a week; others once; still, others who think once a month sufficient. It is exceedingly difficult to lay down any rule in the matter which will be applicable to all men [...]." *Sexual Impotence in the Male*, 128–29, 1883.

22 Though it didn't extend to penectomy or castration, boys weren't spared Kellogg's sadism; he advocated circumcision, without anesthetic, for those who couldn't be "cured" of masturbation by less drastic means. Kellogg, *Plain Facts for Old and Young*, 1881.

23 This oft-cited diary entry may well be apocryphal; see Tréguer, "History of the Phrase 'Close Your Eyes and Think of England,'" 2019.

compromise THE TRUE MISSION OF SEX. Remember that sex was, for husband and wife alike, a solemn duty, for race and country. As Lady Hillingdon allegedly wrote in her journal in 1912,

> **I am happy now that Charles calls on my bedchamber less frequently than of old. As it is, I now endure but two calls a week and when I hear his steps outside my door I lie down on my bed, close my eyes, open my legs and think of England.[23]**

For Acton, this was well and proper; "frigidity" in women wasn't a problem. Male impotence was. Hence the passages from Acton's book I've quoted at length are, counterintuitively, from a chapter on potential causes of *male* sexual dysfunction. Acton thought that fear of women's sexual demands was a common cause of anxiety, impotence, and aversion to marriage among "nervous and feeble" young men—presumably both those who weren't enthusiastic about marital rape, and those who were intimidated by the prospect of needing to satiate a "nymphomaniac" who *did* want sex.

In sum, fear and horror of female desire pervaded the culture on both sides of the Atlantic. The conjugal advice of Acton and his contemporaries seems perfectly calculated to make sex miserable—especially for women, but really, for everyone.

These attitudes have cast a long shadow. I remember, shortly after I moved to the US in the 1980s, being subjected to sex ed at school. Boys and girls were segregated, and the windows were blacked out with construction paper to prevent any salacious information leakage. Cryptic diagrams of internal organs and reproductive processes were projected onto the screen at the front of the classroom. Laughter was forbidden, on pain of being sent to sit out the rest of the period in the hall. The proceedings could not have been less appetizing, or more saturated with shame and dread. Many topics were covered, but most were medical and scary—fibroids, genital warts, teen pregnancy, AIDS, death.

In these classes, it went without saying that boys would try to talk girls into sex; also, that it was wrong, and that girls should listen to Nancy Reagan and "just say no." As with drug use (also on the curriculum in that blacked-out room), the factors that might weaken a girl's resolve and cause her to say "yes" were peer pressure or a self-sacrificing desire to please—never to *be* pleased. The idea of female sexual pleasure literally never came up. Nor is it mentioned in many sex ed programs today.

10   Pronoun wars

Analyzing handedness revealed an often overlooked excluded middle: a sizable population who are neither strictly left- nor strictly right-handed. The survey questions about sex and gender follow the same methodology as the handedness questions, and similarly allow respondents to answer "yes" to both or neither of the questions "Do you identify as female?" and "Do you identify as male?" Here, ambiguous responses are represented by the "Both or neither female/male" curve.

10.0.0 Identifying as both or neither female/male and "they" pronoun use % by age

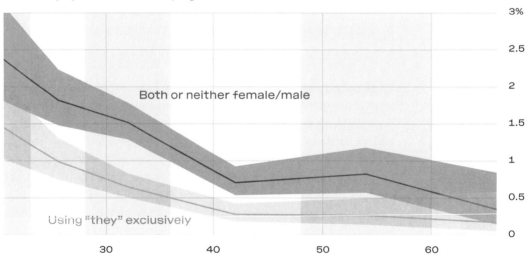

As with handedness and sexual orientation, this is territory where biology, medicine, environment, language, and culture all intersect in complex ways. For handedness, though, the signs of stigma and discrimination are mostly fossilized remains encoded in language, whereas stigmatization based on sex, gender, and *their* excluded middles remains red-hot today. This volcano is active, with the eruption of major debates about reproductive rights, sexuality, sexual equity, non-binariness, and trans rights seemingly every week. As if in a lava flow, the cultural landscape is being shaped and reshaped before our eyes.

In addition to "both or neither," the graph also shows the percentage of people who use the pronoun "they" exclusively, that is, who answer "yes" to "Is the right pronoun for you 'they'?" and "no" to all of the other pronoun choices. Both percentages are much higher among the young, and unsurprisingly, these populations overlap—though the overlap, like the percentages themselves, falls off with age.

10.0.1 Overlap of identifying as both or neither female/male and "they" pronoun use % by age

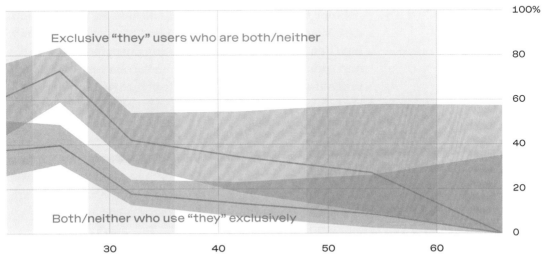

Although, at age 66, only 1 in 250 people do not identify as either strictly male or female, a number of comments from older respondents suggest that they might have responded differently had they been born a generation later:

1 A 60-year-old woman from Grand Junction, Colorado.

I wish I had understood gender fluidity better when I was young.[1]

2 A 66-year-old man from Canyon, Texas.

I'm glad I was born when gender identity was much simpler. You have too many choices today and it would be too hard for me to decide what to be.[2]

At age 18, among those who indeed have "many choices," about 1 in 40 people do not identify as strictly male or female—that's sixfold higher. In the same vein, fewer than 1 in 1,000 66-year-olds use "they" exclusively, but at age 20, about 1 in 70 do—more than a tenfold change.

These are dramatic shifts, and they're likely accelerating, as evidenced by the steepness of the change by age, the increase from year to year, and the comments from younger respondents who are still figuring things out:

I mostly present as female—I'm not out as [nonbinary]/genderfluid/genderqueer. […] I'm generally somewhere in between genders, rarely being 100% male or female. I'm glad I was given a name with a gender-neutral nickname because it makes everything a bit more comfortable. I have never had the courage to reveal my gender identity in relationships.[3]

3 A 30-year-old from Concord, California.

This was a "hard" survey for me. The closest I've come to defining my gender identity is "cis by default." It's just easiest and most comfortable to present as a woman for me, but I don't intrinsically feel like a woman or feminine. And I don't feel comfortable saying I'm non-binary or using pronouns like "they" because I do present as a woman. So yeah, just the normal difficulties with society's rigid gender structure, I guess![4]

4 A 36-year-old woman from Glendale, California.

The increasingly common use of "they" as a singular non-binary pronoun, and the cultural significance of this shift, inspired Merriam-Webster to make it the 2019 Word of the Year. Like many people of my generation, initially I found "they" odd, both impersonal and ungrammatical. Yet its use as a gender neutral pronoun isn't a modern innovation; singular "they" appeared in English as early as the 1300s, only a century after the introduction of the *plural* "they."[5]

5 "They, Pron., Adj., Adv., and N," 2022; Baron, "A Brief History of Singular 'They,'" 2018.

Grumpiness about the singular "they" by style commentators is a much more recent development, dating back only to the mid-18th century, though it has remained in common use anyway. Long before it became a pronoun non-binary people could apply to themselves, it served a useful grammatical function in situations where we need to refer to someone of unknown gender. Of course many other English usages, like the Southern "y'all," have their purposes too (in this case, helpfully differentiating between the singular and plural forms of "you"). Although critics and style guides alike cloak their censure in arguments about utility, the real point is to stigmatize—that is, to reinforce linguistic in- and out-groups.

Human languages aren't like computer languages, which are rigidly engineered and have a strict syntax, with objective "rights" and "wrongs." Our languages are messier than that—and this is a good thing. Messiness allows language to adapt to the changing needs of various populations, and to evolve over time, as the word "queer" has (see the previous chapter). Like anything that propagates under selection, languages are the cumulative Darwinian sum of many generations of such tinkering.

Of course if languages didn't evolve, nobody would be trying to regulate them. Those who *do* try tend to be arguing (or, when emboldened enough, mandating) from a position of privilege. By asserting that certain usages are right and others wrong, they're policing a social boundary and enforcing a value gradient across it—a right and wrong side of the tracks. Often the boundary demarcates class, or race, or both.

A generation ago, gender-neutral "they" tended to be looked down on as colloquial, informal, or even uneducated, not unlike "y'all." On the other hand, disallowing "they" in formal writing without falling back on "he" as a catchall required awkward constructions like "he or she," which had trouble catching on. So, rising acknowledgement of male privilege, and the backlash against that acknowledgement, turned pronouns into a cultural skirmish long before most people were thinking about non-binary or trans identity. In a 2008 jeremiad entitled *Feminism and the English Language*, conservative computer scientist and self-appointed style authority David Gelernter wrote,

> **The fixed idea forced by language rapists upon a whole generation of students, that "he" can refer only to a male, is (in short) wrong. [...] He-or-she'ing added so much ugly dead weight to the language that even the Establishment couldn't help noticing. So feminist authorities went back to the drawing board. Unsatisfied with having rammed their 80-ton 16-wheeler into the nimble sports-car of English style, they proceeded to shoot the legs out from under grammar—which collapsed in a heap after agreement between subject and pronoun was declared to be optional. Can the damage to our mother tongue be undone?6**

6 David Gelernter, "Feminism and the English Language: Can the Damage to Our Mother Tongue Be Undone?," 2008.

Setting aside any critique of Gelernter's own rather steroidal writing style and its mixed automotive-or-equestrian metaphors, this kind of policing follows a familiar pattern. It circles the wagons to protect a virtuous "us" from an invading "them," positing "our way" as an unquestioned, it's-always-been-this-way default and "their way" as radical, foreign, and threatening:

> **Why should I worry about anyone's ideology? [...] Who can afford to allow a virtual feminist to elbow her way like a noisy drunk into that inner mental circle where all your faculties (such as they are) are laboring to produce decent prose?**

But language was already moving on, as it always does. The use of "he" in gender-neutral settings became archaic. By 2016, with the rising popularity of gender-neutral "they" for individuals, David Gelernter's son Josh had taken up the cause of defending the sports-car-horse purity of the English language against those invading pronouns, writing with a familiar sense of righteous grievance:

> **Trying to depluralize "they" is an asinine effort, stemming from a stupid misunderstanding made by stupid people whom the [American Dialect Society] has chosen to indulge rather than to correct. [...] You might ask why it matters one way or the other. Aside from being wrong, and sounding wrong, using "they" as a singular steals precision from the language. It is destructive.[7]**

7 Josh Gelernter, "The War on Grammar," 2016.

It's hard not to conclude that the concerns of the Gelernters, while couched in logical arguments, are more fundamentally political; they're about identity. Hence, war. Where David's beef was with feminists, Josh's was with the new threat: trans and non-binary people. The desire for language to "stay as it is," which is to say, return to the way it was, is hard to tease apart from the Gelernters' broader wish for the world to return to the way it was, perhaps in the 1950s or '60s.[8]

8 Even the Gelernters would be unlikely to argue for a return to the 19th century.

Many modern style commentators harbor more moderate beliefs, and understand that language is always evolving to suit new needs. Steven Pinker, in his 2014 book *The Sense of Style*, wrote,

> **Only a minority [of the Usage Panel] accepts *A person at that level should not have to keep track of the hours they put in*— though the size of that minority has doubled in the past decade, from 20 percent to almost 40 percent, one of many signs that we are in the midst of a historical change that's returning singular *they* to the acceptability it enjoyed before a purist crackdown in the nineteenth century. A slim majority of the panel accepts *If anyone calls, tell them I can't come to the phone* and *Everyone returned to their seats*. The main danger in using these forms is that a more-grammatical-than-thou reader may falsely accuse you of making an error. If they do, tell them that Jane Austen and I think it's fine.[9]**

9 Pinker, *The Sense of Style: The Thinking Person's Guide to Writing in the 21st Century*, 260–61, 2014.

The hat tip to Jane Austen might be a bit embarrassing to David Gelernter, as Gelernter has held up Austen as a paragon of style— seemingly unaware of her frequent use of "they" as a gender-neutral singular pronoun! Still, in Austen's day, "they" never would have been used for a specific, *known* person, or in referring to oneself, because *that kind* of gender ambiguity would have seemed strange, perhaps even freakish. While it certainly existed, it wasn't acknowledged in polite society.

Clearly this is now changing, but the strict gender binary remains very much with us as a cultural default. "Boy or girl?" is still the first question a new parent is likely to get, and the genderedness of language, customs, bathrooms, and so on means that in our daily interactions we continually model each other's gender in ways that are hard to avoid. Many survey respondents evince frustration at this, even when their responses to the questions about sex and gender are unambiguously masculine or feminine: "I hate gendered restrictions and enforcement of binary gender norms";10 "I wish we would eliminate gender from identifying ourselves";11 "gender is exhausting and most of my life trying to present as female in the US has been stressful and uncomfortable, I prefer to just exist without thinking about it and just [be] ME."12 These sentiments most often are expressed by women, for reasons that become clear when we consider who historically has gotten the short end of the stick.

Pronoun pins from a 2016 art and technology festival in Portland, Oregon.

While "they" is an increasingly popular way out of the binary, it's by no means the only alternative brewing in our language's evolutionary cauldron. A few years ago we saw something of a Cambrian explosion of gender neutral pronouns. "Ze," "ey," "hen," "thon," "xe," and even, especially controversially, "it," all have their partisans. Then, there are the nigh-infinite combinations and nuances of usage preferred by individuals. One 26-year-old from Wilkes-Barre, Pennsylvania, wrote,

I identify as both she and he pronouns, never they. They is too much like erasure to me, and sometimes I feel like both she and he, so I don't mind either.

Another wrote,

I identify as gender queer and use she/they pronouns. I do not mind if someone uses "he" but I did not want to select that it was the "right" pronoun.

The responses include many, many more variations.

It may be that this is our new normal: a complex and ever-expanding maze of words between the old traditional neighborhoods of "he" and "she." Future students of English as a second language may need to master such nuances in order to speak respectfully, much the way foreign students of Japanese must struggle through the many honorific forms of address that characterize that language. Or, over time, English usages may settle and "they" (or some alternative) may become commonly enough accepted to displace its competitors and simplify the excluded middle. Or maybe, in the end, "they" will simply become the default pronoun for everybody, with "he" and "she" becoming archaisms like "thee" and "thou." This would certainly make life simpler.[13] With my engineering hat on, it's probably the option I'd pick, if I could make up the rules. But of course that's not anyone's prerogative, because language is not engineered, but evolved. And for now, many people are rolling their own personal pronouns.

13 These shifts aren't limited to English; similar debates are playing out in many other languages too.

This can create a bit of a linguistic minefield. The older or more traditionally minded of us, even those not as ideologically opposed as the Gelernters, tend to be bemused, puzzled, or fearful about misstepping, and can be resentful about suddenly needing to deal with it all. This attitude is typified by a man from Sicklerville, New Jersey:

> **I think that there is so much political correctness in the current time period that it is a little absurd. If someone mistakes someone as a "guy" and they want to really be identified as a "she" how can someone be offended and angry at someone for this? It used to be so simple 50 years ago.**

Ah, the good old late 20th century.

Avoiding such uncomfortable interactions can lead to differing presentations in different contexts; the truth is that most gender-nontraditional people don't relish confrontation either. As a 20-year-old from Austin, Texas, put it, "I use multiple pronouns (she/they) and identify as nonbinary or female depending on who I'm talking to." Complicating things even more (relative forms of address once more recall Japanese honorifics), this dependence on context makes older or more traditional people tend to dramatically underestimate the size of the excluded middle. They aren't confronted with it, even if they are in contact with it. Just as in Jane Austen's time, nuances in gender aren't seen, so, in a self-fulfilling way, they remain invisible.

Linguistic shifts raise profound questions that have become highly charged in today's political and cultural climate, such as: Does rising ambiguity in gender identification reflect an underlying reality that has been with us all along, but has been long suppressed? Or is it a social trend—even, as some have claimed, a fad? (Recall that for sexual orientation, there's evidence of both long-suppressed realities emerging into the open *and* social transmission.) Can we draw a clear line between sex, which many authorities today define as purely biological, and gender, which is often considered purely cultural? Are either sex or gender innate properties, and are either of them inherently binary? Are they fixed for an individual, or can they change (or be changed) over time, or depending on context and environment? There are a variety of strongly held and opposing beliefs regarding all of these questions. If we set aside ideology as best we can, though, it's possible to make headway in answering them by delving more deeply into what the data reveal about excluded middles, just as Chapter 2 described in the simpler domain of handedness.

To be clear, we cannot lean on the handedness analogy too hard. For instance, where "ambidexterity" is a generic catchall term for the excluded middle of handedness, a number of distinct terms map the excluded middle (or middles) of gender. "Non-binary" is the most common, but other variations in common use include "gender queer" and "gender fluid." As with ambidexterity, I didn't include any definitions in the survey, so for now, these terms are best thought of simply as labels for communities people identify with that suggest something nontraditional about their gender.

10.1 Identifying as gender queer, gender fluid, or non-binary % by age

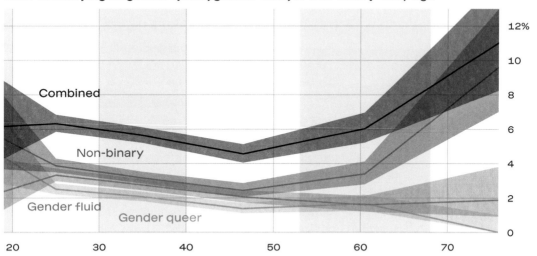

These populations overlap, but their overlap is far from complete, since like gender neutral pronouns, the terms all have their partisans. Hence the total—meaning, people who answer "yes" to any or all of the three questions "Are you non-binary?," "Are you gender

fluid?," or "Are you gender queer?"—is larger than any individually, but smaller than the sum, ranging from 5% to 11% depending on age.

Breakdowns by age show the (by now familiar) rises in non-traditional or minority identities among the young. Some surprising things happen after middle age, though. This is most obvious for the non-binary curve, which is under 3% from ages 40–50, but rises above 5% for younger people, and to near 10% for older people! What's going on here?

The mystery deepens upon further breaking down the non-binary population into three distinct sub-populations: non-binary women (here meaning those who answer "yes" to "Do you identify as female?" and "no" to "Do you identify as male?"), non-binary men ("yes" to "Do you identify as male?," "no" to "Do you identify as female?"), and non-binary people who answer "yes" to neither or both of "Do you identify as female?" and "Do you identify as male?"

10.2 Non-binary identification broken down by female, male, or both/neither % by age

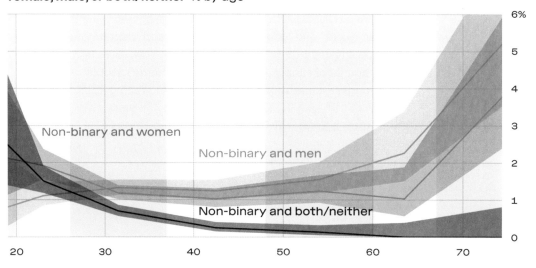

The curious U-shape of the non-binary curve turns out to be a sum of three very different components. First, let's consider those who are both non-binary and respond ambiguously to the questions about their sex ("yes" to both or neither of "Do you identify as male?" and "Do you identify as female?"). Like exclusive users of "they," this curve is high among the young, and low among the older population.

For people over 60, the sex binary reigns absolute: that is, even among older non-binary people, *everyone* answers "yes" to exactly one of "Do you identify as male?" or "Do you identify as female?" Among younger people, though, a rising number are both non-binary and answer "yes" to both or neither male/female. Among 19-year-olds, this applies to about 1 in 40 people. The "both" and "neither" populations appear to be roughly equivalent in other respects. As a 27-year-old non-binary person from Spokane, Washington, put it,

> **I consider myself non-binary, so that's why I answered "yes" to both identification as male and female—but I feel equally correct saying "no" to both as well.**

What are we to make of the other components, though—and especially that the number of people who answer "yes" to "Are you non-binary?" but also identify as male (and not female) *climbs* from about 1% at age 19 to 5% by age 74? This is the exact opposite of the usual age pattern for sexual minorities. Understanding what's going on here requires delving into the complex topic of intersexuality. Intersex people are the *biological* excluded middle of sex—falling somewhere between male and female.

If the concept is new to you, you're not alone. Many survey respondents noted that they had never heard of intersexuality, with some expressing surprise when they Googled it to learn more.[14] Your odds are somewhat higher of having encountered the word "hermaphrodite" at one point or another—a historical and still often-used term for intersex. Even if you *are* familiar with the concept, however, you likely think of it as a rare medical anomaly—perhaps even if you're intersex yourself! The reason: our gender-binary society has rendered intersexuality taboo.

14 It was especially interesting to find this term disproportionately singled out as obscure given the many other niche and in some cases far more recently coined terms on the survey.

Both/neither

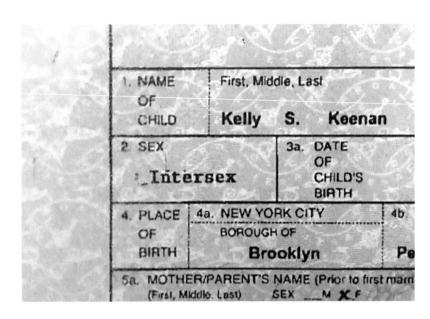

1. NAME OF CHILD	First, Middle, Last		
	Kelly	**S.**	**Keenan**
2 SEX		3a. DATE OF CHILD'S BIRTH	
:_Intersex			
4. PLACE OF BIRTH	4a. NEW YORK CITY		4b.
	BOROUGH OF		
	Brooklyn		Pe
5a. MOTHER/PARENT'S NAME (Prior to first marri			
(First, Middle, Last)	SEX __M ✗ F		

Sara Kelly Keenan's birth certificate, the first in the US to say "Intersex." It was issued in 2016, when she was 55 years old.

Until recently, "male" or "female" were the only options on US birth certificates, allowing (or compelling) parents to always have a binary answer to that inevitable first question: "boy or girl?" In 2012, Ohio became the first state to formally recognize intersexuality on a birth certificate, and New York followed suit in 2016,[1] but such official recognition remains extremely rare.

The lack of recognition is hard to square with the actual incidence of intersexuality in the population, which the survey suggests is close to 2%—a figure consistent with the medical literature, though the range of estimates is broad due to varying definitions, just as with ambidexterity. The rate of reported incidence is far from constant across ages, though; it rises from barely above 0% at 18 years old to near 2% at age 30 or so, but then drops again to below 1.5% in middle age. At first glance, the finding is puzzling. Making sense of it requires a deeper look at both the biology and the medical history of sex determination.

1 Scutti, "'The Protocol of the Day Was to Lie': NYC Issues First US 'Intersex' Birth Certificate," 2016.

11.0 **Intersexuality** % by age

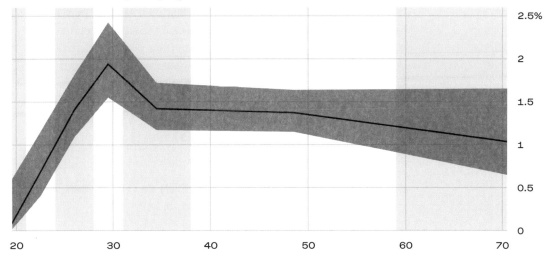

There's much more to intersexuality than genital variations, but those are a good place to start, since for many thousands of years the "boy or girl?" question has been answered within seconds, by visual inspection. For the majority of babies, sex is still determined in a visual snap judgment right after birth, and that determination goes on to influence nearly every aspect of a child's upbringing and place in the world.

Cover art of pulp novel *The Nude Who Did* by Ted Mark, 1970. Artwork by Stanley Borack.

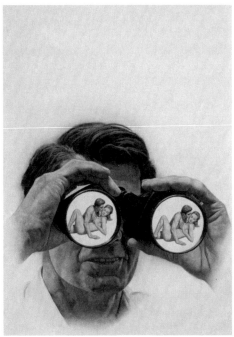

Most people don't see each other naked too often these days—at least, not in real life. We *can* stare all day at a parade of fully sex-differentiated adult genitals on the internet, in unlimited numbers and in high definition. Online, sex differentiation tends to exaggeration, featuring unusually large breasts and penises, dramatically developed muscles for men, extreme hip-to-waist ratios for women, hairy parts strategically lush or smoothly shaven, heavily dimorphic faces selectively enhanced with makeup. (Camera angle turns out to be an important hidden variable, as will be discussed in Chapter 14.) In short, the sex binary in most porn is cartoonish, and visibly intersex genitals are exceedingly rare.

It's unsurprising, then, that most of us have no idea what genitals that are "both," "neither," "a combination," or "somewhere in between" might look like. Of course there *is* plenty of porn featuring trans people, who may have any combination of vulvas, penises, testicles, and breasts. But these bodies don't shed as much light on intersexuality as you might think; in fact their penises and breasts, when present, *also* tend to be highly developed. Trans identity will be explored more deeply in Chapter 12, but for now, suffice it to say that most visibly trans bodies in porn are made possible by modern medicine, often including hormone treatments and surgery, not to mention lucky genes, a careful diet, and lots of time in the gym and at the salon.

EXTERNAL GENITAL DIFFERENTIATION IN THE HUMAN FETUS

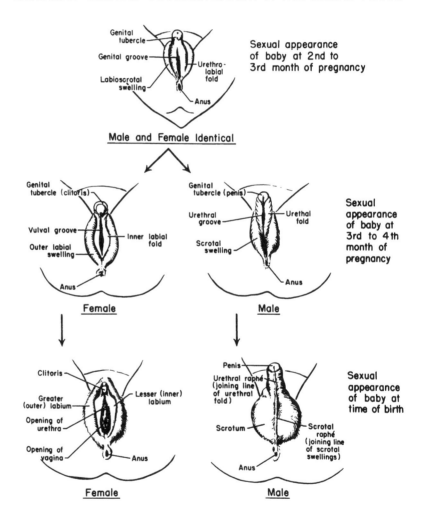

Sexual appearance of baby at 2nd to 3rd month of pregnancy

Sexual appearance of baby at 3rd to 4th month of pregnancy

"Three stages in the differentiation of external genital organs. The male and the female organs have the same beginnings and are homologous with one another." Money, *Man & Woman, Boy & Girl*, 44, 1972.

Sexual appearance of baby at time of birth

Then again, much the same holds for most porn performers, trans or not. It would be optimistic to guess that 1–2% of us look like that with our clothes off. So, intersexuality is both more common than the extreme body types we generally see in porn and, paradoxically, more obscure. Yet intersexuality has been a part of life not only for us, but for every species that reproduces sexually, going back hundreds of millions of years. Shulamith Firestone's "yin and yang" turn out not to be so sharply defined.

As embryos, we don't begin with strongly differentiated genitals, but with primordial structures that can develop either way. The ovaries or testicles (or, if undifferentiated, "ovotestes") start off as a pair of small organs within the abdomen. In female differentiation, a pair of internal structures called the Müllerian ducts develop into the uterus, fallopian tubes, and upper part of the vagina, while in male differentiation the ducts disappear, so that these organs don't develop—though for those with "persistent Müllerian duct syndrome" (PMDS), the ducts remain, resulting in men with uteruses. PMDS is considered a rare disorder, with only 250 cases documented in the medical literature, but the reality is that we have little sense of how common it is, since the uterus is an internal organ and will only be noticed during medical imaging or surgery.[2] We know that PMDS can cause infertility, undescended testes (meaning testicles that remain in the abdomen), and increased risk of eventual cancer in the uterine or testicular tissue, all of which can motivate imaging and surgery. But an unknown number of cases—and, for all we know, it could be a great majority—don't lead to these problems, hence may never be discovered.

When a variation in fetal development affects the *external* genitals, it's harder not to notice. The visible part of the clitoris and the head of the penis are the same structure, but during male development, the inner labia fuse to create the bottom surface of the penis, the outer labia fuse to form the scrotum, and the testes descend into the scrotum. If some of these steps happen but others don't, or some steps happen halfway, the resulting genitals will vary.

2 "Persistent Müllerian Duct Syndrome," 2021.

The Quigley Scale, proposed in 1995, is a phenotypic grading system defining seven classes between "fully masculinized" and "fully feminized" genitals.

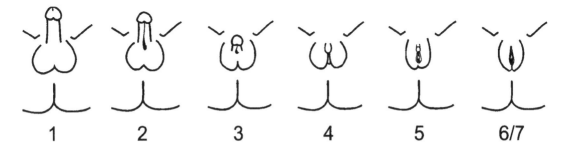

1   2   3   4   5   6/7

A few different diagnostic tools have been developed over the years to help doctors grade these in-between cases, such as the "Prader scale" and the "Quigley scale." The latter is shown here. When pediatric endocrinologist Charmian Quigley and colleagues introduced this

3 Quigley et al., "Androgen Receptor Defects: Historical, Clinical, and Molecular Perspectives," 1995.

scale in a 1995 paper,[3] they explained that "Grades are numbered l–7 in order of increasing severity (more defective masculinization)"; grade 1 is "normal masculinization *in utero*," grade 2 is a "male phenotype with mild defect in masculinization," grade 4 is "severe genital ambiguity," and so on. Such language suggests a value judgment, with the fully differentiated penis as the gold standard and anything else lesser and defective. Is a clitoris really nothing more than a defective and underdeveloped penis?

Before rushing to your own outraged judgment, though, keep in mind that Quigley's article focuses on one particular set of genetic routes to intersexuality, the Androgen Insensitivity Syndromes (AIS). These involve mutations that cause the body to respond less or not at all to androgens, the key virilizing (meaning, "masculinizing") hormones during development. Insofar as AIS is considered a medical condition (an analog would be diabetes caused by insensitivity to insulin, also a hormone), words like "defect" and "severity" make sense— though of course they imply teleology.

People with AIS *are* in fact genetically male, with XY chromosomes. The real biases in this paper and many others like it are not so much about the superiority of the penis, as about the following assumptions:

1   sex is naturally binary, hence

2   intersexuality is a medical disorder, meaning

3   it should be diagnosed and treated by doctors, and finally

4   a person's genes are the ground truth telling us whether they're "really" men or women.[4]

4 Especially in his later work, Quigley himself expressed a more nuanced take, e.g. in Liao et al., "Determinant Factors of Gender Identity: A Commentary," 2012.

These assumptions are widely held by laypeople too, and reflect the way modern medicine and genetics have influenced popular mental models. The belief that sex and gender are binary (and equivalent) is in keeping with many longstanding religious traditions; as a pious 35-year-old woman from Opelika, Alabama, put it,

> **God is the supreme Ruler and Creator of this world. He gets to make the rules, not us. His order of creation was to form male and female. I'm female. That's really all there is to it. People are trying to come up with their own "rules" regarding sexuality, and it's just not our place to do that. Our Holy God is the Sovereign Lord, not us. We get to do things His way, not ours.**

Nettie Stevens (1861–1912), American geneticist who discovered sex chromosones, at the Naples Zoological Station, 1909.

Nettie Stevens and Edmund Beecher Wilson independently discovered the XX (female) and XY (male) sex chromosomes in 1905, putting this religious conviction in binariness on a seemingly rational scientific footing. "I'm a male because I have XY chromosomes, and nothing can change that. There are only 2 genders," per a 36-year-old from Brighton, Colorado. "XX or XY, that's all there is. The rest is BS," agrees a 43-year-old man from Dallas, Texas. The idea that genes are inherently discrete or "digital" fits well with human language, which also deals in discrete identity categories like "man" and "woman." Further, genes are instructions you're born with, a bit like an inner Bible, or prayer scroll, inscribed in the curled-up genetic code of every cell in your body. Choices, malfunctions, complications, and obfuscations might happen afterward, but your God-given DNA must, so the thinking goes, be ground truth—the original instructions. Per a 36-year-old man from Kissimmee, Florida,

While I do not support any discrimination against LGBT or any other life choice people make, and respect any identity someone decides to claim as their own, the fact is that gender is not a social construct. There is a huge amount of variety to human beings, but "male" and "female" are scientific designations that involve the number of chromosomes one has, and someone's biological origin cannot be changed. Leave people to do as they wish as long as it is not hurting anyone, but at the same time, don't ignore science and common sense.

So, does DNA always tell us whether someone is a man or a woman? Firstly, there are a number of fairly common viable chromosomal variations other than XX and XY, including XXX, XXY, and XYY, X0 (only an X chromosome), and rarer variations like XXXY, XXYY, XXXY, and so on. Many people with these variations have intersex characteristics.

But this is just the tip of the iceberg.

I found a curious short comment among the survey responses from a 61-year-old man: "chromosomal mix, xx and xy. fusing of fraternal twin eggs." This remarkable phenomenon is called *chimerism*, after the chimera of Greek mythology, an imaginary creature composed of the parts of other animals (traditionally, a lion's head, a goat's body, and a serpent's tail). The survey respondent was originally a pair of twins in the womb, each a different egg fertilized by a different sperm cell, which fused early in development to form a single fetus. In such cases, there's a 50% chance that the fused fraternal twins won't be the same sex, as happened here. In adulthood, each of his body's cells has a lineage tracing back to one or the other embryo, so genetically, his body is a mosaic of male and female cells! How those cells are distributed throughout the body depends on the timing and details of the fusion. In some cases the result is a sharp boundary between the left and right halves of the body; in others, cell lineages cluster in patches or in whorls.

Chimerism in a rose, a cat, and singer-songwriter Taylor Muhl.

Chimerism is possible for any multicellular organism, including plants. Many calico or tortoiseshell cats are chimeras. So-called *gynandromorphs*, half female and half male, are especially striking in animals that are more sharply sexually dimorphic than humans—that is, where the sexes differ dramatically in size or coloration, as with peacocks and pea hens, or butterflies.

Like PMDS, chimerism in humans is supposedly very rare; there are only about a hundred documented cases.[5] Singer-songwriter Taylor Muhl is one. To raise awareness of the condition, she has posted selfies on social media showing the striking change in coloration between the left and right sides of her abdomen, revealing the different genetic origins of those cells.

If chimerism in humans were really so rare, it would be remarkable luck for one of these near-mythical people not only

5 Wolinsky, "A Mythical Beast. Increased Attention Highlights the Hidden Wonders of Chimeras," 2007.

to have taken my gender survey, but also to have thought to write about their chimerism in the comment field. But wait: a *second* such individual responded too! She's a 26-year-old from Stafford, Texas:

> **FAAB,[6] woman in gender, born with chimeric teste in place of right ovary. I like to joke I ate my twin brother in the womb. I've named this prototeste Conrad the Gonad.**

Gynandromorphic peacock, Sydney, 2007.

6 Female Assigned At Birth.

It's hard not to conclude that the real rate of human chimerism must be far higher than those 100 documented cases suggest, especially since, again like PMDS, the great majority of chimeric people are unlikely ever to find out that they're chimeric, and only half of those with chimeric genes will be gynandromorphic. It's not possible to pin down a real frequency for chimerism from the survey data, but I'd guess that 1 in 1,000 is a better order of magnitude estimate than the "almost never" one would naïvely get by dividing the 100 documented cases by the world population.

All of which is to say that even if one were to assume that genes *were* the ground truth for sex—and there's good reason to doubt this—many more chromosomally ambiguous cases exist than one would think, because quite a few people are walking around with some cellular mixture of Conrad the Gonad and his twin sister.

Intersexuality poses an even more fundamental challenge to the idea of sex being binary in the first place, or being determined by chromosomes. The biological and social machinery of sex and gender differentiation is just complicated; it has many moving parts and feedback loops, all of which can vary from person to person to produce different results. For instance, everybody with an Androgen Insensitivity Syndrome is genetically male, including people with complete insensitivity (grade 7 on the Quigley scale), most of whom are—by their account and pretty much everyone else's—obviously women. Their bodies look female at birth, they are raised as girls and grow into women, and indeed many will never learn that they

Group photo of people with Androgen Insensitivity Syndrome and related intersex conditions, 2010.

don't have uteruses or a second copy of the X chromosome in their cells. Those discoveries typically only take place if they decide to have children, try for a while, and ultimately go to a fertility clinic to understand why they aren't conceiving. (Note, also, that this implies *wanting* children and either living in a country with socialized medicine or belonging to the kind of upper middle class milieu where visiting the fertility clinic is a done thing.)

At the clinic, they will learn that they're sterile. Of course this won't suddenly render them "not women," any more than a hysterectomy would. But they will also now know that they're intersex. Doctor's visits like these are almost certainly why positive responses to "Are you intersex?" rise from near zero to a high water mark during the years between 18 and thirtysomething. After menopause, of course, the odds of finding out will decline.

There's every reason to believe that, insofar as it's meaningful to talk about a "real" rate of intersexuality, it's even higher than the survey's numbers suggest. A 24-year-old woman from Monroe, Louisiana, wrote, for instance, "Sometimes I wonder if I'm genderfluid or intersex, but I'm not confident enough in the former and have never been tested for the latter." A 25-year-old woman from Bella Vista, Arkansas, wrote in more detail about her experience, which is far from uncommon:

> I don't consider myself trans-anything, but I've always been fairly 'masculine' in my attitude, interests, desires and the way I express emotions (though I do have a feminine side). I suspect I have hormone problems, which gave me facial hair and makes me feel very unattractive as a female. I think I'd probably make a better guy because then maybe people

**wouldn't notice the hair, but I don't really 'want' to be a guy.
I just don't want to be an anomaly.**

The fact that almost nobody grows up knowing they're intersex, but some may then find out they are in a doctor's office later in life, goes some way toward explaining the continuing invisibility of intersexuality. Since it's widely understood as a medical diagnosis, being intersex tends to fall under the veil of privacy reserved for medical matters. It's not anyone else's business. Intersex people may seek out support groups, but they're unlikely to "come out" to friends, family, or colleagues, let alone adopt intersexuality as an identity, especially if (as is often the case) they feel themselves to be men or women, and present that way to others too. In some cases, that feeling is unambiguous. In other cases, it isn't, but there's often a desire to "pass" anyway. As a 23-year-old man from Port Huron, Michigan, wrote, "intersex people don't want recognition, it puts a huge target on us for abuse."

Unfortunately this secrecy perpetuates the stigma surrounding intersexuality, as well as the mistaken belief on the part of most people that it's vanishingly rare (if they've even heard of it). At roughly 2%, being intersex is at least as common as having red hair. Almost certainly, you know intersex people. However, very likely, you don't *know* you know them.

It's widely assumed that intersexuality is lifelong, and that it crops up at some constant rate—some fixed number of births out of every thousand. These assumptions are reasonable, but let's hold them only tentatively. For one thing, definitions may be too slippery for any single number to be objectively correct, or to remain constant as our understanding evolves. Also, mounting (though still inconclusive) evidence points to environmental factors altering the odds over time.

Studies have found, for example, that estrogen-mimicking compounds in wastewater have been both changing the sex ratio and increasing the numbers of feminized intersex frogs in suburban neighborhood ponds.[7] Something like that could be happening to humans too. It's one of many ways our reshaping of the environment seems to be coming back around to reshape *us* in a feedback loop of unintended consequences.

Setting this speculation aside, though, let's suppose that people at all times and of all ages have an equal probability of being intersex. If so, the large variability in responses to "Are you intersex?" by age is presumably a function of how many people *know* they're intersex, as opposed to how many of them actually *are*.

7 Lambert et al., "Suburbanization, Estrogen Contamination, and Sex Ratio in Wild Amphibian Populations," 2015.

PREFACE.

As its title shows, this little book relates solely to sexual impotence as it exists in the male.

At some future time I propose to enlarge its scope so as to include the subject of sterility, and to consider both these affections as they occur in men and women.

43 West Fifty-fourth Street, NEW YORK.

May 15th, 1883.

Preface to Hammond, *Sexual Impotence in the Male*, 1883.

The real number of intersex people is then at least as high as the peak of this curve, near 2%. (The incidence probably is higher still, since surely fewer than 100% of intersex 29-year-olds know that they are.) You might suppose older would mean wiser, but from age 42 onward, only about two thirds as many people seem to know as at age 29.

Why does the percentage of people who know they're intersex *drop* among the older population? Presumably they haven't forgotten! The decrease most likely reflects evolving attitudes and practices regarding intersex births, and these changes may have far-reaching implications. To understand them, let's return once again to the 19th century.

In 1883, before the genetic basis of sex was understood, US Army Surgeon General William Hammond published a book called *Sexual Impotence in the Male*. In case the title wasn't clear enough, he noted in the preface that the book "relates solely to sexual impotence as it exists in the male," adding that he might later enlarge it to "include the subject of sterility, and to consider both these affections [disorders] as they occur in men and women."[8] But in describing congenital presentations of the genitals that could result in "sexual impotence in the male," he covers a number of cases we now understand to be intersex. Hammond variously describes Quigley's grades 2 through 4, for example, as "hypospadias" and "suture of the penis."[9] He also describes the absence of testicles, or undescended testicles, and a tendency in some such cases to assume "in many respects the mental and physical attributes of the female sex."[10]

Interestingly, this kind of characterization views nearly every part of the excluded middle as a defective kind of masculinity—just as the Quigley scale would in the next century. While some of Hammond's case studies were probably people with XY chromosomes and an Androgen Insensitivity Syndrome, others were likely people with XX chromosomes and a different set of genetic variations leading to virilizing effects, such as Congenital Adrenal Hyperplasia (CAH)—which is also considered rare but, as with the other conditions mentioned earlier, is likely underreported. Perhaps in the near future some high tech national health system will begin doing full genetic sequencing of all newborns; only then (chimerism aside) will we really know.

[8]   Hammond, *Sexual Impotence in the Male*, 1883.

[9]   Hammond, 220–21.

[10] Hammond, 247.

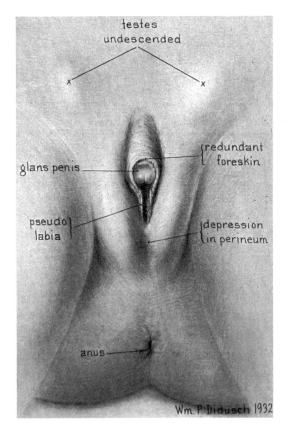

testes
undescended

x   x

glans penis ——

pseudo}
labia

redundant
foreskin

depression
in perineum

anus ——→

Wm. P. Didusch 1932

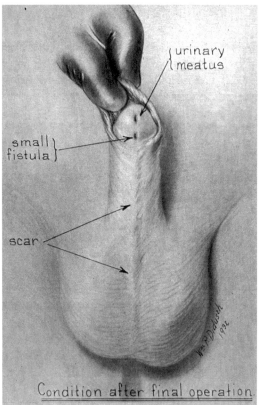

urinary
meatus

small}
fistula}

scar

Wm P Didusch 1932

Condition after final operation.

"Patient reared as female and attended fashionable girls' school until age of 20. Hypo-spadic phallus, with which patient had sexual relations, as a male, with girls in school; then suspected for first time that true sex was male."

→ Numerous operations to cure abnormalities successful. Patient married his hospital nurse; intercourse satisfactory to both." From Young, *Genital Abnormalities, Hermaphroditism and Related Adrenal Diseases*, 52, 1937.

11 Hauser, "Testicular Feminization," 273, 1963.

In any event, when a (usually male) doctor in the late 19th or early 20th century delivered a baby with genitals that looked like a Quigley 2 or 3, the verdict was invariably "it's a boy," with the caveat that cosmetic plastic surgery might be needed to render the baby more "normal looking," not unlike a cleft lip or palate. "Hypospadias surgery" could be quite minor, little more than a bit of sewing up of what would become the lower surface of a penis.

Throughout the 20th century, surgery became increasingly sophisticated and doctors came to better understand the role of hormones in sex differentiation. Administering hormone therapies to either virilize or feminize babies and children became possible. This made it increasingly straightforward to treat many intersex births as boys whose penises simply needed a bit of surgical and hormonal "help" to develop "properly." It was an age of... medical cockiness.

For intersex babies on the far right end of the Quigley scale, though—regardless of chromosomes or other factors—no matter how hard the doctors squinted, they couldn't see a penis. Instead, they saw an oversized clitoris, or "cliteromegaly." And as a 1963 article on intersexuality explains, "In border-line cases with hypertrophy of the clitoris, *amputation* of the clitoris may be necessary for cosmetic reasons."[11]

Brought up in a male orphanage and admitted aged 7 with a "small, hypospadic" penis, patient F.R. was found to have a vagina, uterus, Fallopian tube, and supposed left ovary, leading the doctors to conclude F.R. was "definitely female," with unfortunate consequences: "Child put into girl's clothing; transferred to female orphanage. Developed marked habit of masturbation; on this account enlarged "clitoris" was amputated. At age of 17, operation for hernia: discovery that supposed ovary was testicle. This was removed. Patient again assumed male clothing [... and] has become more masculine in character and interests. He has taken the name of "John," and is employed as a truck driver." From Young, 84–87.

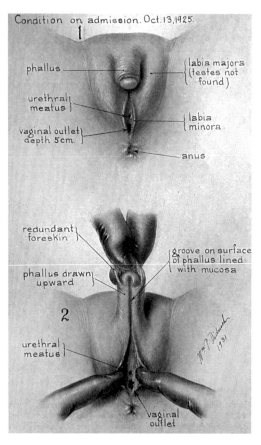

Condition on admission. Oct. 13, 1925.

1

phallus

labia majora (testes not found)

urethral meatus

labia minora

vaginal outlet depth 5cm.

anus

redundant foreskin

groove on surface of phallus lined with mucosa

phallus drawn upward

2

urethral meatus

vaginal outlet

So, a century after Acton's enthusiastic endorsement of surgical removal of the clitoris to deny women pleasure, doctors were still keen on cutting off clitorises—but now just for appearance's sake.

It's telling that upon deciding a baby was female, "normalizing" the way the genitals looked took precedence over any sexual pleasure they might provide.[12] One can't help wondering whether the conclusion would have been the same if a similar procedure were needed to conform to "normal" male appearance? For girls, removal of the clitoris might be a necessary aesthetic sacrifice, but for boys, as we'll soon see, removal of the penis was an unthinkable tragedy.[13]

In cases of so-called testicular feminization (today referred to as Androgen Insensitivity Syndrome), the 1963 article goes on to recommend that children be

> [...] brought up as females in spite of their male gonads
> and chromosomal sex. They should never be told they have
> testes, or that they are hermaphrodites, but we always do
> explain to them that they are sterile, and will remain so, and
> that they will never menstruate. Usually they accept this
> knowledge very well. Most married women either adopt
> children or take part in extra-household activities which
> they often pursue with great success because of their above
> average intelligence.[14]

Passages like these are rife with the biases that pervaded medicine's approach to gender in the 20th century. For one, the throwaway comment about "above average intelligence" is based on the notion that

12 John Money, soon to be introduced, argued for "no evidence of a deleterious effect [on erotic sensation] of clitoridectomy," based on the reported experiences of a dozen women with CAH who underwent the procedure at an older age and consensually. Money, *Venuses Penuses: Sexology, Sexosophy, and Exigency Theory*, 144, 1986. There are, however, some obvious reasons to treat this assertion with a grain (or more) of salt.

13 Similarly, John Harvey Kellogg might have gotten away with cutting off the foreskins of boys who were caught masturbating one too many times, but he certainly couldn't have gotten away with cutting off the whole thing.

14 Hauser, "Testicular Feminization," 273, 1963.

15 A couple of contemporary studies attempted to prove this rather dubious assertion, but they wouldn't pass muster by any modern evidentiary standard. Chapter 15 will offer a more informed perspective.

16 Springer, van den Heijkant, and Baumann, "Worldwide Prevalence of Hypospadias," 2016; Keays and Dave, "Current Hypospadias Management: Diagnosis, Surgical Management, and Long-Term Patient-Centred Outcomes," 2017.

17 Brown and Novick, *Voices from the Edge: Conversations with Jerry Garcia, Ram Dass, Annie Sprinkle, Matthew Fox, Jaron Lanier, & Others*, 38, 1995.

the XY chromosomes would, despite any outward appearance of femininity, result in a more "male," hence more intelligent, brain![15]

Setting this eye roller aside, the article's advice to doctors sheds further light on why young people who are intersex almost never know they are. Standard practice for doctors delivering an intersex baby was to make a measurement with a ruler and, based on clitoris/penis size, decide whether to "sew them up" and (sometimes) administer virilizing hormones, or amputate and (sometimes) administer feminizing hormones.[16] This was all done as young as possible, ostensibly in order to avoid exposing the child to any gender ambiguity growing up—either in their family relationships or in their underwear.

The results could be devastating. In the 1990s, sex activist Annie Sprinkle wrote,

> **In my last workshop, we had a woman who was born with hermaphroditic genitals. At one and a half years old, the surgeons mutilated her. They removed her penis, which was really an enlarged clitoris, and her inner labia. Now she has horrible vaginal and psychological pain, and has never experienced orgasm. [...] She's very angry about having been mutilated, so now she's organizing other people like herself through a newsletter. Unfortunately, this is very common, but rarely addressed. People who are not stereotypically male or female suffer so much.[17]**

Ironically, these practices were based on an idea that seemed progressive in the postwar years: that gender was not innate or biologically predetermined, but was rather an emergent phenomenon, constructed socially and psychologically. The ideological pendulum had swung from pure nature to pure culture.

→ American sexologist, performance artist, former sex worker, and sex work advocate Annie Sprinkle.

Interlude **Ycleptance**

(1) -ive } are suffixes which imply *illustrating* or
    -iveness } *being an example of* the process or source
             designated by the root.

(2) -ivity } are suffixes which imply *manifesting* or
    -uality } *being operated by* powers or capacities
    -ual   } characteristic of the process or source
    -(a/e)nce } designated by the root.
    -(a/e)nt }

"Designative and
Dynamic Words"
from Money, *Venuses
Penuses*, 69, 1986.

Yclept is an Elizabethan word, one form of the past participle of to clepe, meaning to name, to call, or to style. [...] Ycleptance means the condition or experience of being classified, branded, labeled, or typecast. It has its phyletic basis in likeness and unlikeness between individual and group attributes. Human beings have named and typecast one another since before recorded time. The terms range from the haphazard informality of nicknames that recognize personal idiosyncrasies, to the highly organized formality of scientific classifications or medical diagnoses that prognosticate our futures. The categories of ycleptance are many and diverse: sex, age, family, clan, language, race, region, religion, politics, wealth, occupation, health, physique, looks, temperament, and so on. We all live typecast under the imprimatur of our fellow human beings. We are either stigmatized or idolized by the brand names or labels under which we are yclept. They shape our destinies.[1]

1   Money, "Concepts of
Determinism," 1988.

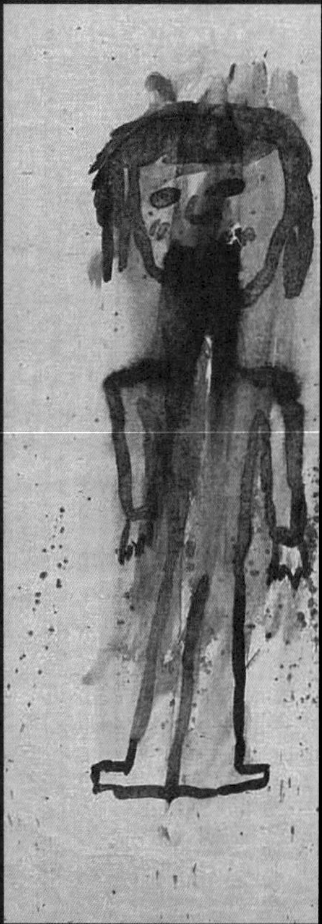

Near noon, Janet awoke with a throbbing head, a roaring in her ears, and a wet feeling under her nose. She touched it: bright blood. It had stained the pillow. On the bedside table, the torn-open packet of Aspros she'd

TURNING THE MIND INSIDE OUT

*Saturday Evening
Post*, 1941.

Drawings on the cover of
Money and Ehrhardt, *Man
& Woman, Boy & Girl*, 1972,
by Sally Hopkins.

Self-portrait
by the young
Bruce/Brenda/
David Reimer.

swallowed the night before, and the empty water glass she'd used to chase all those bitter pills down. Staggering to her feet, she found her face in the mirror, a dusky red. She turned on the tap and vomited, unexpectedly filled with wonder and delight, thankful still to be alive.

→ Portrait of Janet Frame, believed to have been taken by John Money.

By Monday morning, she was feeling better, just a slight headache. She decided she'd have to give up teaching, a commitment that had been weighing her down with crippling anxiety. The problem wasn't the children, whom she loved, but the adults—being scrutinized by the headmaster, dealing with the parents, facing the dreaded afternoon tea with the other teachers. How they all stared at her!

Being a student at the University was easier going, more anonymous. It played to her strengths. For an assignment in her psychology course, she was supposed to submit a short autobiography. Self-disclosure came far more naturally in written sentences. As she wrapped the essay up, Janet added, "Perhaps I should mention a recent attempt at suicide," and described what she'd done, although to make the attempt more impressive, using the chemical term for aspirin—acetylsalicylic acid.

This got the handsome young lecturer's attention. He asked her to stay after class.

Janet's family were working class folk from the country. Though barely three years her elder, John Money exuded all the charm, confidence, and worldliness she as yet lacked. A bit of a heartthrob, really, and quite aware of it. He played the piano beautifully, bantered easily with the students about music and books, and dressed flamboyantly, in tomato-red socks and a rust-colored sports coat. In her head, Janet had

John Money at the University of Otago, Dunedin, New Zealand, 1946.

nicknamed him Ash, after Ashley, the fair young man in *Gone with the Wind*, played by Leslie Howard.

"I enjoyed your autobiography," he said. "All the others were so formal and serious but yours was so natural. You have a talent for writing."

Janet may have felt a flush rising. "Oh I do write. I had a story in the *Listener*—." He was impressed. The *Listener* was hard to get into.

That evening, Mrs. T, her landlady, answering a knock on the door, called up to her, "There are three men to see you. From the University." And there they were: John, another young lecturer, and the head of the psychology department.

The department head spoke first. "Mr. Money tells me you haven't been feeling very well. We thought you might like to have a little rest."

"I'm fine, thank you," answered Janet.

But he insisted, "We thought you might like to come with us down to the hospital—the Dunedin hospital—just for a few days' rest. John will come to visit you."

Thus began eight years in and out of New Zealand mental wards, where Janet Frame, who would eventually be shortlisted for the Nobel Prize in literature, was (incorrectly) diagnosed with

First floor plan of the Seacliff Lunatic Asylum, 1881.

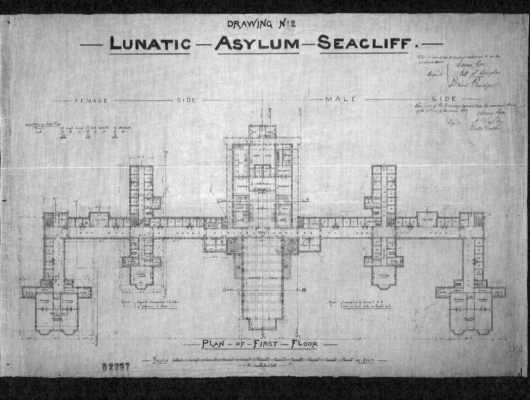

schizophrenia. She underwent the insulin and electroconvulsive shock therapies popular at the time. After being given the "new electric treatment" at Sunnyside Mental Hospital, as she wrote in her autobiography many years later,

> [...] suddenly my life was thrown out of focus. I could not remember. I was terrified. I behaved as others around me behaved. I who had learned the language, spoke and acted that language. I felt utterly alone. There was no one to talk to. As in other mental hospitals, you were locked up, you did as you were told or else, and that was that.[2]

2   Frame, *An Angel at My Table: An Autobiography*, 98, 1984.

Throughout much of this period, though, she did have one person to talk to. Fascinated by her, both professionally and perhaps in other ways, John Money visited regularly. When he learned that she was writing stories and poems, he suggested that she bring them to their therapy sessions for him to keep. He had all the instincts of a great collector, both of art and of people. At some point he showed her stories to Denis Glover of the Caxton Press in Christchurch, who expressed interest in publishing them in a book, with the poems perhaps following.

Though painfully shy and socially anxious, her hand always in front of her mouth to conceal her rotten teeth, Janet craved John's attention and praise. Playing up to his expectations, she tailored her symptoms—and her writing—to the case histories she was reading, keeping the "pure schizophrenia" for the poems, where it was "most at home." There was a dark glamor in the diagnosis. "When I think of you," said Money, "I think of Van Gogh,

Nurses on the front lawn of Seacliff, 1890.

of Hugo Wolf." Looking up these unfamiliar names, Frame found that "all three were named as schizophrenic, with their artistic ability apparently the pearl of their schizophrenia. Great artists, visionaries... My place was set, then, at the terrible feast."

One day, while perusing case histories, Janet read about a woman who was also afraid to visit the dentist, though in her own case, the reluctance was mainly borne of poverty. However, *fear of the dentist* was apparently common among schizophrenics, which, "in the Freudian manner ... [was] interpreted as *guilt over masturbation*, which was said to be one of the causes and a continued symptom of schizophrenia!" Money, "glistening with newly applied Freud," pounced on Frame's ersatz confession of lifelong guilt, hastening to reassure her that masturbation was "perfectly all right, everyone did it." Was that a gleam in his eye? Well, certainly, she was doing it now too, although she had only learned how in the course of her furtive reading a few weeks earlier. Better late than never!

By the end of 1946, Janet was once again living in a boarding-house in Dunedin, her state of mind in fragile equilibrium. But then, John let her know that the "little talks" she so treasured would soon be coming to an end, for he had applied to the Psychiatric Institute at the University of Pittsburgh, and planned to emigrate to America. She tried to conceal her sense of betrayal in the wake of his blithe announcement, and her embarrassment over the asymmetry of their relationship. It hurt.

Perhaps grasping for something consoling to offer, he recommended a therapist friend in Christchurch, who, being of an artistic temperament, was interested in Janet's case. It was an awkward referral, as Christchurch was many hours away by train. But, having no reason now to stay in Dunedin—her abusive family nearby was hardly a draw—Janet resolved to move there. It might make a fresh start.

Soon, she stood waiting on the platform with her few possessions, little more than a folded-up reference from Mrs. T in her pocket ("Polite to the guests at all times, industrious, a pleasure...") and a tiny black kitten, supposedly male but actually female, whom she had first named Sigmund, then corrected to Sigmunde, and finally shortened to the gender-ambiguous Siggy.

After a couple of years' study at the Psychiatric Institute of the University of Pittsburgh, John Money went on to Harvard for a doctorate in Psychology, submitting the dissertation *Hermaphroditism: An Inquiry into the Nature of a Human Paradox*. His career began to take off. Before even being awarded his PhD in 1952, he had already assumed a professorship in pediatrics and medical psychology at Johns Hopkins, a position he would hold onto until his death in 2006. Although his interests were broad and interdisciplinary—some would say unruly— much of his work focused on sexology, endocrinology, and, especially, intersexuality.

He became a giant in his field. The Psychohormonal Research Unit he founded soon after arriving at Johns Hopkins set the standard for the understanding and treatment of trans and intersex people for decades. Money's name is on about 2,000 articles, books, chapters, and reviews; he received dozens of prestigious awards and honors in his lifetime.

He was a prolific coiner of words and phrases, too. Some, like "foredoomance," "behavioron," "gynemimesis," and "ycleptance," never caught on; nor did his own name for his favorite subject: "fuckology." But other terms, like "sexual orientation," "gender role," and "gender identity," have insinuated themselves into everyday English so thoroughly that they no longer sound made up. The word "gender" itself, in its modern usage, owes much to him. Money was the Shakespeare of sexology.

From John Money,
Venuses Penuses, 441,
1986.

TABLE I

Paraphilias

ACROTOMOPHILIA* (Amputee Partner)	MYSOPHILIA (Filth)
	NARRATOPHILIA (Erotic Talk)
APOTEMNOPHILIA* (Self-Amputee)	NECROPHILIA (Corpse)
	PEDOPHILIA (Child)
ASPHYXIOPHILIA (Self-Strangulation)	PICTOPHILIA (Pictures)
	PEODEIKTOPHILIA* (Penile Exhibitionism)
AUTAGONISTOPHILIA* (On Stage)	
AUTASSASSINOPHILIA (Own Murder Staged)	RAPISM or BIASTOPHILIA* (Violent Assault)
AUTONEPIOPHILIA* (Diaperism)	SADISM
COPROPHILIA (Feces)	SCOPTOPHILIA (Watching Coitus)
EPHEBOPHILIA (Youth)	SOMNOPHILIA (Sleeper)
EROTOPHONOPHILIA* (Lust Murder)	STIGMATOPHILIA* (Piercing; Tattoo)
FETISHISM	SYMPHOROPHILIA* (Disaster)
FROTTEURISM (Rub Against Stranger)	TELEPHONE SCATOPHILIA (Lewdness)
GERONTOPHILIA (Elder)	TROILISM (Couple + One)
HYPHEPHILIA (Fabrics)	UROPHILIA or UNDINISM (Urine)
KLEPTOPHILIA (Stealing)	VOYEURISM or PEEPING-TOMISM
KLISMAPHILIA (Enema)	
MASOCHISM	ZOOPHILIA (Animal)

*New term formed from Greek root (in collaboration with Diskin Clay, Professor of Greek, Johns Hopkins University).

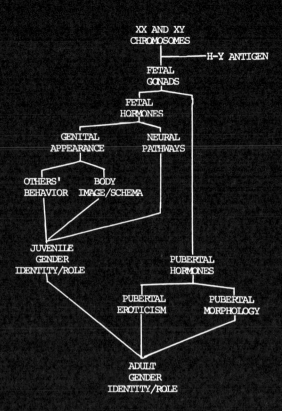

XX AND XY
CHROMOSOMES

H-Y ANTIGEN

FETAL
GONADS

FETAL
HORMONES

GENITAL
APPEARANCE

NEURAL
PATHWAYS

OTHERS'
BEHAVIOR

BODY
IMAGE/SCHEMA

JUVENILE
GENDER
IDENTITY/ROLE

PUBERTAL
HORMONES

PUBERTAL
EROTICISM

PUBERTAL
MORPHOLOGY

ADULT
GENDER
IDENTITY/ROLE

"[...] the sequence of determinants or events that lead to the differentiation of gender identity in childhood or adulthood. [...] With each change in the transmission of the program of gender-identity differentiation, there exists the possibility that an error may be introduced and subsequently transmitted." From John Money, *Venuses Penuses*, 224–25, 1986.

His framework for thinking about sex and gender was sophisticated for the time, synthesizing a wealth of new medical and psychological findings into a coherent theory. Like the Gaian ideas of James Lovelock (and, for that matter, Oberon Zell), it was powerfully influenced by cybernetics, the new science of complex dynamical systems and feedback. Money and his colleagues realized that while most of us think of each individual as intrinsically "male" or "female," in reality there are many variables working in concert to establish "maleness" or "femaleness," with a tangle of causal connections and nonlinear feedback loops linking them all together. There are chromosomes, of course. Then, there are gonads (meaning ovaries or testes), which begin as undifferentiated "sex glands" but, once differentiated, are made up of tissue that looks distinctly ovary-like or testis-like under a microscope. There are internal organs like the vagina, uterus, and fallopian tubes. There's the menstrual cycle. There are external genitals. Breast development. Different patterns of body hair, and, often, of hair loss in middle age. Different patterns of growth, musculature, fat distribution, and bone structure, especially in the face and the pelvis. All of these physical changes are driven by different sex hormone levels during development, both before birth and throughout life; these are secreted not only by the ovaries or testes, but also by the adrenal glands, fat cells, and the pituitary gland in the brain.

Sex hormones also work *on* the brain, both during early development and later on, although given how poorly we understand how the brain works, quite a few unknowns about the timing, nature, and extent of this influence persist. These unknowns are hard to pin down, partially because, as highly social beings, the answer to that first question—"boy or girl?"—determines how a baby is raised, or "socialized," which in turn profoundly influences that child's self-concept or identity.

To further complicate things, out of all of these body, brain, mind, and societal variables, the only one that's arguably binary is chromosomal makeup (and even there, chimerism and chromosomal variations can complicate the picture). Every other item

TABLE 1 *Guide to the Differential Diagnosis of Intersexuality.*

Phenotype	Distribution	Nuclear Sex	Diagnosis	Testes	Adnexal	Müllerian	Wolffian	Ext. Genitalia	Androgens	Oestrogens	Other Features	Familial Association	Incidence amongst Intersexes	Clinical Findings See page
Female		♂	Testicular feminization	+	–		↑ M	↑ F			Pretty females with breasts; usually no pubic or axillary hair	Fairly common	Not uncommon	255
		1 : 1 ♂♀ 3 : 1	Gonadal dysgenesis Turner's syndrome	Rudimentary		↑	↓	↓			No abnormalities / Small stature, webbed neck, cubitus valgus, etc.	Occurs / ? rather rare	Common	290 / 329
		♀	Female adrenogenital syndrome	–	+		↑ M	↑ F			Children: big Adults: small Type as in Fig. 1, p. 183	Fairly common	Common	345
		♀	Female (non-adrenal) pseudo-hermaphrodite	–	+	(+)	↑ M	↑ F			Advanced cases have double urethra (clitoral and vaginal)	Not yet reported	Very uncommon	244
		♂ (♀?)	True gonadal agenesis	–	–		↑	↓			No genital organs	Occurs uncommon	Very uncommon	340
		♀ ♂ 4 : 1	True hermaphroditism	+	+		F M	F M			Urogenital type (see Fig. 1, p. 183)	Occurs	Rare	182
		♂	Male pseudo-hermaphrodite	+	–		↑ M	↓ M				Fairly common	Fairly common	235
		–	So-called male Turner's syndrome	+	–		↑ M	↑ M			Small stature, webbed neck, genu valgum, etc.	Occurs, but very uncommon	Very uncommon	329
	Male	♂	Klinefelter's syndrome	+	–		↑ M	↑ M			Dysplastic type, gynaecomastia, increased Leydig cells, hyaline basement membrane	Occurs, but very uncommon	Common particularly in the debilitated	277

TABLE 2
The sex chromosomes and sex chromatin in the diagnosis of intersexual conditions

Sex chromosome	Sex chromatin	Drumsticks	Phenotype — Female	Phenotype — Male	References [1]
XY				Normal male	l.c.
XX	+	0	Normal female		l.c.
XO	0	0	Turner's syndrome		l.c.; Chapelle (1962), Fraccaro et al. (1960 b), Kosenow et al. (1962), Lüers et al. (1962 b), Maclean et al. (1962), Miller (1962)
XO	0	0	Turner's syndrome (identical twins)		Turner et al. (1962)
XO	0	+	Turner's syndrome with virilization		Lüers et al. (1962 a)
XO	0	0	" Male " Turner's syndrome		House et al. (1960)
XO	0	0	Turner's syndrome (fertile)		l.c. (Bahner)
XO	0	0		Male pseudo-hermaphroditism (True hermaphroditism?)	Atkins et al. (1962)
XO	+	+	Gonadal dysgenesis		l.c., Grumbach (1960)[3]
Xa	+	+	Sexual hypoplasia		Jacobs et al. (1961)
XX	+	+	Sexual hypoplasia, polycystic ovaries		Jacobs et al. (1961)
XX	0	Q	Rudimentary ovaries		l.c. (Jacobs)
XX	+	+	Turner's syndrome with ovaries		Oikawa et al. (1961)
XX	+	+	Gonadal dysgenesis		l.c., Chapelle (1962), Hauser et al. (1960), Jacobs et al. (1961)
XX	+	+	Normal female		l.c.
XX	+	+	Female adrenogenital syndrome		l.c.
XX	+	+	Induced pseudo-hermaphroditism		l.c.
XX	+	+	Female pseudo-hermaphroditism		Dubowitz (1962), Makino et al. (1960), Overzier (1962), Seringe et al. (1960, 1961)
XX	+	+	True hermaphroditism		l.c., Miller (1962), German et al. (1962)
XX	+	+		" Male " Turner's syndrome	l.c., Overzier (1963)
(XX)	+	+	Congenital absence of vagina		Oikawa et al. (1961)
XX	–		Turner's syndrome		Miller (1962)
XX	+	+	Sexual hypoplasia		Bäck (1961), Fraccaro et al. (1960 a), Hamerton et al. (1962), Jacobs et al. (1961)
XXX	+ +	+	Triplo-X-females		Jacobs et al. (1961); l.c., Barr et al. (1960), Carli et al. (1960), Fraser et al. (1960), Hamerton et al. (1960), Johnston et al. (1961), Lüers et al. (1962 b), Maclean et al. (1962), Oikawa et al. (1961), Räis et al. (1960), Sandberg et al. (1960), Uchida et al. (1961)
XXXX	+ + +	+	Mentally defective females		Barr et al. (1960), Carr et al. (1961 a)
XXXX	+ + +	+		"Boy" with cryptorchidism and several malformations	Anders et al. (1960)
Oy(?)	0	0	Girl (gonadal dysplasia) with phallus		Vaharu et al. (1961)
XY	0	0		" False " Klinefelter's syndrome	l.c.; Klotz et al. (1962 a)
XY	0	0		" Male " Turner's syndrome	Fraccaro et al. (1961), Putterweit et al. (1961), Oikawa et al. (1961), Stoiker et al. (1961)
XY	0	0		Male pseudo-hermaphroditism	l.c.; Alexander et al. (1961), Ferguson-Smith (1960)
XY				Male mongol with small and undescended testicles	Bishop et al. (1962)
XY	0	0	Testicular feminization		l.c., Alexander et al. (1961), Chu et al. (1960), Miller (1962), Overzier (1962, 1963)
XY	0	0	Pure gonadal dysgenesis		l.c., Chapelle (1962), Grouchy et al. (1960)
XY	0	0		True hermaphroditism	l.c., Eliacher et al. (1962), Grumbach et al. (1960), Overzier (1961, 1963)
XXY	+	+		True Klinefelter's syndrome with hypospadias	Gray (1961)
XXY	+	+		True Klinefelter's syndrome	l.c., Decourt et al. (1962), Ferguson-Smith (1962), Gropp et al. (1962), Harnden (1961), Kosenow et al. (1961, 1962), Kvenow (1961, 1963), Lüers et al. (1962 b), Maclean et al. (1962), Makino et al. (1960), Miller (1962), Seringe et al. (1961)
XXXY	+ +	+		True Klinefelter's syndrome	l.c.; Barr et al. (1959, 1960), Carr et al. (1961 c), Ferguson-Smith (1962), Johnston (1961), Maclean et al. (1962)
XXXXY	+ + +	+		True Klinefelter's syndrome Hypospadias, bifid scrotum and several other malformations	l.c.; Fraser et al. (1961), Miller et al. (1961 a, b), Fraccaro et al. (1960 c, 1962), Pfeiffer (1962)
XYY	0	0		Normal male, but with defective children	Sandberg et al. (1961)
XXYY	+	+		True Klinefelter's syndrome	l.c.; Barr et al. (1960), Carr et al. (1961 b), Maclean et al. (1962), Muhlal et al. (1960, 1962), Vague et al. (1961)
XXXYY				True Klinefelter's syndrome	Josephine et al. (1962)
⁴X/XO		+	Turner's syndrome		Bänk (1961), Chapelle (1962), Lindsten (1961)
XX/XO		0⁴	Turner's syndrome		l.c.; Fraccaro et al. (1960), Grouchy et al. (1961), Jacobs et al. (1961), Sandberg et al. (1961)
XX/XO		+	Turner's syndrome		l.c.; Chapelle (1962), Ferrier et al. (1961), Grouchy et al. (1961, 1962), Jacobs et al. (1961), Ferrier et al. (1961, 1962)
XX/XO				Similar to Klinefelter's syndrome	Ferrier et al. (1963)
XXX/XO		O	Woman with primary amenorrhea		Maclean (1962)
XX/XO		+ +	Female without vagina or uterus		l.c. (Jacobs); Jacobs et al. (1961)
XXXX/XO⁴		+ +	Turner's syndrome		Sacha et al. (1960)
XXX/XX/XO		+ +	Turner's syndrome		Grumbach et al. (1961), Hayward et al. (1961)
XXX/XX/XO		(+)	Mental defective female		Carr et al. (1962)
XX/XXX			True hermaphroditism		Maclean et al. (1962)
XO/Xyf		+		Male pseudo-hermaphroditism	Waxman et al. (1962) → Gartler et al. (1962)
XO/Xy		0		True hermaphroditism	Ferrier et al. (1962)
XO/Xy/XXXy		0	Atypical Turner's syndrome → True hermaphroditism		Conen et al. (1961)
XO/XYY		0	Atypical Turner's syndrome		Fraccaro et al. (1962)
XO/XY		0	Atypical Turner's syndrome		Bänk et al. (1961), Miller (1962), Judge et al. (1962)
XO/XY		0		" False " Klinefelter's syndrome	Chapelle et al. (1962)
XO/XY		0		True hermaphroditism	l.c., Hirschhorn et al. (1960 a, b), Miller (1960, 1961), Miller et al. (1961)
XO/XY		0		Male pseudo-hermaphroditism	Ferrier et al. (1961), Jacobs et al. (1961), Wilkowson et al. (1962)
XO/XY		0	Turner's syndrome	Congenital anorchism	Miller (1962)
XO/XYY		0		Male pseudo-hermaphroditism	Miles et al. (1962)
XO/XaY		0		Male pseudo-hermaphroditism	Shah et al. (1961)
(XX?/XX.XXY		0		Male pseudo-hermaphroditism	Scheeter et al. (1962)
XX.XY/XO				True Klinefelter's syndrome	l.c., Miller (1962)
XX/XY		+		Normal male	Baikie et al. (1961)
XY/XXY		+		True Klinefelter's syndrome	Klinger et al. (1961)
XY/XXY		0/+	⚖ Fœtus: 60mm	True Klinefelter's syndrome	Lübs (1962), Miller (1962)
XY/XXY		0	Chromatin-negative Klinefelter's syndrome		Sandborg (1961)
XY/XXY		+	Male hypogonadism		Klotz et al. (1962 b)
XY/XXXY + XY		+ +	Mental defective " male "		Maclean et al. (1962)
XX/XXY + XY			Mentally defective male		Barr, Carr et al. (1962)
XO/XY/XXY				True Klinefelter's syndrome	Maclean et al. (1962)
				Normal brother of a Klinefelter case	Miller (1962)
XY/XY,XXY/XXYY?		+	Mental defective " male "		Maclean et al. (1962)
XXXY/XXXY + XY		+	Mentally defective " male "		Maclean et al. (1962)
XAaY,XXY		+		True Klinefelter's syndrome with thalassaemia	Miller (1962)
YO/XY/XXY		+		True Klinefelter's syndrome	Benda et al. (1962)
XO/XX.XY/		+ +		True Klinefelter's syndrome	
XXY + XXXY					
XXXXY/XXXY				True Klinefelter's syndrome	Jacobs et al. (1961), Maclean et al. (1962)
XXY + autosomal				True Klinefelter's syndrome and Down's syndrome	l.c.; Geldren et al. (1961), Hamerton et al. (1962), Lanman et al. (1960), Lehman et al. (1960), Maclean et al. (1962)
XXX + autosomal + del. No. 22, satellite No. 21				Male infant with several malformations	Pfeiffer et al. (1962)
XAO + autosomal			Turner's syndrome		Chapelle (1962)
XXX + autosomal No. 18			Girl with multiple malformations		Uchida et al. (1962)

[1] l.c. = loc. cit. in this book) ² isochromosome for the long arm of X; sex chromatin larger and more numerous than in normal subjects, or deletion of one of the X chromosomes; sex chromatin smaller and less frequent. ³ Now identified as XXX/XX/XO (Grumbach et al. 1961). ⁴ Or vice versa according to the position of the mosaic.

Table mapping many chromosomal variations to intersex diagnoses. From Overzier, *Inter-sexuality*, 173–74, 1963.

3 Money, *Biographies of Gender and Hermaphroditism in Paired Comparisons: Clinical Supplement to the Handbook of Sexology*, 1991.

4 Statistical rigor in medicine has remained a problem. The "evidence-based medicine" movement dates only to the late 1980s, and even today, the evidentiary standards of many papers in medicine (as well as psychology and the social sciences) don't pass muster. Only in recent years has widespread attention been paid to the ensuing replicability crisis in these fields. A reappraisal of standards for data quality and analysis has proven necessary even in "harder" fields, like neuroscience, biology, and physics. Button et al., "Power Failure: Why Small Sample Size Undermines the Reliability of Neuroscience," 2013; Baker, "1,500 Scientists Lift the Lid on Reproducibility," 2016; Junk and Lyons, "Reproducibility and Replication of Experimental Particle Physics Results," 2020.

From John Money, *Venuses Penuses*, 175–76, 1986.

in the list can be modeled as a continuous variable, with plenty of excluded middle. While genes usually kick off the cascade of events that ultimately drive all of the other effects, many factors may contribute to chromosomal sex not aligning with these other variables, all of which are a lot more socially, psychologically, and even anatomically relevant. Imagine these sex and gender variables like a bank of switches (or, more accurately, sliders) in a fuse box. Each influences the others, to different degrees and with time delays ranging from seconds to years. How many of us really have all of these sliders set unambiguously to one side or the other, and when there's ambiguity, how can we talk about any single variable being the definitive one—the one that tells us who we "really" are?

Among the intersex population, and especially the most vexingly ambiguous cases, John Money found individuals with nearly every conceivable configuration of "fuse box settings."[3] As a practicing psychologist who could team up with pediatricians, endocrinologists, and surgeons at Johns Hopkins, he was also far from an armchair observer. Money wanted to make his mark. He could move rapidly from bold hypotheses to grand theories to dogmatic convictions, and didn't shy away from rolling up his sleeves. He put his ideas into practice, often with life-altering procedures on patients of all ages.

TABLE III

Psychologic Healthiness Ratings of 94 Patients

Variety of Hermaphroditism	Healthy	Mild	Nonhealthy Moderate	Severe	Total
1. Adrenal ♀	28	12	7	1	48
2. Nonadrenal ♀	3	—	—	—	3
3. True	1	—	—	—	1
4. ♂, mullerian differentiation	1	—	2	—	3
5. Gonadal agenesis	14	1	1	—	16
6. ♂, simulant ♀	7	—	—	—	7
7. ♂, hypospadiac, breasts	1	—	—	—	1
8. ♂, hypospadiac	8	3	4	—	15
Total	63	16	14	1	94

The whole mid-20th century medical establishment was drunk on its newfound power and overconfident in its burgeoning knowledge about the body. Doctors were less restrained by medical ethics than we are today, less humbled by complexity and unintended consequences, and less schooled in statistical rigor.[4]

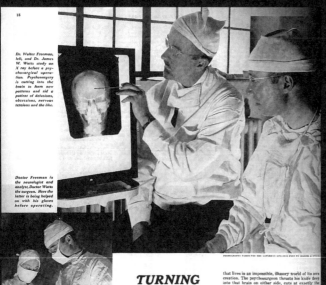

18

Dr. Walter Freeman, left, and Dr. James W. Watts study an X ray before a psychosurgical operation. Psychosurgery is cutting into the brain to form new patterns and rid a patient of delusions, obsessions, nervous tensions and the like.

Doctor Freeman is the neurologist and analyst, Doctor Watts the surgeon. Here the latter is being helped on with his gloves before operating.

TURNING THE MIND INSIDE OUT

By
Waldemar Kaempffert

THERE must be at least two hundred men and women in the United States who have had worries, persecution complexes, suicidal intentions, obsessions, indecisiveness, nervous tensions, literally cut out of their minds with a knife by a new operation on the brain. They are the beneficiaries of psychosurgery, a word which is not yet in the dictionary. From problems to their families and nuisances to themselves, from ineffective and unemployable, many of the two hundred have been transformed into useful members of society. A world that once seemed the abode of misery, cruelty and hate is now radiant with sunshine and kindness to them.

Physically there is nothing abnormal about the brain on which the surgeon of the mind operates. In appearance and structure it is indistinguishable from that of a solid citizen who pays his bills, observes the conventions, belongs to the right clubs, contributes generously to local charities, and lives an irreproachable life. Yet it cannot think logically. It is the brain not of an insane mind but of a mind that lives in an impossible, illusory world of its own creation. The psychosurgeon thrusts his knife deep into that brain on either side, cuts at exactly the right angle in turning an ingrowing and a harassed mind outward and in transforming a personality.

No rash and sudden attempt is psychosurgery, to succeed where kind words, drugs and arguments have failed for centuries. It benefits from all the knowledge ever acquired of the brain as a piece of mechanism. Even the founders of phrenology, F. J. Gall and J. C. Spurzheim, contributed something: for behind their slightly quackish system of feeling bumps on the head and thus judging human character and capabilities lay the sound conception of a brain in which traits of ability and what we call "character" were localized. Since their time every nook and cranny of the brain has been poked into, dissected, examined, blueprinted, named and otherwise identified as if they were components of an automobile. Different parts of the brains of animals were either removed or stimulated with electric currents and the areas and centers discovered that control movement, seeing, hearing, swallowing, winking, breathing, sweating and other activities.

The effect of injuries on human brains was studied—erratic behavior, convulsions, loss of memory and reasoning power, paralysis of the muscles and organs. Dr. Leonardo Bianchi, a famous Italian neurologist, lived and shared his food with monkeys whose forebrains he had removed and noted their loss of what he called "social sense," initiative and memory. The Russian, Pavlov, showed that the mouths of dogs trained to associate the ringing of a bell with eating would water and the

PHOTOGRAPHS TAKEN FOR THE SATURDAY EVENING POST BY HARRIS & EWING

A *Saturday Evening Post* profile of lobotomy pioneers Walter Freeman and James Watts: "The psychosurgeon thrusts his knife deep into that brain on either side, cuts at exactly the right plane and usually succeeds in turning an ingrowing and a harassed mind outward and in transforming a personality." Kaempffert, "Turning the Mind Inside Out," 1941.

→ John Money and Janet Frame at a reunion in Ōtaki, New Zealand, 1987.

A case in point: in 1949, a couple of years after Money emigrated to America, the Nobel Prize in medicine was awarded to António Egas Moniz for his development of the prefrontal lobotomy. Evidence of its efficacy as a cure for mental illness was flimsy at best, though it was true that lobotomized patients tended to become more docile. Perhaps on that account, the procedure was performed enthusiastically throughout the United States over the following decade, not just on mental patients, but on depressed housewives, sullen teenagers, homosexual or supposedly "gender non-conforming" people (see Chapter 6), and unruly children as young as four years old. A six-year-old girl was lobotomized twice, and a twelve-year-old boy died from the procedure.[5]

New Zealand, too, was swept up in the craze. In 1952, back once again in the Seacliff Lunatic Asylum near Dunedin, the troubled Janet Frame was scheduled for her lobotomy, having exhausted the other available therapies. Her mind was complex, restlessly analytical, and almost cripplingly self-reflective. She was embedded in a culture that presumed a clear dividing line between sanity and mental illness, with the various species of illness neatly taxonomized. Yet her detailed knowledge of these disorders, and her desire both to fit in and to stand out, created its own runaway feedback loops. Behavior, physiology, and identity were hard to untangle. It must have been tempting to cut

5   El-Hai, *The Lobotomist:*
A Maverick Medical Genius
and His Tragic Quest to Rid
the World of Mental Illness,
175, 2005.

6   Goldie, *The Man Who In-*
vented Gender: Engaging the
Ideas of John Money, 2014.

7   Frame, "A Night at the
Opera," 2008; Frame, "Gorse
Is Not People," 2008.

the Gordian knot, even if the threads of that knot were her own neu-ral pathways.

She had remained in contact with John Money, and wrote to ask his advice; to his credit, he advised against the procedure. Ultimately, though, the lobotomy was canceled at the last moment not due to his intercession, but because the hospital superinten-dent learned that she had just won one of New Zealand's most pres-tigious literary prizes, the Hubert Church Memorial Award, for *The Lagoon and Other Stories.*[6] The book had finally been pub-lished that year by the Caxton Press in Christchurch. Janet Frame's identity was finally established, once and for all: she was a writer.

Over the next five decades, she went on to write thirteen novels, two collections of poetry, and two more collections of short stories, winning many more awards and honors along the way. Even after her death in 2004, a stream of posthumous publications con-tinued, including two short stories set in mental hospitals published in the *New Yorker* in 2008.[7]

Since Money had first introduced her work to the Caxton Press's founder, he deserves some credit for saving the frontal lobes, if not the life, of the writer many today consider New Zealand's most preeminent—even if his understanding of her situation was muddled by preconceptions, and his professionalism questionable. The same failings would characterize his treatment of many other patients over the years.

The fifties were deeply conservative, a period of social conform-ity and repression, of McCarthyism and J. Edgar Hoover's FBI. While John Money's views on sexuality were in many ways radical, they were also entirely consistent with the era in regarding the idea of a person growing up as anything other than a man or a woman anathema, a recipe for social shunning and mental disorder. Perhaps, in 1950s America, he wasn't far off the mark.

As the years passed, social strictures began to loosen. The mounting backlash against sexual repression, the rise of hippies, and the Summer of Love did nothing to soften Money's position on the binariness of gender, though. In a 1975 article, *Sexual Signatures: On being a man or a woman*, he and his coauthor Patricia Tucker wrote,

> **The irreducible requirement for the survival of humanity**
> **is that men and women cooperate *as* men and women**
> **at least well enough to survive, reproduce, and rear a new**
> **generation. A man's ability to impregnate and a woman's**
> **to menstruate, gestate, and lactate, are not, by them-**

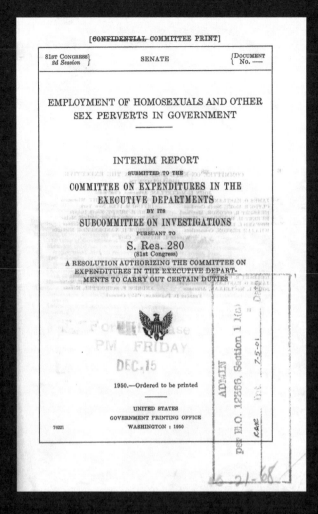

selves an adequate basis for cooperation [...] Gender stereotypes, with all their many more or less arbitrary distinctions, provide the framework for that cooperation.

This was Money's rendition of that hoary old classic, THE TRUE MISSION OF SEX. Given his belief in how essential the gender binary is, not only for the survival of the species but for the individual to fit into *any* kind of society, Money sought to solve the following problem: How could the medical establishment mobilize the array of emerging techniques in surgery, hormone therapy, and psychology to help a person with ambiguous "fuse box" settings become unambiguously a man or a woman, allowing them to take their place in society?

Surgery and hormones turned out to be more reliable tools than psychology. That is, it was a lot harder to convince someone who already thought of themselves in a gendered way to change their mind than it was to resculpt their body. For older patients, then, resculpting the body it was: and so the experts developed and refined the hormonal and surgical techniques known as sex assignment or sex reassignment—later known as gender confirmation. This was pioneering work for treating people we now call trans. Most of the original patients, however, were intersex.

From John Money, *Venuses Penuses*, 155, 1986.

TABLE II

Chromosomes and Rearing Contradictory
19 Cases

CHROMOSOMES	Gonads	Endogenous Hormonal Sex	Internal Accessory Organs	External Genital Morphology	Assigned Sex and Rearing	Gender Role	Type of Ambisexual Development
♂	none	none	♀	♀	11 ♀	11 ♀	Gonadal agenesis (dysgenesis)
♂	♂	♀ 2 juv.	vestigial	♀	3 ♀	3 ♀	simulant female
♂	♂	1 ♂ 3 juv.	vestigial	⚥	4 ♀	4 ♀	cryptorchid male hypospadiac
♀	♀ left ♂ right	⚥	⚥	⚥	1 ♂	1 ♂	true hermaphroditism

TABLE III

Gonads and Rearing Contradictory
20 Cases

GONADS	Chromosomes	Endogenous Hormonal Sex	Internal Accessory Organs	External Genital Morphology	Assigned Sex and Rearing	Gender Role	Type of Ambisexual Development
♀	♀	♀	♀	⚥	2 ♂	2 ♂	female with phallus and ovogenesis
♀	♀	♂	♀	⚥	4 ♂	4 ♂	hyperadrenocortical female
♂	?	1 ♂ 2 juv.	⚥	♀	3 ♀	3 ♀	male with unarrested mullerian differentiation
♂	♂	1 ♀ 2 juv.	vestigial	♀	3 ♀	3 ♀	simulant female
♂	♂	4 ♂ 4 juv.	vestigial	⚥	8 ♀	5 ♀ 1 ♀→♂ 2 ⚦	cryptorchid male hypospadiac

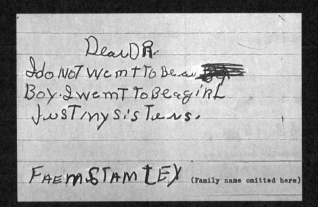

Dear DR
I do NOT wemT To Be a ~~Boy~~
Boy. I wemT To Be a girL
JusT my sisTers.

FAemSTAmLEy (Family name omitted here)

"Unsolicited declaration of desire for sex reassignment given by the boy-to-girl patient [...]" From Money and Ehrhardt, *Man & Woman, Boy & Girl*, 173, 1972.

Many regard Money's greatest error his assertion that gender, as a psychological concept, could arise from a purely psychological origin. He assumed that while gender might be hard to overwrite later in life, it began as a blank slate, and could be freely molded in the first couple of years of life. In other words, if you looked like a girl and were told from infancy that you *were* a girl, then you would *become* a girl, and grow up into a woman; conversely for boys and men. It followed that the best care for intersex people would be to catch them as young as possible, ideally as newborns, decide whether their genitals would be easier to sculpt into a reasonably convincing vulva or penis, quietly do the surgery, and never look back. Money and coauthors spelled out these implications in their 1956 paper *Imprinting and the Establishment of Gender Role*:

Father   andrea Boy

Drawings from Andrea, a patient who "[s]elf-declared as a boy for the first time" from Money and Ehrhardt, *Man & Woman, Boy & Girl*, 288, 1972.

[O]ur findings point to the extreme desirability of deciding, with as little diagnostic delay as possible, on the sex of assignment and rearing when a hermaphroditic baby is born. Thereafter, uncompromising adherence to the decision is desirable. The chromosomal sex should not be the ultimate criterion, nor should the gonadal sex. By contrast, a great deal of emphasis should be placed on the morphology of the external genitals and the ease with which these organs can be surgically reconstructed to be consistent with the assigned sex.

So it was all about the visible genitals, as it has been since time immemorial when we've answered "boy or girl?" in a snap visual judgment at birth. To be a girl, you just needed not to have

anything oversized in your underwear, and to grow breasts after puberty. Being a boy was about being able to stand up to pee, and about not being ridiculed in the locker room. The rest—"gender stereotypes, with all their many more or less arbitrary distinctions"—would simply follow.

Andrea Jackson.

By the 1960s, critics of Money's theory had noticed that his argument for the social flexibility of gender assignment was almost entirely based on accounts of successful gender assignments among intersex people. If the same hormonal processes that shape the body also shape the brain during early development, though, then a lack of strong sexual differentiation in the body might also imply that this population is, on average, unusually gender-flexible psychologically, especially at birth. In fact, those who begin near the center of the gender spectrum may not even *need* so much flexibility to "pass" as either women or men; just a nudge one way or the other, combined with society's powerful bias toward perceiving gender as binary, might be enough.

So, Money needed stronger evidence that gender was socially constructed. In 1966, he got his chance. It came in the form of a desperate letter from Janet and Ron Reimer, the young parents of a pair of baby twins in Winnipeg.

Their story was harrowing.[8] When the twins, Bruce and Brian, were eight months old, they had developed phimosis, a constriction of the foreskin that made it painful to pee. A standard treatment at the time was circumcision. The babies were admitted to St. Boniface Hospital to undergo this minor procedure. Bruce was up first. Instead of a scalpel, an electrocautery machine was used—a device that uses electric current to simultaneously cut and cauterize tissue, instantly sealing the wound and preventing blood loss.

Something went horribly wrong. Whether due to incompetence, malfunction, or some combination, enough electric current was sent through baby Bruce's penis to instantly cook it ("like steak being seared," according to the attending anesthesiologist). The full extent of the damage was not immediately apparent, but

8   Colapinto, *As Nature Made Him: The Boy Who Was Raised as a Girl*, 2000.

the doctors, likely beginning to panic, left Bruce's twin brother, Brian, untouched, and phoned the parents.

In Janet's later account, by the time they were allowed to see Bruce, a couple of days later, his penis was "blackened, [...] sort of like a little string. And it was right up to the base, up to his body." Ron added that it looked "like a piece of charcoal. I knew it wasn't going to come back to life after that."

The doctors wrung their hands, unsure how to proceed. With virtually nothing left to work with, surgical reconstruction was deemed impossible. Dr. G. L. Adamson, head of Winnipeg Clinic's Department of Neurology and Psychiatry, wrote of Bruce, "One can predict that he will be unable to live a normal sexual life from the time of adolescence: that he will be unable to consummate marriage or have normal heterosexual relations, in that he will have to recognize that he is incomplete, physically defective, and that he must live apart."

Bruce's injury was awful by any measure, but this pronouncement highlights the way it was even worse in 1966 than it would be today. Societal expectations of "normality" in all things sexual were so restrictive and judgmental that a boy or man lacking a penis would have been considered a monstrosity who "must live apart."

Months later, deep in despair, Janet and Ron saw John Money on Canadian TV, expounding his theories on the social construc-

Portraits of a young Brenda Reimer.

tion of gender and its implications for intersex babies. Grasping at a faint hope, the Reimers wrote him a letter. Bruce may not have been born intersex, but had the accident not left him in a similar state? He had no penis left to repair, but might surgical *feminization* be an easier route? Since he was still a baby, could he still be raised as a normal girl, if not a normal boy?

Money wrote back promptly: yes, yes, and yes. He encouraged them to bring their child to Johns Hopkins right away. As he would write later on, "Since planned experiments [with babies] are ethically unthinkable, one can only take advantage of unplanned opportunities, such as when a normal boy baby

9 Money and Ehrhardt, *Man & Woman, Boy & Girl: The Differentiation and Dimorphism of Gender Identity from Conception to Maturity*, 162, 1972.

loses his penis in a circumcision accident."[9]

Full advantage was soon taken of this unplanned opportunity. Bruce's testicles were removed, a rudimentary vulva was constructed, and he was given a new name: Brenda. Brenda and Brian (whose phimosis cleared up on its own, underscoring the tragic absurdity of the whole episode) were now a sort of mini, semi-controlled experiment, perfect for putting Money's theory to the test: genetically identical and born male, but being raised as a girl and a boy.

The experiment would take years to unspool. Because Money was both highly invested in the outcome and highly charismatic—coercive, even—it's not clear that the Reimers understood how speculative that theory really was.

There were some inherent tensions at the heart of Money's reasoning. On one hand, he embraced the complexity of cybernetics and systems theory, with its model of the mind and body in terms of multidimensional, continuous, dynamically coupled variables. On the other hand, he also held fast to the binary schema of gender as conceived in the mid-20th century. These ideas were difficult to reconcile. Money assumed that socialization and peer pressure, if applied young enough, have unlimited capacity to steer a person's gender identity in one direction or another; yet he also held that elaborate and arbitrary gender stereotypes are so fundamental to human nature that, in the Flintstones and Jetsons tradition, they transcend culture or era, even if the superficial details might vary. Further, we may begin life arbitrarily "plastic," meaning flexible, able to be pushed toward the masculine or feminine by external social forces during early childhood. Yet somehow, despite the many variables involved, psychological health and "proper functioning" require that by a few years of age we find ourselves firmly on either the masculine or feminine end.

A feedback diagram showing interactions between "the organism and the environment" that lead to behavioral sex differences over time. Reinisch et al., "Sex Differences in Developmental Milestones During the First Year of Life," 1991.

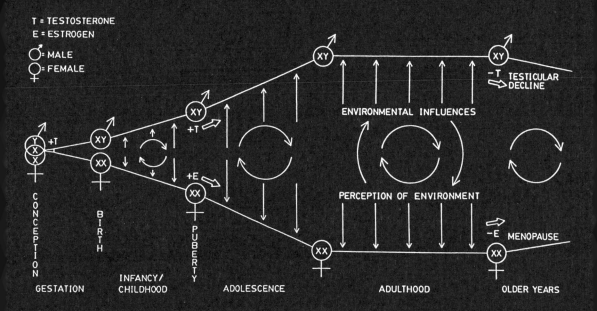

The complexity of the system would—*must*—resolve into a single bit of information.

All of these assumptions are questionable, but taken at face value, they explain why intersex children were almost never told about their condition. As we've seen, they usually aren't told, even today. That's part of Money's legacy.

As a young "girl," Brenda Reimer was similarly in the dark. Janet and Ron knew exactly what had happened to their baby, and made as informed a decision as they could at the time—a decision that included maintaining secrecy. Arguably, they were better informed than most of the parents of intersex babies Money and his colleagues worked with. Although Money didn't necessarily advocate keeping parents entirely out of the loop, he was adamant about controlling the message. If surgical and hormonal treatments could be described in some way that didn't create any gender uncertainty on the parents' part, it would both be more humane for them psychologically (given their presumed horror of the excluded middle) and would ensure their unwavering consistency in socializing their child according to the chosen gender:

Ninety-nine times out of a hundred, the public construes an hermaphrodite as being half boy, half girl. The parents of an hermaphrodite should be disabused of this idea immediately. They should be given, instead, the concept that their child is a boy or a girl, one or the other, whose sex organs did not get completely differentiated or finished.[10]

10 Money, *Venuses Penuses: Sexology, Sexosophy, and Exigency Theory*, 140, 1986.

Many accounts exist of paternalistic doctors following in Money's footsteps over the years, and even, when they could, concealing a newborn's intersexuality from the parents. The less they knew, the better. Especially before the internet and our modern passtime of WebMD doomscrolling, it would have been easy to hide behind technical jargon and the notion of unambiguously male or female genitals that were merely "unfinished" at birth, requiring minor cosmetic surgery to "correct."

Money wrote triumphant accounts of Brenda Reimer's case many times throughout the '70s, withholding her name under medical anonymity. Everything was, reportedly, going swimmingly. Money's yearly psychological evaluations of the twins at Johns Hopkins were relentlessly probing, boundary-violating, and ultimately abusive. They included simulated sexual intercourse he directed them to perform with each other as he watched, ostensibly to reinforce their opposite gender roles. Of course, the children were both traumatized.

BEHAVIORAL SIGNS	PI vs C	AGS vs C	C vs TS
EVIDENCE OF TOMBOYISM			
1. Known to self and mother as tomboy	$p \leq .05$	$p \leq .01$	o
2. Lack of satisfaction with female sex role	o	$p \leq .05$	o
EXPENDITURE OF ENERGY IN RECREATION AND AGGRESSION			
3. Athletic interests and skills	$p \leq .05$	$p \leq .10$	$p \leq .05$
4. Preference of male versus female playmates	$p \leq .05$	$p \leq .01$	o
5. Behavior in childhood fights	o	o	$p \leq .05$
PREFERRED CLOTHING AND ADORNMENT			
6. Clothing preference, slacks versus dresses	$p \leq .05$	$p \leq .05$	o
7. Lacking interest in jewelry, perfume and hair styling	o	o	$p \leq .05$

Legend:
PI = Progestin-induced hermaphroditism (N=10)
AGS = Adrenogenital syndrome (N=15)
TS = Turner's syndrome (N=15)
C   = Matched controls
o   = No significant difference

From Money and
Ehrhardt, *Man &
Woman, Boy & Girl*,
106, 1972.

11 Downing, Morland, and Sullivan, *Fuckology: Critical Essays on John Money's Diagnostic Concepts*, 2014.

12 Money and Tucker, *Sexual Signatures: On Being a Man or a Woman*, 98, 1975.

13 Cavalli-Sforza, *Genes, Peoples, and Languages*, 2000. Although racial categories are often arbitrary and absurd (e.g. the classification of people into "White," "Indian," "Coloured" and "Black" in South Africa under Apartheid), the notion that race is purely a social construct has once again been challenged in recent years by modern full-genome analysis; see Reich, *Who We Are and How We Got Here*, 2018.

Bizarre inconsistencies began to arise in Money's accounts of Brenda's development during this period, sometimes misrepresenting the child's age by years or offering out of date photographic evidence of supposedly "feminine" body language and presentation.[11] At age 12, Brenda began (under protest) to take estrogen pills to induce female puberty, but it was increasingly clear to her that she was not really a girl, even as Money persisted in writing about the case as final proof that "the gender identity gate is open at birth for a normal child no less than for one born with unfinished sex organs."[12] In 1978, Money wrote a final positive account of the Reimer case, though he admitted that Brenda was "tomboyish"; after that, he made no substantial comment on the matter for two decades.

During that time, psychology and sociology textbooks continued to cite Money's research, and the Reimer case in particular, as powerful evidence of the socially constructed nature of gender. This fits into a broader humanist narrative about our being different from other animals due to our near-infinite adaptability and capacity to learn during our lifetimes. In the postwar years the idea of race, as a set of discrete biological categories with objective meaning, was being debunked by historical and genomic evidence; and if race was a cultural construct,[13] why not gender too? Some

David Reimer
(1965–2004).

prominent feminist scholars eagerly embraced this position. A certain strain of the intelligentsia was, in other words, highly receptive to evidence in favor of "nurture" and against "nature," especially in the politically contested realm of gender identity. It was a liberatory idea, promising social progress unconstrained by mere biology.

Meanwhile, shortly after medically induced puberty, the child at the center of this ethically fraught experiment dug in his heels and refused to continue to live as a girl—even prior to learning about his sex reassignment in infancy. When the truth finally came out, he changed his name to David, rejecting both "Brenda" and his original name, "Bruce." In his mid-teens he elected a double mastectomy and phalloplasty (the surgical construction of a penis, a procedure he would undergo again with newly developed techniques a few years later). He began taking testosterone.

By age 25, David was married to a woman and had adopted her children. In 2000, he relinquished his anonymity and collaborated with journalist John Colapinto on a book telling the whole story, largely from the Reimers' point of view. It made quite a stir.

David and Jane on their wedding day, 1990.

Unfortunately, there was no "happily ever after." In 2004, at age 38 and struggling financially, two days after his wife told him she wanted to separate, David Reimer committed suicide by gunshot to the head.

It would be an oversimplification to attribute David's suicide solely to his mutilation and subsequent sex reassignment. In fact his twin brother, Brian, also struggled, and died from an overdose of alcohol combined with antidepressants two years earlier. Still, life would doubtless have gone very differently for the Reimers had the accident never occurred. David experienced intense emotional difficulties from childhood on, facing ceaseless bullying and lack of acceptance from peers, an inability to focus at school, and what we'd now recognize as gender dysphoria. On his last yearly visit to Johns Hopkins at age 13, he fled John Money's office, saying he'd rather kill himself than ever go back. David's relationships with those closest to him—his parents, his brother, and later his wife—were all damaged by the psychological consequences of what had been done to him. His story was deeply unhappy and, once public, struck a profound blow to the idea of gender as a purely social construct.

The publication of the Reimers' story also marked a turning point in Money's career. Although his work had always attracted criticism and troubling rumors circulated, he was still generally lionized in the 1990s, seen as a pioneering polymath, breaking taboos and conducting daring multidisciplinary research in the service of gender and sexual liberation.[14] But by the end of his life, in 2006, Johns Hopkins had been quietly distancing itself for years, pushing him into reluctant retirement. When the department he had founded at the hospital was shuttered, he left under protest, renting a dingy office off-campus and defiantly writing "Psychohormonal Research Unit" on a piece of paper taped to the wall.

14 For instance, in 1991, his friends and colleagues threw him a big party and published *John Money: A Tribute, On the Occasion of His 70th Birthday*. These essays and papers are glowing in their assessment of his contributions to sexology.

John Money's apartment in Baltimore.

Soon funding dried up entirely, and he retreated to his Baltimore apartment, increasingly isolated amid half a century's worth of books, journals, art, erotic magazines, kitsch, and ephemera. Among the papers were the short stories and poems of his old patient, and later friend, Janet Frame. Though never fully at peace, she had escaped both the destructive feedback loops of her early years, and the straightjackets—literal and otherwise—of psychiatric institutions. She died of cancer the same year David Reimer had killed himself, but her artistic legacy was, if anything, still in ascent. She would win New Zealand's top poetry prize three years after her death, for the posthumously published collection *The Goose Bath*. Money's reputation, by contrast, lay in tatters. He had never imagined that he might become a footnote in her biography, rather than the other way round.

Money amassed a collection of over 400 works from Australia, New Zealand, West Africa, and Baltimore.

Once, there had been an unending stream of visitors; no longer. Dust settled on the fierce faces and proud wooden genitals of the Māori and West African sculptures looming from the walls. The tremor in Money's hands turned out to be Parkinson's disease, and as it advanced, dementia began to set in. He wrote about the experience, his graphomania turning inward. Meanwhile, the allegations mounted—not only of over-weening arrogance and questionable clinical judgment, but of ethical monstrosities, scientific fraud, even pedophilia.

Some of his old friends still defended him, pointing out his pathbreaking intellectual achievements. Some of his former patients, too, remained devotedly grateful. In other quarters,

15 Downing, Morland, and Sullivan, "Pervert or Sexual Libertarian?: Meet John Money, 'the Father of F***ology,'" 2015.

16 tvb, "The Death of a 'Pioneer,'" 2006.

though, he was being compared to Josef Mengele, the Nazi physician who had performed unspeakable medical experiments on prisoners in concentration camps.[15] When Money died, on the day before he would have turned 85, an intersex contributor to *Daily Kos* wrote, "I've often joked about the bottle of champagne I have had waiting for this event. [...] It's a good thing I'm not an obituary writer; I'd probably call him the butcher of Baltimore."[16]

It's possible for both of these seemingly contradictory assessments to be valid. Ethical judgment, like sex, gender, and mental health, is often flattened into a binary—good versus evil—but real life resists such simplification. There are few perfect heroes—or perfect villains. John Money was neither.

First, do no harm

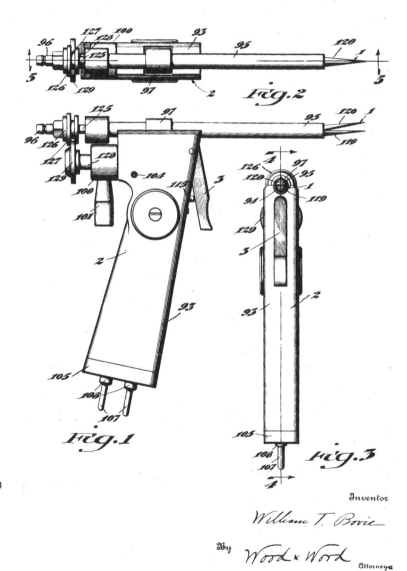

July 14, 1931. W. T. BOVIE 1,813,902

ELECTROSURGICAL APPARATUS

Filed Jan. 18, 1928 3 Sheets—Sheet 1

Fig.2

Fig.1

Fig.3

Inventor

William T. Bovie

By *Wood & Word*

Attorneys

"Another object of this invention is to provide an electro-surgical apparatus adapted to provide a plurality of types of current over a wide power range, [...] with adjustments and controls particularly suited to the convenience of the operating surgeon and his assistants, in order that the proper current may be applied to the patient [...] without danger of confusion [...]".

Had the details of David Reimer's story been more widely known before the late '90s, it would likely have changed the course of treatment for thousands of other children.[1] For one thing, the kind of electrocautery device that injured him continued to be used for circumcision, and led to total destruction of the penis in an unknown number of other infants and small children too.

1   Per Colapinto, "Dr. John Money's misreporting of his case had resulted in similar infant sex reassignments in thousands of other children." *As Nature Made Him: The Boy Who Was Raised as a Girl,* 286, 2000.

Nameplate of a 1930s-era portable Bovie electro-surgical device.

As recently as 2017, a retrospective paper titled *Electrosurgery Use in Circumcision in Children: Is it Safe?* concluded rather belatedly that the kind of "monopolar" device used for Reimer's circumcision was, in fact, not safe. The authors added, "We believe that complications from using monopolar diathermy for circumcision are under-reported."[2] Worse still, parents and doctors of mutilated infants found themselves facing the same quandary that the Reimers had; but now, they thought they had a best practice to follow. Misinformed by the myth of a happy outcome in that case, a 1989 paper in the Journal of Urology[3] was still arguing for making Reimer's treatment standard procedure:

2   Altokhais, "Electrosurgery Use in Circumcision in Children: Is it Safe?," 2017.

3   Gearhart and Rock, "Total Ablation of the Penis After Circumcision with Electrocautery: A Method of Management and Long-Term Followup," 1989.

> **Four patients who had traumatic loss of the penis were managed after the initial injury with a feminizing genitoplasty. Patient reconstruction ranged from 6 months to 3 years. [...] Immediate results were considered to be cosmetically satisfactory in all patients. Followup ranged from 8 months to 23 years [...]. The long-term results have been particularly gratifying in 2 individuals who have been observed for more than**

18 years. Early feminizing genitoplasty offers an excellent method of reconstruction of the external genitalia in the child with traumatic loss of the penis who is assigned a female sex of rearing.

The Reimer story is of course a single anecdote, not real data. The four patients cited in this 1989 article are also far too few for strong conclusions—and I, for one, am leery of nominally expert claims that an outcome is "particularly gratifying," which can paper over the same kinds of methodological and reporting biases Money's claims did. The only people whose "gratification" should matter are the patients themselves, and I'd want to see their unfiltered feedback.

Nonetheless, it's interesting that surgical and hormonal feminization of unambiguously male infants may *sometimes* "work," even if it's far from a best practice for male infants whose penises have been destroyed. The truth about whether a person's eventual gender identification is alterable—whether at birth, in infancy, or even later in life—may depend more on individual circumstances than either John Money or his most vocal opponents would have it.

By the 1990s, narratives about gender identification were shifting, and Money's theories were falling out of favor. In the long tug of war between gendered nature and gendered culture, nature began gaining ground once more. The change had a profound effect on the way doctors manage intersex newborns—and their parents. That shift is evident when intersexuality is broken down by whether respondents were assigned female at birth or male at birth. The resulting pattern is striking.

Respondents between 18 and 24 years old who know they're intersex (so, roughly speaking, Millennials, born around or shortly before the year 2000), were 97% likely to have been assigned female at birth. On the other hand, it's 78% likely that respondents between 58 and 74 years old (roughly corresponding to Baby Boomers, the generation born between 1946 and 1964) who know they're intersex were assigned *male* at birth! The error bars of these curves are substantial, making the exact probability ratios uncertain, but the dramatic reversal from majority male to majority female assignment is unmistakable.

From a pediatric surgeon's point of view, the old male default might have seemed counterintuitive. Gynoplasty was generally considered easier than phalloplasty; as a crude medical maxim from around 1970 held, "It's easier to dig a hole than build a pole."**4** It's true that surgery to create a vagina doesn't need to result in an externally visible structure that can look convincing at locker room distance,

4 Reardon, "The Spectrum of Sex Development: Eric Vilain and the Intersex Controversy," 2016.

12.0.0 **Intersexuality by sex assigned at birth** % by age

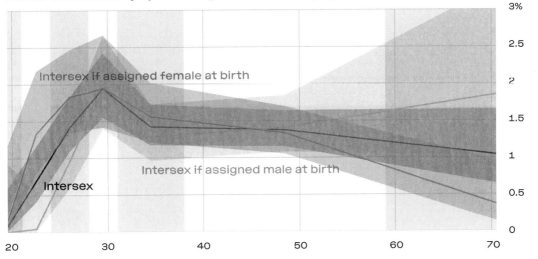

Intersex if assigned female at birth

Intersex if assigned male at birth

Intersex

12.0.1 **Intersex birth assignment** % by age

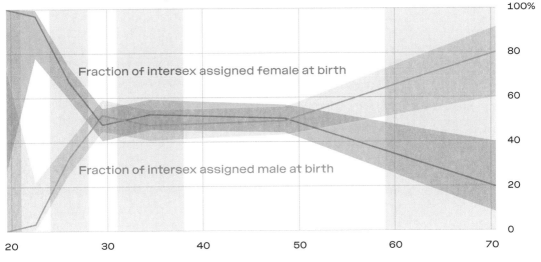

Fraction of intersex assigned female at birth

Fraction of intersex assigned male at birth

pass a stream of urine that allows one to pee standing up, or (most difficult) produce an erection. This is all, as it were, a tall order for plastic surgery, sometimes requiring a suspension of disbelief on the part of the beholder. John Money uncharitably described early attempts at phalloplasty as producing a "lump of meat"[5]—though techniques have since improved.

Focusing on superficial impressions also sets a low bar for surgical vaginas, though. As an intersex adult who underwent feminizing surgery put it in an interview, "I don't look like everyone else does. Not at all." When asked if her vagina carried sensation, she answered, after a long drag on her cigarette, "There's always lack of sensation where there's scarring."[6]

5 Downing, Morland, and Sullivan, *Fuckology: Critical Essays on John Money's Diagnostic Concepts*, 80, 2014.

6 Colapinto, *As Nature Made Him: The Boy Who Was Raised as a Girl*, 227, 2000.

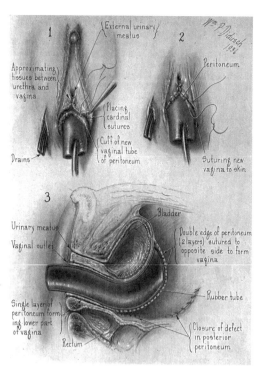

"An individual, 26 years of age, had been brought up as a female. There was a minute penis, a bifid scrotum, undescended testes and a tiny vagina. The patient had female characteristics, was engaged to marry a man and requested the construction of an artificial vagina. The penis was so small that it never could have been used in coitus, and the character of the patient was so typically female that we consented to attempt to make an artificial vagina." From Young, *Genital Abnormalities, Hermaphroditism and Related Adrenal Diseases*, 292–301, 1937.

However, this kind of surgery wouldn't have been the norm for an intersex birth a few decades ago, since, as the data show, intersex babies were almost always assigned male at birth. Indeed, given the multiple surgeries needed for feminization (often spanning childhood and adolescence) it would have been hard to carry such a program out without the patient's understanding—and most intersex Boomers weren't informed of their condition. How *could* a person's intersexuality be kept secret, both from themselves and from their parents?

The key was not starting from scratch. For most Boomers born with genital variations, the doctor's judgment was that relatively minor "corrective" hypospadias surgery of the kind William Hammond described in the 19th century, combined with hormone treatment, could "finish the job" of making a penis out of a micropenis or clitoris, as described in Chapter 11. The surgery could be done well before (the theory went) the infant became self-aware enough to form a fixed gender identity. Regardless of what happened on the inside, any available plasticity in the body was mobilized to nudge the outwardly visible genitals toward unambiguously male, on the presumption that psychological plasticity would allow the child's inner sense of self to follow suit.

Perhaps, also, there was a bias in play whereby answering the first question with "it's a boy" was deemed preferable, all things being equal, to "it's a girl." One sign of that widespread bias is the frequent infanticide or death through neglect of baby girls in many countries, a practice that in recent decades has shifted to include selective abortion of female fetuses. In 1990, Nobel Prize winning economist Amartya Sen shocked the world with his analysis of this phenomenon, suggesting that due to sex-selective abortion and infanticide there were 100 million "missing women."[7]

7 Sen, "More Than 100 Million Women Are Missing," 2017.

12.1 Sex ratios by country

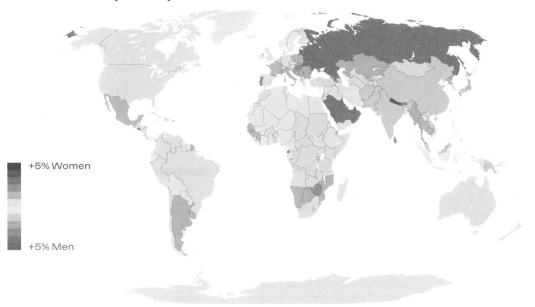

+5% Women

+5% Men

On the other side of the coin, perhaps "noisy feminists" of the kind David Gelernter liked to complain about were starting to make doctors uncomfortable with the idea of cutting off clitorises willy-nilly, despite John Money's oft-repeated claim that it didn't affect a woman's ability to orgasm. (This would have been news to the likes of William Acton and John Harvey Kellogg, on their surgical quests a century earlier to eradicate "nymphomania" through clitoridectomy.)

Human Rights Watch findings are in agreement with the conclusion that intersexuality has historically been "male by default":

8 InterACT and Human Rights Watch, "'I Want to Be Like Nature Made Me': Medically Unnecessary Surgeries on Intersex Children in the US," 2017.

9 The literature sometimes claims the opposite— that female assignment for intersex babies has always been the norm—but that's because hypospadias surgery is often neglected, i.e. the diagnosis of hypospadias (which is common) is understood as a "penis defect" rather than a marker of intersexuality.

> **US government data compiled from several voluntary-reporting databases [...] show that in 2014—the most recent year for which data are available—hypospadias surgery was reported on children 505 times, and clitoral surgery was reported 70 times.[8]**

In other words, when surgery was performed on intersex children, it favored "rounding them up" to male by a factor of 7.2x.[9]

Why, then, is there such a dramatic shift toward *female* assignment at birth for younger intersex people?

Increasing levels of environmental pollutants that disrupt prenatal hormone levels may be part of the answer. In their 2021 book *Count Down*, Shanna Swan and Stacey Colino argue that these pollutants pose a looming fertility crisis, and have been feminizing us all—leading, among other outcomes, to declines over recent decades in testosterone level and sperm count among men.[10] They also argue that prenatal exposure to endocrine disrupting chemicals may be a driver of increasing levels of gender dysphoria and non-binariness.

While these theories can't be ruled out, the way Swan and Colino reach for biological explanations while discounting cultural change seems questionable, given the powerful evidence in the survey data of social transmission (meaning: people being influenced by others). The *Count Down* effect is also unlikely to account for the nearly 180 degree turn in intersex gender assignment that began taking place in 1990 or so.

Something else happened around 1990 that may offer a better explanation: doctors started to change their policies. Furtively performing "corrective" surgery at birth, and keeping children or even parents in the dark about it, at last began falling out of favor. The abstract of that Human Rights Watch article in its entirety reads:

> **Intersex people in the United States are subjected to medical practices that can inflict irreversible physical and psychological harm on them starting in infancy, harms that can last throughout their lives. Many of these procedures are done with the stated aim of making it easier for children to grow up "normal" and integrate more easily into society by helping them conform to a particular sex assignment. The results are often catastrophic, the supposed benefits are largely unproven, and there are generally no urgent health considerations at stake. Procedures that could be delayed until intersex children are old enough to decide whether they want them are instead performed on infants who then have to live with the consequences for a lifetime.**

While it's still the case that vanishingly few intersex 18-year-old Americans know they're intersex, fewer of them are being operated on or given sex hormones as infants nowadays. This reflects a number of converging trends. One is an acknowledgement, based on hard lessons, that John Money was wrong about gender identity being entirely socially determined. Another is the increasing regard for the agency of the children themselves, a sense that they're people whose

10 Swan and Colino, *Count Down: How Our Modern World Is Threatening Sperm Counts, Altering Male and Female Reproductive Development, and Imperiling the Future of the Human Race*, 2022.

rights to self-determination must be protected even—or especially—when they haven't yet developed the self-awareness to make their own decisions.

Leaving their options as open as possible then becomes the priority, and avoiding early surgery or hormones now seems to many more in line with defaulting to female than to male. A large clitoris really isn't the end of the world. Biologically, one can think of the physical development of a fetus as starting out female, with subsequent male development triggered by the addition of hormones; as English endocrinologist Richard Quinton has put it, "the default blueprint is female."[11] There's a degree of flexibility in the timeline for virilization; a micropenis can always be grown or made into a not-so-micro penis later on. As an ahead-of-his-time 66-year-old put it in the survey, "I was born both male and female. Raised female until 6 and then surgically aligned to be all male. Have lived male ever since, and identify as male." Presumably, by 6 years old, this man's sense of his own gender was clear enough that surgery (and probably hormones) could align him with what he felt he was on the inside, rather than having to face David Reimer's lifelong ordeal.

The change taking place now is more profound, though, than just a shift from defaulting to male to defaulting to female. The whole notion that the sex binary is absolute, that the requirements of masculinity and femininity are set in stone, and that either/or choices are mandatory is beginning to dissolve. Leaving options on the table for an intersex child means being honest with them from the beginning about their non-binary status—"both male and female," exactly the ambiguity John Money found so horrifying.

Once we abandon the idea that sex must be either/or, we also need to contend with the question of how big the excluded middle really is. How many people are actually intersex? As will now be clear, this question can't be answered objectively, because most of the variables determining sex aren't discrete. It's like trying to establish how many people are ambidextrous. The only principled approach is to just ask people, and accept that both their answers and their definitions will vary.

Perhaps the percentage isn't so important, as long as we recognize that it isn't negligible. In practice, the only questions we really need to answer are: which infants do we perform sex assignment surgery on, and what pronouns should we default to using with them?

primär · sekundär

A Biblical narrative upended. "Eve first, then Adam! [...] Eve differentiates, unaided, whereas Adam is depicted as needing the help of the archangel who appears with an injection needle loaded with testosterone, the masculizing hormone, shoots up Eve, and lo! Adam comes forth." From Money, *Gay, Straight, and In-Between*, 19, 1988.

11   Saini, *Inferior: How Science Got Women Wrong and the New Research That's Rewriting the Story*, 2017.

Increasingly, the answer to the first question is "none, unless medically necessary" (i.e. except in the very small minority of cases where differences of genital development pose an immediate health risk). And for increasing numbers of young people, the answer to the second question is "they/them," regardless of how their genitals look. For millions of people living in places where the gender binary no longer reigns absolute, not conforming to the binary no longer means "living apart," as it might have in the 1960s.

12.2 Countries protecting intersex children from non-consensual medical intervention

Austria
Spain
Portugal
Greece
Malta

Uruguay

■ Protected
■ Unprotected

12 Trankuility, "Protection of Intersex Children from Harmful Practices," 2016.

Medical practice is well ahead of government regulation with regard to sex assignment surgery for infants, but laws have slowly started to change too. In recent years, a tiny handful of countries[12] — spurred by intersex activists—have made it illegal for medically unnecessary surgeries to be done at birth, or more broadly, non-consensually. In this view, consent is necessary for such surgeries to be regarded as gender confirmation as opposed to genital mutilation. And newborns can't give consent. This is consistent with the most basic statement of the Hippocratic oath, which medical students have been taking in one form or another for millennia: "First, do no harm" (*Primum non nocere*). David Reimer's doctors violated the oath catastrophically, not once, but twice.

Non-binary gender identification is also increasingly available on official forms and documents, though here too, official acknowledgement lags a reality in which one in twenty young Americans identify as non-binary.

Rosie Lohman, born intersex in Ontario in 2012, embodied many of these historic shifts. Although chromosomally XX, Rosie was born with a noticeable genital variation due to the high levels of testosterone common in children with Congenital Adrenal Hyperplasia. A team of specialists attempted to pressure the parents, Stephani and Eric, into signing off on "corrective" surgery, which would have included clitoral reduction as well as the creation of a surgical vagina. But the Lohmans didn't go along with the plan. As a CNN article on their story put it in 2020,

> **Rosie is now in the process of figuring out her gender identity on her own terms. While she says she still likes to use female pronouns for now and wants to keep her name, Rosie says that sometimes she feels like a boy and other times, nonbinary. "Because I am both!" she said. [...] She has one piece of advice for new parents of any intersex baby who might be worried for their future, offered with a smile. "Calm down!"**[13]

13 Neus, "She's 7 and Was Born Intersex. Why Her Parents Elected to Let Her Grow Up Without Surgical Intervention," 2020.

It was a good call: in 2023, Eric Lohman wrote, "Our child no longer uses the name Rosie, nor does he identify as a girl, which I think speaks volumes about our decision to delay surgery."[14]

14 Personal correspondence.

That it's possible to be both public and calm about sex and gender non-binariness is very much a feature of our era. A 2019 article in *Teen Vogue* about intersexuality includes the stories of nine "out" intersex teens, Bria (they/them), Banti (they/them), Johnny (all pronouns), Cat (she/her), Anick (he/him), Francis (he/him), Irene

Intersex rights activists outside the Lurie Children's Hospital of Chicago, 2018.

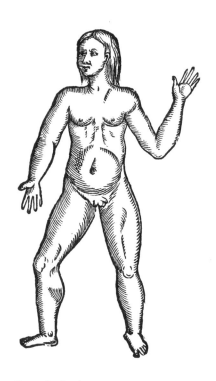

From Ambroise Paré, *Des monstres et prodiges*, 1585.

Hijras in Bangladesh, 2010.

(she/her), Mari (they/them), and Danielle (she/they).[15] Most were kept in the dark throughout childhood and experienced shame, isolation, and confusion before discovering online intersex communities and embracing intersexuality as a component of their identity. These experiences are familiar to many LGBTQ+ people, and the language many young intersex people are using is starting to overlap with these adjacent communities.

The embrace of historically excluded middles seems to be part of a profound and larger shift in the way we think about identity, but it's important to put the rigidity of the 20th century sex and gender binary into a broader historical context. Anthropologists, historians, and social scientists aren't immune to the powerful biases we all encounter when we view other cultures through the lens of modern Western categories and assumptions. Cultural biases lead to a kind of selective blindness, a bit reminiscent of the way we ignore our own noses, despite their occupying a sizeable part of our visual field. For instance, prior to the social strictures of Victorian England, it's not clear that intersexuality (or *any* kind of sexuality) was as taboo as it became in the 19th century. A popular drinking song or "catch" by William Lawes (1602–1645) went:

15 Lindahl, "9 Young People on How They Found Out They Are Intersex," 2019.

16 Peraino, *Listening to the Sirens: Musical Technologies of Queer Identity from Homer to Hedwig*, 206, 2006.

17 Hunter, "Hijras and the Legacy of British Colonial Rule in India," 2019.

18 Flores, "Two Spirit and LGBTQ Idenitites: Today and Centuries Ago," 2020.

19 Bushell, "Los Muxes: Disrupting the Colonial Gender Binary," 2021.

20 Chira, "When Japan Had a Third Gender," 2017.

See, here comes *Robin* Hermaphrodite,
Hot waters, he cryes for his delight:
He got a Child of a Maid, and yet is no man
Was got with childe by a man, and is no woman.[16]

Arguably, colonialism has played a major role in erasing the formerly widespread acknowledgment of non-binary sex or gender in many societies. In South Asia, *hijras* have been long recognized as a third gender, neither male nor female; India, Pakistan, Nepal, and Bangladesh still acknowledge a third gender on official documents, though the legacy of British law in India criminalized non-procreative sexuality until 2018.[17] Many Native American cultures, too, have long recognized non-binary sex and gender in various forms, with the modern umbrella term "Two Spirit" reclaiming a range of such traditions.[18] Among the Zapotecs of modern-day Mexico's Oaxaca valley, the *muxes* were—and and still are—a third gender.[19] Japan had a third gender, *wakashū* (若衆), before the country adopted Western sexual mores in the late 19th century as part of a broader movement to "modernize."[20] There are many more examples in this vein.

For thousands of years, traditional Jewish culture recognized multiple categories of intersexuality, including *androgynos* (אַנְדְּרוֹגִינוֹס), possessing both male and female characteristics, and *tumtum* (טֻומְטוֹם in Hebrew, meaning "hidden"), possessing neither. *Genesis Rabbah*, a Jewish commentary on the Old Testament's creation story written sometime between 500 and 300 BCE, asserts that Adam was created *androgynos* by God, with sex differentiation only occurring when Eve

The late We:wa, a celebrated Zuni textile artist, weaver, and potter. As a Łamana (Two Spirit), they took on a mixture of women's and men's typical roles and skills. In this photograph, they wore traditional women's attire and weaved on a backstrap loom, typically a men's skill. Photo ca. 1871.

was fashioned out of Adam's rib. In short, it may be that the cultural invisibility of non-binariness and intersexuality in recent European and American history is actually a historical anomaly—much like the Nuclear Family.

Even so, we should not fall into the opposite error of thinking that the emerging landscape of diverse gender and sex identities and increasingly broad acceptance of them is a historical norm. Most traditional societies are organized around sexual reproduction and its material requirements, and tend to marginalize those not involved in supporting this central project. This is because, as later chapters of this book will explore, for most people and throughout most of human history, it has been an existential challenge simply to scrape up enough calories to stay alive and propagate.

So, "Robin Hermaphrodite," who may or may not have existed,[21] is celebrated for his extraordinary dual-mode reproductive capacity; but the framing—"got a Child," "was got with childe"—is still very much heteronormative. Ancient Jewish thinking on the subject is framed legalistically, in terms of how marital obligations and patriarchal inheritance laws apply to such cases. *Hijra* communities tend to be marginalized and impoverished; relegated to a low social status, they often depend on survival sex work and suffer violence and abuse with impunity.

For a society to recognize the existence of non-binary and intersex people, in other words, is not the same as to accord them status and respect on their own terms. Today, many young people are willingly embracing non-binary identities with the expectation of equal respect and acceptance by peers.

Our greater modern understanding of the biological and physiological basis of sex is also new, as is our increasingly powerful ability to manipulate it. Ironically, the very techniques John Money and his collaborators marshaled to try to enforce the sex and gender binary of the '50s are now among the tools being used to dismantle it. Emerging communities and changing attitudes have played at least as large a role. With or without medical intervention, sex assigned at birth is no longer the straightjacket it once was.

21 While it's theoretically possible, to be able to impregnate someone else *and* be able to bear a child to term would imply an extremely rare intersex variation; see Bayraktar, "Potential Autofertility in True Hermaphrodites," 2018.

13

The return of Count Sandor

Many believe the trans community is tiny. This misconception became obvious when I ran a small side survey asking respondents for their estimates of some of the statistics the main survey measures— for instance, the percentage of trans people. Trying to keep things simple, I foolishly used a number widget on the web page that didn't allow for responses lower than 1%. Yet 1% was the most common answer, and a number of respondents complained:

I wanted to put a smaller number for the transgender population around my age. (0.01%).[1]

You should have allowed decimals on percentage trans. It is closer to zero than one, but it is above zero. I would say 0.001 percent.[2]

Like any other anonymous identity, the real figure is a moving target. The second respondent above, born in the 1950s, actually would have been close to the mark had he given this answer as a teenager, in 1968. Back then, the US population was around 200 million, and American psychiatrist Ira B. Pauly, known for his research on the topic, estimated that there were just 2,500 transsexual people (as they were then called) in the country.[3]

More recent figures seem to be all over the map. A 2011 study gave a "rough estimate" of around 0.3% of US adults,[4] while several 2016 studies put the number at 0.4–0.6%, though a meta-analysis does note that "Future national surveys are likely to observe higher numbers of transgender people."[5] Indeed they do.

As elsewhere, our intuitive estimates tend to systematically undershoot for two reasons: first, because we form our models of the world when we're young, and are often slow to update them; second, because if we look around at people our own age, we don't see the whole picture. Big national polls, like those run by the Census Bureau, may be thrown off by anonymity concerns. Many studies also estimate overall averages without considering variation as a function of age

1   An 18-year-old man from Fort Lee, New Jersey.

2   A 63-year-old man from Phoenix, Arizona.

3   Pauly, "The Current Status of the Change of Sex Operation," 1968.

4   Gates, "How Many People Are Lesbian, Gay, Bisexual and Transgender?," 2011.

5   Meerwijk and Sevelius, "Transgender Population Size in the United States: A Meta-Regression of Population-Based Probability Samples," 2017.

and time. Yet those variations can be dramatic, as in responses to the question "Do you identify as trans?"

This is another of those cases where the changes in people's responses over time are a lot more radical than a shift to the right by two years from the 2018–19 data to the 2020–21 data. In fact no amount of sliding the 2018–19 curve to the right will make it look like the 2020–21 curve. The effect seems to be accelerating, too; isolating the 2021 data reveals an even sharper rise, especially in the youngest cohort. Given the speed of the change, social transmission seems to be a major factor here—not just among the young, but across all ages.

13.0 Trans identification from 2018 to 2021 % by age

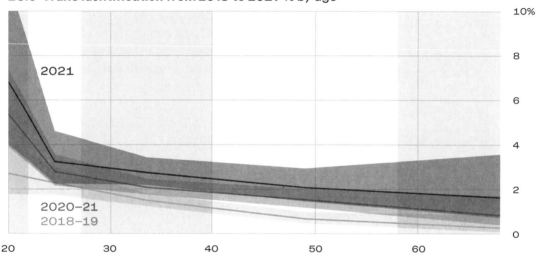

Was David Reimer trans? While he was born a boy, he was raised as a girl. The medical procedures David underwent in his teens and twenties to align his body with his gender—phalloplasty and double mastectomy, plus lifelong hormone treatments—were the same ones undertaken by many trans people who medically transition to masculine bodies. The same is true of less tangible, but also weighty social transitions: name, pronouns, relationships, legal documents. In assessing the relevance of nature versus nurture in David's ordeal, his biographer, John Colapinto, wrote:

> None of this is to suggest that nurture plays no role in gender identity. Virtually every page of *As Nature Made Him* contains an environmental cue or clue that helped to reinforce what Brenda's prenatally virilized brain and nervous system were telling her. [...] I attribute the case's final and complete collapse, however, to the pressing insistence of Brenda's biological maleness—her awakening sexual attraction to girls; her inchoate but adamant

6 Colapinto, *As Nature Made Him: The Boy Who Was Raised as a Girl*, 279–80, 2000.

7 To understand why, consider a population of $N=100$ people, some number X of whom have a property A. X will then be the percentage of people with property A, as shown in many of this book's graphs. The mathematical details of how the uncertainty around X is calculated are described in the Appendix, but let's suppose for simplicity's sake that the uncertainty is 1%, that is, plus or minus one respondent. Given a property that holds for half of the population, a ±1% uncertainty doesn't matter—49% and 51% tell much the same story ("about one in two"). However, if $X=1$, this same ±1% *absolute* uncertainty is a much bigger deal, in *relative* terms; it means the incidence could easily be twice as high ("one in fifty"), or half as high ("one in two hundred"), or even rarer (though given that it *did* occur, it can't be zero). Now, suppose there's a second property B that *also* has a 1% incidence rate. Calculating the percentage of overlap between A and B will be hard. If only one individual out of the 100 has property A, and a different individual is the only one with property B, the real overlap might be zero, or 50%, or something else—nobody can say. The error bar calculations take this uncertainty into account. Making the age bucketing coarser helps by increasing N within each bucket, allowing overlaps between small populations to be sampled better, at the expense of being able to distinguish differences across ages.

aversion to possessing breasts and a vagina. For how many children, at the exquisitely awkward age of fourteen, will insist, upon threat of suicide, that they undergo full sex change, in plain view of neighbors, family, and friends? This almost incomprehensible act of courage on Brenda's part speaks more convincingly than any other piece of evidence to the emphatic demands of our biology, and to the necessity that we—all of us—be allowed to live as we feel we must.[6]

Clearly the entreaty to "be allowed to live as we feel we must" applies to many others. Although the evidence suggests that some intersex people, and some fraction of the population in general, may be quite gender-flexible, this certainly isn't universally the case; and the assignment of intersex babies to a binary gender has often been arbitrary—skewing heavily to "boy" from the 1950s until the 1990s, then skewing heavily to "girl" in more recent years.

Consider the implications: out of the 2% or so of known intersex births, nearly 85% would have been assigned male in the old days, and are being assigned female today. We're talking about a *lot* of people—in the US alone, it works out to about 5.6 million. That's larger than the combined population of Los Angeles and San Diego (or of the seven least populous states—Wyoming, Vermont, Alaska, North and South Dakota, Delaware, and Montana). It seems a safe bet that a significant fraction of these arbitrary assignments have been flat out wrong, just as David Reimer's reassignment in infancy was wrong. So, many people arbitrarily assigned a gender will likely seek to transition later in life, just as he did, making them both intersex *and* trans.

Exploring the overlap between the trans and intersex communities using the survey data is possible, but it requires stretching the analysis to its statistical limit. Only about one in a thousand respondents are both intersex and trans; hence error bars will be large.[7] Moreover, the rate of intersexuality plunges toward zero among the youngest respondents, requiring coarse age bucketing there. Still, the patterns revealed are interesting, and appear to be statistically significant. (Recall that the shaded regions show 90% confidence intervals.)

Between 5% and 15% or so of intersex people are trans, with that percentage rising steadily by age. For reasons that will soon become clear, people in this overlap often struggle for acceptance in either community, as with this 63-year-old woman with XXXY chromosomes assigned male at birth: "even within intersex communities there is great opposition to including transgender people like me." Not all people who are intersex know they are, so the real overlap is probably higher, but this upward trend reflects an increasing number of intersex people who, at some age, feel that their sex assigned at birth wasn't right, and

13.1.0 **Intersexuality compared with trans identification** % by age

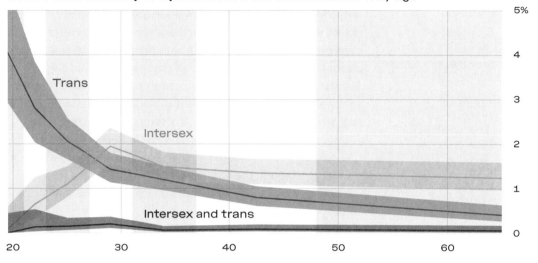

13.1.1 **Overlap of intersex and trans** % by age

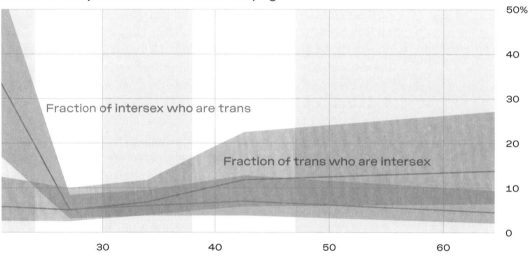

decide to do something about it. They may only learn that they're intersex later, when they seek to transition.

Fifteen percent is not an insignificant effect, especially given the implications among older respondents, vanishingly few of whom (trans or not) are non-binary with respect to their sex. Consider: if, when an intersex baby is born, male or female sex were assigned by flipping a coin, and 30% of the 50% assigned the "wrong" sex feel strongly enough about this to transition—*and* are in a privileged enough position to do so—that would give us 15%. Keep in mind, too, the high stigma associated with being trans, especially among the older generation; this may explain why the number rises only slowly with age. As a 2018 article in the *Guardian* put it, "Meet the trans baby boomers":

8 Hinsliff, "'Age Has Nothing to Do With It': How It Feels to Transition Later in Life," 2018.

[T]here are more than five times as many adult as child gender identity patients in the UK. Some are now having gender reassignment surgery not just in late middle age, but well into retirement. [...] It's perhaps only now that many older people feel comfortable coming out, having grown up in a time when being trans was so steeped in shame and silence that many couldn't even put a name to what they felt.[8]

Remarkably, among the youngest cohort of trans respondents, in their late teens and early twenties, at least 20% and perhaps as many as 50% are (and know they are) intersex. Yet at age 26 and above, that figure is only about 5%. It's likely that more than one factor is in play here. First, only a small fraction of intersex people *know* they are at these young ages. But which fraction? It's likely to include those born with especially non-binary genitals, that is, people from whom their intersexuality (and thus the arbitrariness of their sex assignment at birth) really can't be hidden. Second, both sex and gender non-binariness are more readily embraced by young people, a phenomenon explored more deeply later in this chapter.

In general, being trans means something different for a 20-year-old than for a 60-year-old. The great majority of trans 60-year-olds think of themselves as either men who were assigned female at birth, or women who were assigned male at birth. On the other hand, a large and increasing proportion of young trans people think of themselves as not identifying with their sex assigned at birth—a broader category, since it includes a growing number with non-binary or fluid gender identities, or who reject gender altogether.

This is evident in the pattern of overlap between trans and non-binary identities. Beyond age 60, the overlap is nil; the survey turned up *no* older trans non-binary people, or non-binary trans people. Among 19-year-olds, though, 40% of non-binary people are trans, which likely implies more of a rejection of their (binary) birth gender than an identification with the *opposite* gender. Even more dramatically, fully 80% of 18- to 20-year-old trans people surveyed identify as non-binary.

The overlap between exclusive users of "they" and the trans population follows a similar pattern. Vanishingly few older trans people use "they" pronouns exclusively, while about 20% of 19-year-old trans people do; and while 40% of 19-year-olds exclusively using "they" are trans, this, too, appears to fall off sharply with age—though with so few older respondents in either of these populations, estimating the overlap becomes dicey.

As one might expect, the overlap between "they" users and non-binary people is very high at the younger end, but curiously, by age 70 the overlap is negligible. This is especially noteworthy given that, on

13.2 **Overlap of non-binary and trans** % by age

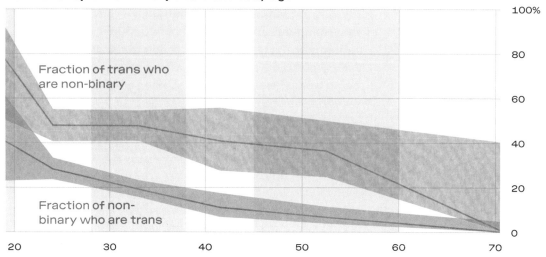

13.3 **Overlap of "they" pronoun users and trans** % by age

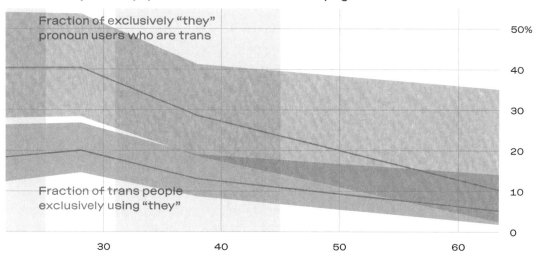

9 As shown at the beginning of Chapter 10, around 1–2% of 20-year-olds identify exclusively with they/them pronouns, a number that only declines for older respondents.

their own, non-binary identification and the use of "they" both follow that U-shaped curve encountered in Chapter 10, with a decline followed by an increase among older respondents.[9] It seems that when older people use "they" (usually *non*-exclusively) or identify with non-binariness (usually *not* to the exclusion of identifying as men or women), they're less consciously part of a social movement in which these answers go together, and imply a more wholesale rejection of gender.

Before delving into the decline in binary sex and gender identification among the young, let's compare the numbers of trans people assigned female at birth versus male at birth.

13.4.0 **"They" pronoun users compared with non-binary identification** % by age

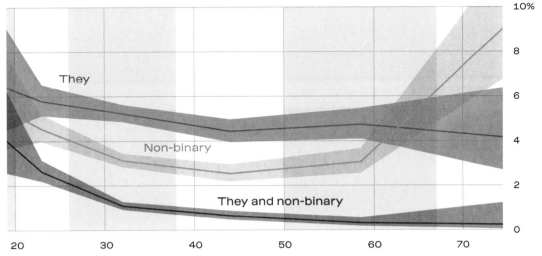

They

Non-binary

They and non-binary

13.4.1 **Overlap of "they" pronoun users and non-binary** % by age

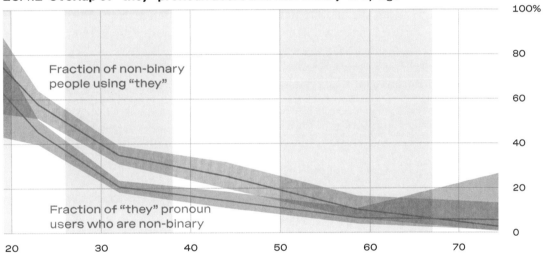

Fraction of non-binary
people using "they"

Fraction of "they" pronoun
users who are non-binary

These curves tell a story at once remarkable and familiar.
Among older people who don't identify with their birth sex assignment (whether they identify as trans or not), male assignment at
birth overwhelmingly predominates, while among younger people
female assignment at birth is much likelier. This pattern should
ring a bell: it's the same as for intersexuality.

Directly comparing the birth sex assignment ratios for intersex
and trans people reveals that they look nearly identical above age 25:
by age 70, assignment is around 80% male at birth, while at age 25, sex
assignment at birth is close to 70% *female*—an astonishing reversal.
At the youngest ages, though, the curves diverge. Virtually *all* intersex
people (at least, those who know they are) are assigned female at birth

13.5 **Trans by sex assigned at birth** % by age

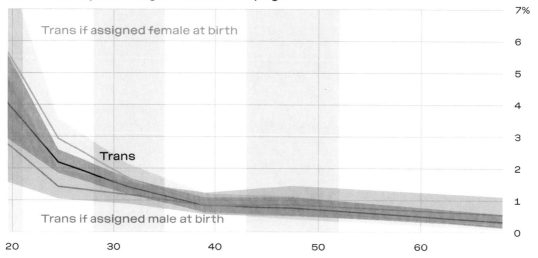

nowadays, for the reasons discussed in the previous chapter. Young trans people also tend to be assigned female at birth, although "only" by a 3:2 majority. I'll return in a moment to the question of why this divergence has appeared among the young.

13.6 **Fraction of intersex and trans people assigned male at birth** % by age

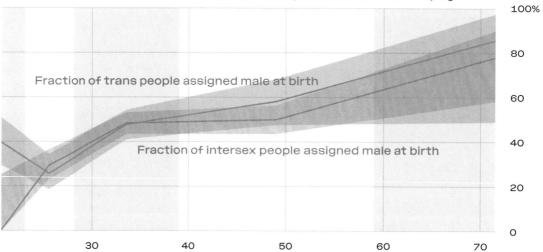

First, though, consider the trans statistics among the older population. These may seem familiar from experience—at least for those of us old enough to remember how things were in the last millennium. When I was a kid, in the 1980s and '90s, words like "cross-dresser," "transvestite," and "transsexual" (which are generally out of favor today, along with some more offensive related terms) were strongly associated with people assigned male at birth who to one degree or another embraced femininity in their clothes, presentation, and identity. One could call the old tendency to assume trans people were assigned male at birth the "Priscilla effect," after the 1994 surprise hit *The Adventures of Priscilla, Queen of the Desert*.[10]

From *The Adventures of Priscilla, Queen of the Desert*, 1994.

"Invertido Sexual" from Gómez, *La Mala Vida en Buenos Aires*, 1908.

As Krafft-Ebing's case history of "Count Sandor V" in the 1880s illustrates (see Chapter 6), there have always been people assigned female at birth who undertook the opposite journey in gender space. There must also be untold numbers of "Count Sandors" throughout history who, escaping the circumstances of their birth, successfully "passed" as men, leaving no medico-legal documentary record. Even so, the survey data confirm the intuition that among the older generation alive today, the "Bernadettes" far outnumber the "Sandors."

Those assigned female at birth may have had less freedom to make choices about gender identity later in life, just as social and economic disadvantage suppressed same-sex attraction among women. It's hard, though, to see the intersex curve overlaid on the trans curve and not suspect a connection. I think the relationship is causal: the reversal from a majority of trans people assigned male at birth to a majority assigned female at birth is, at least in part, a downstream effect of changing intersex medical protocols (though something further is afoot among the youngest cohort, which we'll return to shortly).

It would be surprising *not* to see such an effect, given that in the old days, such an overwhelming majority of intersex babies were assigned male at birth—remember, we're talking about millions of people—and the overwhelming majority are now assigned female at birth. Since John Money's theory that gender can be freely molded by social pressure in the first couple of years of life has been disproven by cases like David Reimer's, one would expect this change in policy to result in major shifts in the trans population—which is just what we see. Hence, among young people today, suddenly "Count Sandors" are handily outnumbering "Bernadettes," though perhaps, in due course, a rising tide of non-binary trans people will outnumber both.

To my knowledge, this relationship has not been quantitatively established elsewhere, though as Jules Gill-Peterson notes in a 2018 book, *Histories of the Transgender Child,*

> **The persistence of the entanglement of intersex and trans life in the bodies of children has been underappreciated; in fact, it endured well into the 1950s, if not later. It lasted nearly as long as we have had the discourse of transsexuality, and yet it has radically faded from contemporary conversations about the plasticity of sex and gender.[11]**

11 Gill-Peterson, *Histories of the Transgender Child*, 17, 2018.

Why hasn't this entanglement been studied more closely in recent decades? One possible reason is discomfort with the topic on the part of both the intersex and trans communities, albeit for different reasons.

Consider intersexuality's *medical* status over the past century. It has widely been thought about as a health condition, like diabetes or gigantism. In this spirit, many intersex people (who know they are) still strongly oppose the excluded middle-embracing approach taken by the Lohmans; they see medical intervention at birth as having allowed them to "grow up normal," and feel thankful in much the way a child born with a cleft lip or palate might feel thankful for early reconstructive surgery.

A modern clinical term for intersexuality is Disorders of Sex Development (DSD), which some people find preferable to the term "intersex" or the older (and even more contested) "hermaphrodite." It feels different to *have* a disorder of sex development than to *be* intersex. Medicine exists to manage or cure disorders—to make them, to the extent possible, go away. Conversely, an identity is emphatically *not* a disorder.[12]

12 Jones et al., *Intersex: Stories and Statistics from Australia*, 95, 2016.

For intersex people who live as men or women but need access to medical care specific to their intersexuality, framing it as a medical condition that isn't anybody else's business makes perfect sense. The word "need" matters here, in that while treatment can occasionally be medically necessary (for example, the so-called "salt-wasting" variety of CAH makes the survival of babies like Rosie Lohman depend on daily medication), in most cases the point of the medical care is to bring an intersex person's presentation in line with the gender binary. So, a self-fulfilling logic is in play here: when a person's "untreated" intersexuality would be socially obvious, managing it as a treatable disorder is precisely what makes it possible for it to be "just" a medical condition— hence *not* socially obvious.

For many trans people, however, the medical framing is offensive. And with good reason. It carries stigma, implying that something is wrong with them—and "wrong" in the head, not "wrong" in the body. Remember that in the 1950s the DSM classified "transvestism" as a perversion, alongside homosexuality, "pedophilia, fetishism, and sexual sadism (including rape, sexual assault, mutilation)," and that these practices were all regarded as criminal. Some of the old "blue laws" criminalizing consensual non-heteronormative acts are still on the books today.[13] While pathologizing lesbian, gay, and bi people is no longer nearly as widespread as it was half a century ago, it's still common to pathologize trans and non-binary people, as reflected in many comments on the survey:

13 Wikipedia, "Sodomy laws in the United States," 2022.

> **I believe confusion about your gender is a mental disease that should be treated instead of encouraged.[14]**

14 A 35-year-old man from Yuma, Arizona.

> **If you actually believe you are anything but male or female you are in fact MENTALLY ILL.[15]**

15 A 33-year-old man from Las Vegas, Nevada.

> **I am normal [...] [I] have female genitalia and chromosomes, no mental illnesses making me think i am not female.[16]**

16 A 47-year-old woman from Nesquehoning, Pennsylvania.

Such views are commonplace even among the young and educated, as per this 22-year-old woman from Hammonton, New Jersey:

> **I don't believe in gender identities opposite of birth gender, outside of those who are intersexual. Not to be rude, but I've been through many Psychology classes and see it just as a trendy misrepresentation of a mental disorder that everyone thinks they relate to.**

This attitude is unsurprising considering that, when the DSM-III-R finished the job of de-pathologizing homosexuality, it merely reclassified transsexuality under a new heading, "Gender Identity Disorders," where it remained until 2013. This dovetails neatly with the fact that John Money and his adherents needed a medical diagnosis to justify their surgical and hormonal meddling with intersex babies and children too young to make medical decisions for themselves. "Fixing" newborns can't be medically justified unless we can claim something is wrong with them.

For trans people, a version of the same conundrum can also surface later in life. Unlike being lesbian, gay, or bi, being trans may in itself involve having expensive medical procedures done—though note that this applies only to a fraction of trans people today. Medical costs impose an especially steep economic barrier in countries lacking free universal access to healthcare—like the US. For insurance to cover a procedure, it needs to be regarded as medically necessary, which is usually interpreted to mean that it must address a medical condition.[17] This has led to rhetorical finessing in which "gender identity disorders" have given way to "gender dysphoria," which is still considered an illness. So, trans people are assigned a status not unlike that of lesbian, gay, and bi people in the wake of the American Psychiatric Association's 1973 memo—the one that threw shade on homosexuality, male chauvinism, and vegetarianism in the same breath (see Chapter 6). Media theorist Sandy Stone described this Catch-22 in an influential 1987 essay:

17 The same argument is taking place in countries that *do* have socialized medicine, where distinctions are still generally made between medically necessary and elective procedures. Elective procedures tend not to be prioritized or even covered by national health plans.

> **When the first academic gender dysphoria clinics were started on an experimental basis in the 1960s, the medical staff would not perform surgery on demand, because of the professional risks involved in performing experimental surgery on "sociopaths." At this time there were no official diagnostic criteria; "transsexuals" were, *ipso facto*, whoever signed up for assistance. Professionally this was a dicey situation. [...] [A] test or a differential diagnosis was needed for transsexualism that did not depend on anything as simple and subjective as feeling that one was in the wrong body. [...] But even after considerable research, no simple and unambiguous test for gender dysphoria syndrome could be developed.[18]**

18 Stone, "The Empire Strikes Back: A Posttranssexual Manifesto," 2006.

As of the last few years, being trans is no longer a disorder, according to the APA—yet getting trans medical care continues to require a diagnosis. It can be a bit head-spinning to think about getting "diagnosed" with something that is not a disorder in order to be "treated" for it.

Nuanced changes in official diagnostic language clearly don't instantly flip the definitions in everyone's minds, either. There's much disagreement even within the trans community; for this 39-year-old man from College Station, Texas, for example, being trans remains strictly a medical issue:

> **Transgender is a medical condition I have, not a freaking identity or a gender in itself. Unlike these little self-diagnosed "genderfluid" snowflakes—aka poseurs—I actually transitioned years ago, complete with medical care and hormones and a name change and not picking a new gender or pronoun every four seconds. I am quite goth/androgynous looking and always have been. I am most definitely male. You don't**

"identify" as trans any more than you "identify" as having diabetes. You get diagnosed with it, ffs.

It seems likely that in the coming years we'll see *this* binary—disorder versus identity—start to dissolve for many.

For starters, medical techniques in general tend to become more sophisticated and safer over time. As that happens, we can start to shift away from thinking of healthcare purely in terms of treating disease. We've already seen a reframing of health broadly in terms of prevention and wellness, but what about proactive agency over our bodies? In years to come, medical choice will surely extend far beyond today's superficial "cosmetic" surgeries. Hormone treatments are of course already more than cosmetic, as they hack the body's own mechanisms for modifying form, function, and even behavior. Still, these remain imperfect technologies. Cross-gender hormones typically limit fertility, and can cause health problems.[19] They also require lifelong medical maintenance.

A more profound change is taking place without any need for transformative medical advances, though. An increasing number of trans people *don't* opt to have medical procedures done; their transition is social and behavioral. This move marks a significant decoupling of identities from bodies—a topic I'll return to in Chapter 15.

Most people in the trans and intersex communities agree that neither being intersex nor trans are "lifestyles," but manifestations of something deeper in one's makeup. Ironically, in this respect, they also agree with a lot of more conservative people in the general population; it's just that those more conservative people tend to think of unchangeable "reality" in terms of sex chromosomes or genitals, whereas many trans and intersex people have a lived experience of unchangeable "reality" being their deeply rooted sense of who they are. As David Reimer could attest, that can't just be ignored or wished away. At the same time, one's sense of gender is an internal, subjective experience, which makes it easy for others to question.

To complicate the picture even further, this internal experience isn't necessarily constant throughout life, or itself binary.[20] A number of survey respondents expressed a nuanced range of sentiments:

I do not consider myself trans, but I have been dealing with mild gender dysphoria.[21]

previously diagnosed with gender identity disorder, I identify as a tomboy.[22]

19 Coleman et al., "Standards of Care for the Health of Transgender and Gender Diverse People, Version 8," 2022; Hembree et al., "Endocrine Treatment of Gender-Dysphoric/Gender-Incongruent Persons: An Endocrine Society Clinical Practice Guideline," 2017; Nahata et al., "Understudied and Under-Reported: Fertility Issues in Transgender Youth—A Narrative Review," 2019.

20 Singh, Bradley, and Zucker, "A Follow-Up Study of Boys With Gender Identity Disorder," 2021.

21 A 28-year-old man from San Jose, California.

22 A 32-year-old woman from Granbury, Texas.

23 A 43-year-old woman from Orange, Texas.

24 A 59-year-old woman from Pensacola, Florida.

I am fine with being a woman. Wish I had been a man. Hated child birth and periods. Hate waxing and shaving and makeup.[23]

wish i had been male.[24]

A wish that things were different doesn't necessarily equate with being trans, nor is it necessarily a disorder, but—either *might* be the case? This is the slipperiness the 1973 APA memo so clumsily struggled with.

To many trans people, the perennial (and possibly unanswerable) "nature versus nurture" question seems beside the point. As Juliet Jacques put it in her 2015 memoir, *Trans,*

> **I had no answer to this question, any more than I could convey to people why I was left-handed, and I didn't think it was fair that I was constantly being obliged to answer it. It wasn't my main concern: I didn't think too much about nature and nurture when I was worrying about the possibility of having my head kicked in if I answered back to any of the people who yelled at me in the street. *The scientists and the sexologists can argue about that*, I thought.**

25 Orange, "Teenage Transgender Row Splits Sweden as Dysphoria Diagnoses Soar by 1,500%," 2020.

It's indeed both unfair and nonsensical to ask trans people to justify their lived reality. Still, just as for handedness, the scientific questions of cause, effect, and mechanism seem worth exploring, both because a better understanding of ourselves is valuable in its own right, and because ignorance breeds just the kind of bigotry Jacques describes.

26 Delahunt et al., "Increasing Rates of People Identifying as Transgender Presenting to Endocrine Services in the Wellington Region," 2018.

27 Irshad, Hashmi, and Aamer, "Between a Rock and a Hard Place – Gender Dysphoria and Comorbid Depression in a Young, Low-Income, Pakistani Transgender Man," 2020.

28 Gentleman, "'An Explosion': What Is Behind the Rise in Girls Questioning Their Gender Identity?," 2022; Smith, "Referrals to the Gender Identity Development Service (GIDS) Level Off in 2018–19," 2019; "Gender Identity Development Service Referrals in 2019–20 Same as 2018–19," 2020.

Recent years have seen a sharp rise in gender dysphoria, especially among young people assigned female at birth. This isn't just an American phenomenon. In March 2020, the *Guardian* reported that "Sweden's Board of Health and Welfare […] confirmed a 1,500% rise between 2008 and 2018 in gender dysphoria diagnoses among 13- to 17-year-olds born as girls."[25] Similar accounts have been reported in countries ranging from New Zealand[26] to Pakistan.[27]

In 2022, England's National Health Service (NHS) reported that its Gender Identity Development Service (GIDS), the UK's only gender identity clinic for people under 18, would need to be shut down and replaced with regional centers to deal with skyrocketing numbers of referrals (more than 5,000 in 2021, doubling the 2019–2020 numbers[28]), which had overwhelmed staff and created unacceptably long waitlists.

Prior to 2011, the majority of referrals had been assigned male at birth, but today, three quarters of referrals were assigned female at birth. This is consistent with the rapid changes evident in the US survey data.

13.7 Referrals to NHS Gender Identity Development Service Number by year

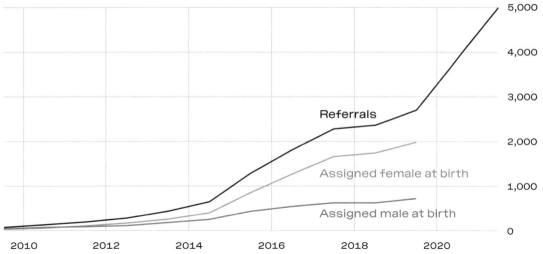

13.8 Referrals to NHS Gender Identity Development Service, share of total by sex assigned at birth % by year

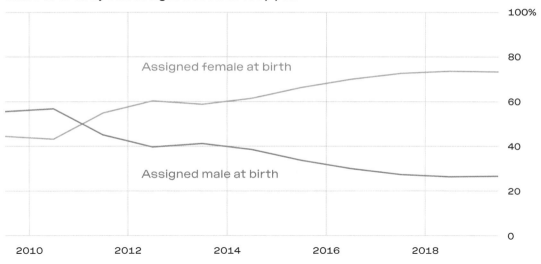

29 Tang et al., "Gender-Affirming Mastectomy Trends and Surgical Outcomes in Adolescents," 2022.

An increasing number of young people are on puberty-blocking hormones, and some have undergone surgeries, occasionally as young as 12.[29] Advocates both within and outside the trans community argue about the appropriate age of consent for these procedures. In some respects, it mirrors the controversy about intersex surgery on infants, but whereas in that case a focus on preserving children's agency militates against early intervention, the situation here is far less clear-cut.

The data offer some insights that push back on ideological arguments made on both sides. First, as we've seen, the shift toward defaulting to female for nearly all intersex babies likely accounts for a significant part of the rise in young people assigned female at birth seeking to transition. The overlap between young trans and intersex people offers an important clue, and the numbers suggest that many young trans men are intersex but unaware of it. This isn't a small effect. However, it's unlikely that latent intersexuality (even defined very broadly) accounts for the nearly 6% of young people assigned female at birth now identifying as trans—nearly half of whom also identify as non-binary. It's important to look at social factors too.

Advocates for early access to medical treatment sometimes argue that gender identity is intrinsic and immutable, because if it were otherwise, it would be harder to justify prescribing life-altering surgery or hormones to children. Such advocacy has led some to deny or minimize accounts of "desisting" or "detransitioning," in which young people change their minds about being trans, or seek to transition back after treatment with hormones or surgery (recall that only a fraction of young trans people undergo medical procedures). But lots of kids going through puberty are uncomfortable in their changing bodies, and many nowadays are identifying as trans, at least for a time. Desisting after puberty appears to be common,[30] and detransitioning sometimes happens too, though unbiased statistics about how often these occur are hard to come by.[31]

Given the powerful evidence of social transmission pretty much everywhere in the survey—including sexual orientation, attraction, and family models—it would be surprising *not* to find such effects. It's thus unfortunate that changing one's mind can be perceived as invalidating, either by trans rights advocates or by their critics. Advocates may find themselves arguing against any element of free will or choice in gender identity, and against any evidence of social transmission—which is hard to square with the data, or with the entire notion of social progress. Conservative critics may argue, on the other hand, that evidence of social transmission proves that "gender nonconformity" is a mere fad or "lifestyle choice," echoing older claims about being gay.

Just as it did then, this conservative argument has real-life consequences. Sonia Katyal, a legal scholar who has updated Kenji Yoshino's 2001 critique of gay "contagion"[32] to address challenges faced by trans parents, notes that custody courts regularly express concerns about "gender contagion—the idea that normalizing gender transition or variance can introduce a level of instability into the child's own gender identity." In one custody case involving a trans parent,

[...] the court was left to wonder, rhetorically, "Was his sex change simply an indulgence of some fantasy?" Whether such evidence would have in fact made a difference in the

30 Drummond et al., "A Follow-up Study of Girls with Gender Identity Disorder," 2008; Steensma et al., "Gender Identity Development in Adolescence," 2013; Wallien and Cohen-Kettenis, "Psychosexual Outcome of Gender-Dysphoric Children," 2008; Steensma et al., "Desisting and Persisting Gender Dysphoria After Childhood: A Qualitative Follow-up Study," 2011. Some researchers, however, have pointed out methodological challenges with desistance studies: Temple Newhook et al., "A Critical Commentary on Follow-up Studies and 'Desistance' Theories About Transgender and Gender-Nonconforming Children," 2018.

31 Expósito-Campos, "A Typology of Gender Detransition and Its Implications for Healthcare Providers," 2021.

32 See Chapter 7.

outcome is unclear, but the court certainly implied that the immutable—or at least unavoidable—character of a parent's gender identity could be entitled to greater consideration than a purely indulgent, selfish "choice" perhaps connected to sexual desire.[33]

33 Katyal and Turner, "Transparenthood," 2019.

It would be helpful to move beyond the either/or argument that animates much of this debate today, and acknowledge that there's no contradiction between people sometimes having "unavoidable" inner drives, exercising free choice, *and* being susceptible to the social transmission of ideas, including both behavior and identity.

Neither is being socially influenced something that only happens to unformed or impressionable young people. Every graph comparing 2018–19 with 2020–21 responses offers evidence that substantial numbers of older people are influenced by social transmission too.[34] Indeed, if they weren't, human progress could only happen "funeral by funeral," as an economist put it in 1975: "the old are never converted by the new doctrines, they simply are replaced by a new generation."[35] Evidently, things don't work this way; humans break the generational speed limit on evolution all the time.

It also seems clear from the data that different people have different degrees of flexibility with respect to their gender identity. Some older survey respondents reflect on how their identities might have differed if they were growing up in today's environment:

34 WEIRD societies place a strong value on personal consistency, which is perhaps why we consider it so embarrassing for our identities and beliefs to be influenced by others as adults. We'd prefer, perhaps, to somehow always be the influencers, yet for the ideas we spread to have sprung into our own minds out of nowhere.

35 O'Toole, "Science Makes Progress Funeral by Funeral," 2017.

> **I sometimes think I would have been happier if I was male. I never thought about this much when I was younger, as transexualism wasn't spoken of much or widely known at the time. I would never want to transition now but I think if I was growing up in today's world I might feel differently. I have always gravitated toward more classically 'masculine' hobbies and tastes. Then again, today there is somewhat less gender stereotyping and being a 'tomboy' is more normal. Even though I'm in my late 40s, I remain a bit confused about gender. I think this is mainly due to social conditioning. I do identify as a woman and very strongly as a lesbian.[36]**

36 A 47-year-old woman from Bridgeport, Connecticut.

Some of these effects are reminiscent of both handedness and sexual orientation. Recall that *exclusively* same-sex attracted people make up a remarkably consistent minority regardless of age; yet the data also reveal a rapidly growing cohort of younger people who are flexible in their attraction, and increasingly identify with the formerly narrower terms "gay" and (especially) "lesbian." Gender identity follows a similar pattern. A rapidly growing cohort of gender-expansive

Buck Angel (1962–), trans porn star, producer, activist, and educator.

young people have embraced the formerly narrower term "trans," whether they opt for medical intervention or not. There is clearly an element of individual choice involved here, and that choice occurs within an evolving social context.

At risk of oversimplifying (for this, too, is not a binary), imagine a "hard core" within the trans community consisting of women born in male-assigned bodies, or (more commonly nowadays) men born in female-assigned bodies—a situation far more prevalent than Ira Pauly's 0.001% estimate in 1968, but likely well below the nearly 6% of young trans people assigned female at birth today. Unless powerful environmental factors are in play (like the estrogen-mimicking pollutants described in *Count Down*), this "hard core" has likely remained fairly constant over time, though evolving intersex protocols seem to have shifted the tide from a majority of trans women to a majority of trans men. This population isn't limited to—but does include—people with rather traditional views about gender:

> **As an older transsexual who had transitioned before the fad, I feel a lot of this stuff these days is invented and find it offensive and unhelpful.[37]**

On the other hand, a sizable and growing number of young people could be described as "gender abolitionists" who reject not only their own binary gender assigned at birth, but the binaries of gender and sexuality altogether:

[37] A 49-year-old man from Traverse City, Michigan.

[38] A 24-year-old from Portland, Oregon.

> **Enby [non-binary], but don't self-id as trans. My entire friend group of 13 or so is all trans or enby. Pansexual is the closest descriptor to my sexuality that was provided, non-gender-differentiated demisexual would probably be more accurate. Also the gender binary is fake.[38]**

Although this is a broad movement, it, too, is especially embraced by young people assigned female at birth. Perhaps this should be unsurprising given the more privileged status of men, and the way campaigns like #MeToo have drawn attention to the stubborn persistence of gender inequality despite centuries of feminist activism.

A view from above

When computing and AI pioneer Alan Turing (1912–1954) first proposed his "Imitation Game" in 1950 as a test of artificial intelligence, it was framed in terms of gender recognition:

> I propose to consider the question, 'Can machines think?' This should begin with definitions of the meaning of the terms 'machine' and 'think'. [...] Instead of attempting such a definition I shall replace the question by another, which is closely related to it and is expressed in relatively unambiguous words.
>
> The new form of the problem can be described in terms of a game which we call the 'imitation game'. It is played with three people, a man (A), a woman (B), and an interrogator (C) who may be of either sex. The interrogator stays in a room apart from the other two. The object of the game for the interrogator is to determine which of the other two is the man and which is the woman. [...]
>
> We now ask the question, 'What will happen when a machine takes the part of A in this game?' Will the interrogator decide wrongly as often when the game is played like this as he does when the game is played between a man and a woman? These questions replace our original, 'Can machines think?'[1]

Alan Turing at age 16, ca. 1928.

1 Turing, "Computing Machinery and Intelligence," 1950.

What we now call the Turing Test takes a gender-neutral form; it involves a human judge trying to determine whether the entity at the other end of an online chat is another human or a machine. It's telling, though, that in his original formulation, Turing's challenge subverted what he regarded as the epitome of human judgment: making a gender determination without relying on physical cues.

There's something very meta about a closeted gay mathematician in postwar Britain proposing to test whether a machine can pass for a man trying to pass for a woman. But of course, in the fifties, binary gender (and heterosexuality) were requirements to be recognized as fully human. So, perhaps Turing was being subversive in more than one way.

In her sharp analysis of the Imitation Game paper, literary critic N. Katherine Hayles wrote,

> **By including gender, Turing implied that renegotiating the boundary between human and machine would involve more than transforming the question of "who can think" into "what can think." It would also necessarily bring into question other characteristics of the [...] subject, for it made the crucial move of distinguishing between the enacted body, present in the flesh on one side of the computer screen, and the represented body [...] in an electronic environment. This construction necessarily makes the subject into a cyborg, for the enacted and represented bodies are brought into conjunction through the technology that connects them. [...] As you gaze at the flickering signifiers scrolling down the computer screens, no matter what identifications you assign to the embodied entities that you cannot see, you have already become posthuman.[2]**

2 Hayles, *How We Became Posthuman: Virtual Bodies in Cybernetics, Literature, and Informatics*, xiii–xiv, 1999.

Certainly, embodiment matters. On the other hand, when we interact with others socially—whether by text, video, or in the flesh—only parts of our bodies are disclosed, while others are covered up. In this, we differ from our primate kin.

Even naked, though, disclosure is incomplete. Aspects of our embodiment remain opaque to our lovers, and even to ourselves, or it wouldn't be possible to grow up intersex and not know it. So, it's not always clear where the boundary lies between a "represented" and "enacted" body.

In an increasingly social and digital world that affords us a growing range of technologies for altering both our bodies and the way we present ourselves to others, it's also no longer clear which (if either) of these is the "real you." Having spent the last several chapters delving into the connections between the biology of sex and gender identification, it's now time to look more carefully at how presentation and behavior relate to identity.

We become Turing's "interrogator (C)" every time we meet someone new and (despite the increasingly strong injunction never to make assumptions) need to guess which pronoun to use. Practically speaking: How do we do it?

Hopefully you're convinced by now that gender isn't something that can be worked out by pure logic, or based on any single variable. It has to be a more holistic (thus necessarily imperfect) judgment, based on the whole "fuse box" of gendered attributes, signals, and behaviors.

Chapter 2 explored handedness from a similarly multidimensional perspective, using optimal linear estimation to correlate dozens of questions about behavior and presentation with personal identity as a left- or right-handed person—or both, or neither. This chapter will apply the same techniques to gender and sexual orientation, allowing us to zoom out from the "trees" of individual responses, which I've focused on so far, to see the whole "forest" of presentation.

Recall how a linear estimator for, say, right-handedness produced the optimal set of question weights for calculating a right-handedness

14.0 Predictors of "Are you female?"
Questions sorted by weight, from most positive to most negative

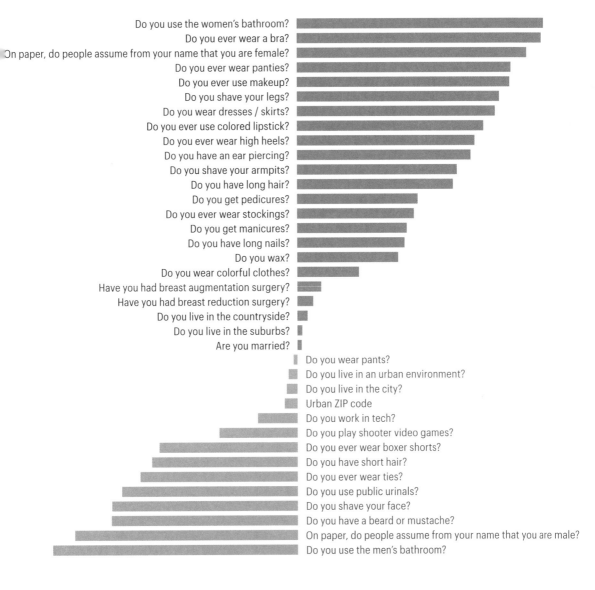

score. The same kind of linear estimator can predict the answer to the question "Are you female?" based on answers to 37 of the survey's behavioral questions. The output is a set of question weights representing the relative importance of each response, ranging from a strong positive correlation (a large positive number), to neutral (near zero), to a strong negative correlation (a large negative number).

Predictably, the question weights for optimally predicting "Are you male?" are virtually identical, but with the positive and negative signs flipped. (Running the same analysis to predict pronoun—exclusively "she" or exclusively "he"—yields nearly identical results.) There are no great surprises in the question weights. Which bathroom someone uses is the single most predictive variable, while long or short hair, manicures, and waxing are more weakly predictive.[3]

3 Keep in mind that the questions and patterns of responses are culturally specific. Long hair, for instance, has been and remains traditional for men in many cultures.

14.1 Predictors of both or neither male/female
Questions sorted by weight, from most positive to most negative

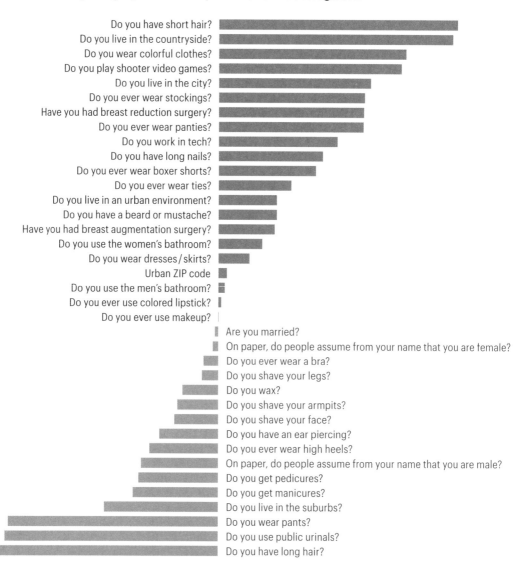

As with handedness, a linear estimator can also be calculated to predict *ambiguous* responses to the gender questions—subjects who answer either "yes" to both, or "no" to both of "Are you female?" and "Are you male?"

Now, hair length becomes far more relevant; short hair is the single most correlated question, while long hair is the most anti-correlated. Bathroom use is no longer so significant, though use of the women's bathroom is somewhat more common than the men's, and the use of urinals is nearly as uncommon as long hair, suggesting a desire for greater privacy. Other signs of androgyny are evident too, such as negative correlations with gendered names.

Clearly there are people in the excluded middle, but is this middle the exception, or the norm, behaviorally speaking? Is the gender binary still alive and kicking? And are "both or neither" people really a "third gender," as has sometimes been claimed?

A mathematical technique called Principal Component Analysis, or PCA, can help address these questions. Using PCA involves taking the set of questions above—which are purely about socially visible behavior and presentation, and don't include "Are you female?" or "Are you male?"—and finding the *internal* correlations among them.

It works as follows. Let's define a "component" as a numerical score calculated just as above: a weighted sum of the answers to the 37 yes/no questions about gender presentation. The "first component" of the PCA is the set of question weights yielding the single most informative score that can be calculated, meaning that knowing this score for any individual would do the best possible job of estimating the answers to *all* 37 questions.[4]

In theory, it could be the case that this one number would suffice to fully describe the data. Imagine, for instance, that we were working with a much smaller set of yes/no questions:

Do you use the women's bathroom?
Do you use the men's bathroom?
Do you have long hair?
Do you have short hair?

As many case studies in this book show, one can never safely assume that a person's response to one of these questions will determine the answer to any other one. There are four variables here, with two potential values each, allowing for $2 \times 2 \times 2 \times 2 = 16$ possibilities of varying popularity. But let's suppose that we were administering this four-question quiz in an imaginary town—call it Stepford,

[4] If you're a math nerd, you may find this language imprecise... and that's true. But I promised there would be no equations, and I'm bending that rule a little bit as it is in the next couple of paragraphs.

Calculating a PCA is a bit like long division from hell—it requires carrying out a complex, repetitive, many-step algorithm, which wasn't practical to do before we had computers. If you're interested in the mechanics, though, check out every old school data scientist's must-have reference manual: William H. Press et al., *Numerical Recipes 3rd Edition: The Art of Scientific Computing*, 2007.

USA—where everyone answers in only one of two equally likely ways: (+1, −1, +1, −1) for Stepford women, and (−1, +1, −1, +1) for Stepford men, where +1 represents "yes" and −1 is "no." If we were to carry out a PCA,[5] the first principal component would then have weights corresponding to (+1, −1, +1, −1), or equivalently, (−1, +1, −1, +1), or any other fixed multiple of these numbers, like (+0.5, −0.5, +0.5, −0.5); only the proportions of the weights relative to each other matter. For a stereotypical woman's responses, this first principal component score would then work out to 0.5×1 + (−0.5)×(−1) + 0.5×1 + (−0.5)×(−1) = +2, while the first principal component value for a stereotypical man's responses would be 0.5×(−1) + (−0.5)×1 + 0.5×(−1) + (−0.5)×1 = −2. This single score, +2 or −2, would tell us how any given respondent answered *all four* questions.

14.2 Gender presentation principal component 1
Questions sorted by weight, from most positive to most negative

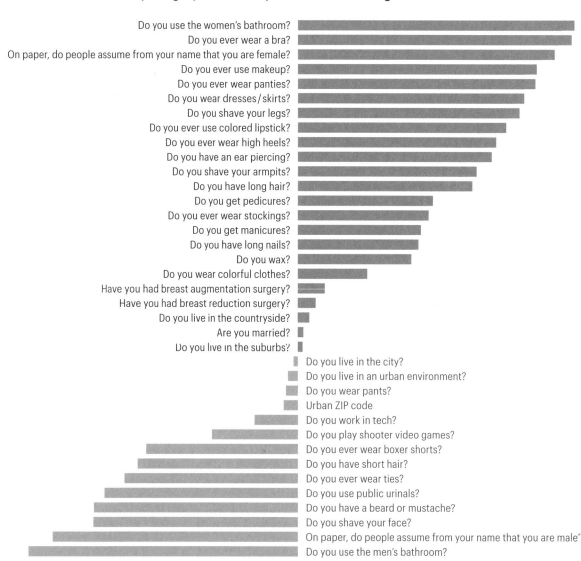

Or maybe not! Even in Stepford, a woman might eventually decide to get a bob at the hairdresser's. The occasional man might even grow his hair out. This would cause a *second* principal component to emerge, with weights (+0.5, −0.5, −0.5, +0.5). As you can check for yourself, this component will be zero for long-haired women or short-haired men, but will produce a +2 for women with bobs, and a −2 for men with long hair. So in this slightly more complex (and slightly more realistic) situation where hair length doesn't always coincide with the gender norm, the original four questions need to be represented by *two* numbers, not just one. The first, and most informative, still encodes gender, while the second is nonzero for anyone with gender-atypical hair length.

So that's Principal Component Analysis. Let's now leave Stepford and enter the real world, where I've recorded valid responses from 9,578 Americans to all 37 gender presentation questions.

The first principal component that emerges looks almost indistinguishable from the gender prediction weights. Maybe this isn't surprising, but it *is* meaningful, since neither sex assigned at birth nor gender identity was an input into the analysis. This result tells us that in the real world, most of the behavioral markers of gender covary in a way that closely mirrors people's identification with a gender. In other words, this one "gender score" emerges organically from the data, and describes more of the variation in it than any other single score would.

Next, let's look at a histogram of everyone's first principal component score, that is, the sum of their answers multiplied by these weights.

14.3 **Histogram of gender presentation principal component 1**
Count by principal component 1 value

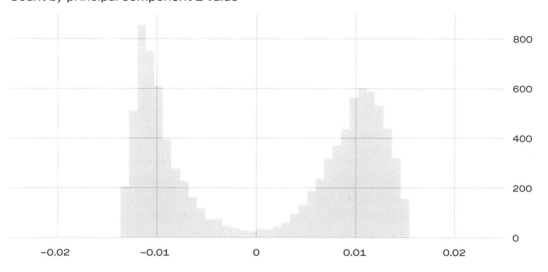

A (two-hump)
Bactrian camel.

This histogram has two humps; it looks like the gender binary is alive and well after all. Though on closer inspection, this can't quite be the full story. For a variable to be described as truly binary, it would have to assume *only* two values, like the +2 and −2 of our Stepford example. Here, there's a whole range or spectrum of values along the "gender axis," from roughly −0.015 to +0.015, with no empty regions along that range.

Nonetheless, there are clearly two peaks, with a less-populated valley in between. The curve looks like the profile of a two-humped camel.

Let's compare this to a histogram of respondents' heights. Men are on average taller than women, so overall, the distribution of human height also looks like a sum of two superimposed bell curves; however, because the random variations *within* the male and female distributions are large compared to the difference between them, no noticeable dip exists in between: the 67 inch or so midpoint (5 feet, 7 inches) remains a common height overall. Hence the sum looks more like a one-hump dromedary (or Arabian camel) than its rarer two-hump cousin.

14.4 **Histogram of respondent height by gender** Count by height in inches

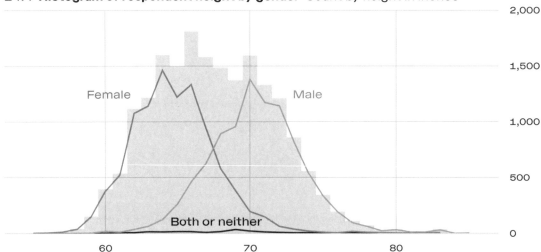

Because height is an easily measured, reasonably clear-cut biological variable while the presentation variables are more squishy and cultural, it's tempting to assume that clear-cut "rational" categories apply to biology but not to culture. For example, in a 2022 book on sex differences, primatologist Frans de Waal writes,

A (one-hump) dromedary.

Differences between the sexes [...] show a bimodal distribution (the famous bell curves), which means that they concern averages with overlapping areas between them. For example, men are taller than women, but only in a statistical sense. We all know women who are taller than the average man, and men who are shorter than the average woman. [...] Gender is a different issue altogether [.... The terms masculine and feminine] refer to social attitudes and tendencies that aren't easily classified. They often mix so that aspects of both are manifested in a single personality. [...] Gender resists division into two neat categories and is best viewed as a spectrum that runs smoothly from feminine to masculine and all sorts of mixtures in between.[6]

6   De Waal, *Different: Gender Through the Eyes of a Primatologist*, 51–52, 2022.

7   De Waal, 67.

Reading this passage, one would guess that height ought to look like a two-hump camel, while a behavioral "gender score" ought to look like a one-hump dromedary, with masculine and feminine traits blending into a featureless continuum; but in fact, it's the other way round. Human bodies are not so strongly sexually dimorphic on average, making the combined height distribution look more *unimodal* than bimodal—notwithstanding de Waal's description of how he and his brothers, like their father, "towered head and shoulders" above their mother.[7] (Though in fairness, adding additional physiological variables, such as weight and muscle mass, would pull the distributions farther apart, up to a point.) A gender presentation score based on those squishy cultural markers, though—clothes, grooming, choice of bathrooms—is clearly bimodal.

Still, while the gender presentation histogram is two-humped, those humps do overlap. So the question of whether gender is binary or not lacks a clear answer. The debate is itself a false binary. Many people, in their presentation, appear to fall clearly into one peak or the other, and the very presence of those distinct peaks suggests categories. Being great pattern recognizers and namers of things, humans would make up names for those peaks if they didn't already exist.[8] However, the peaks *aren't* cleanly separated, so those categories can't account for everyone's presentation. There are people living in the valley too.

8   And of course, in naming them, we would create a feedback loop: with our penchant for anonymous identities, many of us would modify our behavior to fall more clearly into one peak or the other, which would in turn influence our use of language. This describes, in short, how gender is constructed socially, albeit not beginning with a blank slate.

If you're paying close attention, you may have noticed that I haven't yet confirmed whether the two humps in the first principal component histogram actually correspond to sex or gender identification. That question, and more, can be answered by visualizing respondents as points in 2D space, with their coordinates given by their first and second principal component scores—something like a God's eye view of every respondent in a 2D "gender presentation space." (The approach can easily extend to 3D.) Points can then be colored based on the respondent's identification as female, male, both, or neither.

14.5 **Gender presentation space** Leading two principal components

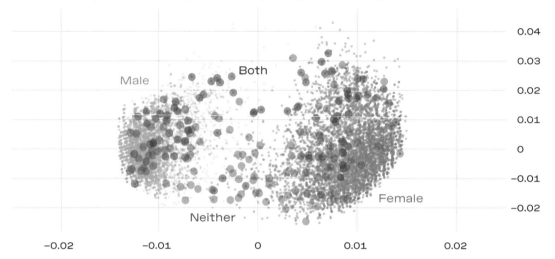

The histogram of respondents' first principal component scores would result from letting all of these points fall onto the horizontal axis and counting them up in bins. It's easy to see that the overwhelming majority of the right-hand hump would consist of orange dots—people who identify exclusively as female—while the left-hand hump would consist mostly of turquoise dots—people who identify exclusively as male. In 2D, these humps look like fairly well-defined clusters. However, if you look closely, you can spot a few people whose identities *wouldn't* be predicted correctly based on how they present. There are orange dots surrounded by turquoise ones, and turquoise dots deep in orange territory. Moreover, a smattering of "both" and "neither" appears across the entire range of presentations (these are drawn with bigger dots for extra clarity, since they're sparser).

Visualizations like these might explain why the idea of a "third gender," as a distinct cluster with specific social markers, has never fully taken off in modern Western culture.[9] "Both" and "neither" points are scattered throughout the whole space, including—but by no means limited to—the excluded middle between conventionally masculine and feminine presentations.

This impression can be confirmed by graphing the likelihoods of female, male, or "both or neither" identification as a function of their

9 Chapter 12 points out the ways in which other cultures have variously defined a "third gender"; it's possible that in certain cultural contexts, and given the right set of questions, a distinct cluster *would* emerge.

score using the optimal linear predictors, just as for left-, right-, and ambiguous-handedness in Chapter 2. Female and male predictors mirror each other, and show near-perfect performance at the extreme ends of the scale, with a transition in between where a greater proportion of "both or neither" people tend to fall. However, "both or neither" is *never* the likeliest option, even at the most ambiguous point in the middle of the scale, where male or female identification is equally likely. Specifically, at that point of "maximum androgyny," a person is about 40% likely to identify as male, 40% likely to identify as female, and 20% likely to identify as both or neither.

14.6 Likelihood of gender identification as a function of "Are you female?" linear predictor % by score

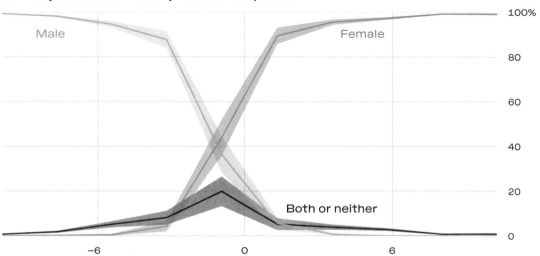

14.7 Likelihood of gender identification as a function of both or neither male/female linear predictor % by score

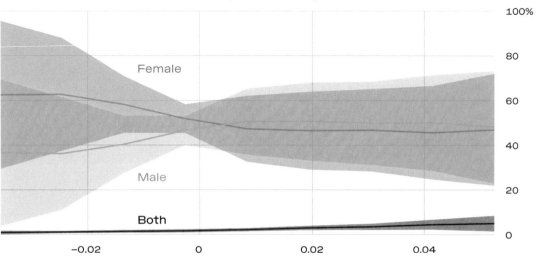

Consistent with this, an optimal linear predictor for "both or neither"-ness doesn't exhibit anything like the reliability of the predictors for binary gender. Even for a person maxing out this score, the likelihood of identifying as "both or neither" is only 5% or so, with the remaining majority of the probability split roughly evenly (with large error bars) between female and male identification. An ambiguous "femaleness vs. maleness" score implies much higher odds of being "both or neither"—closer to 20%—but only because far fewer *binary* respondents fall into that excluded middle. Seen another way, just as many "both or neither" people present the way traditionally female or male people do as present in the excluded middle; it's just that, in that excluded middle, they stand out more clearly against the sparser binary background. So, "both or neither"

14.8 Gender presentation principal component 2
Questions sorted by weight, from most positive to most negative

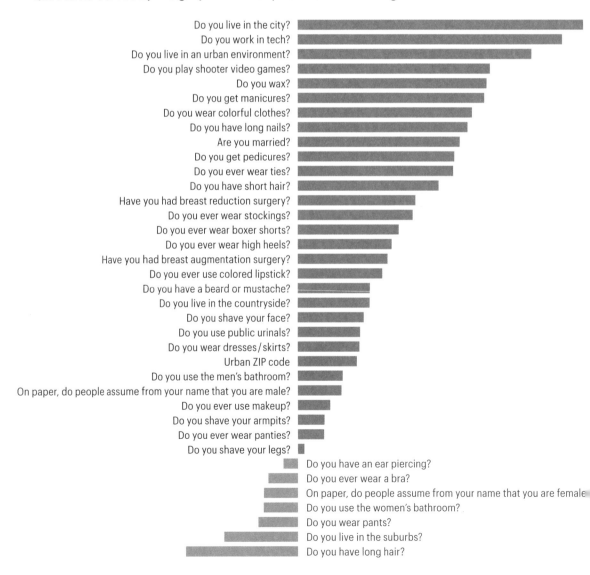

people can look any which way. Most aren't especially androgynous in their presentation.

You may wonder how to interpret "Principal component 2," the vertical axis in the scatter plot. This second component seems relevant to gender identity too, though less straightforwardly. Notice how the clusters tilt slightly: people whose first component is near zero—that is, who are most ambiguous on the horizontal dimension—are more likely to identify as female, and much likelier to identify as "neither," if their second component is less than zero (toward the bottom), but more likely to identify as male if the second component is greater than zero (toward the top). Hence, while most of the information one might use to guess someone's gender is in the first component, knowing the second component would allow for a slightly better guess. (The same is true—though barely—for the third component; a case of diminishing returns.)

High values for this second component correlate with living in the city and working in tech, while low values correlate with living in the suburbs and having long hair. What does it all mean? There may be an interesting story here, but interpretation of second-order effects can start to look more like data art than data science. It all falls in the realm of social signaling, though—in the relevant contexts and communities, people take in this kind of subtle information and use it, often subconsciously, when they make inferences about a stranger's gender. Conversely, we also use an implicit understanding of these patterns when we make decisions about our own presentation (for instance, at the hair salon).

If one were to run a survey including questions about all of the sex-relevant biological, physiological, and anatomical variables discussed in Chapter 11 (on intersexuality), the first principal component of the answers would almost certainly exhibit the same two-hump pattern. Moreover, many of those physiological variables (such as having larger breasts) strongly correlate with behavioral variables (such as wearing a bra), for obvious reasons—though such correlations may be weakening in the disembodied, online world we increasingly inhabit, which has started to look like a giant worldwide Turing Test arena... one which is, incidentally, also full of bots masquerading as people.[10] So, as we all relocate to the internet and (perhaps) gender fades in importance, the two-hump camel pattern *might* start to look more like the height histogram's one-hump dromedary. This idea will be explored further in the next chapter.

As long as we can see each other's real life faces, though, even in a tightly cropped Zoom window, the overlapping but still clearly two-humped pattern of facial sexual dimorphism—the different average shapes of men's and women's faces, allowing reliable classification in

10 Imperva, "2022 Bad Bot Report," 2022; Ikeda, "Bad Bot Traffic Report: Almost Half of All 2021 Internet Traffic Was Not Human," 2022.

a majority of cases—will remain obvious. We'll also continue to make occasional misgendering mistakes, just as if we were to guess at the colors of dots on the survey PCA based on their position alone.

Average face from Pentland, 1991.

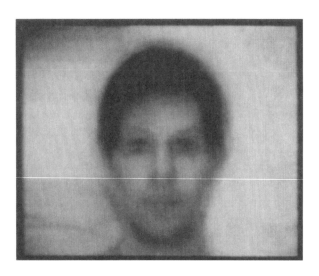

Like the Turing Test, recognizing facial images is a classic problem in machine intelligence. In 1990, Alex "Sandy" Pentland, a computer science professor at MIT and serial entrepreneur, dedicated his lab's attention to face recognition. They began by using precisely the techniques described above, simply replacing the 37 yes/no survey response values with a few tens of thousands of pixel values.[11] The researchers aligned uniformly posed and lit digital images of volunteers' faces, then reduced the resolution to something manage-

[11] Turk and Pentland, "Eigenfaces for Recognition," 1991.

able—256×256 monochrome pixels, each represented by a number between 0 (black) and 1 (white). Averaging those images yields a blurry, indistinct "average face."

Averages can also be made using the faces of people sharing some trait, to generate composite portraits of specific subpopulations. South African artist Mike Mike did this years later in his itinerant photography project *The Face of Tomorrow*,[12] which digitally super-imposed portraits of men and women grouped by age and, somewhat arbitrarily, by geography. By manually aligning the pupils of the

[12] Mike, "The Face of Tomorrow — the Human Face of Globalization," 2004.

Faces of the "average" Sydneysider, by Mike Mike, 2004.

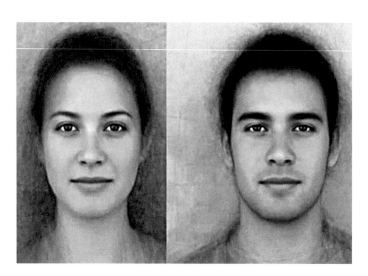

13 There are a few technicalities. For example: the hypothetical Stepford data are arranged so that all responses average to zero over the population. If they didn't, the average response values would need to be subtracted out before calculating weights. (I did so for the handedness and gender presentation analyses.) Similarly, one would need to subtract from a selective facial composite the overall average face to produce the kind of optimal linear estimator described. Then, calculating an estimate involves multiplying the resulting pixel weights by the difference between an unknown portrait's pixels and the average face.

Francis Galton, 71, featured in one of his own anthropometry cards, created on his visit to Alphonse Bertillon's Criminal Identification Laboratory in Paris, 1893.

eyes and other facial features, he was able to make his composites a lot sharper than those of the Pentland Lab in the '90s. The results are striking, and the faces are beautiful in their way, though also bland, since asymmetries and distinctive features (including anything one might consider a blemish) have been averaged away. "Average skin" looks smooth and featureless. "Average hair" looks like a diffuse fuzzy mass, since one subject's individual strands of hair won't match up precisely with those of any other subject.

Though it may not be immediately obvious, these composites are visualizations of exactly the kind of optimal linear estimators I've described for handedness or gender. To understand why, consider how you'd go about calculating the optimal gender weights for the four "Stepford survey" questions earlier in this chapter ("Do you use the women's bathroom?", "Do you use the men's bathroom?", "Do you have long hair?", and "Do you have short hair?"). The basic recipe is to calculate a *conditional average*, meaning that the optimal weights for an "Are you female?" estimator are simply the average of the answers of all of the respondents who said "yes" to "Are you female?"

In the same way, the average face of a young female Sydneysider can serve as a "template for femaleness" among young Sydneysiders. Scoring the relative similarity of a young Sydneysider's face to this template (which can be calculated by summing the products of a subject's facial pixels with the template pixels) will predict the likelihood that the subject is female.**13**

It's a seductively simple and powerful trick. Given the data to make such templates, what else might one be able to predict based on a facial image?

Victorian polymath Francis Galton (1822–1911), a pioneer in the statistical method of correlation, originally invented the facial compositing technique—long before we had digital computers. Galton was less interested in gender, though, than in law and order. Like his contemporary and fellow traveler, our old friend Cesare Lombroso, Galton sought to turn old-fashioned policing into a modern scientific discipline: *criminology.*

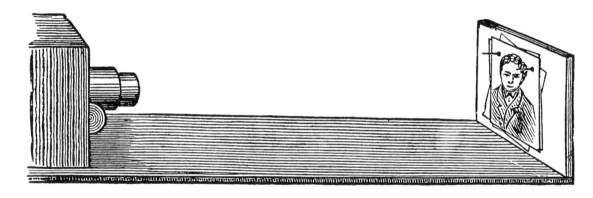

Composite portraiture device from Galton, *Inquiries Into Human Faculty and Its Development*, 1883.

In that spirit, he set out to visually characterize "criminal types" by superimposing exposures of convicts on the same photographic plate,[14] a procedure much like what Mike Mike did digitally more than a century later. Making observations and establishing correlations: the scientific method! But is there really such a thing as an "average criminal face"?

Although Galton's idea contained a kernel of mathematical insight, it suffered from many of the same problems in practice as Lombroso's pseudo-scientific studies of criminality. For starters, super-imposing just a handful of exposures can't yield anything like a real population average. More importantly, though, the selection of people included will determine what the resulting model "predicts"; as a statistician today might say, garbage in, garbage out. If, for instance, the 19th century Irish were economically disadvantaged, hence likelier to turn to crime, and on top of that likelier to be convicted by the British legal system, then the average "criminal face" probably would look Irish. By a feat of circular logic, this "scientific observation" could then be used to justify anti-Irish prejudice: a vicious cycle. This problem isn't merely hypothetical. Predictive policing systems today have been built on the same flawed logic.[15]

Galton's attempts to use multiple exposure portraiture to recon-struct "criminal types."

With computers, it's possible to go beyond the averaged faces Galton could approximate using a hand-ful of exposures on a photographic plate (or Mike Mike's more refined digital composites) and run a full Principal Component Analysis. The equivalent of the "question weights" for each principal component are a set of posi-tive and negative weights on face pixels, each of which, when applied to an individual face image and added up, produces a score. Visualizing the weights, using black for the most negative, white for the most positive, and medium gray for zero, yields ghostly face-like images (so-called "eigenfaces"), which one can think of as

14 Galton, "Composite Portraits," 1878.

15 Agüera y Arcas, Mitchell, and Todorov, "Physiognomy's New Clothes," 2017.

16 Turk and Pentland, "Eigenfaces for Recognition," 1991.

systematically tweaking the average face—adding or subtracting hair in one case, making the forehead and cheekbones more or less prominent in another, and so on.

In this way, just as a questionnaire can be reduced to one or two numbers, a face photo also can be reduced to one or a handful of numerical scores. Forty such numbers (corresponding to the first forty principal components) are enough to uniquely identify an individual, and can easily distinguish feminine-looking faces from masculine-looking ones, much as the first PCA component of the survey does.**16** The result: not just a gender prediction model, but a general system for facial recognition. What could possibly go wrong?

To be sure, face recognition has plenty of valuable and benign uses. Our own brains (or most of them) certainly do face recognition, as do the brains of many other smart visual animals; it powers the capacity for individual recognition described in the Introduction. Neither is there anything inherently sinister about a smart camera that detects faces in the viewfinder to keep them in focus, nor a smartphone with a face unlocking feature uniquely keyed to the phone's owner.

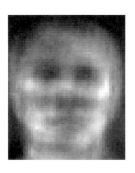

The first four principal components of face images, sometimes called "eigenfaces."

However, early funding for face recognition didn't come from phone or camera manufacturers, but from the Defense Department, which coordinated a number of institutions to accelerate its development, starting in 1993. Based on his lab's promising early results, Sandy Pentland was tapped to help lead this effort. The goal was much the same as that of the revolutionary French government's *Comité de Surveillance*, established in every municipality during the Reign of Terror: to develop techniques whereby the state could monitor the movements of outsiders, dissidents, and suspect individuals in general.**17**

17 "The goal of the FERET program was to develop automatic face recognition capabilities that could be employed to assist security, intelligence, and law enforcement." "Face Recognition Technology (FERET)," 2017.

This French bureaucratic term, *surveillance*, from *sur* (over) and *veiller* (to watch), has since entered the English language too. But whereas blanket surveillance of public spaces used to require vast, shadowy networks of informants, digital face recognition allows it to be automated. Today, the authorities' "view from above" of citizens' movements in security camera-saturated cities like Beijing or London far outdoes the analog police states of the 18th, 19th, and 20th centuries.

18 Reichert, "Clearview AI Facial Recognition Customers Reportedly Include DOJ, FBI, ICE, Macy's," 2020.

19 Kushwaha et al., "Disguised Faces in the Wild," 2018.

20 Harwell, "Facial Recognition Firm Clearview AI Tells Investors It's Seeking Massive Expansion Beyond Law Enforcement," 2022.

Recently, the technology has gotten a lot better, too. Manhattan-based startup Clearview AI uses "deep learning," based on large neural networks rather than simpler "linear" methods like PCA, to supply the FBI, Immigration and Customs Enforcement (ICE), the Department of Homeland Security (DHS), Interpol, and many local police departments (as well as various corporate customers) with truly powerful individual face recognition capability.[18] PCA can be thought of as a simple, "single-layer" artificial neural network; hence, in today's language, a minimal kind of artificial intelligence or AI system. The many stacked layers that give deep learning its name make systems like Clearview's both much more accurate and much more robust, so that face images don't need to be aligned, uniformly posed, or consistently lit, as with PCA. Deep learning can work surprisingly well even when faces are partially hidden, made up, or disguised.[19] Trained on billions of face images scraped from the web and social media, Clearview's system is said to reliably recognize anyone with an online presence from surveillance photos or video.[20]

On one hand, such technology can catch child abusers and foil terrorists. On the other, its indiscriminate deployment can put us all under continuous surveillance, not just by nosy neighbors, but by powerful governments that can mobilize the technology for social control, political repression, or even genocide. Even the US, nominally a democracy whose government must abide by the rule of law, has shown itself perfectly willing to conduct illegal mass surveillance on its own citizens.[21]

21 Snowden, *Permanent Record*, 2019.

Perhaps even more troubling are applications of face recognition that *don't* aim to recognize known individuals, but rather to make inferences about unknown people based on how they look. Some of these systems revive Francis Galton's long-dormant fantasy of recognizing "criminal types." In 2016, for instance, two machine learning researchers, Xiaolin Wu and Xi Zhang, put a paper online, *Automated Inference on Criminality Using Face Images*,[22] claiming that their deep neural net could predict the likelihood that a person was a convicted criminal with nearly 90% accuracy using nothing but a driver's license-style face photo. Their training and testing data consisted of 730 images of men wanted for or convicted of a range of crimes by provincial and city authorities in China, as well as 1,126 face images of "non-criminals [...] acquired from [the] Internet using [a] web spider tool."

Although one can't say for sure what their neural net is *really* picking up on, given the opacity of their data sources, some suggestive clues are offered by the three examples each of "criminals" and

22 Wu and Zhang, "Automated Inference on Criminality Using Face Images," 2016; Wu and Zhang, "Responses to Critiques on Machine Learning of Criminality Perceptions (Addendum of arXiv:1611.04135)," 2017.

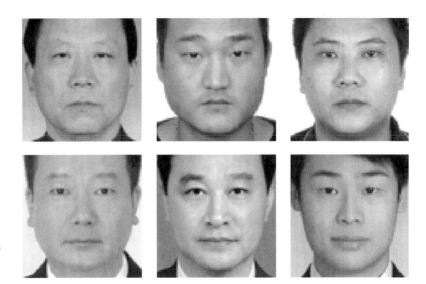

"Criminal" and "Non-criminal" ID card image data samples from Wu and Zhang, 2016.

23 Many facial recognition engines exhibit racial bias. Most commonly, this takes the form of worse recognition performance for minorities underrepresented in the training data. Grother, Ngan, and Hanaoka, "Face Recognition Vendor Test Part 3: Demographic Effects," 2019.

24 Cogsdill et al., "Inferring Character from Faces: A Developmental Study," 2014.

25 Oosterhof and Todorov, "The Functional Basis of Face Evaluation," 2008.

"non-criminals" shown in the paper. For one, the "non-criminals" all wear white-collar shirts, while the "criminals" don't. There may be a racial profiling component in play here too.[23] The main difference, though, is most likely the frowny faces of the "criminals," and the smiley faces of the "non-criminals." (This interpretation is also consistent with measurements the authors offer of average differences in facial landmark positions between the two groups.)

That's right: the "criminals" look meaner, and the "non-criminals" look nicer! But is that a cause, or an effect? We develop biases against "mean-looking" people early in childhood. Even 3- and 4-year-olds can reliably distinguish "nice" from "mean" face images.[24] Physiognomists, too, have long held the perfectly reasonable-sounding position that nice people have nice faces, and mean people have mean faces.

What, exactly, do these stereotypically "nice" and "mean" faces look like? Researchers studying the social perception of faces in recent years[25] have used (you guessed it) Principal Component Analysis to explore not only this question, but how people's first impressions of faces work in general. In one experiment, a video game-like face renderer produces a wide range of artificial faces based on 50 numerical measurements; experimental participants then describe their impressions of randomly generated faces, or rate them according to some perceived personality trait. PCA can capture most of the variability in people's first impressions using just a few components, three of which the researchers have named "dominance," "attractiveness," and "valence." The first two are fairly self-explanatory. The third, "valence," is associated with positive impressions like "trustworthy" and "sociable."

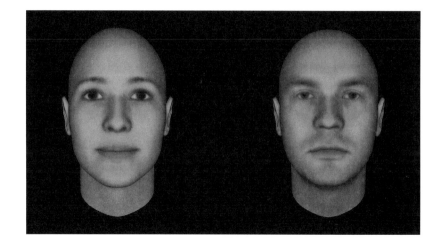

Computer reconstructions of "nice" (left) and "mean" (right) faces based on experimental data, courtesy of Alex Todorov.

↓ Courtroom drawing of Patrick Eugene Joseph Prendergast, 1894.

→ From Victor G. Rocine, "The Seat of Love, and the Story that Lips Tell," 1907.

An optimal linear predictor lets us visualize what a stereotypically "trustworthy" or "untrustworthy" face looks like, as shown here for white males. Notice how the "trustworthy" face has a more smiley expression—and reads as more feminine—while the "untrustworthy" face is more frowny and more masculine. It's likely no coincidence that the supposedly "criminal" faces in Wu and Zhang's paper look a lot like the "untrustworthy" face, while the "non-criminal" faces are more like the "trustworthy" face.

ASSASSIN PATRICK EUGENE JOSEPH PRENDERGAST. TO BE HANGED TODAY

Lips of Judge Cooley

TALK PRINCIPLE.

Honesty is seen in these lips, but not affection Compare these lips with those of Mrs. Meyer.

Mouth and Lips of Prendergast, the Murderer.

A protruding under lip is a bad sign. Such an under lip denotes crime and vicious instincts. Compare this mouth with that of Judge Cooley.

TALK BRUTALITY.

Lips of Mrs. Meyer

A loving mouth has large and full lips. The lips of Mrs Meyer in-

TALK RELIGION.

d cat : mission-ary tendencies, a love for the public and public work. Compare these lips with those of Mr. Depew. Colonel Ingersoll's lips and those of Mrs. Meyer indicate oratory.

Galton's composites of "criminal types" also look more like the "untrustworthy" face. They resemble "Prendergast, the Murderer," a mentally disturbed Irish-born newspaper distributor who assassinated five-term Chicago Mayor Carter Harrison, Sr. on October 28th, 1893.

The following year, an iconic courtroom drawing of Patrick Eugene Prendergast with a downturned mouth made it into the *Chicago Tribune*. The dour mouth, disembodied like that of a homicidal Cheshire cat, was subsequently immortalized in several American books on physiognomy, warning the reader to beware any bearer of such lips. Perhaps this was indeed Prendergast's resting face, though given the circumstances—summarized by the caption under the newspaper portrait, "TO BE HANGED TODAY"—it's hard to be sure.

People make instinctive, automatic judgments about character traits like trustworthiness after seeing a face for less than one tenth of a second.[26] Author Malcolm Gladwell wrote effusively about snap judgments like these in his 2005 bestseller, *Blink: The Power of Thinking Without Thinking*. It does seem that such judgments do a remarkable job of predicting important life outcomes,[27] ranging from political elections to economic transactions to legal decisions.

The question is, are these *good* judgments? Either answer would be interesting. If they *are* good judgments, then the physiognomists are right—we really do advertise our essential character traits on our faces. On the other hand, if those judgments are arbitrary, then that they do such a good job of predicting outcomes tells an even more disturbing story: that unwarranted prejudice based on resting facial appearance plays a decisive role in human affairs.

A large body of research favors the latter interpretation.[28] For example: in 2015, Brian Holtz, of Temple University, published the results of a series of experiments[29] in which facial "trustworthiness" was shown to strongly influence experimental participants' judgment. The participants were asked to decide, after reading a vignette, whether a hypothetical CEO's actions were fair or unfair. While the judgment varied (as one would hope) depending on how fair or unfair the actions described in the vignette were, it also varied depending on whether the CEO's face looked "trustworthy" or "untrustworthy" in the profile photo.

In another study,[30] participants played an online investment game with what they believed were real partners, represented by "trustworthy" or "untrustworthy" faces. Participants were more likely to invest in "trustworthy" partners even in the presence of more objective reputational information about the past investment behavior of their partners.

[26] Peterson et al., "Deep Models of Superficial Face Judgments," 2022.

[27] Olivola, Funk, and Todorov, "Social Attributions from Faces Bias Human Choices," 2014.

[28] Todorov et al., "Social Attributions from Faces: Determinants, Consequences, Accuracy, and Functional Significance," 2015.

[29] Holtz, "From First Impression to Fairness Perception: Investigating the Impact of Initial Trustworthiness Beliefs," 2015.

[30] Rezlescu et al., "Unfakeable Facial Configurations Affect Strategic Choices in Trust Games With or Without Information About Past Behavior," 2012.

31 Wilson and Rule, "Facial Trustworthiness Predicts Extreme Criminal-Sentencing Outcomes," 2015.

Even more chillingly, another study[31] found that among prisoners convicted of first degree murder, the unlucky defendants with "untrustworthy" faces were disproportionately more likely to be sentenced to death than to life imprisonment. This was also the case for people who were falsely accused and subsequently exonerated.

So, we're not endowed with some subconscious *Blink*-like genius for making snap judgments about people's characters based on how they look. Unfortunately, we make those snap judgments anyway, sometimes to our own detriment: for instance, studies in which the trustworthiness of economic behavior was measured show that relying on face judgments can make our decisions *less* reliable than if we were making them, literally, blind.[32]

32 Efferson and Vogt, "Viewing Men's Faces Does Not Lead to Accurate Predictions of Trustworthiness," 2013.

The worst consequences, though, fall upon anyone who happens to have an "untrustworthy" face. For example, it seems that they'll be significantly more likely, all things being equal, to end up convicted of a crime, while a guilty party with a "trustworthy" face is likelier to get away with their misdeeds. In sum, the facial "criminality detector" tells us more about our own pervasive biases than about the subject's character.

In the Fall of 2017, a year after the "resting criminal face" paper came out, a higher-profile study[33] began making the rounds claiming that sexual orientation could be reliably guessed based on a facial image. The *Economist* featured the study on the cover of their September 9th magazine;[34] on the other hand, two major LGBTQ+ organizations, The Human Rights Campaign and GLAAD, immediately labeled it "junk science."[35]

33 Wang and Kosinski, "Deep Neural Networks Are More Accurate than Humans at Detecting Sexual Orientation from Facial Images," 2018.

34 "Advances in AI Are Used to Spot Signs of Sexuality," 2017.

35 Anderson, "GLAAD and HRC Call on Stanford University & Responsible Media to Debunk Dangerous & Flawed Report Claiming to Identify LGBTQ People Through Facial Recognition Technology," 2017.

Michal Kosinski, who co-authored the study with fellow researcher Yilun Wang, initially expressed surprise, calling the critiques "knee-jerk" reactions. However, he then doubled down with even bolder claims: that similar approaches will soon be able to measure the intelligence, political orientation, and—you guessed it—criminal inclinations of people from their faces alone.[36]

36 Levin, "Face-Reading AI Will Be Able to Detect Your Politics and IQ, Professor Says," 2017.

Once again, this echoes the old claims of Cesare Lombroso and Richard von Krafft-Ebing: physiognomy, but now dressed in the "new clothes" of AI. However, while Wu and Zhang seemed well outside the mainstream in tech and academia, Kosinski is a faculty member of Stanford's Graduate School of Business, and the new study was accepted for publication in the respected *Journal of Personality and Social Psychology*. Much of the ensuing scrutiny focused on ethics, implicitly assuming that the science was valid. As with the previous year's result, however, there's reason to believe otherwise.

Composite heterosexual faces   Composite gay faces

Male

Female

Facial composites from Wang and Kosinski, 2018.

37 Clearly this is an incomplete accounting of sexual orientations, as well as presuming a gender binary. The problems inherent in AI systems that make such discrete classifications of people are well described in Katyal and Jung, "The Gender Panopticon: AI, Gender, and Design Justice," 2021.

The authors trained and tested their "sexual orientation detector" using 35,326 images from public profiles on a US dating website. Composite images of the lesbian, gay, and straight men and women in the sample,**37** reminiscent of Galton's composites, reveal a great deal about the patterns in these images.

According to Wang and Kosinski, the key differences between the composite faces are in their physiognomy, meaning that sexual orientation tends to correlate with a characteristic facial structure. However, you'll notice right away that some of these differences are more superficial. For example, the "average" straight woman appears to wear eyeshadow, while the "average" lesbian doesn't. Glasses are clearly visible on the gay man, and to a lesser extent on the lesbian, while they seem absent in the heterosexual composites.

14.9 **Women's responses to "Do you ever use makeup?"** % by age

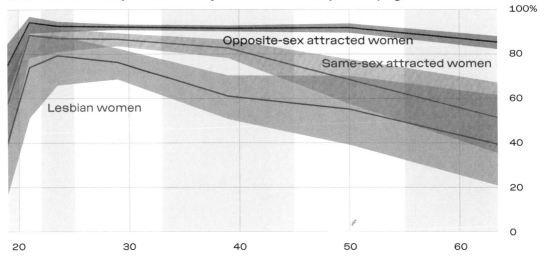

14.10 **Women's responses to "Do you wear eyeshadow?"** % by age

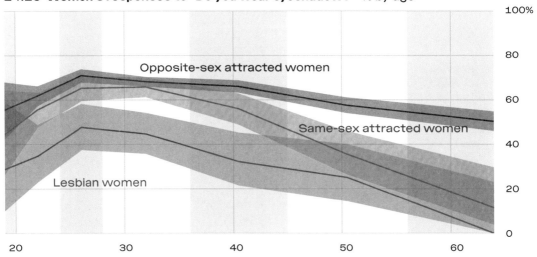

38 Margaret Mitchell is an AI researcher, and Alex Todorov is a world expert on the social perception of faces. Todorov co-authored several papers cited in this chapter, and has published a book on the topic: Todorov, *Face Value: The Irresistible Influence of First Impressions*, 2017. I also went back on the Savage Lovecast to talk about this work in November of 2017; see Savage, "Episode #579," 2017.

Might it be the case that the algorithm's ability to detect orientation has less to do with facial structure than with grooming, presentation, and lifestyle?

When the study was published, I was already running the Mechanical Turk surveys that would eventually turn into this book, so I teamed up with a couple of colleagues, Margaret Mitchell, then at Google, and Alex Todorov, then faculty at Princeton's Psychology Department, to run an extra survey that might shed some light on Wang and Kosinski's findings.**38** In addition to the usual questions about sexual orientation and attraction, we added a few, like "Do you wear eyeshadow?" and "Do you wear glasses?"; "Do you have a beard or mustache?" and "Do you ever use makeup?" were already on there.

14.11 Women's responses to "Do you like how you look in glasses?" % by age

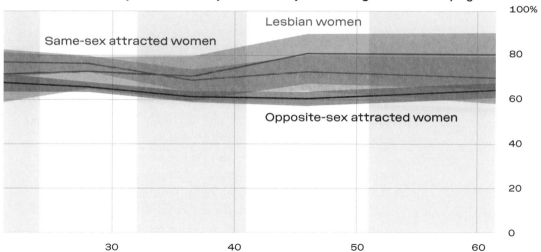

14.12 Men's responses to "Do you like how you look in glasses?" % by age

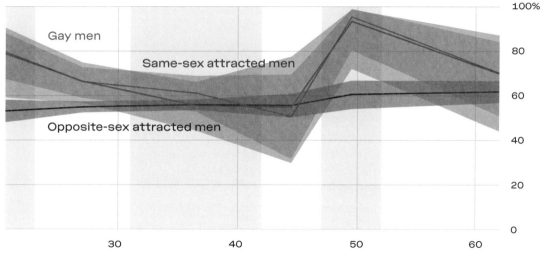

14.13 Men's responses to "Do you have stubble on your face?" % by age

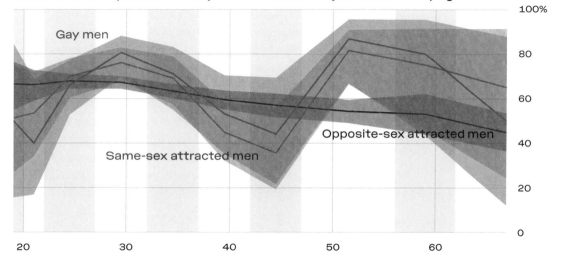

These graphs break down responses by sexual orientation, based both on behavior and identity. "Opposite-sex attracted women" are people who answer "yes" to "Are you female?," "no" to "Are you male?," and "yes" to "Are you sexually attracted to men?" and "Are you romantically attracted to men?"; a very similar sub-set of women answer "yes" to "Are you heterosexual or straight?" "Same-sex attracted women" are those who answer "yes" to "Are you sexually attracted to women?" and "Are you romantically attracted to women?" The curves for men follow the same pattern.

It will surprise no one that, at all ages, straight women tend to wear more makeup and eyeshadow than same-sex attracted and (even more so) lesbian-identifying women—although seen another way, the curves also show that these stereotypes are often violated. Even among opposite-sex attracted women, between a third and half *don't* wear eyeshadow, while around half of lesbians in their mid-20s *do*.

That same-sex attracted people of most ages wear glasses significantly more than exclusively opposite-sex attracted people do might be less obvious, but it is so. What should one make of this? A physiognomist might cook up a theory about gay people having worse eyesight.

It's unlikely, though. Answers to the question "Do you like how you look in glasses?" reveal that wearing glasses is probably more of a fashion statement, with the fashion trend varying by age. The pattern holds both for women and for men, though the trends seem to be at their most variable among gay (and more generally same-sex attracted) men. Perhaps Elton John had something to do with it?

Answers to the question "Do you have stubble on your face?" also tell an interesting story about trends. Gay and same-sex attracted men under the age of 45, who contributed the majority of the facial images in the dataset, are somewhat less likely on the whole to have stubble than those who are opposite-sex attracted, despite a peak around age 30. There's another peak around age 55. In their paper, Wang and Kosinski speculate that the relative faintness of the beard and mustache in their gay male composite might be due to feminization as a result of prenatal underexposure to androgens (male hormones). But the fact that 30- and 55-year-old gay and same-sex attracted men have stubble *more often* than straight men of the same age tells a different story, in which fashion trends and cultural norms are once again the determining factor.

Among gay and same-sex attracted men, those trends seem to be oscillating as a function of age, and I'd bet that they oscillate over time too. It's what one would expect to see if the point were to look a bit different, and to set or quickly follow a trend among your peers. This is social signaling in a dynamic environment. As always, cultural evolution allows us to differentiate our behavior and appearance to create, evolve, and sometimes subvert anonymous identities that are often designed to be obvious to our fellow humans at a glance.

Wang and Kosinski also note that the heterosexual male composite has darker skin than the other three composites. Once again, the authors reach for a hormonal explanation: "While the brightness of the facial image might be driven by many factors, previous research found that testosterone stimulates melanocyte structure and function leading to a darker skin." A simpler explanation: opposite-sex attracted men are 29% more likely to work outdoors, and among men under 31, this rises to 39%; of course, spending time in the sun darkens skin.

None of these findings prove that there's no physiological basis for sexual orientation; on the contrary, lots of evidence supports the view that orientation runs much deeper than a presentation choice or a "lifestyle." (For one thing, if it *were* simply a "lifestyle," gay conversion therapy wouldn't be such a spectacular failure.) It follows that if researchers dig deeply enough into human physiology and neuroscience, they may eventually find factors that reliably correlate with sexual orientation—but this is a tautology, really just boiling down to "your body and brain make you who you are." How could it be otherwise?

The survey has little to offer as far as such correlates go, though there *is* one tantalizing statistic: very tall women are significantly overrepresented among lesbian-identifying respondents. However, while the correlation is interesting, it's very far from a useful *predictor* of women's sexual orientation. To get a sense of why, let's look at the numbers. The way Wang and Kosinski measure the performance of their "AI gaydar" is equivalent to choosing a straight and a gay or lesbian face image, both from data "held out" during the training process, then asking how often the algorithm correctly guesses which is which. 50% performance would be no better than random chance. Guessing that the taller of two women is the lesbian achieves only 51% accuracy—barely above random chance. Despite the statistically meaningful overrepresentation of tall women among the lesbian population, the great majority of lesbians are *not* unusually tall.

By contrast, the performance measures in the paper, 81% for gay men and 71% for lesbian women, seem impressive.[39] However,

39 These figures rise to 91% for men and 83% for women if 5 images are considered.

we can get comparable results simply by using a handful of yes/ no survey questions about presentation. For example, for pairs of women, one of whom is lesbian, the following trivial algorithm is 63% accurate: if neither or both wear eyeshadow, flip a coin; otherwise guess that the one who wears eyeshadow is straight, and the other lesbian. Making an optimal linear estimator using six more yes/no questions about presentation ("Do you ever use makeup?," "Do you have long hair?," "Do you have short hair?," "Do you ever use colored lipstick?," "Do you like how you look in glasses?," and "Do you work outdoors?") as additional signals raises the performance to 70%. Given how many more details about presentation are available in a face image, 71% performance no longer seems impressive.

Several studies[40] have shown that human judges' "gaydar" is no more reliable than a coin flip when the judgment is based on pictures taken under well-controlled conditions (head pose, lighting, glasses, makeup, etc.). However, it's well above chance if these variables *aren't* controlled for, because as noted above, a person's presentation—especially if that person is out—involves social signaling.

Wang and Kosinski argue against this interpretation on the grounds that their algorithm works on Facebook selfies of users who make their sexual orientation public, as well as profile photos from a dating website. The issue, however, isn't whether the images come from a dating website or Facebook, but whether

40 Cox et al., "Inferences About Sexual Orientation: The Roles of Stereotypes, Faces, and the Gaydar Myth," 2016.

14.14 **Legality of homosexuality by country**

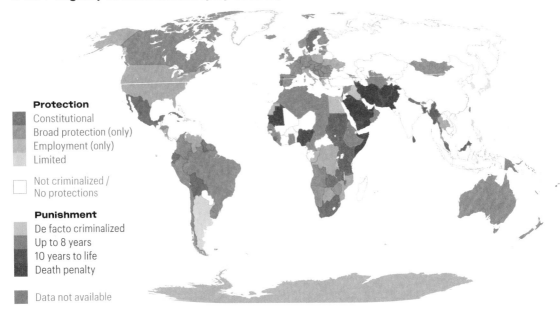

Protection
Constitutional
Broad protection (only)
Employment (only)
Limited

Not criminalized /
No protections

Punishment
De facto criminalized
Up to 8 years
10 years to life
Death penalty

Data not available

41 Rule and Ambady, "Brief Exposures: Male Sexual Orientation Is Accurately Perceived at 50ms," 2008.

they are self-posted or taken under standardized conditions. In one of the earliest "gaydar" studies using social media,[41] participants could categorize gay men with about 58% accuracy in a fraction of a second; but when the researchers used Facebook images of gay and heterosexual men posted by their friends (still an imperfect control), the accuracy dropped to 52%.

From a human rights perspective, it's a lucky thing that "AI gaydar" doesn't work so well, since as of 2022, homosexuality remains a criminal offense in 67 countries. In a number of them (Iran, Saudi Arabia, Yemen, Afghanistan, Brunei, Mauritania, Pakistan, Qatar, the United Arab Emirates, Nigeria, Uganda, and Somalia), it may be punishable by execution. Hence, in these countries, an accurate "gaydar camera" (together with the kind of ubiquitous surveillance increasingly common in public spaces) would amount to a dragnet technology for rounding up gay people, who are by definition "criminals," for mass incarceration—or worse.

Remember that homosexuality was also criminalized in most Western countries until very recently. In England, it was punishable by death under the Buggery Act of 1533, which codified "sodomy" as a "detestable and abominable vice." The 1861 Offences against the Person Act reduced the punishment to life imprisonment, and remained in force until 1967.

42 Estimates range from 2 to more than 20 million lives. Drury, "Alan Turing: The Father of Modern Computing Credited with Saving Millions of Lives," 2019; Copeland, "Alan Turing: The Codebreaker Who Saved 'Millions of Lives,'" 2012.

43 McCann, "Turing's Law: Oscar Wilde Among 50,000 Convicted Gay Men Granted Posthumous Pardons," 2017.

Both Oscar Wilde and Alan Turing were convicted under this law. At the time of Turing's trial in 1952, he was not only a computer science pioneer, but also a war hero, having secretly cracked the Nazis' Enigma codes, saving untold numbers of Allied lives.[42] Turing was sentenced to so-called "chemical castration" (feminizing estrogen injections, like those David Reimer underwent) as an alternative to prison. Like Oscar Wilde, Turing died in his forties, possibly of suicide. The British government had done its best to ruin both of their lives. Queen Elizabeth only officially "pardoned" Turing in 2013, nearly 60 years after his death. Wilde was "pardoned" in 2017, along with 50,000 other gay men on the far side of the grave.[43]

Subtle biases in image quality, expression, and grooming can be picked up on by humans, so these biases can also be detected by AI. While Wang and Kosinski acknowledge grooming and style, they believe that the chief differences between their composite images relate to face shape, arguing that gay men's faces are more "feminine" (narrower jaws, longer noses, larger foreheads) while lesbian faces are more "masculine" (larger jaws, shorter noses, smaller foreheads). As with less facial hair on gay men and darker skin on straight men, they suggest that the mechanism is gender-atypical hormonal exposure during development. This echoes the widely discredited 19th century "sexual inversion" model of homosexuality, as illustrated by Krafft-Ebing's "Count Sandor V" case study among many others.

More likely, though, the differences are a matter of shooting angle. A 2017 paper on the head poses heterosexual people tend to adopt when they take selfies for Tinder profiles is revealing.[44] In this study, women are shown to be about 50% likelier than men to shoot from above, while men are more than twice as likely as women to shoot from below.

Shooting from below will have the apparent effect of enlarging the chin, shortening the nose, and attenuating the smile. This view emphasizes dominance—or, maybe more benignly, an expectation that the viewer will be shorter. On the other hand, shooting from above simulates a more submissive posture, while also making the face look younger, the eyes bigger, the face thinner, and the jaw smaller—though again, this can also be interpreted as an expectation or desire[45] for a potential partner (the selfie's intended audience, after all) to be taller. If you're seeking a same-sex partner, the partner will tend on average to be of the same height, so one would expect the average shot to be neither from below nor from above, but straight on.

44 Sedgewick, Flath, and Elias, "Presenting Your Best Self(ie): The Influence of Gender on Vertical Orientation of Selfies on Tinder," 2017.

45 Per Fink et al., "Variable Preferences for Sexual Dimorphism in Stature (SDS): Further Evidence for an Adjustment in Relation to Own Height," 2007.: "[...] evidence suggests that females prefer taller over shorter males, indeed taller males have been found to have greater reproductive success [...] relative height is also important [...] people adjust their preferences [...] in relation to their own height in order to increase their potential pool of partners." The finding held in all three countries studied—Austria, Germany, and the UK—as well as in an earlier Polish study.

Selfies of the author, showing variations in camera angle, beardedness, and glasses.

And this is just what we see. Heterosexual men on average shoot from below, heterosexual women from above, and gay men

46 Although the authors use a face recognition engine designed to try to cancel out effects of head pose and expression, my research group confirmed experimentally that this doesn't work, a finding replicated by Tom White, a researcher at Victoria University in New Zealand. White, "I expected a 'face angle' classifier using vgg-face features would perform well, but was still floored by 100% accuracy over 576 test images," 2017.

47 Parr and Waller, "Understanding Chimpanzee Facial Expression: Insights into the Evolution of Communication," 2006.

48 Dunbar, *Friends*, 186, 2021.

Supposed "[d]egeneracy seen in [the] eyes, eyebrows, nose, lips, jaw, hair and pose," from Rocine, 1910.

and lesbian women from closer to eye level.**46** Notice that when a face is photographed from below, the nostrils are prominent (as in the heterosexual male face), while higher shooting angles hide them (as in the heterosexual female face). A similar pattern can be seen in the eyebrows: shooting from above makes them form more of a V shape, but they get flatter, and eventually caret-shaped (^) as the camera is lowered. Shooting from below also makes the outer corners of the eyes seem to droop. In short, the changes in the average positions of facial landmarks match what you'd expect to see from differing selfie angles.

Let's turn this observation on its head: might the human smile and frown have their origins in dominant (taller, looking downward) and submissive (shorter, looking upward) head poses? If so, these expressions may originally have evolved, at least in part, to mimic the way facial appearance varies based on height and posture.**47**

Indeed, there's strong evidence that smiling is the human version of the "bared teeth face" or "fear grin" in monkeys, associated with submission or appeasement.**48** Submissive postures also tend to involve crouching and making one's body look small, while dominant postures involve looking big and towering over others, or at least using head angle to *seem* taller—hence expressions like "acting superior" or "looking down your nose at some-one." I find it suggestive, also, that arching one's eyebrows (which shortens the forehead and changes the eyebrow shape) is associated with a superior attitude.

Whatever the reasons, when we look at human faces today—especially static, two-dimensional photos of strangers taken under uncontrolled conditions—there's a degree of visual ambiguity between head pose, the shapes of facial features, and affect (i.e. smiling or frowning).

In the heterosexual context, this may also explain the stereotypically more feminine look of the average "nice" or "trustworthy" face, and the more masculine character of the average "mean" or "untrustworthy" face. As researchers put it in a 2004 paper, *Facial Appearance, Gender, and Emotion Expression,*

[A] high forehead, a square jaw, and thicker eyebrows have been linked to perceptions of dominance and are typical for men's faces […],

49 Hess, Adams, and Kleck, "Facial Appearance, Gender, and Emotion Expression," 2004.

whereas a rounded baby face is both feminine and perceived as more approachable [...] and warm [...], aspects of an affiliative or nurturing orientation. This leads to the hypothesis that—regardless of gender—individuals who appear to be more affiliative are expected to show more happiness, and individuals who appear to be more dominant are seen as more anger prone. As cues to gender and cues to affiliation/dominance are highly confounded, this would lead to more women being expected to be happiness prone and more men to be anger prone.[49]

50 Rocine, 171.

This brings us back once more to physiognomy. A woman with what appears to be an unsmiling, perhaps defiant expression, photographed in V.G. Rocine's 1910 physiognomy primer *Heads, Faces, Types, Races*, supposedly illustrates "Degeneracy seen in [the] eyes, eyebrows, nose, lips, jaw, hair and pose."[50] As with a collection of similar mugshots from Lombroso's *The criminal woman*, a great majority of the female "crime" in question was either non-violent and associated with poverty, or just reflected behavior that didn't conform to prevailing gender and sexual norms. With so many biases in play, it's hard to know which was judged first— women's faces, or their actions.

Table IV, "Fisionomie di criminali Russe" [Physiognomies of Russian criminals] from Lombroso, *La donna delinquente, la prostituta e la donna normale*, 1893.

15   Postgender

From Abi Bechtel's tweet, June 1, 2015.

Abi Bechtel, a teaching assistant at the University of Akron and mother of three, was fed up. It was 3:36pm on the first of June, 2015. She was standing in front of aisle E11 in the toy department, phone raised, taking a picture of the sign: "Building Sets," and… "Girls' Building Sets." Abi tweeted the photo alongside four words: "Don't do this, @Target."[1]

It worked. A couple of months and many retweets later, Target responded by announcing they'd be phasing out unnecessary gendered signage. In the following years, they built on the policy by introducing gender-neutral bathrooms, children's bedding, and clothes.[2]

Toca Boca, the clothing company Target partnered with to help drive the change, was making its first foray into brick-and-mortar retail. Originally a casual game company, it was known for its popular gender stereotype-defying apps, Toca Boca Hair Salon and Toca Robot Lab. Much of the colorful imagery featured on the kids' clothes—from "a coral-colored T-shirt of a mean-mugging sloth donning a baseball cap, with the word 'Fast' printed underneath" to "a purple pile of poop"—were "characters ripped straight from the apps of Toca Life, […] digital games that emphasize role playing and are set in common locales such as farms or city streets."[3]

The hyper-gendered world of children's clothing had long been dominated by franchised media relentlessly flogging a pink/blue, unicorn/dinosaur binary. Many of the big brands used to be anchored by prime time TV shows and cartoons targeting either girls or boys. The media landscape had been changing, though, crumbling into a demographic fractal of competing channels, content streams, and social feeds. Among a generation growing up "digitally native," as the marketers put it, something new seemed to be afoot, a gender-neutral aesthetic spreading from the online to the offline world.

1   Bechtel, "Don't do this, @Target," 2015.

2   ABC News, "Target Moves Toward Gender-Neutral Store Signage," 2015; Suhay, "Target Experiments with Gender Neutrality in Its Stores," 2016; Lang, "Target to Install Gender-Neutral Bathrooms in All of Its Stores," 2016.

3   Miller, "Target Debuts An All-Gender Product Line For Kids," 2017.

Of course parents are the ones who need to open their wallets
to buy this stuff for their kids, so mounting frustration from people
like Abi Bechtel doubtless played a role. However, Toca Boca wasn't
just following an ideological premise, or responding to the demands
of parents. They were, per their digital roots, data-driven, using obser-
vational testing to understand "what characters users most like and
identify with, as well as the most appealing colors, what kids think
is funny, and what scenarios skew too heavily toward a certain gender
or seem to exclude some players." The more inclusive a design, the
more universal its appeal. Online, "scale the user base" has always
been the mantra. Target doubtless saw the business sense in this idea.

Predictably, though, the retailer's new policies stoked controversy among social conservatives. Writing for conservative media
outlet *TheBlaze*, Matt Walsh lamented,

> **Progressives see the toy industry like they see everything:
> an ideological battleground, another politicized arena to
> defeat traditional concepts of gender and usher in this new
> ambiguous dystopia where kids can live as amorphous, gen-
> derless, pansexual blobs of nondescript matter. […] I won't
> attempt to defend every gender stereotype or "gender norm,"
> but I do subscribe to the radical theory that boys and girls
> are different and distinct from one another in complex, con-
> crete, and important ways, and many of the dreaded "norms"
> are, well, normal and biological. It is precisely our role as
> parents to help our kids "conform" to their gender, to their**

4 Walsh, "Yes, Target, I Do Want My Daughter to Conform to Her Gender," 2015.

identity, and grow from boys and girls into well adjusted, confident masculine men and feminine women.[4]

Walsh dramatizes just how central the gender binary can be to traditional ideas about identity—or mere personhood—by describing those who don't hew to the binary as "amorphous [...] blobs of nondescript matter." Yet curiously, he also implies that children need to be socialized or taught to be masculine or feminine—that "nature" needs to be propped up and reinforced by culture. This view is reminiscent of John Money's discredited (and at the time, progressive) theory of the gender binary as socially constructed. Money's whole clinical pediatric practice was dedicated to the project of helping kids "conform," so that they could grow up to become "well adjusted, confident masculine men and feminine women."

A phrenological bust from Pacheco, *Esposición sumaria del sistema frenológico del doctor Gall*, 1835.

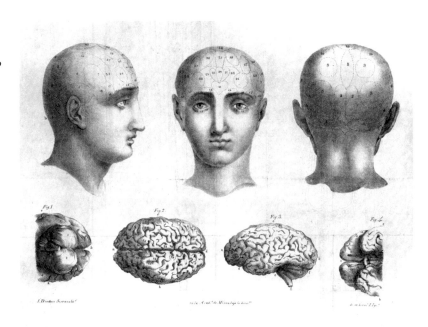

5 Among the larger studies with statistically meaningful datasets are Ruigrok et al., "A Meta-Analysis of Sex Differences in Human Brain Structure," 2014; Ritchie et al., "Sex Differences in the Adult Human Brain: Evidence from 5216 UK Biobank Participants," 2018.

As our deepening understanding of intersexuality has made obvious, the biology of sex is more complex than a binary either/or, but it's still the case that most of our bodies can be meaningfully classified along this axis. The big question is whether the same applies to the brain. Is there, in any quantifiable sense, such a thing as a "female brain" or "male brain," independent of learning and socialization?

This remains hotly contested. A whole scientific literature shows that both the absolute and relative sizes of various brain regions do vary, on average, by sex.[5] Some studies have attempted to relate these differences to cognitive skills, but here the results are murky, generally showing weak or inconclusive results, relying on small numbers of subjects, and using highly artificial tasks. Drawing firm conclusions is nearly impossible since, in the real world, nature and nurture are inseparable.

In her 2019 book *Gender Mosaic: Beyond the Myth of the Male and Female Brain*,[6] Israeli neuroscientist Daphna Joel points out that individual variability in both skills and brain structures is far larger than the average difference between the sexes, with a majority of people exhibiting what she calls a "mosaic" of more typically masculine or feminine brain regions and cognitive traits.[7] In other words, at least on the basis of today's coarse physical and functional measurements, most of us have an "intersex brain."

Using these findings as a springboard, Joel makes the radical-sounding case for gender abolition in most areas of life. She doesn't deny that our bodies (and, to a lesser extent, our brains) vary by sex, but she believes we attribute far too much importance to this particular axis of variation—with profoundly negative consequences.

For instance, she finds it frustrating—as do many, myself included—that a phrase like "woman scientist" can be used to describe *her*, while "man scientist" sounds redundant in describing *me*; I enjoy the privilege of simply being a "scientist." The situation is a grown-up analog to "Building Sets" versus "Girls' Building Sets." When I type "woman scientist" into Google, I get 10.2 million hits, but only 2.4% as many—247 thousand—for "man scientist." "Man scientist" is just not a thing. Of course the search result doesn't reflect that 97% of scientists are women; quite the opposite. It's just that qualifiers in language always attach to minorities, as described for handedness back in Chapter 2.[8]

Transfeminist author Julia Serano calls this the "marked/unmarked" distinction, noting that one doesn't even have to be in the minority to be "marked":

> **[W]omen make up slightly over fifty percent of the population, and yet we are marked relative to men.[9] This is evident in how people comment on, and critique, women's bodies and behaviors far more than men's, and how things that are deemed "for women" are often given their own separate categories (e.g., chick lit, women's sports, women's reproductive health), whereas things that are "for men" are seen as universal and unmarked.[10]**

There's often an insinuation implied. It would sound odd to describe an acquaintance as a "blue-eyed scientist," for instance—although

6 Joel and Vikhanski, *Gender Mosaic: Beyond the Myth of the Male and Female Brain*, 2019.

7 Joel's work implies that the distribution of values for each individual brain measurement is, in the previous chapter's vocabulary, dromedary-like, or one-humped, like the distribution in body height. It still may be the case, however, that a predictor combining many individually unreliable measurements together would yield a more distinctly two-humped distribution.

8 These numbers are changing. In some scientific fields, women now outnumber men. Language tends to be a lagging indicator, though.

9 As with handedness (see Chapter 3), etymology tells this story: "woman" derives from the Old English *wifmann*, a compound of *wif*, meaning female—whence "wife" in modern English—and *mann*, meaning person or human being—whence "man" in modern English. Hence a woman is a female man (marked), while a man is just a *mann* (unmarked).

10 Serano, *Excluded: Making Feminist and Queer Movements More Inclusive*, 2013.

blue eyes are also a minority—because eye color, being unmarked, isn't deemed relevant to anything else—such as being a scientist.[11] Every time we use the phrase "woman scientist," we're admitting that, in our minds, being a woman *is* somehow relevant to, and perhaps even in tension with, being a scientist.

For some, the underlying bias is explicit. At a 2005 conference hosted by the National Bureau of Economic Research, Lawrence Summers, then president of Harvard University, argued that female scientists were underrepresented due to biological factors—meaning, women simply aren't as interested in or as good as men at doing science.[12] Software engineer James Damore floated a similar claim about the underrepresentation of women in engineering in a widely circulated memo at Google in 2017.[13]

Charles Babbage.

→ Augusta Ada King, Countess of Lovelace.

These are old claims. They used to take more extreme forms; in the 19th century, women were commonly held to be incapable of abstract or creative thought. This was one rationale for barring them from higher education in fields like mathematics—for what would the point be?

Consider the intellectual partnership between Charles Babbage (1791–1871), inventor of the Analytical Engine (a steampunk precursor to the modern computer) and Ada Byron King, Countess of Lovelace (1815–1852), who wrote the first ever computer program.[14] As a woman, Lovelace's only route to higher math was private tutoring. (Being a countess did have its benefits; social class introduces a whole other dimension of inequality.) Yet even her relatively progressive math tutor, Augustus De Morgan, expressed his skepticism that she could make a real contribution in a cautionary letter to Ada's mother, Lady Byron, in 1844: "[T]he very great tension of mind which [wrestling with mathematical difficulties requires] is beyond the strength of a woman's physical power of application."[15] Astonishingly, he wrote this letter soon

11 The irrelevance of such physical features doesn't stop science journalists from habitually playing physiognomist, as in, "The distinguished old scientist has a shock of white hair, and a protruding, yet somehow also majestic, pair of ears."

12 Goldenberg, "Why Women Are Poor at Science, by Harvard President," 2005.

13 The memo got Damore fired: Damore, "Google's Ideological Echo Chamber: How Bias Clouds Our Thinking About Diversity and Inclusion," 2017.

14 Sadly, neither lived to see such a machine built, let alone a program run.

15 Hollings, Martin, and Rice, "The Lovelace–De Morgan Mathematical Correspondence: A Critical Re-Appraisal," 2017.

16 Lombroso and Ferrero, *La donna delinquente, la prostituta, e la donna normale*, 1893.

17 Quotes are from the translation by Nicole Hahn Rafter and Mary Gibson of Lombroso and Ferrero, *Criminal Woman, the Prostitute, and the Normal Woman*, 2004.

18 "Why can't a woman be more like a man?," Cukor, *My Fair Lady*, 1964.

after Lovelace's seminal publication describing how to program the Analytical Engine, a masterwork of mathematical creativity and arguably the founding document of the entire field of computer science!

So, between low expectations and lack of access to higher education, Victorian women encountered great difficulty contributing to science, technology, engineering, or math, yet the near-absence of women in these fields was considered the very evidence that they weren't capable. When, against all odds, women *still* managed to excel, as Lovelace and a few others did, their successes went unacknowledged, or were regarded as freakish.

Cesare Lombroso attempted to put these attitudes on a "scientific" footing in his 1893 followup to *The Criminal Man*, entitled *The Criminal Woman, the Prostitute, and the Normal Woman*.**16** Echoing commonly held beliefs at the time, he asserted not only that "Compared to male intelligence, female intelligence is deficient,"**17** but also that "woman is always fundamentally immoral." Further,

"Criminal" lesbian couple from Lombroso, *La donna delinquente, la prostituta e la donna normale*, 423, 1893.

Normal woman has many characteristics that bring her close to the level of the savage, the child, and therefore the criminal (anger, revenge, jealousy, and vanity) and others, diametrically opposed, which neutralize the former. Yet her positive traits hinder her from rising to the level of man, whose behavior balances rights and duties, egotism and altruism, and represents the peak of moral evolution.

Ugly as this characterization is, it might seem like it could at least have afforded an enterprising woman a route up the patriarchal ladder by being, as Rex Harrison drawled in *My Fair Lady*, "more like a man";**18** but this wasn't the case. If a woman failed to be submissive or to conform to gendered expectations, then her "masculine" character made her a degenerate, just as "feminine" traits would for a man:

Degeneration induces confusion between the two sexes, as a result of which

one finds in male criminals a feminine infantilism that leads to pederasty. To this corresponds masculinity in women criminals, including an atavistic tendency to return to the stage of hermaphroditism. [...] To demonstrate the presence of innate virility among female prisoners, it is enough to present a photograph of a couple whom I surprised in a prison. The one dressed as a male is simultaneously so strongly masculine and so criminal that it is difficult to believe she is actually female.

It was a no-win situation.

Gender bias has diminished since the 19th century, but by how much? Recall that intersex medical literature from the 1960s still took for granted that "Most married [chromosomally male] women [...] take part in extra-household activities which they often pursue with great success because of their above average intelligence."[19]

Violinist Hilary Hahn (1979–).

While recent literature on sex-based cognitive differences hasn't reached any clearcut conclusion, the lingering effects of low expectations, social pressure, and discrimination remain obvious—not just anecdotally, but in large-scale, real world findings. Perhaps most famously, a shift toward gender equality in orchestras began taking place after "blind" auditions became the norm some decades ago, raising the percentage of women in the United States's five highest-ranked orchestras from 6% in 1970 to 21% in 1993.[20] Today, women make up half of the New York Philharmonic.[21] Clearly it wasn't the case that men make better violinists, though that claim would have seemed plausible in 1970.

A similar real-world experiment has been conducted in the field of software engineering using GitHub, the world's largest social coding platform.[22] When an engineer adds code to a project—a process that requires approval from a project owner—their gender may be either visible or invisible, depending on their user profile. A 2016 study of 3 million code contributions from 1.4 million coders found that women's code was accepted more often than men's... *unless* the contributors were outsiders to a project and their gender was visible. Under those conditions, men's contributions were accepted more often.

A more recent study at Google found that "pushback" on code contributions, meaning requests for additional work before the contribution would be accepted, were more extensive not only for women,

19 See Chapter 11.

20 Goldin and Rouse, "Orchestrating Impartiality: The Impact of 'Blind' Auditions on Female Musicians," 2000.

21 Tommasini, "To Make Orchestras More Diverse, End Blind Auditions," 2020.

22 Think of GitHub as a social media platform, except that every post consists of a chunk of code contributed to one of the more than 100 million software projects hosted there, rather than a drunk selfie you'll regret tomorrow morning. GitHub-hosted software powers much of our digital lives.

23 Murphy-Hill et al., "The Pushback Effects of Race, Ethnicity, Gender, and Age in Code Review," 2022.

but also for older and nonwhite engineers.[23] Unfortunately, in a corporate setting where teammates all tend to know each other, gender-blind coding is a lot harder to pull off than on worldwide social coding projects with many contributors.

Academia is no better. A sweeping 2021 review identified sources of gender bias in science at every career stage, noting among many other effects that "several studies where the identity of the authors was experimentally manipulated demonstrated that conference abstracts, papers, and fellowship applications were rated as having higher merit when they were supposedly written by men."

So, women (along with other historically underrepresented minorities) still struggle against powerful bias in fields like science and engineering. Yet when we're able to measure their real-world contributions on a level playing field, under gender-blind conditions, we don't see evidence of the inferiority Summers, Damore, and others insinuate. The insistence that such insinuations are harmless questions or mere "food for thought" angers many advocates for gender equality, as such insinuations reinforce the biases that pose the greatest obstacles to equality.

Musical performance, science, and engineering in the modern world have something in common: an increasing degree of disembodiment relative to the more physical presence, and the more physical kind of labor, that predominated in centuries past. Today, many humans are information workers, and many of our relationships with each other are pure information relationships; our genitals, and more broadly, the sexual differences between our bodies, just aren't relevant anymore to these forms of work or relationships.

I'm not denying the raw physicality of live music, the way you can feel it in your body, the way it can move you to get up and dance. In the end, though, if you're a violinist, what really counts is what comes out of the violin—not what's on the album cover, or under your clothes. In evaluating code or a scientific paper, the irrelevance of sex and gender is even more obvious.

While sex and gender *aren't* irrelevant in many more traditional forms of physical labor, historical accounts about the genderedness of such labor are often overstated or misleading. For instance, when prominent anthropologists (at the time, overwhelmingly male) convened at the University of Chicago in 1966 for a symposium called "Man the Hunter," their "synthesis" of a range of biased ethnographic studies led them to conclude that intelligence itself was, literally, a product of men's work.[24] In most traditional cultures, parties of men go out on big hunting expeditions, presumably because of their

24 Lee and DeVore, *Man the Hunter: The First Intensive Survey of a Single, Crucial Stage of Human Development—Man's Once Universal Hunting Way of Life*, 1968.

greater average size and strength. The theory held that increasingly sophisticated and cooperative hunting strategies lay at the heart of advances in technology and culture, which in turn produced an increasing surplus of high quality protein from big game, giving us more energy to grow bigger brains, and more leisure to develop better technology: a virtuous cycle.

Timucan men cultivating the land while Timucan women sow maize or beans. From Le Moyne de Morgues, *Brevis narratio eorum quae in Florida Americai provincia Gallis acciderunt*, XXI., 1591 with engravings by Theodor de Bry (1528–98).

25 Sterling, "Man the Hunter, Woman the Gatherer? The Impact of Gender Studies on Hunter-Gatherer Research (A Retrospective)," 2014; Gurven and Hill, "Why Do Men Hunt? A Reevaluation of 'Man the Hunter' and the Sexual Division of Labor," 2009; Haas et al., "Female Hunters of the Early Americas," 2020.

26 In the 1960s, as for orchestras, the overwhelming majority of anthropologists were male. There are now two female PhD graduates in anthropology for every male, and the majority of faculty hires in anthropology are women. Speakman et al., "Market Share and Recent Hiring Trends in Anthropology Faculty Positions," 2018.

The many problems with this "Man the Hunter" narrative have been dissected in detail elsewhere;[25] I'll just mention a few here. In traditional societies, gathering, scavenging, gardening, and small animal hunting—all of which are more typically "women's work"—turn out to provide more calories, more consistently, than big game hunting. Also, archeological inventories of technological development skew toward weaponry (which often features hard stone or metal points) at the expense of wooden tools, basketry, and early farming technologies, which tend to leave less physical evidence but are just as important. Finally, although cooperation was indeed central to the development of humanity as a social species, the idea that cooperation evolved from men's activities seems dubious, given the sophistication of cooperative practices among women in traditional societies—likely beginning with cooperative child rearing. In sum, women have played a central role in the development of human civilization, but historical biases in the scholarship marginalized their role prior to a more balanced assessment of the evidence in recent decades.[26]

It's important to acknowledge, though, that men and women have meaningfully different physical capabilities, reflected in strongly gendered divisions of labor in nearly all traditional societies—whether

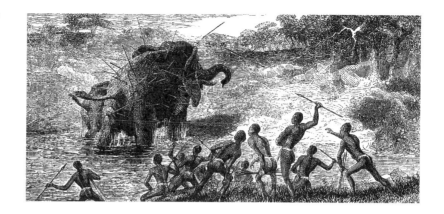

The "Man the Hunter" trope as depicted by David Livingstone in *Missionary Tales and Researches in South Africa*, 1857.

27 Mazur and Booth, "Testosterone and Dominance in Men," 1998; Muñoz-Reyes et al., "The Male Warrior Hypothesis: Testosterone-Related Cooperation and Aggression in the Context of Intergroup Conflict," 2020.

28 Tiller et al., "Do Sex Differences in Physiology Confer a Female Advantage in Ultra-Endurance Sport?," 2021; Lieberman et al., "Running in Tarahumara (Rarámuri) Culture: Persistence Hunting, Footracing, Dancing, Work, and the Fallacy of the Athletic Savage," 2020.

29 I'm about 6 feet tall, which, in ordinary life, is on the taller side. When I first attended the TED conference and found myself surrounded by CEOs and other high-status people, I was struck by a sense of suddenly being shorter than everyone (with the exception of Jeff Bezos). A number of studies have confirmed a powerful height bias, especially among men, in the corporate world. Judge and Cable, "The Effect of Physical Height on Workplace Success and Income: Preliminary Test of a Theoretical Model," 2004.

or not this has been accompanied by patriarchy. In old fashioned, gender-binary terms: women have babies and nurse; men don't. Men are usually more muscular than women, giving them an edge when it comes to heavy lifting. Warfare, too, is usually associated with men, perhaps not just because of physical differences, but due to testosterone-fueled aggression, a sex-linked trait found in many other animals too.[27] Women, on the other hand, are better equipped than men for endurance running, which has played a key role in some traditional societies;[28] they also tend to be healthier and, as we've seen, live longer.

These differences are real, and for certain kinds of physical labor, they still matter. However, in a corporate environment or on Zoom, they're irrelevant. Desk work involves little physical exertion, which has its downsides (our bodies probably aren't well adapted to sitting for eight hours each day), but is also equalizing. It means that physical prowess no longer confers any advantage. Today, unless you belong to a street gang, it's either impossible or unacceptable to resolve disputes or establish hierarchies through physical combat. Sexual aggression and rape, too, are unacceptable, as is bringing any kind of sexual behavior into the workplace. The rise of remote work, the #MeToo movement, and the COVID era have all played a role in accelerating this shift, not just by reducing physical contact, but in subtler ways too—for instance, by making it impossible to tell how tall anyone is on a Zoom call.[29]

Compared to our 200,000+ year history as a species, all of these changes are very recent, and many are technologically enabled. Charles Babbage, who was not only the inventor of the computer but was obsessed with automation in all its forms, described the effect of technology on laborers in the British textile industry in his 1832 book *On the Economy of Machinery and Manufactures*:

Power-loom weaving, 1835.

[From 1822 to 1832], the number of hand-looms in employment has diminished to less than one-third, whilst that of power-looms has increased to more than five times its former amount. The total number of workmen has increased about one-third; but the amount of manufactured goods (supposing each power-loom to do only the work of three hand-looms) is three and a half times as large as it was before.

In considering this increase of employment, it must be admitted, that the two thousand persons thrown out of work are not exactly of the same class as those called into employment by the power-looms. A hand-weaver must possess bodily strength, which is not essential for a person attending a power-loom; consequently, women and young persons of both sexes, from fifteen to seventeen years of age, find employment in power-loom factories.[30]

In other words, industrialization—in this case, using steam to power weaving looms—turned what had been men's work into anyone's work. And in an era when women and children were paid far less,[31] and workers had become interchangeable, this meant women's work and children's work.

Nowadays, a wide array of technologies similarly decouple labor from bodies, with all their here-and-now limitations and particularities, age and sex included. Cars and trucks, motorized wheelchairs, power saws, forklifts, tractors, robotic manipulators, and many other machines extend the effect Babbage described into all areas of farming, industry, and life in general. The increasing role of military drones may even do the same for warfare.[32]

[30] Babbage, *On the Economy of Machinery and Manufactures*, 339, 1832.

[31] For instance, in writing about pin manufacturing, Babbage writes, "It is usual for a man, his wife, and a child, to join in performing these processes; and they are paid at the rate of five farthings per pound. They can point from thirty-four to thirty-six and a half pounds per day, and gain from 6s. 6d. to 7s., which may be apportioned thus; 5s. 6d. the man. 1s. the woman, 6d. to the boy or girl." If you're unfamiliar with old British money, this works out to 66 pence for the man, 12 pence for the woman, and 6 pence for the child for a full day of labor. Child labor nowadays is largely illegal, and this kind of pay discrepancy gives us a sense of what the gender pay gap statistics in Chapter 4 looked like farther back.

[32] Westerman, "Ukrainian Women Have Started Learning a Crucial War Skill: How to Fly a Drone," 2022.

While this makes many historically "male" forms of labor more accessible to women (and children, if allowed), technofeminist writers in the 1980s also wrote about many other modern developments that break the mold of traditionally "female" labor, like washing machines, showers, kitchen appliances, and vacuum cleaners. In accounts of labor-saving or -democratizing technologies we tend to forget about essential labor in the household; the subjugated status of women under patriarchy has meant that such labor has traditionally been considered a wifely duty, unpaid and taken for granted. Such domestic injustice animated the International Wages for Housework Campaign,[33] launched in 1972 by activists Mariarosa Dalla Costa, Silvia Federici, Brigitte Galtier, and Selma James—part of the larger struggle for women's agency and economic independence touched on in Chapter 4. Although caring and caretaking remain largely uncompensated today, they're slowly becoming less gendered, due both to changing attitudes and evolving technologies.

[33] Federici, *Wages Against Housework*, 1975.

Bettye Lane, *Wages for Housework at International Women's Day March*, New York, March 12, 1977.

I remember, as a young father, changing a lot of diapers and spending many, many hours walking with a baby strapped to my chest in a BabyBjörn carrier. Back in 2002, this still attracted stares and double takes sometimes; usually delighted ones from women, occasionally uncomfortable ones from men. There's deep muscle memory connected with that time; as I type, I find my hands, arms, and shoulders contorting to rehearse those old familiar tucking, buckling, and strap-testing gestures.

Twenty years later, carrier designs have apparently gotten a bit more ergonomic. Hundreds of baby carriers compete on the market now; Swedish BabyBjörn competitor Najell, under a photo of a hipster

A Najell AB baby carrier as advertised on Najell.com.

couple with "his and hers" twins in carriers, advertises that they're "Designing baby carriers that fit both parents!," adding,

An "artificial uterus" from Emanuel M. Greenberg, US Patent No. 2,723,660, 1955.

Nov. 15, 1955   E. M. GREENBERG   2,723,660
ARTIFICIAL UTERUS

Filed July 22, 1954   2 Sheets—Sheet 1

FIG. I

EMANUEL M. GREENBERG
INVENTOR

BY *Ralph H. Bitner*
ATTORNEY

Fathers are increasingly taking an equal part and responsibility in parenting and raising their children. A very positive development that we love and want to encourage. In Sweden, it's common to share the paternity leave, often both parents take at least a few months off work to stay at home with the newest family member. [...] We have designed the Najell Original Baby Carrier so there are no buckles in the back that are hard to reach. Of course, some men can be flexible, just as women can be stiff. But the fact is that most women are used to buckling bras in the back and are in general more flexible. Buckling in the back can be close to impossible for men, and there is no need for extra trouble when putting on a baby carrier. It should be easy, simple and comfortable.[34]

Carriers are only the tip of an unacknowledged technological iceberg. Baby bottles, breast pumping, and refrigeration allowed my wife to leave me equipped to "nurse" our baby when she traveled for international conferences. We supplanted breast milk with formula when we needed to. Umbrella strollers let us get around the city easily, and a clever portable folding playpen let us instantly create a safe, toy-filled pop-up environment anywhere.

34 Najell, "Designing Baby Carriers That Fit Both Parents!," 2021.

35 *The Dialectic of Sex: The Case for Feminist Revolution*, chap. 10, 1970.

36 Usuda et al., "Successful Use of an Artificial Placenta to Support Extremely Preterm Ovine Fetuses at the Border of Viability," 2019.

37 Cederstrom, "Are We Ready for the Breastfeeding Father?," 2019; Wamboldt, Shuster, and Sidhu, "Lactation Induction in a Transgender Woman Wanting to Breastfeed: Case Report," 2021.

Such technologies are important but unsung, much like the wooden farming and domestic tools overlooked by so many archaeologists in the mid-20th century. The radical sex abolition politics envisioned by Shulamith Firestone in 1970 called for artificial wombs,[35] and in the coming decades we may indeed get there.[36] There's a recent resurgence of interest in male and trans breastfeeding, a possibility available to more people than one might think—breasts aren't nearly as sexually differentiated as genitals.[37] But it's easy to forget how far we've come with much simpler social and material innovations like strollers, bottles, formula, breast pumping, unisex carriers, perinatal care, and universal parental leave. Such low-tech hacks can already bring us a fair way toward gender equality in the reproductive realm.

Of course, with biological reproduction in sharp decline, reproductive gender equality is relevant to fewer and fewer of us— a topic we'll return to in Part III.

In many ways, our move online, in which computers increasingly mediate our every interaction with the world and with each other, continues the job of dethroning gender, turning it into an opt-in form of anonymous identity with only a tenuous connection to the shape of one's genitals.

15.0 Trans, non gender-typical genitals, and male/female flipped from birth assignment % by age

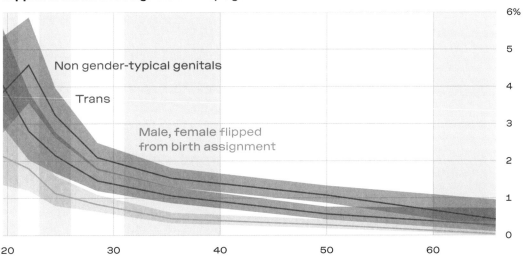

This is apparent in responses to the questions "Are you female?," "Are you male?," "Do you have a vagina?," and "Do you have a penis?" Even among respondents who answer "yes" to only one of the first two

questions, an increasing number of young people don't answer the other two questions the way social conservatives like Matt Walsh would expect. That is, there are an increasing number of women with penises and/or without vaginas, and men with vaginas and/or without penises; these numbers follow the same pattern as "Are you trans?," but are even higher across all ages, peaking at 4.6% among 20–23-year-olds.[38]

Romantic and sexual relationships are increasingly happening online, too, potentially beginning to decouple even this intimate aspect of life from physical bodies. At the same time as it started to become commonplace to see noses and mouths disappearing behind protective masks in the "real world," our digital faces have been undergoing a virtual makeover. Avatars, augmented reality makeup, and neural nets can re-render us completely—our gender, voice, age, race, and pretty much anything else. This puts a literal spin on N. Katherine Hayles' claim that we're becoming cyborgs, with our "enacted and represented bodies [...] brought into conjunction through the technology that connects them."

A split sense of self—in your own head one way, and in your presentation another—brings with it a risk of painful misalignment. Italian psychiatrist Enrico Morselli (1852–1929) first described this phenomenon as *dysmorphophobia* in an 1891 paper: "the sudden onset and subsequent persistence of an idea of deformity: the individual fears he has become or may become deformed (δύσμορφος) and feels tremendous anxiety (φόβος, fear) of such an awareness."[39] Morselli believed the condition to be a common problem; he documented 78 cases.

It may not be coincidental that mirrors had only become affordable enough for the general public earlier in the 19th century, thanks to a glass silvering process invented by a German chemist in 1835. Advertising and modeling were also in rapid ascent. As people—especially girls and young women—were confronted with an onslaught of idealized female bodies in mass media throughout the 20th century, the inevitable comparison of images in the mirror with models in print and on TV (first airbrushed, then photoshopped) led to a rise in what the DSM-III-R renamed *body dysmorphia*, along with associated behaviors like anorexia.

With selfie filters on social media today, we've managed to create the perfect storm: combining the self-reflection of mirrors, the idealized (often hypersexualized) bodies of mass media, and an increasing dissociation from "meatspace." British science communicator Liv Boeree has vividly described the ensuing phenomenon of "Snapchat dysmorphia,"[40] in which young people identify strongly with their Insta-filtered images and feel unhappy with or dissociated from their bodies. It has become a trend for young women to seek cosmetic surgery to bring their physical selves into closer alignment with their social media.[41]

[38] Per Chapter 13, this also speaks to the way increasing numbers of trans people, especially among the young, don't see being trans as implying or requiring medical treatment.

[39] Morselli, "Sulla Dismorfofobia E Sulla Tafefobia," 1891. See also Fava, "Morselli's Legacy: Dysmorphophobia," 1992.

[40] Boeree, "In my experience, all the furore over Instagram & Facebook causing teenage depression is overlooking the bigger issue: beauty filters. I mean just look at this absurdity," 2021.

[41] Walker et al., "Effects of Social Media Use on Desire for Cosmetic Surgery Among Young Women," 2021.

Selfies of Liv Boeree without (left) and with (right) beauty filters applied, 2021.

While accounts of "Snapchat dysmorphia" tend to emphasize hyper-feminization in young women, many other virtual body modifications are possible too. People may alter themselves to appear more masculine online, or younger. Even without explicit digital alteration, an androgynous, hoodie-wearing young person may look gender-neutral within the tightly cropped frame of a Zoom call, but less so in person. The rise in gender dysmorphia might be the tip of an iceberg. Maybe we need a proper Greek name for "online versus offline dysmorphia."

We shouldn't think of this phenomenon only in the negative terms of dysmorphia, though. As social creatures, our world really is each other, and in this sense, what matters to us is how we live in our own imaginations and those of others. And our imaginations are expanding. For many young people, an embrace of fluidity and rejection of either/or categories can be liberatory.

Wherever older respondents might harbor assumptions about mutually exclusive answers on the survey, growing numbers of younger respondents violate such assumptions. For instance, 2.7%

15.1 Younger respondents are more likely to reject either/or characterizations of gender and sexuality % by age

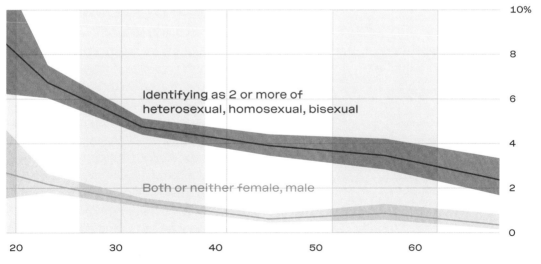

Identifying as 2 or more of heterosexual, homosexual, bisexual

Both or neither female, male

of 19-year-olds identify as both or neither male and female, and more than 8% answer "yes" to more than one of the questions "Are you heterosexual?," "Are you homosexual, gay or lesbian?" and "Are you bisexual?" When these are just social concepts, or profile settings that can be toggled on a dating or social media app, there's no need to box yourself in. Our inherent flexibility finally has free rein.

How far will the cyborg-like digital dissociation between bodies and identities go? At this point, it's unclear. Neural nets can transform our digital selves in any conceivable way—far beyond anything surgery can approximate. New deepfake-like techniques aren't limited, the way Photoshop was in the old days, to smoothing a bit here or slimming a bit there. The language we're speaking can be altered, we can become skilled singers, we can be rendered as cartoons, we can look like elves or pixies. Or even nonhuman entities.

The old adage, "On the Internet, nobody knows you're a dog" was coined by *New Yorker* cartoonist Peter Steiner in 1993, in an era when social interaction online consisted of a handful of nerds at universities typing text into chat windows. Online culture has come a long way in the three decades since. While the actual "internet of animals"**42** still hasn't taken off, it's now commonplace for humans to present as other species online—though cats are more popular than dogs. It's also becoming increasingly difficult to tell humans from AIs. Online, Daphna Joel's vision of "gender abolition" seems almost quaint in restricting itself to that one old-fashioned variable.

42 Curry, "The Internet of Animals That Could Help to Save Vanishing Wildlife," 2018.

In Chapter 4, I cited science fiction writer Kim Stanley Robinson's visionary novel *2312*, which describes a distant future in which we acquire a degree of control over our bodies that renders us posthuman. I added that even Robinson's vision was conservative compared to the "uploading" scenario, in which we become virtual beings unconstrained by bodies altogether. Yet this is exactly what we're already doing digitally, without any of the fuss, downtime, commitment, risk, and expense of surgery, hormones, or gene splicing. Even clothes shopping, haircuts, and grooming become optional when equivalent (or better) effects can be applied directly to pixels.

"On the Internet, nobody knows you're a dog."

The *New Yorker*, July 5, 1993.

Is this just a superficial fad, or is it something more profound? It really depends on which we consider the real world—the flesh and blood one, or the one we're creating for ourselves online. Of course

Selfies of the author unmodified and with various FaceApp filters, 2021.

the virtual world depends on the physical world to exist, but then again, the Earth depends on the sun, and the city on the countryside. The question is: where do *we* live? That is, who are we now?

The answer varies—partly, by age. Some of us are in constant contact with the physical, still making a living by pushing brooms, nursing or caretaking, pulling shots of espresso, picking fruit or painting houses; still spending our time with clients, coworkers, friends, and lovers in the flesh. For others, reality is online. As always, there's no binary; most of us are dual citizens. But if we're honest with ourselves, especially since COVID, many of us have been online more than not. Does this mean we've already been uploaded... without even noticing?

Part III
Humanity

16   Ignition

The universal need to connect with others has brought the world online. That same force has been attracting us together in space since long before the internet. It's human physics. Gravity caused the sparse clouds of hydrogen gas that characterized the early universe to coalesce over time into stars and galaxies; attraction between people does the same. We call the structures that emerge villages, towns, and cities. Just as a collapsing hydrogen cloud ignites at a certain density and begins to burn with nuclear fusion, when human populations condense into cities they, too, begin to glow—with new ideas, traditions, technologies, economies, arts, and culture.

"Ignition" is the overarching story of much of the past 10,000 years or so of human development, and because developing culture and increasing population density create potent feedback loops, urbanization has greatly accelerated in recent history. History itself has in turn accelerated. While the overwhelming majority of us used to gather, hunt, or farm, living in nomadic bands or in small settled communities, in the 2000s we've reached a milestone: Today over half of humanity lives in a city.

Urbanization also gives rise to another, subtler feedback loop. We've seen that identity, gender, and attraction are partly built into our genetic inheritance, but are also partly cultural, environmental, and volitional. So attraction brings people together, which creates culture and subculture, which in turn alters the way we identify and creates new patterns of attraction.

Luke and C-3PO enter the Mos Eisley cantina in *Star Wars Episode IV: A New Hope*, 1977

View of Tataouine, Tunisia at night, 2012. The city inspired the name of Luke Skywalker's fictional home planet of Tatooine.

Cultural innovation also leads to specialization, sorting, and something like speciation; cities act as cultural reactors for the rapid evolution of new practices and norms.[1] That's why prudes like William Acton (see Chapter 9) tend to express moral panic about "sex in the city," where seemingly anything goes; their so-called "immoral haunts" are invariably urban bars and clubs, not country barns hosting square dances. The "perverse" is, in effect, the unfamiliar.

The "immoral haunt" trope is a classic.[2] We can watch it retreaded a century later—or, if you'd prefer, a long time ago and in a galaxy far, far away—at the Mos Eisley Cantina on the planet Tatooine in *Star Wars* (1977). In the movie, Jedi master Obi-Wan Kenobi primly characterizes the Cantina as a "wretched hive of scum and villainy." On the other hand, this interplanetary urban dive is clearly *the* place to go for decent music (in real life, a jazz composition by John Williams featuring Afro-Caribbean instruments for added "exoticism"). In the *Star Wars* novelization, Obi-Wan offers more nuance:

> **Most of the good, independent freighter pilots frequent this place, though many can afford better. They can talk freely here. [...] Watch yourself though. This place can be rough.[3]**

Walking inside, Luke Skywalker, our wide-eyed country bumpkin, is "astonished at the variety of beings making use of the bar":

> **There were one-eyed creatures and thousand-eyed, creatures with scales, creatures with fur, and some with skin that seemed to ripple and change consistency according to their feelings of the moment.**

1　This, too, has a physics analog: as collapsing hydrogen clouds begin fusing in the crush of a star's heart, they begin to form the whole alphabet soup of elements in the periodic table—each with its own patterns of attraction, repulsion, and reactivity.

2　Historical echoes of it go back at least to ancient Rome.

3　George Lucas (ghostwritten by Alan Dean Foster), *Star Wars: From the Adventures of Luke Skywalker*, 93, 1976. Given Alan Dean Foster is a lifelong travel enthusiast with, perhaps, a more cosmopolitan outlook than George Lucas, it's tempting to interpret Foster's markedly different tone in the novelization as a small act of subversion.

Hovering near the bar itself was a towering insectoid that Luke glimpsed only as a threatening shadow. It contrasted with two of the tallest women Luke had ever seen. They were among the most normal-looking of the outrageous assemblage of humans that mixed freely among alien counterparts. Tentacles, claws, and hands were wrapped around drinking utensils of various sizes and shapes. Conversation was a steady babble of human and alien tongues.[4]

"A cosplay of Jabba's slave, Oola" at the Anaheim Star Wars Celebration, 2015.

4 Lucas, 94.

Variety, sensuality, food and drink, unfamiliar scents and languages, foreign accents, trade and commerce, music and art, style and fashion—in short, *culture*. Such complexity emerges from the convergence and density of the city (or "spaceport"), its busy, high-speed cross-pollination. Contrast this state of affairs with the monkish asceticism of the few remaining Jedi, or the bland Midwestern isolation of Luke's uncle's farm—cultural environments where small numbers and low density conspire to ensure that nothing much ever changes. Hence, traditional values.

Alfred Kinsey and colleagues noticed the powerful effect of population density in producing a sharp contrast between "sex in the city" and "sex in the countryside." In their analysis, they sought to disentangle the biological universals of human attraction from the queer particulars of urban life, while dispelling the idea that homosexuality (for instance) is some kind of uniquely urban "disorder":

There is a wide-spread theory among psychologists and psychiatrists that the homosexual is a product of an effete and over-organized urban civilization. The failure to make heterosexual adjustments is supposed to be consequent on the complexities of life in our modern cities; or it is a product of a neuroticism which the high speed of living in the city imposes upon an increasing number of individuals. The specific data on the particular rural and urban groups […] do seem to suggest that there is something in city life which encourages the development

of the homosexual. But the distinctive thing about homosexuality in the city is the development of a more or less organized group activity which is unknown in any rural area.

Domenico (il Passignano) Cresti, *Bathers at San Niccolò*, 1600.

← "Lost, lonely, boyishly appealing—this is Beebo Brinker—who never really knew what she wanted—until she came to Greenwich Village and found the love that smoulders in the shadows of the twilight world." From the cover of lesbian pulp fiction novel *Beebo Brinker* by Ann Bannon, 1962. Art by Robert McGinnis.

5 Kinsey, Pomeroy, and Martin, *Sexual Behavior in the Human Male*, 455, 1948.

Large cities have taverns, night clubs, restaurants, and baths which may be frequented almost exclusively by persons interested in meeting homosexual friends [...]. In this city group, the development of an elaborate argot gives a sense of belonging which may defend a minority group against the rest of society; but it also intensifies a feeling which the group has that it stands apart from the rest of the population. Moreover, it is this city group which exhibits all the affectations, the mannerisms, the dress and the other displays which the rest of the population take to be distinctive of all homosexual persons, even though it is only a small fraction of the males with homosexual histories who ever display such characteristics. None of these city-bred homosexual institutions is known in rural areas [...].[5]

Kinsey's main observation here was that many mannerisms we think of as "gay" aren't about being gay in itself, but reflect a particular gay urban culture. A number of survey respondents acknowledge this cultural dimension, and one even points out the feedback effect of culture back *onto* attraction:

Not only does my sexuality/sexual attraction fluctuate, but culture has a big influence on it. I travel around the world

6   A 38-year-old man from Pearisburg, VA.

7   Per historian Cynthia Enloe: "Feminists have shown [...] that ideas about what constitutes acceptable behavior by men can [...] vary in surprising ways across cultures. [...] In fact, tourists, traveling executives, overseas troops, aid technocrats, migrant workers—everyone who moves between cultures watches for signs of what constitute appropriate ways to be manly in different societies. Sometimes men try to mimic those forms of masculinity; at other times they view the alternatives with contempt and go home with a renewed sense of the superiority of their own home-grown formulas for being 'real men.'" *The Morning After: Sexual Politics at the End of the Cold War*, 5, 1993.

8   See Brakefield et al., "Same-Sex Sexual Attraction Does Not Spread in Adolescent Social Networks," 2014. "[P]eer influence has little or no effect on the tendency toward heterosexual or homosexual attraction in teens, and [...] sexual orientation is not transmitted via social networks."

getting paid to have adventures. There are women and men that I meet who I only find attractive within the particular culture. Take the same person and let them assimilate into a different culture and my attraction fades. Somehow the social dynamics make a big difference for me.[6]

Of course, the same could be said of "being straight"; heterosexual masculinity, for instance, can manifest in many ways in different cultures, potentially resulting in different patterns of attraction.[7] However, minorities, sexual or otherwise, can only concentrate their numbers to achieve "cultural ignition" in big cities. That's why gay cultures tend to be urban—whether in ancient Greece, Victorian London, or the East Village in New York—even though, as far as we know, homosexual attraction exists everywhere and has existed in every historical era.[8]

How relevant is this urban phenomenon to the United States, though? You might not think of the US as a particularly urban country. Its founding myth featured wide-open spaces, attractive to rugged homesteaders seeking escape from a corrupt, overcrowded, citified Old World. Thus the Skywalker farm evokes the American heartland, while the Mos Eisley cantina (its exterior footage was filmed in Tunisia) reads as dangerous and foreign—literally, alien.

Thomas Jefferson would have shared this anti-urban sensibility; his United States was a land of gentleman-farmers, self-sufficient and incorruptible. Of course there was a certain cognitive dissonance in the Jeffersonian utopia, relying as it did on a steady supply of urban goodies for the library and the drawing room... not to mention plenty of slave

Thomas Jefferson's vegetable garden at Monticello, Virginia, 2005.

labor. Also, let's not forget that the Americas were far from uninhabited when European colonists first arrived, having supported both nomadic and settled societies for many thousands of years.[9]

"Relief traffic map of the recommended interregional system. The height of the traffic bands indicates approximately the average density of traffic [...]. The mounting spires at the principal cities picture the great increases of traffic to be expected on sections of routes traversing the cities." From the 1944 *Interregional Highways* report.

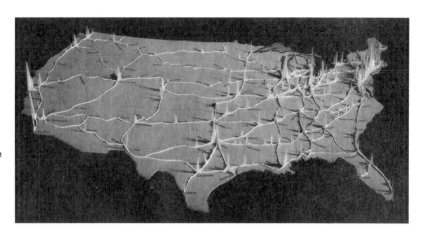

In more recent memory, the US has often been described as suburban, home to a Flintstones lifestyle of low-slung residential neighborhoods dotted with lawns, backyard barbecues, swing sets, and two-car garages, a short drive from some freeway entrance ramp. Suburban sprawl *is* real. It mushroomed during the Cold War, partly owing to a massive federally funded plan to make the country harder to wipe out with targeted nuclear strikes on its cities.[10]

Mass relocation to the suburbs required a kind of urban erasure in the American imagination. It helped that many Americans had long been suspicious of life in the city, that "wretched hive of scum and villainy"; but the rural alternative was no longer attractive for most, or even viable. As geographic historian Mathew Farish has put it,

> [T]he antithesis of the degraded city was the small, independent farm; but by 1950 this image [...] was an anachronism, replaced by the high modernist pastoralism of the postwar suburbs—peripheral, expansive and architecturally, racially and (largely) economically homogeneous. It was these suburban 'citadels' that infiltrated the discourse of Cold War geopolitics: they were the quintessential sites of American life [...]. Suburbs embodied order, safety and a deeply gendered consumerism [...].[11]

Farish describes Soviet premier Nikita Khrushchev's visit to the US in 1959. President Eisenhower took Khrushchev to see Levittown, an ur-suburb completed in 1947 whose builder, William Levitt, had

9 There's evidence of human habitation in the Americas going back at least to the last glacial maximum. By the 13th century, Cahokia, a settlement of the now lost Mississippian culture, may have had a population larger than that of contemporary London.

10 Lapp, *Must We Hide?*, 1949; Lapp, "The Strategy of Civil Defense," 1950. See also Farish, "Disaster and Decentralization: American Cities and the Cold War," 2003; Kargon and Molella, "The City as Communications Net: Norbert Wiener, the Atomic Bomb, and Urban Dispersal," 2004.

11 Farish, "Disaster and Decentralization: American Cities and the Cold War," 2003.

proclaimed that "no man who owns his own house and lot can be a Communist... he has too much to do."

Or, perhaps, too *little* to do! For the vaunted safety of the suburbs wasn't only about staying outside the lethal radius of a hypothetical nuclear strike downtown. According to George Kennan, one of the architects of the US's Cold War policy of Soviet containment, the groups most susceptible to communist infiltration included "labor unions, youth leagues, women's organizations, racial societies, religious societies, social organizations, cultural groups, liberal magazines, publishing houses, etc."[12] All were vectors for social transmission—hence the erosion of traditional values.

Foreigners, artists, latchkey kids, and homosexuals joined communists on the menu of national security concerns. Undercover FBI agents even snuck onto women's softball teams to keep tabs on the lesbian menace.[13] Hence, the city itself was regarded as an enemy within, and like communism, it, too, needed to be contained. The suburbs were that containment vessel, bland and culturally impenetrable.

So went the rhetoric. But what do the data tell us?

Census Bureau figures show how many people live in every ZIP code, and ZIP codes can be mapped. Technically, the official maps show "ZIP Code Tabulation Areas" (ZCTAs), since ZIP codes were originally designed for mail delivery, and until the year 2000 they didn't correspond to areas on the map with defined borders. With ZCTAs, though, the ground area of every ZIP code can be calculated, making it possible to create a detailed map of population density. Coloring in the ZIP code areas from densest to sparsest, stopping when 62.7% of the population has been covered, makes the country's fundamentally urban character obvious.

The headline: by area, only 3.23% of the country is colored in. In other words, an extraordinarily large fraction of the American population lives on a very small percentage of the land.[14]

The 62.7% cutoff is arbitrary, but for now, think of the colored-in ZIP codes as "urban," and the others as "rural"; I'll soon quantify the excluded middle of this binary—the suburbs. (White areas, mostly representing mountainous and wild terrain where there are no mail delivery routes, have—at least officially—no permanent population.) The resulting density map looks a lot like NASA's "Black Marble," the Earth as imaged by satellite at night, since terrestrial light sources and cities generally coincide.

As its name implies, NASA's Black Marble covers the whole planet. It's a powerful image, rendering the simile of cities as stars in the night sky almost literal—as above, so below. Civilization radiates light. If we

12 Kennan, "The Long Telegram," 1946.

13 Enloe, *The Morning After: Sexual Politics at the End of the Cold War*, 1993.

14 I originally picked 62.7% to corroborate the headline of a 2015 press release from the US Census Bureau, "U.S. Cities Are Home to 62.7 Percent of the U.S. Population, but Comprise Just 3.5 Percent of Land Area," 2015. My calculation, based on more recent data, suggests that urbanization is still advancing.

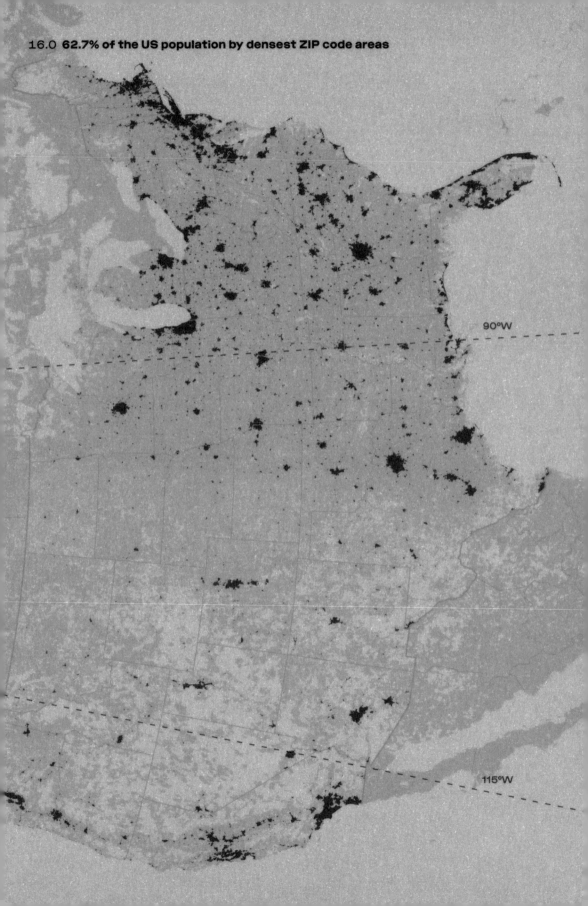

16.0 **62.7% of the US population by densest ZIP code areas**

90°W

115°W

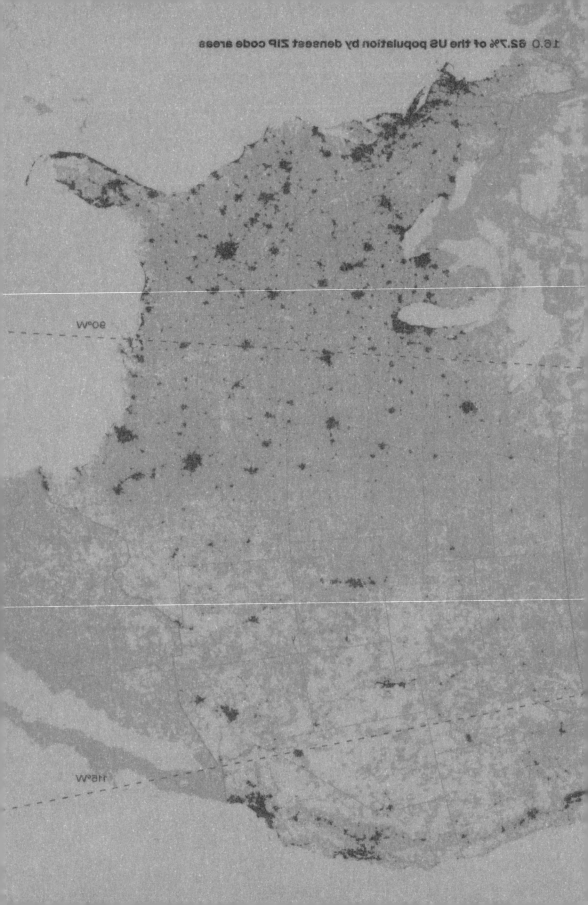

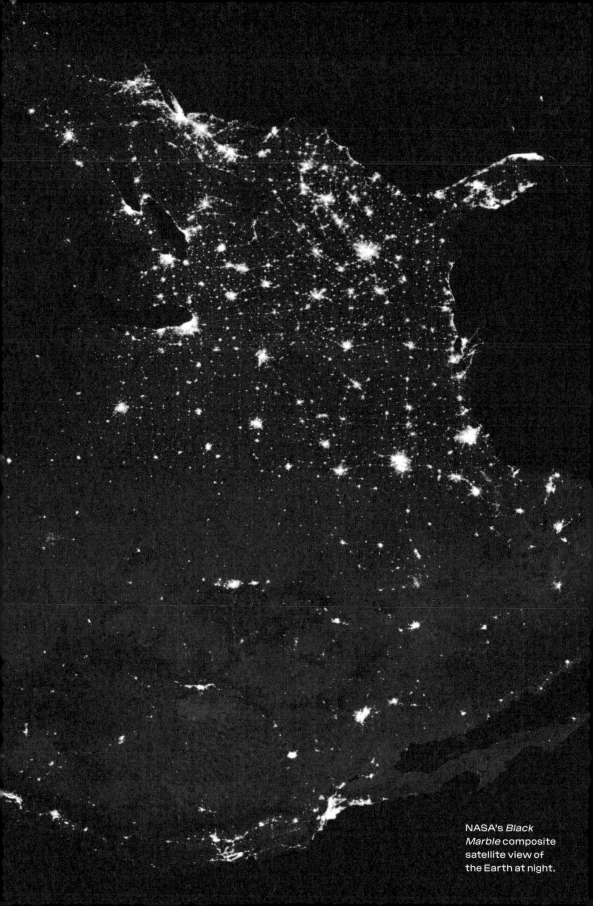

NASA's *Black Marble* composite satellite view of the Earth at night.

could see this image in time lapse over the past few centuries, we'd indeed witness cities "ignite" as their populations coalesce, first very faintly with firelight, then with gaslight, then much more brightly with electrification.**15**

15 Excessively so, as much of this energy expenditure is wasteful light pollution.

As we'll explore in this third and final part of the book, the dark regions of the map are critically important too. At risk of belaboring the obvious, the city and the countryside are interdependent. Cities have always relied on a much larger hinterland for food, water, and other natural resources, and on the farmers, miners, woodcutters, wagon or truck drivers, and so on who do essential work needed to keep the city alive, yet don't live in cities themselves.

Small-scale agriculture in Vietnam, 2005.

On the other hand, the vision of a bucolic countryside that could get by just fine without the city is also a fantasy. Given Jefferson's beautiful study at Monticello, full of books and gadgets purchased in New York, London, and Paris, and his general obsession with scientific advancement, he probably was well aware of this—in private. We couldn't farm at today's scale using anything like the backbreaking techniques of pre-industrial homesteaders (or slave plantations) anymore, or keep livestock in the traditional ways of the Maasai in East Africa. Such techniques have been characterized by the word "subsistence" because they allow agriculturalists or pastoralists to feed themselves, but they don't produce the superabundance needed to *additionally* feed an urban population orders of magnitude larger.

Of course that would be fine if there *were* no cities to feed. However, even the most committed anti-urbanists would agree that the very high infant mortality and low life expectancy of 18th century peasants is a legacy we're glad to have left behind. Life in the countryside today depends deeply on the technology, goods, expertise, services, and culture that come from the city.

Precisely these technologies and services not only have allowed cities to grow bigger, but have caused the countryside to become far more sparsely populated than it used to be. Today's gigantic farms rely on intensive mechanization, hence far less human labor, than in the past. High-technology farming explains why so much of the population lives in such a small fraction of the country's land area today.

Keeping this in mind, it may come as less of a surprise that the United States, with its advanced economy and relatively recent colonial reformatting, is *especially* urbanized relative to the rest of the world. In fact, one can argue that the US has been the world's leading economy over the past century or so as a direct result of its urban density and overall scale, not due to some uniquely American character trait. Achieving such scale and density was in turn a product of the timing and manner of American colonial settlement—by the very people who were pioneering the key enabling technologies for large scale urbanization.

16.1 **Urbanization since 1700 CE** % by year

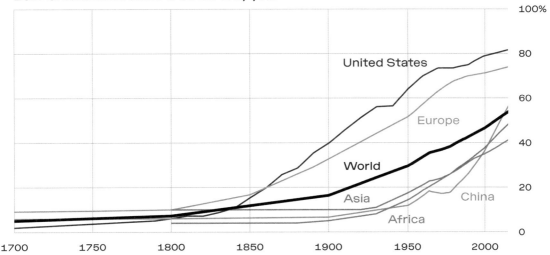

Trends over time tell this story clearly. In 1800, around 10% of Europeans lived in cities; in the United States, the figure was under 5%.[16] Farming efficiency only needed to be marginally above subsistence level to support such comparatively small urban populations. Then, the technologies of the Industrial Revolution, first invented in Britain and Europe, began to take root in the US, especially in the northern states, following the abolition of slavery there.

The new country was short on labor, but had plenty of space and natural resources—thanks to (at times genocidal) land seizure on a breathtaking scale. Hence mechanized practices that saved labor, even if they were profligate with energy or raw materials, were more economically viable in the American context than elsewhere. Also, such innovations met little resistance from the artisans and organized workers who had long pushed back against automation in the Old World.

Once introduced, mechanization put businesses on a path toward ever-increasing productivity. Even when first-generation

16 Our World in Data, "Urbanization over the Past 500 Years," 2018.

17 Habakkuk, *American and British Technology in the Nineteenth Century: The Search for Labour-Saving Inventions*, 1962.

18 Notice how the Great Depression in the US (1929–1939) parallels a similar temporary slowdown in urbanization during the even more devastating "Great Leap Forward" in China (1958–1962), which, ironically, sought to transform the country from an agrarian economy into a technologically advanced communist society. In reality, the technological base for shifting away from an agrarian economy was already developing in China, and attempting to speed up the transformation through wishful thinking and mandated social upheaval appears to have slowed things down instead, in the process causing the death by famine of tens of millions.

industrial technology proved wasteful, balky, or of questionable quality, it established a baseline. Any subsequent improvements through the investment of intellectual or economic capital increased operating profit; thus, "automation culture" is friendly to the kind of entrepreneurial tinkering and relentless optimization that would come to characterize American industrial capitalism.[17]

Applied to agriculture, mechanization greatly scaled up farming efficiency. This drove urbanization so quickly that by 1860, the US and Europe had both risen to 20% urban, with the US, on a steeper upward slope, surging ahead of the rest of the world over the next century. Urbanization marched onward, slowed only momentarily by the Great Depression,[18] until the countryside started to run out of people who *could* fuel this great migration into cities. Even then, American cities continued to grow thanks to an influx from abroad; with such a dynamic economy, the country had become an attractive destination for immigrants from all over the world. So, by 1920, half of Americans lived in cities; by the 1960s, two out of three; and by the 2000s, four out of five.

The Black Marble shows how west of the Mississippi, later European settlement, which could take advantage of more advanced technologies from the start, resulted in an especially sparse countryside, with the great majority of people there settling into a handful of dense urban pockets. East of the Mississippi, earlier settlement yielded a more typically Old World pattern, full of small and mid-sized towns, but even there (with the exception of a dense corridor from Washington, DC to New York) most of the land is quite sparsely populated—and becoming more so every year.

16.2 Cumulative US population by cumulative area of ZIP codes sorted by decreasing population density Population (millions) by area (square miles)

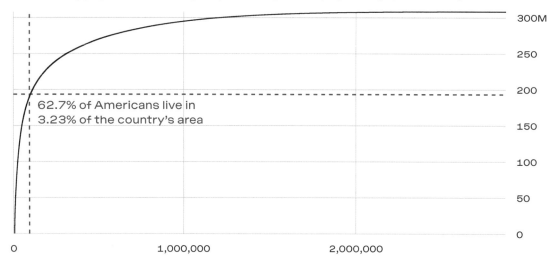

62.7% of Americans live in 3.23% of the country's area

Plotting the relationship between cumulative population and cumulative land area offers a more complete sense of today's population distribution. The 100 million people living in the densest places occupy only about 18,000 square miles—equivalent to a square 130 miles on a side, or 0.63% of the total area of the US. Dashed red crosshairs show 62.7% of the US population, a bit under 200 million people; they occupy just 3.23% of the total area. These remarkable statistics highlight an effect that, while obvious, is still worth dwelling on: the growth of cities, driven as it is by migration from the countryside, both implies and creates vast, sparsely inhabited hinterlands.

I asked survey respondents for their ZIP code so that it would be possible to break down their answers not only by age, but also by population density. In addition, the surveys included the seemingly redundant questions, "Do you live in the city?", "Do you live in the suburbs?", and "Do you live in the countryside?" Responses to these questions offer us a chance to compare a physical measurement—population density based on ZIP code, which varies continuously—with the subjective labels people use when describing themselves as city, suburb, or countryside dwellers.

The horizontal axis shows ZIP code density, measured in square meters per person. Because this quantity varies over such a vast range, from only about 10 square meters per person in dense cities (where people might be living literally on top of each other in apartment buildings) to more than 100,000 square meters per

16.3 Respondents living in the "city," "suburbs," or "countryside" as a function of population density % by square meters per person

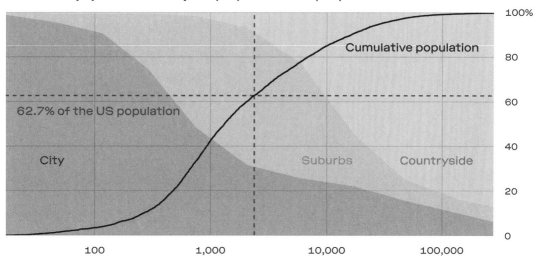

person (think Montana), a logarithmic axis is needed to make out the curves clearly, meaning the evenly spaced tick marks are 100, 1,000, 10,000, 100,000 rather than 100, 200, 300, 400.

The vertical axis breaks down, at each density, the fraction of people answering "yes" to precisely *one* of the questions "Do you live in the city?", "Do you live in the suburbs?", and "Do you live in the countryside?" A cumulative percentage of the total US population as a function of density is also shown, as in the previous plot, in black. Keep in mind that without a logarithmic horizontal axis, most of the area shown would be countryside; recall that the entire half of the plot to the left of the dotted red crosshairs, again representing about 62.7% of the population, covers only 3.23% of the country's area, while the right half covers the remaining 96.77%. As you can see, the 62.7% population threshold evenly splits the suburbs into a more urban half and a more rural half.

Now, we have an objective answer to the subjective question of what the terms "city," "suburb," and "countryside" actually mean to people. Unsurprisingly, this objective answer doesn't feature sharp thresholds in terms of population density (or, it seems safe to assume, in terms of any other measurable quantity). One could choose to define such thresholds by popular vote (e.g., cities as places with less than about 1,000 square meters per person, suburbs between about 1,000 and about 10,000, and countryside above 10,000), but those cutoffs are just the densities at which disagreement between people is at its highest.

Dallas suburbs and skyline, 2009.

As in every other situation where you might suppose answers to be mutually exclusive, some people respond to the three yes/no questions ambiguously. It's just like handedness and sexual orientation. People who answer "no" to all, or "yes" to more than one of the three, probably have a story as to why that makes sense for them, as with a woman from San Clemente, California, who wrote, "I'm not certain if I live in a suburb or a city, I believe I'm on the edge of both."

So once again, we have excluded middles. And once again, we could wonder whether some kind of objective right answer might exist, perhaps based on an official city map. But even here, ground truth is elusive. Many maps of cities have boundaries drawn on them in one place or another, and some of those boundaries matter, determining who your state representative is, or whether you have to pay a city tax. To people living on those borders, though, they often feel arbitrary. And, in fact, they change all the time, as cities grow (and, sometimes, shrink). Those who redraw borders tend to acknowledge that the new border better reflects "reality."

When they do so, they acknowledge that city boundaries are socially constructed. This doesn't imply that there *are* no such boundaries, or that they're an illusion, or that they don't correlate with any underlying physical property—obviously they do, as NASA's Black Marble makes clear. For them to be socially constructed means that they're a necessarily imperfect, somewhat fuzzy, and ever-shifting consensus arising from both direct observation and continual tugs in different directions—politics, in other words.

Inevitably, feedback loops arise. For instance, at some point, an official map might be drawn based on some person or committee's opinion or political interest. If the map actually matters (say, because of differing tax rates or zoning codes), then that map will shape how *future* development occurs. Development affects local population density. Local density affects people's mental models as to where the city ends. Those models in turn affect what subsequent officials think, and how they amend future maps. People also affect each other's mental models all the time, through their everyday use of language, and sometimes through arguments about definitions, either with regard to specific instances (your house isn't *really* in the city!) or general principles (if you live in a high rise apartment it *must* be part of the city!).

I live in a city that could be classified as the suburbs, but city officials are trying to get away from that term so I consider where I live Urban.[19]

19 A 19-year-old man from Arlington, Texas.

So, the push and pull of opinions will affect physical reality, and reality will affect opinions. Those feedback loops can work to bring people into greater agreement, but they can also—and even simultaneously—create opposing camps, sharpen disagreements, and foster tribalism.

By now, these themes will all sound familiar. Our reality is both grounded in the observable world and deeply social; further, our beliefs shape our present and future reality. Or, perhaps more accurately, "realities," since outside the realm of pure math, reality can't be fully pinned down or seen from an entirely objective point of view. It's fuzzy and plural. And "measuring" it tends to affect it, a bit like quantum physics.

I carried out a fun experiment with the data to illustrate how the definitions of words like "city" and "countryside" vary socially. As Black Marble shows, the coasts of the continental US are particularly dense. Segregating ZIP codes by longitude shows how the term "city" is defined differently for people on the coasts as opposed to the heartland. I arbitrarily defined the "Central USA" as ZIP codes that lie between 90°W and 115°W, and "Coastal USA" as ZIP codes lying outside this band. (Those lines of longitude are marked on the population density map.)

On the coasts, the population density has to be a good deal higher, on average, for people to consider themselves city dwellers! If you were to slide one curve over to match the other, you'd find that the difference amounts to more than a threefold change in density. That is, on the coasts, the land area per person has to be one third of what it would have to be in the central US before an "average" person would consider themselves to be a city dweller. The same pattern holds for suburbs and for the countryside (also, there are fewer suburbanites overall in the central US, which makes sense, since the cities tend to be smaller).

If the meanings of "city" and "countryside" change from the coast to the heartland, it's easy to imagine that will be even truer of more contested terms like "trans" and "queer." To reiterate a point I've made in Parts I and II, this book doesn't argue for the correctness of *any* particular definition; I agree with gender and technology researcher Os Keyes, who has written:

> **What does it mean to say someone is queer? What does it mean to say someone is trans? In both cases, there really *isn't* a fixed definition that holds everywhere. Trans identity is contextual, and fluid; it is also autonomous. There's no test that you give someone to determine they're "actually" trans [...].[20]**

20 Keyes, "Counting the Countless," 2019.

One 33-year-old survey respondent from San Francisco offered a definition of "queer" expansive enough to accommodate nearly anybody:

16.4.0 **"Do you live in the city?" responses in central vs. coastal USA**
% by square meters per person

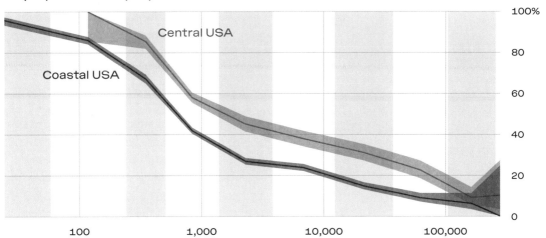

16.4.1 **"Do you live in the suburbs?" responses in central vs. coastal USA**
% by square meters per person

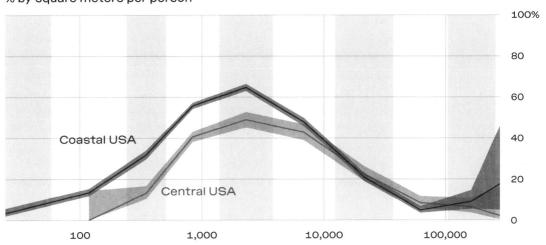

16.4.2 **"Do you live in the countryside?" responses in central vs. coastal USA**
% by square meters per person

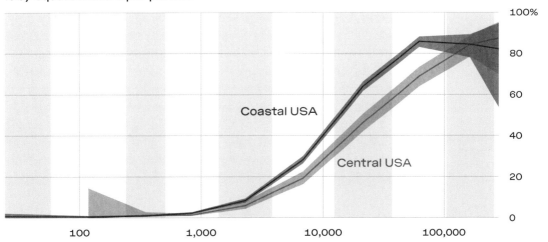

Castro District,
San Francisco, 2006.

"Queer" simply means "different," I have always been different, I've always loved being different, I mesh well with my fellow, harmless, polite, outcasts of the world, proudly. Also, San Francisco.

One might guess that a more conservative respondent—perhaps from one of the squarer states between the coasts—would define "queer" differently.

Rather than comparing the center to the coasts, in this chapter and the next, I'll break down survey responses by density itself, contrasting "city people," defined as those who both say that they live in the city and are in ZIP codes corresponding to the densest 62.7% of the American population, with "country people," who both say they live in the countryside and are in ZIP codes corresponding to the sparsest 37.3%.

As usual, the distinction is both arbitrary and noisy around the edges. It also excludes some respondents. However, it does a reasonable job of highlighting meaningful differences between urban and rural populations. I'll argue that these differences are both the natural result of the "population physics" sketched at the beginning of this chapter, and the key drivers of the political polarization that characterizes our time.

In the popular imagination, that polarization has often been framed geographically, in terms of "coastal elites" versus "flyover country," but this view isn't accurate. The coasts are of course more "citified" on average, and the heartland more "countrified," but in today's geography of ideas, Manhattan is much closer to Chicago, Houston, or Los Angeles than to upstate New York.

So, how does this play out for queerness? First: fewer queer people live in the countryside than in the city. The gap is insignificant among young people, about 15% of whom are queer regardless of where they live; but by age 65, nearly threefold more city-dwellers identify as queer: one in twenty in the city, and one in fifty in the country. (Keep in mind that curves swooping downward nearly in parallel may be maintaining a roughly constant difference in absolute terms, but in relative terms, their difference becomes far more meaningful at lower percentages.)

In part, the greater percentage of heteronormatively attracted people[21] in the countryside explains the lower percentage of queer people living there. Once again, young people are similar, but there's a marked divergence with age. There's more to this story, though.

21 As defined earlier: women sexually and romantically attracted exclusively to men, and vice versa.

16.5 "Do you identify as queer?" in the city vs. countryside % by age

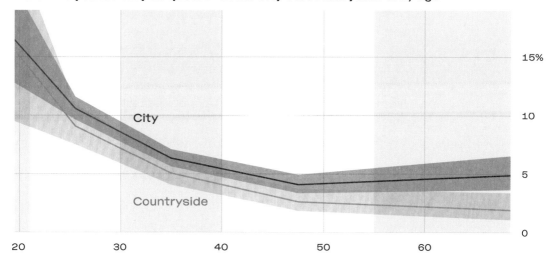

City

Countryside

20 30 40 50 60

15%

10

5

0

16.6 Heteronormative attraction in the city vs. countryside % by age

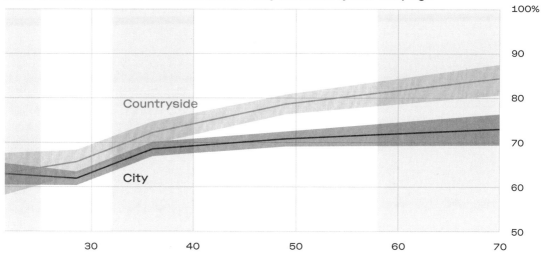

Countryside

City

30 40 50 60 70

100%

90

80

70

60

50

16.7 "Homosexual, gay, or lesbian" people who are queer in the city vs. countryside % by age

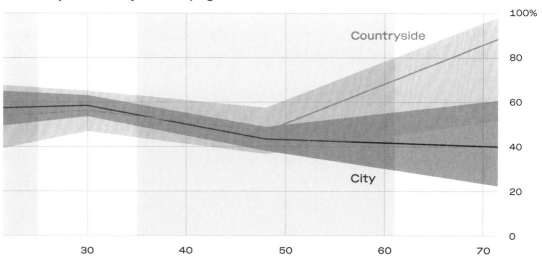

Countryside

City

30 40 50 60 70

100%

80

60

40

20

0

The *definition* of queerness also appears to vary between these populations in interesting ways. In the country-side, a large majority of older gay and lesbian people—perhaps 90%—consider themselves queer, while this is true of less than half of urban 70-year-old gay and lesbian people. This gap illustrates the way older people in the countryside tend to use terms like "queer" in a manner more consistent with its older mid-20th century usage—which, remember, wasn't just "different," but tended to mean specifically gay or lesbian. Hence, both self-reported attraction *and* the use of identity language are more traditional in the countryside, especially among older people.

16.8 "Are you polyamorous?" in the city vs. countryside % by age

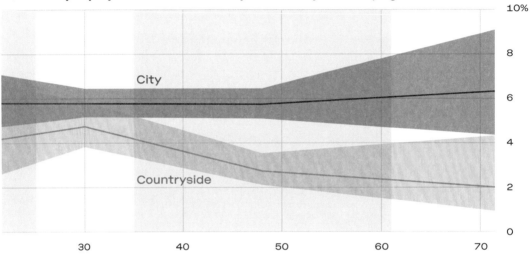

16.9 "Are you non-monogamous?" in the city vs. countryside % by age

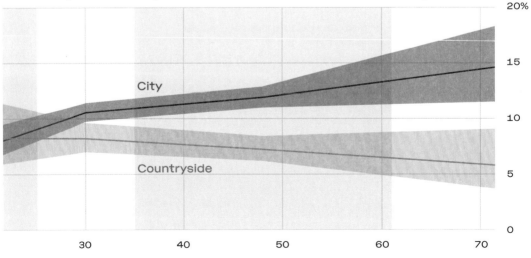

It would be exhausting to reproduce all of the plots in Part II in their city/countryside versions, so let's stick to a few representative highlights, illustrating the following broad observations:

1   The countryside is more conservative.

2   Young people in the city and countryside differ less, while older people differ more.

3   Hence older people in the countryside tend to be extra-conservative.

Non-monogamy and polyamory, for instance, are far more common in the city, again showing modest differences among the young, but an increasing divergence with age.

Non-monogamy looks similar for city and countryside dwellers in their 20s, but in the city, it increases with age, while in the countryside, it decreases a bit with age, until by age 65 the city rate is double the countryside rate. Recall from Chapter 5 that the pattern of overall increase with age probably stems from people in long-term relationships eventually seeking additional sexual or romantic outlets. In the city, such opportunities are more plentiful, and perhaps pursuing them is also less stigmatized.

Similar patterns show up in the lesbian, gay, and bi populations. As with the other trends, the pattern probably owes to several effects: first, young people live online more, which does a lot to erase the geographic distinctions between city and countryside; but also, young people are likelier to live where they were born. As we get older, we

16.10 Gay or bi men in the city vs. countryside % by age

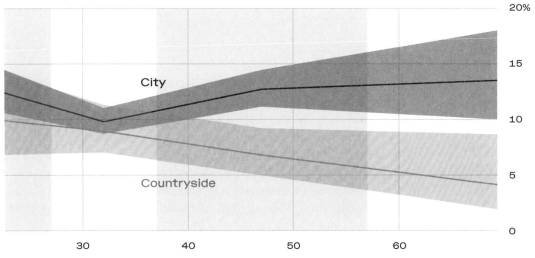

16.11 Lesbian or bi women in the city vs. countryside % by age

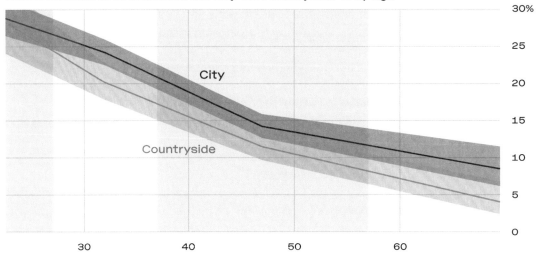

16.12 "Are you homosexual, gay or lesbian?" in the city vs. countryside % by age

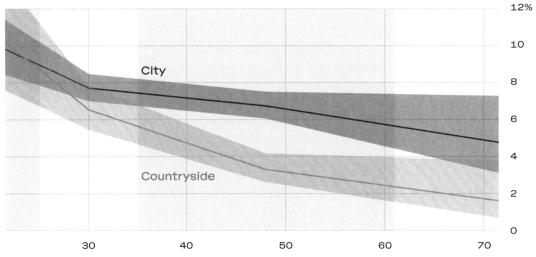

often move, especially in the US. This results in a geographic sorting of the population, an effect we'll return to.

Finally, insofar as people have some degree of flexibility with respect to their gender or sexuality (or any other aspect of their behavior and identity), they'll be biased by their environment. Social transmission is just as likely to suppress a latent minority orientation or identity in the countryside as to amplify it in the city.

It's hard to overstate the divergent results of these effects on people's mental models of what is "normal." For instance, 10% of young people identify as "Homosexual, gay or lesbian," but among older people in the countryside, the number drops below 2%; for the earliest data from 2018, the figure is closer to 1%. A minority trait shared by one in ten

16.13 Trans if assigned female at birth in the city vs. countryside % by age

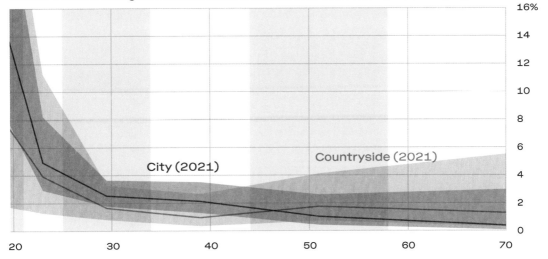

City (2021)

Countryside (2021)

16.14 "Do you identify as non-binary?" in the city vs. countryside % by age

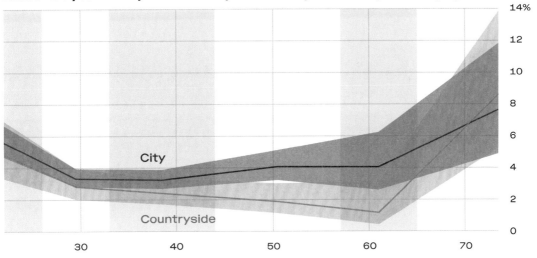

City

Countryside

people feels very different, psychologically, from one you believe to hold for only one in a hundred.

As described in Chapter 13, the number of young people assigned female at birth identifying as trans is rising dramatically. Being young, being assigned female at birth, responding to the most recent survey (2021), and (it turns out) living in the city all increase the odds, to the point where about 14% of 18- to 21-year-olds satisfying these criteria identify as trans. Both the difference between the city and the countryside and the sharp rise from 2018 to 2021 suggest that social transmission is a significant factor.

Unlike the usual trend toward greater frequency of minority identification among the young, remember that non-binary

16.15 "Are you intersex?" in the city vs. countryside % by age

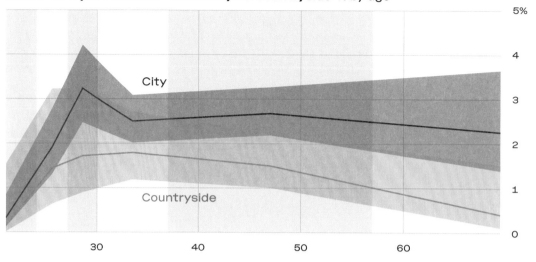

16.16 Intersex if assigned male at birth in the city vs. countryside % by age

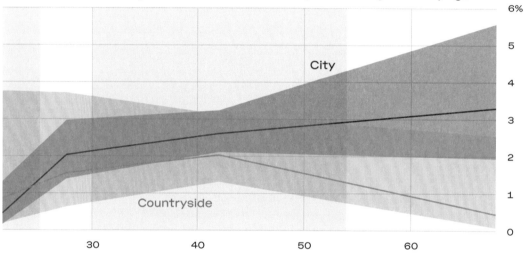

16.17 Intersex if assigned female at birth in the city vs. countryside % by age

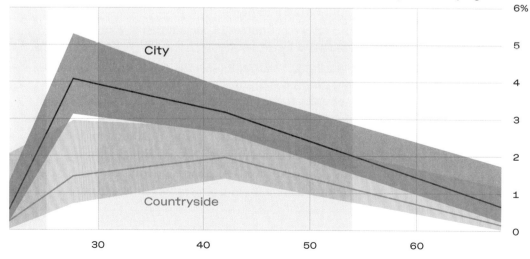

identity exhibits an unusual, U-shaped age pattern (see Chapter 10). Exploring its origin led us to an investigation of intersexuality and the recent reversal in intersex medical protocols. Breaking the non-binary curve down by urban vs. rural populations adds more color to this story.

As you might expect, more non-binary people live in the city than in the countryside—at *almost* all ages, though the relative difference is negligible at the younger end of the scale. Among the older cohort in the countryside, however, there's an even sharper upward turn than in the city; the error bars are large, but it might be that even *more* 73-year-olds in the countryside identify as non-binary than city-dwellers—perhaps over 8%!

Recall that one likely driver of this rise in non-binariness late in life is the large cohort of intersex people who used to be arbitrarily assigned male at birth. Looking at intersex statistics may help clarify what's going on.

Although, once again, the error bars are large, these data are consistent with the broader idea that changes in culture and practices begin in the city, then propagate over time to the countryside. Most noticeably, self-reported intersexuality is *much* more prevalent in the city than in the countryside, over all ages and regardless of sex assigned at birth. We can probably assume that the underlying rate of intersexuality isn't different—but the rate of diagnosis is.

As the physician and sexologist David Oliver Cauldwell pointed out as far back as 1948 (albeit using language that is no longer current),

> **The hermaphrodite is not always easy to recognize. The positive hermaphrodite condition of a large number of individuals has not been determined until after the death of the individual. Diagnoses have been made, however, through deliberate biopsy, and through accidental discovery upon the initiation of surgical procedures for other reasons.[22]**

22 Cauldwell, *Bisexuality in Patterns of Human Behavior: A Study of Individuals Who Indulge in Both Hetero-Sexual and Homosexual Practices, with Comparative Data on Hermaphrodites, the Human Intersex*, 6, 1948.

23 As noted in Chapter 13, intersexuality contributes significantly to the trans population, but doesn't seem sufficient to account for the sharp rise in trans identification among the young.

What was true in 1948 remains true today, especially among populations with less access to medical care or to intersex and trans communities—which is to say, outside the city. Even when they recognize an intersex birth, many more doctors in the countryside still might be following John Money's advice to keep that person (and perhaps even their parents) in the dark.

The shift toward assigning more intersex babies female at birth also seems to have taken place earlier and more decisively in the city.[23]

The General Motors "Futurama" exhibit, New York World's Fair, 1939.

Assuming that the city numbers are more accurate, this should also cause us to revise our estimate of the "real" rate of intersexuality (with the caveat that "reality" here is hard to define) upward yet again, to at least 4% of those assigned female at birth! All of those unacknowledged intersex people—as well as trans and gender-expansive people—are likely contributors to the outsized increase in non-binariness among older people in the countryside, as with a 35-year-old from Walla Walla, Washington, who wrote, "I've wondered if I'm intersex or closet trans." Even to be able to formulate that question, and potentially have a conversation about it with a doctor, implies an awareness of these traits that older people, especially in the countryside, are less likely to possess.

In the broadest strokes, all of these patterns can be summarized as follows: older people, especially in the countryside, are living in the past. Or, as cyberpunk author William Gibson memorably observed, the future is already here— it's just not very evenly distributed.[24]

24 O'Toole, "The Future Has Arrived—It's Just Not Evenly Distributed Yet," 2012.

Country and blues

A 1786 bid to establish monarchy in the United States included an offer to Prince Henry of Prussia to become king.

Differences in culture and outlook between the city and the countryside manifest themselves in political struggle. Broadly speaking, politics are about the push and pull of interests, ideologies, and identities. In a democratic country with established institutions and the rule of law, those laws and institutions form a *status quo*, and in response to the populace's push and pull, the *status quo* evolves over time.

Think of the "first principal component" of politics in terms of that trajectory—specifically, as gas pedal and brakes. Progressive people want to step on the gas, pushing forward with change, while conservative people want to step on the brakes, slowing the rate of change.

Obviously, politics are a lot more complicated than this one-dimensional gas versus brakes cartoon. The variety of answers to the optional, vaguely worded "essay question" on the political surveys I ran in 2016 and 2020 reveal the complexity (and occasional zaniness) of people's ideological convictions:

1   A 26-year-old white man from Citra, Florida.

2   A 35-year-old woman from Columbus, Ohio, who in describing herself notes, "My father is Nigerian and my mother is Native American and Black European. I do consider myself African American, not Black."

3   A 36-year-old man from Oxford, Mississippi.

i want to dissolve the two party system, legalize all drugs and end the drug war, then use that money to provide rehab and drug awareness. Stop bombing overseas and start rebuilding, help local groups fight back against terrorism and tyranny by funding and equipping them rather than direct intervention. i think we should all have guns, free healthcare, and welfare for the poor but take government out of it as much as possible.[1]

I am a conservative liberal. People have the right to do and be who they are as long as it does not physically harm another person who has been born.[2]

I'm a monarchist. We're misunderstood by liberal whites.[3]

Independent thought seems to be alive and well!

Still, the "progressive versus conservative" dimension does appear to capture the lion's share of variation in people's political positions, both in the US and in many other countries; hence the universal distinction between "left wing" (progressive) and "right wing" (conservative). The Baron de Gauville, a deputy at the National Assembly during the French Revolution, explained how the association with left and right came to be: "Those who were loyal to religion and the king took up positions to the right of the chair so as to avoid the shouts, oaths, and indecencies that enjoyed free rein in the opposing camp." We can hear echoes of the same old themes in the name of the progressive grassroots organization MoveOn.org—gas pedal!—and on the right, the rallying cry—

4 A 56-year-old man from Laramie, Wyoming.

make america great again![4]

—which goes beyond brakes, and calls for reverse.

The simple "gas versus brakes" model of politics, combined with the idea that population density drives cultural evolution, yields a prediction: local population density will play a bigger role than any other single factor in determining a person's politics—and, more broadly, identity. Put another way, "who we are" is in no small part a function of *where* we are. This was one of the main hypotheses I set out to test when I first began running Mechanical Turk surveys in 2016. The surveys included not only questions about voting, but also about current social issues, including:

> **Do you believe that global warming is an imminent threat?**
> **Are you in favor of a woman's right to an abortion?**
> **Do you consider yourself a supporter or ally of LGBT rights?**
> **Are you a supporter of same sex marriage rights?**
> **Are you a supporter of the Black Lives Matter movement?**
> **Are you in favor of federally funded universal healthcare?**
> **Is the imposition of Sharia law within the US a threat?**
> **Should the US be more aggressive in deporting**
> **illegal immigrants?**
> **Are white Americans being systematically undermined**
> **or discriminated against?**
> **Do you believe that enacting gun control measures**
> **is a bad idea?**
> **Do you consider homosexuality morally wrong?**
> **Should the US put a halt to the immigration of Muslims?**

Indeed, both in 2016 and in 2020, the answers to these dozen questions follow one of two patterns as a function of population density. The first six generate an overwhelming "yes" (typically 90–100%) from people in the densest ZIP codes, but drop down dramatically in the countryside.

Climate change, marriage equality, and abortion rights are broadly popular causes; support for these only drops below half in the most sparsely populated places, and even there, not by much. LGBT rights, Black Lives Matter, and universal healthcare are more divisive, with support in the countryside dropping to 20–30%—though even for these issues, support in the great majority of ZIP codes, covering

17.0 Social issues more popular in densely populated areas
% by square meters per person

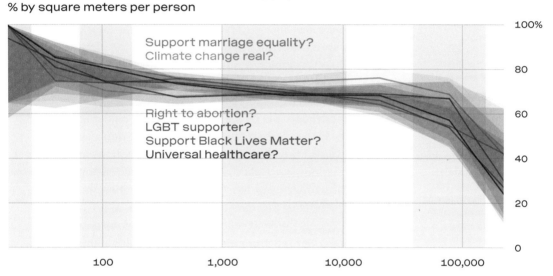

17.1 Social issues more popular in sparsely populated areas
% by square meters per person

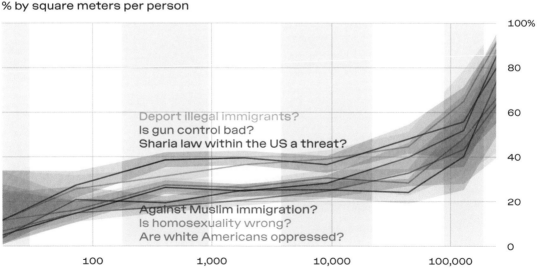

not only the cities and suburbs but even much of the countryside, remains a robust 60–70%. Again, big dropoffs occur only in the most sparsely populated places.

The remaining six questions follow the opposite pattern: only 10% or so of people in the densest urban ZIP codes say "yes," but upward of 50% of those in the deep countryside do, with concern about gun control, Sharia law, and deporting illegal immigrants reaching as high as 80–90%.

Consider the question, "Is the imposition of Sharia law within the US a threat?" Sharia (شريعة) meaning "Islamic law," is a religious law forming part of the Islamic tradition.[5] According to the US Constitution, no religious tradition can be used as the basis for *any* law, though Christian beliefs and values have clearly shaped popular opinion, hence law, on a variety of issues—such as abortion. Muslim Americans are a small minority, though, making the idea that Muslim religious traditions could gain enough political traction to shape US law anytime soon far-fetched.

This question's relationship with the presence of Muslims in the neighborhood is especially interesting. Considerably fewer Muslims live in the US than Jewish people. In the densest ZIP codes, the Jewish population exceeds 13%—though the imposition of Jewish religious law, Halakha (הֲלָכָה) seems less of a popular concern.[6] Muslim Americans, too, tend to live near cities, though their numbers are greatest just *outside* the urban core. At no density does their concentration exceed 4% or so. In the deep countryside, they disappear entirely from the population. Yet it's in these very places, where there are no Muslims for miles around, that people are most concerned about Muslim immigration and Sharia law.

5 Hence technically "Sharia law" is a redundant phrase, like "pizza pie" or "panini sandwich." Pro tip for non-Italian speakers: *pizza* already means "pie," and *panino*, the singular of *panini*, already means "sandwich."

6 Though in fairness, at least half of American Jews are secular to the point of being agnostic or atheist, and only a small minority take Jewish law seriously. (See Pew, "Jewish Americans in 2020," 2021.) Antisemitism nonetheless still exists, and may even be resurgent, as suggested by the substantial number of people, both urban *and* rural, answering "yes" to the question "Are Jewish interests overrepresented in Washington?"

17.2 **Muslim and Jewish populations by density** % by square meters per person

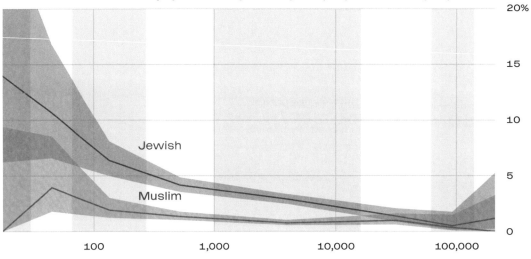

"Were you born in the US?" and race % by square meters per person

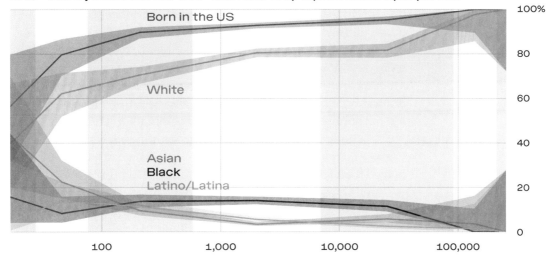

Similarly, graphing answers to the questions "Were you born in the US?" and "Do you identify as White / European American?" reveals a powerful sorting effect. Fewer than half of those living in inner cities identify as white, and fewer than 60% were born in the US. In the most rural ZIP codes, though, virtually everyone is white and native-born. Yet 60% of this same rural population answers "yes" to "Are white Americans being systematically undermined or discriminated against?" That number is close to 0% in the city. Why?

Perhaps because, in a bustling city full of immigrants, people of different races, ethnicities, and religions live cheek by jowl and are familiar with each other. Neighbors walk by one another on the street, mix socially, and eat together; they might become friends, go on dates, become partners, end up raising families. Whatever your background, other races and ethnicities aren't a mystery in the city, and given firsthand exposure to non-white people, most white people find it hard to cling to a conviction that *they* are singled out or structurally disadvantaged, or that immigrants in the neighborhood pose an existential threat to their way of life.

On the other hand, many rural Americans *do* feel that their way of life is under threat—and with good reason. Their communities have been

Lower East Side of New York, ca. 1890.

7   Cross, Califf, and Warraich, "Rural-Urban Disparity
in Mortality in the US From
1999 to 2019," 2021. Native
Americans were the only other
American demographic group
studied whose mortality also
increased from 1999 to 2019.

economically hollowed out, unemployment and poverty are endemic, infrastructure is crumbling, public transit and education are inade-quate, and on top of that, opioid drugs are ravaging the social fabric. Improvements in healthcare have led to steadily declining mortal-ity in the city, but the countryside has been left behind; among rural Americans aged 25–64, mortality hasn't just failed to decrease, but has *increased* from 1999 to 2019.[7] It was rising even before COVID hit, but naturally, the pandemic made the situation even worse.

While questionable policy decisions, the misdeeds of Oxy-Contin® manufacturer Purdue Pharma, and plain bad luck have all played their part, it's hard not to see the confluence of crises in the rural US as connected to an underlying cause: the demographic emptying-out of end stage urbanization. It's unsurprising that con-ditions in rural areas and small towns can generate resentment, or, given a largely homoge-neous racial makeup, that the resentment can become racially (or ethnically, or religiously) charged. The easiest "other" to resent is someone who isn't present, someone you can imagine enjoying a better life elsewhere. And indeed, by many measures, life in the big city—where all those "other" people live—*is* better.

Abandoned factories
of the former Packard
Automotive Plant,
Detroit, 2009.

Why is the countryside so overwhelmingly white? There are
a few reasons. First, European colonists systematically dispossessed native populations, moving them off lands they declared "public" and selling the parcels to white agriculturalists.[8] Then came Jim Crow era racist land policies, and associated waves of so-called "white flight" to the suburbs throughout the 20th century. One of the more infamous practices, often referred to as "redlining," involves federal and local governments drawing racial boundaries on maps, and either denying services to people within certain areas or using selective pricing to enforce *de facto* segregation. For instance, in the 1980s, Pulitzer Prize winning investigative reporter Bill Dedman showed how, in Atlanta, banks often financed mortgages for lower-income whites, but not for middle- or even upper-income Black people, in effect excluding them from certain neighborhoods while creating urban ghettos.[9]

8   Deloria, *Custer Died for
Your Sins: An Indian Manifesto*,
1969; Banner, *How the Indians
Lost Their Land: Law and
Power on the Frontier*, 2007;
Farrell et al., "Effects of Land
Dispossession and Forced
Migration on Indigenous Peo-
ples in North America," 2021.

9   Dedman, "The Color of
Money," 1988.

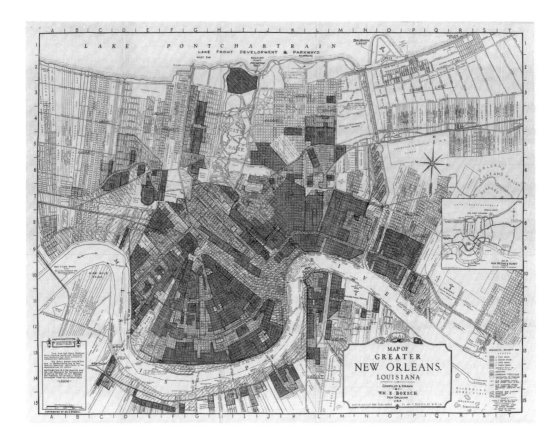

Map of New Orleans created by the US Federal Government's Home Owners' Loan Corporation between 1935 and 1940, illustrating redlining. Color-coded grades were assigned to neighborhoods reflecting their "mortgage security," from "A" (green–deemed safe by banks and mortgage lenders) to "D" (red–"hazardous"). The race and class of residents was factored into the calculation of risk grades. See Nelson et al., "Mapping Inequality," 2021.

When immigrants come to the US, they also typically arrive in—and remain in—the cities. Not only are cities where the educational and economic opportunities tend to be; they're also, as we've seen, the places to go for minorities of all kinds to find community. That probably explains why, at the rural extreme of the density scale, there isn't a single survey respondent who was born outside the US!

From the above it's clear why inner cities and suburbs tend to be ethnically mixed, and why people in the countryside tend to be native-born. Most Black Americans aren't recent immigrants, though. Why, then, do so few of them live in rural places?

Redlining is usually understood as a city and suburb phenomenon, but equally unfair practices have victimized Black farmers. The *Counter*, a "nonprofit, independent, nonpartisan newsroom investigating the forces shaping how and what America eats," published an investigative piece in 2019 detailing a century-long history of systematic discrimination against Black farmers by the US Department of Agriculture (USDA):

USDA and federal farm policy are largely responsible for driving black people out of farming almost entirely.

"Farmer waiting for supplies which he is buying cooperatively at Roanoke Farms, North Carolina," 1938.

Black farmers lost around 90 percent of the land they owned between 1910 and 1997, while white farmers lost only about 2 percent over the same period.[10]

Structural inequalities aren't limited to discrimination against Black people. In the US, 86% of farm owner-operators are male, and only 6% are Hispanic. Meanwhile, 80% of farm laborers are Hispanic. While a number of factors might contribute to this discrepancy, one stands out: exclusionary policies have targeted them too. Asian landowners have also been systematically disenfranchised, and, of course, Native Americans.[11]

The countryside's homogeneity—and the near absence of any immigrant influx, other than seasonal labor—has had another effect as well: the rural population today is considerably older than the urban population. As societies industrialize, their birth rates plummet, a topic I'll take up in more detail in the next chapter. In countries with advanced economies but very low immigration rates, like Japan, low birth rates have led to a population strongly skewed toward older people. The same has happened in the American countryside, as revealed by Census Bureau statistics.[12]

17.4 **Age distribution of urban and rural populations** % by age

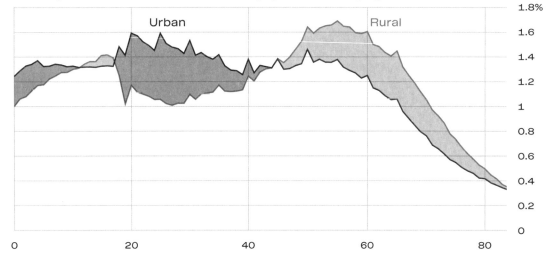

Around age 18, many young adults who grew up in the countryside move to the city, whether to go to college, find work, or find their community. Relative to the national average, this results in an urban overrepresentation of young adults and a corresponding rural underrepresentation of young adults. It also leads to an overrepresentation of older adults in the countryside, since these curves are distributions, meaning that they add up to 100%: like lumps on a carpet, pushing down on one spot moves the lump elsewhere.

Remember that, in every breakdown by age, being older proved to be a powerful predictor of conservatism. So is living in the countryside, even when age is held constant. So, the higher proportion of older people in the countryside creates a compounding effect. Rural places end up older, whiter, more conservative, and more heteronormative. People living in rural areas aren't exposed to much diversity, and that makes them even more afraid of the invisible "other." It also makes them feel outnumbered, threatening their long-held belief that they are the majoritarian norm. Indeed, they're right to believe that they no longer are.

If you *are* living in a rural place and you're "other"—whether that means Black, queer, non-monogamous, or for that matter just not so conservative—it also means you're likelier to move to the city if you can, because you probably won't find community in the countryside. Consequently we've found ourselves in a feedback loop, with the rural places becoming ever more conservative, even as the cities become more progressive.

Although these are long-term trends, evidence of them can be seen by comparing responses to the survey in 2016 and in 2020, when I re-ran it with many of the same questions. For example, graphing support for the Black Lives Matter (BLM) movement as a function of density illustrates the way social change originating in cities tends to be slow in percolating into rural places.

Support for BLM was always higher in the city than in the countryside, but in 2016 the differences were a bit less stark— around 80% in the city, and about 15% in the deep countryside, a 65% gap. By 2020, BLM had gained huge support overall, rising 20% nearly everywhere to reach virtually 100% in the densest neighborhoods. However, at the lowest densities, support remained unchanged; the rural-urban gap had grown to an extraordinary 85%. The increased polarization wasn't a case of people in the countryside becoming *more* conservative; they just stayed put—as best we can tell given those large error bars (due to small numbers) in the most rural places.

10 Rosenberg and Stucki, "How USDA Distorted Data to Conceal Decades of Discrimination Against Black Farmers," 2019.

11 Horst and Marion, "Racial, Ethnic and Gender Inequities in Farmland Ownership and Farming in the U.S.," 2019.

12 Smith and Trevelyan, "The Older Population in Rural America: 2012–2016: American Community Survey Reports," 2019.

17.5 "Are you a supporter of the Black Lives Matter movement?"
% by square meters per person

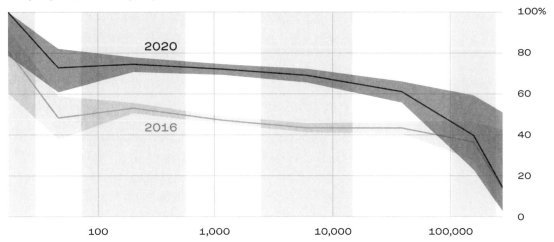

A similar pattern in mirror image holds for responses to the question "Are white Americans being systematically discriminated against?" This conservative talking point was a minority view in the city and suburbs in 2016, and became even more so by 2020. However, it's a majority perspective in the deep countryside, where opinion remained unmoved over those four years.

It would be wrong to conclude that the countryside doesn't change over time, though (a point I'll unpack further in Chapter 20). Over these four years, so many more people have become aware of racially biased policing that "staying put" on questions of race arguably looks more like swimming against the tide. The surveys show evidence of actively rising rural conservatism in the answers about climate change, deporting illegal immigrants, and banning Muslim immigration.

In 2016 there was broad consensus on climate change being a problem—a solid majority across all population densities. By 2020, everybody in the cities knew it was a problem, but in the most rural places, astonishingly, that had become a fringe position. 2020, remember, was a year of record-setting wildfires in California; more than 4% of the state's land area had burned, with the August Complex fire alone incinerating over a million acres across seven counties. On the other side of the planet, Australia had just endured its own extreme climate event, the Black Summer, a relentless onslaught of bushfires in which over a billion animals are estimated to have died.

As the cities and suburbs liberalize, the countryside is not only digging in its heels, but becoming increasingly conservative, xenophobic, and aggrieved.

17.6 "Are white Americans being systematically undermined or discriminated against?" % by square meters per person

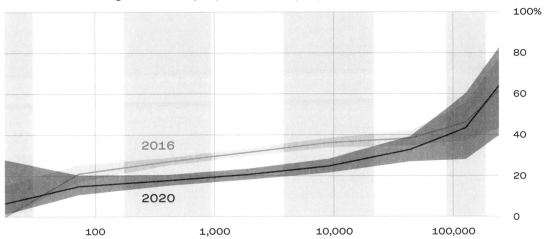

17.7 "Do you believe that global warming is an immiment threat?"
% by square meters per person

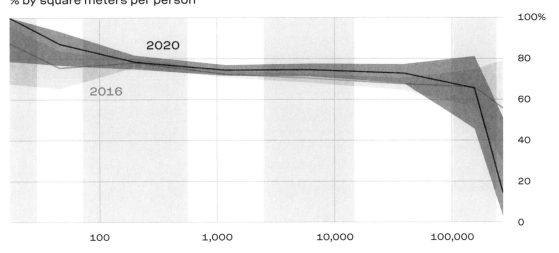

17.8 "Should the US be more aggressive in deporting illegal immigrants?"
% by square meters per person

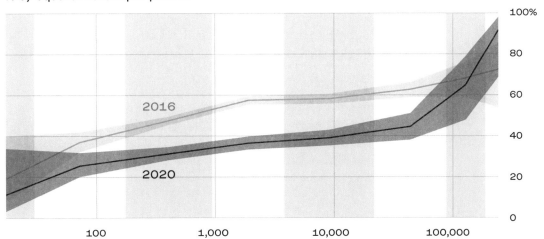

13 A 33-year-old man from Aurora, Colorado.

14 A 46-year-old man from Niagara Falls, New York.

15 As usual when the error bars are large, these percentages are far from exact; still, the qualitative difference between 2016 and 2020 is obvious and dramatic.

16 Even New England's famously bucolic liberal arts colleges behave, in effect, like small, dense, cosmopolitan cities: They bring together young people from a wide geographic area (including international students) and concentrate them in a small area. Predictably, the resulting politics are very progressive, as the close-up voting map of Ithaca, New York (the home town of Cornell University), later in this chapter illustrates.

17 Azrael et al., "The Stock and Flow of U.S. Firearms: Results from the 2015 National Firearms Survey," 2017.

I'm a proud white nationalist.[13]

I am a white male and thus hated in my own country.[14]

The xenophobia goes beyond race, also targeting other minorities, as is evident in the changing response to "Do you consider homosexuality morally wrong?" While these curves look similar in the city and suburbs from 2016 to 2020, rising steadily from zero to around 30%, moral disapproval of homosexuality in the most rural places has tripled over these four years, rising from around 20% to likely above 60%.[15] It's easy to see why, if you're queer and grow up in the countryside, you'll probably want to move to the city as soon as you can, especially nowadays—which will, in turn, amplify the political urban/rural sorting effect.

Recall, from the Census Bureau's urban/rural age distribution, how the rural population takes an immediate dive and the urban population rises by about the same percentage right at age 18, when kids become legal adults in the US. That's also the age at which many young people go to college, and most colleges and universities aren't rural.[16] It's a safe bet, though, that the incentive to move to the city, whether to go to college or to take your chances on the job market there, will be a lot higher if you don't fit in where you grew up. And if you *do* find your community in the city, it's unlikely that you'll be eager to return to the countryside later in life.

The increasingly pro-gun stance of rural Americans disquiets many progressives. This trend likely goes along with higher rates of armament, not just with handguns or hunting rifles but with arsenals of long guns and machine guns associated with tactical assault or warfare.[17] Whether such weapons can be considered reasonable investments in "self-defense" depends on whether one is talking about defending a home against an intruder or a village against an invading army. In cities, where most deaths from gun violence occur, well under 10% of the population feels that it would be a bad idea to enact stronger gun control measures. Yet the sense of needing armed protection from "those other people" is highest in the most rural places. In 2016, fewer than half felt that stricter gun control was a bad idea, but by 2020, that figure had risen above 80%.

At the end of Part II, noting the way so many of us spend most of our time online nowadays, I posed the half-serious question, "Does this mean we've already been uploaded?" Put another way, does where we live matter anymore, or are we all living virtually, in a kind of simulated social life where the constraints of physical space have

17.9 "Should the US put a halt to the immigration of Muslims?"
% by square meters per person

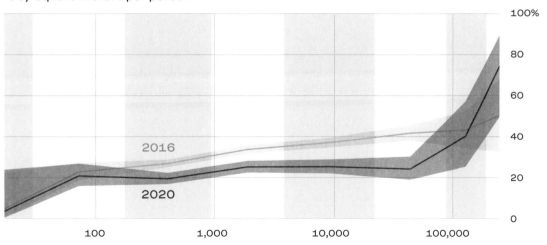

17.10 "Do you consider homosexuality morally wrong?"
% by square meters per person

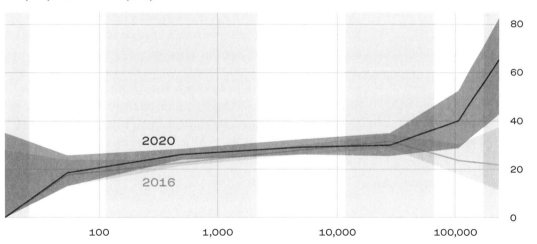

17.11 "Do you believe that enacting gun control measures is a bad idea?"
% by square meters per person

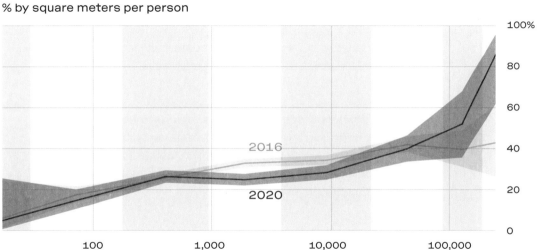

been nullified? The findings in this chapter suggest that, despite living online, where we make our home *physically* still matters—a lot. Otherwise, there wouldn't be such dramatic variations in attitudes and values by ZIP code.

At least in part, the geographic "sorting hat" effect, in which certain subpopulations end up better represented in the countryside and others in the city, accounts for such variations. However, this is unlikely to be the whole story. We've seen the power of social transmission in determining our perspectives, attitudes, and identities: Our friends influence us. Our friends also tend to be nearby, even in this era of ubiquitous online communication. In his 2021 book *Friends*, British anthropologist Robin Dunbar summarizes a wealth of evidence showing the correlation between friendship and physical proximity:

> **There is an unwritten law in the study of social networks known as the 'Thirty-Minute Rule': you will make the effort to see someone, and view them as important to you, if they live within thirty minutes' travel time of where you live. [...] That being so, you might suppose that you would be more inclined to phone or text those who live beyond the thirty-minute limit to make up for the fact that you can't get round to see them in person. In fact, it seems that you don't. You are more likely to phone the friends that live near you, as Hang-Hyun Jo was able to show from an analysis of phone-call patterns[18] [...]. [Y]ou phone most often the people you see most often. [...] When people move away and don't have the opportunity to meet up so often, friendships seem to flag surprisingly quickly [...] [A] friendship of high strength will decline to no more than a mere acquaintance-ship in just three years.[19]**

So social proximity explains why geography continues to matter when it comes to our beliefs and identities. We may spend many hours each day online, interacting with friends and scrolling through social media; but who those friends are, hence which social media, will depend in no small part on where we live.

The stark and rising polarization in worldview created by these social sorting effects paints an alarming picture for observers on either side of the political divide. Many feel under threat, and may even seek to cut any remaining ties with the "other" camp. For instance:

[18] Jo et al., "Spatial Patterns of Close Relationships Across the Lifespan," 2014.

[19] Dunbar, *Friends*, 100–101, 2021.

I think European Americans need to hold a referendum to cut our losses. We can separate into two groups, those who are loyal to the Caucasian race and those who are not, aka white race traitors. Those who are disloyal can get out. They can take their Jewish conspirators with them for the 1965 Immigration Reform Act and the Federal Reserve. First order of business; civil war to establish a new "whites only" nation. Second on the list; nuke Israel for 9/11. The researchers might think European Americans and members of the Caucasian race are unaware we are experiencing genocide. We are. And white leadership, across the board, is directly responsible for it. My guess, think the French Revolution on acid is what is coming our way.[20]

20 A 55-year-old from Raleigh, North Carolina.

It has become commonplace to characterize the growing divide as a possible prelude to civil war. Today's situation is very different from the one preceding the US Civil War, though; that war was fought between a bloc of northern emancipated states and a bloc of southern slave states. That's not how it breaks down now. It's hard to imagine a civil war between the cities and the countryside— because they are so mutually dependent, and the "borders" don't look like country borders at all.

The Jesusland map, a popular meme satirizing political polarization at the state level during the 2004 US presidential election.

An early "culture wars" meme from the 2004 presidential election depicted a satirical "Jesusland map," with Jesusland consisting of the states in the heartland and south, and a "United States of Canada" combining the more liberal coasts with their low-key, progressive neighbor to the north. This state-by-state political picture is inaccurate, though. The real "Jesusland map" looks more like NASA's Black Marble— and that just doesn't look like a map of two countries in any conventional sense. It looks like an increasingly interconnected network of "United Cities" pitted against a vast, sparsely populated, and increasingly conservative hinterland. This explains the analogous polarization happening in many other

17.12.0 **The 2016 presidential election vote** % by square meters per person

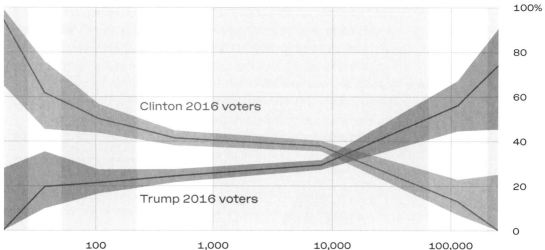

17.12.1 **The 2020 presidential election vote** % by square meters per person

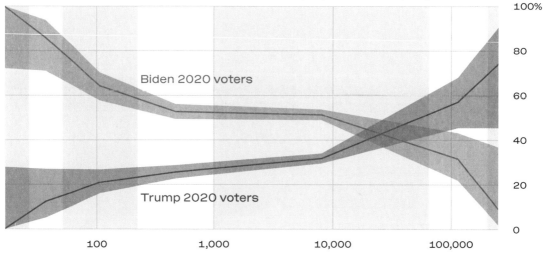

countries too, even those that have nothing comparable to the American Civil War in their histories.

An entrenched two-party system, which has in recent years shifted to align itself almost perfectly with the rural-urban axis, has exacerbated the political divide in the US. In 2016, ZIP code density already did a better job of predicting voting for Trump or Clinton at the urban or rural end of the spectrum than any other obvious variable (e.g. race, gender, education, wealth). *Zero* survey respondents in the densest ZIP codes answered "yes" to "Did you vote for Donald Trump in the November 2016 presidential election?" while about 95% answered "yes" to "Did you vote for Hillary Clinton in the November 2016 presidential election?" In the sparsest ZIP codes, three quarters of the respondents had voted for Trump, while the Clinton vote dropped to zero. This degree of political sorting by population density is astonishing.

In June 2020, the conservative voting pattern remained virtually unchanged, especially among conservative voters in the sparsest ZIP codes. On the other hand, the progressive vote in urban and suburban ZIP codes—where a larger (and, in the end, decisive) fraction of people said they would vote for Joe Biden—shifted much more. Many of these people had voted for a third-party candidate in 2016, so in this sense, the punditry's view that Biden was less divisive than Clinton was correct. However as a consequence, if anything, the overall polarization between city and countryside *increased* between 2016 and 2020 as the left finally coalesced.

For better or worse, democracy, and especially its American two-party variant, is inherently biased toward inertia. Put another way, there is a conservative bias. The arrow of time itself works against progressivism. Many possible paths take us forward, while the past (even if we mythologize it) is easier to pin down, hence easier to form a coalition around. Relatedly, conservatives tend to evolve more slowly in their positions—or they wouldn't be called "conservative." They're also a more homogeneous population, which makes them more coherent in their cultural values and positions; conservatives can effectively align and push for a stable agenda over many years, while diverse, faster-evolving progressives with divergent visions of the future spend more time infighting. Conservatives are "dog people," loyal and able to hunt effectively in packs (or PACs!), while progressives are more like "cat people," individualistic and impossible to herd.

This observation bears more weight than a snappy cliché. Psychological research has shed light on systematic differences between the way liberals and conservatives evaluate moral

Percent
difference

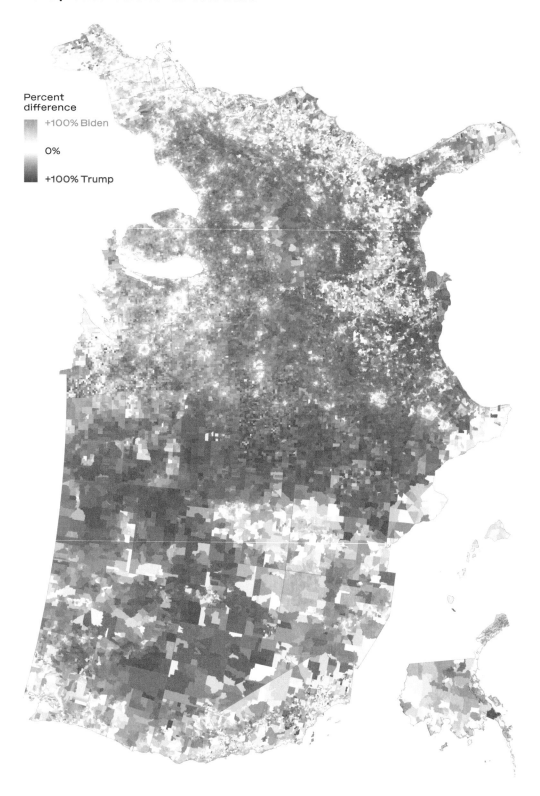

+100% Biden

0%

+100% Trump

17.13.1 **Democratic voting density in the 2020 presidential election**
Democratic votes per square mile

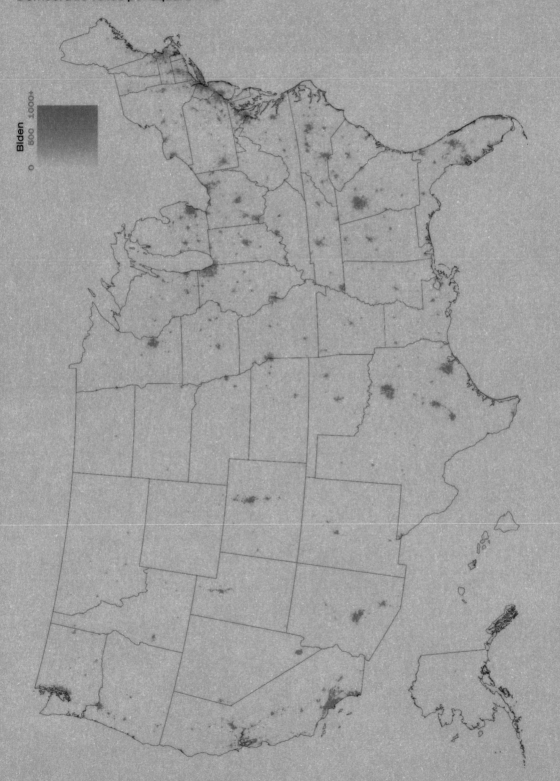

Biden

0 500 1,000+

17.13.1 Democratic voting density
in the 2020 presidential election
Democratic votes per square mile

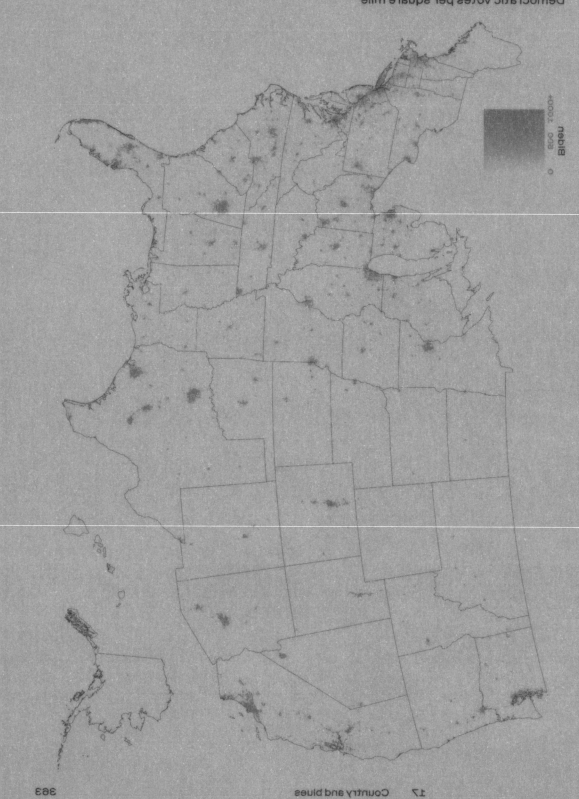

Biden

0   800   2,000+

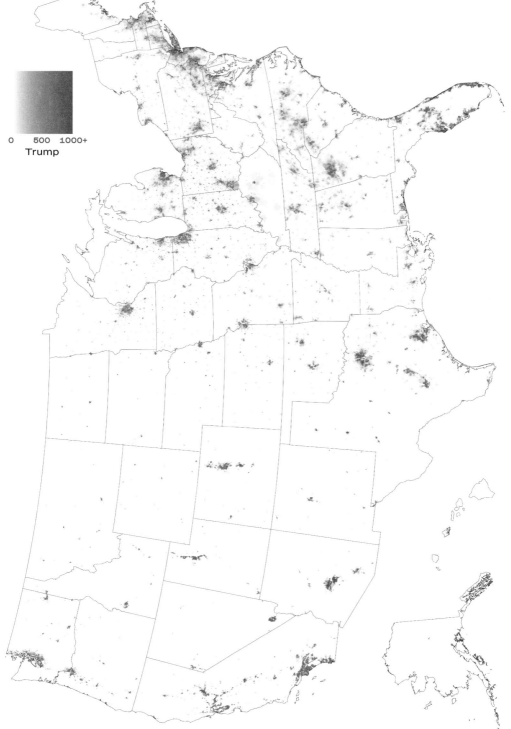

Trump

0   500   1000+

17.13.3 Close-ups of combined Republican and Democratic voting densities in the 2020 presidential election Votes per square mile

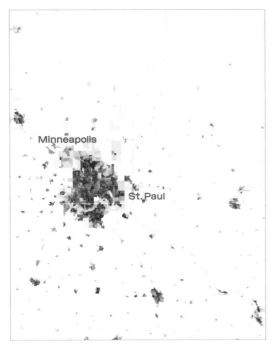

Minnesota

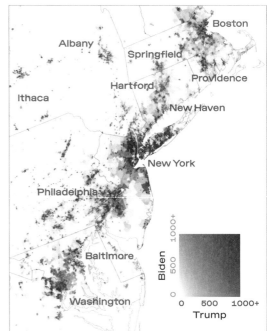

Northeast Corridor

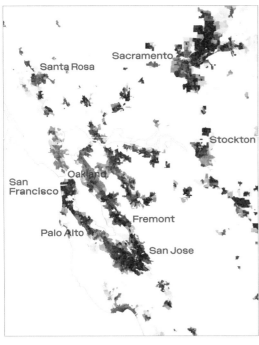

Bay Area

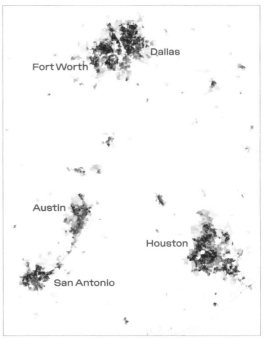

Texas

choices. As Jonathan Haidt and colleagues wrote in a highly influential 2009 paper,

> We [...] do not think of political ideology—or morality—as a strictly one-dimensional spectrum. In fact, we consider it a strength of [our] theory that it allows people and ideologies to be characterized along five dimensions. Nonetheless, we expect that the individualizing–binding distinction can account for substantial variation in the moral concerns of the political left and right, especially in the United States, and that it illuminates disagreements underlying many "culture war" issues.[21]

21 Graham, Haidt, and Nosek, "Liberals and Conservatives Rely on Different Sets of Moral Foundations," 2009.

The five dimensions of the researchers' "Moral Foundations Theory" are harm/care, fairness/reciprocity, ingroup/loyalty, authority/respect, and purity/sanctity. The first two are "individualizing" or, as I've put it, cat-like. The last three are "binding," or dog-like. Liberals rely far more on the individualizing values in making their judgments, while conservatives rely on all five. More recent work from the University of Birmingham in the UK supports the connection between moral foundations and politics:

> Individualizing-Ingroup Preference and Binding-Ingroup Preference scores predicted more Attitude Bias and more Negative Attitude Bias toward immigrants [...], more Implicit Bias [...], and more Perceived Threat from immigrants [...]. We also demonstrated that increasing liberalism was associated with less Attitude Bias and less Negative Bias toward immigrants [...], less Implicit Bias [...], and less Perceived Threat from immigrants [...].[22]

22 Stewart and Morris, "Moving Morality Beyond the In-Group: Liberals and Conservatives Show Differences on Group-Framed Moral Foundations and These Differences Mediate the Relationships to Perceived Bias and Threat," 2021.

Beyond the inherent challenges to progressive change, considering this chapter's graphs alongside the population density curves from the previous chapter brings to light something odd and perhaps undemocratic. About 90% of the US population lives below 30,000 square meters per person (about halfway between 10,000 and 100,000 on the logarithmic axis), which is roughly where the voting curves cross over each other. And indeed, the Democrats garnered more votes than the Republicans in both the 2020 *and* the 2016 elections. But all votes aren't equal.

By land area, the country looks "red," as seen in now-familiar voting maps that color in precincts based on their popular vote. However, by population count, the US has already tipped decisively to "blue." The precinct-level voting map looks the way it does—overwhelmingly red by area—precisely because of the combined effects of intensive urbanization and political sorting by population density.

Arguably, a more informative way to visualize voting is to divide Democratic and Republican precinct votes by area. This is a more faithful rendition of the popular vote—approximating the pointillist image we'd see if every person were represented by a tiny red or blue dot.[23] Red and blue votes can be visualized separately, or overlaid to form a single image, with the two colors mixing to produce purple in the most contested areas. Although both red *and* blue votes are scarce in the deep countryside (because people are!), red votes are comparatively far more common in rural places, giving them a diffuse red hue—as is especially evident east of the Mississippi, where more of the countryside is settled. Major cities, though, are invariably more blue than red, whether they're on the East or West Coast, in the Midwest or in Texas. Small towns are typically much redder, though, with occasional exceptions like Ithaca, New York (not coincidentally, home to Cornell University).

Unfortunately for progressive people, by apportioning representative voting and legislative power by geographical area, the American electoral system gives a lot more political power to the rural population. Unless the rules change, US politics will always lag significantly behind the country's demographics.

The unequal weight of the urban and rural vote also paints a stark picture of the real legacy of white supremacy in the United States. When Black, Native, Asian, and Hispanic people were systematically excluded from or pushed out of farming to create a "white countryside," they were not only deprived of income, the ability to accumulate wealth, and a legacy to pass on to future generations; they and their descendants were also excluded from political representation in the very places where votes carry disproportionate weight. In cities and suburbs, a long history of voter suppression and disenfranchisement targeting Black and other minority communities has been well documented. But even if a Black person manages to vote in the city, their ballot counts for only a fraction of what it would have had they cast it in the countryside. Hence, rural "whitening" has had an even more profound effect on national politics than urban redlining. And as the countryside continues to empty

23 To math nerds: This normalization allows a sum or integral over any given area to faithfully count up the number of votes within that area. Equivalently, it makes the map's overall appearance *not* depend on the spatial resolution over which vote counts are aggregated.

THE GEORGETOWN ELECTION—THE NEGRO AT THE BALLOT-BOX.—[See page 162.]

Political cartoon by Thomas Nast for *Harper's Weekly*, March 16, 1867.

out, the relative voting power of the more homogeneous populations remaining there only continues to increase.

> ive seen several examples of the electoral college proving that not every vote matters. how can someone get more votes by the people who politics is supposed to serve yet the person with less real votes ends up being the winner. it taught me that voting is pointless and my opinion doesnt matter.[24]

24 A 35-year-old from East Windsor, Connecticut.

18

Checking our numbers

This chapter is about death. Throughout the book, we've been steadily zooming out, both in space and in time, to consider human identity from an increasingly holistic perspective. Now, it's time to connect the observations about sexuality, urbanization, identity, and politics to the longer arc of human population

18.0 Age distribution of respondents
Average (and median) age by square meters per person

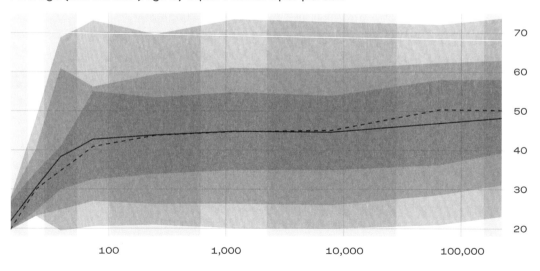

1   The plot actually
shows postmenopausal
people assigned female
at birth, to ensure all child-
births are captured.

2   Craig, "Replacement
Level Fertility and Future
Population Growth," 1994.

growth, and that means exploring the balance between reproduction and mortality. Shifts in that balance over time are both
caused by and drive the most dramatic changes we're undergoing,
as a species *and* as a planet. Those shifts have brought us to an
unprecedented tipping point: a time of great sensitivity to small
differences, when a nudge this way or that could take us to very
different futures.

Let's begin by considering where babies come from—not
anatomically, but geographically! Recall that Americans are having fewer children today than it would take to replace the
population from one generation to the next (see Chapter
5). This is especially true in the city, where the number of
births drops precipitously. Partly, this is because cities
skew toward younger people. There are likely a number of
reasons; one is the American tradition in which couples
move to the suburbs to have kids.

However, even considering only the number of
children born to post-menopausal women (I've picked ages
44–64), the contrast between rural and urban fertility is
stark.[1] Below about 100 square meters per person, women
average fewer than one child. Below about 1,000 square
meters per person, the threshold above which most people
think of themselves as living in the suburbs, the figure is 1.5 or
fewer. Only at the most rural extreme, around 100,000 square
meters per person, does the number of children per female, normally called the "total fertility rate" or TFR, approach replacement
rate, which is about 2.1 in the developed world.[2]

18.1 Children born to 44–64-year-olds assigned female at birth
Average (and median) by square meters per person

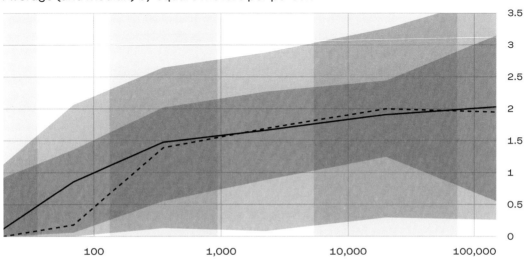

There's an obvious and striking conclusion here: cities are not even *remotely* demographically self-sustaining. They're population sinks. Not only must they draw on the material resources of the countryside to survive; they also need a continual influx of young people from elsewhere. Without immigration, a city will age rapidly and then collapse, like a star running out of nuclear fuel to burn.

Replacement TFR isn't exactly two because women and men aren't born in precisely equal proportions, and more importantly, because early deaths before or during a person's fertile years have to be taken into account. Without modern medicine, replacement TFR is *well* above two, as infant and childhood mortality are especially high. (While this factor isn't generally considered, I think that in advanced economies, a good deal of the excess above two is also due to the not so tiny percentage of intersex children![3])

In any case, in a closed community with no immigration or emigration, constant mortality, and a TFR of precisely the replacement rate, a population's size will remain constant. If the potential mothers average fewer than two children each over their reproductive years, the population will shrink exponentially; if they have more than two-point-something children on average, it will grow exponentially. Replacement rate represents a knife's edge between exponential growth and exponential decline. Unless actively maintained somehow, stability is elusive.

To get a sense of *how* elusive, let's do some rough calculations. Assume for the moment that a "generation" is 30 years, and for simplicity's sake, let's pretend that replacement TFR is precisely two, ignoring premature mortality and other corrections. Then, under steady conditions, a total fertility rate of 5, which was roughly the world average from 1950–1970,[4] leads to a doubling of the population every 23 years or so. Over a century, population would grow by 21-fold! Such calculations offer some perspective on sensational book titles of that era, like *The Population Bomb* (1968).[5]

On the other hand, a TFR of one, as we see in the densest ZIP codes, works out to a halving of the population every 30 years; or, a TFR of 1.5 works out to a halving every 72 years, and a drop to 10% of the original population size after 240 years. At that rate, 2,300 years from now, only two people would be left.[6] Compared to human history so far, which extends back hundreds of thousands of years, 2,300 years is no time at all.

Given the runaway logic of exponential growth or decline, it may seem astonishing that we're still around after so many millennia. How could we have stayed balanced on the knife's edge for such a long time? It seems that either we should have gone extinct long ago,

3 Today, the odds of an American woman dying under the age of 44 are only about 3%, so intersexuality (which often implies diminished fertility or sterility) is at least as likely, and will thus be as large a contributor to raising replacement TFR above two. Office of the Chief Actuary, Social Security Administration, "Period Life Table, 2019, as Used in the 2022 Trustees Report," 2022.

4 United Nations, Department of Economic and Social Affairs, Population Division, "World Population Prospects 2022, Online Edition," 2022.

5 Ehrlich and Ehrlich, *The Population Bomb*, 1968.

6 People do of course live longer than a single "generation," so at least initially, the drop wouldn't be quite so quick.

or our numbers should have exploded until we suffered a die-off from overpopulation, at which point, presumably, the cycle would repeat.

It's the second. This is, in fact, how life works in general. Historically, human population has been subject to the same dynamics as any other animal on Earth: We've mated and produced offspring, or tried to, at a healthy clip—well above replacement, for otherwise we'd continually teeter on the brink of extinction. Our reproductive powers are not as impressive as those of some species (a male seahorse releases up to 1,000 young), but we're certainly capable of explosive growth—much more so than our primate cousins, the chimpanzees and bonobos, for whom nursing and infancy are more protracted due to a lack of alloparental help (see Chapter 4).

The country with the highest current fertility rate, Niger, has a TFR of nearly 7. That works out to a population doubling time of 17 years. Unchecked, such high fertility would mean rapid exponential growth, and a planet stacked neck deep with human bodies—literally—in a couple of dozen generations. In the past, that hasn't happened for the same reasons the planet isn't stacked neck deep with any other animal: malnutrition and starvation, disease, violence, and predation.

In 1798, the English Reverend Thomas Robert Malthus (1766–1834) published just this observation in his famous *Essay on the Principle of*

Michael Wolgemut, *Dance of Death*, leaf from *The Nuremberg Chronicle*, 1493.

Population, noting how fundamental a force such miseries have been in shaping our numbers over time:

Thomas Robert Malthus, 1834.

Population, when unchecked, increases in a geometrical ratio. Subsistence increases only in an arithmetical ratio.[7] A slight acquaintance with numbers will shew the immensity of the first power in comparison of the second.

    By that law of our nature which makes food necessary to the life of man, the effects of these two unequal powers must be kept equal.

    This implies a strong and constantly operating check on population from the difficulty of subsistence. This difficulty must fall somewhere and must necessarily be severely felt by a large portion of mankind.[8]

Put this way, it's a bleak but basic observation; yet it came as a shock to many of his readers. Why did it take until 1798 for someone to notice this?

It turns out that others were, in fact, making the same observation around the same time, seemingly independently. Five years earlier, unbeknownst to Malthus, Chinese scholar Hong Liangji (洪亮吉) had written the essays "Reign of Peace" and "Livelihood," sounding a similar alarm about overpopulation:

Some may ask: Do Heaven and Earth have remedies? The answer is that their remedies are in the form of flood, drought, sicknesses, and epidemics. But those unfortunate people who die from natural calamities do not amount to more than 10 or 20 percent of the population.

    Some may ask: Does the government have remedies? The answer is that its methods are to exhort the people to develop new land, to practice more intensive farming, to transfer people from congested areas to virgin soils, to reduce the fiscal burden, to prohibit extravagant living and the consumption of luxuries, to check the growth of land-lordism, and to open all public granaries for relief when natural calamities strike [...]. In short, during a long reign of peace Heaven and Earth

7 In modern language, we would say that population grows exponentially, while the food supply only increases linearly. Malthus's arguments for linear growth in the food supply are less than airtight, but his conclusion would follow more directly simply by noting that the Earth's food production capacity is finite. An exponential will exceed any finite threshold, and more quickly than you'd think.

8 Malthus, *An Essay on the Principle of Population*, 1798.

could not but propagate the human race, yet their resources that can be used to the support of mankind are limited. **During a long reign of peace the government could not prevent the people from multiplying themselves, yet its remedies are few.**[9]

The timing wasn't coincidental. Consider the preconditions for a Hong Liangji or Thomas Malthus to make and pass on the observations they did on exponential population growth and the role of starvation in limiting it:

1   Literacy.

2   The leisure to ponder and write treatises, and an intelligentsia to read them.

3   Enough knowledge of math to understand exponential growth and its "immensity" in comparison to any finite limit.

9   Ho, *Studies on the Population of China, 1368–1953,* 271–72, 1959.

4   Observation of exponential population growth within their own lifetimes.

5   Observation of starvation at work to limit the population.

Before looking more closely into why scholars on opposite sides of the world might have ticked all five boxes for the first time at the close of the 18th century, let's consider the situation today. Despite persistent social inequities, a majority of 21st century Americans meet the first four conditions—including many who work multiple jobs and didn't go to college. Literacy and numeracy are widespread, most of us have enough leisure to spend hours daily watching TV or scrolling through social media, and we've seen extraordinary rises in population within our lifetimes. Almost no Americans today tick the fifth box, though, since starvation and child mortality are no longer significant forces keeping the US population in check. It's telling that poverty in much of the modern world correlates with obesity rather than skinniness.

Until very recently, conditions could not have been more different. The website *Our World in Data* is a great resource for demographic data and analysis, and offers a startling historical perspective on extreme poverty.

18.2 World distribution of population by income from 1820 to 2018 % by year

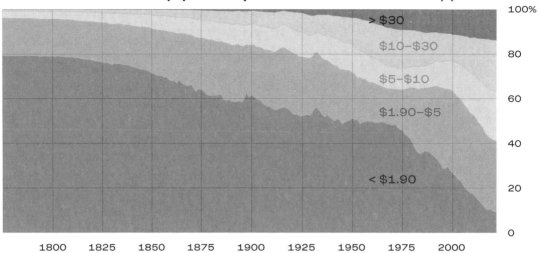

18.3 Total world population by income from 1820 to 2018
Population (billions) by year

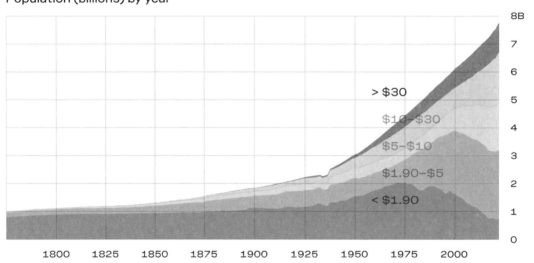

What counts as "extreme poverty" is a subject of intense debate (like the terms "city" and "countryside," it has no objective definition), but the scale of this worldwide transition over the past 200 years is breathtaking, no matter where the line is drawn. If you live in extreme poverty, that means, in practice, your time and energy throughout the day are spent in a struggle to get enough calories to survive and reproduce.

There are still people in the world living under such conditions, but not only are they a minority; fewer people, in absolute numbers, live in extreme poverty than in 1820, when our population was *one eighth* of its size today. Back in 1820—and at every time up until then, to the best of our knowledge—the overwhelming majority of human beings lived in extreme poverty.

All of which is to say: Thomas Malthus and Hong Liangji were privileged members of tiny elites in their respective countries with the leisure and education to do the kind of scholarship that got them Wikipedia entries a couple of centuries later. At the same time, neither they nor their (also privileged) readers had to venture far from the front gates of their estates to encounter the other 99%—a population that had begun to grow explosively, yet was still visibly constrained by starvation and other "positive checks," as Malthus calls them:

"The Plowman"
from Hans Holbein's
*Simolachri,
Historie, e Figure
de la Morte*, 1549.

The positive check to population, by which I mean the check that represses an increase which is already begun, is confined chiefly, though not perhaps solely, to the lowest orders of society.

[...] I believe it has been very generally remarked by those who have attended to bills of mortality that of the number of children who die annually, much too great a proportion belongs to those who may be supposed unable to give their offspring proper food and attention, exposed as they are occasionally to severe distress and confined, perhaps, to unwholesome habitations and hard labour. [...] [It] seems difficult to suppose that a labourer's wife who has six children, and who is sometimes in absolute want of bread, should be able always to give them the food and attention necessary to support life. The sons and daughters of peasants will not be found such rosy cherubs in real life as they are described to be in romances. It cannot fail to be remarked by those who live much in the country that the sons of labourers are very apt to be stunted in their growth, and are a long while arriving at maturity. Boys that you would guess to be fourteen or fifteen are, upon inquiry, frequently found to be eighteen or nineteen. And the lads who drive plough, which must certainly be a healthy exercise, are very rarely seen with any appearance of calves to their legs: a circumstance which can only be attributed to a want either

10 Malthus, *An Essay on the Principle of Population*, 1798.

of proper or of sufficient nourishment.[10]

"The Child" from Holbein, 1549.

Such conditions date back a long way. With malnutrition and disease keeping the death rate up—especially among children, who are the most vulnerable—being an average parent in virtually any premodern agricultural society would have been very different from parenthood in the US today. It would have been a parade of loss and grief; perhaps also, out of necessity, a time of less emotional investment in the lives of individual children. That's why, in many traditional cultures, babies aren't even named until they make it to a certain age.[11] It's remarkable that we can now assume that every child will grow to adulthood, and that it's such an unexpected shock when that doesn't happen. This is a consequence of recent medical and social technologies having disarmed Malthus's "positive checks."

By "medical technologies," I don't so much mean MRIs and bone marrow transplants, but the basics, like safer childbirth, hygiene, antibiotics, and vaccines. By "social technologies," I mean the laws, norms, and institutions that greatly reduce the murder rate, make honor killings unacceptable, provide a basic level of universal food, clothing, and shelter, and in other ways prevent many of the deaths that would have happened in an earlier era.

To be sure, none of these benefits are fully universal, let alone fairly distributed. Black infants in America, for instance, are more than twice as likely to die before their first birthday as white infants.[12] However, none of these discrepancies even approaches normal conditions in Malthus's day, when childhood mortality was magnitudes higher for everyone, nobles and peasants alike.

Still, by the 18th century, positive checks on population had started to lift, and the ensuing population explosion became suddenly obvious. The same was happening in Qing Dynasty China; per Hong Liangji,

Our society has been stable for more than a hundred years. In terms of the number of households, it is five times more than thirty years ago, ten times more than six decades ago and twenty times more than a hundred years ago [...]. Farms and houses are always scarce, and they are not enough for the excessive population growth [...]. Floods, droughts, and plagues are the means Heaven uses to mitigate the tension.[13]

11 McCormick, "Infant Mortality and Child-Naming: A Genealogical Exploration of American Trends," 2010.

12 K. F. Foundation, "Infant Mortality Rate by Race/Ethnicity (2019)," 2022.

13 Hu, "A Micro-Demographic Analysis of Human Fertility from Chinese Genealogies, 1368–1911," 2020.

To put this population growth in context, we'll need to look at long-term historical data. What follows is necessarily simplified, and the numbers involve guesswork as we venture deep into the past, but the outlines of the story are clear and uncontested.

Beginning with a zoomed-out view of the world's total population since the dawn of agriculture, we see something that barely looks like a graph at all. It's more like a flat line indistinguishable from zero, followed by a near-vertical spike at the very end. Entrepreneurs like to fantasize about "hockey stick" plots showing money or customers growing slowly, then exploding upward; this is the mother of all hockey sticks.

18.4 World population from 10,000 BCE to 2100 CE (projected)
Population (billions) by year

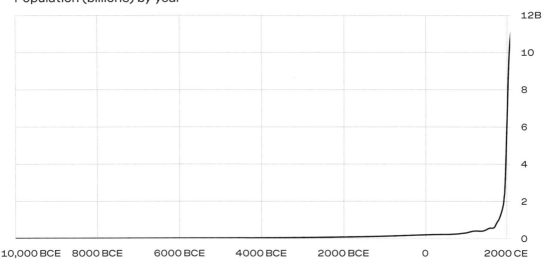

18.5.0 World population from 10,000 BCE to 2100 CE (projected)
Population by year

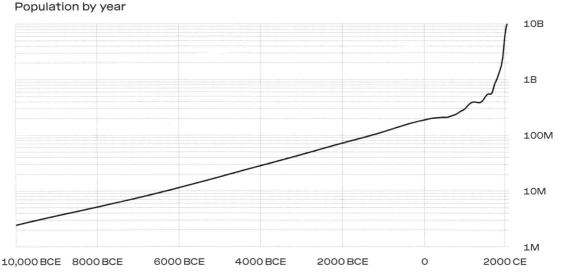

Making sense of it requires a logarithmic population axis. Seen this way, an exponential increase over time looks like a straight line, where the slope of the line measures the growth rate.

Even on a logarithmic scale, there's a leap upward near the end of the timeline, but now we can see that what looked like a flat line over the 10,000+ years during which increasing numbers of humans began to practice traditional agriculture was already characterized by steady exponential growth. Despite being invisible on a linear scale because the population was so much smaller than today's, during those 10,000 years, our numbers grew about 70-fold.

"Adam Tills the Soil" from Holbein, 1549.

Was traditional agriculture in itself a significant positive-check-eliminating technology? This turns out to be a tricky question. Clearly agriculture supplied enough calories for the population to grow 70 times larger than it had been under the hunting and gathering regime, but as Malthus points out, driving the plough by hand and eating the produce from your traditional family farm won't put a lot of meat on your calves. This is true even without accounting for the levies imposed on peasants by the patriarchal warlords, headmen, clergy, or nobility that tend to parasitize[14] agricultural societies.

A convincing case has been made that the hunter-gatherer lifestyle was healthier— at least, for the survivors—than subsistence farming.[15] The diets and activities of most hunter-gatherers were varied, they had plenty of time for art and leisure, and their social structures tended to be quite egalitarian.

On the other hand, while our hunter-gatherer ancestors might have been physically impressive in adulthood, they suffered high infant and childhood mortality. Moreover, high mortality (by any modern standard) continued into adulthood due to violence, accidents, infections, and the dangers of childbirth. Less depressingly, prolonged breastfeeding, common among hunter-gatherers, suppressed women's fertility; we'll get to the birth control side of the population equation in the next chapter. My point here, though, is that death was a constant stalker. Even strong, healthy adults walked a tightrope of positive checks, and could die suddenly of myriad causes. We know this, in part, because that same mortal precarity still holds among the few remaining traditional hunter-gatherer societies today.[16]

[14] Or organize, depending on your politics.

[15] Sahlins, "The Original Affluent Society," 1972; Berbesque et al., "Hunter-Gatherers Have Less Famine than Agriculturalists," 2014.

[16] Hill, Hurtado, and Walker, "High Adult Mortality Among Hiwi Hunter-Gatherers: Implications for Human Evolution," 2007.

Mothers of the San-speaking people, Namibia.

A Sámi family in Finland, 1936.

Farming got started after the last Ice Age ended, the glaciers retreated, and Earth's climate entered a long, stable, mild period. Newly exposed fertile soils could support subsistence agriculture, enabling higher population density. In such environments, farming began to supplant hunting and gathering. This may have been less a matter of the agriculturalists out-reproducing the hunter-gatherers than of slowly crowding them out as more and more land fell under cultivation.[17] Hence many remaining hunter-gatherers today, like the Khoesān people in southern Africa, have been displaced over time into the least productive land, too marginal to be worth farming.

A 70-fold population increase may seem impressive—and it is—but keep in mind how slowly it happened. Assuming, as we did earlier,

17 Bettinger, "Prehistoric Hunter-Gatherer Population Growth Rates Rival Those of Agriculturalists," 2016.

18 Historical generation
times would likely have
been shorter, which given
a known doubling time,
would drive our estimate of
each generation's fertility
lower still.

30 years per generation, this amounts to an "effective" fertility rate
of only 2.025 children per potential mother surviving into adulthood—barely above two—for a doubling time of about 1,600 years.[18]
Traditional farming, in other words, provides enough calories for the
population to grow, but just barely. Until very recently, malnutrition
and starvation were at least as common among farmers as among
hunter-gatherers; it was just that productive land could support many
more farmers on a per-area basis, and so, like any other species
stumbling upon a new niche, we eventually filled it.

The niche may have been large, but it was also miserable. To
get a sense of how grim traditional subsistence farming is, and how
recently most of us were still stuck in its Malthusian grip, we need
only look at economic data in countries where reliable record keeping
goes back a few centuries. For instance, Irish economist Morgan
Kelly and economic historian Cormac Ó Gráda have made a detailed
study of the positive check under traditional farming in England.
In a 2014 paper, they wrote:

19 Kelly and Ó Gráda,
"Living Standards and
Mortality Since the Middle
Ages," 2014.

> **[W]hile average living standards in England were high by
> contemporary standards, a substantial fraction of the
> population nonetheless lived in deep poverty. Gregory King,
> in 1688, estimated that one-fifth of England's population
> had annual incomes of £2, placing them at the edge of biolog-
> ical survival.[19]**

Seen this way, farming looks less like a triumphal evolutionary step in
which humans achieve mastery over nature, and more like a virus or
curse wherein a malevolent suite of specially adapted plant and animal
species enslave humanity, cultivating *us* in concentrated labor camps.
The very concept of labor can be understood as a product of this traumatic event. The Book of Genesis seems to echo the trauma in the story
of Adam and Eve's expulsion from the garden of plenty:

20 Gen 3:17–19 (New
Living Translation).

> **I have placed a curse on the ground. All your life you will
> struggle to scratch a living from it. It will grow thorns
> and thistles for you, though you will eat of its grains. All your
> life you will sweat to produce food, until your dying day.[20]**

In the Hindu tradition, the ancient Ramayana of Valmiki is even
more explicit:

> **In the Golden Age, agriculture was abomination. In the
> Silver Age, impiety appeared in the form of the agriculture.
> In the Golden Age, people lived on fruits and roots that**

21 Mehta, "Did Agriculture Reduce Human Lifespan?," 2001.

were obtained without any labor. For the existence of sin in the form of cultivation, the lifespan of people became shortened.[21]

So, agricultural life ground on miserably. With some significant wobbles up and down due mainly to the Black Death, population growth remained in low gear up until about a century before Malthus and Hong Liangji wrote their essays, with the effective fertility rate averaging only 2.06 between 600 CE and 1700 CE.

18.5.1 **World population from 600 to 2100 CE, highlighting three epochs of exponential growth** Population by year

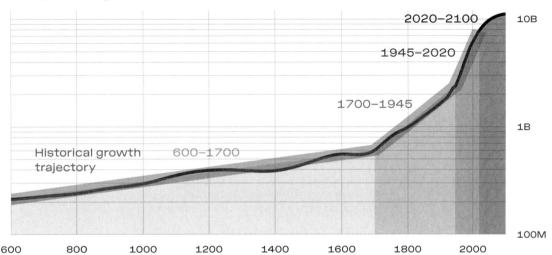

Let's pause to take stock of the Black Death, or Bubonic Plague. It was the deadliest pandemic in recorded history, making COVID look insignificant by comparison. The *Yersinia pestis* bacterium, treatable today with antibiotics, may have killed up to 200 million people in Europe, Asia, and North Africa in epidemic waves from the Middle Ages up to the 17th century (though its deep history appears to go much farther back into antiquity). It was a major positive check, resulting in periods of global population *decline* even as farming technologies slowly improved.

Tellingly, the unevenness of harvests was a key factor in plague mortality. Hunger interacted with disease in ways that are less obvious to us nowadays than they would have been back then. Per Kelly and Ó Gráda:

[I]t is only with improved public health in the 20th century that people began literally to starve to death: before this

The Great Plague
of Marseille in 1720
as depicted by
Michel Serre in 1721.

22 Kelly and Ó Gráda,
"Living Standards and
Mortality Since the Middle
Ages," 2014.

most famine victims succumbed to epidemic disease. That epidemics followed poor harvests was not simply because of hunger [... but due to] the interaction between malnutrition and vagrancy. As hungry people took to the roads in search of work or charity, the combination of malnutrition, poor hygiene, exposure to the elements, and psychological stress turned them into both victims and vectors of contagious disease.[22]

Black Death notwithstanding, between 600 CE and 1700 CE, the worldwide population doubling time works out to about 700 years. Although this growth rate is formidable when compounded over a few centuries, it still only amounts to a 5% increase over an average 50 year period. So, by fits and starts, in a slow increase unnoticed by contemporary observers, the world population crept up to about 600 million by the year 1700.

To be clear, this is a worldwide average. At certain times and places over those centuries some populations thrived for a time and grew far more quickly. On the other hand, if the Black Death

*The Triumph of
Death* by Pieter Bruegel
the Elder, 1562.

had just decimated the country and one couldn't zoom out to see the big picture, it would hardly have been obvious on the ground that life was slowly winning out over death. An overpopulation argument like Malthus's would have seemed like a mathematical abstraction, far removed from reality. The next war, famine, or plague was always just around the corner, and despite endless childbirth, having more than two children survive to have children of their own would have counted as a blessing.

Patrick Bell's reaping machine, 1851.

Around the year 1700, though, something remarkable happens. The exponential slope becomes *much* steeper, with the effective fertility rate jumping to 2.36, for a doubling time of only 124 years. With plague-scale pandemics on pause (due in no small part to better harvests), the increase in population would have been noticeable for the first time over a single human lifespan. Hence the near-simultaneity of the observations by Hong Liangji and Thomas Malthus about a hundred years later—when the new trend had been firmly established—both seems inevitable, and could not have happened earlier. Suddenly, evidence of a population explosion was all around. Multiplying like rabbits, now *we* were the plague!

Why 1700? The big changes taking place in Europe around then were the Scientific and Industrial Revolutions.[23] They gave rise to a cascade of new technologies that made farming more productive, as well as improving medical care and social systems for resource redistribution and risk pooling. Chinese farming technologies had undergone their own period of rapid development as well, and were starting to reap the benefits of energy-intensive

23 It has been argued (e.g. by Steven Shapin, in his influential book *The Scientific Revolution*, 1996.) that these weren't properly "revolutions," but gradual accumulations of evolutionary changes upon which we only impose a "revolutionary" narrative in later historical accounts. There's some truth to this. On the other hand, the sharp turn in the population curve suggests that the term "revolution" isn't mere hyperbole for what happened around 1700.

24 Although the Chinese and European cultures may have seemed worlds apart, remember that they shared a single continent, and were webbed together by the silk routes, where both goods and ideas flowed continually back and forth. The importance of New World crops in China also speaks to the way the technological and agricultural histories of Europe and China were closely coupled.

New World crops, especially corn.**24** Many more people could be fed—and they were. In the century leading up to Hong Liangji's essay, the Chinese population had tripled, from about 100 million to about 300 million. And that was just the beginning.

In 1945, population growth leaps again, stepping into overdrive. This is the baby boom. Boomers are often thought of as an American post-World War II phenomenon; indeed, the war did delay a cohort of pregnancies that otherwise would have been conceived while the men were at the front, thus creating a bulge in the postwar birthrate in the US and many other countries. However, the population curve reveals this demographic turn to be a sustained worldwide transition in effective fertility lasting well over a generation—more of an ongoing roar than a boom.

What happened? As with the Scientific and Industrial Revolutions, developments in public health and agriculture drove the growth.

During the Second World War, antibiotics started to be mass-produced, eliminating a great deal of death from bacterial infection. That had important consequences for injuries on the battlefield, of course, but it also meant that soldiers contracting gonorrhea, chlamydia, or that old Victorian bogeyman, syphilis, could now easily be treated. Rather than vainly trying to impose moral strictures on sex, publicity campaigns began to encourage anyone with symptoms to visit a doctor. For once, ads promising miracle cures delivered.

In civilian life, everyday infections became treatable too. Many of us alive today have caught bugs that would have killed us in an earlier era, either in childhood or in adulthood. Bacteria, from plague-causing *Yersinia pestis* to *E. coli* in contaminated food to *Staphylococcus* from cuts, were an important positive check on human population throughout our entire history—until antibiotics. Indoor plumbing and improved sanitation also prevented disease that would otherwise have killed untold numbers of people, especially in childhood.

Babies born in a maternity hospital in Paris on January 1, 1946.

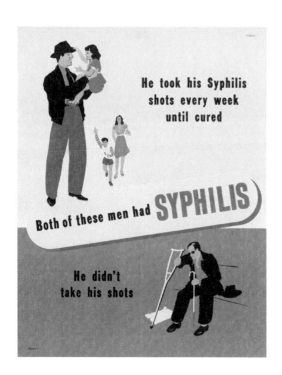

He took his Syphilis shots every week until cured

Both of these men had SYPHILIS

He didn't take his shots

By 1943, doctors had learned to use penicillin to treat syphilis. This World War II era poster promotes its benefits.

25 A slogan chemical giant DuPont adopted in 1935, then quietly dropped in 1982.

26 Blaser and Falkow, "What Are the Consequences of the Disappearing Human Microbiota?," 2009; Rook, "Hygiene and Other Early Childhood Influences on the Subsequent Function of the Immune System," 2011; Vandegrift et al., "Cleanliness in Context: Reconciling Hygiene with a Modern Microbial Perspective," 2017.

Arable land use under different productivity scenarios, from LtG, 50, 1972.

Around the same time, farming techniques further revolutionized, not just due to increasingly powerful fuel-powered tractors and farm equipment, but through widespread adoption of oil-derived chemical fertilizers and new generations of hyper-efficient, scientifically engineered crops. The now-boutique practices we file nostalgically under "organic" farming—cultivation of heirloom varieties, avoidance of chemical fertilizers and pesticides—used to be *all* farming, and it was a lot less efficient. "Better living through chemistry"[25] may sound like a dubious motto to our ears, but synthetic chemicals and genetically modified crops have certainly allowed more of us to live—*many* more.

The pharmaceutical and agricultural developments of the 20th century have also brought us a bevy of sustainability problems, though. Factory farming depletes the soil, pollutes freshwater, destroys biodiversity, poisons pollinating insects, and relies heavily on nonrenewable, climate-destroying fossil fuels. We're only beginning to understand subtler, more insidious downsides as well. For instance, routine use of antibiotics has led to widespread antibiotic resistance, while modern hygienic practices may be responsible for weakening our immune systems and devastating our microbial biome.[26]

Figure 10 ARABLE LAND

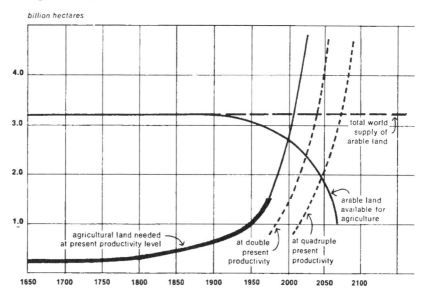

billion hectares

total world supply of arable land

arable land available for agriculture

agricultural land needed at present productivity level

at double present productivity

at quadruple present productivity

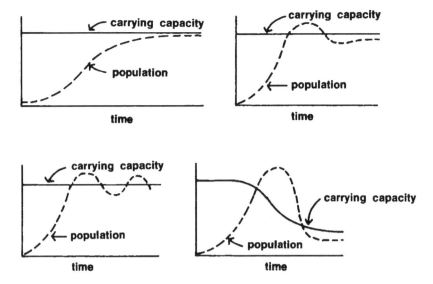

27 Meadows et al., *The
Limits to Growth: A Report
for the Club of Rome's
Project on the Predicament
of Mankind*, 1972.

At the root of every other ecological problem of our own making, super-exponential human population growth is in itself unsus-
tainable on a finite planet—obviously. The baby boom led to an
urgent revival of this Malthusian anxiety, most famously in a 1972
report, *The Limits to Growth* (LtG), commissioned by an interdisciplinary group of intellectuals styling themselves the "Club of
Rome."**27** The LtG modeling team, led by pioneering environmental scientist Donella Meadows (1941–2001), used the fancy, newly
invented technique of computer simulation to try to quantify
Malthus's intuitions under a range of hypothetical scenarios, taking
into account not only population growth and arable land area, but

18.6 Glaciation cycles over the past 800,000 years
Atmospheric carbon dioxide (ppmv) by thousands of years before present

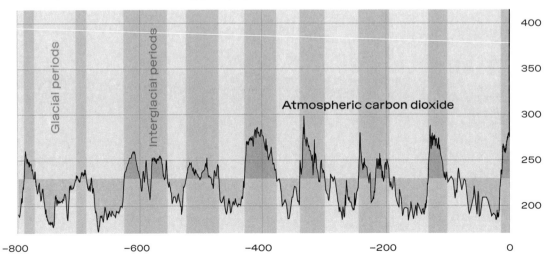

Model of carbon dioxide concentration in the atmosphere based on measurements at Mauna Loa, Hawaii. From LtG, 72, 1972.

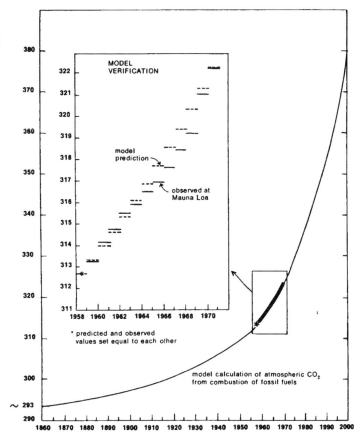

MODEL VERIFICATION

model prediction

observed at Mauna Loa

* predicted and observed values set equal to each other

model calculation of atmospheric CO_2 from combustion of fossil fuels

28 The most cogent critiques were leveled at the report's predictions of imminent resource depletion based on known reserves (e.g. of chromium); subsequent resource exploration based on the market demand increased reserve estimates a good deal, making predictions that we'd run out of chromium look alarmist. This isn't a compelling argument for dismissing the report or the model, though, given that its whole point was to allow researchers to explore the implications of different assumptions about reserves and technology improvements.

29 These time lags can be thought of as a kind of inertia or momentum in many key variables, such as pollution and population.

30 Meadows et al., 73.

growth in *per capita* industrial output, pollution, non-renewable resource depletion, and a number of other interrelated variables.

Although in the ensuing half century the model has been heavily critiqued—even ridiculed—its basic premises and methods are reasonable.**28** It makes the key observation, too, that straining Earth's carrying capacity degrades the ecosystem, which in turn decreases carrying capacity; especially when this effect is combined with rapid population overshoot, "business as usual" social and economic policies, and the inevitable time lag in the dynamics of a system with feedback loops,**29** the prognosis looks grim: a return to immiseration, and die-off on a catastrophic scale. A great reset.

Remarkably—remember, this is 1972—*The Limits to Growth* specifically calls out global warming as a cause for concern, noting that based on 14 years of carbon dioxide measurements at the observatory on Mauna Loa, CO_2 concentrations would reach 380 parts per million by the year 2000, "an increase of nearly 30 percent of the probable value in 1860." The authors add that a transition to nuclear power could stop CO_2 emissions, hopefully "before it has had any measurable ecological or climatological effect."**30**

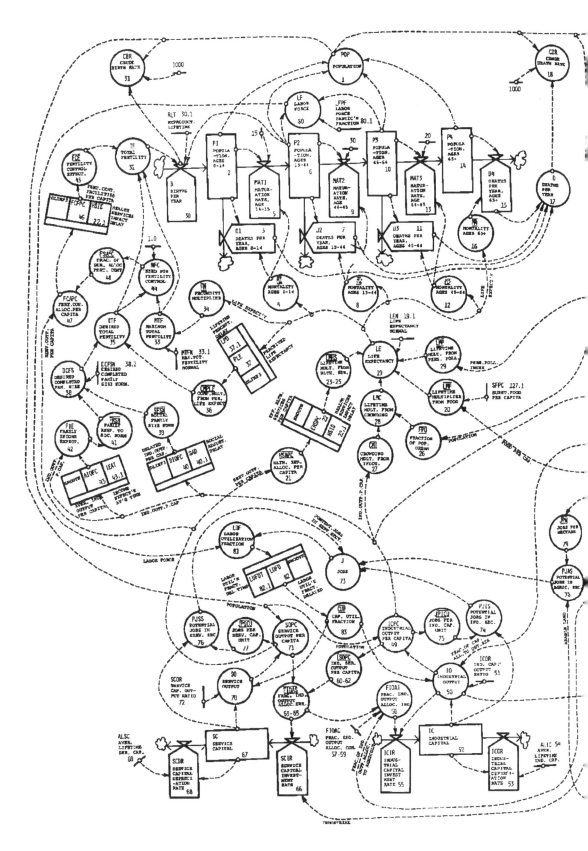

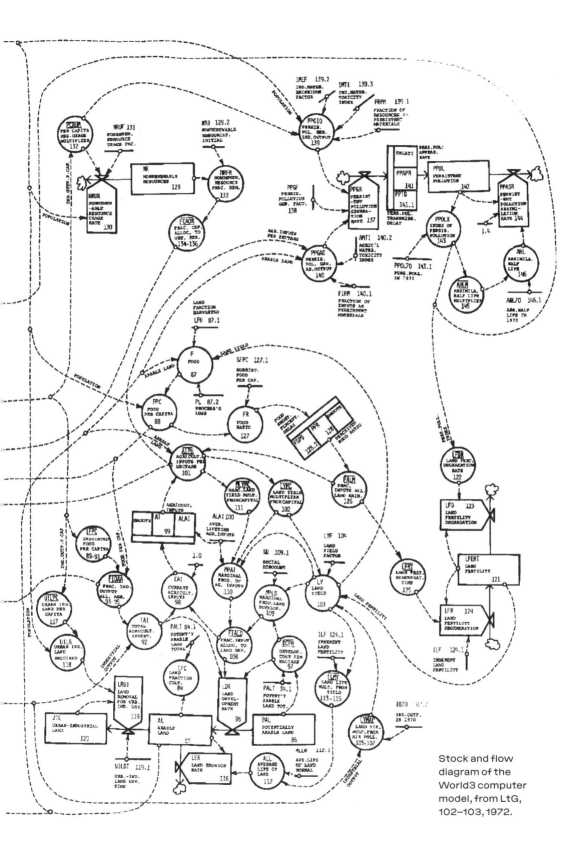

Stock and flow diagram of the World3 computer model, from LtG, 102–103, 1972.

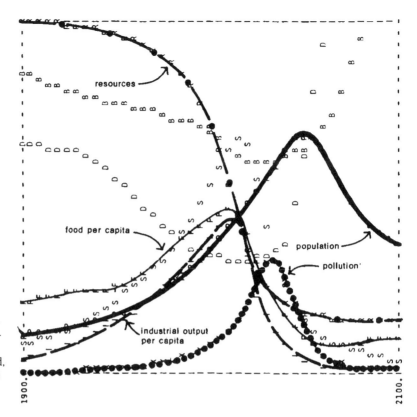

"The 'standard' world model assumes no major changes in the physical, economic, or social relationships that have historically governed the development of the world system. [...] Population growth is finally halted by a rise in the death rate due to decrease in food and medical services." LtG, 124, 1972.

31 Also unfortunately, nuclear power has become unpopular due to high-profile accidents (Three Mile Island, Chernobyl, and Fukushima) and an association with Cold War nuclear anxieties, despite being an excellent complement to solar energy. The environmental impacts, health risks, and fatalities associated with nuclear power are all orders of magnitude lower than those of the fossil fuel plants needed to meet demand following the widespread closures of nuclear reactors. Shellenberger, "Testimony Before the United States Senate Committee on Energy and Natural Resources," 2021.

32 Tans and Keeling, "Carbon Cycle Greenhouse Gases, Trends in CO2," 2022.

33 Bardi, "Cassandra's Curse: How 'The Limits to Growth' Was Demonized," 2008.

34 Piccioni, "Forty Years Later. The Reception of the Limits to Growth in Italy, 1971–1974," 2012.

Unfortunately, that ship has sailed.**31** We first reached 380 parts per million in 2004, and today, we're seeing arable land area shrink as global warming turns once-fertile equatorial land into desert—which is indeed decreasing the Earth's carrying capacity, starting in those (often already poor) regions.

As of this writing, in 2022, CO_2 levels have shot up to 420 parts per million, a value far higher than it has reached in millions of years, and over a great many glacial cycles. It will continue to rise for at least as long as we remain dependent on fossil fuels, or until our civilization crashes—potentially due to a climate gone haywire.**32** But in the 1970s, public awareness of climate change still lay far in the future.

Stepping on the same rake Al Gore's climate activism would in the 2000s, *The Limits to Growth* first became a surprise bestseller, then sparked an immune response from an array of powerful interests, who mounted a largely successful campaign to deny, dispute, and discredit it.**33** The Vatican worried that limits to growth, like condoms, are incompatible with being fruitful and multiplying.**34** The business lobby pushed back because they saw LtG as an unwelcome prelude to regulation. Economists were outraged by the very *idea* that exponential growth can't continue

35 Turner, "A Comparison of The Limits to Growth with 30 Years of Reality," 2008; Hall and Day, "Revisiting the Limits to Growth After Peak Oil," 2009; Pasqualino et al., "Understanding Global Systems Today—A Calibration of the World3-03 Model Between 1995 and 2012," 2015; Herrington, "Update to Limits to Growth: Comparing the World3 Model with Empirical Data," 2021.

36 In Greek mythology, Cassandra was a Trojan priestess fated to utter true prophecies nobody would believe. Chicken Little refers to an old European morality tale about a foolish chicken whose false cries of "The sky is falling!" lead to unwarranted panic.

forever. The left was also not having it, believing LtG to promote eugenics, or to be an elitist scam to trick the proletariat into believing that a workers' paradise was unattainable. So, capitalism and Marxism, supposedly sworn enemies, found common ground: growth *must* continue, and "degrowth" is heresy.

The smear campaign worked. Almost everyone for whom *The Limits to Growth* still rings a bell today remembers it vaguely as a Chicken Little scare, debunked long ago. And yet, LtG's model did a surprisingly solid job of tracking the actual numbers over the following decades.[35] Perhaps it resembled Cassandra more than Chicken Little.[36]

Luckily for our entire planet, we aren't seeing yet another upward kink in the exponential growth rate of the human population. Instead, in the most dramatic transition yet, population growth is now screeching to a halt, and soon we'll see it start to fall—just as *The Limits to Growth* predicted. This turn away from population growth marks a profound, historic shift for humanity, and we're right on the cusp of it.

Also luckily, the impending population decline hasn't been the acute die-off due to resource scarcity that the authors of LtG warned us to expect in their original "business as usual" scenario; we've simply been opting to have fewer children. Yay!

18.7 **Total fertility rate** Live births per woman by year

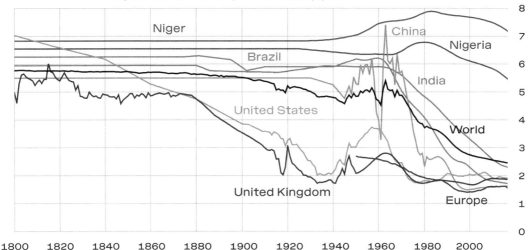

But before we breathe a sigh of relief: the LtG model *did* factor in declining fertility; the decline has just happened quickly enough, and food production has improved quickly enough, to avoid a return of the positive check—so far.

We're by no means out of the woods, though. None of the LtG scenarios predicted increased mortality before 2020. The authors have always been quick to point out that their model isn't meant to forecast precise dates or numbers, which is well nigh impossible for a complex nonlinear system like our planet's ecology/demography/political economy. Rather, they aimed to sketch out, in broad strokes, how the major variables are likely to interact, and what the resulting overall trajectories might look like qualitatively. Still, let's play along.

Scenario[37]	Description	Why growth stops
BAU (Business As Usual)	No assumptions added to historic averages	Collapse due to natural resource depletion
BAU2	Double the natural resources of BAU	Collapse due to pollution (e.g. climate change)
CT (Comprehensive Technology)	BAU2 + exceptionally high technological development and adoption	Rising costs eventually lead to declining industrial output and some increased mortality
SW (Stabilized World)	CT + changes in societal values and priorities	Population is stable by the mid-21st century, with human welfare remaining high

[37] Adapted from Herrington, "Update to Limits to Growth: Comparing the World3 Model with Empirical Data," 2021 and Meadows, Randers, and Meadows, *The Limits to Growth: The 30-Year Update*, 2004, though Herrington uses the LtG authors' scenario 9 for SW, while I use scenario 10.

The original BAU ("Business As Usual") scenario was based purely on historical data available in 1972, and assumed "no major change" in "physical, economic, or social relationships." It predicted a collapse starting around 2020 due to natural resource depletion. Remember all that talk about Peak Oil back in the early 2000s? Everything about modern society depends on oil. Scarcity was the cliff we seemed to be headed over.

Then, fracking technologies saved the day,[38] opening up vast and previously inaccessible oil and gas reserves in shale deposits—starting in the US. So we won't be running out of gas anytime soon after all. An updated BAU2 scenario, which doubles the natural resource assumptions of BAU, became a better fit.

[38] DeCarolis and LaRose, "Annual Energy Outlook 2023 with Projections to 2050," 2023.

The bad news: in BAU2, collapse still comes, but due to pollution rather than resource depletion. The research community is in broad agreement on this point: just because we could in principle extract vast reserves of additional shale oil doesn't mean we can afford to burn it. We have to leave that carbon in the ground. Moreover, if we want to return to anything like our historic levels of atmospheric CO_2, we'll have to use enormous amounts of energy in the future to put the carbon we've already released into the atmosphere *back* into the ground—and, of course, the energy to do so will have to come from some other source.

The CT ("Comprehensive Technology") scenario is techno-optimistic, assuming BAU2 resources along with rapid development and adoption of new, clean, efficient technologies across the board. CT delays most impacts and greatly softens our landing, avoiding a general collapse in our average living standard. By contrast, BAU and BAU2 both foretell a worldwide return to a 30 year average life expectancy this century, due to mortality rates rising back up to levels we haven't seen since 1900.

18.8 **World life expectancy from 1900 to 2100, by LtG scenario**
Life expectancy by year

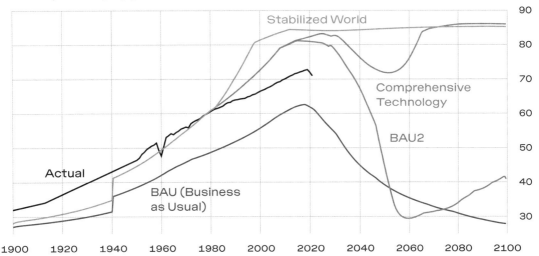

We appear to be somewhere in BAU2 or CT territory, so things could be worse... though they could also have been better, in that we're gambling our future on further technological rabbits popping out of hats just in time.

The best of all worlds, SW ("Stabilized World"), reaches and sustains a high standard of living for all, but it would have required a much sharper reduction in population growth, targeting a sustained 6 billion people, starting back in 1982. We blew right past that target; it looks like our numbers have well and truly overshot.

The social changes needed to achieve a stabilized population have often been equated with China's "one child" policy, which was indeed inspired by the Malthusian panic of the 1970s (not least *The Limits to Growth*) and went into effect in 1980. Birth rates had already been falling in China just as they had been elsewhere, due to economic development. Numerous exceptions to "one child" were also granted beginning in the 1980s. While the policy may not have made any great difference to long term population trends, it did bring human rights abuses, including forced contraception, abortion, and sterilization. It also contributed substantially to the vast number of "missing women" worldwide due to sex-selective abortion or infanticide, as under patriarchy it was deemed preferable for the "one child" to be a boy (see Chapter 12).

After many years of international criticism and internal debate, the "one child" policy was finally eased to allow for two children in 2015. All limits were removed in 2021. Today, China's fertility rate is nonetheless well below two, and still falling—a trajectory broadly similar to those of other countries making the transition out of poverty. The moral: we could have achieved a Stabilized World decades ago, not by instituting China's draconian "one child" policy globally, but by greatly accelerating the economic development of the world's poorer countries, as the next chapter will explore.

Further technological jackpots that avoid the pollution-induced crash of BAU2 are still possible, of course. As I'm making final revisions to this chapter, news is breaking that at Lawrence Livermore National Laboratory, scientists have used lasers to finally achieve nuclear fusion that releases more energy than it consumes. This is a major milestone. Cheap, large-scale fusion power would change everything, allowing us to stop burning fossil fuels and even power a massive carbon recapture effort. However, the news is full of disclaimers and caveats. Real fusion power plants still seem to be many decades away.[39] We know of no magic bullets that can get us out of our pickle quickly or painlessly.

The scenarios that haven't already been ruled out suggest that a hard time for humanity, our overshoot "correction," may lie just ahead. On the other hand, technology is still advancing, continuing to offer cleaner and more efficient ways for us to thrive. It's a high-stakes race between overshoot and innovation. Perhaps as soon as the late 2020s or 2030s, we'll have a clearer picture of which kind of scenario—hard landing or soft—we'll need to contend with. In this book's final chapters, we'll explore some of the social and technological developments that are likely to determine the outcome.

Despite the LtG authors' injunction not to take their modeled dates too seriously, it's interesting to see that after so many decades of declining mortality, we've witnessed worldwide death rates rising again from 2020 through 2022—right on schedule. But, you'll object, that's COVID-19! Pandemics just *happen*; their timing has nothing to do with limits to growth![40]

It's true that a pandemic can strike at any time. Before dismissing COVID as random bad luck irrelevant to the big picture, though, consider that, as with the Black Death, COVID mortality *isn't* random; it's strongly correlated with underlying health factors, both at the

39 Chang, "Scientists Achieve Nuclear Fusion Breakthrough With Blast of 192 Lasers," 2022.

40 The only other comparable dip marring the upward trend in worldwide life expectancy over the last two centuries occurred between 1958–1961, due to the 15–55 million people estimated to have died during China's Great Leap Forward. The World Health Organization estimates that COVID-19 has been responsible for 14.9 million excess deaths in 2020–21. WHO Technical Advisory Group for COVID-19 Mortality Assessment, "14.9 Million Excess Deaths Associated with the COVID-19 Pandemic in 2020 and 2021."

41 Timmons, "U.S. Poor Died at Much Higher Rate from COVID than Rich, Report Says," 2022; "A Poor People's Pandemic Report: Mapping the Intersections of Poverty, Race and COVID-19," 2022.

individual and at the community level. That's why people in poor counties in the US died of COVID at nearly twice the rate as those in rich counties,[41] and during the especially deadly Delta wave, at *five times* the rate.

Just as in the Middle Ages, we would not expect the *direct* causes of death during a widespread resurgence in mortality to be starvation, but rather, war, epidemic disease, and the general poor health that tends to accompany poverty. Moreover, even before COVID, the decline in mortality in the developed world had already been slowing, and even, as noted in the previous chapter, starting to increase again in the American countryside—a function not only of poverty in the traditional sense, but of disconnection and eroding social capital. Rising economic inequality is doubtless a factor as well, since it prevents available resources from reaching those who most need them, even as aggregate wealth rises.

At any rate, we'll soon find out whether COVID-19 is a blip or the start of a larger reversal in the long-running decline in mortality. I hope it's just a blip.

Like Lynn Margulis, that other pioneering theorist of planetary-scale thinking, Donella Meadows stirred up great controversy yet somehow still labored in relative obscurity throughout most of her career. She died young, in 2001. Dennis Meadows, Donella's partner and LtG co-author, carried on with the work. In 2022, he was interviewed for the 50th anniversary of the original report. In response to the usual "So what's ahead?" wrap-up question, he said,

42 Heinberg and Meadows, "Dennis Meadows on the 50th Anniversary of the Publication of The Limits to Growth," 2022.

Donella Meadows.

I'm an old activist. I'm 80 years old. […] I don't know what's coming. I look at those downward sloping curves […] and I honestly don't know what it's going to look like on the ground over the next 40 to 50 years. But my guess is that some people may come through this period not even being much aware of collapse, whereas others, of course, are already far into the decline of their personal situation, their culture, their community, and so forth.[42]

19   **Choice**

In the Middle Ages, humanity was resource-constrained. As ever, the ruling class had a lot more than its fair share, but redistributing their extra food among all of the hungry people still would have left everyone hungry—indeed, during famines, even the nobility tended to starve.

Today, aggregate wealth doesn't constrain human well-being, but uneven wealth distribution does. This much is widely understood—nobody would need to go hungry anymore, if only the resources could quickly get to where they are most needed. What's less widely understood, though, is the profound effect of uneven wealth distribution on birth rate, which is arguably even more important to human welfare today than hunger.

The negative correlation between wealth and fertility was obvious even in Malthus's time. He noticed that the aristocracy had fewer children than the poor, but whereas he framed the difference in moral terms,[1] in reality the effect is demographic and economic. As *Our World In Data* puts it when comparing national statistics,

> **In all countries we observed the pattern of the demographic transition, first to a decline of mortality that starts the population boom and then a decline of fertility which brings the population boom to an end. The population boom is a temporary event.**
>
> **In the past the size of the population was stagnant because of high mortality, now country after country is moving into a world in which the population is stagnant because of low fertility.[2]**

The US, in other words, is typical among rich countries. Indeed, when the UN runs population size simulations based on historical data for the more economically developed regions of the world, they conclude that as of now, population in these places has already peaked and will likely not increase further.[3] Nearly

[1]   This sentiment has been echoed by many moralizers before and since, e.g. in William Acton's characterization of the lower classes as lustful and lacking in self-control—see Chapter 9.

[2]   Roser et al., "World Population Growth," 2013.

[3]   We can take the "medium fertility" scenario as a reasonable best guess, though the most recent data seem more consistent with the even faster population decline of the "low fertility" curve.

[4]   Malthus, *An Essay on the Principle of Population*, 1798.

[5]   These would be supplanted by thick rubber sheaths in the 19th century, which, while cheaper, were... distancing.

[6]   Casanova, *History of My Life*, 1966–1971.

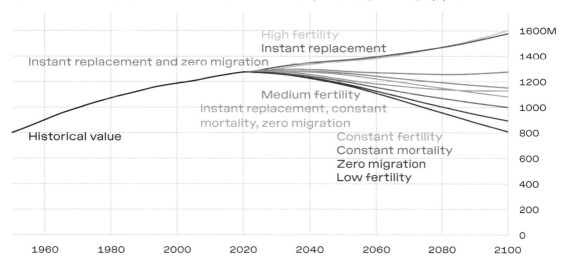

19.0 Total population of more economically developed regions with UN forecast variants from 2022 to 2100 Population (millions) by year

High fertility
Instant replacement

Instant replacement and zero migration

Medium fertility
Instant replacement, constant
mortality, zero migration

Historical value

Constant fertility
Constant mortality
Zero migration
Low fertility

1600M
1400
1200
1000
800
600
400
200
0

1960 1980 2000 2020 2040 2060 2080 2100

Giacomo Casanova, the famous Italian adventurer, entertaining sex workers by blowing up condoms to check for holes, 1872.

all remaining worldwide population increases will come from the less economically developed parts of the world, and the rate at which *their* fertility declines in turn will be a function of how quickly they develop economically.

But why is this happening? The availability of birth control in advanced economies is clearly part of the story. Malthus assumed that inextinguishable "passion between the sexes"[4] automatically led to serial pregnancies and an endless parade of offspring, which could only be stemmed through heavy-handed intervention by church or state—much as China eventually tried with the "one child" policy. At the time, he may not have been far off the mark: sexual impulses *are* powerful, patriarchy suppresses women's choices, and in 1798, birth control options left much to be desired. Reusable condoms did exist, typically made from chemically treated linen or animal gut.[5] They could be bought at chemist shops, barbershops, and theaters, but they weren't cheap. In his memoirs, the infamous libertine Giacomo Casanova (1725–1798) describes blowing up his condom before use to inspect for holes.[6] This was very much a gentleman's game. It would have been regarded as scandalous for a

7 Collier, *The Humble Little Condom: A History*, 120–21, 2007.

woman—either married or unmarried—to buy one, and for a typical sex worker, such a condom might have cost several months' pay.[7]

Condoms are instances of what Malthus called "preventive checks," which lead to fewer births, as opposed to "positive checks" that kill the young. While positive checks *decrease* when social and medical technologies improve, preventive checks *increase*. The Pill, which first became available in 1960, was without a doubt the single most important such technology. It put contraception in women's hands; it was discreet, safe, reversible, reliable, affordable, and non-invasive; and it didn't involve doing anything special during or immediately before sex. It was a dream come true. No prior method had even come close to fulfilling all of these desiderata.

A woman holding a package of birth control pills, New York, 1972.

Of course, condoms have also gotten a lot cheaper and better, and we now have a number of other good contraceptive options too. Abortion and elective sterilization (increasingly, vasectomy for men, as it's a far less invasive procedure than sterilization for women) have been important preventive checks.

Birth control technologies aren't the whole story, though. They have emerged alongside the suite of social innovations described in Chapter 9—changes in the workforce, economy, laws, and customs that make it possible (and attractive) for people to live fulfilling lives with few or no children.

Until recently, it's been extremely difficult for women to stay independent and single, or to divorce. Plenty of older female survey respondents describe being trapped in marriages they don't really want, due to some combination of social pressure, the obligations of motherhood, and economics (again, see Chapter 9). Being a single woman has gotten a lot easier, though, and that also has lowered birth rates.

Birth Control Review,
November 1923, in
*The Selected Papers
of Margaret Sanger.*

Then, there's the greater social acceptance of lesbian and gay couples, or the many other configurations in which love, sex, and companionship aren't necessarily geared toward producing kids. Of course same-sex couples *can* have kids, but it won't "just happen" due to a missed pill or a slipup in the bedroom. It's something they have to want, choose, and work for. Today, even for heterosexual couples, having children is increasingly seen as a deliberate choice, rather than an unexamined default.

For that matter, the same is true of being partnered at all. The sociologist Eric Klinenberg wrote a book about this phenomenon in 2013 whose title pretty much gives away the plot: *Going Solo: The Extraordinary Rise and Surprising Appeal of Living Alone.*

8 Klinenberg, *Going Solo: The Extraordinary Rise and Surprising Appeal of Living Alone*, 3–4, 2013.

[O]ur species has embarked on a remarkable social experiment. For the first time in human history, great numbers of people—at all ages, in all places, of every political persuasion—have begun settling down as singletons. [...] [T]oday, for the first time in centuries, the majority of all American adults are single. The typical American will spend more of his or her adult life unmarried than married, and for much of this time he or she will live alone.[8]

19.1 **"Are you married?" in the city vs. countryside** % by age

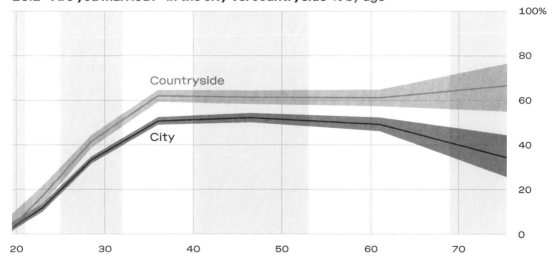

9 Like the graphs themselves, these figures are calculated by weighting the averaged responses from groups of survey participants to match the overall demographics of the United States (see the Appendix for details).

10 Klinenberg, 4–5.

11 U.S. Census Bureau, "Census Bureau Releases New Estimates on America's Families and Living Arrangements," 2022.

As Klinenberg notes and the survey data confirm, this is, foremost, an urban phenomenon. About 47.5% of Americans over 18 are married.[9] While a solid majority of countryside dwellers at all ages over 35 are married, for city dwellers, the average barely reaches half between ages 35–60; only a minority are married outside that 25 year window. This pattern is very different from the midcentury Flintstones era, when being an unmarried adult caused one to be seen as odd or a failure; even in the countryside, that's obviously no longer the case. In 1950, only 9% of American households consisted of single adults.[10] By 2022, the figure had risen to 29%.[11]

Klinenberg is at pains to point out that for many, "going solo" doesn't imply a lonely life, nor is it about prioritizing freedom and lack of commitment over intimacy. In this sense, "solo" is a misnomer: "Living alone gives us time and space to discover the pleasures of being with others." Singletons often have multiple close connections, whether social, sexual, or romantic. These may be stable for long periods and may involve long-term commitments, or they may shift over time, but there's no indication that singletons are as a population less connected or emotionally healthy than married people. Social fulfillment while single is easier in the city, though, where there'll tend to be a lot more of "your people" around, whomever they are. Presumably that's why this trend started in cities, and is so much more pronounced there.

Sexuality itself seems to be evolving in a related way. People are deciding what (and who) they want to do more intentionally, rather than just acting out a received script. Being intentional only works, however, if the economic and social conditions allow for it. In particular, it only works in a sexually egalitarian society where women are able to survive and thrive without being dependent on a man—a change from the *status quo* for most agricultural societies for thousands of years, in both monogamous and polygynous variants. A happy irony results: Letting go of patriarchy makes men freer too.

Reproductive choice is key to self-determination for both women and men. It's especially important for women, though, given that the costs and risks of labor, childbirth, nursing, and child care are disproportionately theirs to bear, even with the "post-gendering" technologies described in Chapter 15. That so many women, including an increasing number who are unpartnered, still willingly choose to take these burdens on speaks to the fact that having kids remains intrinsically rewarding for many (though by no means all).

Why do we do it? As economic sociologist Viviana Zelizer puts it, "A national survey of the psychological motivations for having children confirms their predominantly sentimental value." A child,

12 Zelizer, whose work focuses on the attribution of cultural and moral meaning to the economy, wrote these rather tart words in her 1985 book, *Pricing the Priceless Child.* Perhaps her son, Julian, took them as a challenge; in 2007 he joined her at Princeton's Department of History and Public Affairs, to form the first mother-son professorial team in Princeton's history. Zelizer, *Pricing the Priceless Child: The Changing Social Value of Children*, 1985; Rubin, "Prof: Election Dynamic Bodes Well for the Jews," 2008.

13 See Chapter 7.

14 Our World in Data, "Children per Woman vs. Number of Children Wanted," 2023.

15 Zelizer, *Pricing the Priceless Child: The Changing Social Value of Children*, 3, 1985.

she wryly observes, "is expected to provide love, smiles, and emotional satisfaction, but no money or labor."[12] These intangibles do count for something. But despite the delights of having children, as we've seen, few potential mothers in rich countries with reproductive choice decide to have *large* numbers of them: the average is below two.

Can we trust that this average truly reflects women's uncoerced choices? Reproductive choice isn't ideal in the US, especially in the wake of successful multi-decade campaigns from conservative and religious groups to roll back *Roe v. Wade*. Thus the US fertility rate may still be skewing high, as plenty of American women today with limited access to social support, money, information, health care, contraception, and abortion will suffer unwanted births. On the other hand, financial precarity prevents some women from having *wanted* babies. Which effect is bigger remains uncertain.

Overall, the US fertility rate is in the same ballpark as that of many other developed countries, such as France and the UK, which have full national access to healthcare, including abortion and subsidized childcare. Perhaps, then, we *are* starting to get a sense of how many babies potential mothers choose to have on average when they can make that choice freely—although, given the inevitable role of social transmission,[13] an unbiased measurement would be difficult, even in principle. The World Bank has run surveys asking mothers in many countries how many births they ideally would have wanted, and how many babies they've actually had, to get a sense of unmet demand for contraception; almost inevitably, the wanted births are fewer, but only by a bit.[14] In the 2019 data, mothers in Colombia, for instance, wanted 1.6 babies, and had 1.86; in Mali, they wanted 5.5 babies, and had 5.88. As ever, desires, norms, and realities are connected by social feedback loops.

In the developed world, poorer families have more children on average; the converse holds as well, though: large numbers of children further impoverish those families. As Zelizer observes, nowadays kids don't just fail to bring money into the household—"They are also expensive."[15] This can lead to long-running intergenerational cycles of poverty. Or, to turn the situation on its head, having *fewer* children can mean substantially *more* resources per child, as well as a better life for the parents.

So, here's a puzzle. Why do poor people have so many kids? Or historically, if kids cost their parents so much money, why would we have been raising so many more of them back when *everybody* was so much poorer? Could it be that we were impoverished *because of* our high fertility?

19.2 **Total fertility rate by country** Live births per woman

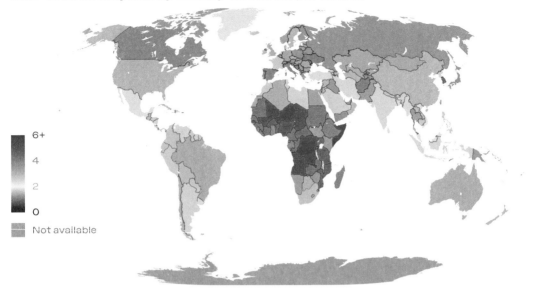

6+

4

2

0

Not available

Eight-year-old Jennie Camillo is pictured picking cranberries in Turkeytown, New Jersey, during the summer of 1910. Photo by Lewis Hine.

In fact, it was the opposite. Children used to enrich families, not impoverish them:

In sharp contrast to contemporary views, the birth of a child in 18th century rural America was welcomed as the arrival of a future laborer and as a security for parents later in life. The economic value of children for agricultural families has been well documented by anthropologists.[16]

Urbanization during the Industrial Revolution didn't immediately change this calculus, either. With their nimble fingers and modest needs, children could be good little factory workers too, back in the days before that was frowned upon![17]

Agricultural child labor has always been more common, though, due to correlations among economic development, automation, and the shift away from subsistence agriculture. The pattern still holds today. Among Niger's 17 million citizens, for example, agriculture remains the primary economic activity, and 43% of children between the ages of 5 and 14 work.[18] Recall that Niger has a world-topping total fertility rate of about 7 children per woman. Overall, about one fifth of all African children, or 72 million, are laborers—a higher proportion than on any other continent—and 85% of this child labor is agricultural.[19]

Photographer Lewis Hine notes: "Many youngsters here. Some boys were so small they had to climb up on the spinning frame to mend the broken threads and put back the empty bobbins." At the Bibb Mill in Macon, Georgia in January, 1909.

16 Zelizer, 5.

17 See Babbage's notes on child factory labor in *On the Economy of Machinery and Manufactures* in Chapter 15.

18 Bureau of International Labor Affairs, "2021 Findings on the Worst Forms of Child Labor: Niger"; Wikipedia, "Agriculture in Niger," 2020.

19 International Labour Organization, "Global Estimates of Child Labour: Results and Trends, 2012–2016," 2017.

20 Stanton, *Sex: Avoided Subjects Discussed in Plain English*, 47, 1922.

Today, only 1% or so of American women have as many children as the average in Niger, but remember that this wasn't always so. Back in 1922, Henry Stanton considered seven kids entirely reasonable, though he cautioned against fourteen, "of whom seven are likely to die, while the numerous successive births wear out and age the unfortunate mother."[20]

Urbanization was less advanced in 1922, but its inverse correlation with fertility had been noticed long before Stanton's day. He and his contemporaries still thought of children as generators of wealth, though, and so concluded that the trend toward fewer children must have been cultural—moreover, a deplorable "perversion," made possible only by the cushiness of life in a rich country:

"Mrs. Cecilia Wega, 39, of Castle Shannon [...] has 13 children yet finds time and energy to put in 48 hours a week hard work as a laborer for the Pennsylvania Railroad." Pittsburgh, Pennsylvania, 1943.

Material changes have taken place in the birth rate of a number of countries during the past fifteen or twenty years which [...] do not seem to depend on such things as trade, employment and prices; but on the spread of an idea or influence whose tendency must be deplored, that of "birth control," a phrase much heard in these days.

The fact that a decline in human fertility and a falling birth rate are most noticeable in the relatively prosperous countries is a proof that it does not proceed from economic causes; but is due rather to the spread of the doctrine that it is permissible to restrict or control birth. In such countries as the United States, England, and Australasia, where the standards of human comfort and living are notoriously high, the decline in the birth rate has been most noticeable.[21]

21 Stanton, 48–9.

Stanton was thoroughly mistaken; the reality is both cultural *and* economic. Birth control technologies and women's rights are part of the picture. But also, as societies transition away from agriculture, children go from being an economic asset to a costly choice—which means opting to have fewer of them, and perhaps, accordingly, thinking of them as more precious: a luxury, rather than an investment.

If we need any further evidence of how fundamental economics are to fertility, we need only consider the fertility rates of the richest oil states: Kuwait, Qatar, the United Arab Emirates, Norway, Saudi Arabia, and Bahrain.[22] Norway, the outlier here, is a Scandinavian liberal democracy and has had a fertility rate below two since 1975. The Gulf states, though, were economically undeveloped religious patriarchies

22 These are the top ranking oil producers per capita, less Brunei, Oman, Libya, and Guyana, which have significantly lower mean and median wealth.

19.3 **Total fertility rate in oil-rich countries from 1960 to 2017**
Live births per woman by year

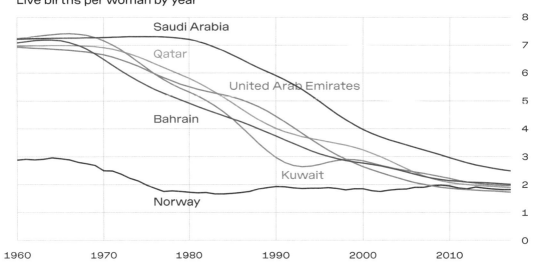

III   Humanity

before oil money began flowing in—which was practically yesterday. They all had fertility rates of around 7—higher than the poorest countries today—as recently as 1960. By 2017, their fertility rates were comparable to that of Norway, despite *still* being religious patriarchies with few women's rights.

Let's consider the political implications of the inverse relationship between wealth and fertility. Based on what we now know, we'd expect lower fertility in the city than in the countryside, and indeed, as we've seen, this is the case. Breaking down fertility rate by age reveals that not only do women in the countryside have children at a faster pace, but also that they start having children younger. Remember that to calculate a rate of population growth, one needs to take into account not only how many children women have on average by menopause, but also the generation time, which I've arbitrarily fixed at 30 years. Since urban mothers tend to have children later in life, though, their typical generation time is longer. This decreases urban fertility relative to the countryside still further.

Even in the American countryside, though, the fertility rate is far from that of the old days—or of the developing world. The average only exceeds two for women well beyond menopause, highlighting how the average number of children per potential mother in the countryside (and, indeed, everywhere in the US) has been in decline for decades. The generation that has just reached menopause had children at a rate well below replacement, both in the city and in the countryside. Hence people with high TFRs in sparsely populated ZIP codes are a small

19.4 Children born to people assigned female at birth in the city vs. countryside Average (and median) by age

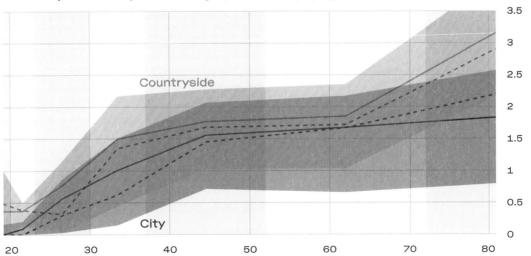

minority, and are "living in the past" in several senses: their cultural norms belong to an earlier generation, they themselves are typically older, and as a result their average fertility rate reflects that of a previous generation.

Running the fertility calculations for all white women in the US yields an even lower total fertility rate of 1.27. Once again, this is unsurprising, since lower fertility correlates with wealth and privilege. It also implies that even if the US were to stop admitting immigrants, its population would still be rapidly becoming less white over time.

Demonstrators at the "Unite the Right" rally in Charlottesville, Virginia, on August 12, 2017.

There are some political ironies here. If the ethno-nationalist right is concerned about being demographically "replaced" by non-white people, they should advocate for robust foreign aid, racial equity, and abortion rights. More foreign aid would lower fertility rates abroad, reducing immigration from poorer countries (both by lowering their populations over time and by increasing their quality of life, making their inhabitants less keen to leave); and greater racial equity in the US, together with freer access to abortion, would more quickly lower the fertility rate of non-white people at home.

This last was, in fact, one of the arguments marshaled by Margaret Sanger (1879–1966), the founder of Planned Parenthood and the driving force behind the development of the Pill. Sanger worked relentlessly for women's reproductive rights, but was also associated with the eugenics movement and enthusiastically cited demographic studies by Nazi researchers. (Another good reminder, regardless of one's politics today, that it's hard to find either perfect heroes or perfect villains—especially when we judge historical figures by today's moral yardstick.) In her 1920 book *Woman and the New Race*, Sanger wrote,

Margaret Sanger, 1916.

23 Sanger, *Woman and the New Race*, 44–5, 1920.

24 Planned Parenthood, "Opposition Claims About Margaret Sanger," 2021.

If we are to develop in America a new race with a racial soul, we must keep the birth rate within the scope of our ability to understand as well as to educate. We must not encourage reproduction beyond our capacity to assimilate our numbers so as to make the coming generation into such physically fit, mentally capable, socially alert individuals as are the ideal of a democracy.

The intelligence of a people is of slow evolutional development—it lags far behind the reproductive ability. It is far too slow to cope with conditions created by an increasing population, unless that increase is carefully regulated.

We must, therefore, not permit an increase in population that we are not prepared to care for to the best advantage—that we are not prepared to do justice to, educationally and economically. We must popularize birth control thinking. We must not leave it haphazardly to be the privilege of the already privileged. We must put this means of freedom and growth into the hands of the masses.**23**

"A new race with a racial soul" is a very unfortunate turn of phrase, though its connotations would have been somewhat different at the time. Such passages, along with Sanger's ambiguous attitude toward eugenics, have led to a great deal of belated soul-searching, apology, and disavowal on the part of Planned Parenthood.**24** Still, Sanger's main point here is that birth control should not remain the prerogative of the Casanovas of the world; it must be accessible to the poor, who, in a post-agricultural society, can least afford to raise large families. She understood clearly that birth control is both enabled by, and enables, economic mobility and development, particularly in the city.

Sanger's idea has withstood the test of time. While the project of universal access to birth control is unfinished, we've now reached a point where preventive checks are doing more to decrease our numbers than positive checks used to—not only among Americans, but soon, worldwide. The exponential logic of the population bomb has been disarmed, drawing our brief period of unchecked growth to a close. Now, we have an unprecedented choice: What will a post-growth humanity look like?

Terra incognita

Here be dragons.
From the Psalter World
Map, ca. 1260.

↓ Rockport Harbor,
Rockport, Maine,
ca. 1930–45.

→ Western Clock
Factory, La Salle,
Illinois, E.C. Kropp Co.,
ca. 1920.

As we turn toward the future, we can't overlook the blank expanses on the map, where an old time cartographer might have inked in dragons or other symbols of the unknown. Today, pretty much every corner of Earth has been explored, surveyed, and imaged from space, so those blanks might seem more boring than mysterious. They're the places where few or no people live. I've argued that cultural and technical innovations in cities have fueled the accelerating pace of social change; this, too, can tempt us to focus exclusively on urban life, where we're presumably getting a glimpse of things to come. Yet as we'll see, the changing countryside is its own kind of science fiction.

Let's examine the term "countryside" more carefully. I've used the word in an indiscriminate way to refer to something like 95% of our planet's landmass—everywhere that isn't brightly lit on the NASA Black Marble view of Earth's night side. In rough order of decreasing

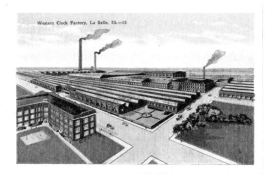

human occupancy, those darker places can be broken down like this:

A   Villages and towns. These are the small human settlements that haven't, and in general won't, tip into the kind of exponential growth and "ignition" that results in cities.

B   Industrial zones, including ports, pipelines and railways, warehouses, power plants, sewage treatment plants, dams, reservoirs, oil wells, mines, and factories. These make up the globe-spanning technical life-support infrastructure cities require.

C   Farms, orchards, and plantations. These are the expansive cultivated areas that supply cities with most of their food.

D   Wilderness. Although no part of Earth's surface is free of humanity's effects, there are large areas of uncultivated land where nobody lives or works full-time. These include mountains and deserts, forests, jungles, national parks, prairies and scrublands, swamps and backwoods. The oceans, also, mostly fit into this category.

City dwellers like me tend to have mental pictures of such places, sometimes dating back to childhood. I grew up in Mexico City in the 1970s and early '80s, and didn't see much of the countryside as a kid, but I do remember being deeply impressed by a collection of stereoscopic View-Master slides mounted on cardboard reels, a kind of early all-analog VR developed by the US's largest producer of scenic postcards. Holding the bright red View-Master up to a window for

A View-Master stereo viewer.

↓ "Home of J.E. Ranch, Waverly, N.Y.," Asheville Postcard Company, ca. 1912.

→ "A Mountain Stream In Autumn," Asheville Postcard Company, ca. 1912.

backlight and peering into its plastic lenses, I gawked at commanding views of places with iconic faraway names, like Bryce Canyon and the Grand Tetons; also, the majestic Hoover Dam, a cattle ranch, and a beautifully turned out Main Street in small town America.

The View-Master reels were highly curated, of course, and might even have had a whiff of Cold War propaganda about them. Still, those were real photos of real places. If you don't live there, it's easy to imagine that such antique images of life outside the big city remain accurate today. After all, we've seen that people living in rural places tend to be older and more conservative—I've argued that they're in this sense "living in the past"—and this seems consistent with the postcard pictures: old-timey and changeless.

In reality, life outside the city is utterly different now, and many rural residents are deeply uncomfortable with a lot of the changes they're seeing; hence the desire for those changes to stop, and even for the clock to turn back. It's not just about an opioid crisis, an economic downturn, or other "weather phenomena" of the moment. The changes are immense and systemic, climate-like (indeed, some are climate-driven). Renowned architect and urban theorist Rem Koolhaas has put it like this: "The countryside is now the frontline of transformation [...] more volatile than the most accelerated city."[1]

1   Koolhaas, "Countryside," 2012.

Abandoned homes in Detroit, 2017.

Let's turn over these postcards one by one and consider real life there today, beginning with villages and towns. As we've seen, the countryside is emptying out as young people move to the city (or suburbs near the city) for education, opportunity, and community, leaving behind an aging, shrinking, and increasingly homogeneous rural population. While some small towns remain vibrant (often by

Giuseppe Spagnuolo has for a quarter century been the last remaining inhabitant of Roscigno Vecchia, a village in the Cilento area of Campania, southern Italy.

thriving on tourism, preserving and capitalizing on the "postcard look"), many more are shrinking and ultimately turning into ghost towns and ruins. Moss covers roofs, animals nest in attics, mold peels back wallpaper, tree roots twist their way through floorboards, blackberry brambles pull down walls. Life goes on, but without people.

This process is well underway in most countries with advanced economies, where urbanization and declining birth rates combine to erase smaller settlements. As of 2021, 6,000 villages lay abandoned in Italy. Another 15,000 Italian villages had lost more than 95% of their residents. By the time you read this, the numbers will be higher. An entire medieval hamlet, Pratariccia, was sold on eBay for $3.1 million in 2012, but more recently, asking prices for abandoned villages have been far more modest. It's a buyer's market—and even in the picturesque Italian countryside, few people are interested in buying.[2]

In fact, the price has probably gone negative. In 2017, the desperate mayor of Bormida, a small town in Liguria, posted to Facebook apparently offering $2,100 to anyone willing to move there, though he beat a hasty retreat when 17,000 inquiries flooded into his inbox; lots of people were strapped for cash, but so, apparently, was the regional government.[3] So, the town's demographic collapse has continued unabated. As of 2022, Bormida is home to 12 people over 90 years old, but only 10 young people between the ages of 10 and 19.[4]

Japan, similarly, has an epidemic of *akiya* (空き家), or abandoned homes, and has set up special banks to try to sell them off, but supply is far outpacing demand. The phenomenon began with the abandonment of old-fashioned country houses of the *Spirited Away* variety,[5] but given Japan's exceptionally low birth rate, aging population, low immigration, and already maxed-out urbanization, abandonment is spreading into higher-density places too. Whole islands have been abandoned, some of which, like Hashima, off the coast of Nagasaki,

2 Marchetti, "An Entire Tuscan Village Is Being Sold on Italian eBay for $3 Million," 2012.

3 Craggs, "The Italian Village of Bormida Won't Actually Pay You $2,100 to Move There," 2017.

4 Brinkhoff, "Bormida," 2022.

5 Miyazaki, *Spirited Away*, 2001.

Derelict homes in Wajima, Japan.

6 Martin, "Japan's Glut of Abandoned Homes: Hard to Sell but Bargains When Opportunity Knocks," 2017; Chandran, "Here's How Japan Is Breathing New Life into Its 'Ghost Towns,'" 2019.

7 Such was the trendiness of ruins in the 18th century that some landowners had them built to order. Cooper, "Europe Was Once Obsessed With Fake Dilapidated Buildings," 2018.

have become tourist destinations—though such sights are increasingly commonplace. Even in Tokyo, more than 10% of the housing stock stands empty today. By 2033, the Nomura Research Institute projects that about one third of Japanese houses will be uninhabited, and by 2040, the country's unclaimed land will reach 28,000 square miles—roughly the area of Ireland.**6** The process will speed up over time.

There's an undeniable post-apocalyptic romance in this abandonment and decay. We're not the first generation to notice it. The French romantic painter Hubert Robert (1733–1808) loved this motif so much that his friends nicknamed him *Robert des ruines*. His paintings featured peasants grazing cattle among imaginary Roman ruins, as well as the imagined future ruins of real places, like the grand gallery of the Louvre. Just as the artistic contemplation of a skull gives us the spooky, pleasurable shiver of *memento mori* ("remember Death"), images like Robert's remind us that all things must pass, and there's a special grandeur in the passing of great things—monumental galleries, cities, entire lost civilizations.**7**

A Hermit Praying in the Ruins of a Roman Temple by Hubert Robert, ca. 1760.

Now, let's turn over the farm postcard. Many smaller family farms
have succumbed to similar forces, and are now rewilding: reverting to
forest, scrubland, or prairie. Where the land was agriculturally marginal
to begin with, or the soil degraded, the return to nature isn't always
quick, and the species mix may not look much like it did before farming,
but it's a return to nature nonetheless.

We've already touched on the root cause of this abandonment in
Chapters 16 and 18: the transition from subsistence agriculture to large-
scale agriculture. In Colonial America, agriculture was the primary
livelihood for 90% of the population, and most farms were subsistence
operations. By the year 2000, only about 2% of Americans farmed for
a living, and today, that number is even lower. Most of us are no longer
connected to the land in the traditional way—yet we still very much
depend on it to stay alive. Farmed goods now tend to travel to the cities
along international supply chains from large, highly automated farms
far from any city.

Consider the story of hog farming in the US over the past century.
In 1900, there were 4.3 million hog farms, which works out to one hog
operation per 18 people. Since 40% of the population lived in cities and
families were large, that pretty much meant that if you lived in the countryside, your family kept hogs, or if not, your neighbor did. The average
farm kept a dozen animals or so. By 2017, there were only 66 thousand
hog farms left, a 65-fold reduction, but the total number of animals had
grown slightly—from 63 million in 1900 to 72 million in 2017. Now, a
thousand-hog operation is on the small side.[8]

Economies of scale mean that the total area devoted to hog farming is much smaller than it used to be, though. The "factory farming"
practices on many large farms are both cruel and unhealthy, but even
if they all went free-range, the area saved relative to millions of family

8 Given that the US
population has more than
quadrupled since 1900,
this also suggests that we
eat a lot less pork than we
used to.

20.0.0 Share of labor force employed in agriculture from 1400 to 2019 % by year

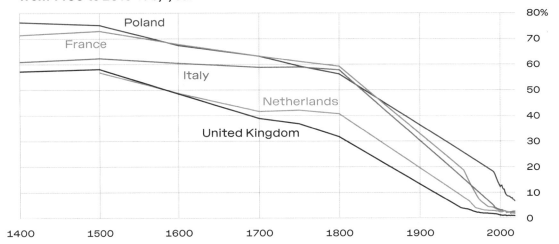

20.0.1 Share of labor force employed in agriculture from 1950 to 2019 % by year

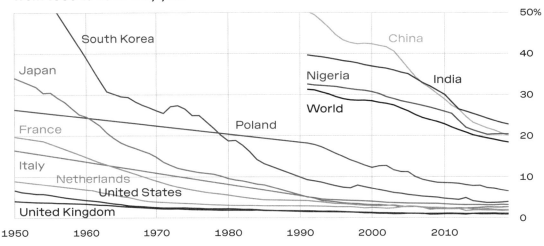

20.1 Consolidation of hog farms from 1900 to 2017
Number by year

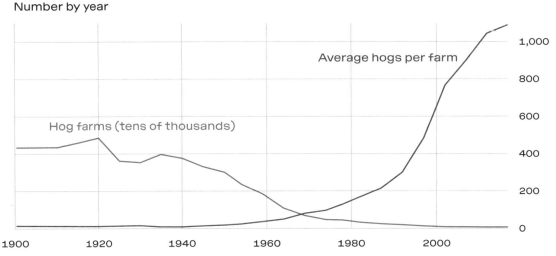

operations would still be vast—as are the savings in other resources. In effect, pigs have urbanized, just as humans have.

A similar pattern of consolidation of larger farms and decreasing total agricultural area over the past 20 years holds not only in the US, but also in the industrialized economies of most rich countries. Yet all this consolidation has happened at the same time as an overall increase in population size. Cities today need more food than ever, but the need is being met with a decreasing amount of land under cultivation. Since 1982, the land used for farming in the US has decreased by an area equivalent to Washington State.[9] In fact, we appear to have reached the worldwide peak in our total demand for agricultural land; even in Africa, one of the last remaining regions where the area under cultivation is still rising, its growth has slowed, and looks likely to start falling within the next few years, well before the continent's population peaks.

This is a remarkable turnaround. When children's book author Bill Peet wrote *Farewell to Shady Glade* to build ecological awareness among young readers in 1966, cities and factories were pouring untreated effluent into streams, and earth movers were plowing places like Shady Glade into the ground, though by that point, usually to build new suburbs—the area under cultivation in the US had been declining since 1950.

Illustration by Garth Williams from E.B. White, *Charlotte's Web*, 1952.

9 McAfee, *More from Less: The Surprising Story of How We Learned to Prosper Using Fewer Resources—and What Happens Next*, 184, 2019.

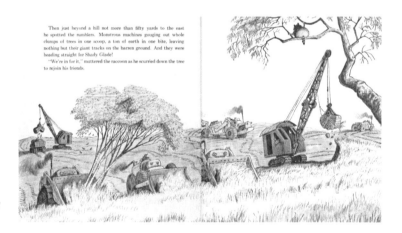

Then just beyond a hill not more than fifty yards to the east he spotted the rumblers. Monstrous machines gouging out whole clumps of trees in one scoop, a ton of earth in one bite, leaving nothing but their giant tracks on the barren ground. And they were heading straight for Shady Glade!
"We're in for it," muttered the raccoon as he scurried down the tree to rejoin his friends.

From Bill Peet, *Farewell to Shady Glade*, 1976.

Environmental regulation, some of it probably written by policymakers who read Bill Peet as kids, has helped with pollution; but the fact that rewilding is now happening at a faster clip than bulldozing owes less to regulation than to urbanization and efficiencies of scale.

20.2 Total area for agricultural land use from 1600 to 2016
Area (millions of hectares) by year

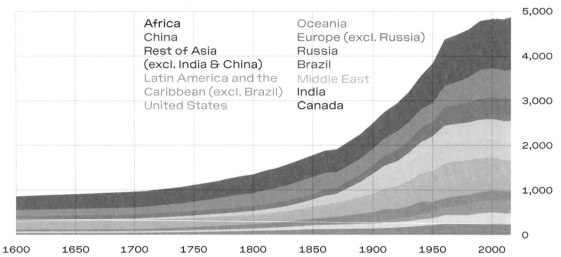

Africa
China
Rest of Asia
(excl. India & China)
Latin America and the
Caribbean (excl. Brazil)
United States

Oceania
Europe (excl. Russia)
Russia
Brazil
Middle East
India
Canada

20.3 Crop productivity gains % of 1961 crop productivity by year

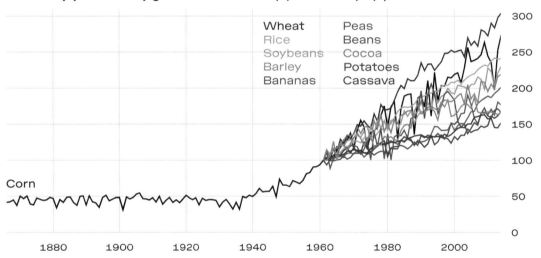

Wheat
Rice
Soybeans
Barley
Bananas

Peas
Beans
Cocoa
Potatoes
Cassava

Corn

The emptying-out of the countryside and decrease in agricultural footprint has only been possible because the technologies of food production have become vastly more efficient. This, too, is a long-term trend spanning centuries, but it has sped up in recent times. As described in Chapter 18, engineered crops and industrial fertilizer are key factors, but just as importantly, humans have been mostly taken out of the agricultural production loop and replaced by machines with much higher throughput. In the US, we can no longer find Malthus's "lads who drive plough," or even animals who do. Robots are doing the job now.

"Robots taking jobs" still seems like a Jetsonian fantasy in the city. I certainly don't see much evidence of a robot invasion in Seattle. It's true that slowly, over decades, ATMs have taken over certain tasks that bank tellers used to do, and the self-checkout scanners at Safeway seem to be processing quite a few customers with "15 items or less." On the other hand, Amazon has decided to close its 68 experimental fully automated shops, where you used to be able to grab items and just walk out, while unblinking robotic eyes added charges to your Prime account.[10] Undoubtedly these technologies will continue to advance and eventually become commonplace (indeed, the same technology is now showing up in Amazon Fresh stores), but the changes seem modest and gradual.

10 Dastin, "Amazon to Shut Its Bookstores and Other Shops as Its Grocery Chain Expands," 2022.

Robots at work at Tesla's Fremont factory, 2017.

As Koolhaas notes, though, the frontline of the transformation is the countryside, not the city. The reason is simple: so far, robots are still not very good at interacting with people, and cities are all about interactions with people. That's why, even at the self-checkout line in the supermarket, the biometric security checkpoint at the airport, the computerized conveyor belt sushi restaurant, or the automated check-in kiosk at a trendy "robotic hotel,"[11] there are employees standing by to help when—inevitably—the human-machine interaction goes awry. By contrast, the large-scale infrastructure in the countryside needed to support humanity today is increasingly robotic and hands-free—to the degree that its machinic nature makes much of the land humans directly depend on, paradoxically, a "human exclusion zone." That's one reason most of us are unaware of the dramatic changes. We're simply not around to see them.[12]

11 HTN Staff, "Dutch Hotel Brand CitizenM Launches a Technology-Enabled 'Corporate Subscription' Plan," 2020.

12 There's strong evidence that an aging workforce accelerates the robotic automation trend; see Acemoglu and Restrepo, "Demographics and Automation," 2021. Hence, the older demographics of rural places may also be a significant driver of the accelerated turn to automation in the countryside.

Lights-out production facility.

Human exclusion zones have mostly been written about in the context of so-called "lights-out manufacturing": factories so fully automated that they can forgo the expense of keeping the lights on. The Japanese robotics company FANUC, for example, has been a lights-out operation since 2001. Heating and air conditioning are turned off in FANUC plants too, since there's no need to cater to the fussily narrow environmental envelope humans prefer. In the whirring darkness, freezing or stifling, FANUC industrial robots build *more* industrial robots, working around the clock to churn out their brethren without human intervention for up to a month at a time.[13] The system works because every step in the manufacturing process is precise, reliable, and repeatable. Unlike us, in other words.

13 Null and Caulfield, "Fade to Black: The 1980s Vision of 'Lights-out' Manufacturing, Where Robots Do All the Work, Is a Dream No More," 2003.

Fully automated straddle carriers (AutoStrads) move shipping containers at the Port of Los Angeles, the busiest shipping port in the US, 2016.

While most factories are still early in their transition to these kinds of practices, the container ship ports that global commerce relies on so heavily are well on their way to becoming fully robotic, surrounded by chain link fencing that excludes everyone save a

14 Globally, only 4% of shipping ports were automated as of 2022, and port automation in the US lags many other countries due to union pressure. However, although the nation has hundreds of ports, the largest—in Los Angeles, Long Beach, and New York / New Jersey—process about half of all imported goods, and are now automated; as elsewhere, automation and consolidation go hand in hand. Hsu, "Before the Holiday Season, Workers at America's Busiest Ports Are Fighting the Robots," 2022; Schmidt, "Why Does the U.S. Lag Other Nations so Badly in the Automation of Its Ports?," 2022.

handful of technicians and security guards.[14] The geometric, Lego-like landscapes of automated ports are a far cry from the bustling ant-hills of human activity characterizing traditional ports, from antiquity through most of the 20th century. Indeed, in centuries past, such ports, along with the businesses that sprang up to cater to their sailors, long-shoremen, traders, and merchants, seeded many of today's coastal cities. Now, the connection between trade and cities has become abstract.

Maersk Line container ships in port, Rotterdam, 2019.

Increasingly intensive automation extends to the vessels carrying the cargo, too. The first container ship, the Clifford J. Rogers, completed in 1955, was crewed by 15 people and could carry the equivalent of roughly 65–70 modern shipping containers or "TEUs" (twenty-foot equivalent units). The Ever Alot, a 2022 container ship, carries 24,004 TEUs, and is crewed by 25 people—a more than two hundred fold decrease in the need for human labor.[15] Much the same is true of

15 "The Evolution of Container Ships and Their Sizes," 2022.

Inside a Google data center in Douglas County, Georgia.

wind farms, oil pipelines, mines... all of these basic industries are undergoing a rapid transition to full automation, or something close to it.

Even information processing is becoming increasingly automated. Giant datacenters of the kind run by Google, Microsoft, and Amazon (they used to be called "server farms") have pretty much been human exclusion zones for years, with a lone technician going in now and then to swap out a broken part. In 2011, Apple, for instance, built a billion dollar datacenter in Maiden, North Carolina, once a thriving manufacturing town. The community, initially overjoyed at the prospect of a big new employer, soon learned that only 50 full time employees would be hired. Residents "[couldn't] comprehend how expensive facilities stretching across hundreds of acres [could] create so few jobs," as the *Washington Post* put it; "[I]n the newer digital economy, capital investments that a generation ago would have created thousands of new positions often equal only a handful today, with computers and software processing the heavy lifting [...]."[16] Since 2011, datacenter automation has advanced considerably.

16 Rosenwald, "Cloud Centers Bring High-Tech Flash but Not Many Jobs to Beaten-down Towns," 2011.

Barriers divide this Amazon warehouse so that humans and robots may safely work together.

Amazon's warehouses are increasingly robotic too, which doesn't create great working conditions for the humans remaining there doing as-yet-unautomated jobs. Multidisciplinary researcher-activists Kate Crawford and Vladan Joler have written poetically about the uncanny valley characteristic of such workplaces:

> **At Amazon distribution centers, vast collections of products are arrayed in a computational order across millions of shelves. The position of every item in this space is precisely determined by complex mathematical functions that process information about orders and create relationships between products. The aim is to optimize the movements of the robots**

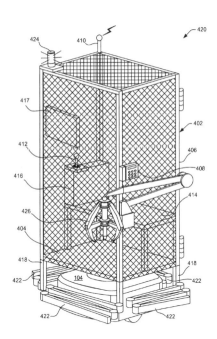

and humans that collaborate in these warehouses. With the help from an electronic bracelet, the human worker is directed through warehouses the size of airplane hangars, filled with objects arranged in an opaque algorithmic order.

Hidden among the thousands of other publicly available patents owned by Amazon, U.S. patent number 9,280,157 represents an extraordinary illustration of worker alienation, a stark moment in the relationship between humans and machines. It depicts a metal cage intended for the worker, equipped with different cybernetic add-ons, that can be moved through a warehouse by the same motorized system that shifts shelves filled with merchandise. Here, the worker becomes a part of a machinic ballet, held upright in a cage which dictates and constrains their movement.[17]

"Disclosed herein is a human transport device and associated system to transport a user within an active workspace." From Amazon employees Wurman et al., US Patent No. 9,280,157, 2016.

17 Crawford and Joler, "Anatomy of an AI System: The Amazon Echo as an Anatomical Map of Human Labor, Data and Planetary Resources," 2018.

Of course, the inventors would doubtless argue that these metal cages aren't designed to imprison people, but to keep them safe from heavy machinery in an environment well on its way to becoming a human exclusion zone. Then again, one could argue that since cities are wildlife exclusion zones, the only safe way to keep a wild animal in the city is in a zoo cage. Outside human enclaves, will *we* be tomorrow's wildlife, caged for our own safety amid our robotic infrastructure?

Most farmland in the industrialized world is a human exclusion zone now, too. Great tracts of the Midwest that used to be divided up into family farms are now tilled, planted, and harvested by hulking agricultural robots whose smaller ancestors we used to call, quaintly,

An Agrobot robotic strawberry harvester, 2019.

"tractors." Needless to say, none of these robots looks anything like the droids on the Skywalker family farm.

In fact *no* working robots today are anthropoid, like the Star Wars "protocol droid" C-3PO, because they don't really *do* human protocol; why would they speak our languages, or have arms and legs, or person-like dimensions at all, if their environment is entirely non-human? Why would they sense the world as we do, or operate on our timescales? We tend not to recognize robots as such because we bring in so many anthropomorphic assumptions. Even the beepily articulate R2-D2 turns out to be a human-enough shaped chap (as evidenced by the fact that he could be operated from the inside by 3-foot-8-inch English actor Kenny Baker). Droids were buddies—not only because they could communicate with you,[18] but because they could share spaces with you, go where you go. With a bit of Jedi persuasion to overcome human prejudice, they could even accompany you into an interplanetary dive bar.

18 Notwithstanding that R2-D2 seems to have been a better communicator than C-3PO—perhaps because C-3PO was more *obviously* British?

You don't want to try walking into a bar with a bright yellow, twelve foot tall, eleven tonne FANUC M-2000*i*A. Oops, you can't—it'll be bolted down. Little pick-and-place machines that solder circuit boards at high speed might be more compact, but they're generally fully integrated into an assembly line—it might not even be obvious where one robot ends and another begins. Perhaps a bright green autonomous John Deere 8R tractor, then?[19] It may be highly mobile, but it, too, wants you to keep your distance. Its beeps aren't the friendly dialtones of R2-D2, but loud, monotonous, garbage-truck-backing-up sounds telling any nearby human to stay well clear. If you, or anything else out of the ordinary, are in the advancing path of this behemoth, it will stop in its tracks and call for supervisor assistance, just like a grocery checkout robot when you forget to put your scanned item on the scale. As Doug Nimz, a fourth generation corn and soybean farmer from Minnesota, puts it in a promotional video,

The FANUC M-2000*i*A, demonstrating its 1.7t payload capacity.

19 "John Deere Reveals Fully Autonomous Tractor at CES 2022," 2022.

I can pull up the app, I can monitor the tractor, see how much of the field it's gotten tilled. I can check the fuel level. I can check the app to see how much of the field is left. If there was something in the field that it wasn't sure about the tractor will stop and alert me [...]. Autonomy will help because we will be able to put a tractor out in the field and let it run for 24 hours a day because it's not manned. But it also helps us with the weather because we can run so hard when soil conditions are fit.[20]

Superficially, autonomous tractors resemble driverless cars— and autonomous driving is one domain in which city dwellers have expressed real anxiety about job loss to automation. There are millions of truck, taxi, and Uber drivers in the US. It's interesting, though, that despite many years of incremental progress, real adoption of driverless car technology always seems like it's still a few years off. In the meantime, driverless tractors, ports, container ships, and mines are already here, largely unnoticed. They differ in that, once more, these applications can take place in human exclusion zones!

In a hypothetical New York where the streets were given over *entirely* to robotic cars, passengers could be whisked anywhere at great speed. There would be no need for traffic lights, stop signs, or indeed any traffic signs, as vehicles could coordinate the timing of their flows and turns through each intersection with the precision of a zipper's interlocking teeth. We might finally have the personal freedom of movement and speed that car manufacturers have been promising in their advertising for a hundred years. As economist Judy Wajcman snarks,

A Waymo self-driving car in suburban Mountain View, California, 2017.

21 Wajcman, *Pressed for Time: The Acceleration of Life in Digital Capitalism*, 50, 2015.

The incongruity of the automobile's promise of freedom of movement with the actuality of a largely sedentary existence in a landscape dominated by traffic-overloaded motorways is [...] pronounced today. However, it is the speed of information flows rather than of motorcars that is at the forefront of our imagination.[21]

Information flow would in fact be the key to fulfilling the promise of real autonomous mobility. With communication at near light speed across the street grid and nose-to-tail "trains" of cars forming and splitting at need, jams and delays would be a rarity. Lanes could be much narrower and street parking would not be needed, letting café tables and gardens spill out onto wide sidewalks. Residential and shopping streets could fully pedestrianize, as many of the cuter towns in Europe have done. No idling, no stop-and-go traffic, and far higher utilization would mean fewer cars and a lower ecological footprint. Electric charging or battery swapping could be fully automated, decreasing the need for resource-intensive long-range batteries. Public transit would have to up its game to remain competitive—or perhaps ride sharing and public transit could merge into a single system.

A cow and traffic share the road in Jaipur, India, 1999.

22 Specifically: the tunnels and elevated tracks of metro systems like the London Underground are human exclusion zones. Hence robotic trains, with passengers safely sealed up inside, can zip through them at high speed.

23 Wajcman, 55.

It's an attractive picture. None of it is likely to happen at scale anytime soon, though. Driving in a real city during rush hour is a mess, whether for a human or for a robot. That's why the London Underground will remain popular for a long time to come.[22] Indeed, today, "riding a Victorian technology in central London—the bicycle—during peak hours is faster than traveling by car."[23] This is the issue: driving involves constant interaction and social negotiation with other drivers, motorcyclists, bicyclists, pedestrians, and sometimes other animals—all of which have their own agendas, places to be, good or

Traffic in Mumbai, India, 2016.

bad attitudes, and sometimes, horrifyingly, little screens they're looking at instead of the road. A competent driver is aware of everyone else, conscious of what they're paying attention to, and modeling what they might do next. There's constant give and take, occasional risk taking and boundary pushing.

As density rises, the social component of driving becomes increasingly challenging. Sometimes honking needs to happen. That's why, even as robotic Ubers glide through the eerily depopulated suburbs of Phoenix, we're still nowhere close to having effective driverless vehicles in Mumbai. New York and London might fall somewhere in the middle… but probably more on the Mumbai side.

A few years ago, many of us who worked in the various subdisciplines of AI believed that the fundamental challenge for autonomous driving was perceptual: machines' inability to make sense of a complicated environment reliably, the way people can. However, the problem turns out not to be an inability to program machines to perceive cows, people, and bikes. While no sensor system is perfect, modern AI can perform all of these tasks, and with better reliability than distractible human drivers with our measly two eyes pointing in just one direction out of our heads. The problem is negotiating social interactions in a mixed human-machine environment, without the machine coming to a standstill. Safe and effective urban driving simply can't be reduced to a set of preprogrammed rules, even given complete and accurate information about everything on the road.

At very high density, human social modeling of robots becomes a major challenge too. If people don't consider a robotic driver a social entity deserving of respect—and perhaps even posing a credible threat to one's own safety if suddenly cut off, or angered—then cautious, well-behaved autonomous vehicles simply won't be able to make any headway during rush hour. They'll be frozen in place as bolder, pushier pedestrians and mopeds swerve and swarm around them, confident in the machine's unlimited patience and (presumably) near-zero tolerance for risk to human life.

Paradoxically, then, introducing autonomous cars can make traffic worse. It's possible that driverless vehicles simply *can't* be made to work in dense human environments unless they become

24 Personally, I'm a fan of just pedestrianizing the densest places in cities. I agree with Wajcman that cars there make quality of life worse, regardless of who or what is at the wheel.

25 "Pioneering Autonomous Road Trains Achieve World First," 2022.

convincingly social "persons"—or manual driving is banned altogether, and the street becomes a human exclusion zone.[24]

This contrasts dramatically with conditions in the Australian outback, where massive and increasingly autonomous[25] "road trains" of trucks have been doing long-distance ore hauling for many years. It's cheaper, faster, more fuel-efficient, and doubtless has saved the lives of truckers who might otherwise have nodded off somewhere between Tanami and Yuendumu—although many of those truckers might have preferred dosing up on Red Bull and taking their chances rather than being out of a job.

A road train, Northern Territory, Australia, 2005.

The outback and Mumbai differ, of course, in that the interior of Australia is one of the least populated places on the planet, while India is one of the densest.

Somebody is still directing those "autonomous" vehicles in the outback, of course. Originally, that person was driving the lead truck. Now, that somebody might be directing fleet operations remotely from 750 miles away. Autonomy and human exclusion zones mean that the human-machine interface becomes higher-level, more abstract and removed from the action. Ironically, it means that most of us—even when we're "operators"—have less direct contact with technology than we used to. For example, a single farmer can operate (or, increasingly, just monitor) their agricultural robots on a tablet from the farmhouse—or from a Starbucks in town. Robotic tractor paths get overlaid on robotic drone-mapped fields showing crop growth and health. It's like real-life Farmville.

For Rem Koolhaas, this abstraction takes on an almost metaphysical quality:

A fleet harvesting soybeans in Mato Grosso state, Brazil, 2008.

26 Koolhaas, "Countryside," 2012.

27 Dutch manufacturer Lely's Astronaut A5, for instance, is a self-service cow milking robot. Cows roam freely, and go to the machine when they're ready to be milked. Lely also makes robots that automate grazing, feeding, and monitoring.

You could even say that the landscape and iPad have become identical. That the iPad is now the earth and the farmer works with it. And that on the iPad the ground is now defined. And every single action from planting to weeding is specified for the smallest pixel to create the largest possible yields.[26]

Agricultural fields are increasingly becoming digital, abstract surfaces.

28 "The Netherlands Are Almost the World's Largest Exporter of Agricultural Products! How Did That Happen?," 2020.

Cattle management and dairy milking, pigpens and chicken farms are similarly being run increasingly robotically nowadays.[27] For the moment, fruit picking is delicate work that requires real humans with depth perception, hand-eye coordination, and nimble fingers, but lots of startups are working on that problem. Greenhouses of truly astonishing scale are now run in a way that looks a lot like lights-out manufacturing, with air mixtures and light spectra designed for maximum plant output—and decidedly not for human occupancy. Within greenhouses, we carry out a kind of localized terraforming, engineering the landscapes of alternative planets where tomatoes or lettuces are at home, but people must wear environment suits.

The Netherlands, with its high population density, low birth rate, and limited arable land area, has been a big innovator here. As a result, they've become—despite their tiny size—the world's second biggest food exporter by volume![28]

Aerial photograph of Dutch greenhouses by German photographer Tom Hegen, 2019.

Since so much of the farmer's work is now information work, it's hard to imagine that the farmer's physical presence will be needed at all in the future. Perhaps soon the farm will be managed entirely from afar, with just the occasional tech crew or veterinarian going out to debug a machine or animal. Eventually even *those* crews may be robotic. Seasonal migrant laborers, who today are needed to harvest certain crops, may no longer be needed as automation progresses. Food farms will start to look a lot like server farms.

A farmer's home sits at the helm of a fleet of greenhouses, the Netherlands, 2017.

If you're a city dweller, this may all sound pretty weird—discovering that the View-Master is just a historical VR fantasy, and you're now living in a habitable bubble on an otherwise alien planet.

Well, that's not entirely true. The traditional "farm postcard" still does exist in places, just as some picturesque villages still survive; though like villages, artisanal farms aren't "load bearing" today. They don't, and couldn't, supply much of humanity's caloric needs. However, as technology for intensifying agriculture continues to improve and population starts to decline, that may change. Small-scale farming can also serve meaningful social purposes, and shouldn't be dismissed merely as supplying "organic" luxuries for the rich. Food isn't just about sustenance, but also about identity, dignity, and community.

Cadillac Urban Gardens in Southwest Detroit, 2012.

29 The effect is especially pronounced for staples like rice, which require the whole community to come together to harvest each farmer's crop in turn. In China, for instance, collective social values vary by region based on whether the staple crop is rice or wheat (which requires less neighborly help); see Talhelm et al., "Large-Scale Psychological Differences Within China Explained by Rice Versus Wheat Agriculture," 2014.

Lufa Farms' rooftop greenhouses in Montreal, 2013.

Small-scale farming remains inherently communal; even in the Malthusian days of subsistence agriculture, it knit together the social fabric.[29] Now that subsistence is less at issue but lack of social connection has emerged as a major problem, supplanting large-scale commercial food production with small-scale farming or gardening makes sense. Modern small-scale farming and gardening don't focus so much on yield as on participation, connectedness to our food, and human interaction. People will pay extra for these things, or, given the opportunity, will invest time and love in them even when they don't have that economic "extra." That's why small farms tend not to be in the deep countryside, but nearer to towns and cities, or even inside them. We see such practices today in many parts of Europe, at farmer's markets, and for that matter on urban micro-farms in Detroit and in community gardens in Baltimore. The future of small-scale farming is

An automated vertical farm in Pittsburgh, Pennsylvania, 2021.

30 This change in mindset is like the one that has already taken place in our thinking about exercise. The idea of "taking exercise" used to be something only for the eccentric, and then for the rich; the poor had no spare time (or calories) to burn on such "pointless" activity. When even poor and working class people became rich enough to have spare time and calories— and then began to suffer epidemic diabetes—it became clear that exercise isn't a frivolous pastime, but important for everyone.

already here—it's just, like the other futures described in this book, not evenly distributed.[30]

There's also more to eating well than meeting a minimum calorie count. Fresh herbs, beautiful tomatoes, lettuces, and many other non-staple crops can be grown in small plots or on rooftops. Still, big farming operations are here to stay, and it's clear that we're not going back to a world where those great tracts of land (or urban farms, or greenhouses) are worked by a peasant class. Automation and efficiencies of scale will remain essential.

Over time, sophisticated robotics and AI should allow even large-scale, highly automated farming to become more varied and organic. Swarms of smaller drones and robots with better sensors and brains can replace today's steamroller-like iron giants. Instead of endless fields formatted like circuit boards with rows of identical plants, more nimble, intelligent cultivation of multi-species ecosystems will be able to take better care of the soil and produce more food per acre. Hopefully, individualized medicine for animals will do away with indiscriminately mixing large doses of antibiotics and antifungal agents into feed. Similarly, "precision agriculture" is increasingly allowing fertilizers and pesticides to be applied to individual plants, adaptively microdosing them rather than blanketing the earth with chemicals mostly destined to run off into groundwater. Especially in combination

A wildlife crossing in Sudbury, Ontario, completed in 2012.

The formerly militarized border separating East and West Germany has been converted to a nature reserve known as the German Green Belt.

31 We can't lose sight of the challenge imposed by energy inputs, though. Plants harvest energy through photosynthesis. In traditional farming, sunlight is the energy source. In a high-tech greenhouse, far greater density can be achieved, but only by illuminating the plants with LEDs, which must themselves be powered somehow. Fixing nitrogen to create fertilizer likewise requires energy. So everything comes back to energy, and hence to the fundamental problem of weaning ourselves off of fossil fuels.

32 Wilson, *Half-Earth: Our Planet's Fight for Life*, 2017.

33 Dreifus and Wilson, "In 'Half Earth,' E.O. Wilson Calls for a Grand Retreat," 2016.

34 Ellis, "To Conserve Nature in the Anthropocene, Half Earth Is Not Nearly Enough," 2019.

with greenhouse technologies, methods like these will likely result in further dramatic decreases in the land area needed to feed the world, as well as a much lighter ecological footprint.[31]

We desperately need conservation and rewilding of the land freed up to arrest and begin to reverse our planet's ecological free-fall. Taking a hands-on approach (both human *and* machine "hands") to rewilding former farmlands may become necessary, as we may not be able to afford to wait the decades or centuries it'll take for some of these degraded landscapes to recover on their own.

In one of his last books, the legendary biologist E.O. Wilson (1929–2021) advocated for half of the Earth's surface to be designated a human-free reserve, to restore the planet's biodiversity.[32] While the *New York Times* called Wilson's plan a "grand retreat"[33]—and it is, relative to land use today—some environmental scientists who have studied this topic closely believe that, to quote the title of one paper from 2019, "To Conserve Nature in the Anthropocene, Half Earth Is Not Nearly Enough."[34]

Automation and human exclusion zones, then, aren't dystopian, but necessary: just the kinds of rabbits we must pull out of hats to avoid ecological collapse. Fortunately, key large-scale trends are moving us in the right direction already. We *are* retreating from large areas of the planet as we urbanize. Technical systems, including intensive automation, are giving us the means to do it.

There's something missing from Wilson's picture, though. The sense that we have been ruining nature, so must now wholly withdraw from it for the Earth to heal, rests on the idea that humanity is *separate* from nature, even in opposition with it—the exact belief that has caused so much of our self-inflicted harm. When economists, even conservation-minded ones, talk about "natural resources," "ecosystem services," or pollution as an "externality," they reinforce this worldview. So do the romantics who see, in abandoned villages and family farms gone to seed, a "return to nature."

In reality, nature is all around us, and includes us. It has been here all along. Human activity hasn't only extinguished species, but has also been giving rise to them at a furious pace, both through agricultural engineering and through the unwitting creation of novel ecosystem niches. New kinds of mosquitoes have made homes in subway tunnels; rodents of all kinds have specialized to take advantage of human infrastructure; certain insect populations respond differently to light now, and have changed their appearance to blend in against new surfaces; urban birds have evolved to eat novel foods and sing different songs in cities, which are loud yet full of tasty snacks.[35]

Of course we should do everything in our power to protect the remaining Himalayan snow leopards and spotted owls, but it's a mistake to consider them "natural" and the new species (including ourselves) "unnatural," or to turn from despoiling the environment without a second thought to setting it apart from us on a pedestal— a pattern curiously akin to what Freud called the "Madonna-whore complex," in which a man insists on seeing women as either saintly or debased. The genderedness of the metaphor is hardly accidental, for we've once again encountered the Baconian vision of scientific patriarchy: "man" raping a feminized "nature," albeit in these more enlightened times, withdrawing after the deed in shame and remorse rather than triumph.

Can one respect nature without treating it as a saintly, untouchable "other"? Absolutely: Native Americans, Aboriginal people, and many other indigenous populations were active, constructive participants in their ecologies for thousands of years, until their ways of life were disrupted by colonialism and globalization. For instance, many cultures traditionally use controlled fire to manage forests and scrubland, enhancing biodiversity and decreasing the likelihood of catastrophic uncontrolled burns; this is far more sophisticated than Smokey the Bear's doctrine, which presumes that the ideal interaction between people and the forest is to "leave no trace."

Similarly, in her 2013 book *Braiding Sweetgrass*,[36] Robin Wall Kimmerer, an environmental biologist and member of the Potawatomi tribe, cites many examples of the "honorable harvest," in which the interdependence

35 Schilthuizen, *Darwin Comes to Town: How the Urban Jungle Drives Evolution*, 2018.

36 Kimmerer, *Braiding Sweetgrass: Indigenous Wisdom, Scientific Knowledge and the Teachings of Plants*, 20, 2013.

Robin Wall Kimmerer (1953–).

between humans and other species goes far beyond "sustainability." Sweetgrass, black ash, and a number of other plant species have been shown to thrive *better* in environments where they continue to be harvested traditionally than where the harvesting has stopped.

Far from being an oddity, such mutualism between species, including humans, is normal. Fur trappers who practice their trade thoughtfully increase the local populations of the animals they hunt.[37] So, too, do modern, gun-toting game hunters. Ducks Unlimited, founded by duck hunters in 1937, has conserved more than 15 million acres in North America[38]—roughly the area of West Virginia—and the organization's efforts seem to be working. While North American bird populations in general have declined alarmingly since 1970, waterfowl have increased by over 50%.[39] Trout Unlimited, Salmon Unlimited, Pheasants Forever, and other similar groups have mobilized to protect many other species people are invested in preserving.[40]

There should be no surprise here, for this is how everything else in nature works: coevolution, co-adaptation, and interdependence, even between predators and prey. The whole ecosystem flourishes as each species finds new tricks to eke more out of its own niche, in the process providing increased inputs or services to neighboring species, and helping them to thrive in turn. In nature, relationships are paramount.

The animist worldviews of many indigenous people reflect a practical understanding of this principle. They often attribute personhood to other species; Kimmerer describes her elders referring to beavers as "Beaver people," bears as "Bear people," and even trees as "standing people."[41] If you're committed to the modern Western idea that beavers, bears, and trees are *not* people, you might think of it as a mind hack, analogous to what anthropologists call "fictive kinship" (see Chapter 4). Fictive kinship can socially extend relationships like brother-sister to entire clans or moieties, both strengthening social bonds and discouraging inbreeding by generalizing the incest taboo. "Fictive personhood" can similarly extend our instinctual empathy and reciprocity to the nonhuman, mobilizing both our emotions and our ingenuity on behalf of companion species.

Clearly, fictive kinship and fictive personhood are useful concepts, but do they rest on lies, or reflect deeper truths? Is that even the right question? We once more grapple with the quandaries of authoritative definition that have come up throughout this book—with handedness and ambidexterity in Part I, sex and gender in Part II, and cities, suburbs, and countryside earlier in Part III. If

37 Kimmerer, 190–94.

38 Wyatt, "Texas Helps Ducks Unlimited Reach 15 Million-Acre Conservation Milestone," 2021.

39 Rosenberg et al., "Decline of the North American Avifauna," 2019.

40 McAfee, *More from Less: The Surprising Story of How We Learned to Prosper Using Fewer Resources—and What Happens Next*, 261, 2019.

41 Kimmerer, 58.

Europeans and Aboriginal people define kinship differently, what makes the European definition "real," and the Aboriginal version "fictive"? If the Potawatomi consider the trees people, who has the standing to tell them they're mistaken, and why? They clearly have better ideas about forestry than the colonists did.

This is not a matter of pitting science against animism, but rather, a matter of how we understand categories and identity, and the consequences of that understanding. Insofar as identity affects real world outcomes, we might all benefit by learning something about kinship and personhood from Native elders. In time, we may look back on today's Western ideas about personhood and find them as provincial as the 19th century belief that living things are governed by a different chemistry from inanimate ones, or that humans have no common ancestry with the other great apes.

Similarly provincial thinking has given rise to the idea of so-called "invasive species"—a term coined at the height of the Cold War by English zoologist Charles Sutherland Elton.[42] The notion that nature comes packaged into a predefined taxonomy, with every species native to a certain place and anything discovered *out* of its place an "enemy alien," is reminiscent of the old "Great Chain of Being" cosmology wherein God, as the universe's CEO, assigned every living thing a spot on His org chart (see Planetary Consciousness, between Chapters 4 and 5).

In fact, species evolve and differentiate continuously. Moreover, they migrate all the time, both seasonally and as a result of shifting ecological conditions. The checkerspot butterfly, which flies only a few paces from its cocoon before laying eggs, is about as sedentary as a flying animal can get, yet its range has been creeping steadily northward and uphill as the climate warms. Trees, which seemingly don't move at all, have been shifting their territorial ranges too. Between bird droppings spreading seeds from one continent to another and rafts of vegetation ferrying creatures across oceans, it turns out that life on Earth has never respected geographical boundaries; it's *always* on the move.[43]

Yes, cruise ships, muddy shoes, and undeclared veggies sneaking through customs have sped up and assisted the migrations of many species. Migrations have at times been disruptive, and occasionally catastrophic, especially on remote islands, where highly specialized, long-undisturbed bird and mammal populations have been decimated by cats, rats, and pathogens introduced by human colonists. The global war on "invasive species" has been waged on the strength of a few such ecological horror stories.

42 Elton, *The Ecology of Invasions by Animals and Plants*, 1958.

43 Shah, *The Next Great Migration: The Beauty and Terror of Life on the Move*, 2020.

However, as French ecologist Audrey Muratet has noted, on the entire European continent, not one documented extinction can be attributed to an "invasive species"; in fact, in most cases, their introduction *increases* biodiversity—as one might expect, given that every introduced species creates new relationships, niches, and opportunities for others.

We've gotten the story wrong, Muratet argues, because the "construction of knowledge about [invasive] species is marred by ideological values that bias scientific reasoning and experiments." Moreover:

> **It is difficult not to draw a parallel between exotic species and immigration. [...] The long history of racism and xenophobia, whether in the United States or in Europe, has contributed to the denigration of what appears to be "foreign." In ecology, the restoration of native landscapes through the control or elimination of alien species is predicated on a discourse [...] similar to xenophobic nativist sentiments aimed at human populations. [...] [Such] arguments, like those against immigration in the human sphere [...], are devoid of scientific rigor but not of nauseating ideologies.[44]**

44 Muratet, "Postface: Une Querelle," [Afterword: An Argument,] 2021; translation mine.

Muratet's arguments should not be taken as a call to stop worrying about biodiversity. Many wild plant and animal populations have gone into dangerous decline as human populations have exploded. The main drivers have not been "invasive species" as usually defined, but rather people, domesticated animals, crops, and technologies terraforming the landscape at high speed—shrinking or destroying some niches, creating others, and, of course, altering the climate everywhere.[45] We cannot expect the rest of nature to remain static amid such dynamic upheaval. Migration has always been the way living organisms escape worsening conditions and seek out better ones, and during times of great change, great migrations are bound to occur.[46]

45 Disruptions to the ocean's temperature and pH are especially worrisome.

46 The camel family, whose history has long been intertwined with that of humans, offers a case in point. Usually considered "native" to the Middle East, its greatest diversity occurs in the Americas, and today, it thrives in the wild only in Australia. See Thompson, *Where Do Camels Belong?: Why Invasive Species Aren't All Bad*, 2014.

We humans are no different. A 2020 ProPublica and *New York Times* report entitled "Where will everyone go?" describes conditions at the leading edge of an unfolding crisis, in regions of Central America where climate change and poverty intersect:

> **Even as hundreds of thousands of Guatemalans fled north toward the United States in recent years, in [...] a state**

called Alta Verapaz, where precipitous mountains covered in coffee plantations and dense, dry forest give way to broader gentle valleys—the residents have largely stayed. Now, though, under a relentless confluence of drought, flood, bankruptcy and starvation, they, too, have begun to leave. Almost everyone here experiences some degree of uncertainty about where their next meal will come from. Half the children are chronically hungry, and many are short for their age, with weak bones and bloated bellies. [...] The odd weather phenomenon that many blame for the suffering here—the drought and sudden storm pattern known as El Niño—is expected to become more frequent as the planet warms. Many semiarid parts of Guatemala will soon be more like a desert. Rainfall is expected to decrease by 60% in some parts of the country, and the amount of water replenishing streams and keeping soil moist will drop by as much as 83%. Researchers project that by 2070, yields of some staple crops [...] will decline by nearly a third.[47]

47 Lustgarten, "Where Will Everyone Go?," 2020.

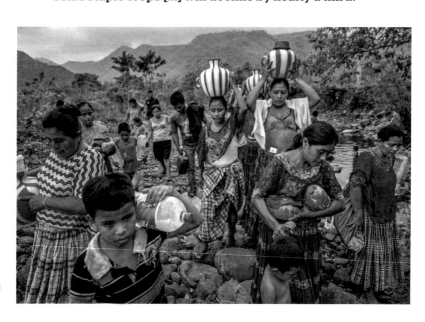

"The river that once flowed through the Nuevo Paraiso Indigenous community is now just a stream. Residents depend on it for all their water needs and are afraid it will completely dry up soon." Alta Verapaz, Guatemala. From Lustgarten, "Where Will Everyone Go?", 2020.

As less habitable or even uninhabitable zones open up around the equator and habitable zones shift toward the poles, life, both human and nonhuman, will do what it has always done: migrate. Over a billion people are likely to be displaced by 2050.[48] Humans today, though, face a new barrier to migration both unique to our species and, despite our tendency to unthinkingly accept it, only a couple of centuries old: the legally regulated form of personal identity known as "national citizenship."

48 Institute for Economics and Peace, "Over One Billion People at Threat of Being Displaced by 2050 due to Environmental Change, Conflict and Civil Unrest," 2020.

As a formalized proxy for language, culture, and values, citizenship is very imperfect. Nearly all countries have become multilingual and multicultural to one degree or another, precisely because of accelerated human migrations (voluntary and not) from the colonial period onward. Globalized media mixes cultures up even further. Ensuing diasporas have created widely dispersed populations with shared cultures and languages.

Pushing against such emerging complexity in the 20th century, colonial administrations created many countries out of whole cloth, especially in Africa and the Middle East, with arbitrary borders insensitive to cultural realities on the ground. Yet arbitrary lines drawn on a map matter when people's movement across them is prevented by force. Then too, our human tendency to embrace identities and undergo divergent cultural evolution often paves a road to nationalism. The partition of India and Pakistan, or of North and South Korea, shows how quickly this process can operate. At any rate, in many economically less-developed parts of the world under climate stress, from Myanmar to Afghanistan to Guatemala, the old nation-state model seems broken.

Using a computer simulation, ProPublica ran two potential scenarios for Central American regions like Alta Verapaz over the coming decades. In the grimmer of the two, northern countries like the United States seal their borders, resulting in the immiseration and early death of tens of millions of climate refugees. Under such stress, local governments may topple, preventing investment in infrastructure and embroiling the region in resource conflict and civil war. The numbers of the dead and starving will balloon, due to the powerful correlation between poverty and birth rate. From the viewpoint of the rich and secure, having more children under these conditions seems irrational, irresponsible, or even inhumane, but as we've seen, this view is out of touch with reality. When child mortality is high and survival depends on subsistence agriculture, we have more children. Or in Malthus's terms, negative checks only come in response to a decline in positive checks.

In the more optimistic ProPublica scenario, the United States allows the flow of climate migrants across the border. Although a porous border would be a major political challenge, it would be the better choice by far. Firstly, it would save many people, avoiding the worst of a humanitarian catastrophe. But also, immigrants are needed north of the border, where the highly urbanized United States is undergoing a demographic crash. Without an influx of young people, soon there won't be a workforce to carry out many important jobs, both skilled and unskilled. The nursing and hospice needs of aging Americans alone are a cause for concern in the coming years, especially since such "caring labor" is less automatable than information work. In his book *The New Nomads*, author and activist-entrepreneur Felix Marquardt makes the case that countries with advanced economies like the US would do well to distribute refugees throughout their territories, including into their less-populated countrysides, as these are the places with the most urgent need for an influx of a younger workforce in essential services. Additional benefits would include avoiding the urban ghettoization and isolation of immigrant communities, and allowing organic cross-cultural contact to gradually soften fears of foreign invasion.[49]

49 Marquardt, *The New Nomads*, 2021.

    While such measures can delay the inevitable, demographic collapse will ultimately cause the growth-based engine of capitalism to sputter. We've seen a preview in the countryside, where the emptying-out is already well advanced. Sooner or later, we will need to rethink the economy in terms that optimize for collective wellbeing rather than for unending growth; but in the richer countries, that day of reckoning will come sooner without immigration, as an aging (and increasingly post-reproductive) population shrinks. Delaying such rethinking has great human costs, as it appears that the growth economy has tipped from one that raised many boats during the baby boom to one that is more zero-sum today, both within countries and between them.

21 Who are we becoming?

The central themes of this book have all revolved around human identity: how we think of ourselves and others, how we form communities, and how we propagate through time. Answering the question "Who are we now?" requires us to reflect on a more basic question: Who do we mean by "we"?

In her book *Twilight of Democracy*, Anne Applebaum emphasizes the urgency of both questions given the recent worldwide turn toward authoritarianism—even in countries, like the US, whose democratic institutions seemed solid at the close of the 20th century. Whether they arise from the political right or left, authoritarian leaders and their enablers invariably weaponize identity politics in the service of us-versus-them nationalism. We've seen how urbanization, especially in countries open to immigration, can create politically polarizing feedback loops that pit cities against rural communities. Yet at a party she threw in the Polish countryside for her friends, both left- and right-leaning, younger and older, Applebaum noticed the

> [...] false and exaggerated division of the world into "Somewheres" and "Anywheres"—people who are supposedly rooted to a single place versus people who travel; people who are supposedly "provincial" versus those who are supposedly "cosmopolitan" [...]. [P]eople with fundamentally different backgrounds could get along just fine, because most people's "identities" stretch beyond this simple duality. It is possible to be rooted to a place and yet open to the world. It is possible to care about the local and the global at the same time.

Applebaum felt especially hopeful about the young:

> They mixed English and Polish, danced to the same music, knew the same songs. No deep cultural differences, no profound civilizational clashes, no unbridgeable identity gaps appeared to divide them. Maybe the teenagers who feel both Polish and European, who don't mind whether they

are in the city or the country, are harbingers of something else, something better, something that we can't yet imagine. Certainly there are many others like them, and in many countries.[1]

1 Applebaum, *Twilight of Democracy*, 180, 2020.

The data in Chapter 16 support Applebaum's view. Young people from the city and from the countryside are far more alike in their outlook than older people. Technology, double-edged as always, can take both credit and blame—credit for connecting far-flung people together into global communities (especially the young), and blame for enabling the mass surveillance, disinformation, and polarization campaigns that empower authoritarianism and create social division.

2 See Chapter 20.

The social challenges posed by driverless cars[2] suggest that technology will soon have an even more profound role to play in our answer to the question "Who are we now?" AI enables machines to exhibit agency, and as such, requires us to think of them as more than mere "engines" performing rote computational tasks, or passive "media" helping humans to communicate at a distance. Our reluctance to imagine that anything nonhuman could exhibit agency has far deeper roots than the AI debate; it has much to do with how Western thought has conceived of the nonhuman natural world as an "externality," that is, as also lacking agency.

3 See the first interlude.

I believe that "we" ought to expand to include not only the nonhuman life on our planet, but also all of its factories, tools, and robots—that they are no less "natural" than the farm, or the forest, or our own human bodies. James Lovelock, of Gaia hypothesis renown,[3] agreed:

> [N]either Newcomen's [steam] engine nor a nuclear power plant looks or behaves much like a zebra or an oak tree; they appear to be utterly different in every respect. Nevertheless [...] the Anthropocene is a consequence of life on Earth. It is a product of evolution; it is an expression of nature.[4]

4 Lovelock, *Novacene*, 70, 2019.

As a wise systems thinker, Lovelock was alive to the way ecosystems are built out of webs of interdependence. Technology is no exception:

> We shall not descend into the kind of war between humans and machines that is so often described in science fiction because we need each other. Gaia will keep the peace.

This isn't a plea for granting personhood as usually understood, with its attendant rights and responsibilities, to giant yellow FANUC robots and autonomous John Deere tractors. Nor does it make sense to ask squirrels and rivers to vote in our elections. We're having a hard enough time

5 For instance: philosopher and polymath Justin Smith-Ruiu has written, "AI is [...] a massive kick in the balls to humanity. I will continue to kick back for as long as I am alive—not in combat against the "pathetic fallacy" [the attribution of human feelings and responses to inanimate things or animals], the very notion of which I reject, but in defense of the ecumene of true beings against the encroachment of spurious ones." Smith-Ruiu, "Cull the Robo-Dogs, Cherish the Dirt-Clods: On AI, the Pathetic Fallacy, and the Boundaries of Community," 2023.

6 See Chapters 12 and 13.

7 See Chapters 18 and 19.

Stelarc, *Third Hand*, Tokyo, Yokohama, Nagoya, 1976–1980.

securing human rights (and the vote) for all humans! Soon enough, we probably *will* have robots with something akin to feelings, consciousness, and a sense of self we can relate to socially, and this will inevitably complicate our thinking, but that's a topic for a whole different book. In any case such questions about personhood, social status, and agency seem irrelevant for the kinds of robots described in Chapter 20—asocial machines that do intensive, repetitive life support labor far away from human beings, on farms, at ports, and in production lines. We probably don't need to discuss robot rights for irrigation systems.

However, the habit of "othering," which we've encountered so many times throughout this book, is troubling both when we apply it to each other, *and* when we apply it to nature or technology. It's not coincidental that in this period of increasingly fractious identity politics, many of us are also distancing ourselves from our own technologies—asserting that they're separate from us, or even at odds with us, rather than an integral part of who we are.**5** Intersex surgeries, hormone therapies, birth control, in vitro fertilization, and other medical technologies of the postwar era have been key to the emergence of many of the identities explored in Part II.**6** Technology has allowed us to emancipate ourselves from the Malthusian trap of subsistence agriculture, and has enabled us to start dismantling the patriarchy that has accompanied it.**7** The technologies that allow large cities to form have been

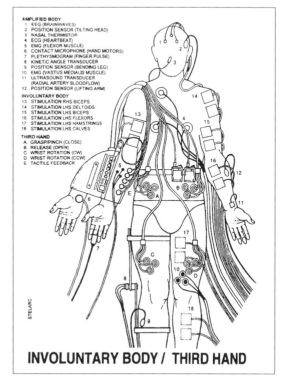

INVOLUNTARY BODY / THIRD HAND

prerequisites for the rich cultures and minority identities that emerge in urban conditions, as Kinsey pointed out and the survey data confirm.[8] And, of course, most of us wouldn't exist at all had it not been for the technological revolutions that so dramatically increased our numbers starting around 1700, and stepping up further around 1945.

Clearly then, technology is fundamental to who we are; but more than that, it's a mistake to see it as a mere "tool" or "resource," for the same reason that it's wrong to consider nature an "externality." The Australian performance artist Stelarc put this beautifully in an interview about his work in 2002:

> **The body has always been a prosthetic body. Ever since we evolved as hominids and developed bipedal locomotion, two limbs became manipulators. We have become creatures that construct tools, artefacts and machines. We've always been augmented by our instruments, our technologies. Technology is what constructs our humanity; the trajectory of technology is what has propelled human developments. I've never seen the body as purely biological, so to consider technology as a kind of alien other that happens upon us at the end of the millennium is rather simplistic.[9]**

8 See Chapter 16.

9 Zylinska and Hall, "Probings: An Interview with Stelarc," 2002.

In other words, with our use of fire, clothes, medicines, and so on, technology has *always* been part of us, not an "other." Long before modern AI, Donna Haraway made a similar point in even more striking terms:

> **The machine is not an *it* to be animated, worshipped, and dominated. The machine is *us*, our processes, an aspect of our embodiment. We can be responsible for machines; they do not dominate or threaten us. We are responsible for boundaries; we are they.[10]**

10 Haraway, "A Cyborg Manifesto: Science, Technology, and Socialist-Feminism in the Late Twentieth Century," 1991.

This is why the idea that robots are "taking our jobs," as if robots are some kind of alien invading force, doesn't make a lot of sense. Robots aren't an "other" that competes with us—like any technology, they're part of us. They may not exactly be *alive* according to most definitions,[11] but they grow out of civilization the same way hair and nails grow out of a living body. They're part of humanity... and we're partly machine.

Granted, this may seem like cold comfort to human seasonal laborers who lose their livelihood to robotic fruit pickers that can, in Doug Nimz's words,[12] "run for 24 hours a day [when] conditions are fit"—perhaps picking the fruit at peak ripeness with a flurry of precision manipulators, operating in an eerily lit greenhouse with an unbreathable high-CO_2 atmosphere.

11 Although by a more expansive definition of life, they are; see Walker, "AI Is Life," 2023.

12 See Chapter 20.

At issue is not the machine, but inequality among human beings. Too many of us haven't understood yet that we're also interdependent. We're all in it together; we need to share our gains as we develop in order for the center to hold. By "othering" the robot and thinking of it as a competitor that has won a zero-sum game of efficient fruit picking, we take our eyes off the real problem: the person picking the fruit had no stake in the success of the farm, let alone the survival of the planet, and is considered disposable by the farm's owners and by society when no longer "useful" at that job. When a government engages in mass surveillance of its citizenry, a similar breach in solidarity takes place, whether the mechanism involves ubiquitous networks of human informants (as in communist East Germany) or ubiquitous networks of AI-enabled cameras (as in Xinjiang).**13**

13 See Chapter 14.

This is the situation we live in today: alienation. It implies that the human citizen or laborer was *already* being treated like a non-person—that is, like a machine. Conversely, we're in the untenable position of "othering" the machine because we were already in the untenable position of "othering" each other.

The underlying inequalities cut in well-documented ways across lines of race, ethnicity, gender, and class. In the American context, the owners of large farms, like big businesses in many sectors of the American economy, tend to be older, white, and male.**14** They may be worried about cultural upheaval or having their guns taken away, but they're not generally the ones worried about robots taking their jobs. On the contrary, they're the ones installing and upgrading those robotic systems, to improve the profitability of their farms. (In

14 In other countries, equivalent majoritarian biases apply.

Woolworth's employees on strike, New York, 1937.

fairness, they may feel they have little choice to remain competitive, if all the neighbors are upgrading.) It's the largely Hispanic farm laborers whose livelihoods are threatened. Cycles like this lead to amplification of inequalities over time, and the hardening of identity groups in the face of struggle and grievance.

Of such a struggle in the coal mines of Harlan County, Kentucky, in the 1930s, songwriter-activist Florence Reece sang,

Which side are you on? Which side are you on?
They say in Harlan County, There are no neutrals there.
You'll either be a union man, Or a thug for J.H. Blair.
Oh, workers can you stand it? Oh, tell me how you can.
Will you be a lousy scab, Or will you be a man?

Eventually, union solidarity worked, and not just for coal miners (or men). The labor movement secured important rights and dignities many of us take for granted today; we can thank those organizers for the five day, 40-hour work week.

Organizing relies on the creation of anonymous identities, as described in the Introduction; that's why popular movements like the Harlan County worker's strike have historically only taken off once urbanization is in full swing. Peasant farmers in agricultural societies are too spread out to create concentrated "people power," especially without modern communication technologies. When workers gather at the coal mine or in the factory, though, the situation changes. Even if initially underpaid and overworked, they can form an anonymous identity and take collective action.

Commenting on an earlier people's movement during the Industrial Revolution, radical British orator John Thelwall wrote,

> **[M]onopoly, and the hideous accumulation of capital, in a few hands, [...] carry, in their own enormity, the seeds of cure. Man is, by his very nature, social and communicative—proud to display the little knowledge he possesses, and eager, as opportunity presents, to encrease his store. Whatever presses men together, therefore, though it may generate some vices, is favourable to the diffusion of knowledge, and ultimately promotive of human liberty. Hence every large workshop and manufactory is a sort of political society, which no act of parliament can silence, and no magistrate disperse.[15]**

15 Thelwall, *The Rights of Nature Against the Usurpations of Establishments*, 1796.

Seen this way, unions, collective bargaining, and labor politics are social technologies, and as always, the spark of an idea requires a sufficient concentration of people to ignite. The function of such social technologies is to more equitably distribute the wealth generated by efficiencies of scale.

The trouble, though, is that the adversarial nature of class struggle combines in-group solidarity with out-group othering. It implies that life is zero-sum, us-versus-them. It creates a binary identity around being either a "worker" or an "owner," with neither side necessarily incented to do the right thing from a planetary perspective. Should coal mining still be practiced today? If we believe in the importance of efficiency, technology, and environmental regulation for continued human survival

In 1960s animated sitcom *The Jetsons*, patriarch George Jetson regularly complains of his heavy work load: pushing a button on and off as many as five times for three hours, three days a week.

on Earth, a traditional union whose mission is to protect labor from disruption will be pitted against this greater goal. On the other hand, traditional owners who instrumentalize their human "workforce" have no incentive to redistribute the economic benefits of efficiency—or to worry about the planet.

Ultimately, this process of commodifying others doesn't put the farmer or mine owner on top either. It ends with complete financialization—the takeover of economic, cultural, and political concerns by, quite literally, money itself. Businesses become rows in a spreadsheet, enriching financial institutions and speculators far removed from realities on the ground. These speculators' stakes will be purely abstract and economic; they'll become "pixel farmers" in the most thorough sense, optimizing cash crops or maximizing extraction for commodity markets while workers fall back into poverty and the planet overheats.

Even the jobs of the "pixel farmers" aren't safe. Remember, AI can "run for 24 hours a day," working the virtual marketplace just as an autonomous tractor can till the field—faster and better than any human can. Financialization looks a bit like a pyramid scheme, but nobody really wins—not even the finance people at the top of the pyramid. Their children may inherit a large number on a spreadsheet, but with a wrecked planet and the hatred of every other survivor, they'll be unhappy in their bunkers. And then, the staff will mutiny! Money can obfuscate and anonymize our interdependence, but can't magic it away.[16]

So, it turns out that we're *all* members of the precariat: a social class whose survival is precarious at every level, lacking in physical, psychological, or economic security—not because we lack the means for everyone to thrive, but because we lack solidarity at the needed scale. In an interdependent world, we can only achieve safety through mutual care, empathy, and trust. The overarching challenge of our century is to become a very big "we," including all humans, our technologies, and the plants, and animals, and every other lifeform on the planet. They are not just our kin, but our self. We'll need a planet-sized umbrella identity.

16 Rushkoff, *Survival of the Richest*, 2022.

Appendix for data nerds

1 When other datasets were used (e.g. for long term and international statistics like human population over the last 10,000 years), you can find a pointer to the original source under the plot's ↓ button in the online version of this book.

Most of the plots in this book were generated from the responses to a series of surveys I conducted using Amazon's Mechanical Turk service ("MTurk") between 2016 and 2022. This Appendix describes how I processed the data to generate the plots.[1]

But first, a word on the demography of MTurk workers. They represent a fairly broad cross-section of Americans. They're certainly more varied and representative than the respondents that used to make up the mainstay of academic surveys in the social sciences: undergraduates on college campuses. However, there are some significant statistical differences between MTurk workers as a population and the US as a whole. The biggest are age and sex.

To create an account, you have to be at least 18 years old, so children aren't represented at all. It would be interesting to know how the under-18 crowd would respond to some of the questions, but this would require different tools (and a careful ethics review). People over 50 are also underrepresented, while younger adults

22.0.0 Age distributions of USA and Mechanical Turk populations
Probability density by age

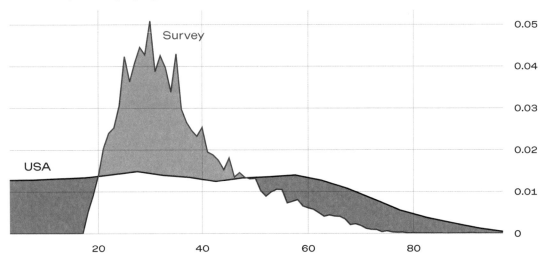

are overrepresented. Few respondents are over 70, and almost nobody is over 80—much like a typical young professional workforce.

The age and race distributions of MTurk workers are quite stable over time. Separately plotting age distributions for the 2018, 2019, 2020, and 2021 surveys on gender and sexuality (which are, remember, distinct sets of respondents) shows that, except for random noise due to limited sample size, the curves are all the same. This gives us a rare instance of a variable that changes purely as a function of age, and not as a function of time (see Chapter 7), unlike any of the personal identity or behavioral traits explored throughout this book. Not coincidentally, unlike those traits, age isn't subject to social transmission. But more to the point, the stable age distribution tells us that people at every age are entering and leaving the Mechanical Turk workforce, "mixing" with the larger population in a way that leaves this key demographic property unaffected. Hence, year-to-year changes in other traits can be fairly confidently attributed to real changes in the US population, as opposed to unrelated changes in the demographics of Mechanical Turk workers.

22.0.1 Age distributions of survey respondents, 2018–2021
Probability density by age

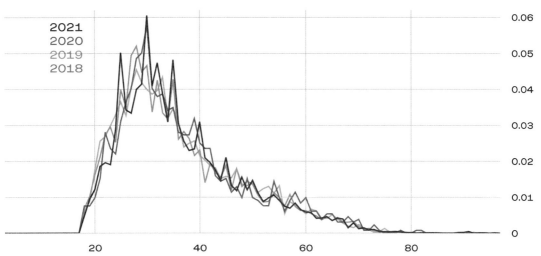

As described in Chapter 5, women's longer lifespan affects the sex balance in the US; at 18 years old, they're a slight minority, while by age 75 they represent 55% of the population, and rising. Among survey respondents, women are a significant majority across almost all ages. Women may be the majority because, although Mechanical Turk is a bit like Uber, you can take online surveys without needing to leave home, own a car, or let strangers into your space. So at least physically, it's a safe way to participate in the gig economy. It also requires no

22.1 Comparison of female representation between USA and Mechanical Turk % by age

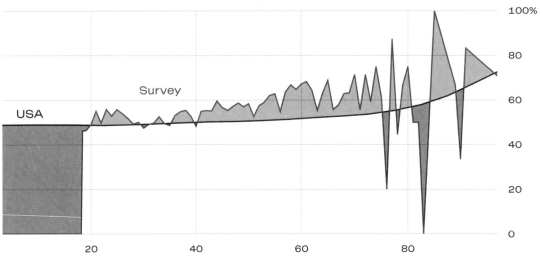

resources other than access to the internet, and is compatible with being a homemaker. Hence Uber workers skew male, and Mechanical Turk workers skew female, especially among the older respondents—arguably, further evidence of male privilege.

Many of the plots in this book break down respondents by age, which (mostly[2]) sidesteps the differences in representation by age; there are just larger error bars where there's less MTurk representation. Plots that break down respondents by (binary) sex similarly sidestep any non-representative sampling by sex.

You may have noticed something different about the age histograms in this Appendix: they're unbinned, or more accurately, the bins are all a single year,[3] unlike similar plots throughout the rest of the book where I've binned age ranges more coarsely to produce a smoother curve. Unbinned, the data are noisy, even when including the whole population of respondents. Above age 80, there are so few respondents that some data points are entirely missing.

A degree of judgment is needed to interpret noisy histograms. Is the apparent rise in female respondents after middle age real? Almost certainly. Are the drops below 50% at some ages above 70 real? Probably not, but the response counts are too low to say so with high confidence. There's no unbiased, optimal, and "fully automatic" way to make such judgments. I tried several fancy ideas from the statistics literature, but they introduce problems of their own.[4] Almost all have one or more parameters, making them *not* "fully automatic." Some generate output with discrete steps, creating the illusion that the underlying percentages change discontinuously at precise ages. Others generate smooth curves, but these curves still

2 One might still worry about the differing distribution shapes within an age bin, especially if the age bin is broad; in practice, however, this isn't a major effect.

3 The questions about birth month actually allow somewhat better age precision.

4 Shimazaki and Shinomoto, "Kernel Bandwidth Optimization in Spike Rate Estimation," 2010; Jensen, "Kernel Probability Estimation for Binomial and Multinomial Data," 2015; Scargle, "Studies in Astronomical Time Series Analysis. V. Bayesian Blocks, a New Method to Analyze Structure in Photon Counting Data," 1998.

have up-and-down wiggles that aren't statistically significant—yet judging the significance of those wiggles becomes less intuitive when the data have already been heavily processed. Getting rid of the wiggles is possible, but only at the cost of washing out a lot of interesting and statistically meaningful variation by age.

At the heart of the problem is the tradeoff between bin size and sample size. A small bin (in the limit, a single year) will let us finely resolve changes in percentage by age, but then the sample size within each bin will be low, making the percentage itself highly uncertain. A large bin will include more samples, hence improve our estimate of the percentage, but at the cost of washing out any changes by age.

Remember that each sample is just one bit of information, a yes/no, or in the language of statistics, a "binomial variable." If a bin has no samples in it, our uncertainty is complete. If it has a single sample, then the only possible values are 0% and 100%. If it has two samples, the only possible values are 0%, 50%, and 100%. As the number of samples grows, the number of possible values increases, and our confidence in the accuracy of the measured value increases too— that is, the error bar gets smaller. Quantifying this relationship relies on making some statistical approximations, which I'll only sketch here. Consult the sources I cite for derivations and more details.

If n^+ is the number of "yes" responses and n^- is the number of "no" responses, for a total of $n = n^+ + n^-$ samples, then the probability of a "yes" is easily calculated: $p = n^+/n$. We can express it as a percentage by multiplying by 100.

But what about the error bars? Often, error bars are described as "plus or minus" some fixed measurement error ε, which we'd write $p \pm \varepsilon$, but this can't work here, as any probability p must remain between zero and one. So, for instance, if we had a sample size of three and all three responses were "no," then we'd have $p = 0$, but with such a small sample the uncertainty should be high; yet zero would still have to be the *lower* bound on the confidence interval, because a probability can't be less than zero. Hence the error bars can't be symmetric. Put another way, the midpoint of the confidence interval can't in general be p.

American mathematician Edwin Bidwell Wilson (1879–1964) derived an elegant, often-used formula for the asymmetric error bars of a binomial variable.[5] In a 2006 paper, biostatisticians Jake Olivier and Warren May[6] give the following modified form of this "Wilson interval":

5 Wilson, "Probable Inference, the Law of Succession, and Statistical Inference," 1927.

6 Olivier and May, "Weighted Confidence Interval Construction for Binomial Parameters," 2006.

$$(1 - w)p + (w)\frac{1}{2} \ \pm \ Z_{\alpha/2}\sqrt{(1 - w)\frac{p(1 - p)}{n + Z^2_{\alpha/2}} + (w)\frac{1}{4(n + Z^2_{\alpha/2})}}$$

where

$$w = \frac{Z_{\alpha/2}^2}{n + Z_{\alpha/2}^2}$$

and $Z_{\alpha/2}$ is the "probit" (or $1 - \frac{1}{2}\alpha$ quantile of the normal distribution) corresponding to the target error rate α. Throughout the book, I've used a 90% confidence interval, which works out to

$$Z_{\alpha/2} = \sqrt{2}\,\mathrm{erf}^{-1}(1 - \alpha) \approx 1.64485$$

with $\alpha = 1 - 0.9 = 0.1$.

Olivier and May's form of the Wilson interval is useful in a couple of ways. First, it shows that the midpoint of the confidence interval interpolates between 0.5 and p with coefficient w. If $n = 0$, $w = 1$, the midpoint is 0.5, and the confidence interval ranges from zero to one, indicating complete uncertainty as one would expect. As n increases, w goes toward zero, the midpoint gets closer to p, and the uncertainty shrinks. Practically, the formulation allows us to use weighted averaging to calculate p.[7] I'll get to how survey respondents are weighted in a moment.

First, though, let's finish with binning. One option would have been to do something dead simple: use a fixed bin size—say, 6 years—for all plots. However, there is no single optimal bin size. Using a single value produces huge error bars and poor estimates in some places, while washing out important and statistically significant detail in others. Rather than using either fixed bins or fancy but still imperfect automatic binning techniques, I've chosen the bins manually for each plot, sizing them adaptively to bring out finer detail where the data support doing so, and using larger bins to get rid of fluctuations I judged likely to be spurious. I tried to err on the side of larger bins to keep the plots as legible as possible and avoid adding visual noise to them. As often as possible, I've also combined multiple series in the same plot (hence with the same binning), to allow for apples-to-apples comparisons. I believe the result is a reasonable balance between clear storytelling, simplicity, and statistical rigor.

Avoiding fancy techniques and showing the binning clearly on the plots also allows one to read off data points, like "about 20% of 18–20 year-old female respondents are lesbian" (see Chapter 8), with confidence that this statistic is accurate, easily reproducible, and "what it says on the tin," that is, based solely on the weighted responses of all 18–20-year-old female respondents. However, the exact percentage, the shape of the curve,

[7] One could take this further and calculate a correction to w based on the variation in sample weights contributing to each estimate; when the stratified sampling weights vary widely, n is effectively reduced.

8   I'm not making raw survey data available, as this would require very careful vetting to avoid any possibility of de-anonymization. Narayanan and Shmatikov, "Robust De-Anonymization of Large Sparse Datasets," 2008.

and the error bars will all change if the youngest age bin is instead set to 18–19, or 18–21. That's why, in the freely available online version of this book, the binning is editable. If you tap on the ↔ button, you can drag bin boundaries to move them, and add or remove bins by tapping. You can also download the unbinned data behind each plot, allowing for a more open-ended re-analysis.[8]

22.2 **"Do you identify as non-binary?" binned randomly** % by age

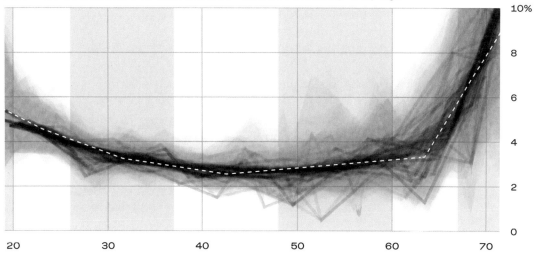

To illustrate visually how varying the binning can affect the curves, we can try superimposing many randomly binned versions of the same data—here, as an example, responses to the question "Do you identify as non-binary?" as a function of age, per figures 10.1 and 10.2 in Chapter 10. (Averages are rendered in semi-transparent black, while error bars are rendered in yellow; the binning used in figure 10.2 is also shown superimposed.) These many superimpositions make a good case that the U shape is real, and not an artifact of any specific choice of bins. Still, the exact profile of the U can vary substantially depending on binning, and some bin choices introduce additional artifacts.[9] In the plots throughout the book, I've tried to bin conservatively, to reveal the stable underlying pattern while keeping the counts in each bin as large as possible.

9   You may wonder whether this superimposition technique could itself have been used to render "objective consensus" curves throughout the book. Unfortunately, even here there are "editorial" choices: each random binning is created by picking a constant number of bin boundaries (I've chosen 10), uniformly distributed over the range of ages (here, 18–76). These (or any other) choices, and the underlying non-uniformity of the data, mean that the distribution of different curves visualized is still not free of statistical bias.

I've used a technique commonly called "stratified sampling" to non-uniformly weight the answers of different respondents. The concept is straightforward. Suppose we're estimating the number of people who answer "yes" to a question like "Are you heterosexual?" between the ages of 50 and 70. To use round numbers, suppose that 52% of Americans in that age range are women, but 65% of survey respondents in the same age range are women. (For purposes of this calculation let's also assume a sex binary, i.e. that 48% of Americans in this age range are men, and 35% of our survey respondents are.) Since women and men vary systematically in how they respond to the question, we'd want to weight our survey respondents' answers in such a way that the average will reflect the US population as a whole. Specifically, the mens' answers should be overweighted by the ratio $0.48/0.35 \approx 1.37$ while the womens' answers should be under-weighted by $0.52/0.65 = 0.8$. I've done this kind of reweighting based not only on sex, but on a handful of crude demographic character-istics measured by the 2017 US Census:

1   Age, broken down into four ranges: 18–24, 25–34, 35–49, and 50+.

2   Sex, binary and based on assignment at birth.

3   Race, broken down into four categories: White or "Caucasian," Black, Asian, and all others, this last including Native American, Asian and Pacific Islander, and any non-categorized response.

4   Urban vs. rural, based on population density calculated from ZIP code.

This works out to $4 \times 2 \times 4 \times 2 = 64$ demographic buckets in total. It's important to emphasize that these categories are arbitrary and should not be interpreted as meaningful in their own right. As many plots in this book make clear, there's nothing special about any particular choice of age ranges, and neither sex nor urban/rural distinctions are binary in real life. The four racial categories, too, are not only arbitrary, but poorly defined and reductive, not unlike those used in South Africa under Apartheid. I've broken the data down into these 64 buckets for reweighting because when one uses stratified sampling, it's import-ant to keep the total number of categories for reweighting small, and the occupancy of each category non-negligible, lest one end up with overly large weights for small or undersampled populations (which would produce a noisy result). The 2017 US Census provided fairly reliable estimates of the total sizes of these particular buckets, and our MTurk survey respondents could also be sorted into them based on their answers to specific questions (some of which, e.g. for race, mir-rored the anachronistic language used in the Census precisely to make a direct comparison possible). Regardless of how arbitrary the buckets are, when populations are sorted in this way, their answers to other survey questions do vary systematically by bucket, and re-weighting the buckets to conform to the overall US population is likely to make our statistics more representative.[10]

10 I've also generated versions of all of the sur-vey-based plots in this book using raw, unweighted data; in general, the results are not qualitatively differ-ent from the weighted ones, though of course precise percentages and curve shapes do vary. The down-loadable data in the online version of this book provides stratified sampling weights independently, allowing data nerds to reproduce unweighted plots if desired.

In Chapter 1, I mentioned that there were a few "traps" laid in the surveys to exclude from the analysis most people who responded by clicking randomly. These included:

A   Checking six questions about birth month: "Were you born in January or February?", "Were you born in March or April?", "Were you born in May or June?", "Were you born in July or August?", "Were you born in September or October?", and "Were you born in November or December?". Exactly one of these six questions should be answered with a "yes," and the other five with a "no." Since there are $2^6 = 64$ possible responses, clicking at random will yield a valid combination only $6/64 = 9.375\%$ of the time.[11] Recall also that the questions are interspersed with many others in random order. In addition to asking for the respondent's age, some surveys asked the yes/no question "Were you born before 1983?". I picked this year because it divided respondents fairly evenly in half based on their median age (at least, at the time I wrote the question). Random clicking will thus be inconsistent with age about half the time.[12]

B   Answering the same way to both "Were you born in the US?" and "Were you born outside the US?" is inconsistent, and will happen 50% of the time for a random clicker.

C   Answering "yes" to "Do you menstruate?" but "no" to "Have you ever menstruated?" is inconsistent, and will happen 25% of the time for a random clicker.

D   Answering "no" to "Have you ever been pregnant?" but claiming to have personally given birth to more than zero children is inconsistent. Age, number of children, height, and weight (when present) are checked against generous upper and/or lower bounds.[13] In the politics surveys, voting for multiple presidential candidates in the same November election is disallowed, as is claiming to have voted for a 2016 candidate while answering "no" to "Did you vote in the November 2016 presidential election?" or claiming to be planning to vote for a 2020 candidate while answering "no" to "Do you plan to vote in the November 2020 presidential election?". ZIP codes are verified.

In general, around 10–20% of respondents were weeded out by these "traps," though the majority appear to have been honest mistakes or misunderstandings rather than random clicking. *Not* being weeded

[11] In practice, considerably less often, as when humans "click at random" the result isn't really random—it usually consists either of straight "no"s, straight "yes"es, or a more-balanced-than-truly-random mix of "no" and "yes." In other words, confronted with six binary questions and told to answer them randomly, few people will answer five one way, and just one the other way, because the result doesn't "look random enough."

[12] Birth month and the exact date the survey is taken both figure into the calculation.

[13] Think: Guinness World Records.

22.3.0 **Time taken to complete survey** % of peak by minutes

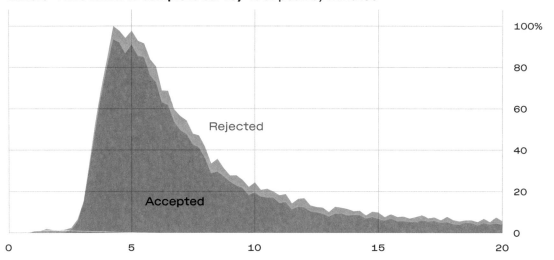

22.3.1 **Acceptance rate as a function of time taken to complete survey**
% by minutes

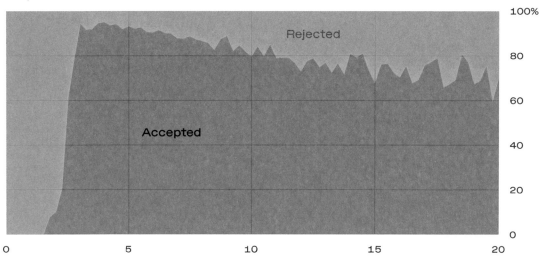

14 These histograms are binned uniformly by 15 second increments.

out doesn't guarantee honesty, but it means that a respondent would have needed to go to some effort to invent a consistent fake persona.

A histogram of survey completion time is revealing.**14** Most commonly, respondents took about 5 minutes to do the gender and sexuality survey, which had the largest number of questions. (The completion time statistics were broadly similar for the other surveys.) Very few people finished in fewer than 2.5 minutes, and we can see that the acceptance rate of these very fast respondents is 0%—either they were clicking randomly, or they were sloppy. Notice, though, that super-speedy respondents are a tiny minority. Those who took between 3 and 5 minutes had acceptance rates above 90%.

Interestingly, beyond 5 minutes, the longer respondents took to finish, the lower the rate of acceptance, dropping steadily to 60% by about 20 minutes. It's possible that taking a long time to finish is correlated with being distracted, cognitively impaired, or simply not being fluent in English. I've occasionally used quotes from the free-text answers of weeded-out respondents who had clearly made an honest mistake but had something interesting to say (though their quantitative data are excluded from the plots).

In Chapters 2 and 14, linear methods are used to combine the responses of multiple yes/no questions into numerical scores—in Chapter 2, $D = 30$ questions about handedness, and in Chapter 14, $D = 37$ questions about gender presentation. Responses are modeled as D-dimensional vectors of zeros (for "no") and ones (for "yes"). The overall average response is first calculated and subtracted from each individual response, so that response vectors are zero-centered. Each component is then normalized by its standard deviation. Zero-centered and normalized response vectors are used for linear regression and, in Chapter 14, Principal Component Analysis (PCA). Errorbars for linear regression are calculated empirically, by holding out a random 30% of the responses to serve as the test set, while evaluating optimal question weights using the remaining 70% of the data. This process is repeated 600 times. Histograms of linear estimator performance show average values and 90% confidence intervals for the held-out test data over these 600 runs.

A final note. In plots showing the medians of nonnegative integers, such as number of children (e.g. in Chapter 18), uniform random values in the range $(-\frac{1}{2}, +\frac{1}{2})$ are added to individual samples, then these are clipped to avoid going negative, before calculating medians and quantiles. This is done to allow the medians and quantiles to vary continuously, revealing underlying trends in the data rather than stair-stepping between integer values. (Means, drawn as solid lines, are calculated using the raw data without any added noise.) The method isn't perfect, but it's simple, it makes the plot more informative, and it produces unbiased quantile estimates.

Acknowledgments

***Who Are We Now?* died and came back to life** several times. In its earliest incarnation, it was a side project based on one of the lectures I gave for a course at the University of Washington, *Intelligent Machinery, Identity, and Ethics*. My first thanks go to Adrienne Fairhall and Benjamin Bratton, for encouraging me to put that course together as a way to organize my thoughts into something that could turn into a book. Thanks also to my students, whose questions and after-class discussion often challenged and refined my thinking.

"Just record and transcribe the lectures, then edit them," said Benjamin. I complained that there was too much material. "Then find a self-contained piece and start with that," he advised. It worked, but it wasn't as easy as he made it sound!

The (more or less) self-contained piece in question, focusing on the "identity" element of the course, originally consisted of a slideshow of plots based on my first Mechanical Turk surveys, each revealing something non-obvious and accompanied by a caption one or two sentences long. In my quest to contextualize these findings, stories about evolutionary biologists, sexologists, criminologists, witches and wizards, and eco-prophets began entering the mix. It seemed, for a while, that *Who Are We Now?* was destined to become a comic book, something like xkcd meets the OkCupid data blog.[1] (That might still happen one day.) Lucy Bellwood drew some beautiful comix treatments, as well as providing helpful editorial input.

As more surveys and more background material accumulated, and as the stakes of evolving human identity came into focus and the text lengthened, it became clear that this needed to become a "real" book. Warm thanks to Lesley Hazleton for making that abundantly clear one overcast afternoon on the deck of her houseboat. I began another rewrite and shopped the manuscript around, but had trouble finding a traditional publisher who both believed in the idea and was willing to include all of the graphics, let alone invest in the design that would be needed to do justice to the visual material. Never mind putting it all on the web for free.

[1]   If you don't know what either of these are, you should stop reading and go check them out.

The solution turned out to be near at hand: the crew I had worked with to publish my novella, *Ubi Sunt*, were game to reunite. Profound thanks to JC Gabel of Hat & Beard Press, for his unhesitating boldness in taking this unconventional project on, and to multitalented design geniuses James Goggin, Marie Otsuka, and Minkyoung Kim, who dove into ambitious parallel treatments of *Who Are We Now?* as both an interactive web book and a print book. Johan Michalove, my polymathic *Intelligent Machinery* TA, undertook workflow engineering, fact checking, reference wrangling, captioning, editing, image rights securing, and when needed, eyebrow-raising, with timely assistance from David Michalove. The maps rock because we were fortunate to enlist cartographer extraordinaire Scott Reinhard to make them. Laurie Aguera-Arcas was an exacting copy editor, applying her red pen to the manuscript in a hundred or so places per chapter (thank you, Mom). Sybil Perez at Hat & Beard was our final proofreader. My deepest gratitude to this globe-spanning dream team, who dedicated a painstaking year to turning *Who Are We Now?* from an unruly collection of text, code, and pixels into a beautiful finished whole.

Some of the material in Chapters 3 and 14 first appeared in essays I co-authored with Margaret Mitchell and Alex Todorov; my warm thanks to them for that intellectual partnership.

Eleanor Drage, Geoff Keeling, Adrienne Fairhall, Justin Smith-Ruiu, Sonia Katyal, and Emily French provided close readings and major editorial input into large sections of the text. This would have been a different and lesser book without them. My heartfelt thanks also to: Maikoiyo Alley-Barnes, Dylan Baker, Genevieve Bell, Rebecca Brown, Kristen Carney, Ted Chiang, Patricia Churchland, Kate Devlin, Ellen Forney, Nancy Hartunian, Katie Herzog, Tim Keck, Rem Koolhaas, Danielle Krettek, Alison Lentz, Kerry Mackereth, Andrew McAfee, Phoenix Meadowlark, K Allado-McDowell, Audrey Muratet, Peter Norvig, Tim O'Reilly, Irene Pepperberg, Dan Savage, Oliver Siy, Troy Conrad Therrien, Chai Vasarhelyi, Judy Wajcman, Lawrence Weschler, and Oberon Zell-Ravenheart. As with any project of this size, the roster of friends and colleagues whose intellectual input and encouragement mattered over the years is long, and I'm sure my recollection is incomplete—so apologies to anyone I've missed. And of course, any errors and all opinions expressed are strictly my own.

Bibliography

Preface

Bermon, Stéphane, and Pierre-Yves Garnier. "Serum Androgen Levels and Their Relation to Performance in Track and Field: Mass Spectrometry Results from 2127 Observations in Male and Female Elite Athletes." *British Journal of Sports Medicine* 51, no. 17 (September 2017): 1309–14.

Bermon, Stéphane, Angelica Lindén Hirschberg, Jan Kowalski, and Emma Eklund. "Serum Androgen Levels Are Positively Correlated with Athletic Performance and Competition Results in Elite Female Athletes." *British Journal of Sports Medicine*. bjsm.bmj.com, December 2018.

Edelman, Lee. *No Future: Queer Theory and the Death Drive*. Durham: Duke University Press, 2004.

Herbenick, Debby, Molly Rosenberg, Lilian Golzarri-Arroyo, J. Dennis Fortenberry, and Tsung-Chieh Fu. "Changes in Penile-Vaginal Intercourse Frequency and Sexual Repertoire from 2009 to 2018: Findings from the National Survey of Sexual Health and Behavior." *Archives of Sexual Behavior* 51, no. 3 (April 2022): 1419–33.

Jensen, Marisa, Jörg Schorer, and Irene R. Faber. "How Is the Topic of Intersex Athletes in Elite Sports Positioned in Academic Literature Between January 2000 and July 2022? A Systematic Review." *Sports Medicine — Open* 8, no. 1 (October 20, 2022): 130.

Kulu, Hill. "Why Do Fertility Levels Vary Between Urban and Rural Areas?" *Regional Studies* 47, no. 6 (June 1, 2013): 895–912.

Ortiz-Ospina, Esteban, and Max Roser. "Marriages and Divorces." *Our World in Data*, 2020. https://ourworldindata.org/marriages-and-divorces.

Roser, Max. "Fertility Rate." *Our World in Data*, 2014. https://ourworldindata.org/fertility-rate.

Introduction: Anonymous identity

Barras, Colin. "Only Known Chimp War Reveals How Societies Splinter." *New Scientist*, May 7, 2014. https://www.newscientist.com/article/mg22229682-600-only-known-chimp-war-reveals-how-societies-splinter/.

Bellafante, Ginia. "Why the Big City President Made Cities the Enemy." *New York Times*. July 24, 2020. https://www.nytimes.com/2020/07/24/nyregion/trump-cities.html.

Cuboniks, Laboria. *The Xenofeminist Manifesto: A Politics for Alienation*. London: Verso Books, 2018.

Dennis, Patricia, Stephen M. Shuster, and C. N. Slobodchikoff. "Dialects in the Alarm Calls of Black-Tailed Prairie Dogs (*Cynomys ludovicianus*): A Case of Cultural Diffusion?" *Behavioural Processes* 181 (December 2020): 104243.

D'Ettorre, Patrizia, and Jürgen Heinze. "Individual Recognition in Ant Queens." *Current Biology* 15, no. 23 (December 6, 2005): 2170–74.

Diamond, Jared. *Guns, Germs, and Steel: The Fates of Human Societies*. New York: W. W. Norton & Company, 2005.

Everett, Daniel Leonard. *Don't Sleep, There Are Snakes: Life and Language in the Amazonian Jungle*. New York: Pantheon Books, 2008.

Filatova, Olga A., Volker B. Deecke, John K. B. Ford, Craig O. Matkin, Lance G. Barrett-Lennard, Mikhail A. Guzeev, Alexandr M. Burdin, and Erich Hoyt. "Call Diversity in the North Pacific Killer Whale Populations: Implications for Dialect Evolution and Population History." *Animal Behaviour* 83, no. 3 (March 1, 2012): 595–603.

Firestone, Shulamith. *The Dialectic of Sex: The Case for Feminist Revolution*. New York: Morrow, 1970.

Fournier, Denis, and Serge Aron. "Evolution: No-Male's Land for an Amazonian Ant." *Current Biology* 19, no. 17 (September 15, 2009): R738–40.

Goodheart, Adam. "The Last Island of the Savages." *The American Scholar* 69, no. 4 (2000): 13–44.

Graeber, David, and David Wengrow. *The Dawn of Everything: A New History of Humanity*. New York: Farrar, Straus and Giroux, 2021.

Haldane, John B. S. "Population Genetics." *Nature: New Biology* 18, no. 1 (1955): 34–51.

Hamilton, W. D. "The Genetical Evolution of Social Behaviour. II." *Journal of Theoretical Biology* 7, no. 1 (July 1964): 17–52.

Lewis, Sophie. "Shulamith Firestone Wanted to Abolish Nature—We Should, Too." *The Nation*, July 14, 2021. https://www.thenation.com/article/society/shulamith-firestone-dialectic-sex/.

Lovelock, James. *Novacene: The Coming Age of Hyperintelligence*. London: Allen Lane, 2019.

Lowie, Robert H. "Some Aspects of Political Organization Among the American Aborigines." *The*

Journal of the Royal Anthropological Institute of Great Britain and Ireland 78, no. 1/2 (1948): 11–24.

Man, E. H. "On the Aboriginal Inhabitants of the Andaman Islands. (Part II.)." *The Journal of the Anthropological Institute of Great Britain and Ireland* 12 (1883): 117–75.

Marquardt, Felix. *The New Nomads: How the Migration Revolution Is Making the World a Better Place.* London: Simon & Schuster, 2021.

Moffett, Mark W. "Human Identity and the Evolution of Societies." *Human Nature* 24, no. 3 (September 2013): 219–67.

——. *The Human Swarm: How Our Societies Arise, Thrive, and Fall.* New York: Basic Books, 2019.

Wikipedia. "Overview effect," May 29, 2020. https://w.wiki/5XuL.

Patterson, F. G. "The Gestures of a Gorilla: Language Acquisition in Another Pongid." *Brain and Language* 5, no. 1 (January 1978): 72–97.

Pepperberg, Irene Maxine. *The Alex Studies: Cognitive and Communicative Abilities of Grey Parrots.* Cambridge, MA: Harvard University Press, 2002.

Rosling, Hans, Ola Rosling, and Anna Rosling Rönnlund. *Factfulness: Ten Reasons We're Wrong About the World — and Why Things Are Better Than You Think.* New York: Flatiron Books, 2018.

Sapolsky, Robert M. *Behave: The Biology of Humans at Our Best and Worst.* New York: Penguin, 2017.

Savage, Dan, and Blaise Agüera y Arcas. "The Sex Robots Are Coming!!! (Episode #526)." Podcast. *Savage Lovecast*, November 22, 2016. https://savage.love/lovecast/2016/11/22/the-sex-robots-are-coming/.

Scott, James C. *Seeing Like a State: How Certain Schemes to Improve the Human Condition Have Failed.* New Haven: Yale University Press, 1998.

Sheehan, Michael J., and Elizabeth A. Tibbetts. "Specialized Face Learning Is Associated with Individual Recognition in Paper Wasps." *Science* 334, no. 6060 (December 2, 2011): 1272–75.

Smith, J. Maynard. "Group Selection and Kin Selection." *Nature* 201, no. 4924 (March 1964): 1145–47.

de Waal, Frans. *Chimpanzee Politics: Power and Sex Among Apes.* New York: Harper & Row, 1982.

——. *Different: Gender Through the Eyes of a Primatologist.* New York: W. W. Norton & Company, Inc., 2022.

——. *Our Inner Ape: A Leading Primatologist Explains Why We Are Who We Are.* New York: Riverhead Books, 2005.

——. *The Bonobo and the Atheist: In Search of Humanism Among the Primates.* New York: W. W. Norton & Company, 2014.

Wissler, Clark. "The Culture-Area Concept in Social Anthropology." *The American Journal of Sociology* 32, no. 6 (1927): 881–91.

——. "The North American Indians of the Plains." *Popular Science Monthly* 82 (May 1913). https://w.wiki/6MLv.

Chapter 1:
Whom to believe?

Hardyck, C., and L. F. Petrinovich. "Left-Handedness." *Psychological Bulletin* 84, no. 3 (May 1977): 385–404.

Jensenius, John S., Jr. "A Detailed Analysis of Lightning Deaths in the United States from 2006 Through 2019." National Lightning Safety Council, February 2020.

Papadatou-Pastou, Marietta, Maryanne Martin, Marcus R. Munafò, and Gregory V. Jones. "Sex Differences in Left-Handedness: A Meta-Analysis of 144 Studies." *Psychological Bulletin* 134, no. 5 (September 2008): 677–99.

Porac, Clare. *Laterality: Exploring the Enigma of Left-Handedness.* Elsevier Scicnce, 2016.

Rodriguez, Alina, Marika Kaakinen, Irma Moilanen, Anja Taanila, James J. McGough, Sandra Loo, and Marjo-Riitta Järvelin. "Mixed-Handedness Is Linked to Mental Health Problems in Children and Adolescents." *Pediatrics* 125, no. 2 (February 2010): e340–48.

Sorenson, Susan B. "Gender Disparities in Injury Mortality: Consistent, Persistent, and Larger than You'd Think." *American Journal of Public Health* 101 Suppl 1 (December 2011): S353–58.

Ziegler-Graham, Kathryn, Ellen J. MacKenzie, Patti L. Ephraim, Thomas G. Travison, and Ron Brookmeyer. "Estimating the Prevalence of Limb Loss in the United States: 2005 to 2050." *Archives of Physical Medicine and Rehabilitation* 89, no. 3 (March 2008): 422–29.

Chapter 2:
The excluded middle

Brydum, Sunnivie. "John Paulk Formally Renounces, Apologizes for Harmful 'Ex-Gay' Movement." *Advocate*, April 24, 2013. https://www.advocate.com/politics/religion/2013/04/24/john-paulk-formally-renounces-apologizes-harmful-ex-gay-movement?page=0,1.

Forney, Ellen. *Marbles: Mania, Depression, Michelangelo, and Me: A Graphic Memoir.* New York: Gotham Books, 2012.

Herron, and James. *Neuropsychology of Left-Handedness.* Academic Press, 1980.

Chapter 3: Stigma and inferiority

Anders, Valentin. "Etimología de Izquierda." Etimologías de Chile. Accessed July 1, 2022. http://etimologias.dechile.net/?izquierda.

Assandri, Fabrizio. "Il Cranio Del 'Brigante' Villella Può Restare Al Museo Lombroso." *La Stampa.* May 17, 2017. https://www.lastampa.it/torino/2017/05/17/news/il-cranio-del-brigante-villella-puo-restare-al-museo-lombroso-1.34601404/.

Darwin, Charles. *The Descent of Man, and Selection in Relation to Sex.* New York: D. Appleton, 1871.

Fausto-Sterling, Anne. *Myths of Gender: Biological Theories About Women and Men, Revised Edition.* New York: Basic Books, 2008.

Fliess, Wilhelm. *Der Ablauf des Lebens: Grundlegung zur exakten Biologie.* Leipzig and Vienna: Franz Deuticke, 1906.

Freud, Sigmund. "The Interpretation of Dreams." In *The Basic Writings of Sigmund Freud*, edited and translated by A. A. Brill. New York: Modern Library Random House, 1938.

Gruner, Wolf. "The Forgotten Mass Destruction of Jewish Homes During 'Kristallnacht.'" *New Frame*, November 19, 2019. https://www.newframe.com/the-forgotten-mass-destruction-of-jewish-homes-during-kristallnacht/.

Hildén, K. "Studien über Das Vorkommen Der Darwinschen Ohrspitze in Der Bevölkerung Finnlands." *Fennia* 52 (1929): 3–39.

Lombroso, Cesare. *Criminal Man*. Edited by Mary Gibson and Nicole Hahn Rafter. Duke University Press, 2006.

——. *L'uomo delinquente*. Milano: Hoepli, 1876.

Lombroso, Gina, and Cesare. *Criminal Man, According to the Classification of Cesare Lombroso, Briefly Summarised by His Daughter Gina Lombroso Ferrero*. New York: G.P. Putnam's Sons, 1911.

Rubio, O., V. Galera, and M. C. Alonso. "Anthropological Study of Ear Tubercles in a Spanish Sample." *Homo: Internationale Zeitschrift Für Die Vergleichende Forschung Am Menschen* 66, no. 4 (August 2015): 343–56.

Shafer, Daniel R. *Man and Woman; Or, Creative Science and Sexual Philosophy*. St. Louis: J.H. Chambers & Co., 1882.

Singh, P., and R. Purkait. "Observations of External Ear—an Indian Study." *Homo: Internationale Zeitschrift Für Die Vergleichende Forschung Am Menschen* 60, no. 5 (September 11, 2009): 461–72.

Wikipedia. "Social stigma," April 15, 2020. https://w.wiki/5XuK.

Stekel, Wilhelm. *Die sprache des traumes: Eine darstellung der symbolik und deutung des traumes in ihren bezeihungen zur kranken und gesunden seele, für ärzte und psychologen*. Wiesbaden: J. F. Bergmann, 1911.

Tyler, Imogen. *Stigma: The Machinery of Inequality*. London: Zed Books Ltd., 2020.

Wiktionary. "右," December 9, 2020. https://w.wiki/5ZEV.

Wiktionary. "左," January 19, 2021. https://w.wiki/5ZEU.

Chapter 4: Family models

Brooks, David. "The Nuclear Family Was a Mistake." *Atlantic*, March 2020. https://www.theatlantic.com/magazine/archive/2020/03/the-nuclear-family-was-a-mistake/605536/.

Chused, Richard H. "Married Women's Property Law: 1800–1850." *Geo. LJ* 71 (1982): 1359.

Dominus, Susan. "The Fathers' Crusade." *New York Times*. May 8, 2005. https://www.nytimes.com/2005/05/08/magazine/the-fathers-crusade.html.

Fuchs, Rachel Ginnis, and Stephanie McBride-Schreiner. "Foundlings and Abandoned Children." *Oxford Bibliographies Online Datasets*. Oxford University Press, January 13, 2014. https://doi.org/10.1093/obo/9780199791231-0075.

Henrich, Joseph, Steven J. Heine, and Ara Norenzayan. "The Weirdest People in the World?" *The Behavioral and Brain Sciences* 33, no. 2–3 (June 2010): 61–83; discussion 83–135.

Hrdy, Sarah Blaffer. *Mothers and Others: The Evolutionary Origins of Mutual Understanding*. Cambridge, MA: Belknap Press, 2009.

Hunter, D. *Chav Solidarity*. London: Lumpen, 2018.

Inequality.org. "Gender Economic Inequality." Institute for Policy Studies. Accessed July 12, 2022. https://inequality.org/facts/gender-inequality/#gender-wealth-gaps.

International Labour Organization, Walk Free, and International Organization for Migration. "Global Estimates of Modern Slavery: Forced Labour and Forced Marriage," 2022. https://www.walkfree.org/reports/global-estimates-of-modern-slavery-2022/.

Leonardi, Michela, Pascale Gerbault, Mark G. Thomas, and Joachim Burger. "The Evolution of Lactase Persistence in Europe. A Synthesis of Archaeological and Genetic Evidence." *International Dairy Journal / Published in Association with the International Dairy Federation* 22, no. 2 (February 2012): 88–97.

Lewis, Sophie. *Abolish the Family: A Manifesto for Care and Liberation*. London: Verso Books, 2022.

McCammon, Holly J., Sandra C. Arch, and Erin M. Bergncr. "Early US Feminists and the Married Women's Property Acts." *Social Science History* 38, no. 1–2 (2014): 221–50.

McDermott, Rose, and Jonathan Cowden. "Polygyny and Violence Against Women." *Emory LJ* 64, no. 6 (2015): 1767.

Nichols, Thomas Low, and Mary Sargeant Gove Nichols. *Marriage: Its History, Character, and Results*. New York: T.L. Nichols, 1854.

Pagel, Mark, and Walter Bodmer. "The Evolution of Human Hairlessness: Cultural Adaptations and the Ecto-parasite Hypothesis." In *Evolutionary Theory and Processes: Modern Horizons: Papers in Honour of Eviatar Nevo*, edited by Solomon P. Wasser, 329–35. Dordrecht: Springer Netherlands, 2004.

Pew Research Center. "The Rise in Dual Income Households," June 18, 2015. https://www.pewresearch.org/ft_dual-income-households-1960-2012-2/.

Robinson, Kim Stanley. *2312*. London: Orbit, 2012.

Ryan, Christopher, and Cacilda Jethá. *Sex at Dawn: The Prehistoric Origins of Modern Sexuality*. New York: Harper Collins, 2010.

Ryan, Michael. *The Philosophy of Marriage: In Its Social, Moral, and Physical Relations. With an Account of the Diseases of the Genito-Urinary Organs Which Impair or Destroy the Reproductive Function, and Induce a Variety of Complaints; with the Physiology of Generation in the Vege-table and Animal Kingdoms; Being Part of a Course of Obstetric Lectures Delivered at the North London School of Medicine, Charlotte Street, Bloomsbury Square*. London: John Churchill, 1837.

Solis, Marie. "We Can't Have a Feminist Future Without Abolishing the Family." *VICE*, February 21, 2020. https://www.vice.com/en/article/qjdzwb/sophie-lewis-feminist-abolishing-the-family-full-surrogacy-now.

Starkweather, Katherine E., and Raymond Hames. "A Survey of Non-Classical Polyandry." *Human Nature* 23, no. 2 (June 2012): 149–72.

U.S. Bureau of Labor Statistics. "Highlights of Women's Earnings in 2020." *Labor Force Statistics from the Current Population Survey*, September 8, 2022. https://www.bls.gov/cps/earnings.htm#womensearnings.

White, D. R., and M. L. Burton. "Causes of Polygyny: Ecology, Economy, Kinship, and Warfare." *American Anthropologist* 90, no. 4 (1988): 871–87.

Wrangham, Richard. "Control of Fire in the Paleolithic: Evaluating the Cooking Hypothesis." *Current Anthropology* 58, no. S16 (August 1, 2017): S303–13.

Interlude: Planetary consciousness

Apicella, Coren, Ara Norenzayan, and Joseph Henrich. "Beyond WEIRD: A Review of the Last Decade and a Look Ahead to the Global Laboratory of the Future." *Evolution and Human Behavior: Official Journal of the Human Behavior and Evolution Society* 41, no. 5 (September 1, 2020): 319–29.

Cole, Logan W. "The Evolution of Per-Cell Organelle Number." *Frontiers in Cell and Developmental Biology* 4 (August 18, 2016): 85.

Farrington, Benjamin. "Temporis Partus Masculus; an Untranslated Writing of Francis Bacon." *Centaurus; International Magazine of the History of Science and Medicine* 1, no. 3 (1951): 193–205.

Haraway, Donna J. "Cyborgs and Symbionts: Living Together in the New World Order." In *The Cyborg Handbook*, edited by Chris Hables Gray, xi–xx. New York: Routledge, 1995.

Henrich, Joseph, Steven J. Heine, and Ara Norenzayan. "Beyond WEIRD: Towards a Broad-Based Behavioral Science." *Behavioral and Brain Sciences; New York* 33 (June 20, 2010): 2–3.

——. "Most People Are Not WEIRD." *Nature*, June 30, 2010, 29–29.

——. "The Weirdest People in the World?" *The Behavioral and Brain Sciences* 33, no. 2–3 (June 2010): 61–83; discussion 83–135.

Kaishian, Patricia, and Hasmik Djoulakian. "The Science Underground: Mycology as a Queer Discipline." *Catalyst* 6, no. 2 (November 7, 2020). https://doi.org/10.28968/cftt.v6i2.33523.

Kothe, Erika. "Tetrapolar Fungal Mating Types: Sexes by the Thousands." *FEMS Microbiology Reviews* 18, no. 1 (March 1996): 65–87.

Lane, Nick. *Transformer: The Deep Chemistry of Life and Death*. New York: W. W. Norton & Company, 2022.

Lovejoy, Arthur O. *The Great Chain of Being: A Study of the History of an Idea*. Cambridge, MA: Harvard University Press, 1964.

Lovelock, J. E. "Gaia as Seen Through the Atmosphere." *Atmospheric Environment* 6, no. 8 (January 1, 1972): 579–80.

Margulis, Lynn. "Gaia Is a Tough Bitch." In *The Third Culture*, edited by John Brockman, 129–47. New York: Touchstone, 1995.

Margulis, Lynn, and Ricardo Guerrero. "Two Plus Two Equals One: Individuals Emerge from Bacterial Communities." In *Gaia 2: Emergence: The New Science of Becoming*, edited by William Irwin Thompson, 50–67. Hudson, NY: Lindisfarne Press, 1991.

Marinetti, Filippo Tommaso. *L'alcòva d'acciaio: romanzo vissuto*. Milan: Casa Editrice Vitagliano, 1921.

Nichols, Mary Sargeant Gove. *Mary Lyndon, Or, Revelations of a Life: An Autobiography*. New York: Stringer and Townsend, 1855.

Nichols, Thomas Low. *Esoteric Anthropology*. Post Chester, NY: N.Y. Stereotype Association, 1853.

"Obituary: Lynn Margulis." *Daily Telegraph*. December 13, 2011. https://www.telegraph.co.uk/news/obituaries/science-obituaries/8954456/Lynn-Margulis.html.

Sagan, Dorion. *Lynn Margulis: The Life and Legacy of a Scientific Rebel*. White River Junction, Vermont: Chelsea Green Publishing, 2012.

Sheldrake, Merlin. *Entangled Life: How Fungi Make Our Worlds, Change Our Minds & Shape Our Futures*. Random House Publishing Group, 2020.

"The Grey School of Wizardry." Accessed July 1, 2022. https://www.greyschool.net/.

Tuttle, Elaina M., Alan O. Bergland, Marisa L. Korody, Michael S. Brewer, Daniel J. Newhouse, Patrick Minx, Maria Stager, et al. "Divergence and Functional Degradation of a Sex Chromosome-like Supergene." *Current Biology* 26, no. 3 (February 8, 2016): 344–50.

Wayland-Smith, Ellen. *Oneida: From Free Love Utopia to the Well-Set Table*. New York: Picador, 2016.

Wilden, Anthony. *System and Structure: Essays in Communication and Exchange*. London: Tavistock Publications, 1972.

Zell, Oberon. *GaeaGenesis: Conception and Birth of the Living Earth*. Edited by Haleigh Isbill. Cincinnati, Ohio: Left Hand Press, 2022.

——. "Oberon Zell – Master Wizard." oberonzell.com, 2018. https://oberonzell.com/.

——. "TheaGenesis: The Birth of the Goddess." *Green Egg* V, no. 40 (July 1, 1970).

Zell-Ravenheart, Morning Glory. "A Bouquet of Lovers: Strategies for Responsible Open Relationships." *Green Egg* 23, no. 89 (1990): 228–31.

Zell-Ravenheart, Oberon. *Green Egg Omelette: An Anthology of Art and Articles from the Legendary Pagan Journal*. Franklin Lakes, NJ: New Page Books, 2008.

Chapter 5: Nuclear meltdown

Allred, Colette A. "Marriage: More than a Century of Change, 1900–2016." *Family Profiles* 17 (2018).

Ausubel, Jacob. "Globally, Women Are Younger than Their Male Partners, More Likely to Age Alone." Pew Research Center, January 3, 2020. https://www.pewresearch.org/fact-tank/2020/01/03/globally-women-are-younger-than-their-male-partners-more-likely-to-age-alone/.

Barker, Meg-John. *Rewriting the Rules: An Integrative Guide to Love, Sex* and Relationships. Abingdon, Oxon: Routledge, 2012.

Caruso, Calogero, Giulia Accardi, Claudia Virruso, and Giuseppina Candore. "Sex, Gender and Immunosenescence: A Key to Understand the Different Lifespan Between Men and Women?" Immunity & Ageing: I & A 10, no. 1 (May 16, 2013): 20.

Conley, Terri D., Amy C. Moors, Jes L. Matsick, and Ali Ziegler. "The Fewer the Merrier?: Assessing Stigma Surrounding Consensually Non-Monogamous Romantic Relationships." Analyses of Social, 2013. https://doi.org/10.1111/j.1530-2415.2012.01286.x.

Conley, Terri D., Ali Ziegler, and Amy C. Moors. "Backlash From the Bedroom: Stigma Mediates Gender Differences in Acceptance of Casual Sex Offers." Psychology of Women Quarterly 37, no. 3 (September 1, 2013): 392–407.

Fern, Jessica. Polysecure: Attachment, Trauma and Consensual Nonmonogamy. Portland, OR: Thorntree Press LLC, 2020.

Hamilton, W. D. "The Moulding of Senescence by Natural Selection." Journal of Theoretical Biology 12, no. 1 (September 1966): 12–45.

Haupert, M. L., Amanda N. Gesselman, Amy C. Moors, Helen E. Fisher, and Justin R. Garcia. "Prevalence of Experiences With Consensual Nonmonogamous Relationships: Findings From Two National Samples of Single Americans." Journal of Sex & Marital Therapy 43, no. 5 (July 4, 2017): 424–40.

Hrdy, Sarah Blaffer. Mothers and Others: The Evolutionary Origins of Mutual Understanding. Cambridge: Belknap Press, 2009.

Jia, Haomiao, and Erica I. Lubetkin. "Life Expectancy and Active Life Expectancy by Marital Status Among Older U.S. Adults: Results from the U.S. Medicare Health Outcome Survey (HOS)." SSM — Population Health 12 (December 2020): 100642.

Klein, Sabra L., and Katie L. Flanagan. "Sex Differences in Immune Responses." Nature Reviews. Immunology 16, no. 10 (October 2016): 626–38.

Locker-Lampson, Frederick. Patchwork. London: Smith, Elder, & Co., 1879.

Manzoli, Lamberto, Paolo Villari, Giovanni M. Pirone, and Antonio Boccia. "Marital Status and Mortality in the Elderly: A Systematic Review and Meta-Analysis." Social Science & Medicine 64, no. 1 (January 2007): 77–94.

Mitchell, Kirstin R., Catherine H. Mercer, Philip Prah, Soazig Clifton, Clare Tanton, Kaye Wellings, and Andrew Copas. "Why Do Men Report More Opposite-Sex Sexual Partners Than Women? Analysis of the Gender Discrepancy in a British National Probability Survey." Journal of Sex Research 56, no. 1 (January 2019): 1–8.

Oertelt-Prigione, Sabine. "The Influence of Sex and Gender on the Immune Response." Autoimmunity Reviews 11, no. 6–7 (May 2012): A479–85.

Ortiz-Ospina, Esteban, and Max Roser. "Marriages and Divorces." Our World in Data, 2020. https://ourworldindata.org/marriages-and-divorces.

Osterman, Michelle, Brady Hamilton, Joyce A. Martin, Anne K. Driscoll, and Claudia P. Valenzuela. "Births: Final Data for 2020." National Vital Statistics Reports: From the Centers for Disease Control and Prevention, National Center for Health Statistics, National Vital Statistics System 70, no. 17 (February 2022): 1–50.

Perel, Esther. Mating in Captivity: Sex, Lies and Domestic Bliss. London: Hodder, 2007.

Pollet, Thomas V., Sophia E. Pratt, Gracia Edwards, and Gert Stulp. "The Golden Years: Men from the Forbes 400 Have Much Younger Wives When Remarrying than the General US Population." Letters on Evolutionary Behavioral Science 4, no. 1 (June 23, 2013): 5–8.

Rubin, Jennifer D., Amy C. Moors, Jes L. Matsick, Ali Ziegler, and Terri D. Conley. "On the Margins: Considering Diversity Among Consensually Non-Monogamous Relationships." Special Issue on Polyamory. Journal für Psychologie 22, no. 1 (2014): 19–37.

Ryan, Michael. The Philosophy of Marriage: In Its Social, Moral, and Physical Relations. With an Account of the Diseases of the Genito-Urinary Organs Which Impair or Destroy the Reproductive Function, and Induce a Variety of Complaints; with the Physiology of Generation in the Vegetable and Animal Kingdoms; Being Part of a Course of Obstetric Lectures Delivered at the North London School of Medicine, Charlotte Street, Bloomsbury Square. London: John Churchill, 1837.

Savage, Dan. American Savage: Insights, Slights, and Fights on Faith, Sex, Love, and Politics. New York: Dutton, 2013.

Schweizer, Valerie. "Marriage: More than a Century of Change, 1900–2018." Family Profiles 21 (2020).

Wei, Lan-Hai, Shi Yan, Yan Lu, Shao-Qing Wen, Yun-Zhi Huang, Ling-Xiang Wang, Shi-Lin Li, et al. "Whole-Sequence Analysis Indicates That the Y Chromosome C2*-Star Cluster Traces Back to Ordinary Mongols, Rather Than Genghis Khan." European Journal of Human Genetics 26, no. 2 (February 2018): 230–37.

Chapter 6: The true mission of sex

American Psychiatric Association. Diagnostic and Statistical Manual: Mental Disorders (DSM-I). DSM Library. Arlington, VA: American Psychiatric Association, 1952.

——. "Homosexuality and Sexual Orientation Disturbance: Proposed Change in DSM-II, 6th Printing, Page 44, Position Statement (retired)." APA Document Reference No. 730008. Arlington, VA: American Psychiatric Association, 1973.

Bagemihl, Bruce. Biological Exuberance: Animal Homosexuality and Natural Diversity. New York: St. Martin's Press, 2000.

Bergler, Edmund. Homosexuality: Disease or Way of Life? New York: Hill & Wang, Inc., 1956.

——. One Thousand Homosexuals: Conspiracy of Silence, or Curing and Deglamorizing Homosexuals? Paterson, New Jersey: Pageant Books, 1959.

Blackwell, Elizabeth. *The Human Element in Sex: Being a Medical Inquiry into the Relation of Sexual Physiology to Christian Morality*. London: J. & A. Churchill, 1894.

Dock, Lavinia L. *Hygiene and Morality: A Manual for Nurses and Others, Giving an Outline of the Medical, Social, and Legal Aspects of the Venereal Diseases*. New York: G. P. Putnam's sons, 1910.

Goode, Erica. "On Gay Issue, Psycho-analysis Treats Itself." *New York Times*. December 12, 1998. https://www.nytimes.com/1998/12/12/arts/on-gay-issue-psychoanalysis-treats-itself.html.

Heath, Robert G. "Pleasure and Brain Activity in Man: Deep and Surface Electroencephalograms During Orgasm." *The Journal of Nervous and Mental Disease* 154, no. 1 (January 1972): 3–18.

Katz, Jonathan Ned. *Gay American History: Lesbians and Gay Men in the U.S.A.; A Documentary*. New York: Crowell, 1976.

Krafft-Ebing, Richard von. *Psychopathia Sexualis with Especial Reference to Contrary Sexual Instinct: A Medico-Legal Study; Authorized Translation of the Seventh Enlarged and Revised German Edition*. Translated by Charles Gilbert Chaddock M. D. Philadelphia: F. A. Davis, 1893.

Mak, Geertje. "Sandor/Sarolta Vay: From Passing Woman to Sexual Invert." *Journal of Women's History* 16, no. 1 (2004): 54–77.

Mbũgua, Karori. "Reasons to Suggest That the Endocrine Research on Sexual Preference Is a Degenerating Research Program." *History and Philosophy of the Life Sciences* 28, no. 3 (2006): 337–57.

"Medicine: The Strange World." *Time*, November 9, 1959. https://content.time.com/time/magazine/article/0,9171,811384,00.html.

O'Neal, Christen M., Cordell M. Baker, Chad A. Glenn, Andrew K. Conner, and Michael E. Sughrue. "Dr. Robert G. Heath: A Controversial Figure in the History of Deep Brain Stimulation." *Neurosurgical Focus* 43, no. 3 (September 2017): E12.

"Robert Heath Society," November 6, 2013. http://www.heathsociety.org/.

Schneider, David. *The Invention of Surgery: A History of Modern Medicine: From the Renaissance to the Implant Revolution*. New York: Pegasus Books, 2021.

Stanton, Henry. *Sex: Avoided Subjects Discussed in Plain English*. New York: Social Culture Publications, 1922.

Wells, Samuel Roberts. *Wedlock; Or, the Right Relations of the Sexes: Disclosing the Laws of Conjugal Selection, and Showing Who May, and Who May Not Marry*. New York: Fowler & Wells Co., 1884.

Chapter 7: Nature-cultures of attraction

Blackmore, Susan J. *The Meme Machine*. Oxford: Oxford University Press, 2000.

Chokshi, Niraj. "Yes, People Really Are Eating Tide Pods. No, It's Not Safe." *New York Times*. January 20, 2018. https://www.nytimes.com/2018/01/20/us/tide-pod-challenge.html.

Hale, Anne, Lindsay B. Miller, Jason Weaver, Sarah Quinn Husney, and Regina Henares. "The Dual Scales of Sexual Orientation." *Journal of Bisexuality* 19, no. 4 (October 2, 2019): 483–514.

Henrich, Joseph, Steven J. Heine, and Ara Norenzayan. "The Weirdest People in the World?" *The Behavioral and Brain Sciences* 33, no. 2–3 (June 2010): 61–83; discussion 83–135.

Kinsey, Alfred C., Wardell B. Pomeroy, and Clyde E. Martin. *Sexual Behavior in the Human Male*. Philadelphia: W. B. Saunders Co., 1948.

Malone, Nicholas, and Kathryn Ovenden. "Natureculture." In *The International Encyclopedia of Primatology*, 1–2. Hoboken, NJ, USA: John Wiley & Sons, Inc., September 14, 2016. https://doi.org/10.1002/9781119179313.wbprim0135.

Serb, Jeanne M., and Douglas J. Eernisse. "Charting Evolution's Trajectory: Using Molluscan Eye Diversity to Understand Parallel and Con-vergent Evolution." *Evolution: Education and Outreach* 1, no. 4 (September 25, 2008): 439–47.

Yoshino, Kenji. "Covering." *The Yale Law Journal* 111, no. 4 (January 2002): 769.

Chapter 8: Female flexibility

Coffman, Katherine B., Lucas C. Coffman, and Keith M. Marzilli Ericson. "The Size of the LGBT Population and the Magnitude of Antigay Sentiment Are Substantially Underestimated." *Management Science* 63, no. 10 (September 1, 2017): 3168–86.

Wikipedia. "Gray asexuality," September 18, 2021. https://w.wiki/5Zdk.

Hensley, Christopher, and Richard Tewksbury. "Inmate-to-Inmate Prison Sexuality: A Review of Empirical Studies." *Trauma, Violence, & Abuse* 3, no. 3 (July 1, 2002): 226–43.

Chapter 9: Pressure to conform

Acton, William. *Prostitution, Considered in Its Moral, Social, and Sanitary Aspects, in London and Other Large Cities: With Proposals for the Mitigation and Prevention of Its Attendant Evils*. London: J. Churchill, 1857.

—. *The Functions and Disorders of the Reproductive Organs: In Childhood, Youth, Adult Age, and Advanced Life; Considered in Their Physiological, Social, and Moral Relations*. 3rd ed. Philadelphia: Lindsay and Blakiston, 1867.

Bergler, Edmund. *Homosexuality: Disease or Way of Life?* New York: Hill & Wang, Inc., 1956.

Blackwell, Elizabeth. *Essays in Medical Sociology*. London: Ernest Bell, 1902.

Burton-Cartledge, Phil. "Zombies and Ideology." *All That Is Solid …* (blog), November 6, 2010. http://averypublicsociologist.blogspot.com/2010/11/zombies-and-ideology.html.

Compton, Julie. "A Year into Pandemic, America's Remaining Lesbian Bars Are Barely Hanging On." *NBC News*, April 4, 2021. http://www.nbcnews.com/feature/nbc-out/year-pandemic-america-s-remaining-lesbian-bars-are-barely-hanging-n1262936.

Flanders, Judith. "80,000 Prostitutes? The Myth of Victorian London's Love Affair with Vice." History News Network. Accessed December 23, 2022. https://historynewsnetwork.org/article/156189.

Graham, Sylvester. *A Lecture to Young Men on Chastity: Intended Also for the Serious Consideration of Parents and Guardians*. Boston: G.W. Light, 1838.

Hammond, William Alexander. *Sexual Impotence in the Male*. New York: Bermingham & Company, 1883.

Kellogg, John Harvey. *Plain Facts for Old and Young*. Burlington, IA: Segner & Condit, 1881.

Kimmel, Michael S. *The History of Men: Essays on the History of American and British Masculinities*. SUNY Press, 2005.

Robb, Graham. *Strangers: Homosexual Love in the Nineteenth Century*. New York: W. W. Norton & Company, 2004.

Savage, Dan. "Savage Love: Fresh Starts." *Stranger*, September 18, 2018. https://www.thestranger. com/savage-love/2018/09/18/325 26908/fresh-starts.

Stekel, Wilhelm. *Frigidity in Woman: In Relation to Her Love Life*. Translated by James S. Van Teslaar. Disorders of the Instincts and the Emotions: The Parapathiac Disorders. New York: Horace Liveright, 1926.

The Lesbian Bar Project. "The 21 Bars —The Lesbian Bar Project." Accessed August 12, 2022. https://www.lesbianbarproject. com/.

Tréguer, Pascal. "History of the Phrase 'Close Your Eyes and Think of England.'" Word histories, November 27, 2019. https:// wordhistories.net/2019/11/27/ close-eyes-think-england/.

Chapter 10: Pronoun wars

Baron, Dennis. "A Brief History of Singular 'They.'" Oxford English Dictionary, September 4, 2018. https://web.archive.org/ web/20230127031004/https:// public.oed.com/blog/a-brief-history-of-singular-they/.

Gelernter, David. "Feminism and the English Language: Can the Damage to Our Mother Tongue Be Undone?" *Weekly Standard*, March 3, 2008. https://web.

archive.org/web/20080510073058/ http://weeklystandard.com/ Content/Public/Articles/ 000/000/014/783lvmtg.asp?pg=1.

Gelernter, Josh. "The War on Grammar." *National Review* (blog), October 8, 2016. https://www. nationalreview.com/2016/10/ gender-pronouns-job-titles/.

Pinker, Steven. *The Sense of Style: The Thinking Person's Guide to Writing in the 21st Century*. New York: Penguin, 2014.

"They, Pron., Adj., Adv., and N." In *OED Online*. Oxford: Oxford University Press, March 2022. https://www.oed.com/view/ Entry/200700#eid18519864.

Chapter 11: Both/neither

Brown, David Jay, and Rebecca McClen Novick. *Voices from the Edge: Conversations with Jerry Garcia, Ram Dass, Annie Sprinkle, Matthew Fox, Jaron Lanier, & Others*. Freedom, CA: Crossing Press, 1995.

Hammond, William Alexander. *Sexual Impotence in the Male*. New York: Bermingham & Company, 1883.

Hauser, G. A. "Testicular Feminization." In *Intersexuality*, edited by Claus Overzier, 255–76. London and New York: Academic Press, 1963.

Keays, Melise A., and Sumit Dave. "Current Hypospadias Management: Diagnosis, Surgical Management, and Long-Term Patient-Centred Outcomes." *Canadian Urological Association Journal* 11, no. 1–2 Suppl. 1 (January 2017): S48–53.

Lambert, Max R., Geoffrey S. J. Giller, Larry B. Barber, Kevin C. Fitzgerald, and David K. Skelly. "Suburbanization, Estrogen Contamination, and Sex Ratio in Wild Amphibian Populations." *Proceedings of the National Academy of Sciences of the United States of America* 112, no. 38 (September 22, 2015): 11881–86.

Liao, Lih-Mei, Laura Audi, Ellie Magritte, Heino F. L. Meyer-Bahlburg, and Charmian A. Quigley. "Determinant Factors of Gender Identity: A Commentary." *Journal of Pediatric Urology* 8, no. 6 (December 2012): 597–601.

Money, John. *Venuses Penuses: Sexology, Sexosophy, and Exigency Theory*. Buffalo, NY: Prometheus Books, 1986.

Money, John, and Anke A. Ehrhardt. *Man & Woman, Boy & Girl: The Differentiation and Dimorphism of Gender Identity from Conception to Maturity*. Baltimore, London: Johns Hopkins University Press, 1972.

"Persistent Müllerian Duct Syndrome." In *GARD: Genetic and Rare Diseases Information Center*. Gaithersburg, MD: NIH National Center for Advancing Translational Sciences, November 8, 2021. https://rarediseases. info.nih.gov/diseases/8435/ persistent-mullerian-duct-syndrome.

Quigley, Charmian A., Alessandra De Bellis, Keith B. Marschke, Mostafa K. el-Awady, Elizabeth M. Wilson, and Frank S. French. "Androgen Receptor Defects: Historical, Clinical, and Molecular Perspectives." *Endocrine Reviews* 16, no. 3 (June 1995): 271–321.

Scutti, Susan. "'The Protocol of the Day Was to Lie': NYC Issues First US 'Intersex' Birth Certificate." *CNN*, December 30, 2016. https://www.cnn. com/2016/12/30/health/intersex-birth-certificate/index.html.

Springer, A., M. van den Heijkant, and S. Baumann. "Worldwide Prevalence of Hypospadias." *Journal of Pediatric Urology* 12, no. 3 (June 2016): 152.e1–7.

Wolinsky, Howard. "A Mythical Beast. Increased Attention Highlights the Hidden Wonders of Chimeras." *EMBO Reports* 8, no. 3 (March 2007): 212–14.

Young, Hugh Hampton. *Genital Abnormalities, Hermaphroditism and Related Adrenal Diseases*. Baltimore: Williams & Wilkins, 1937.

Interlude: Ycleptance

Adkins, Judith. "'These People Are Frightened to Death': Congressional Investigations and the Lavender Scare." *Prologue Magazine*, August 15, 2016. https://www.archives.gov/ publications/prologue/2016/summer/ lavender.html.

Baker, Monya. "1,500 Scientists Lift the Lid on Reproducibility." Nature Publishing Group UK, May 25, 2016. https://doi.org/10.1038/533452a.

Button, Katherine S., John P. A. Ioannidis, Claire Mokrysz, Brian A. Nosek,

Jonathan Flint, Emma S. J. Robinson, and Marcus R. Munafò. "Power Failure: Why Small Sample Size Undermines the Reliability of Neuroscience." *Nature Reviews. Neuroscience* 14, no. 5 (May 2013): 365–76.

Cavalli-Sforza, Luigi Luca. *Genes, Peoples, and Languages*. New York: North Point Press, 2000.

Colapinto, John. *As Nature Made Him: The Boy Who Was Raised as a Girl*. London: Quartet, 2000.

Coleman, Eli, ed. *John Money: A Tribute, On the Occasion of His 70th Birthday*. New York: The Haworth Press, 1991.

Downing, Lisa, Iain Morland, and Nikki Sullivan. *Fuckology: Critical Essays on John Money's Diagnostic Concepts*. Chicago: University of Chicago Press, 2014.

——."Pervert or Sexual Libertarian?: Meet John Money, 'the Father of F***ology.'" *Salon*, January 4, 2015. https://www.salon.com/2015/01/04/pervert_or_sexual_libertarian_meet_john_money_the_father_of_fology/.

El-Hai, Jack. *The Lobotomist: A Maverick Medical Genius and His Tragic Quest to Rid the World of Mental Illness*. Hoboken: Wiley, 2005.

Frame, Janet. *An Angel at My Table: An Autobiography*. New York: G. Braziller, 1984.

——."A Night at the Opera." *New Yorker*. May 26, 2008. https://www.newyorker.com/magazine/2008/06/02/a-night-at-the-opera-fiction-janet-frame.

——."Gorse Is Not People." *New Yorker*. August 25, 2008. https://www.newyorker.com/magazine/2008/09/01/gorse-is-not-people.

Goldie, Terry. *The Man Who Invented Gender: Engaging the Ideas of John Money*. Vancouver, BC: UBC Press, 2014.

Junk, Thomas R., and Louis Lyons. "Reproducibility and Replication of Experimental Particle Physics Results." *arXiv [physics.data-An]*, September 15, 2020. arXiv. http://arxiv.org/abs/2009.06864.

Money, John. *Biographies of Gender and Hermaphroditism in Paired Comparisons: Clinical Supplement to the Handbook of Sexology*.

Amsterdam, New York: Elsevier, 1991.

——."Concepts of Determinism." In *Gay, Straight, and In-Between: The Sexology of Erotic Orientation*, 114–19. New York, Oxford: Oxford University Press, 1988.

——. *Venuses Penuses: Sexology, Sexosophy, and Exigency Theory*. Buffalo, NY, US: Prometheus Books, 1986.

Money, John, and Anke A. Ehrhardt. *Man & Woman, Boy & Girl: The Differentiation and Dimorphism of Gender Identity from Conception to Maturity*. Baltimore, London: Johns Hopkins University Press, 1972.

Money, John, and Patricia Tucker. *Sexual Signatures: On Being a Man or a Woman*. Boston: Little, Brown, 1975.

Overzier, Claus Von. "Methods of Clinical Investigation." In *Intersexuality*, edited by Claus Von Overzier. London and New York: Academic Press, 1963.

Reich, David. *Who We Are and How We Got Here: Ancient DNA and the New Science of the Human Past*. New York: Pantheon Books, 2018.

Reinisch, June M., Leonard A. Rosenblum, Donald B. Rubin, and M. Fini Schulsinger. "Sex Differences in Developmental Milestones During the First Year of Life." In *John Money: A Tribute, On the Occasion of His 70th Birthday*, edited by Eli Coleman, 19–36. New York: The Haworth Press, 1991.

tvb. "The Death of a 'Pioneer.'" *Daily Kos*, July 9, 2006. https://www.dailykos.com/stories/2006/07/09/225943/-the-death-of-a-pioneer.

Chapter 12:
First, do no harm

Altokhais, Tariq Ibrahim. "Electrosurgery Use in Circumcision in Children: Is it Safe?" *Urology Annals* 9, no. 1 (January 2017): 1–3.

Bayraktar, Zeki. "Potential Autofertility in True Hermaphrodites." *The Journal of Maternal-Fetal & Neonatal Medicine: The Official Journal of the European Association of Perinatal Medicine, the Federation of Asia and Oceania Perinatal Societies, the International Society of Perinatal Obstetricians* 31, no. 4 (February 2018): 542–47.

Bushell, Alice. "Los Muxes: Disrupting the Colonial Gender Binary." *Human Rights Pulse*, June 11, 2021. https://www.humanrightspulse.com/mastercontentblog/los-muxes-disrupting-the-colonial-gender-binary.

Chira, Susan. "When Japan Had a Third Gender." *New York Times*. March 10, 2017. https://www.nytimes.com/2017/03/10/arts/design/when-japan-had-a-third-gender.html.

Colapinto, John. *As Nature Made Him: The Boy Who Was Raised as a Girl*. London: Quartet, 2000.

Downing, Lisa, Iain Morland, and Nikki Sullivan. *Fuckology: Critical Essays on John Money's Diagnostic Concepts*. Chicago: University of Chicago Press, 2014.

Flores, Ana. "Two Spirit and LGBTQ Idenitites: Today and Centuries Ago." Human Rights Campaign, November 23, 2020. https://www.hrc.org/news/two-spirit-and-lgbtq-idenitites-today-and-centuries-ago.

Gearhart, John P., and John A. Rock. "Total Ablation of the Penis After Circumcision with Electrocautery: A Method of Management and Long-Term Followup." *The Journal of Urology* 142, no. 3 (September 1989): 799–801.

Hunter, Sophie. "Hijras and the Legacy of British Colonial Rule in India." Engenderings, June 17, 2019. https://blogs.lse.ac.uk/gender/2019/06/17/hijras-and-the-legacy-of-british-colonial-rule-in-india/.

InterACT, and Human Rights Watch. "'I Want to Be Like Nature Made Me': Medically Unnecessary Surgeries on Intersex Children in the US." Human Rights Watch, 2017. https://www.hrw.org/report/2017/07/25/i-want-he-nature-made-me/medically-unnecessary-surgeries-intersex-children-us.

Lindahl, Hans. "9 Young People on How They Found Out They Are Intersex." *Teen Vogue*, October 25, 2019. https://www.teenvogue.com/gallery/young-people-on-how-they-found-out-they-are-intersex.

Neus, Nora. "She's 7 and Was Born Intersex. Why Her Parents Elected to Let Her Grow Up Without Surgical Intervention." *CNN*, January 10, 2020.

https://www.cnn.com/2020/01/10/us/intersex-surgeries-gothere/index.html.

Peraino, Judith A. *Listening to the Sirens: Musical Technologies of Queer Identity from Homer to Hedwig*. University of California Press, 2006.

Reardon, Sara. "The Spectrum of Sex Development: Eric Vilain and the Intersex Controversy." *Nature* 533 (May 10, 2016): 160–63.

Saini, Angela. *Inferior: How Science Got Women Wrong and the New Research That's Rewriting the Story*. Boston: Beacon Press, 2017.

Sen, Amartya. "More Than 100 Million Women Are Missing." In *Gender and Justice*, edited by Ngaire Naffine, 219–22. 1990. Reprint, London: Routledge, 2017.

Swan, Shanna H., and Stacey Colino. *Count Down: How Our Modern World Is Threatening Sperm Counts, Altering Male and Female Reproductive Development, and Imperiling the Future of the Human Race*. New York: Scribner, 2022.

Trankuility. "Protection of Intersex Children from Harmful Practices." Wikimedia Commons, October 2016. https://commons.wikimedia.org/wiki/File:Protection_of_intersex_children_from_harmful_practices.svg.

Young, Hugh Hampton. *Genital Abnormalities, Hermaphroditism and Related Adrenal Diseases*. Baltimore: Williams & Wilkins, 1937.

Chapter 13: The return of Count Sandor

Colapinto, John. *As Nature Made Him: The Boy Who Was Raised as a Girl*. London: Quartet, 2000.

Coleman, E., A. E. Radix, W. P. Bouman, G. R. Brown, A. L. C. de Vries, M. B. Deutsch, R. Ettner, et al. "Standards of Care for the Health of Transgender and Gender Diverse People, Version 8." *International Journal of Transgender Health* 23, no. S1 (August 19, 2022): S1–259.

Delahunt, John W., Hayley J. Denison, Dalice A. Sim, Jemima J. Bullock, and Jeremy D. Krebs. "Increasing Rates of People Identifying as Transgender Presenting to Endocrine Services in the Wellington Region." *The New Zealand Medical Journal* 131, no. 1468 (January 19, 2018): 33–42.

Drummond, Kelley D., Susan J. Bradley, Michele Peterson-Badali, and Kenneth J. Zucker. "A Follow-up Study of Girls with Gender Identity Disorder." *Developmental Psychology* 44, no. 1 (January 2008): 34–45.

Expósito-Campos, Pablo. "A Typology of Gender Detransition and Its Implications for Healthcare Providers." *Journal of Sex & Marital Therapy* 47, no. 3 (January 10, 2021): 270–80.

Gates, Gary J. "How Many People Are Lesbian, Gay, Bisexual and Transgender?" The Williams Institute, April 1, 2011. https://web.archive.org/web/20150425174542/http://williamsinstitute.law.ucla.edu/wp-content/uploads/Gates-How-Many-People-LGBT-Apr-2011.pdf.

The Tavistock and Portman NHS Foundation Trust. "Gender Identity Development Service Referrals in 2019–20 Same as 2018–19." Tavistock and Portman NHS Foundation Trust, May 29, 2020. https://tavistockandportman.nhs.uk/about-us/news/stories/gender-identity-development-service-referrals-2019-20-same-2018-19/.

Gentleman, Amelia. "'An Explosion': What Is Behind the Rise in Girls Questioning Their Gender Identity?" *Guardian*. November 24, 2022. https://www.theguardian.com/society/2022/nov/24/an-explosion-what-is-behind-the-rise-in-girls-questioning-their-gender-identity.

Gill-Peterson, Jules. *Histories of the Transgender Child*. University of Minnesota Press, 2018.

Hembree, Wylie C., Peggy T. Cohen-Kettenis, Louis Gooren, Sabine E. Hannema, Walter J. Meyer, M. Hassan Murad, Stephen M. Rosenthal, Joshua D. Safer, Vin Tangpricha, and Guy G. T'Sjoen. "Endocrine Treatment of Gender-Dysphoric/Gender-Incongruent Persons: An Endocrine Society Clinical Practice Guideline." *The Journal of Clinical Endocrinology and Metabolism* 102, no. 11 (November 1, 2017): 3869–3903.

Hinsliff, Gaby. "'Age Has Nothing to Do With It': How It Feels to Transition Later in Life." *Guardian*. November 17, 2018. https://amp.theguardian.com/society/2018/nov/17/age-nothing-do-with-it-transition-later-life-transgender.

Irshad, Usama, Ali Madeeh Hashmi, and Irum Aamer. "Between a Rock and a Hard Place – Gender Dysphoria and Comorbid Depression in a Young, Low-Income, Pakistani Transgender Man." *Cureus* 12, no. 9 (September 2, 2020): e10205.

Jacques, Juliet. *Trans: A Memoir*. Brooklyn: Verso Books, 2015.

Jones, Tiffany, Bonnie Hart, Morgan Carpenter, Gavi Ansara, William Leonard, and Jayne Lucke. *Intersex: Stories and Statistics from Australia*. Cambridge, UK: Open Book Publishers, 2016.

Katyal, Sonia K., and Ilona M. Turner. "Transparenthood." *Michigan Law Review*, no. 117.8 (2019): 1593.

Meerwijk, Esther L., and Jae M. Sevelius. "Transgender Population Size in the United States: A Meta-Regression of Population-Based Probability Samples." *American Journal of Public Health* 107, no. 2 (February 2017): e1–8.

Nahata, Leena, Diane Chen, Molly B. Moravek, Gwendolyn P. Quinn, Megan E. Sutter, Julia Taylor, Amy C. Tishelman, and Veronica Gomez-Lobo. "Understudied and Under-Reported: Fertility Issues in Transgender Youth—A Narrative Review." *The Journal of Pediatrics* 205 (February 2019): 265–71.

Orange, Richard. "Teenage Transgender Row Splits Sweden as Dysphoria Diagnoses Soar by 1,500%." *Guardian*. February 22, 2020. https://amp.theguardian.com/society/2020/feb/22/ssweden-teenage-transgender-row-dysphoria-diagnoses-soar.

O'Toole, Garson. "Science Makes Progress Funeral by Funeral." Quote Investigator, September 25, 2017. https://quoteinvestigator.com/2017/09/25/progress/.

Pauly, Ira B. "The Current Status of the Change of Sex Operation." *The*

Journal of Nervous and Mental Disease 147, no. 5 (November 1968): 460–71.

Singh, Devita, Susan J. Bradley, and Kenneth J. Zucker. "A Follow-Up Study of Boys With Gender Identity Disorder." *Frontiers in Psychiatry / Frontiers Research Foundation* 12 (March 29, 2021): 632784.

Smith, Michael. "Referrals to the Gender Identity Development Service (GIDS) Level Off in 2018–19." The Tavistock and Portman NHS Foundation Trust, June 28, 2019. https://tavistockandportman. nhs.uk/about-us/news/stories/ referrals-gender-identity-development-service-gids-level-2018-19/.

Wikipedia. "Sodomy laws in the United States," September 10, 2022. https://w.wiki/5ijZ.

Steensma, Thomas D., Roeline Biemond, Fijgje de Boer, and Peggy T. Cohen-Kettenis. "Desisting and Persisting Gender Dysphoria After Childhood: A Qualitative Follow-up Study." *Clinical Child Psychology and Psychiatry* 16, no. 4 (October 2011): 499–516.

Steensma, Thomas D., Baudewijntje P. C. Kreukels, Annelou L. C. de Vries, and Peggy T. Cohen-Kettenis. "Gender Identity Development in Adolescence." *Hormones and Behavior* 64, no. 2 (July 2013): 288–97.

Stone, Sandy. "The Empire Strikes Back: A Posttranssexual Manifesto." *The Transgender Studies Reader*, 2006.

Tang, Annie, J. Carlo Hojilla, Jordan E. Jackson, Kara A. Rothenberg, Rebecca C. Gologorsky, Douglas A. Stram, Colin M. Mooney, Stephanie L. Hernandez, and Karen M. Yokoo. "Gender-Affirming Mastectomy Trends and Surgical Outcomes in Adolescents." *Annals of Plastic Surgery* 88, no. 4 (May 2022): S325.

Temple Newhook, Julia, Jake Pyne, Kelley Winters, Stephen Feder, Cindy Holmes, Jemma Tosh, Mari-Lynne Sinnott, Ally Jamieson, and Sarah Pickett. "A Critical Commentary on Follow-up Studies and 'Desistance' Theories About Transgender and Gender-Nonconforming Children." *Inter-national Journal of Transgenderism* 19, no. 2 (April 3, 2018): 212–24.

Wallien, Madeleine S. C., and Peggy T. Cohen-Kettenis. "Psychosexual Outcome of Gender-Dysphoric Children." *Journal of the American Academy of Child and Adolescent Psychiatry* 47, no. 12 (December 2008): 1413–23.

Chapter 14: A view from above

"Advances in AI Are Used to Spot Signs of Sexuality." *Economist*. September 9, 2017. https:// www.economist.com/science-and-technology/2017/09/09/ advances-in-ai-are-used-to-spot-signs-of-sexuality.

Agüera y Arcas, Blaise, Margaret Mitchell, and Alexander Todorov. "Physiognomy's New Clothes." Medium, May 6, 2017. https:// medium.com/@blaisea/ physiognomys-new-clothes-f2d4b59fdd6a.

Anderson, Drew. "GLAAD and HRC Call on Stanford University & Responsible Media to Debunk Dangerous & Flawed Report Claiming to Identify LGBTQ People Through Facial Recognition Technology." GLAAD, September 8, 2017. https://web.archive. org/web/20170910172214/ https://www.glaad.org/blog/ glaad-and-hrc-call-stanford-university-responsible-media-debunk-dangerous-flawed-report.

Cogsdill, Emily J., Alexander T. Todorov, Elizabeth S. Spelke, and Mahzarin R. Banaji. "Inferring Character from Faces: A Developmental Study." *Psychological Science* 25, no. 5 (May 1, 2014): 1132–39.

Copeland, Jack. "Alan Turing: The Codebreaker Who Saved 'Millions of Lives.'" *BBC*, June 19, 2012. http://www.bbc.co.uk/news/ technology-18419691.

Cox, William T. L., Patricia G. Devine, Alyssa A. Bischmann, and Janet S. Hyde. "Inferences About Sexual Orientation: The Roles of Stereotypes, Faces, and the Gaydar Myth." *Journal of Sex Research* 53, no. 2 (2016): 157–71.

Drury, Colin. "Alan Turing: The Father of Modern Computing Credited with Saving Millions of Lives." *Independent*. July 15, 2019. https:// www.independent.co.uk/news/ uk/home-news/alan-turing-ps50-note-computers-maths-enigma-codebreaker-ai-test-a9005266.html.

Dunbar, Robin. *Friends: Understanding the Power of Our Most Important Relationships*. London: Little, Brown Book Group, 2021.

Efferson, Charles, and Sonja Vogt. "Viewing Men's Faces Does Not Lead to Accurate Predictions of Trustworthiness." *Scientific Reports* 3 (January 10, 2013): 1047.

NIST. "Face Recognition Technology (FERET)," July 13, 2017. https:// www.nist.gov/programs-projects/ face-recognition-technology-feret.

Fink, Bernhard, Nick Neave, Gayle Brewer, and Boguslaw Pawlowski. "Variable Preferences for Sexual Dimorphism in Stature (SDS): Further Evidence for an Adjustment in Relation to Own Height." *Personality and Individual Differences* 43, no. 8 (December 1, 2007): 2249–57.

Galton, Francis J. "Composite Portraits." *Nature* 18 (1878): 97–100.

Grother, Patrick, Mei Ngan, and Kayee Hanaoka. "Face Recognition Vendor Test Part 3: Demographic Effects." Gaithersburg, MD: National Institute of Standards and Technology, December 2019. https://doi. org/10.6028/nist.ir.8280.

Harwell, Drew. "Facial Recognition Firm Clearview AI Tells Investors It's Seeking Massive Expansion Beyond Law Enforcement." *Washington Post*. February 16, 2022. https:// www.washingtonpost.com/ technology/2022/02/16/clearview-expansion-facial-recognition/.

Hayles, Nancy Katherine. *How We Became Posthuman: Virtual Bodies in Cybernetics, Literature, and Informatics*. Chicago: University of Chicago Press, 1999.

Hess, Ursula, Reginald B. Adams Jr, and Robert E. Kleck. "Facial Appearance, Gender, and Emotion Expression." *Emotion* 4, no. 4 (December 2004): 378–88.

Holtz, Brian C. "From First Impression to Fairness Perception:

Investigating the Impact of Initial Trustworthiness Beliefs." *Personnel Psychology* 68, no. 3 (September 2015): 499–546.

Ikeda, Scott. "Bad Bot Traffic Report: Almost Half of All 2021 Internet Traffic Was Not Human." *CPO Magazine*, May 25, 2022. https://www.cpomagazine.com/cyber-security/bad-bot-traffic-report-almost-half-of-all-2021-internet-traffic-was-not-human/.

Imperva. "2022 Bad Bot Report." Imperva Resource Library, May 16, 2022. https://www.imperva.com/resources/resource-library/reports/bad-bot-report/.

Katyal, Sonia K., and Jessica Y. Jung. "The Gender Panopticon: AI, Gender, and Design Justice." *UCLA Law Review* 68 (2021): 692.

Kushwaha, Vineet, Maneet Singh, Richa Singh, Mayank Vatsa, Nalini Ratha, and Rama Chellappa. "Disguised Faces in the Wild." In *2018 IEEE/CVF Conference on Computer Vision and Pattern Recognition Workshops (CVPRW)*, 1–9. IEEE, 2018.

Levin, Sam. "Face-Reading AI Will Be Able to Detect Your Politics and IQ, Professor Says." *Guardian*. September 12, 2017. https://amp.theguardian.com/technology/2017/sep/12/artificial-intelligence-face-recognition-michal-kosinski.

McCann, Kate. "Turing's Law: Oscar Wilde Among 50,000 Convicted Gay Men Granted Posthumous Pardons." *Daily Telegraph*. January 31, 2017. https://www.telegraph.co.uk/news/2017/01/31/turings-law-thousands-convicted-gay-bisexual-men-receive-posthumous/.

Mike, Mike. "The Face of Tomorrow — the Human Face of Globalization," August 19, 2004. https://artbase.rhizome.org/wiki/Q2002.

Olivola, Christopher Y., Friederike Funk, and Alexander Todorov. "Social Attributions from Faces Bias Human Choices." *Trends in Cognitive Sciences* 18, no. 11 (November 2014): 566–70.

Oosterhof, Nikolaas N., and Alexander Todorov. "The Functional Basis of Face Evaluation." *Proceedings of the National Academy of Sciences of the United States of America* 105, no. 32 (August 12, 2008): 11087–92.

Parr, Lisa A., and Bridget M. Waller. "Understanding Chimpanzee Facial Expression: Insights into the Evolution of Communication." *Social Cognitive and Affective Neuroscience* 1, no. 3 (December 2006): 221–28.

Peterson, Joshua C., Stefan Uddenberg, Thomas L. Griffiths, Alexander Todorov, and Jordan W. Suchow. "Deep Models of Superficial Face Judgments." *Proceedings of the National Academy of Sciences of the United States of America* 119, no. 17 (April 26, 2022): e2115228119.

Reichert, Corinne. "Clearview AI Facial Recognition Customers Reportedly Include DOJ, FBI, ICE, Macy's." *CNET*, March 2, 2020. https://www.cnet.com/news/privacy/clearview-ai-facial-recognition-customers-reportedly-include-ice-justice-department-fbi-macys/.

Rezlescu, Constantin, Brad Duchaine, Christopher Y. Olivola, and Nick Chater. "Unfakeable Facial Configurations Affect Strategic Choices in Trust Games With or Without Information About Past Behavior." *PloS One* 7, no. 3 (March 28, 2012): e34293.

Rocine, Victor Gabriel. *Heads, Faces, Types, Races*. Chicago: Vaught-Rocine Pub. Co, 1910.

Rule, Nicholas O., and Nalini Ambady. "Brief Exposures: Male Sexual Orientation Is Accurately Perceived at 50ms." *Journal of Experimental Social Psychology* 44, no. 4 (July 1, 2008): 1100–1105.

Savage, Dan. "With Google Powerhouse, Blaise Agüera y Arcas (Episode #579)." Podcast. *Savage Lovecast*, November 28, 2017. https://savage.love/lovecast/2017/11/28/with-google-powerhouse-blaise-aguera-y-arcas/.

Sedgewick, Jennifer R., Meghan E. Flath, and Lorin J. Elias. "Presenting Your Best Self(ie): The Influence of Gender on Vertical Orientation of Selfies on Tinder." *Frontiers in Psychology* 8 (April 21, 2017): 604.

Snowden, Edward. *Permanent Record*. New York: Henry Holt and Company, 2019.

Todorov, Alexander. *Face Value: The Irresistible Influence of First Impressions*. Princeton University Press, 2017.

Todorov, Alexander, Christopher Y. Olivola, Ron Dotsch, and Peter Mende-Siedlecki. "Social Attributions from Faces: Determinants, Consequences, Accuracy, and Functional Significance." *Annual Review of Psychology* 66 (January 3, 2015): 519–45.

Turing, Alan Mathison. "Computing Machinery and Intelligence." *Mind; a Quarterly Review of Psychology and Philosophy* LIX, no. 236 (October 1, 1950): 433–60.

Turk, Matthew, and Alex Pentland. "Eigenfaces for Recognition." *Journal of Cognitive Neuroscience* 3, no. 1 (Winter 1991): 71–86.

de Waal, Frans. *Different: Gender Through the Eyes of a Primatologist*. New York: W. W. Norton & Company, Inc., 2022.

Wang, Yilun, and Michal Kosinski. "Deep Neural Networks Are More Accurate than Humans at Detecting Sexual Orientation from Facial Images." *Journal of Personality and Social Psychology* 114, no. 2 (February 2018): 246–57.

White, Tom (@dribnet). "I expected a 'face angle' classifier using vggface features would perform well, but was still floored by 100% accuracy over 576 test images." Twitter, September 14, 2017. https://twitter.com/dribnet/status/908521750425591808.

William H. Press, Saul A. Teukolsky, William T. Vetterling, and Brian P. Flannery. *Numerical Recipes 3rd Edition: The Art of Scientific Computing*. Cambridge University Press, 2007.

Wilson, John Paul, and Nicholas O. Rule. "Facial Trustworthiness Predicts Extreme Criminal-Sentencing Outcomes." *Psychological Science* 26, no. 8 (August 2015): 1325–31.

Wu, Xiaolin, and Xi Zhang. "Automated Inference on Criminality Using Face Images." *arXiv [cs.CV]*, 2016. arXiv. https://arxiv.org/abs/1611.04135v1.

—."Responses to Critiques on Machine Learning of Criminality Perceptions (Addendum of arXiv:1611.04135)." *arXiv [cs.CV]*, May 26, 2017. arXiv. https://arxiv.org/abs/1611.04135.

Chapter 15: Postgender

ABC News. "Target Moves Toward Gender-Neutral Store Signage." *ABC News*, August 10, 2015. https://abcnews.go.com/Lifestyle/target-moves-gender-neutral-store-signage/story?id=32982682.

Babbage, Charles. *On the Economy of Machinery and Manufactures*. London: Charles Knight, 1832.

Bechtel, Abi. "Don't do this, @Target." Twitter, June 1, 2015. https://web.archive.org/web/20220518120023/https://twitter.com/abianne/status/605503223575781376#.

Boeree, Liv (@liv_boeree). "In my experience, all the furore over Instagram & Facebook causing teenage depression is overlooking the bigger issue: beauty filters. I mean just look at this absurdity." Twitter, October 6, 2021. https://twitter.com/liv_boeree/status/1445868089539588100.

Cederstrom, Carl. "Are We Ready for the Breastfeeding Father?" *New York Times*. October 18, 2019. https://www.nytimes.com/2019/10/18/opinion/sunday/men-breastfeeding.html.

Cukor, George. *My Fair Lady*. Warner Bros., 1964.

Curry, Andrew. "The Internet of Animals That Could Help to Save Vanishing Wildlife." Nature Publishing Group UK, October 16, 2018. https://doi.org/10.1038/d41586-018-07036-2.

Damore, James. "Google's Ideological Echo Chamber: How Bias Clouds Our Thinking About Diversity and Inclusion." Google Diversity Memo, July 2017. https://web.archive.org/web/20170809021151/https://diversitymemo.com/.

Fava, Giovanni A. "Morselli's Legacy: Dysmorphophobia." *Psychotherapy and Psychosomatics* 58, no. 3–4 (1992): 117–18.

Federici, Silvia. *Wages Against Housework*. Bristol: Published jointly by the Power of Women Collective and the Falling Wall Press, 1975.

Firestone, Shulamith. *The Dialectic of Sex: The Case for Feminist Revolution*. New York: Morrow, 1970.

Goldenberg, Suzanne. "Why Women Are Poor at Science, by Harvard President." *Guardian*. January 18, 2005. https://www.theguardian.com/science/2005/jan/18/educationsgendergap.genderissues.

Goldin, Claudia, and Cecilia Rouse. "Orchestrating Impartiality: The Impact of 'Blind' Auditions on Female Musicians." *The American Economic Review* 90, no. 4 (September 2000): 715–41.

Gurven, Michael, and Kim Hill. "Why Do Men Hunt? A Reevaluation of 'Man the Hunter' and the Sexual Division of Labor." *Current Anthropology* 50, no. 1 (February 2009): 51–62; discussion 62–74.

Haas, Randall, James Watson, Tammy Buonasera, John Southon, Jennifer C. Chen, Sarah Noe, Kevin Smith, Carlos Viviano Llave, Jelmer Eerkens, and Glendon Parker. "Female Hunters of the Early Americas." *Science Advances* 6, no. 45 (November 2020). https://doi.org/10.1126/sciadv.abd0310.

Hollings, Christopher, Ursula Martin, and Adrian Rice. "The Lovelace–De Morgan Mathematical Correspondence: A Critical Re-Appraisal." *Historia Mathematica* 44, no. 3 (August 1, 2017): 202–31.

Joel, Daphna, and Luba Vikhanski. *Gender Mosaic: Beyond the Myth of the Male and Female Brain*. New York: Little, Brown, 2019.

Judge, Timothy A., and Daniel M. Cable. "The Effect of Physical Height on Workplace Success and Income: Preliminary Test of a Theoretical Model." *The Journal of Applied Psychology* 89, no. 3 (June 2004): 428–41.

Lang, Nico. "Target to Install Gender-Neutral Bathrooms in All of Its Stores." *Advocate*, August 18, 2016. https://www.advocate.com/transgender/2016/8/18/target-install-gender-neutral-bathrooms-all-its-stores.

Lee, Richard Borshay, and Irven DeVore, eds. *Man the Hunter: The First Intensive Survey of a Single, Crucial Stage of Human Development—Man's Once Universal Hunting Way of Life*. Chicago: Aldine De Gruyter, 1968.

Lieberman, Daniel E., Mickey Mahaffey, Silvino Cubesare Quimare, Nicholas B. Holowka, Ian J. Wallace, and Aaron L. Baggish. "Running in Tarahumara (Rarámuri) Culture: Persistence Hunting, Footracing, Dancing, Work, and the Fallacy of the Athletic Savage." *Current Anthropology* 61, no. 3 (June 1, 2020): 356–79.

Lombroso, Cesare, and Guglielmo Ferrero. *Criminal Woman, the Prostitute, and the Normal Woman*. Translated by Mary Gibson and Nicole Hahn Rafter. Duke University Press, 2004.

—. *La donna delinquente, la prostituta, e la donna normale*. Torino: L. Roux, 1893.

Mazur, A., and A. Booth. "Testosterone and Dominance in Men." *The Behavioral and Brain Sciences* 21, no. 3 (June 1998): 353–63; discussion 363–97.

Miller, Meg. "Target Debuts An All-Gender Product Line For Kids." *Fast Company*, July 10, 2017. https://web.archive.org/web/20220923194349/https://www.fastcompany.com/90132191/target-debuts-an-all-gender-kids-product-line.

Morselli, Enrico. "Sulla Dismorfofobia E Sulla Tafefobia." *Boll. Reale Accad. Med. Genova* 6 (1891): 3–14.

Muñoz-Reyes, J. A., P. Polo, N. Valenzuela, P. Pavez, O. Ramírez-Herrera, O. Figueroa, C. Rodriguez-Sickert, D. Díaz, and M. Pita. "The Male Warrior Hypothesis: Testosterone-Related Cooperation and Aggression in the Context of Intergroup Conflict." *Scientific Reports* 10, no. 1 (January 15, 2020): 375

Murphy-Hill, Emerson, Ciera Jaspan, Carolyn Egelman, and Lan Cheng. "The Pushback Effects of Race, Ethnicity, Gender, and Age in Code Review." *Communications of the ACM* 65, no. 3 (February 23, 2022): 52–57.

Najell. "Designing Baby Carriers That Fit Both Parents!" Najell — Urban Dreamers, 2021. https://web.archive.org/web/20210418120231/https://najell.com/urban-dreamers/

designing-baby-carriers-that-fit-both-parents/.

Ritchie, Stuart J., Simon R. Cox, Xueyi Shen, Michael V. Lombardo, Lianne M. Reus, Clara Alloza, Mathew A. Harris, et al. "Sex Differences in the Adult Human Brain: Evidence from 5216 UK Biobank Participants." *Cerebral Cortex* 28, no. 8 (August 1, 2018): 2959–75.

Ruigrok, Amber N. V., Gholamreza Salimi-Khorshidi, Meng-Chuan Lai, Simon Baron-Cohen, Michael V. Lombardo, Roger J. Tait, and John Suckling. "A Meta-Analysis of Sex Differences in Human Brain Structure." *Neuroscience and Biobehavioral Reviews* 39 (February 2014): 34–50.

Serano, Julia. *Excluded: Making Feminist and Queer Movements More Inclusive.* Berkeley, California: Seal Press, 2013.

Speakman, Robert J., Carla S. Hadden, Matthew H. Colvin, Justin Cramb, K. C. Jones, Travis W. Jones, Isabelle Lulewicz, et al. "Market Share and Recent Hiring Trends in Anthropology Faculty Positions." *PLoS One* 13, no. 9 (September 12, 2018): e0202528.

Sterling, Kathleen. "Man the Hunter, Woman the Gatherer? The Impact of Gender Studies on Hunter-Gatherer Research (A Retrospective)." In *The Oxford Handbook of the Archaeology and Anthropology of Hunter-Gatherers,* edited by Vicki Cummings, Peter Jordan, and Marek Zvelebil, 151–74. Oxford University Press, 2014.

Suhay, Lisa. "Target Experiments with Gender Neutrality in Its Stores." *Christian Science Monitor,* February 9, 2016. https://www.csmonitor.com/USA/Society/2016/0209/Target-experiments-with-gender-neutrality-in-its-stores.

Tiller, Nicholas B., Kirsty J. Elliott-Sale, Beat Knechtle, Patrick B. Wilson, Justin D. Roberts, and Guillaume Y. Millet. "Do Sex Differences in Physiology Confer a Female Advantage in Ultra-Endurance Sport?" *Sports Medicine* 51, no. 5 (May 2021): 895–915.

Tommasini, Anthony. "To Make Orchestras More Diverse, End Blind Auditions." *New York Times.* July 16, 2020. https://www.nytimes.com/2020/07/16/arts/music/blind-auditions-orchestras-race.html.

Usuda, Haruo, Shimpei Watanabe, Masatoshi Saito, Shinichi Sato, Gabrielle C. Musk, Erin Fee, Sean Carter, et al. "Successful Use of an Artificial Placenta to Support Extremely Preterm Ovine Fetuses at the Border of Viability." *American Journal of Obstetrics and Gynecology* 221, no. 1 (July 2019): 69.e1–69.e17.

Walker, Candice E., Eva G. Krumhuber, Steven Dayan, and Adrian Furnham. "Effects of Social Media Use on Desire for Cosmetic Surgery Among Young Women." *Current Psychology* 40, no. 7 (July 1, 2021): 3355–64.

Walsh, Matt. "Yes, Target, I Do Want My Daughter to Conform to Her Gender." theblaze.com, August 13, 2015. https://www.theblaze.com/contributions/yes-i-do-want-my-daughter-to-conform-to-her-gender.

Wamboldt, Rachel, Shirley Shuster, and Bikrampal S. Sidhu. "Lactation Induction in a Transgender Woman Wanting to Breastfeed: Case Report." *The Journal of Clinical Endocrinology and Metabolism* 106, no. 5 (April 23, 2021): e2047–52.

Westerman, Ashley. "Ukrainian Women Have Started Learning a Crucial War Skill: How to Fly a Drone." *NPR.* November 26, 2022. https://www.npr.org/2022/11/26/1135633681/ukraine-women-drones-russia-war.

Chapter 16: Ignition

Brakefield, Tiffany A., Sara C. Mednick, Helen W. Wilson, Jan-Emmanuel De Neve, Nicholas A. Christakis, and James H. Fowler. "Same-Sex Sexual Attraction Does Not Spread in Adolescent Social Networks." *Archives of Sexual Behavior* 43, no. 2 (February 2014): 335–44.

Cauldwell, David O. *Bisexuality in Patterns of Human Behavior: A Study of Individuals Who Indulge in Both Hetero-Sexual and Homosexual Practices, with Comparative Data on Hermaphrodites, the Human Intersex.* Edited by E. Haldeman-Julius. Girard, Kansas: Haldeman-Julius Publications, 1948.

Enloe, Cynthia H. *The Morning After: Sexual Politics at the End of the Cold War.* University of California Press, 1993.

Farish, Matthew. "Disaster and Decentralization: American Cities and the Cold War." *Cultural Geographies* 10, no. 2 (2003): 125–48.

Habakkuk, Hrothgar John. *American and British Technology in the Nineteenth Century: The Search for Labour-Saving Inventions.* Cambridge: Cambridge University Press, 1962.

Kargon, Robert, and Arthur Molella. "The City as Communications Net: Norbert Wiener, the Atomic Bomb, and Urban Dispersal." *Technology and Culture* 45, no. 4 (2004): 764–77.

Kennan, George. "The Long Telegram." In *Containment: Documents on American Policy and Strategy, 1945–1950,* edited by Thomas H. Etzold and John Lewis Gaddis. 1978. Reprint, Columbia University Press, 1946.

Keyes, Os. "Counting the Countless." ironholds.org, March 24, 2019. https://ironholds.org/counting-writeup/.

Kinsey, Alfred C., Wardell B. Pomeroy, and Clyde E. Martin. *Sexual Behavior in the Human Male.* Philadelphia: W. B. Saunders Co., 1948.

Lapp, Ralph E. *Must We Hide?* Cambridge, MA: Addison-Wesley Press, 1949.

—."The Strategy of Civil Defense." *The Bulletin of the Atomic Scientists* 6, no. 8–9 (August 1, 1950): 241–43.

Lucas, George. *Star Wars: From the Adventures of Luke Skywalker.* New York: Ballantine Books, 1976.

O'Toole, Garson. "The Future Has Arrived —It's Just Not Evenly Distributed Yet." Quote Investigator, January 24, 2012. https://quoteinvestigator.com/2012/01/24/future-has-arrived/.

Our World in Data. "Urbanization over the Past 500 Years." Our World in Data, August 21, 2018. https://ourworldindata.org/grapher/urbanization-last-500-years.

U.S. Census Bureau. "U.S. Cities Are Home to 62.7 Percent of the U.S. Population, but Comprise Just 3.5 Percent of Land Area." PR Newswire, March 4, 2015. https://www.prnewswire.com/news-releases/us-cities-are-home-to-627-percent-of-the-us-population-but-comprise-just-35-percent-of-land-area-300045436.html.

Chapter 17: Country blues

Azrael, Deborah, Lisa Hepburn, David Hemenway, and Matthew Miller. "The Stock and Flow of U.S. Firearms: Results from the 2015 National Firearms Survey." *RSF: The Russell Sage Foundation Journal of the Social Sciences* 3, no. 5 (2017): 38–57.

Banner, Stuart. *How the Indians Lost Their Land: Law and Power on the Frontier*. Cambridge, MA: Belknap Press, 2007.

Cross, Sarah H., Robert M. Califf, and Haider J. Warraich. "Rural-Urban Disparity in Mortality in the US From 1999 to 2019." *The Journal of the American Medical Association* 325, no. 22 (June 8, 2021): 2312–14.

Dedman, Bill. "The Color of Money." *Atlanta Journal-Constitution*, 1988. http://powerreporting.com/color/.

Deloria, Vine. *Custer Died for Your Sins: An Indian Manifesto*. New York: Macmillan, 1969.

Dunbar, Robin. *Friends: Understanding the Power of Our Most Important Relationships*. London: Little, Brown Book Group, 2021.

Farrell, Justin, Paul Berne Burow, Kathryn McConnell, Jude Bayham, Kyle Whyte, and Gal Koss. "Effects of Land Dispossession and Forced Migration on Indigenous Peoples in North America." *Science* 374, no. 6567 (October 29, 2021): eabe4943.

Graham, Jesse, Jonathan Haidt, and Brian A. Nosek. "Liberals and Conservatives Rely on Different Sets of Moral Foundations." *Journal of Personality and Social Psychology* 96, no. 5 (May 2009): 1029–46.

Horst, Megan, and Amy Marion. "Racial, Ethnic and Gender Inequities in Farmland Ownership and Farming in the U.S." *Agriculture and Human Values* 36, no. 1 (March 1, 2019): 1–16.

Jo, Hang-Hyun, Jari Saramäki, Robin I. M. Dunbar, and Kimmo Kaski. "Spatial Patterns of Close Relationships Across the Lifespan." *Scientific Reports* 4 (November 11, 2014): 6988.

Nelson, Robert K., Ladale Winling, Richard Marciano, and Nathan Connolly. "Mapping Inequality." Edited by Robert K. Nelson, Edward L. Ayers, et al. *American Panorama*, 2021. https://dsl.richmond.edu/panorama/redlining/#loc=12/29.889/-90.089&city=new-orleans-la.

Pew Research Center. "Jewish Americans in 2020," May 11, 2021. https://www.pewresearch.org/religion/2021/05/11/jewish-americans-in-2020/.

Rosenberg, Nathan, and Bryce Wilson Stucki. "How USDA Distorted Data to Conceal Decades of Discrimination Against Black Farmers." *Counter*, June 26, 2019. https://thecounter.org/usda-black-farmers-discrimination-tom-vilsack-reparations-civil-rights/.

Smith, Amy Symens, and Edward Trevelyan. "The Older Population in Rural America: 2012–2016: American Community Survey Reports." U.S. Census Bureau, September 2019. https://www.census.gov/content/dam/Census/library/publications/2019/acs/acs-41.pdf.

Stewart, Brandon D., and David S. M. Morris. "Moving Morality Beyond the In-Group: Liberals and Conservatives Show Differences on Group-Framed Moral Foundations and These Differences Mediate the Relationships to Perceived Bias and Threat." *Frontiers in Psychology* 12 (April 21, 2021): 579908.

Chapter 18: Checking our numbers

"A Poor People's Pandemic Report: Mapping the Intersections of Poverty, Race and COVID-19." Poor People's Campaign: A National Call for Moral Revival, April 2022. https://www.poorpeoplescampaign.org/pandemic-report/.

Bardi, Ugo. "Cassandra's Curse: How 'The Limits to Growth' Was Demonized." The Oil Drum: Europe, March 9, 2008. http://theoildrum.com/node/3551.

Berbesque, J. Colette, Frank W. Marlowe, Peter Shaw, and Peter Thompson. "Hunter-Gatherers Have Less Famine than Agriculturalists." *Biology Letters* 10, no. 1 (January 2014): 20130853.

Bettinger, Robert L. "Prehistoric Hunter-Gatherer Population Growth Rates Rival Those of Agriculturalists." *Proceedings of the National Academy of Sciences of the United States of America* 113, no. 4 (January 26, 2016): 812–14.

Blaser, Martin J., and Stanley Falkow. "What Are the Consequences of the Disappearing Human Microbiota?" *Nature Reviews. Microbiology* 7, no. 12 (December 2009): 887–94.

Chang, Kenneth. "Scientists Achieve Nuclear Fusion Breakthrough With Blast of 192 Lasers." *New York Times*. December 13, 2022. https://www.nytimes.com/2022/12/13/science/nuclear-fusion-energy-breakthrough.html.

Craig, J. "Replacement Level Fertility and Future Population Growth." *Population Trends*, no. 78 (Winter 1994): 20–22.

DeCarolis, Joseph, and Angelina LaRose. "Annual Energy Outlook 2023 with Projections to 2050." U.S. Energy Information Administration, March 16, 2023. https://www.eia.gov/outlooks/aeo/pdf/AEO2023_Release_Presentation.pdf.

Ehrlich, Paul Ralph, and Anne Howland Ehrlich. *The Population Bomb*. New York: Ballantine Books, 1968.

Hall, Charles A. S., and John W. Day Jr. "Revisiting the Limits to Growth After Peak Oil." *American Scientist* 97, no. 3 (2009): 230–37.

Heinberg, Richard, and Dennis L. Meadows. "Dennis Meadows on the 50th Anniversary of the Publication of The Limits to Growth." Post Carbon Institute, February 23, 2022. https://www.postcarbon.org/dennis-meadows-on-the-50th-anniversary-of-the-publication-of-the-limits-to-growth/.

Herrington, Gaya. "Update to Limits to Growth: Comparing the World3 Model with Empirical Data." *Journal of Industrial Ecology* 25, no. 3 (June 1, 2021): 614–26.

Hill, Kim, A. M. Hurtado, and R. S. Walker. "High Adult Mortality Among Hiwi Hunter-Gatherers: Implications for Human Evolution." *Journal of Human Evolution* 52, no. 4 (April 2007): 443–54.

Ho, Ping-Ti. *Studies on the Population of China, 1368–1953*. Cambridge, MA: Harvard University Press, 1959.

Hu, Sijie. "A Micro-Demographic Analysis of Human Fertility from Chinese Genealogies, 1368–1911." PhD thesis, London School of Economics and Political Science, 2020. https://doi.org/10.21953/lse.00004223.

Kelly, Morgan, and Cormac Ó Gráda. "Living Standards and Mortality Since the Middle Ages." *The Economic History Review* 67, no. 2 (May 2014): 358–81.

K. F. Foundation. "Infant Mortality Rate by Race/Ethnicity (2019)." KFF State Health Facts, April 27, 2022. https://www.kff.org/other/state-indicator/infant-mortality-rate-by-race-ethnicity/.

Malthus, Thomas Robert. *An Essay on the Principle of Population*. London: J. Johnson, 1798.

McCormick, Al. "Infant Mortality and Child-Naming: A Genealogical Exploration of American Trends." *The Journal of Public and Professional Sociology* 3, no. 1 (2010): 2.

Meadows, Donella H., Dennis L. Meadows, Jørgen Randers, William W. Behrens III, and Club of Rome. *The Limits to Growth: A Report for the Club of Rome's Project on the Predicament of Mankind*. New York: Universe Books, 1972.

Meadows, Donella H., Jørgen Randers, and Dennis L. Meadows. *The Limits to Growth: The 30-Year Update*. White River Junction, VT: Chelsea Green Publishing Company, 2004.

Mehta, Narendra G. "Did Agriculture Reduce Human Lifespan?" *Nature* 409 (January 2001): 131–131.

Office of the Chief Actuary, Social Security Administration. "Period Life Table, 2019, as Used in the 2022 Trustees Report," 2022. https://www.ssa.gov/oact/STATS/table4c6_2019_TR2022.html.

Pasqualino, Roberto, Aled W. Jones, Irene Monasterolo, and Alexander Phillips. "Understanding Global Systems Today—A Calibration of the World3-03 Model Between 1995 and 2012." *Sustainability: Science Practice and Policy* 7, no. 8 (July 23, 2015): 9864–89.

Piccioni, Luigi. "Forty Years Later. The Reception of the Limits to Growth in Italy, 1971–1974." The Donella Meadows Project, July 3, 2012. https://donellameadows.org/archives/forty-years-later-the-reception-of-the-limits-to-growth-in-italy-1971-1974/.

Rook, Graham A. W. "Hygiene and Other Early Childhood Influences on the Subsequent Function of the Immune System." *Digestive Diseases* 29, no. 2 (July 5, 2011): 144–53.

Sahlins, Marshall. "The Original Affluent Society." In *Stone Age Economics*, 1–39. Chicago: Aldine-Atherton, 1972.

Shapin, Steven. *The Scientific Revolution*. Chicago: University of Chicago Press, 1996.

Shellenberger, Michael D. "Testimony Before the United States Senate Committee on Energy and Natural Resources," March 11, 2021. https://www.energy.senate.gov/services/files/B3F496B5-ADF4-457F-94C8-4257680DCB32.

Tans, Pieter, and Ralph Franklin Keeling. "Carbon Cycle Greenhouse Gases, Trends in CO2." NOAA, Earth System Research Laboratories, Global Monitoring Laboratory, October 5, 2022. https://gml.noaa.gov/ccgg/trends/.

Timmons, Heather. "U.S. Poor Died at Much Higher Rate from COVID than Rich, Report Says." *Reuters*. April 4, 2022. https://www.reuters.com/world/us/us-poor-died-much-higher-rate-covid-than-rich-report-2022-04-04/.

Turner, Graham M. "A Comparison of The Limits to Growth with 30 Years of Reality." *Global Environmental Change: Human and Policy Dimensions* 18, no. 3 (2008): 397–411.

United Nations, Department of Economic and Social Affairs, Population Division. "World Population Prospects 2022, Online Edition," 2022. https://population.un.org/wpp/Download/Standard/Fertility/.

Vandegrift, Roo, Ashley C. Bateman, Kyla N. Siemens, May Nguyen, Hannah E. Wilson, Jessica L. Green, Kevin G. Van Den Wymelenberg, and Roxana J. Hickey. "Cleanliness in Context: Reconciling Hygiene with a Modern Microbial Perspective." *Microbiome* 5, no. 1 (July 14, 2017): 76.

WHO Technical Advisory Group for COVID-19 Mortality Assessment. "14.9 Million Excess Deaths Associated with the COVID-19 Pandemic in 2020 and 2021." World Health Organization, May 5, 2022. https://www.who.int/news/item/05-05-2022-14.9-million-excess-deaths-were-associated-with-the-covid-19-pandemic-in-2020-and-2021.

Chapter 19: Choice

Wikipedia. "Agriculture in Niger," April 13, 2020. https://w.wiki/5tub.

Bureau of International Labor Affairs. "2021 Findings on the Worst Forms of Child Labor: Niger." U.S. Department of Labor. Accessed October 28, 2022. https://www.dol.gov/agencies/ilab/resources/reports/child-labor/niger.

Casanova, Giacomo. *History of My Life*. Translated by Willard R. Trask. 12 vols. New York: Harcourt, Brace & World, 1966–1971.

Collier, Aine. *The Humble Little Condom: A History*. Amherst, NY: Prometheus Books, 2007.

International Labour Organization. "Global Estimates of Child Labour: Results and Trends, 2012–2016." ILO Geneva, 2017. https://www.ilo.org/africa/areas-of-work/child-labour/lang--en/index.htm.

Klinenberg, Eric. *Going Solo: The Extraordinary Rise and Surprising Appeal of Living Alone*. New York: Penguin Books, 2013.

Malthus, Thomas Robert. *An Essay on the Principle of Population*. London: J. Johnson, 1798.

Our World in Data. "Children per Woman vs. Number of Children Wanted." Our World in Data, March 31, 2023. https://ourworldindata.org/grapher/fertility-vs-wanted-fertility?time=2019.

Planned Parenthood. "Opposition Claims About Margaret Sanger." Planned Parenthood Federation of America, April 2021. https://www.plannedparenthood.org/uploads/filer_public/cc/2e/cc2e84f2-126f-41a5-a24b-43e093c47b2c/210414-sanger-opposition-claims-p01.pdf.

Roser, Max, Hannah Ritchie, Esteban Ortiz-Ospina, and Lucas Rodés-Guirao. "World Population Growth." Our World in Data, 2013. https://ourworldindata.org/world-population-growth.

Rubin, Debra. "Prof: Election Dynamic Bodes Well for the Jews." *New Jersey Jewish News*, October 16, 2008. Internet Archive. https://web.archive.org/web/20130916150555/http://njjewishnews.com/njjn.com/101608/njProfElectionDynamic.html.

Sanger, Margaret. *Woman and the New Race*. Edited by Carrie Chapman Catt. New York: Brentano's, 1920.

Stanton, Henry. *Sex: Avoided Subjects Discussed in Plain English*. New York: Social Culture Publications, 1922.

United Nations, Department of Economic and Social Affairs, Population Division. "World Population Prospects 2022, Online Edition," 2022. https://population.un.org/wpp/Download/Standard/Fertility/.

U.S. Census Bureau. "Census Bureau Releases New Estimates on America's Families and Living Arrangements." United States Census Bureau Newsroom, November 17, 2022. https://www.census.gov/newsroom/press-releases/2022/americas-families-and-living-arrangements.html.

Zelizer, Viviana A. *Pricing the Priceless Child: The Changing Social Value of Children*. New York: Basic Books, 1985.

Chapter 20: Terra incognita

Acemoglu, Daron, and Pascual Restrepo. "Demographics and Automation." *The Review of Economic Studies* 89, no. 1 (June 10, 2021): 1–44.

Brinkhoff, Thomas. "Bormida." City Population, August 8, 2022. https://www.citypopulation.de/en/italy/liguria/savona/009014__bormida/.

Chandran, Rina. "Here's How Japan Is Breathing New Life into Its 'Ghost Towns.'" World Economic Forum, July 2, 2019. https://www.weforum.org/agenda/2019/07/doing-the-i-turn-japan-taps-tourism-to-lure-city-dwellers-to-emptying-villages/.

Cooper, Paul. "Europe Was Once Obsessed With Fake Dilapidated Buildings." *Atlantic*, April 18, 2018. https://www.theatlantic.com/science/archive/2018/04/fake-ruins-europe-trend/558293/.

Craggs, Ryan. "The Italian Village of Bormida Won't Actually Pay You $2,100 to Move There." *Condé Nast Traveler*, May 11, 2017. https://www.cntraveler.com/story/the-italian-village-of-bormida-wants-to-pay-you-2100-dollars-to-move-there.

Crawford, Kate, and Vladan Joler. "Anatomy of an AI System: The Amazon Echo as an Anatomical Map of Human Labor, Data and Planetary Resources." *AI Now Institute and Share Lab*, September 7, 2018. https://anatomyof.ai/.

Dastin, Jeffery. "Amazon to Shut Its Bookstores and Other Shops as Its Grocery Chain Expands." *Reuters*. March 2, 2022. https://www.reuters.com/business/retail-consumer/exclusive-amazon-close-all-its-physical-bookstores-4-star-shops-2022-03-02/.

Dreifus, Claudia, and Edward O. Wilson. "In 'Half Earth,' E.O. Wilson Calls for a Grand Retreat." *New York Times*. February 29, 2016. https://www.nytimes.com/2016/03/01/science/e-o-wilson-half-earth-biodiversity.html.

Ellis, Erle C. "To Conserve Nature in the Anthropocene, Half Earth Is

Not Nearly Enough." *One Earth* 1, no. 2 (October 25, 2019): 163–67.

Elton, Charles S. *The Ecology of Invasions by Animals and Plants*. London: Methuen, 1958.

Epstein, Eli. "An Entire Tuscan Village Is Being Sold on Italian eBay for $3 Million." *Business Insider*, June 28, 2012. https://www.businessinsider.com/tuscan-village-pratariccia-on-sale-for-3-million-2012-6.

Hsu, Andrea. "Before the Holiday Season, Workers at America's Busiest Ports Are Fighting the Robots." *NPR*. September 11, 2022. https://www.npr.org/2022/09/11/1121243540/supply-chain-dockworkers-ilwu-union-workers-automation.

HTN Staff. "Dutch Hotel Brand CitizenM Launches a Technology-Enabled 'Corporate Subscription' Plan." *Hotel Technology News*, September 22, 2020. https://hoteltechnologynews.com/2020/09/dutch-hotel-brand-citizenm-launches-a-technology-enabled-corporate-subscription-plan/.

Institute for Economics and Peace. "Over One Billion People at Threat of Being Displaced by 2050 due to Environmental Change, Conflict and Civil Unrest." the Institute for Economics and Peace, September 9, 2020. https://www.economicsandpeace.org/wp-content/uploads/2020/09/Ecological-Threat-Register-Press-Release-27.08-FINAL.pdf.

John Deere. "Autonomous 8R Tractor | John Deere Precision Ag." Youtube, January 4, 2022. https://www.youtube.com/watch?v=QvFoRk4JsPc.

John Deere News. "John Deere Reveals Fully Autonomous Tractor at CES 2022," January 4, 2022. https://www.deere.com/en/news/all-news/autonomous-tractor-reveal/.

Kimmerer, Robin Wall. *Braiding Sweetgrass: Indigenous Wisdom, Scientific Knowledge and the Teachings of Plants*. Minneapolis, MN: Milkweed Editions, 2013.

Koolhaas, Rem. "Countryside." Stedelijk Museum Amsterdam, Amsterdam, The Netherlands, April 25, 2012. https://www.oma.com/lectures/countryside.

Lustgarten, Abrahm. "Where Will Everyone Go?" ProPublica and the *New York Times Magazine*, July 23, 2020. https://features.propublica.org/

climate-migration/model-how-climate-refugees-move-across-continents/.

Marchetti, Silvia. "Opinion: Why Italy Must Put Its Forgotten 'Ghost Towns' up for Sale—or Risk Losing Them Forever." *Local*, August 26, 2021. https://www.thelocal.it/20210826/opinion-why-italy-must-put-its-forgotten-ghost-towns-up-for-sale-or-risk-losing-them-forever/.

Marquardt, Felix. *The New Nomads: How the Migration Revolution Is Making the World a Better Place*. London: Simon & Schuster, 2021.

Martin, Alex K. T. "Japan's Glut of Abandoned Homes: Hard to Sell but Bargains When Opportunity Knocks." *Japan Times*, December 26, 2017. https://www.japantimes.co.jp/news/2017/12/26/national/japans-glut-abandoned-homes-hard-sell-bargains-opportunity-knocks/.

McAfee, Andrew. *More from Less: The Surprising Story of How We Learned to Prosper Using Fewer Resources—and What Happens Next*. New York: Scribner, 2019.

Miyazaki, Hayao. *Spirited Away*. Japan: Studio Ghibli, 2001. https://www.imdb.com/title/tt0245429/.

Muratet, Audrey. "Postface: Une Querelle." In *Ailanthus altissima: une monographie située de l'ailante*, edited by Simon Boudvin, translated by Blaise Agüera y Arcas. Paris: Éditions B42, 2021.

Null, Christopher, and Brain Caulfield. "Fade to Black: The 1980s Vision of 'Lights-out' Manufacturing, Where Robots Do All the Work, Is a Dream No More." *Business 2.0 Magazine, CNN Money*, June 1, 2003. https://web.archive.org/web/20110606100012/http://money.cnn.com/magazines/business2/business2_archive/2003/06/01/343371/index.htm.

Mineral Resources. "Pioneering Autonomous Road Trains Achieve World First," April 13, 2022. https://www.mineralresources.com.au/news-media/pioneering-autonomous-road-trains-achieve-world-first/.

Rosenberg, Kenneth V., Adriaan M. Dokter, Peter J. Blancher, John R. Sauer, Adam C. Smith, Paul A. Smith, Jessica C. Stanton, et al. "Decline of the North American Avifauna." *Science* 366, no. 6461 (October 4, 2019): 120–24.

Rosenwald, Michael S. "Cloud Centers Bring High-Tech Flash but Not Many Jobs to Beaten-down Towns." *Washington Post*. November 24, 2011. https://www.washingtonpost.com/business/economy/cloud-centers-bring-high-tech-flash-but-not-many-jobs-to-beaten-down-towns/2011/11/08/gIQAccTQtN_story.html.

Schilthuizen, Menno. *Darwin Comes to Town: How the Urban Jungle Drives Evolution*. New York: Picador, 2018.

Schmidt, Emily. "Why Does the U.S. Lag Other Nations so Badly in the Automation of Its Ports?" APM Research Lab, November 3, 2022. https://www.apmresearchlab.org/10x-port-automation.

Shah, Sonia. *The Next Great Migration: The Beauty and Terror of Life on the Move*. New York: Bloomsbury, 2020.

Talhelm, T., X. Zhang, S. Oishi, C. Shimin, D. Duan, X. Lan, and S. Kitayama. "Large-Scale Psychological Differences Within China Explained by Rice Versus Wheat Agriculture." *Science* 344, no. 6184 (May 9, 2014): 603–8.

Allyn International. "The Evolution of Container Ships and Their Sizes," June 29, 2022. https://logisticslearning.com/largest-container-ships/.

Global De Heus News. "The Netherlands Are Almost the World's Largest Exporter of Agricultural Products! How Did That Happen?," January 23, 2020. https://www.deheus.com/articles/news/the-netherlands-are-almost-the-worlds-largest-exporter-of-agricultural-products-how-did-that-happen.

Thompson, Ken. *Where Do Camels Belong?: Why Invasive Species Aren't All Bad*. Vancouver, BC: Greystone Books, 2014.

Wajcman, Judy. *Pressed for Time: The Acceleration of Life in Digital Capitalism*. Chicago: University of Chicago Press, 2015.

Wilson, Edward O. *Half-Earth: Our Planet's Fight for Life*. New York: Liveright, 2017.

Wyatt, Matt. "Texas Helps Ducks Unlimited Reach 15 Million-Acre Conservation Milestone." *Houston Chronicle*, March 26, 2021. https://www.houstonchronicle.com/texas-sports-nation/general/article/Texas-helps-Ducks-Unlimited-reach-15-million-acre-16055998.php.

Chapter 21: Who are we becoming?

Applebaum, Anne. *Twilight of Democracy: The Seductive Lure of Authoritarianism*. New York: Knopf Doubleday Publishing Group, 2020.

Haraway, Donna Jeanne. "A Cyborg Manifesto: Science, Technology, and Socialist-Feminism in the Late Twentieth Century." In *Simians, Cyborgs, and Women: The Reinvention of Nature*, edited by Donna Jeanne Haraway. New York: Routledge, 1991.

Lovelock, James. *Novacene: The Coming Age of Hyperintelligence*. London: Allen Lane, 2019.

Rushkoff, Douglas. *Survival of the Richest: Escape Fantasies of the Tech Billionaires*. New York: W. W. Norton & Company, 2022.

Smith-Ruiu, Justin. "Cull the Robo-Dogs, Cherish the Dirt-Clods: On AI, the Pathetic Fallacy, and the Boundaries of Community." Justin Smith-Ruiu's Hinternet, April 15, 2023. https://justinehsmith.substack.com/p/cull-the-robo-dogs-cherish-the-dirt.

Thelwall, John. *The Rights of Nature Against the Usurpations of the Establishments: A Series of Letters to the People of Britain on the State of Public Affairs and the Recent Effusions of the Right Honourable Edmund Burke*. London: H.D. Symonds and J. March, 1796.

Walker, Sara. "AI Is Life." *Noēma*, April 27, 2023. https://www.noemamag.com/ai-is-life/.

Zylinska, Joanna, and Gary Hall. "Probings: An Interview with Stelarc." In *The Cyborg Experiments: The Extensions of the Body in the Media Age*, edited by Joanna Zylinska. New York: Continuum, 2002.

Appendix for data nerds

Jensen, Greg. "Kernel Probability Estimation for Binomial and Multinomial Data." PeerJ PrePrints, June 2, 2015. https://doi.org/10.7287/peerj.preprints.1156v1.

Narayanan, Arvind, and Vitaly Shmatikov. "Robust De-Anonymization of Large Sparse Datasets." In *2008 IEEE Symposium on Security and Privacy (sp 2008)*, 111–25, 2008.

Olivier, Jake, and Warren L. May. "Weighted Confidence Interval Construction for Binomial Parameters." *Statistical Methods in Medical Research* 15, no. 1 (February 2006): 37–46.

Scargle, Jeffrey D. "Studies in Astronomical Time Series Analysis. V. Bayesian Blocks, a New Method to Analyze Structure in Photon Counting Data." *The Astrophysical Journal* 504 (September 1, 1998): 405–18.

Shimazaki, Hideaki, and Shigeru Shinomoto. "Kernel Bandwidth Optimization in Spike Rate Estimation." *Journal of Computational Neuroscience* 29, no. 1–2 (August 2010): 171–82.

Wilson, Edwin B. "Probable Inference, the Law of Succession, and Statistical Inference." *Journal of the American Statistical Association* 22, no. 158 (1927): 209–12.

Data Sources

4.0 U.S. Bureau of Labor Statistics, *Labor Force Statistics from the Current Population Survey*, "Highlights of Women's Earnings in 2020," https://www.bls.gov/cps/earnings.htm#womensearnings; **4.1** ILGA World: Lucas Ramon Mendos, Kellyn Botha, Rafael Carrano Lelis, Enrique López de la Peña, Ilia Savelev and Daron Tan, "State-Sponsored Homophobia 2020: Global Legislation Overview Update" (Geneva: ILGA, December 2020); **Lesbian Bar Map** https://www.lesbianbarproject.com/; **12.1** World Bank. "Female Population as a Percentage of Total Population (SP.POP.TOTL.FE.ZS)." World Development Indicators. Accessed July 7, 2023. Available at: https://data.worldbank.org/indicator/SP.POP.TOTL.FE.ZS; **12.2** Wikipedia contributors. "Protection of intersex children from harmful practices" Map. In Wikipedia, The Free Encyclopedia. Last modified June 28, 2023, 17:20 (UTC), CC0 1.0, https://w.wiki/6k$w; **13.7–13.8** Gender Identity Development Service, "Number of Referrals to GIDS," https://gids.nhs.uk/about-us/number-of-referrals/; **14.14** ILGA World: Lucas Ramon Mendos, Kellyn Botha, Rafael Carrano Lelis, Enrique López de la Peña, Ilia Savelev and Daron Tan, "State-Sponsored Homophobia 2020: Global Legislation Overview Update" (Geneva: ILGA, December 2020); **16.0** U.S. Census Bureau, "ZIP Code Tabulation Area Gazetteer File [based on the 2020 Census tabulation blocks]," https://www.census.gov/geographies/reference-files/time-series/geo/gazetteer-files.html; U.S. Census Bureau, "P1: Total Population (DECENNIALDHC2020.P1)" in "2020 Census Demographic and Housing Characteristics File (DHC)", retrieved from https://data.census.gov/; Center for International Earth Science Information Network (CIESIN), Columbia University. 2018. "Documentation for the Gridded Population of the World, Version 4 (GPWv4), Revision 11 Data Sets." Palisades NY: NASA Socioeconomic Data and Applications Center (SEDAC). https://doi.org/10.7927/H45Q4T5F Accessed 07 July 2023; Black Marble 2016, NASA Earth Observatory images by Joshua Stevens, using Suomi NPP VIIRS data from Miguel Román, NASA GSFC. Story by Michael Carlowicz; **16.1** Our World in Data, "Urbanization Over the Past 500 Years, 1500 to 2016," CC BY 4.0, https://ourworldindata.org/grapher/urbanization-last-500-years; **16.2–16.4.2, 17.0–17.3, 17.5–17.12.1, 18.0–18.1** U.S. Census Bureau, "ZIP Code Tabulation Area Gazetteer File [based on the 2020 Census tabulation blocks]," https://www.census.gov/geographies/reference-files/time-series/geo/gazetteer-files.html; U.S. Census Bureau, "P1: Total Population (DECENNIALDHC2020.P1)" in "2020 Census Demographic and Housing Characteristics File (DHC)", retrieved from https://data.census.gov/; **Jesusland** Wikipedia contributors. "Jesusland map.svg." Map. In Wikipedia, The Free Encyclopedia. Last modified May 5, 2023, 02:42 (UTC), CC BY-SA 2.5, https://w.wiki/6$bn; **2020 Voting Density Maps (17.13.0–17.13.3)** "2020 National Precinct Boundary Shapefile and Presidential Election Results," Redistricting Data Hub; **18.2–18.3** Our World in Data, "Distribution of Population Between Different Poverty Thresholds, World, 1820 to 2018," CC BY 4.0, https://ourworldindata.org/grapher/distribution-of-population-between-different-poverty-thresholds-historical?country=~OWID_WRL; **18.4–18.5.1** Our World in Data, "Population, 10,000 BCE to 2021," CC BY 4.0, https://ourworldindata.org/grapher/population; **18.6** Tomruen, "Co2 glacial cycles 800k," 27 July 2017, CC BY-SA 3.0, https://w.wiki/7Fe3; Dieter Lüthi et al., "High-Resolution Carbon Dioxide Concentration Record 650,000–800,000 Years before Present," *Nature* 453, no. 7193 (May 2008): 379–82; **18.7** Our World in Data, "Fertility Rate: Children Born per Woman, 1800 to 2022," CC BY 4.0, https://ourworldindata.org/grapher/children-born-per-woman; **18.8** Gaya Herrington, "Update to Limits to Growth: Comparing the World3 Model with Empirical Data," *Journal of Industrial Ecology* 25, no. 3 (June 1, 2021): 614–26; Donella H. Meadows, Jørgen Randers, and Dennis L. Meadows, *The Limits to Growth: The 30-Year Update* (White River Junction, VT: Chelsea Green Publishing Company, 2004); **19.0** United Nations, Department of Economic and Social Affairs, Population Division. "World Population Prospects 2022, Online Edition," 2022. https://population.un.org/wpp/Download/Standard/Fertility/; **19.2** World Bank. "Total Fertility Rate (SP.DYN.TFRT.IN)." World Development Indicators. Accessed July 7, 2023. Available at: https://data.worldbank.org/indicator/SP.DYN.TFRT.IN; **19.3** Our World in Data, "Fertility Rate: Children Born per Woman, 1960 to 2022," CC BY 4.0, https://ourworldindata.org/grapher/children-born-per-woman; **20.0.0–20.0.1** Our World in Data, "Share of the Labor Force Employed in Agriculture," CC BY 4.0, https://ourworldindata.org/grapher/share-of-

the-labor-force-employed-in-agricultur
e?tab=chart&time=1300..latest&
country=ITA-FRA-NLD-POL-GBR;
Our World in Data, "Number of People
Employed in Agriculture, 1801 to 2019,"
CC BY 4.0, https://ourworldindata.
org/grapher/number-of-people-
employed-in-agriculture; Our World
in Data, "Population, 1800 to 2021,"
CC BY 4.0, https://ourworldindata.
org/grapher/ population?time=1800..
latest&country=CHN-IND-NGA-
USA-OWID_WRL-POL-KOR-JPN-ITA-
FRA-NLD-GBR; **20.1** U. S. Bureau of
the Census. *U. S. Census of Agriculture:
1950.* Vol. II, General Report, Statistics
by Subject. U. S. Government Printing
Office, Washington, D. C., 1952;
USDA, National Agricultural Statistics
Service. *1987 Census of Agriculture*;
USDA, National Agricultural Statistics
Service. *2012 Census of Agriculture*;
USDA, National Agricultural Statistics
Service. *2017 Census of Agriculture*;
20.2 Our World in Data, "Agricultural
Area Over the Long-Term, 1600 to 2016,"
CC BY 4.0, https://ourworldindata.org/
grapher/total-agricultural-area-over-
the-long-term; **20.3** Our World in Data,
"Crop Yields, World, 1961 to 2021," CC
BY 4.0, https://ourworldindata.org/
grapher/key-crop-yields.

Index

Image Credits

Museum; **65:** Gallery Bilderwelt/ Hulton Archives via Getty Images; **66:** United States Marshal branding the author, RC12181, Reference Collection, State Library and Archives of Florida, 1870, https://supremecourt.flcourts. gov/content/download/243675/file/ Evolution-of-Justice-2021.pdf; **66:** Southworth & Hawes, "The Branded Hand of Captain Jonathan Walker," August 1845, The Massachusetts Historical Society, https://w.wiki/6k$T; **67:** Basilica of Sant'Apollinare Nuovo, ca. 6th century, https://seeinggodart. wordpress.com/2015/02/23/sheep-or-goat/; **68:** Bettman/Bedman via Getty Images; **69:** Romano Cagnoni/ RETIRED/Hulton Archives via Getty Images; **69:** "Large and Small Intellects" in L. Fowler and Orson Squire Fowler, *The Illustrated Self-Instructor in Phrenology and Physiology*, 1855, https://www.gerda-henkel-stiftung.de/Lorenz_Menschenzucht; **70:** Fig. I. in Gina Lombroso Ferrero, *Criminal Man*, 39, 1911, https:// wellcomecollection.org/works/ xs639uwk/items?canvas=39; **72:** Fig. 2. in Charles Darwin, *The Descent of Man, And Selection in Relation to Sex*, 17, 1874, https://w.wiki/6sVK; **72:** Andre Ueberbach, Eigene Aufnahme, 2007, CC BY-SA 2.0 DE, https://w. wiki/6k$U; **72:** Fig. 28 in Gina Lombroso Ferrero, *Criminal Man*, 280, 1911, https://wellcomecollection.org/ works/xs639uwk/items?canvas=280; **73:** Fig. 1, Fig. 2. in Cesare Lombroso, *L'Uomo Delinquente*, 28, 1876, https:// archive.org/details/luomodelinquente 00lomb/page/28/; **75:** Anonymous, Sigmund Freud and Wilhelm Fliess, 1890, https://w.wiki/6k$V.

Part II: Sex and gender **78–79:** iStock.com/LYagovy.

Chapter 4: Family models **82:** Heinz Haber, *The Walt Disney Story of Our Friend the Atom*, 1956; **83:** Allstar Picture Library Limited/ Alamy; **83:** Jetsons, Everett Collection, Inc; **84:** Printed by permission of the Norman Rockwell Family Agency Copyright ©1943 the Norman Rockwell Family Entities; **86:** Thomas Low Nichols, Portrait of Mary Gove Nichols, 1887, https://w.wiki/6k$W; **89:** CBS

Photo Archive/CBS via Getty Images; **89:** Walter Fischer/ullstein bild via Getty Images; **90:** Tamarin, SWNS, 2021; **90:** Anonymous, The New Poor Law poster, 1837, The National Archives, UK; **91:** duncan1890 via Getty Images; **92:** Anonymous, Fela Women, https://www.nigerianeye. com/2013/10/i-cant-understand-why-my-father-married.html; **92:** Raja Ravi Varma, Draupadi and Pandavas, 1910, https://w.wiki/6k$X; **93:** King Naser al-Din al-Qajari, Selfie, 1923, https://twitter.com/leiloonm/ status/541429849106423808; **96:** Rick Guidice, NASA ID Number: AC75-1086, 1970s, NASA Ames Research Center, https://space.nss.org/settlement/ nasa/70sArtHiRes/70sArt/art.html.

Interlude: Planetary consciousness **98:** Fabbula TV, Donna Haraway / Speculative Fabulation, May 24, 2016, CC BY 3.0, https://www.youtube.com/ watch?v=zFGXTQnJETg; **98–99:** Alexander von Humboldt, "Idealer Durchschnitt von der Bildung der Erdrinde," 1850, https://w.wiki/6n9F; **99:** Alexander von Humboldt, "Selbstportrait in Paris," 1814, https:// w.wiki/6k$Y; **100:** "Great chain of being" in Didacus Valades, *Rhetorica christiana*, 1579, https://w.wiki/6k$Z; **101:** Jcmurphy at English Wikipedia, "Lord Bacon Stamp," 1910, https://w. wiki/6k$a; **101:** Gian Lorenzo Bernini, "Rape of Proserpina," 1621–1622, photo by Int3gr4te, January 20, 2007, CC BY-SA 3.0, https://w.wiki/6k$b; **102:** Heinrich Berghaus, "Umrisse Der Pflanzengeographie," 1838, David Rumsey Historical Map Collection, CC BY-NC-SA 3.0, https://www. davidrumsey.com/luna/servlet/detail/ RUMSEY-8-1-1526-160064:Umrisse-Der-Pflanzengeographie; **103:** Emblem 2d: "Nutrix ejus terra est." in Michael Maier, *Atalanta Fugiens*, 1618, https://w.wiki/6k$e; **103:** NASA/ Bill Anders, "Earthrise," December 24, 1968, https://w.wiki/6k$d; **104:** © Oberon Zell www.TheMillennialGaia. com; **105:** © Zell; **107:** Bernard Spragg, "Schizophyllum commune (Split gill)," March 14, 2017, CC0 1.0, https://w.wiki/6k$f; **108:** "Lynn Margulis at her Boston University Lab

in the early 1970s." Used by permission of the estate of Lynn Margulis; **109:** © Zell; **109:** © Zell; **110:** © Zell; **111:** Anonymous, "Stirpicults," 1887, https://tontine255.files.wordpress. com/2011/01/eugneics-children-c1887. jpg, **112:** Dr. John B. Ellis, "The upper sitting-room, Oneida Community, 'the childrens hour'," 1870, https://www. loc.gov/pictures/item/2022636499/; **112:** Elizabeth Dodson Gray, "The world-map of patriarchy," 1982 in Zell-Ravenheart, *Green Egg Omelette: An Anthology of Art and Articles from the Legendary Pagan Journal*, 111, 2008; **113:** © Zell; **115:** © Zell.

Chapter 5: Nuclear meltdown **119:** Salar Arkan — سالار ارکان, "A grandma and her grandchild watching 'Nowruz' ceremony," March 26, 2017, CC BY-SA 4.0, https://w.wiki/6TwM; **122:** Anonymous, "Vintage Gay," 1918, https://bosguydotcom.files. wordpress.com/2021/02/vintage-gay-3.25.21-oldmasc-ig.png; **123:** Anonymous, "This Is The Life," ca. 1910, https://w.wiki/6k$g; **123:** PopTech, PT5_4589, October 20, 2017, CC BY-SA 2.0, https://www.flickr.com/ photos/poptech/26512715299/; **123:** Roman Robinson, Portrait of Dan Savage; **126:** Rory Midhani, "The Bloomsbury Group," http://www. rorymidhani.com/; **129:** Bisexual Resource Center, "Bidentification Card," 2014, https://images.app.goo.gl/ vw7oVKuTX99uSTYf6.

Chapter 6: The true mission of sex **130:** Anonymous, "[Elizabeth Blackwell, 1821–1910, oval bust, wearing wedding veil]", ca. 1877, Library of Congress, https://www. loc.gov/pictures/item/2005679734/; **132:** Anonymous, "Lavinia Lloyd Dock," https://w.wiki/6o3j; **133:** M.W. Ridley, "Her majesty Queen Victoria and the members of the royal family," July 14, 1877, https://www.loc.gov/ pictures/item/2003679744/; **134:** Manchester Libraries, Information and Archives; **134:** Bain News Service, "Syrian children," ca. 1910–15, https:// www.loc.gov/item/2014698957/; **134:** T. Bell, *Kalogynomia: or, The Laws of Female Beauty Being the Elementary*

Principles of that Science, 407, 1899; **135:** Lehmann, "Richard v. Krafft-Ebing," 1903, https://w.wiki/6k$h; **135:** Wiener Tagblatt, "Comtesse Sarolta Vay," Wellcome Collection, CC BY 4.0, https://wellcomecollection.org/works/fwvqptww/items; **137:** Sueddeutsche Zeitung Photo/Alamy; **138:** Lafayette Photo, "Portrait of Sarah Bernhardt as Hamlet," July 1899, https://w.wiki/6k$i; **139:** AP Photo/John F. Urwiller; **141:** Photo by Kay Tobin © Manuscripts and Archives Division, The New York Public Library; **142:** © Bolerium Books Inc; **144:** Otis Historical Archives National Museum of Health and Medicine, "Bergonic chair," CC BY 2.0, https://w.wiki/6k$j; **145:** Figure XII-7, Figure XII-8, Heath, Robert G., Hal C. Becker, Leona Bersadsky, Robert M. Corrigan, Arthur W. Epstein, Warren L. Founds, Francisco Garcia Bengochea et al. *Studies in Schizophrenia: A Multidisciplinary Approach to Mind-Brain Relationships*. Harvard University Press, 1954, as cited in O'Neal, Christen M., Cordell M. Baker, Chad A. Glenn, Andrew K. Conner, and Michael E. Sughrue. "Dr. Robert G. Heath: A Controversial Figure in the History of Deep Brain Stimulation." *Neurosurgical Focus* 43, no. 3 (2017): E12. https://doi.org/10.3171/2017.6.FOCUS17252.

Chapter 7: Naturecultures of attraction 152: Copyright © 2017, The Trustees of Indiana University on behalf of the Kinsey-Institute. All rights reserved; **153:** Blaise Agüera y Arcas; **154:** Kay Tobin, "Germantown couple on porch #1," 1977, New York Public Library Digital Collections, Manuscripts and Archives Division, https://digitalcollections.nypl.org/items/510d47e3-b5c0-a3d9-e040-e00a18064a99; **155:** Anonymous, "Vintage Lesbian Couples," ca. 1890, https://i0.wp.com/themindcircle.com/wp-content/uploads/2016/05/Vintage-Lesbian-Couples-1.jpg; **160:** Clément Ader, "Clément Ader Avion III," 1897, photo by Roby CC BY-SA 2.0 BE, https://w.wiki/6k$k; **160:** Manchester Daily Express/SSPL via Getty Images; **161:** iStock.com/panda3800.

Chapter 8: Female flexibility 166: Blaise Agüera y Arcas; **169:** Frank McCarthy, "Cosmopolitan," 1971

https://pulpcovers.com/wp-content/uploads/2011/01/20395179-mccarthy_cosmo_aug711.jpg; **173:** Johann Friedrich Overbeck, "Italia und Germania," 1811–1828, https://w.wiki/6n9J.

Chapter 9: Pressure to conform 174: Wilde Douglas British Library B20147-85, Gillman & Co, May 1893, https://w.wiki/6k$m; **177:** Kay Addams, Cover of *Warped Desire*, 1960, https://pulpcovers.com/wp-content/uploads/2016/02/Beacon-B289-1960.jpg; **178:** Lesbian Bar Project LLC; **180:** Hon F L G, *Swell's Night Guide Through the Metropolis*, 1841, https://www.thelondoneconomic.com/entertainment/revealing-guide-to-victorian-londons-secret-brothels-and-prostitutes-unearthed-107489/; **181:** E. J. Bellocq, Accession No. 36.2004, International Center of Photography, https://www.icp.org/browse/archive/objects/storyville-portrait-new-orleans-2; **182:** Christopher D'Alton, Watercolour drawing, 1862. Wellcome Collection, Public Domain Mark, https://wellcomecollection.org/works/ydfz8zpr; **183:** CCI ARCHIVES / SCIENCE PHOTO LIBRARY; **184:** Albert V. Todd, Surgical Appliance, May 29, 1903, US patent 745,264, https://patents.google.com/patent/US745264A/en.

Chapter 10: Pronoun wars 191: AWang (WMF), "Gender recognition pins cropped," September 9, 2016, CC BY-SA 4.0, https://w.wiki/6k$n.

Chapter 11: Both/neither 196: Sam Levin / *Guardian*, Sara Kelly Keenan's birth certificate, 2017, https://www.theguardian.com/world/2017/jan/11/intersex-rights-gender-sara-kelly-keenan-birth-certificate; **197:** Ted Mark, *The Nude Who Did*, 1970, With permission from Penguin Random House LLC; **198:** John Money, "External Genital Differentiation in the Human Fetus" in *Man & Woman, Boy & Girl: The Differentiation and Dimorphism of Gender Identity from Conception to Maturity*, 44, 1972; **199:** Quigley, Charmian A., Alessandra De Bellis,

Keith B. Marschke, Mostafa K. El-Awady, Elizabeth M. Wilson, and Frank S. French. "Androgen Receptor Defects: Historical, Clinical, and Molecular Perspectives." *Endocrine reviews* 16, no. 3 (1995): 271–321. Scan by Jonathan. Marcus, "Quigley Scale," September 9, 2010, CC BY-SA 3.0, https://w.wiki/6k$o. Animation by Mrityunjay Marol, https://jaymarol.com/; **201:** Anonymous, "Nettie Stevens," 1909, Bryn Mawr College Special Collections, http://triptych.brynmawr.edu/cdm/singleitem/collection/BMC_photoarc/id/165/rec/1; **202:** Raquel Baranow, "Two Colored Rose Chimera," January 25, 2020, CC BY-SA 4.0, https://w.wiki/6k$p; **202:** fyOh18wxd9c51, https://www.instagram.com/gataquimera/; **202:** Taylor Muhl, "Chimerism self portrait," https://www.livescience.com/61890-what-is-chimerism-fused-twin.html; **203:** Victor, "Albino Peacock," December 7, 2007, https://www.flickr.com/photos/thebeeb/2137844739/in/dateposted/; **204:** Ksaviano, "Orchids," August 1, 2010, CC BY 3.0, https://w.wiki/6k$q; **206:** Hammond, *Sexual Impotence in the Male*, 1883; **207–208:** Fig. 33. Case 1; Fig. 55. Case 3; Fig. 61. Case 5. in Hugh Hampton Young. *Genital Abnormalities, Hermaphroditism and Related Adrenal Diseases*. Baltimore: Williams & Wilkins, 1937. Drawings by William P. Didush; **209:** Randal Alan Smith, "Annie headshot," April 10, 2005, GNU Free Documentation License, https://w.wiki/6k$r.

Interlude: Ycleptance 210: John Money, *Venuses Penuses: Sexology, Sexosophy, and Exigency Theory*, 69, 1986; **210:** Bruce/Brenda/David Reimer, Drawing, https://www.healthyplace.com/gender/inside-intersexuality/the-true-story-of-john-joan; **211:** Waldemar Kaempffert, Harris A Ewing, page 18, *Saturday Evening Post*, May 24, 1941, https://w.wiki/6k$u; **211:** John Money and Anke A. Ehrhardt, *Man & Woman, Boy & Girl: The Differentiation and Dimorphism of Gender Identity from Conception to Maturity*, 1972; **212:** Anonymous, Janet Frame, https://www.textpublishing.com.au/authors/janetframe; **212:** Fig. 4., photo by Theo Schoon in Eli Coleman, *John Money:*

A Tribute (on the occasion of his 70th birthday), 72, 1991; **213:** Robert Lawson, "Plan of Seacliff Hospital," 1902, https://w.wiki/6k$s; **214:** Archives New Zealand, "Picture of Nurses," June 15, 2020, https://w.wiki/6k$t; **216:** Table 1, John Money, Paraphilias, in *Venuses Penuses*, 441, 1986; **217:** John Money, *Venuses Penuses*, 225, 1986; **218:** C. Overzier, *Intersexuality*, Mainz, 173–74, 1963; **219:** Table III, John Money, *Venuses Penuses*, 176, 1986; **220:** Waldemar Kaempffert, Harris A Ewing, page 18, *Saturday Evening Post*, May 24, 1941, https://w.wiki/6k$u; **220:** Eli Coleman, David Suisted, *John Money: A Tribute (on the occasion of his 70th birthday)*, 78, 1991; **222:** Hoey committee, "Employment of Homosexuals and Other Sex Perverts in Government," December 15, 1950, https://www.archives.gov/publications/prologue/2016/summer/lavender.html; **223:** Table II, III, John Money, *Venuses Penuses: Sexology, Sexosophy, and Exigency Theory*, 155, 1986; **224:** Fig 8.8, John Money, Anke A. Ehrhardt, *Man & Woman, Boy & Girl*, 173, 1972; **224:** Fig. 9.13, Fig. 9.14: Case #2., John Money and Anke A. Ehrhardt, *Man & Woman, Boy & Girl*, 288, 1972; **225:** Fig. 9.10: Case #2., John Money and Anke A. Ehrhardt, *Man & Woman, Boy & Girl*, 286, 1972; **225:** Anonymous, Portrait of Janet Reimer with Bruce and Brian, https://www.dailystar.co.uk/news/world-news/tragic-life-boy-raised-girl-24473250; **226:** Anonymous, Portrait of Bruce/Brenda Reimer, https://medium.com/lessons-from-history/this-boy-committed-suicide-because-he-was-raised-as-a-girl-for-a-scientific-experiment-d18a99888dd7; **227:** Fig. 1., Reinisch et al., "Sex Differences in Developmental Milestones during the First Year of Life," in Eli Coleman, *John Money: A Tribute (on the occasion of his 70th birthday)*, 31, 1991; **229:** Table 6.1, John Money, Anke A. Ehrhardt, *Man & Woman, Boy & Girl*, 106, 1972; **230:** Anonymous, Portrait of David Reimer, In Memory of David Reimer, Facebook; **230:** Anonymous, David and Jane Reimer, https://www.dailystar.co.uk/news/world-news/tragic-life-boy-raised-girl-24473250; **231–32:**

Anonymous, John Money's apartment, https://www.esgallery.co.nz/john-money-collection.

Chapter 12: First, do no harm 234: W. T. Bovie, "Electro-surgical Apparatus," January 18, 1928, US patent 1,813,902 https://patents.google.com/patent/US1813902A/en; **235:** Down Home Auctions LLC, "Vintage Portable Bovie electro surgical unit," August 29, 2018, https://www.proxibid.com/Art-Antiques-Collectibles/Collectibles/Vintage-Portable-Bovie-electro-surgical-unit/lotInformation/43856716; **238:** Hugh Hampton Young, *Genital Abnormalities, Hermaphroditism and Related Adrenal Diseases*, 1937; **241:** Fig. 1., John Money, *Venuses Penuses: Sexology, Sexosophy, and Exigency Theory*, 194, 1988; **243:** Kat Jercich, Rewire News Group, Originally published August 13, 2018; **244:** Ambroise Paré, "An hermaphrodite in Des monstres et prodiges," 1585, https://juliamartins.co.uk/they-seemed-neither-and-yet-both-hermaphroditism-and-binary-categories; **244:** United States Agency for International Development, "A group of Hijra in Bangladesh," February 7, 2010, https://w.wiki/6k$x; **245:** John K. Hillers, "We-Wa, a Zuni berdache, weaving," https://w.wiki/6t98.

Chapter 13: The return of Count Sandor 255: Courtesy of MGM Media Licensing; **255:** Eusebio Gómez, *La Mala Vida en Buenos Aires*, 184, 1908; **264:** Buck Angel, "Buck Angel Headshot," October 26, 2010, CC BY-SA 3.0, https://w.wiki/6nWM.

Chapter 14: A view from above 265: Anonymous, "Alan Turning Aged 16," ca. 1928, https://w.wiki/oZx; **272:** J. Patrick Fischer, "Bactrian Camel in Shanghai Zoo," December 30, 2011, CC BY-SA 3.0, https://w.wiki/6nWN; **273:** Florian Prischl, "Camelus dromedarius in Nuweiba," October 28, 2007, CC BY-SA 3.0, https://w.wiki/6nWP; **278:** Turk, Matthew A., and Alex P. Pentland. "Face Recognition Using Eigenfaces." In Proceedings. 1991 IEEE computer society conference on computer vision and pattern recognition, pp. 586–587.

IEEE Computer Society, 1991; **278:** Karen Donnelly, Raimond de Weerdt and Tony Nott, "The 'average' Sydneysider," 2006, https://www.smh.com.au/technology/technology-plots-the-average-face-of-sydney--and-the-rest-of-the-world-20110211-1ap3w.html; **279:** Galton Papers, (GALTON/1/2/5/4/2), UCL Special Collections, UCL Archives, London; **280:** Francis Galton, *Inquiries Into Human Faculty and Its Development*, 342, 1883; **280:** Francis Galton, *Inquiries Into Human Faculty and Its Development*, frontispiece, 1883; **281:** AT&T Laboratories Cambridge, "Eigenfaces," December 01, 2005, https://w.wiki/6nWQ; **283:** Wu, Xiaolin, and Xi Zhang. "Automated inference on criminality using face images." arXiv preprint arXiv:1611.04135 (2016): 4038-4052; **284:** Alexander Todorov/Social Perception Lab; **284:** *Chicago Tribune*, "Patrick Eugene Joseph Prendergast," July 13, 1894, https://w.wiki/6nWR; **284:** V. G. Rocine, *Heads, Faces, Types, Races*, 181, 1910, https://archive.org/details/headsfacestypes00roci/page/180/mode/2up; **287:** Wang, Yilun, and Michal Kosinski, Composite images of gay and straight subjects, "Deep Neural Networks Are More Accurate than Humans at Detecting Sexual Orientation from Facial Images." *Journal of personality and social psychology* 114, no. 2 (2018): 246; **294:** Blaise Agüera y Arcas, Selfies; **295:** V. G. Rocine, *Heads, Faces, Types, Races*, 171, 1910, https://archive.org/details/headsfacestypes00roci/page/170/mode/2up; **296:** C. Lombroso, "Physiognomies of Russian criminals," *La donna delinquente: la prostituta e la donna normale*, Tav. VII, 1893.

Chapter 15: Postgender 298: Abi Bechtel, "Don't do this, @Target," June 2, 2015, https://twitter.com/abianne/status/605503223575781376; **299:** Toca Boca, Toca Life Stories, 2020, https://kidscreen.com/2020/02/21/toca-boca-launches-first-animated-series/; **300:** Jose Ramon Pacheco, "Phrenology," 1835, https://w.wiki/6nWT; **302:** Antoine Claudet, Daguerreotype of Charles Babbage, ca. 1847–51 https://w.wiki/6nWU; **302:** Margaret Sarah Carpenter, Portrait of Ada Lovelace,

1836, https://w.wiki/4rnk; **303:** C. Lombroso and E.G. Ferrero, *Donna delinquente*, 423, 1893; **304:** OJ Slaughter, Violinist Hilary Hahn; **306:** Theodor de Bry, *Brevis narratio eorum quae in Florida Americae provincia*, XXI., 1591; **307:** David Livingstone, "Female Elephant Pursued with Javelins," 1857, https://w.wiki/7Agk; **308:** Sir Edward Baines, "Power loom weaving," 1835, CC-BY-4.0, https://w.wiki/6nWV; **309:** Bettye Lane, Schlesinger Library, Harvard Radcliffe Institute; **310:** Najell AB, najell.com; **310:** E. M. Greenberg, "Artificial Womb," July 22, 1954, https://w.wiki/6nWW; **313:** Liv Boeree, https://twitter.com/liv_boeree/status/1445868089539588100; **314:** Peter Steiner, *New Yorker*, July 5, 1993, www.CartoonStock.com; **315:** Blaise Agüera y Arcas, FaceApp portraits.

Part III: Humanity 316–17: Ingmar Bergman, "Antonius Block plays chess with Death," *The Seventh Seal*, 1957, Svensk Filmindustri.

Chapter 16: Ignition 318: PictureLux / The Hollywood Archive / Alamy Stock Photo; **319:** Averater, "Tataouine by night," December 25, 2012, CC BY-SA 3.0, https://w.wiki/6nWX; **320:** William Tung, "A cosplay of Jabba's slave," Oola, April 18, 2015, CC BY-SA 2.0, https://w.wiki/6nWY; **320:** Ann Bannon, Robert McGinnis, Cover of *Beebo Brinker*, 1962, https://pulpcovers.com/beebo-brinker/; **321:** Domenico Passignano, "Bathers at San Niccolo," 1600, https://w.wiki/6nWZ; **322:** Moofpocket, "Monticello veggie garden," October 13, 2005, CC-BY-SA 3.0, https://w.wiki/6nWa; **323:** National Interregional Highway Committee, *Interregional Highways*, 1944, https://archive.org/details/interregional-highways/page/n53/mode/1up; **327:** NASA Earth Observatory images by Joshua Stevens, using Suomi NPP VIIRS data from Miguel Román, NASA's Goddard Space Flight Center; **328:** Dennis Jarvis, Vietnam-2145, February 1, 2009, CC BY-SA 2.0, https://www.flickr.com/photos/22490717@N02/3554229659; **332:** Andreas Praefcke, "Dallas skyline and suburbs," 2009, CC BY 3.0, https://w.wiki/6nWb; **336:**

Matthew McPherson, "Castro San Francisco flag," September 6, 2006, CC BY-SA 2.5, https://w.wiki/6nWc; **344:** Bettmann/Bettmann via Getty Images.

Chapter 17: Country and blues 345: Antoine Pesne, Portrait of Prince Henry of Prussia, 1745, https://w.wiki/6nWd; **349:** Nelson, Robert K., Ladale Winling, Richard Marciano, and Nathan Connolly. "Lower East Side street," dsc_ls_092, DOS: Sanitation & Street Cleaning, 1890–1900, https://nycma.lunaimaging.com/luna/servlet/detail/RECORDSPHOTO UNITARC-36-36-1282781-163070; **350:** Albert duce, "Abandoned Packard Automobile Factory Detroit," October 25, 2009, CC BY-SA 3.0, https://w.wiki/6nWe; **351:** Nelson, Robert K., Ladale Winling, Richard Marciano, and Nathan Connolly. "Mapping Inequality." Edited by Robert K. Nelson and Edward L. Ayers. American Panorama, 2021. https://dsl.richmond.edu/panorama/redlining/#loc=12/29.889/-90.089&city=new-orleans-la, licensed under CC BY-NC-SA 4.0; **352:** John Vachon, "Farmer waiting for supplies which he is buying cooperatively at Roanoke Farms, North Carolina," 1938, Library of Congress, FSA/OWI collection, https://www.loc.gov/pictures/collection/fsa/item/2017762423/; **369:** Harper & Brothers, Harper's Weekly, Vol. 11., 1857, https://archive.org/details/harpersweeklyv11bonn/page/172/mode/1up.

Chapter 18: Checking our numbers 370–71: Bernt Notke, "Danse Macabre in Tallinn," 1475/1499, https://w.wiki/6nWf; **373:** The Nuremberg Chronicle of Hartmann Schedel, "Nuremberg chronicles — Dance of Death (CCLXIIIIv)," 1440–1514, https://w.wiki/6nWg; **374:** John Linnell, Portrait of Thomas Robert Malthus, 1834, Wellcome Collection, Public Domain Mark, https://wellcomecollection.org/works/yaa9pmyb; **375:** 余集 绘, "Hong Liangji," Qing Dynasty, https://w.wiki/6nWj; **377:** "The Plowman" from Hans Holbein's *Simolachri, Historie, e Figure de la Morte*, 1549; **378:** Hans Holbein the Younger, "Holbein Danse Macabre

39," 1497, https://w.wiki/6nWk; **380:** Hans Holbein, "The Dance of Death: Expulsion from Paradise; Adam Cultivating the Ground," CC0 1.0, https://w.wiki/6nWm; **381:** Aga Szidlick, Namibia— San Tribe, 2016; **381:** Kortcentralen Helsingfors, "Sami family Finland," 1936, https://w.wiki/6nWr; **384:** Michel Serre, "Chevalier Roze à la Tourette," 1720, https://w.wiki/6nWn; **384:** Pieter Brueghel the Elder, "The Triumph of Death," 1526, Museo del Prado, https://w.wiki/6nWo; **385:** George Heriot Swanston, "Patrick Bell's reaping machine," 1851, https://w.wiki/6nWp; **386:** Keystone-France/Gamma-Keystone via Getty Images; **387:** Anonymous, "Both of these men had syphilis," 1941–1945, National Archives Catalog, NAID 513979, https://w.wiki/6nWq; **387–92:** Donella H. Meadows, Dennis L. Meadows, Jørgen Randers, William W. Behrens III, *The Limits to Growth, A Report for the Club of Rome's Project on the Predicament of Mankind*, 1972; **397:** The Donella Meadows Project.

Chapter 19: Choice 399: Anonymous, "Casanova and the Condom," 1872, Library of Congress, http://www.loc.gov/item/2004665384/; **400:** Bettmann/Bettmann via Getty Images; **401:** Margaret Sanger, "Birth Control Review," November 1923, in The Selected Papers of Margaret Sanger. HQ764.S3 A25 2003, CSUN University Library, Special Collections & Archives; **404:** Lewis Wickes Hines, "Eight year old Jennie Camillo lives in West Maniyunk, Pa., September 1910," The U.S. National Archives, https://www.flickr.com/photos/usnationalarchives/7496183108/; **405:** Lewis Wickes Hine, "488 Macon, Ga. Lewis W. Hine 1-19-. Bibb Mill No. 1 Many youngsters here. … ," 1909. Photograph. https://www.loc.gov/item/2018674998/; **405:** Bettmann/Bettmann via Getty Images; **408:** Anthony Crider, "Charlottesville 'Unite the Right' Rally," August 12, 2017, CC BY 2.0, https://w.wiki/6k$8; **409:** Bettmann/Bettmann via Getty Images.

Chapter 20: Terra incognita 410: Anonymous, "Psalter World Map," ca.1265, https://w.wiki/6k$A; **410:** Asheville Postcard Company, "Rockport Harbor, Rockport, Maine," ca. 1930–1945, https://w.wiki/6k$E; **410:** Anonymous, "West Clock Factory, La Salle, Ill.," ca. 1920s, https://www.ebay.com/itm/255829266948; **411:** Courtesy of The Strong, Rochester, New York; **411:** Asheville Postcard Company, "Home of J. E. Ranch, Waverly, N. Y.," ca. 1912, https://www.etsy.com/listing/1222264610/wavery-ny-farm-postcard-vintage-color; **411:** Asheville Postcard Company, "A Mountain Stream In Autumn When Nature Paints A Perfect Picture," ca. 1912, https://www.ebay.com/itm/324963005638; **412:** NurPhoto/NurPhoto via Getty Images; **413:** Katrinshine/Alamy Stock Photo; **414:** Toby Howard/Shutterstock; **414:** Hubert Robert, "A Hermit Praying in the Ruins of a Roman Temple," 1760, https://w.wiki/6k$F; **415:** B137, "Abandoned farmhouse, overgrown," May 4, 2010, CC BY-SA 4.0, https://w.wiki/6k$G; **417:** E. B. White, *Charlotte's Web*, 1952. Illustrated by Garth Williams; **417:** Bill Peet, *Farewell to Shady Glade*, 1976; **419:** Tesla Motors, "Tesla Fremont Factory," https://insideevs.uol.com.br/news/498262/biden-plano-incentivos-carros-eletricos/; **420:** CNC Industries, "Fastem 8760 Multi Level System," https://cncind.com/flexible-manufacturing-system/; **420:** Tim Rue, www.timrue.com; **421:** Kees Torn, Maersk McKinney Möller & Marseille Maersk, September 6, 2019, CC BY-SA 2.0, https://www.flickr.com/photos/68359921@N08/48694054418/; **421:** "Douglas County servers" by Google LLC; **422:** Watchara Phomicinda/MediaNews Group/The Press-Enterprise via Getty Images; **423:** Amazon Technologies Inc, "System and Method for Trans-porting Personnel Within An Active Workspace," 2016, US Patent 9,280,157 B2 https://patents.google.com/patent/US9280157B2/en; **423:** AGROBOT, "agrobot," 2019, https://grist.org/food/self-driving-tractors-robot-apple-pickers-witness-the-high-tech-future-of-farming/; **424:** Anonymous, "R2D2 and C3PO," 1982, https://www.corriere.it/tecnologia/19_maggio_31/history-moments-profilo-twitter-che-ci-riporta-indietro-tempo-7bb413da-8378-11e9-89bd-2f20504508c1-bc_11.shtml; **424:** FANUC, "M-2000iA/1700L," https://ia-robotics.com/fanuc-m-2000-1700l-car-lift/; **425:** Grendelkhan, "Waymo self-driving car front view," February 24, 2017, CC BY-SA 4.0, https://w.wiki/6k$J; **426:** Frans Lemmens/Corbis Unreleased via Getty Images; **427:** iStock.com/polybutmono; **428:** Thomas Schoch, "Road Train Australia," August 3, 2005, CC BY-SA 3.0, https://w.wiki/6k$K; **429:** Paulo Fridman/Corbis Historical via Getty Images; **429:** e-agro.tech, Agricultural field, https://e-agro.tech/; **430:** Tom Hegen, No. TGS06, Greenhouse Series, https://www.tomhegen.com/collections/the-greenhouse-series; **430:** Luca Locatelli/Institute; **431:** John F. Martin for General Motors, "Cadillac Urban Gardens," August, 2012; **431:** Lufa Farms, "Aerial view of Lufa Farms," July 13, 2013, CC BY-SA 3.0, https://w.wiki/6k$L; **432:** Fifth Season, "Vertical farm," https://www.governing.com/next/robots-take-vertical-farming-to-new-heights; **432:** Skyward Kick Productions/Shutterstock; **433:** Klaus Leidorf, "European Green Belt," August, 2003; **434:** Dale Kakkak; **438:** 2019 Meridith Kohut.

Chapter 21: Who are we becoming? 443: *Third Hand*, Tokyo, Yokohama, Nagoya, 1976–1980, Photo: T. Ike, Diagram: Stelarc; **445:** Underwood Archives/Photo Archive via Getty Images; **447:** IMAGO / United Archives.

Who Are We Now?
Blaise Agüera y Arcas

First North American Edition 2023

ISBN 978-1-955125-30-7

10 9 8 7 6 5 4 3 2 1

Design (print and web editions):
    James Goggin (Practise),
    Minkyoung Kim, and Marie Otsuka
Development (web edition):
    Minkyoung Kim and Marie Otsuka
Editorial Coordinator: Johan Michalove
Images and Permissions:
    David Michalove
Cartography: Scott Reinhard
Copyeditor: Sybil Perez

Type: Chroma ST (Selina Bernet,
Source Type, 2023), CMU Serif (Donald
Knuth, 1984, converted from Metafont
by Andrey V. Panov), Graphik and
Graphik Compact (Christian Schwartz,
Hrvoje Živčić, Ilya Ruderman,
Commercial Type, 2009/2017), Produkt
(Christian Schwartz, Berton Hasebe,
Ilya Ruderman, Commercial Type, 2014),
Produkt Condensed (Kara Gordon,
Berton Hasebe, Christian Schwartz,
Commercial Type, 2022)

Paper: Winter & Company Wibalin
Finelinen Terracotta/Cherry/Sapphire
Blue 115gsm, Igepa Maxioffset
120gsm, Fedrigoni Golden Star K 110gsm

Printed and bound in Belgium
at die Keure Printing, Bruges

Hat & Beard, LLC
713 N La Fayette Park Place
Los Angeles, CA 90026
www.hatandbeard.com

H&B